Developmental Psychology Today

SECOND EDITION

Developmental Psychology Today

SECOND EDITION

CRM/RANDOM HOUSE

Second Edition   9876543

Copyright © 1975 by Random House, Inc.
All rights reserved under International and Pan-American
Copyright Conventions. No part of this book may be
reproduced in any form or by any means, electronic or
mechanical, including photocopying, without permission in
writing from the publisher. All inquiries should be addressed to
Random House, Inc., 201 East 50th Street, New York, N.Y.
10022. Published in the United States by Random House, Inc.,
and simultaneously in Canada by Random House of Canada
Limited, Toronto.
Library of Congress Catalog Card Number: 74–21783
ISBN: 0–394–31074–8
Manufactured in the United States of America

PREFACE

In many ways, DEVELOPMENTAL PSYCHOLOGY TODAY, Second Edition, is a brand-new book. Although it retains the most positive features of the first edition, we have made many changes on the basis of our experiences in publishing the first edition and in response to the vast amount of feedback that we have received from instructors, students, and reviewers who read and evaluated the first edition.

When we started the second edition, we had two major goals in mind: to organize coherently and to summarize the current concerns of and knowledge in developmental psychology and to present these materials as an effective teaching/learning resource.

The materials in this edition of DEVELOPMENTAL PSYCHOLOGY TODAY are almost totally new and have been organized to present the information logically and clearly. We have broadened the scope and depth of coverage, included appropriate cross-referencing among chapters, expanded the nature and amount of citations, and attributed theoretical and practical positions to their major proponents. We have added such study aids as outlines at the beginning of each chapter, chapter summaries and suggested readings at the end of each chapter, a rewritten and expanded glossary and index, and a film appendix. To increase the text's effectiveness, we have prominently identified the key concepts and terms through the use of **boldface** and *italic* and have tried to write in a style and at a level of difficulty that will seize and maintain reader interest. In addition, we have recast the graphic elements to supplement and complement the text.

Through the combined efforts and expertise of many professionals, the second edition of DEVELOPMENTAL PSYCHOLOGY TODAY has become, in our opinion, an authentic and attractive approach to the study of developmental psychology. We hope that you agree.

Harvey A. Tilker, Ph.D.
Director and Publisher
Psychology Publishing Group
CRM Books

CONTENTS

UNIT I
The Meaning of Development

Developmental Psychology Today

SECOND EDITION

Babies grow into adult human beings, full of the qualities and imperfections typical of humanity. But the behavior of an adult man or woman is very different from the behavior of a relatively helpless infant. A person watching a young baby gazing intently at his fist would be unable to predict whether that baby would grow into an adult who was honest or dishonest, rash or careful, confident or insecure. Developmental psychologists attempt to describe how the baby develops into the adult he will become and to explain why he develops into one kind of adult and not another. Heredity, culture, and personal experience all play their parts in that development, and different psychologists have explained their influences in different ways. When you finish this unit, you will begin to see that no one approach can answer every question and that there is more than one path to an adequate description of human development.

UNIT I
The Meaning
of Development

Throughout life, all aspects of
development are interdependent.

1

THE CONCEPT OF DEVELOPMENT

The development of a human being may seem mysterious—even magical. Can we possibly explain how a one-cell fertilized egg develops into a
fully human newborn, a linguistically accomplished kindergartner, a
budding engineer, a competent parent, and an involved citizen? The
human life cycle is the subject of developmental psychology. This branch
of psychology explores the ways in which human physical growth and
intellectual and social behavior change over time, and it seeks to find how
growth and behavior relate to each other.

Developmental psychology has a perspective on human development.
It sees human behavior as a changing system that includes both biological
and sociocultural determinants, which work together to produce behavioral development. At no time is a person without an environment, nor is
he ever without biological systems that affect his behavior. Rather, a
developing person is an integration of biological and environmental
forces that act together in an organized way. That integration changes
over time. A person's development poses some of the most fascinating
questions that one can ask about the nature of humanity.

In this chapter we will see how the concept of childhood emerged as a
separate stage of life, when the idea of adolescence was born, and how
the social and economic structure of a society shapes the way its members
view the life span. We will discover that developmental psychology
draws on different disciplines, on different types of information, and on
different levels of explanation to describe changes in behavior over the
life span. We will find out that research leads to statements that are good
for describing average development but that these statements fail to
predict the behavior of many individuals. We will learn that development
is an orderly, ever-increasing, and more complex change in a consistent
direction. In addition, we will find that it is helpful to regard behavior as
proceeding through phases of development. When you finish reading this
chapter, and the rest of the book, you may find yourself looking at the
behavior of yourself and others around you in a different way.

HISTORICAL BACKGROUND

The contemporary student of developmental psychology may believe that the life span, from conception to death, has always been seen as we now see it. In the twentieth century, we recognize distinctions among the prenatal period, infancy, childhood, adolescence, and adulthood. But the human life span has not always been divided into these periods, nor need it be.

Philippe Ariès (1962) has examined the concept of the life cycle as it has been seen from the Middle Ages to the present. He has concluded that in the Middle Ages even the concept of childhood as it is defined today was virtually unknown. There was a clearly admitted infancy, lasting until approximately the age of seven. But thereafter, people whom we would consider children were simply assimilated into the adult world. The art and social documents of the Middle Ages show children and adults mingling together in one unified community, wearing the same clothes, and performing the same functions. Society made no distinction among them on the basis of age or phase of psychological development. The vast majority of children—and adults—were, of course, totally unschooled. But even those who obtained the minimal schooling required to become priests or clerks learned in ungraded schools where children, adolescents, and adults intermingled.

Emergence of Childhood

It was only in the seventeenth and eighteenth centuries that the concept of childhood as a separate stage of life slowly began to appear. A new and sentimental view of childhood sprang up along with new theories of education that were concerned with promoting the child's moral and intellectual development, protecting him from the evils and corruptions of adult society, and preserving his real or imagined childhood virtues. At the same time, schools became increasingly graded by age, and both the average length of schooling and the number of children who received formal education increased.

From historical evidence it seems clear that childhood became a separate stage of life only when large numbers of people entered the middle class, the amount of leisure time increased, and the rate of infant mortality decreased. As the middle class prospered, there was less need for their children to work in order to ensure the family's economic survival. The lowered rate of childhood mortality meant that more children would live to reach puberty; therefore, parents could devote themselves less cautiously to each child. And the new mercantile capitalism required that a larger portion of the citizenry be literate and fluent with numbers; thus, more children had to go to schools.

Ariès's analysis of the emerging concept of childhood has had far-reaching implications for understanding the relationship between historical change and psychological development. Ariès has spoken explicitly about concepts of childhood, but the experience of childhood changed as well, although perhaps less dramatically. In the Middle Ages, many children died before the age of six, and those who survived were apprenticed out or put to work. Both parents and masters often treated them with what we would consider a shocking lack of tenderness, protectiveness, attention, and care. Parents seem to have invested little emotional energy in their children; children were rarely spoken of as precious possessions to be cherished and protected.

But as a stage of childhood began to emerge, a larger proportion of those betweeen the ages of six and fourteen were deliberately segregated into schools. Such segregation increasingly sheltered them from the demands of adult work. Children found new freedom to play and to experiment and had systematic opportunities to develop new interpersonal and technical skills. In advanced Western societies, segregation of childhood is now virtually complete, but it has been only in this century that it has finally been extended to the working and lower classes. The mark of this full institutionalization of childhood is univer-

Figure 1.1 Although divisions in the life cycle, such as childhood, adolescence, and old age, are now commonplace, these periods of development were not recognized during earlier times. They emerged as more people survived childhood and lived longer and as societies became industrialized and segregated into socioeconomic levels and age-graded roles.

sal primary education. It has taken four centuries for us to move from an era in which childhood was unrecognized to an era in which we take it completely for granted and protect it with an array of legal, social, and educational institutions.

Emergence of Adolescence

The concept of adolescence is of more recent origin. Only after childhood had been marked off from adulthood was adolescence interposed between them. Adolescence as we think of it today emerged only in the nineteenth and twentieth centuries, and the extension of adolescence as a stage of psychological growth is far from complete even today. Puberty in the sense of biological maturation occurs, of course, in all societies, but in early Western societies, it seemed to go largely unnoticed. When children are considered neither innocent nor importantly different from adults, the fact of puberty constitutes neither a fall from innocence nor a change in status, and it therefore has little special meaning.

When a postpuberty stage of life was first noted in the eighteenth and nineteenth centuries, concepts of adolescence centered on two images: the cherubino (the androgynous youth) or the recruit (the young soldier in training). Only in our century did the modern concept of adolescence appear. And even today, images of adolescence are fluid and changing. Media that portray adolescents still alternate between earlier images of the adolescent as awkward, acned, and anguished and newer images that view the adolescent either as deviant, wild, and uncontrolled or else as an idealistic and accurate critic of society, the repository of the future's hope.

The recent emergence of the concept of adolescence does not mean that no one ever had an adolescence before society formulated the concept. Clearly, the potential for this experience is part of our endowment as human beings, and in previous centuries many men and women passed through what would now be recognized as an adolescent experience. But three things have changed in the last century. First, adolescence as a stage of life has been socially recognized and acknowledged. Second, society has begun to sanction and support adolescence, increasingly buttressing it with educational, familial, institutional, and economic resources. Third, these new resources, coupled with other changes in society, have given an ever larger proportion of young people the possibility of continuing psychological growth during the years from thirteen to eighteen. This opportunity arose when society granted them protection from adult responsibilities, created educational institutions to fill their duty-free time, and developed a positive image of a postchildhood, preadulthood stage of life: adolescence.

As with the recognition of childhood, the emergence of adolescence is closely related to social, economic, and historical changes. Increasing industrialization has freed young people past the age of puberty from the requirements of farm and factory labor. Indeed, the rising standards of economic productivity today make the adolescent, especially the uneducated adolescent, almost impossible to employ. The new attitudes toward adolescence are expressed in laws that make full-time employment before the age of sixteen or eighteen illegal. Growing affluence provides most families and the larger society with the wealth needed to support these economically unproductive adolescents in school. And all these changes have happened, on a mass scale, almost within living memory; even our child labor laws were passed only in the twentieth century. However, one must always remember that descriptions of the general society necessarily ignore pockets of poverty, such as that surrounding migratory farm laborers, in which financial considerations force children and adolescents to work in defiance of law.

Emergence of Late Adulthood

The period of late adulthood is also a recent phenomenon because until this century most people died before they reached the age of seventy or seventy-five. Today more adults are living until their physical capacities and economic self-sufficiency are threatened. In some societies older adults are venerated as wise, experienced advisers. Unfortunately, in the United States many younger adults view older people as irrelevant. Because older adults acquired their experiences during an era that no longer exists, the young regard them as passé and perhaps as uncomfortable reminders of their own fates. Like children and adolescents, older adults are often segregated into special institutions that keep them out of view and out of the minds of younger people. The many problems this experience creates for older adults will be brought out in Chapter 22.

Today we divide development into phases that are marked by *social* events, such as the beginning of meaningful speech (the end of infancy and the start of childhood, at about the age of two) or the achievement of adult roles in employment, marriage, and reproduction (the end of adolescence and the start of adulthood, in the early twenties for many people).

Other markers we attach to the life span are *biological:* birth (the end of the prenatal period and the start of infancy) and reproductive maturity at puberty (the end of childhood and the start of adolescence). We are not consistent in choosing markers for periods in the life span, and our markers are by no means universal. Other contemporary societies divide life into three periods—such as infancy, childhood, and adulthood—or even only two—infancy and adulthood (Mead, 1968).

The way in which people in a society view the life span depends largely on its social and economic system. If the preparation for adult roles is gradual and continuous from early childhood and if the necessary technology can be acquired by apprenticeship, then adulthood is likely to begin shortly after a person reaches reproductive maturity. On the other hand, if full participation in the economic system depends on years of technical education, then a period of adolescence is likely to be recognized. Toward the end of the life span, when participation in the economic system becomes less active, older adults may be forced to retire from their jobs, creating a period that some call "old age." Older adults are, of course, still adults, but the loss of social and economic roles can drastically change the experience of later adulthood.

STUDYING DEVELOPMENTAL PSYCHOLOGY

Unlike other areas of psychology, which tend to be organized by content areas, such as learning, motivation, and psychopathology, the concerns of developmental psychology cut across content areas to describe and to explain the changes that occur over time in learning, motivation, and so forth.

The field attempts to *describe* and to *explain* changes in human behavior across the years of the life span. The first step toward such an understanding of behavioral development must be an accurate and detailed description of the changes that occur. The second step, or series of steps, concerns explanations for the observed changes.

A **behavior** is defined as an observable act that can be described or measured reliably. **Reliability** means that two or more scientists can agree on the measurement. Behaviors can be measured in many ways, some simply by watching and others by using instruments of various kinds, such as recordings of heart rates, questionnaires, and films of children's interactions. Developmental psychologists do not pick any behavior at random to measure and describe; nor do they attempt to study the universe of all possible

behaviors. To describe every possible behavior and every individual variant of it is an impossible task. Instead, psychologists select for detailed study those theoretically or practically important behaviors.

Use of Theory

To explain how and why behavior develops, psychologists have constructed sets of logically related statements about the nature of development called **theories.** A theoretical statement is usually abstract and does not refer directly to what is observed. For example, Erik Erikson's (1963) theory of psychosocial development says that young children around the age of two to four need to develop **autonomy,** a feeling of self-control and self-determination. One cannot observe autonomy directly, but if Erikson is correct about the young child's need to direct his own behavior, we should see behavioral evidence, such as the two-year-old's emphatic "No" to parental requests, the verbal response "Me do it" to proffered help, the temper tantrums that sometimes occur when a child's goals are thwarted, and so forth. Erikson's theoretical statement about autonomy *predicts* these diverse behaviors.

Theories should lead to testable hypotheses or predictions about observable behavior. If the statements of a theory predict a great deal that is observed about human behavior, then we say that the theory is a useful explanation of human development. Thus far no theory has satisfactorily covered all aspects of human development. Rather, as Chapter 2 shows, theories tend to be restricted to some part of development, such as social behavior or intellectual development or language acquisition.

As a part of psychology, developmental psychology uses scientific methods and procedures to study human behavior. Researchers emphasize the testing of hypotheses derived from theories, using methods that can be described and applied by other investigators. Studies must lead to results that others can repeat and confirm. However appealing children and adolescents are, no description of their actions can adequately explain their behavior.

The prediction and explanation of behavior are two important goals of psychology. Another is *control.* For example, the control of behavior through rewards and punishments is of theoretical importance to psychologists and of practical importance to parents, teachers, and other adults who have responsibility for rearing children. Today, one major approach to changing behavior in this way is **behavior modification.** For example, schools and other institutions use ''behavior mod'' to increase the frequency of desirable behaviors among their charges and to reduce the frequency of undesirable ones.

Because developmental psychologists are interested in development across the life span, information on behavioral changes in all periods is important. However, researchers have collected relatively more information on school-aged children and newborn babies than on older infants and adults. This situation has come about because of the difficulties involved in studying people who are not yet or are no longer in an institution such as a maternity hospital or a school. Because the subjects of study are gathered conveniently together in them, institutions have provided excellent opportunities for investigations of human development.

Contributions of Other Disciplines

Several other scientific fields are also concerned with human development: biology, sociology, and anthropology. Developmental psychologists depend on information on the individual's biological history and maturation, on social organization, and on cultural influences, which comes from these other disciplines. They need such information to explain behavior because psychologists see the developing human as a changing system that integrates biological factors and experience. The kinds of experiences a person has in growing up depend largely on what kind of family and society he lives in (for example, how many brothers and sisters he has, how punitive his parents are, how his society divides people by age, what kinds of institutions exist) and on cultural values that distinguish right from wrong, good from bad. What a person learns in the sociocultural context depends on both his readiness to learn and the availability of materials and ideas for him to acquire. In the case of children, maturational level has a profound influence on what they select from the world around them; a child's environment determines what is available for him to learn.

Take language, for example. The ability to learn a language is one of humankind's evolved characteristics. All normal members of the species learn to speak. But developmentalists know that the child is not able to talk until he has attained a certain level of neurological development (Lenneberg, 1967). No six-month-old speaks in sentences. At the same time, a child living in a relatively unstimulating, unresponsive environment begins to speak later than a child reared in a more stimulating home. In the first case, the child is not biologically ready to speak; in the

second, the child's world does not offer adequate speech models for him to learn from. The time and rate at which language develops in a particular child are the result of both his level of maturity and his previous experience in vocalizing, in listening to language, and in being rewarded for the use of language. The language he learns to speak fluently is that of his cultural group.

Evolutionary biologists have given insightful accounts of humanity's evolutionary history, which have set the stage for understanding individual development. After all, children develop into human adults, not into chimpanzees. All children have more in common with one another than any one of them has with any other species. Despite our individual differences, as human beings we share much in common.

Developmental biologists have provided detailed descriptions of embryological development that can serve as a model for understanding all development. The complex integration of genetic and environmental influences across the life span, and from the level of the single cell to that of the whole organism, has made psychologists aware of the need to consider both classes of influences on human behavioral development.

Sociologists and cultural anthropologists have emphasized the importance of understanding development within a sociocultural context. A child is always a member of a human group, particularly his family, his neighborhood group, his school class, and so forth. Much of his behavior is influenced by his

Figure 1.2 The field of developmental psychology draws on information from other fields in order to understand, predict, and explain human behavior. Biological knowledge of cell division and studies of cross-cultural differences in human development exemplify the important contributions made by other disciplines.

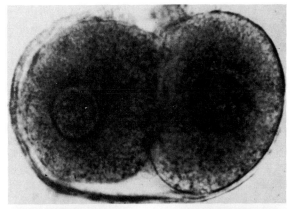

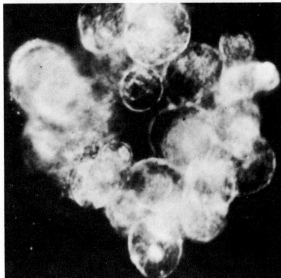

setting, both his immediate circumstances and his longer-range memberships in various groups. As shown in the historical perspective on childhood and adolescence, the ways in which a culture interprets the life span can have profound influences on the expectations that others have for a person's behavior at different times in his life.

EXPLAINING HUMAN DEVELOPMENT

Developmental psychology adds the information drawn from other fields to the basic psychological principles of other areas of psychology. The explanation of a human behavior often includes elements from these various fields. But one must be very careful to adopt a level of explanation that is appropriate for that behavior.

Levels of Explanation

One frequent criticism of behavioral studies that emphasize biological variables, such as those explaining behavioral differences between males and females in terms of hormone levels, is that their explanations are **reductionist.** That is, they reduce the causes of a complex behavior to a simple explanation. For example, the level of male hormones may contribute (greatly or little) to sex differences in behavior, but they are not a sufficient explanation for the observed behavioral differences. As later chapters show, many other factors—such as different parental responses to boys and girls, rewards for appropriate sex-role behavior, and so forth—may also play important roles in shaping sex differences in behavior. To explain the differences we observe, we must consider the effects of hormone differences along with other prenatal and postnatal environmental differences. In this example hormones are only one component in the behavioral system; how important they are can be determined by research that varies hormone and rearing conditions separately (Money and Ehrhardt, 1972).

Psychological phenomena are not adequately explained by sociological or anthropological principles either. Most statements in these fields apply to average tendencies among groups of people, not to individuals. For example, a sociological study of reproduction among subgroups in a society may lead to statements about the relative fertility of married versus unmarried persons, Catholics versus Protestants, younger versus older couples, and so forth. The sociological explanation of fertility does not describe individual people's behavior or their motives for having or not having children. To explain why certain people in a subgroup (for example, married persons) reproduce whereas others do not usually requires a psychological explanation. On the other hand, a psychological explanation of why some people want children and others do not does not adequately explain the declining birth rate in the United States; that requires a socioeconomic-cultural set of factors that psychology cannot provide.

In short, we need to draw on information from other fields, be it hormone levels or social-class effects, but if we expect to explain behavior, we must be careful to integrate this information at the level at which behavior is influenced.

Types of Knowledge

Most developmental psychologists gather information on (1) behavior at different ages; (2) behavioral changes as people grow older; (3) environmental events that influence behavior; and (4) variations among individuals in their development. These four kinds of information make up most of the knowledge in developmental psychology.

One must first gather descriptions of behavior before he can evaluate explanations and theories. The sucking patterns of newborns (Type 1 information), for example, have been extensively described by Lewis Lipsitt (1967a) and Arnold Sameroff (1968). All normal newborns show the components of sucking, which they combine in a rhythmic alternation of bursts and rests. Additional descriptions of later sucking behavior in one-month-olds allow us to eval-

uate the changes that occur with increasing maturity and experience (Type 2 information). Intensive investigations of the effects of rewards on rates of sucking have demonstrated that newborns will alter their sucking patterns to get sweetened water (Type 3 information). Finally, other studies show that individual babies have distinctive patterns of sucking, which, when recorded, identify them at least as well as their footprints. The individual baby's sucking pattern is a kind of "signature" (Type 4 information). Whereas all normal babies suck in bursts interrupted by rests, individual babies have different numbers of sucks per burst and shorter or longer rests between. The four types of knowledge are complementary and valuable, each in its own way. No explanation of behavior could be complete unless it took all of them into account.

Two additional kinds of information play a role in the field of developmental psychology: case histories of individuals and research on other species. Case histories of unusual patterns of development can sometimes give us insights about normal development. For example, Dorothy Baruch's (1964) case history of a boy who developed extreme fears illustrates how early parent-child relations affect later development. Around the turn of the century, a number of ardent parents kept diaries that described every change in their infant's behavior over the early years. Psychologists found these baby biographies useful in describing sequences and individual differences in development. Although the diaries were not

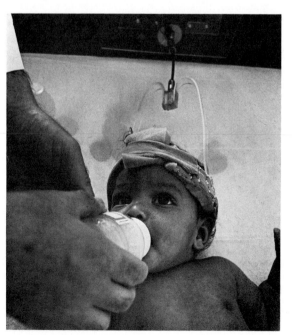

Figure 1.3 Laboratory studies of the sucking patterns of newborns illustrate the four types of information that are widely sought and used in developmental psychology: A particular behavior is identified (Type 1); changes in its occurrence with age are described (Type 2); environmental events that alter its occurrence are noted (Type 3); and individual variation in its development is determined (Type 4).

objective, scientific descriptions, they provided a basis for further scientific study. Case histories by scientific observers, such as Jean Piaget's (1926) observations of his own three children, have provided a rich source of ideas for further investigation.

Research on nonhuman species has a long history in psychology. Although the albino rat has played a much smaller role in developmental than in some other areas of psychology, primates such as chimpanzees and rhesus monkeys have provided valuable information. For ethical reasons, some theoretically interesting ideas about development cannot easily be tested with human beings. No psychologist would deprive a human baby of his mother in order to observe the effects of isolation on his development. But Harry Harlow and his associates (Harlow and Harlow, 1966; Harlow and Zimmermann, 1959) have conducted just such research with rhesus and other monkeys. Their results, which are discussed in Chapters 9 and 13, demonstrate the importance of contact comfort for the normal social development of monkeys. Because monkey and human babies have similar periods of close infant-mother relationships, we can infer that human babies who are deprived of close contact with a caretaker will also show distorted social development. These inferences from research on other primates are supported by naturally occurring "experiments" on babies reared in large impersonal institutions and by occasional case histories of babies who have been isolated by neglectful mothers (L. Yarrow, 1961).

Individual Variation

Most research in developmental psychology leads to conclusions that are general statements about the behavior or developmental change under investigation. The general statements summarize what was found to be true for the largest number of subjects or for the "average" subject in an experiment. But the behavior or development of some subjects may have been different from that of the majority. For example, William Rohwer's (1971) study of children's learning showed that categorically organized materials are easier to remember than randomly ordered lists. That is, the list "car, boat, plane; chair, table, bed" is easier to remember than the list "car, bed, table; plane, chair, boat." Most elementary-school children will look at the first list and think "three transports, three furnitures," which helps them recall the individual items. Some children, however, do not use categories to help them remember and thus recall as few items from the first list as from the second.

Figure 1.4 Individual differences are manifest in all aspects of human development and behavior. Developmental psychologists usually allow for and make use of this variation among people in evaluating and discussing their research.

Developmental psychologists acknowledge that the results shown for most people do not apply to all individuals. Thus, one can say that elementary-school children are likely to use categories to help them remember lists of items, even if all children do not use that strategy. Or a developmental psychologist may say that young adolescents generally become self-conscious about their appearances without being proved wrong by the example of your best friend, who remained an unconscious slob until he was eighteen.

It is often important to study individual variation in behavior for clues about the many possible ways of behaving in the same situation. Children who learn to read successfully in the first grade seem to do so in a variety of ways. Choosing a single method to teach reading to less successful readers has been nearly impossible because no one method has been successful with all children who have reading problems. Studies indicate that some children learn more quickly with a phonic approach, whereas others learn best using a sight, or look-say, method (Chall, 1967). Individual differences in aptitudes for reading are only one example of normal variation.

The fact of individual differences in almost all behavior does not keep developmental psychologists from testing general hypotheses about development or from making general statements about their results. One must be aware, however, that whereas individual exceptions exist, general statements are often useful in practical as well as theoretical ways. We know, for example, that good day care does not harm most children (Fein and Clarke-Stewart, 1973). The development of young children in day care is as normal on the average as the development of children at home with their mothers. That statement has obvious practical implications. However, we must always realize that some day-care placements are not good and that some children are more upset than others about leaving their mothers. But on the average, day care has no effects different from those of home care.

On the other hand, researchers might study a day-care center that by chance alone had a large number of unhappy children. It would be incorrect to conclude, on the basis of this study, that day-care centers and unhappy children go together.

The best safeguard against accepting such a chance finding as typical is to have other investigators study other children in other day-care centers in the same way to see if they find the same thing. This is called a **replication** study. Because so many factors can influence a study of behavior—including the investi-

gator's own bias (R. Rosenthal, 1968)—it is important that others who do not have exactly the same ideas can repeat the results.

THE NATURE OF DEVELOPMENT

All normal infants grow first into children and then into adults, which is no surprise. This sequence implies several characteristics about development, however: (1) development is orderly change; (2) it is directional; (3) it is cumulative to a large extent; and (4) it is characterized by increasing differentiation and complex organization.

Anyone who has watched children develop knows that changes in their behavior occur more frequently and more rapidly during infancy than later. The changes in behavior over the life span are neither accidental nor random. There is an orderly sequence to behavioral development, whether we talk about language acquisition, social play, or moral judgment. Each kind of behavior can be described in a series of developmental steps. When children first use words, around eleven to fourteen months of age, they typically use one word at a time. Later, at about twenty-one to twenty-four months, they begin to put two or three words together. By three to three and one-half years, most children use complex sentences and can tell brief stories. But no child begins by speaking in sentences and then develops to a one-word phase. The orderly sequence of language acquisition is directional and predictable.

The same sort of predictable development occurs in social play. One-year-olds hardly notice each other, whereas preschool children generally play side by side but not together. By the early school years, most children can interact in games that have specific rules and that require each child to play a role. The sequence is the same for all children.

These sequences of development often proceed from simpler, more global behaviors to increasingly differentiated but integrated sets of behaviors. As children mature and incorporate more of the social world around them, they increasingly organize separate behaviors into such complex sets. For example, moral judgments of young children are often based on global concepts of "right" and "wrong." Their ideas of rightness and wrongness depend more on the outcome of an act than on the intentions of the actor. A child of four or five may feel that a boy who breaks the cookie jar in the act of stealing a cookie is no worse than another who breaks the jar while reaching for a cookie his mother told him to get. In both cases the boy broke the cookie jar. But most older children and adults would separate the two cases and base their moral judgments on the boys' intentions. Older children can also differentiate shades of wrongdoing. Many adolescents and adults base specific moral judgments on complex ideals that they have abstracted from experience in concrete situations. The development of moral judgment closely parallels changes in children's thinking, which becomes more hypothetical from childhood to maturity.

Sequences

The notion of sequences of development pervades developmental psychology. Most theorists have acknowledged that behavioral development proceeds in an orderly fashion, and many have pointed to the increasing differentiation and complex organization of behavior at later ages (Erikson, 1963; Flavell, 1972; McNeill, 1970b; Piaget, 1926; Werner, 1957). One must specify the exact nature of the sequences of development for each kind of behavior, whether cognition, language, perception, social interaction, or personality.

John Flavell (1972) has examined the sequences of intellectual development in search of "meaningful" relationships among behaviors. Although children acquire many behaviors at the same time, not all the behaviors are related to each other logically, socially, or biologically. Some are simply coincidental. It is not very interesting to notice that the average child's foot reaches size 12 before his vocabulary approximates 6,000 words. No one thinks that the two events

Figure 1.5 The growth of a plant from seedling to maturity illustrates a gradual and continuous process of development. The plant's foliage and roots develop at the same pace and are interdependent: As the plant grows more leaves, it needs more support from its roots, and root growth is partially dependent on the number of leaves drawing energy from the sun.

are related, except by some tortuous and unlikely maturational links between skeletal growth and language acquisition. Flavell has suggested that "interesting" sequences in development result from one of three possible factors: (1) the structure of the organism; (2) the structure of the environment; or (3) the structure of the task. Some developmental sequences occur because of biological maturation; others, because children's experiences increase as they get older; and still others, because some skills are logically related in ordered sequences, such as the one-word to multiple-word utterance.

If earlier behaviors are related in any meaningful, formal, or causal way to later ones, then we can describe the relationship between the earlier and later behaviors as developmental. According to Flavell, sequences in intellectual development can be classified into five types: addition, substitution, modification, inclusion, and mediation.

1. In **addition,** the later-emerging skill is added to the earlier one and supplements but does not replace it. For example, a child learns to count by rote before he learns the concept of number. That is, he knows the names of the numbers before he learns that the number 6 refers to any collection of six objects. Children do not replace their counting ability with number concepts; they simply add the new skills to their other behavior.

2. In **substitution,** the later-emerging item replaces the earlier one completely or almost completely. For example, young children often believe that dreams are real, external events that happen while they are asleep. Dreams can have the same reality for children as wide-awake experiences. By middle childhood, however, most children realize that dreams are subjective, internal experiences. Their recognition of the nature of dreams replaces their earlier belief.

3. In **modification,** the later-emerging behavior represents a differentiation or a generalization of a more stable form of an earlier skill. For example, children in the primary grades progressively change their understanding of the physical world. They gradually come to realize that quantities (numbers, lengths, volumes) do not change if only certain perceptual properties change. The number of coins in a row of five coins six inches in length is still five coins, whether the row is spread out to cover ten inches or is reduced to three inches. Children of seven or eight can tell the difference between essential changes (like addition and sub-traction) and nonessential changes (like the length and density of the row). Children also generalize this operation to continuous quantities such as water, realizing that a quantity remains the same when poured from a narrow glass to a squat one, and to other qualities such as weight. In the process of applying such ideas to many situations, a child becomes more sure of his ideas and more efficient in solving problems that depend on these skills; in short, his use of the logical operation becomes more stable.

4. In **inclusion,** the earlier item becomes incorporated (included) as an integral part of a later item. For example, naming skills that children develop in the second to third years of life become incorporated into all later language development. Adults use names to talk about people and objects and continue to acquire names of additional objects and people, which they incorporate into symbolical reasoning about them. In fact, it is hard to imagine symbolic operations that do not use earlier skills of some kind.

5. In **mediation,** the earlier-developed item serves as a bridge or stepping stone to the later one. For example, a child must have the ability to count before he understands that five coins remain five coins, no matter how they are spread out; counting mediates the development of this notion, but it is not incorporated wholly into it. An older child does not depend on counting to know that spreading a row of coins so that it covers ten inches instead of six does not change the number of coins in a row. He knows that the number remains the same because no coins were added or subtracted.

When intellectual behaviors can be related by one of these methods, they are considered part of a developmental sequence.

Stages

The idea of stages in development is different from that of sequences. Whereas sequences imply that some behaviors precede others in a meaningfully related way, stages imply additional qualities that are more difficult to define.

The idea of stages of development is popular with most people. Parents often refer to a two-year-old's "negative" stage, meaning that their child often says "No," refuses to do what is asked of him, and generally defies parental authority. Sometimes adolescents are said to be in a "rebellious" stage because they sometimes defy parental values, attitudes, and authority. Used in this loose way, the term "stage" is nothing more than a label characterizing a dominant theme in the behavior of a certain age group.

Developmental psychologists give a more exact meaning to the term "stage." When they call a period in the life span a stage, they mean that the organization of behavior at that time is qualitatively different from its earlier or later organization. Further, they mean that changes in many behaviors occur simultaneously and reach their maximum likelihood of occurrence as soon as a person enters the stage. Let us examine the usefulness of a strict stage theory of development.

A stage is characterized, first, by the *organization* of behaviors that occur at the same time. Abilities, motives, and other kinds of behavior must be related to each other in a psychologically cohesive pattern. For example, the two-year-old who is said to be in a "negative" stage should display his negativism in many ways (which many do), and negativism must characterize most of his behavior (which it does not). Two-year-old behavior also suggests curiosity, affectionate ties to parents, increasing mastery of symbolic representation, and many other characteristics that no one would call negative. Thus, it is difficult to see any usefulness in calling the second year of life a "negative" stage when so many other behavioral themes are also evident.

Second, a stage must represent *qualitative* changes in behavior from that of earlier periods. Quantitative

Figure 1.6 The metamorphosis of an insect from one form to another illustrates a discontinuous process of development. The development of a butterfly from egg to larva to pupa to adult involves a set sequence of stages, each with a distinct organization.

changes, or changes in amounts, occur throughout the life span and give no evidence for stages. People gradually obtain more information, learn more words, gain experiences of all kinds. Qualitative shifts may also occur, such as the change from no language to meaningful speech and the shift from finding members of the opposite sex repulsive (or at least neutral) to finding them attractive. In some cases behavior changes dramatically over a short period of time, and we tend to call these qualitative changes, especially if the later behavior had not occurred earlier.

The evidence for qualitative changes in behavior is mixed. Often a closer look at the earlier "stage" will reveal antecedents of the later behavior that seemed to pop up, full-blown. In number concepts, for example, Rochel Gelman (1972) has shown that three- and four-year-olds possess many parts of later skills. Indeed, when small numbers are used, they can count accurately, and they are not fooled by changes in the length of an array of three to five chips. Although most children do not easily manipulate large numbers until they are in the early school grades, preschool children already have many of the component skills. What appears to be a dramatic qualitative shift to a new "stage" of logical reasoning probably involves some important quantitative changes as well.

The third requirement for a stage, that many behaviors change *simultaneously,* appears to be met only rarely in the life span. The case of adolescence is perhaps the strongest. In a period of three or four years, children become adult in several senses: They become reproductively mature, they grow rapidly at first and then nearly stop growing, their thinking reaches adult levels of logic, and they apply their reasoning skills to introspection about themselves in ways that few children do. The hormonal changes around puberty may play a major role in the simultaneous maturation of the sexual, physical, intellectual, and self-descriptive aspects of adolescence. In addition, the social experiences of adolescents are qualitatively different from those of children by virtue of the adolescents' new bodies and new interests. In the sense that many behaviors change simultaneously, therefore, adolescence may qualify as a stage. There is much less evidence for such coordinated shifts in behaviors at other ages.

The fourth requirement, that behavior characteristic of the new stage reaches its *maximum likelihood of occurrence* immediately after the stage begins, is not met at all. There are always quantitative changes in a person's ability to use new behavior. Both laboratory evidence (Lipsitt, 1967b) and common experience point to the different degrees to which children of different ages acquire new behavior. John Flavell (1971) refers to two classes of problems in deciding whether a child has a new kind of behavior. One class of problem refers to how easily the child can recall it and attempt to use it. The second class refers to the child's ability to use the new behavior effectively once he has recalled it. For example, the preschool children studied by Gelman (1972) displayed advanced number concepts when only small numbers were involved. With some difficulty they could recall the strategies and apply them effectively to arrays of three to five items. They could not handle the concepts, however, when larger quantities were involved. Although they possessed the strategies for some problems, they did not possess them for similar but more complex problems. Gelman's research indicates that such skills do not reach their maximum likelihood of occurrence immediately after they first appear in the child's behavior. The requirement that behaviors in a new stage reach maximum efficiency soon after they develop is probably never met.

The concept of stage in development, when strictly defined, is not the best way to view the life span, although in many cases it continues to be useful. Behavioral changes are not strictly qualitative, do not always occur simultaneously across many kinds of behavior, and do not reach maximum usefulness as soon as they appear. The stage concept is used by theorists like Erik Erikson and Jean Piaget to cover some parts of behavioral development, but their stage concepts, when applied rigidly, are contradicted by important recent evidence (Flavell, 1971). Most developmental psychologists are not considered strict stage theorists.

Phases

This book will use the concept of phases to describe periods of the life span. As you have already read, there is no one right way to divide up the life span. The ways in which periods have been conceived in the past and in other cultures differ considerably. In addition, it is impossible to use a strict stage concept of development. Thus, we have chosen to use five chronological periods or phases that roughly correspond to our cultural usage.

The *prenatal* phase begins at conception and ends at birth. *Infancy* begins at birth and continues until approximately age two. By the end of the second year, most children have begun to acquire language and symbolic thought. In addition, most adults think of two-year-olds as children rather than as infants,

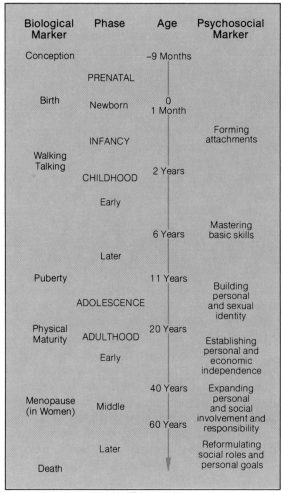

Biological Marker	Phase	Age	Psychosocial Marker
Conception		–9 Months	
	PRENATAL		
Birth	Newborn	0 1 Month	
	INFANCY		Forming attachments
Walking Talking			
	CHILDHOOD	2 Years	
	Early		
		6 Years	Mastering basic skills
	Later		
Puberty		11 Years	
	ADOLESCENCE		Building personal and sexual identity
Physical Maturity	ADULTHOOD	20 Years	
	Early		Establishing personal and economic independence
		40 Years	Expanding personal and social involvement and responsibility
Menopause (in Women)	Middle		
		60 Years	
	Later		Reformulating social roles and personal goals
Death			

Figure 1.7 The five phases of development reflect chronological divisions based on cultural usage. This drawing shows examples of biological and psychosocial markers, subperiods of development, and approximate age ranges that are likely to be considered characteristic of each phase.

which corresponds to the developmental shift from nonlinguistic to linguistic communication. Of course, other important changes occur in social and emotional behavior from infancy to childhood.

The third phase, *childhood,* begins an early period around age two and continues through late childhood at around age twelve. Puberty is usually accepted as the end of childhood and the beginning of adolescence. *Adolescence,* the fourth phase, is a less definite period because its end is not defined as well as the end of other phases of development. Adolescents are generally accepted as adults when they acquire adult economic and social roles. *Adulthood,* the fifth phase, generally begins in the late teens or early twenties and continues until death. This is clearly the longest phase, spanning early adulthood, the middle years, and late adulthood until death. There are many social and biological changes in adulthood, although the rate of development is much slower than in the earlier years.

These five phases are only one way to segment development, but such a division makes the discussion of concurrent behavioral changes more comprehensible. One should never forget that development is continuous across the life span. Although each person goes through periods of relatively rapid or slow development, his life shows a continuity from conception to death.

USES OF DEVELOPMENTAL PSYCHOLOGY

When a student enrolls in a course on developmental psychology, he may first want to know *how* people develop. He may want a description of how children and adults behave at different ages. The average person tends to think of developmental psychology as a source of data about average development: When should children know their colors? When does the adolescent growth spurt begin? What differences are there in the IQ scores of people from different ethnic and socioeconomic backgrounds? Does intelligence really decline as people age? Developmental psychology answers many questions about how development occurs.

More interesting than descriptive questions are questions that ask *why* development occurs as it does. Why do most children know primary-color names by kindergarten? (Why not earlier or later?) Why does the adolescent growth spurt begin and end so regularly? Why do people differ in IQ scores? And so forth.

As the field has matured, developmental psychologists have turned their attention to building theories of development and to testing their theories empirically.

To test the implications of a theory, developmental psychologists have used scientific methods, including laboratory experiments, field studies, educational interventions, and a multitude of other observational and experimental techniques. These methods will be explained in Chapter 3.

Questions about the hows and whys of development have given us a sound basis for describing and explaining much about development. This book relies heavily on the results of scientific studies of development, and it interprets these results in terms of various theoretical positions. This book is neither a long narrative of the changes in behavior that occur across the life span, nor is it an exposition on how to rear children or how to lead "the good life." As scientists, psychologists learned long ago that their primary mission is to provide sound and useful sets of information for consumers to evaluate rather than an arbitrary set of rules for them to follow. True, psychologists are always interested in and alert to the applications of psychological data and theories. Even so, they are more likely, for example, to discuss the effects of praise on a person's behavior than to tell employers that they must compliment their employees.

This book may well provide you with a new way of looking at the development of human behavior. It is easy to view lower organisms with detachment, for their behavior is removed from anything you have experienced. It is more difficult, at first, to look at the behavior of a human being in a similarly objective fashion. But a major message of psychology is that human behavior has its antecedents and its consequences, that there is a regularity and a degree of lawfulness in development. With appropriate analysis and objective study you should be able to discover why certain types of behavior occur and how conditions may influence later behavior. After reading this book you should no longer be content, for example, to ascribe aggressive behavior to meanness, but you should demand (and should be able to begin to formulate) a more penetrating analysis of why a person so often fights with others.

The consumers of information from developmental psychology are students, parents, teachers, pediatricians, social workers, government planners, and many others who need to understand how people's development can be enhanced or improved by life circumstances, how best to plan programs for the citizenry, young and old, and how to improve everyone's chances for optimum development. Parents face problems in the management and rearing of their own children. Teachers are confronted with difficulties in instructing their students. Pediatricians are more aware today of the relationship of behavior to physical problems in their young patients. Social workers must make decisions that affect the future successes of people in their charge. Government planners need to know what kinds of programs will best serve young children in day care, teen-agers in work-study programs, older adults in nursing care, and so forth.

Some questions about human development cannot be answered at present, but there is enough sound information and incisive theory for developmental

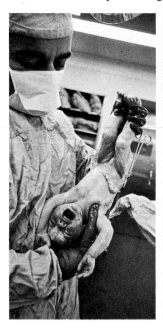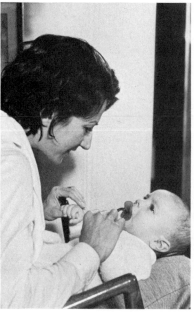

psychology to offer exciting possibilities to anyone interested in understanding and influencing the development of human behavior.

SUMMARY

1. In the twentieth century, we generally divide the life span into the prenatal period, infancy, childhood, adolescence, and adulthood. But societies with different social and economic systems have viewed the life span differently. The concept of a separate childhood emerged with the rise of the middle class; adolescence, with rising industrialization; and late adulthood, with increased life expectancy.

2. The field of developmental psychology attempts to reliably describe, to understand, and to explain changes in human behavior across the life span. Developmental psychologists construct theories, using information from psychology as well as from biology, sociology, and anthropology, to help them understand, predict, and explain human behavior.

3. Developmental psychologists are careful to use an appropriate level of explanation to explain a given behavior. They search for a complete explanation of behavior by studying behavior at different ages, behavioral changes as people grow older, environmental events that influence behavior, and variations among individuals, as well as by conducting research on nonhuman species and studying case histories of individuals. Replication studies are the best safeguard against accepting a chance finding as typical.

4. Development from infancy to adulthood involves orderly change that is directional, is largely cumulative, and involves increasing complexity and organization. Several concepts have been used to explain the relationship among developmental changes in behavior: sequences indicate that some behaviors precede others in a meaningfully related way; stages indicate that the organization of behavior is qualitatively different from one stage to the next; phases indicate that development is continuous across the life span and that the divisions are culturally determined.

5. Developmental psychologists' questions about the hows and whys of development have led to much useful information about the regularity and lawfulness of human development. Although some questions about human development cannot yet be answered, what is known offers insight into and understanding of many facets of human development.

SUGGESTED READINGS

Ariès, Philippe. *Centuries of Childhood: A Social History of Family Life.* Robert Baldick (tr.). New York: Vintage Books, 1965.

Bruner, Jerome S. "The Growth of Mind," *American Psychologist,* 20 (1965), 1007–1017.

Hall, Elizabeth. "Conversation with D. O. Hebb: Hocus-Pocus," *Psychology Today,* 3 (November 1969), 20–27.

Homans, George C. *The Nature of Social Science.* New York: Harcourt Brace Jovanovich, 1967.

Watson, Robert I. "History of the Study of the Child," in R. E. Bergman (ed.), *Children's Behavior.* New York: Exposition Press, 1968.

Figure 1.8 Developmental psychology provides knowledge of the many changes that take place during each phase of life. This information is of great value to, and widely used by, all those who have an interest in understanding and furthering human development.

All psychological views of human development are attempts to describe and explain the processes and influences involved in the shaping of human life from one point in time to another.

2
THEORIES OF DEVELOPMENT

A couple is waiting in line to buy tickets to a concert when two adolescents push in front of them. "I'd like to talk to the parents of those kids," says the man, "and tell them how to raise children"; the woman responds, "Boys are just like that." Then the woman behind them pipes up: "These teen-agers are all alike. They're like animals."

Each of us has a personal theory of how and why people behave as they do. Unfortunately, we rarely agree in our explanations of human behavior, and there is no easy way to decide which of us (if any) is correct. Private theories of development are derived from our personal experiences (which may be radically different from the experiences of others), the books and magazines we read, the motion pictures and television programs we watch, and the common assumptions of our culture, which may be contradictory in themselves and different from the assumptions of other cultures. Furthermore, what passes for explanation in casual conversation would not usually satisfy the scientific requirements for an explanation.

Our private, naive "theories" of development are not really theories in a formal sense. They are often internally inconsistent, and they are seldom specified clearly enough to generate testable predictions. The statement "Boys are just like that" does not readily suggest any ways of testing the truth or falsity of the statement or of finding out whether the personal "theory" is correct.

In this chapter we will discuss the various models of man that have influenced theories of human development. We will explore the major types of developmental theories and learn the common assumptions that theories within each type share. We will investigate theories that assume that the environment is all-powerful, theories that rely on the evolutionary history of the human species as the reigning force, and theories that spring from Sigmund Freud's insights into human motivations. Finally, we will show that, whereas no one group of theories can explain the development of all human behavior, each can make a useful contribution.

PHILOSOPHICAL MODELS OF MAN

Naive and scientific observers, past and present theorists—indeed, everyone—make assumptions, often unstated, about the nature of human development. In developmental psychology, these assumptions frequently focus on the ease or difficulty of changing behavior (*malleability*), on the *active versus passive* role of man in his own development, on the *innate* goodness or evil of humanity, and on the *relationship of child to adult behavior.*

Malleable Man?

Extreme positions have always existed on the issue of malleability, or how much human behavior can change in response to environmental changes. Theorists such as William McDougall (1923) believed that behavior results from many instincts that pre-ordain the development of such traits as aggression and competition. According to this view, environmental influences could only increase or decrease the frequency of certain traits. Thus, aggressive acts are bound to appear because of man's "aggressive instinct."

Other theorists, such as B.F. Skinner (1974) and Albert Bandura (1969a), emphasize the extreme malleability of development. They believe that an adult is primarily the product of his environment and that, for example, his family, his friends, and his society begin teaching him to be aggressive or competitive while he is still a baby in his crib. Learning, not instinct or maturation, is the key to development of behavior.

Still other theorists, such as Jean Piaget (1970), Erik Erikson (1963), and Heinz Werner (1957), have taken intermediate positions on the issue of malleability. They see the environment as important in human development, but only in the context of a person's ability to organize his experience.

Active or Passive Man?

The view of man as an active agent in his own development contrasts with the other view of him as a passive recipient of stimulation from the environment. The active view emphasizes the human being as a seeker of stimulation, as a filter, organizer, interpreter, and storer of experiences. Contemporary developmentalists such as Jean Piaget and his followers subscribe to this view.

The developing person is frequently seen as a more or less passive recipient of environmental stimulation by learning and behavioral theorists in the traditions of B.F. Skinner, Clark Hull, and Ivan Pavlov. According to this behavioral-learning tradition, among the ways a person's behavior can change are through association of a stimulus with a response, reward for his actions, and imitation of another's actions.

Naturally Good or Evil?

Another set of important assumptions about the nature of man concerns his innately good or evil nature. Instinct theories and Freudian psychoanalytic theory (Freud, 1905) are among those that have emphasized the "animal" drives of sex and aggression that supposedly motivate much human behavior. If children are basically wild, they must be tamed. Therefore, parents and society must train children to express their instinctive urges in socially acceptable forms. It is socially acceptable to "tell someone off"; it is not all right to assault and mutilate a person who angers you.

Other theorists have stressed that human beings are basically good and that society corrupts them. Jean Jacques Rousseau (1762) believed that man is peaceful and compassionate until turned from his good nature by an evil society. Rousseau, an eighteenth-century French thinker, is the philosophical forefather of John Dewey (1916), the American educational philosopher who stressed that children are basically curious, exploratory creatures who seek to learn above all else. Contemporary proponents of open schools (Kohl, 1968; Kozol, 1970) follow Rousseau and Dewey in their beliefs about the wisdom and basic goodness of the child.

Miniature or Inferior Adults?

Finally, the relationship of the child's behavior to adult behavior is an issue in developmental theories. As noted in Chapter 1, in earlier times children were often seen as miniature adults. They were assumed to be quantitatively but not qualitatively different from adults. In recent years, others have seen children as deficient adults, less able to think, feel, or understand than mature human beings are. Holding up adult standards as the goal of development, some psychologists charted children's intelligence according to "mental age." By this measure children were usually viewed as less adequate than adults, as not quite all there.

Cognitive theorists such as Jean Piaget (1952b, 1970) and Jerome Bruner (1964), who describe intellectual development, and Roger Brown (1973), who describes early language behavior, have proposed that child behavior must be understood in its own right. They assume that child behavior is or-

Figure 2.1 Stills from *The Wild Child*, a film about Jean Itard's efforts to civilize and educate Victor, one of a large number of so-called wild or feral children discovered and described from time to time throughout the recorded history of man. Although such children have often been viewed as a test case of man's basic nature and development, scientists generally have found that accounts of a feral child's background and prior development are suspect and unreliable.

ganized in a different way from adult behavior and that it is neither correct nor profitable to compare children directly to adults. Although young children do not understand the world in adult terms, they do have effective but different ways of gaining information and of making things happen. A baby who cries to be fed can be just as effective in getting food as an adult who says "Please" and "Thank you."

These assumptions about human nature are combined in various ways by contemporary developmental psychologists. Present theories of development fall into three broad categories that may be labeled in a number of ways. We will call them behavior-learning theories, evolved-primate theories, and psychodynamic theories. Each set of theories is based on different assumptions about human beings, and each generates testable hypotheses about the development of behavior. They manage to exist simultaneously largely by avoiding one another.

BEHAVIOR-LEARNING THEORIES

Many learning and behavior theories tend to see the newborn baby as a relatively empty organism prepared to react to stimulation from the environment but with few organizing properties of his own. His behavior develops gradually as he receives and processes input from the environment.

Most developmental psychologists who subscribe to a learning theory see development as a continuous process over the life span. New behaviors are learned partly because they are rewarded. For example, children learn to imitate their parents because parents reward attempts to behave in socially acceptable ways. Children learn the names that language gives to objects; they learn to count, to follow directions, and to acquire thousands of other behaviors that are part of "growing up." As adults, they continue to learn new responses to the environment—new work skills, new information about the social world. Development, then, is the result of cumulative learning. The learning process has no developmental stages.

In general, unless there is definite evidence to the contrary, most behavior-learning theories assume that all classes of behavior are learned. However, allowance is made for possible internal, maturational changes in people that affect the responses they are capable of giving. Obviously, a baby of six months cannot walk no matter how much encouragement or practice he gets. There is a definite limit to his ability to learn to walk, and behavior-learning theories do not deny this. On the other hand, most would assume that experiences such as being held up on his feet and being rewarded for attempts to walk play a part in the baby's eventual mastery of the skill.

The Learning Tradition

Learning theories see the human being as an organism that has learned to behave in uniquely human ways. In this tradition, most of what a person becomes is a matter of what he has experienced or learned, and his learning begins even before he leaves the womb.

Most behavior or learning theories concentrate on observable behaviors and avoid inner events that cannot be observed. Some theories, for example, consider mental concepts such as love, maturity, intelligence, and personality as meaningless apart from the behaviors that define them and the situations in which they occur. They point out that it is not useful to say that a child is dependent. One must always specify the kind of behaviors that are called dependent and the situations in which particular dependent behaviors do and do not occur. This approach has provided a useful corrective to the vague, unscientific use of mental concepts that characterized some earlier theories.

Why, in the behavior-learning theory view, do people behave at all? Some earlier views assumed that all motivation to behave was based on drives to reduce tension by acquiring food, water, sexual satisfaction, and so forth. When applied to human behavior, these drives include the needs for security, approval, and other social rewards. Recently, some views have expanded motivation to include curiosity and exploratory drives. In such views, boredom may lead to a state of arousal that is rewarded by the organism's explorations (Berlyne, 1960). For example, many animals, as well as human beings, will give required responses just for the pleasure of exploring a new place or seeing interesting events. It is generally recognized that food and water are not the only effective rewards for human behavior (most children are not kept hungry and thirsty); praise and such symbolic rewards as money and tokens work just as well. Even the correct answer is a reward in problem-solving situations.

Over the years, adherents to learning theories have come to agree that at least two major types of processes are important in understanding how people learn. One process is called classical conditioning, and the other, operant conditioning.

Classical Conditioning

Studies of classical, or respondent, conditioning grew out of the work of Ivan Pavlov (1927) in Russia.

Pavlov demonstrated that certain behaviors, which he called **reflexes,** were responses to external stimuli. There are two kinds of reflexes: unconditioned reflexes and conditioned reflexes. **Unconditioned reflexes** are responses that—before any learning takes place—a person naturally pairs with a specific stimulus, such as blinking one's eye when a puff of air strikes the eyeball or salivating when food is placed in one's mouth. **Conditioned reflexes** are established when one associates a neutral stimulus, such as a bell or light, with the unconditioned stimulus. If the conditioned stimulus occurs repeatedly just before the unconditioned stimulus, a person comes to respond to the conditioned stimulus much as he originally did only to the unconditioned stimulus.

Emotions are particularly subject to classical conditioning. For example, a child can come to fear the sight of an object that is associated with something that earlier caused him pain or startled him. It is a common observation that, by the time he is a year old, an infant begins to cry when he sees a pediatrician who has previously been paired with painful injections. A child who has been bitten by a dog may come to fear the house or the whole city block in which the attack occurred. Furthermore, the child may generalize his fear. The infant who has been given injections by the pediatrician may come to fear all people in white coats or all rooms that look like a doctor's office. The child bitten by a dog may come to fear all four-legged creatures.

Operant Conditioning

A basic learning mechanism that is associated with B.F. Skinner (1938) is operant conditioning, also called instrumental conditioning. It changes the frequency of a response as a result of **reinforcement.** For example, when a child receives a reward like candy or social approval immediately after he responds in a certain way, he is likely to repeat that response. The candy or praise acts as reinforcement.

If the child gets no reward, or if he is punished, he will not repeat the response so often. Responses that are not reinforced decrease in frequency or may even be eliminated (**extinguished**). Responses that are punished appear to be extinguished, but they are only suppressed; once the punishing stimuli are gone, the response may reappear.

For example, a father who wants his daughter to quit chewing her nails can use operant-conditioning techniques. He might decrease the frequency of nail-biting by offering praise when the child goes without biting her nails for ten minutes. Gradually, as

Figure 2.2 A comparison of the major concepts and terms, emphasis, and areas of application of three viewpoints representative of behavior-learning theories.

BEHAVIOR-LEARNING THEORIES

B. F. Skinner

Major Concepts and Terms

Operant Behavior: behavior determined by its effect on the environment
Functional Analysis: linking a behavior to the precise conditions that determine it
Contingency: the relationship between a behavior and its consequences
Reinforcement: any stimulus that increases the likelihood of a behavior occurring

Emphasis

Concern with overt behavior—what the individual does, how he behaves
Determination of precise environmental conditions or situational events that control or determine behavior
Rejection of inferred dynamics or other internal motivational forces
Application of basic conditioning principles to complex behaviors

Areas of Application

Programed instruction, self-control, control of institutions, social and environmental engineering

Albert Bandura

Major Concepts and Terms

Observational Learning: learning without any direct rewards or reinforcements
Imitation: learning and performance of a behavior as a consequence of observing another person
Model: a person who provides information about a behavior by performing that behavior
Acquisition Versus Performance: the distinction between learning a behavior and its actual commission

Emphasis

Concern with overt behavior—what the individual does, how he behaves
Consideration of internal, cognitive events only in relation to their behavioral referents
Focus on learning in the absence of overt performance and reinforcement
Concern with complex current social behavior, such as skill acquisition

Areas of Application

Acquisition of social behaviors, effects of television, learned aggression and fear, therapeutic intervention

Todd Risley

Major Concepts and Terms

Applied Behavior Analysis: the experimental study of the real-life conditions that determine behavior
Multiple Baseline Design: experimental observation of several behaviors while influencing only a few of those behaviors
Incidental Teaching Procedure: a method using normal activities (such as play) for learning
Living Environment: the total stimulus situation in which an individual lives and learns

Emphasis

Concern with overt behavior—what the individual does, how he behaves
Experimental examination of behavior in real-life (applied) settings
Development of methods, techniques, and technology for change over time
Manipulation, design, and modification of the environment to increase its effectiveness in determining behavior

Areas of Application

Teaching language, teaching social behavior, increasing effectiveness of school environment, designing more effective learning environments

she regularly goes for longer periods without chewing her nails, the father might offer praise at longer intervals. He must also ignore any nail-biting that he sees in order to allow the objectionable behavior to become extinguished. He should not punish the child for nail-biting, because she may only suppress her biting in her parent's presence and continue it when he is out of sight.

The application of operant principles has been remarkably successful in changing many kinds of behavior, such as overeating or disrupting the classroom, and in teaching the retarded to read. Developmental psychologists who wish to use this technique search for the functional relationships that exist between responses and stimuli (including reinforcers). The functional or experimental analysis of behavior also concentrates on how various ways of providing reinforcement change the frequency of observable responses, regardless of what mediating or other internal links may or may not occur.

These timetables for reinforcing behavior are called **schedules of reinforcement.** A child who is reinforced for each correct response is on a schedule of **continuous reinforcement.** But once a behavior is established, such a schedule is not necessary. Numerous studies have shown that one can maintain responses just as effectively, or more so, on schedules of **partial reinforcement** of two types: **interval reinforcement,** in which a person is reinforced for his first response after a specified time has passed, and **ratio reinforcement,** in which a person is reinforced only after he has responded a certain number of times. These schedules of reinforcement have real-life examples: Some children are on an interval schedule of reinforcement (they must do their chores, but they get an allowance only once each week), whereas other children are on a ratio schedule (they get paid after they have completed a certain number of chores).

Different schedules of reinforcement have somewhat different effects on the rate of responding. For example, continuous reinforcement keeps a person responding at a steady, moderate rate. Under interval reinforcement, a person tends to respond only at the end of the interval. On a ratio schedule, a person tends to respond at a relatively high constant rate to get the reward that comes after a set number of responses.

Another important procedure in operant learning concerns the development of new behavior. Some responses are infrequently given. However, by rewarding **successive approximations,** or behavior that resembles more and more closely the final desired response, it is possible to shape behavior. Using this technique, for example, some experimenters have taught pigeons to play ping-pong and to guide missiles (Skinner, 1960), and others have taught various cognitive, social, and language skills to children and adults (Semb, 1972).

Extensions of Learning Principles

Psychologists who apply behavior-learning theories to development have directed their efforts toward analyzing a variety of developmental tasks. Tasks in concept and social learning illustrate how learning principles may be extended to these areas.

Concept Learning.   Many conceptual tasks, such as spelling skills in English, are to a considerable extent based on arbitrary associations that must be learned. But there is more to learning than simple associations. Once a person learns a given task, he can often solve similar problems by a process called **stimulus generalization;** that is, he responds to similar situations with the same responses he learned earlier. But a child can also learn to learn. Instead of learning merely to respond in the same way in similar situations, the child often learns a strategy that will help him find the correct answer in different situations. In other words, he **transfers** what he learns in one situation to the next.

Learning strategies and stimulus generalization are both processes by which learning goes beyond the stimulus situation. There are, however, even more

Figure 2.3 Concept learning often involves the development of a particular understanding or strategy. In this example, after observing her teacher use a stethoscope with a rabbit, the child transfers her understanding of the stethoscope's use from a breathing rabbit to a piano that is being played.

29

complex ways in which people learn. It is clear from many studies that human beings "think" about their environments when given a chance to do so. Many developmental and learning psychologists, therefore, assume the existence of **mediating mechanisms,** or internal cues, to account for the internal processing that people do when faced with a problem. Being asked to choose between two items in a discrimination task is a stimulus that evokes a response in a person. His first response of looking may then act as a stimulus for an internal response, such as using the label "square," which leads to choosing the square, which gets him a reward. Older children and adults can learn complex strategies such as "Two left, two right, two left, and so on," and "Small blue triangle, not large or red or nontriangular figure." Not all mediated strategies are verbal, but verbal labels provide an easy way for older children and adults to increase the likelihood of giving the correct response.

Social Learning. A number of concepts and principles from behavior-learning theory, commonly referred to as social-learning theory, have made a major contribution in describing and explaining the development of personality characteristics and social behavior.

For example, the concept of **imitation** plays a key role in most social-learning accounts of human development. Many studies have now been carried out that demonstrate, for example, the increasing resemblance of the child's social behavior to that of adult models.

Some researchers have discovered that if a child is rewarded for imitating a model, the child will tend to imitate the model even when the child is not rewarded (Bandura, 1969b). If the child sees that the model is rewarded for its actions, he will tend to copy the behavior.

Over the years there have been several different but supplementary social-learning interpretations regarding the role and importance of imitation. Some time ago, for example, Neal Miller and John Dollard (1941) proposed that the nurturance from parents becomes the motivating force for the child's imitations. That is, as parents satisfy the child's needs for food, warmth, and affection, they become associated with the satisfaction of those needs and take on reinforcing properties themselves. Because the parents' behaviors are reinforcing, the child imitates them to reward himself. Jerome Kagan (1958) and John Whiting (1960) pointed out somewhat later that parents also have more power and control more possessions than the child does and that the child envies their status and therefore copies his parents in the hope that his imitations will enable him to acquire their influence and status. More recently, Albert Bandura and Richard Walters (1963) have stressed that children can learn new responses from merely watching a model and that a child also is likely to imitate any observed behavior that he sees rewarded.

In general, most developmental psychologists who adhere to this kind of theory view the growth of new behavior through imitation as a continuous proc-

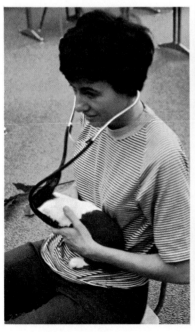

ess; they see no qualitative shifts in development. If the child can give the response at all, one presumably can selectively reward it so that it will occur in new situations with new associations. According to social-learning theory, such processes as these produce most personality characteristics and social behaviors.

EVOLVED-PRIMATE THEORIES

The group of theories loosely classified under the label "the evolved primate" view human development from an evolutionary perspective. Man, as a primate (a class shared with chimpanzees and other apes), has evolved to behave in uniquely human ways. Just as the internal organs and the external limbs have evolved to certain forms, so human behavior has characteristic patterns.

The Interactionist Tradition

Evolved-primate theorists all recognize the necessary *interactions* that must occur between the developing person and his environment. The present state of his development always depends on his internal structures (which result from past maturation and experience) and on what is available to him in his environment. Development is strongly cumulative but not continuous. These are stage theories of development.

Evolutionary theorists also recognize that people are more likely to respond in certain ways than in others. Evolutionary history strongly influences these probabilities. For example, people ordinarily learn to speak, whereas chimps do not. At any particular age, people are likely to learn in some ways but not in others. As Chapter 14 will show, it is difficult to get an eight-year-old to think abstractly about impossible propositions. If you ask him, "What would happen if the world were flat?" he will likely respond, "But the world is not flat." An adolescent is potentially capable of reeling off the hypothetical consequences of a flat world. In other words, some types of responses are more likely at each phase of development.

According to evolved-primate theories, behavior at each phase of development is uniquely organized. Development is not a continuous process from conception to death but one marked by shifts from one way of thinking and behaving to another. From an adult perspective, preschool children often explain concepts in amusing ways. A four-year-old may believe that fire is alive because it moves. His concept of life is based on the characteristic of self-initiated movement. Adults know that movement is one

property of life but that movement alone is not sufficient. A closer examination of the young child's thought in Chapter 11 will show that he possesses a coherent logic—his is not adult logic, but he has an organized way of dealing with the world. This recognition of children as different from adults is a distinguishing mark of evolutionary theories.

In the last fifty years, two important theorists have emerged to represent the evolved-primate position: Jean Piaget (1952b, 1970b) and Noam Chomsky (1972). Piaget's theory centers on the development of intelligence; Chomsky's, on language. Both theories are structuralist views of human behavior. Piaget's **genetic epistemology** has produced an enormous surge of research in recent years. Epistemology is the study of knowledge—how we know what we know. The term "genetic" here means developmental. Piaget's theory covers the development of intelligence (ways of knowing) over the life span. Chomsky's theory of language has also led to a great deal of research. His theory deals with the human ability to acquire a language and to generate regular but unique utterances. The rules that people use to make sentences and how they acquire these rules are the major concerns of his theory.

Piaget's Theory

Piaget's theory gives a meaningful continuity to the development of human understanding, and it has strongly influenced much research in the field of perceptual and intellectual development. These topics will be considered in detail in Chapters 7, 11, and 14.

For Piaget, all knowledge comes from action. For example, the baby acts on objects around him—feels, turns, bangs, mouths them—and grows in his knowledge of those objects through structuring his experience. The baby's knowledge grows neither from the objects themselves nor from the baby himself but from the interaction of the two and the consequent links between actions and objects.

Schemes. Piaget sees the child's understanding of his world (as opposed to the mere recording of it) as arising from the coordination of actions and the interrelationships of objects: He is a **constructionist.** Both relationships—of actions and of objects—are the baby's constructions of reality, not something given by the actions or the objects alone. For example, an infant can throw a ball and roll it; he can apply those same actions to an orange. He learns that both objects roll (are round) but that, when thrown, the ball bounces and the orange goes "thud." From his

EVOLVED-PRIMATE THEORIES

Jean Piaget

Major Concepts and Terms

Constructionism: the individual's understanding of the world, which arises from patterns of relationships or schemes between objects and actions

Adaptation: the tendency for an organism to maintain equal balance between the processes of assimilation (absorbing and organizing experiences around existing activity patterns) and accommodation (modifying existing activity patterns to allow incorporation of new knowledge)

Stages of Intellectual Development: periods that are not continuous and that are distinctly different over life

Scheme: a pattern of mental action that helps the individual understand the world

Emphasis

Primary concern with understanding how we know what we know; focus on cognitive or mental structure

Belief that knowledge grows from the interaction between the genetically determined cognitive structure of organism and the environment

Emphasis on limitations caused by cognitive structural development

De-emphasis of environmentally produced changes and individual differences

Areas of Application

Education, intelligence, problem solving, communication

Jerome Bruner

Major Concepts and Terms

Representation: the translation of experience into an understanding of the world

Enactive Mode: the representation of objects and past events in terms of their appropriate actions

Iconic Mode: the representation of objects and past events in terms of images that summarize and represent action

Symbolic Mode: the representation of objects and past events in terms of linguistic symbols

Emphasis

Concern with thinking

Belief that knowledge grows out of the interaction between maturational development and environment

Attention to environmentally produced changes in the development of capabilities

Focus on individual's capabilities, not his limitations

Areas of Application

Education, instruction, design and construction of instructional materials, problem solving

Noam Chomsky

Major Concepts and Terms

Linguistic Competence: the system of linguistic knowledge that underlies speech behavior but is not realized in a direct or simple way in performance

Transformational Grammar: a system of rules, presumed to be internalized by the user, that relates underlying structures of the language to surface structures

Surface Structure: the grammatical arrangement of a spoken sentence

Underlying Structure: the underlying grammatical arrangement of a sentence, which plays a central role in determining the meaning of a sentence

Emphasis

Concern with language, focusing on innate, fixed structure common to all languages and on how we learn and use language

Belief that rules of transformation are critical to language development

Rejection of associational learning of language

De-emphasis of environmental factors and imitation in learning language

Areas of Application

Communication, language training, linguistics, artificial languages

Figure 2.4 A comparison of the major concepts and terms, emphasis, and areas of application of three viewpoints representative of evolved-primate theories.

apparently ordinary and simple actions on objects, an infant comes to know some effects of his actions and some properties of objects. He also learns to coordinate his actions—he cannot throw and roll the same object simultaneously, but he can finger it first and then throw or roll it. Action patterns, which Piaget calls **schemes,** are built up and coordinated throughout development. In the infant, they are like concepts without words.

Older children and adults have more internalized action schemes, which they use to gain and structure their knowledge. Later schemes can be mental actions. Although the actions of thinking are internal, they derive from earlier concrete experiments that the infant performs on the world. Mental arithmetic replaces the physical act of counting; logical sequences of thought like "If . . . then" statements replace the younger child's concrete manipulations of cause-effect relations. An older person need no longer literally try out the solution to every problem.

For example, most adults have come to understand the principle of gravity: When released from an elevated position, objects fall. But a ten-month-old baby explores gravity by dropping bits of dinner from the highchair tray and watching intently as the green bean hits the floor. (He also discovers that cups fall, spoons fall, cookies fall.) Fortunately, a baby's scheme of dropping objects in space soon becomes coordinated with many objects, so that he no longer creates the same mess over and over again. Furthermore, dropping food is antithetical to eating it, so that

a hungry baby comes to recognize that eating and dropping the same object are not compatible schemes.

Assimilation and Accommodation. In Piaget's theory, children's thinking develops through two processes: assimilation and accommodation. **Assimilation** refers to the incorporation of new knowledge through the use of existing schemes. For example, a child can bang a large variety of objects and assimilate to his existing scheme whether or not "banging" is a primary attribute of each object. Some objects make loud noises, others, soft; some break, others squeak; and so forth. **Accommodation** refers to the modification of the child's existing schemes to incorporate new knowledge that does not fit them.

The processes of assimilation and accommodation always work together in complementary fashion. To assimilate is to use what one already knows how to do; to accommodate is to acquire a new way of doing something. Both processes continue to function throughout the life span. For example, in the United States we are being asked to convert our thinking to the metric system. In essence, we are being asked to restructure our existing schemes (accommodation). After we have learned the metric units of weight, volume, and linear measure, we will have to assimilate much of what we knew under the old scheme to the new one. Does one wear a sweater outdoors at 30° C? (No.) Is 80 kilometers per hour too fast a speed to drive on a freeway? (Probably not.) Is $3.50 per kilogram too much to pay for pork chops? (No.) In

Figure 2.5 This sequence, viewed from a Piagetian perspective, illustrates the complementary and ongoing processes of assimilation and accommodation. The infant applies (assimilates) a grasping scheme to reach the toy. She then accommodates that scheme, turning the toy so that it will fit through the bars of her crib.

Figure 2.6 Illustration of Piaget's three major stages of cognitive development. (*top*) During the sensorimotor period, the infant manipulates objects but does not understand their function or the basis of his actions. (*middle*) During the first of two periods of representational thought, the preoperational period, the child comes to mentally represent people, objects, and events when these are absent. He understands, for example, that an airplane flies, and he can imitate its flight. (*bottom left*) During the second period of representational thought, the concrete-operational period, the child increasingly classifies objects and events into categories and becomes able to coordinate his thinking in terms of such categories. He now, for example, can assemble the components of a kite into a complete and functional unit. (*bottom right*) During the formal-operational period, the individual becomes capable of more formal thought involving hypothetical possibilities and several alternative reasons for an event. He now, for example, may understand the principles of the functioning of an airplane and perhaps use this understanding to design a new type of airplane.

other words, any new way of acquiring knowledge will have to be applied to what we have already learned in a different way under other schemes.

At any given time, the developing person can change his cognitive structures only to a limited extent. There must always be some continuity. The balance, or equilibrium, between assimilation and accommodation changes over the life span in the direction of greater balance. **Equilibration** is the most general developmental principle in Piaget's theory; it states that the organism always tends toward biological and psychological balance and that development is a progressive approximation to an ideal state of equilibrium that it never fully achieves. A child's equilibrium at any one stage may be upset by external events such as new information he cannot readily assimilate or by internal processes that bring him to a new "readiness" to accommodate. In both cases, the child's previous temporary equilibrium is upset, and development advances to a new, higher level of organization.

Stages. According to Piaget's theory, intellectual development goes through a series of stages, and the organization of behavior is qualitatively different at each stage. Although, as you may recall from Chapter 1, a strict stage theory may be indefensible, it is useful when applied to what Piaget calls "the major structures." The two conditions that Piaget sets for his stage theory are: (1) stages must be defined to guarantee a constant order of succession, and (2) the definition must allow for the progressive development of mental structures without relying totally on either heredity or environment.

Piaget proposes three major stages of intellectual development: a **sensorimotor** period, a period of **representational** thought (subdivided into **preoperational** and **concrete-operational** periods), and a **formal-operational,** or propositional, period. The sensorimotor period, which is discussed in Chapter 7, begins at birth and extends through the first two years of life. The period of representational thought begins around the age of two with the preoperational stage, when children start to record experiences symbolically. This period is discussed in Chapter 11. Beginning at about seven or eight, children enter the concrete-operational period, discussed in Chapter 14, when they begin to understand new kinds of logical operations involving reversible transformations. By eleven or twelve, young adolescents begin to develop a formal logic that consists of propositions ("If . . . then" statements); at this time they enter the formal-

operational period, which is covered in both Chapter 14 and Chapter 18.

Chomsky's Theory

Noam Chomsky's theory of language attempts to account for the fact that every human being speaks in unique sentences that in his view adhere to a deep, underlying structure common to all human language. Many developmental psychologists have used Chomsky's theory to explain the rapid mastery of language that takes place during a child's first four years. Their work is discussed in detail in Chapters 8 and 12.

Chomsky's theory proposes that language is based on a generative or productive process, not on an imitative one. Children and adults use rules to generate sentences. Childhood rules are different from adult rules, and it is not clear how children acquire them. When a two-year-old wants to signal his wish to leave the house, he may say "Go bye-bye." If his mother says, "Do you want to go bye-bye in the car?" the toddler can respond "Bye-bye car," but he probably cannot repeat the whole adult utterance. Note that the toddler's choice of words to express his version of the adult sentence is selective. He uses those words that carry the action meaning of the adult sentence. He does not say "You . . . in the . . . ," a phrase that carries little of the original meaning. Children's sentences usually have action words, objects, and subjects of the action before they have prepositions or adverbs. Chomsky recognizes that children do imitate some aspects of adult speech, particularly vocabulary, but he maintains that children's speech can never be accounted for without assuming that their brains are predisposed to discover the abstract grammatical rules of language.

Psycholinguists have noticed the amazing speed with which children become proficient speakers of their native languages; in about two years, from ages two to four, the average child develops from the one- or two-word utterance to almost complete command of adult grammar. The rapidity of this process suggests that a maturational process underlies language acquisition.

The issue of maturation of "innate" potential for language has been hotly debated. Chomsky and many psycholinguists maintain that the human brain has evolved a capacity for language, which matures rapidly between birth and three or four years. Thus, children learn whatever language they hear during this period. Of course, if a child is totally deaf or isolated from human speech, he will not acquire spoken language. In the psycholinguistic view, language acquisition depends on both the underlying maturation of the brain and on exposure to a language.

Because speech is acquired so rapidly during the preschool period, Chomsky has challenged the behavior-learning account of language acquisition as too cumbersome and time-consuming. Most of the structuralist–behavior-learning battle has been waged over how a child acquires the rules for constructing utterances. Chomsky and other structuralists have argued convincingly that the ability to acquire grammar is part of man's evolved capacity for language, which matures rapidly in early childhood. They generally acknowledge, however, that many vocabulary items are acquired through learning principles, because words are arbitrary associations between sounds and objects. Learning principles can also account for the acquisition of meaning. Both cognitive and learning theories agree that word meaning comes from experience within contexts that give meaning to a verbal concept. The discussions of language development in Chapters 8 and 12 rely on both theories.

The New Ethologists

In the past few years, a small group of dedicated naturalists who have sought to observe development in its real-life settings have become an emerging force in developmental psychology. Their methods come from behavioral biology; their ideas, from Darwin. The new ethologists translate biological evolutionary concepts into behavioral terms to study human development. The trend toward ethological-genetic thinking is increasing at a rapid rate. As we will see at various points throughout this book, observational techniques, so rigorously developed by ethologists, are gaining favor in all areas of developmental psychology.

These new ethologists are primarily interested in the role that behaviors play in survival and reproductive success. **Adaptation** is a key concept; man (and every other species) has evolved in environmental contexts that are as important to understand as the nature of man himself. The necessity for man to be in harmony with his environment leads ethologists of human behavior to look at development as adaptation. They see social behaviors as related to group cohesion, to the competition for mates, to survival of the young, and so forth. Intelligence is a prime mechanism for adaptation; those individuals who can solve problems in their world are more likely to leave offspring for the next generation.

One of the most useful ethological notions is that of **releasing stimuli,** those events that regularly evoke certain behavior in all members of a species, which can explain regularities in mating patterns, aggression, appeasement, and some other typical behaviors. For example, observers have noted that children's play groups have "dominance hierarchies" much like troops of baboons or chimpanzees. Usually, the children in the group agree on who is "toughest," who is "smartest," and so forth. By the time children are six or seven, their groups are often structured with well-established roles of leader and follower. The followers seldom challenge the leaders, but when

Figure 2.7 Dominance hierarchies are patterns of interaction based on power considerations, which characterize the structure of groups of many species. Such hierarchies may be more or less resistant to change depending on the activities of the group and other features of its organization.

they do there are ritualized ways to settle the issue, short of physical combat. These descriptions also apply to baboon troops in the wild. The new ethologists have noted the remarkable similarities in the social behaviors of man and his nearest primate relatives (N. Jones, 1972).

Courtship and greeting behaviors also show apparently universal ritualized aspects. Irenäus Eibl-Eibesfeldt (1970) has studied such behavior extensively in groups around the world. He has discovered amazing similarities in the facial expressions that people use; for example, in flirtatious greetings by females, the eyebrows go up, the head tilts, the gaze lowers, and the eyelids drop. No matter which cultural tradition a woman comes from, she seems to display this form of greeting to the opposite sex. Both sexes usually employ the eyes and eyebrows in greeting other people, no matter where they live.

And no matter where they live, all human beings respond to cuteness in babies and baby animals by wanting to pick them up and cuddle them. What makes baby forms of a species "cute"? Young animals are cute because they have relatively large heads, particularly foreheads, and foreshortened facial features. The toy industry takes advantage of this to make cute dolls with very small features embedded in large heads and small bodies. In other species, the baby forms elicit caretaking from adults, whereas adult forms do not. In human beings, the usual adult response to babies is also affectionate. Perhaps cuteness is a releasing stimulus for human caretaking as well, and perhaps human beings have evolved the response to cuteness because it improves the chances of adequate infant care and survival (Lorenz, 1943).

Jerome Bruner (1972) has speculated on the uses of the long period of immaturity in human development. Human educability is a prime species characteristic. The baby and child are easily taught many skills, and they yearn to explore and to learn. Play is an important way in which the young practice skills without suffering adult consequences, as when they play house or doctor or soldier or any adult role. Evolution has guaranteed that during the years between birth and adulthood, children will want to learn the many skills required of adults who will survive and leave offspring. According to Bruner, language, playfulness, curiosity, and the need to master one's environment appear to be evolved characteristics that make human development what it is.

In general, then, the evolved-primate theories suggest that behavior grows out of biological development. Human behavior is the end product of man's evolutionary history. The structure of behavior is inherent in genetic-biological development; the development of behavior occurs in interaction with the environment.

PSYCHODYNAMIC THEORIES

Most psychodynamic theories discuss and analyze human development in terms of various confrontations between the growing individual and the demands of his social world. They stress how the individual must accommodate to society while obtaining gratification for his basic drives. Most also emphasize that the child gradually develops a sense of self, an identity against which to judge his own behavior.

As a group, psychodynamic theorists have centered their attention on personality development. Their concern has been to understand and explain the development of both rational and irrational feelings and behavior. To some extent, all psychodynamic theories have tried to account for human development by looking for early experiences, usually emotional, that may influence later behavior.

Psychodynamic theories are generally concerned with inner development and view man as motivated by various internal and external forces. These forces in turn are considered to be determining factors in human behavior. Some psychodynamic theories view these internal forces as benign or positive growth forces that can be either impeded or facilitated by environmental events. In other psychodynamic theories, the internal forces are irrational or nongrowth forces, which must be controlled by various socialization practices and cultural standards.

The Self-Social Tradition

The idea that there is a "me" or a "self" intuitively makes sense to most people. In most psychodynamic theories, the concept of a self is a major construct. It manages to capture each person's feeling of realness and uniqueness as well as to bring together, and seemingly to explain, a number of observations about a person that might otherwise appear meaningless.

Of equal importance to the concept of self is the significance ascribed to other people in most psychodynamic theories. For example, the ways in which people relate to others and the difficulties of interpersonal development have been the subject of such social-psychodynamic theories as those of Karen Horney (1937) and Harry Stack Sullivan (1953). These and other theories emphasize the fact that people need other people but that they do not always learn to express their needs in socially acceptable

Figure 2.8 A comparison of the major concepts and terms, emphasis, and areas of application of three viewpoints representative of psychodynamic theories.

PSYCHODYNAMIC THEORIES

Sigmund Freud

Major Concepts and Terms

Psychic Structure: the organization of the personality, consisting of id, ego, and superego

Anxiety: the experience of discomfort as a consequence of conflict among parts of the psychic structure

Defense Mechanisms: responses that an individual makes in an attempt to cope with and reduce anxiety

Psychosexual Stages: stages of personality development based on different zones of pleasure—oral, anal, phallic, and genital

Emphasis

Concern with intrapsychic dynamics; why people are driven to do what they do

Explanation of behavior through analysis of conflicts among instincts, reality, and society

Belief that instincts and maturational development precede environmental effects

De-emphasis of rational cognitive processes

Areas of Application

Psychotherapy, parent-child relations, abnormal behavior, education

Erik Erikson

Major Concepts and Terms

Psychosocial Development: human development viewed in terms of its dependence on interaction with others

Crisis: the critical conflict that an individual experiences as he grows emotionally

Stages of Growth: crucial periods in development, each consisting of unique conflicts that an individual must deal with

Ego Identity: the accumulated, integrated experiences of the individual's view of himself

Emphasis

Concern with psychosocial development throughout life and with the role of society and interpersonal relationships in individual development

Belief that growth occurs out of the confrontation between an individual's needs and the demands of society

Belief that an individual's social view of himself is more important than his sexual urges

Emphasis on continuity between the stages of development

Areas of Application

Psychotherapy, parent-child relations, psychiatry, education

Harry Stack Sullivan

Major Concepts and Terms

Personification: a group of related attitudes, feelings, and concepts about oneself or another, which have been acquired from extensive experience

Dynamism: an enduring pattern of learned behaviors that recur in an individual's interpersonal relations

Self-structure: defensive behaviors that are learned to avoid or minimize anxiety arising from interpersonal relationships

Experience: events that the individual participates in and that become more distinct and ordered during development

Emphasis

Focus on individual as a product of the interpersonal environment; distinctly human qualities are the consequence of social interaction

Belief that development is sequential, that the individual passes through a series of phases, accumulating experiences from predominant relationships

Belief that tension and anxiety arise from the individual's interaction with his environment

Equal emphasis on rational cognitive processes and on irrational emotional processes

Areas of Application

Psychotherapy, interpersonal communication, parent-child relations, education

ways. Some people move away from others out of fear; others move against people in anger. The infant legitimately demands adult attention, but the adult must engage in mutually satisfying relationships to get his needs met. Unless one learns how to deal with others as an adult, one can end up isolated or angry.

All psychodynamic theories also stress that how one feels about oneself is of paramount importance in relationships with others and in effective everyday behavior. It is easier to analyze these feelings if we separate self-concept from self-esteem. **Self-concept** is the sum of ideas one has about oneself; **self-esteem** is how one evaluates oneself: Am I good or bad, smart or dumb, worthwhile or useless? People with poor self-esteem are unhappy with themselves and usually have difficulty forming good relationships with others. High self-esteem is associated with self-confidence, moderate risk taking, and good interpersonal skills. Unless one has a reasonably good opinion of himself, he can doubt his abilities to do anything well.

Because there are many major psychodynamic theories, this section will discuss only those of Sigmund Freud and Erik Erikson in detail. In later chapters on personality, we will return to their work as well as that of such others as Alfred Adler, Harry Stack Sullivan, and Erich Fromm.

Freud's Theory

Sigmund Freud (1905) is the father of psychodynamic theories and the founder of psychoanalysis. Whether or not one accepts his theory of man's development, his influence on psychology, the arts, and literature has been enormous. In a prim Victorian Age, he put forth a theory of unconscious motivation, human sexuality, and instinctual aggression.

As Freud saw it, from earliest infancy man is motivated by his irrational urges toward pleasure. Rational behavior develops out of conflict between social demands and the young child's instincts, which are **sublimated** (altered in socially acceptable ways) in the course of the child's adaptation to his environment. Intelligence or adaptation is secondary to a sensuality that has become socialized.

Freud proposed three conflicting aspects of human personality: the id, the ego, and the superego. In the **id** reside all of the **unconscious** impulses (the person is unaware of these forces). The **superego** is his conscience, which develops in early childhood as he internalizes parental values and standards of conduct. The **ego** guides a person's realistic coping behavior and mediates the eternal conflicts between what he wants to do (the province of his id) and what he must or must not do (the province of his superego).

Freud's view of man's development is in part an evolutionary one. Man's biological urges are part of his evolved animal nature. His development proceeds through interaction with external reality, which transforms him, and with further maturation he continues to interact with reality, which again transforms him, and so forth. Almost inevitably, the cost of man's coming to terms with rational behavior is a loss of

Figure 2.9 Freud emphasized that developmental tasks, such as feeding and toilet training, not only force the young child to master his own body needs and functions but force him to do so in a socially prescribed way. Because these demands are often conflicting and stressful, Freud proposed that they may become associated with anxiety, hostility, and guilt and result in various disturbances in further development.

contact with his basic impulses and a denial of their direct gratification. As a consequence, most civilized men are anxious. In contrast, infants are not anxious until they begin to differentiate themselves from their caretaking environments and begin to cope with the demands of reality.

Freud believed that development is an unfolding of genetic stages in which instinctual impulses become attached to various pleasure centers of the body. He described the life cycle of man in sexual terms, tying psychological development to the resolution of the conflicts that characterize each stage of life. Current psychodynamic theories are elaborations and modifications of Freud's thought or reactions to it.

Erikson's Psychosocial Theory

Erik Erikson (1963), one modifier of Freud's psychoanalytic theory, has developed an elaborate stage theory. Erikson describes emotional development across the life span, which makes his theory particularly important to understand.

In Erikson's psychosocial theory, personality develops according to steps predetermined by the human organism's readiness to be driven toward, to be aware of, and to interact with a widening social world, a world that begins with a dim image of mother and ends with an image of humankind. Erikson saw development as consisting of the progressive resolution of conflicts between the child's needs and social demands. At each of eight stages, conflicts must be resolved, at least partially, before progress can be made on the next set of problems. The failure to resolve problems at any stage can result in psychological disorders that affect the rest of the life span.

From Trust to Industry. A baby needs to develop a relationship in which he can get what he requires from a mother who is ready and able to provide it. He needs to develop feelings of comfort with his mother and needs to know that a consistent caretaker will be there when he needs her. Constant, reliable care promotes the baby's sense of *trust.* This consistency in care enables a baby to learn to tolerate frustrations and to delay immediate gratifications, because he knows that adults around him care and can be trusted to meet his needs. If a baby's needs are not consistently met, he can develop a sense of mistrust and will react to frustration with anxiety and upset.

After the infant begins to walk and to exercise some self-direction, he runs into social restraints. During this second stage, he increasingly demands to determine his own behavior ("Me do it!"), but

because he has little judgment about his actual capabilities, he needs to be gently protected from excesses while granted *autonomy* in those matters that he can handle. It is particularly important at this stage, Erikson suggests, that parents not shame a child into feeling that he is incompetent. Shame can be a devastating experience for anyone, and it is particularly difficult for young children who are struggling for autonomy and who are not yet sure that they can develop competent self-regulation.

After the child has gained a relatively secure sense of autonomy, he enters the third stage of development and is ready to take the initiative in planning his own activities. As Erikson sees it, *initiative* adds to autonomy the quality of undertaking, planning, and attacking a task for the sake of being active and on the move. In the preceding stage, self-will often inspired acts of defiance. In the third stage, the child is ready for positive, constructive activities under his own initiative. The potential problem at this period is guilt; the child may come to feel that his intrusiveness and activity have evil consequences. This is the period of sexual attraction to the opposite-sex parent: of seductive behavior by little girls toward their fathers and of assertive, manly behavior of little boys toward their mothers. As a child resolves these hopeless attractions, he identifies with the same-sex parent and develops a conscience. Harsh parental responses to a child's sexual overtures and other initiatives, however, can lead to an overdeveloped, harsh conscience that may always plague the person with guilt.

Erikson theorizes that, when the child has come to terms with his family by identifying with the same-sex parent, he enters the fourth stage and is ready to move into the larger world. About this time, in our culture, he goes to school. Before the child can become an adult in any society, he must become a worker; he learns that he will gain recognition by producing things (*industry*). The child, therefore, wants to learn the technical skills that characterize adults—be they literacy or hunting or herding. The potential problem in this period lies in a sense of inadequacy and inferiority, which can develop if a child is not praised for his accomplishments. In Erikson's theory, this is a decisive stage, for the child must prepare for effective adult roles.

From Identity to Ego Integrity. In the fifth stage, the adolescent questions all of his previous resolutions to problems of trust, autonomy, initiative, and industry. Rapid body growth and genital maturity create a "physiological revolution" within him at the time that he faces adult life. According to Erikson, the adolescent searches for continuity and sameness within himself—a sense of *identity*—and in his search he has to refight the battles of earlier years, usually casting his parents in the role of adversaries. He tries and discards roles and ways of behaving, then reformulates them and tries them again. The potential problem at this period is that the adolescent's identity will fail to become consistent and that he will have a sense of personal diffusion. Some adolescents cannot seem to develop a sense of who they are as people, as sexual beings, as adult workers, as potential parents. If a sense of role diffusion lasts into adulthood, the person may never be able to make consistent decisions about who he is and where he is going in life.

The young adult, emerging from the search for identity, is eager and willing to fuse his identity with that of others. In terms of Erikson's sixth stage, he is ready for *intimacy,* for relationships with others in which he is strong enough to make sacrifices for another's welfare and to not lose himself in another's identity. It is at this point that true sexual love can emerge. The young adult has the job of putting work and love together. The potential problem at this period is isolation from others, a failure to commit oneself to loving relationships because of competition or fear.

Generativity characterizes the seventh stage and refers to the adult's concern with establishing and guiding the next generation. According to Erikson, productivity in work and creativity in one's life are important concepts in this period. Having a sense of accomplishment in adult life depends on giving loving care to others and regarding one's own contributions to society as valuable. Merely producing children does not give a person a sense of generativity; one must see one's role in rearing them as a contribution to humankind and the larger society. The possible dangers of this period are self-absorption and a sense of stagnation, a sense of going nowhere, doing nothing important.

In Erikson's theory, the final stage of the life cycle should result in a sense of wholeness, of purposes accomplished and a life well lived. If one "had it to do over again," he would change little about the choices he has made, about the way he has lived. In such a final consolidation of life's stages, death loses its sting. The potential problem in the final stage is regret and despair over wasted chances and unfortunate choices. A person in this stage who feels despair fears death in an ironic way that those with *ego integrity* do not. Although the despairing person expresses disgust over his life, he yearns for another chance. The person with integrity accepts death as the end of meaningful trip.

Ego Psychology

Compared to Freud's theory, Erikson's psychosocial theory places greater emphasis on the development of adaptive behaviors. A few contemporary psychodynamic theorists have been even more concerned than

Erikson's Stages of Development								
Stage	1	2	3	4	5	6	7	8
Maturity								Ego Integrity vs. Despair
Adulthood							Generativity vs. Stagnation	
Young Adulthood						Intimacy vs. Isolation		
Puberty and Adolescence					Identity vs. Diffusion			
Latency				Industry vs. Inferiority				
Locomotor/Genital			Initiative vs. Guilt					
Muscular/Anal		Autonomy vs. Shame						
Oral/Sensory	Trust vs. Mistrust							

Figure 2.10 (*opposite*) Erikson's proposed sequence of psychosocial stages of development and the types of possible outcomes often associated with each stage. Beginning with the oral/sensory stage, Erikson's first four stages are, respectively, extensions of Freud's oral, anal, phallic, and latency stages. In the remaining four stages, Erikson has elaborated on Freud's approach by adding dimensions of interpersonal relationships. (Adapted from E. H. Erikson, *Childhood and Society*, 2nd rev. ed., copyright © 1963 by W. W. Norton & Company, Inc.)

(*left*) Pictorial representation of Erikson's eight stages. In sequence from left to right and from top to bottom, the major task in each succeeding stage is developing a sense of (1) trust, (2) autonomy, (3) initiative, (4) industriousness, (5) identity, (6) intimacy, (7) generativity, and (8) ego integrity.

Erikson with ego functions and adaptive intelligence. Robert White (1960), for example, puts forth a theory of "competence" motivation. White proposes that after the child becomes, in Erikson's terms, concerned with industry, his motives to learn and to be effective become independent of his earlier impulses for sensual gratification. White and a number of other ego psychologists disagree with Freud's position that throughout life man is motivated only by his basic instincts.

Abraham Maslow (1954) believed that theories of motivation and personality should stress healthy development. He proposed a hierarchy of needs to describe a person's developmental progression from physiological-instinctive motives to more rational, intellectual ones. Figure 2.11 shows the hierarchy. Maslow believed that human beings are **self-actualizing**—that they tend toward becoming all that they can be. He proposed that realizing one's potential in work and love is a basic human need. Before a person can become self-actualized, however, his more fundamental needs for food, security, esteem from others, and self-esteem must be met. If a person is chronically hungry or if his life is constantly threatened, he cannot be self-actualizing. His energies are tied up with survival. The final need in Maslow's hierarchy is to know and to understand in a cosmic sense, to feel oneself part of the larger order of the universe. Only a person who has accomplished his own actualization can strive for such understanding.

All the psychodynamic theorists mentioned and others whose work will appear in later discussions of personality and identity make important statements about the developmental course of human drives to become a complete person. Complete human beings have not only fulfilled their needs, but they cope, resolve conflicts, give support to others, and contribute to their societies. It is this sense of wholeness in ego functions that all these theorists have stressed.

OVERVIEW AND EVALUATION

Although the three groups of theories presented in this chapter may appear to have nothing in common, they are largely complementary. All believe that human growth and development is regular, and all agree that behavior is at least potentially predictable. But, as hinted earlier, they have usually avoided each other's company in two senses: They often attend to different behaviors (even if they give them the same label, like "learning"), and they often explain different aspects of the developmental process.

For example, behavior-learning theories do not take into account developmental shifts in cognitive behavior over the life span. One might think, therefore, that children at all ages are as intellectually capable as adults in learning. But the research evidence discussed in Chapters 11 and 14 supports the view that important developmental shifts in understanding and learning do occur around the ages of five to seven (S. White, 1970) and at puberty.

Differences also show clearly in each group's approach to sex differences (Maier, 1965). In behav-

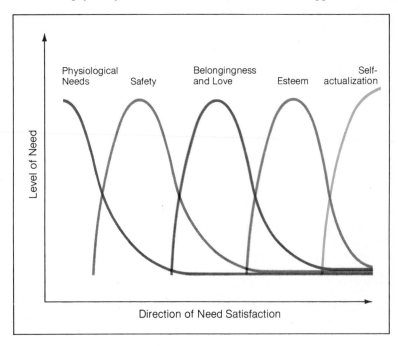

Figure 2.11 Maslow's proposed hierarchy of human needs. The relative saliency of the five main classes of needs changes progressively, as the graph shows: The peak of an earlier main class of needs must be passed (needs satisfied) before the next higher need can begin to assume a dominant role. (Adapted from Maslow, 1954)

ior-learning theories, it is the reaction of other people and of the culture in general to maleness or femaleness that sets up differences in the personality and social development of boys and girls. A cognitive theory like Piaget's makes no distinction between the sexes, but a psychodynamic theory generally considers biological sex differences essential to an explanation of personality development.

As you read this book, you will notice that different sections stress different theories. Work that implements cognitive theories will be discussed most heavily in chapters on language and intellectual development; psychodynamic theories will appear most often in the discussions of personality. Because behavior-learning theories regard all behavior as learned and because their techniques of study are used by psychologists of all persuasions, their work or their methods will appear throughout the book. Theories developed by the new ethologists, whose evolutionary approach is exciting, if unfulfilled, will appear wherever they seem to contribute to an explanation of human development.

SUMMARY

1. Theories of human development are based on different assumptions about the nature of man.

2. Behavior-learning theories view man's behavior as quite malleable, his role in his development as more or less passive, and the development of behavior as continuous over the life span. There are two major types of learning: In classical conditioning, conditioned reflexes are established by the association of one stimulus with another stimulus that is known to cause an unconditioned reflex. In operant conditioning, the frequency of a response can be increased or decreased, depending on when, how, and to what extent it is followed by reinforcement or punishment. Learning principles are used to analyze many phenomena, among which are concept learning and social learning.

3. Evolved-primate theories see man's behavior as relatively changeable, his role in development as active, and the development of behavior as progressing by stages. Piaget's theory, which is consistent with such a view, sees the child as constructing an understanding of the world and suggests the notion of schemes, with which the child assimilates and accommodates new knowledge, maintaining equilibrium between his internal schemes and the outside world. Intellectually, the child progresses through the sensorimotor, the representational, and the formal-operational stages. Another theory consistent with this view is Chomsky's, which proposes that language is based on a generative process and that the child's brain is predisposed to discover language's underlying structure. Central to ethological theories, which are another example of this view, are notions of man's adaptation to his environment and the existence of releasing stimuli.

4. Psychodynamic theories see man's behavior as relatively fixed, his role in development as generally more active than passive, and the development of behavior as a somewhat discontinuous process involving the interplay between various internal and external forces. For Freud, the unconscious forces of the id are tempered and sublimated by the ego and the superego. For Erikson, personality develops according to steps predetermined by the organism's readiness to interact with the external world. In general, psychodynamic theories stress that the development of how one feels about oneself is of great importance and that the individual follows a developmental course toward becoming an active, complete person.

5. Although focusing on different aspects of the developmental process, the three groups of theories are largely complementary, and all can be useful in different ways.

SUGGESTED READINGS

Erikson, Erik. *Childhood and Society.* New York: Norton, 1963.

Hall, Elizabeth. "Conversation with Jerome Bruner: Bad Education," *Psychology Today,* 4 (December 1970), 50–57+.

Hall, Elizabeth. "Conversation with Niko Tinbergen: Ethology's Warning," *Psychology Today,* 7 (March 1974), 65–76+.

Maier, Henry W. *Three Theories of Child Development.* New York: Harper & Row, 1965.

Skinner, B. F. *About Behaviorism.* New York: Knopf, 1974.

Similarities and differences in development depend on common heritage and conditions in the prenatal and postnatal environment.

3

DETERMINANTS OF DEVELOPMENT

If a child in the second grade has difficulty learning to read, her teacher may say that she has poor eyesight, or that her parents tried to teach her reading too early, or that she is lazy, or that she is of low intelligence. The teacher seldom considers that all four factors could have been involved and that each one could have contributed to the child's reading disability. Human beings, including those of us who pride ourselves on our ability to understand the complexities and nuances of life, are often in search of a single answer when it comes to explaining behavior. In fact, however, few facets of behavior and development can be fully understood by looking at the relationship between a single developmental effect and a single cause.

In this chapter, we will explore some of the different causes of human behavior and the ways that developmental psychologists set about studying those causes. We will see that heredity and environment always work together to shape behavior and that maturation plays an important part in the process. We will discover that genetic research with animals can help us to understand heredity in human beings, and we will discuss some of the ways that researchers go about exploring genetic influences on individual differences. We will look at environments and will see how they influence the developing person. We will see that developmental psychologists use different kinds of studies and that each type gives them a different amount of control over the investigation of various biological or environmental determinants. We will find that no one type of study can supply all the necessary information about development and that all kinds are needed for a full account.

CLASSES OF DETERMINANTS

If a single cause rarely explains behavior, then any understanding of human development must involve the exploration and documentation of multiple, interacting causes. Yet before one can consider the way that causes interact, it is necessary to separate them and talk about different *classes* of causes. Thus, it is convenient to speak of hereditary influences (genetic and biological) on behavior, even though heredity cannot operate without the collaboration of the environment. The physical environment, such as the mother's uterus in the prenatal period, is another class of developmental determinant. And there are social influences on a child's behavior, even though the same environmental influences may work differently on persons of different body types, different skin colors, different ages, and even different generations.

Developmental psychologists are especially aware that behavior depends on both the person and his environment. Whereas other psychologists have been content to study behavior at one particular time, developmentalists study changes across time. As we noted in Chapter 1, most developmentalists appeal to both biological and environmental determinants to explain the changes that occur in the developing person. Both **nature** and **nurture** play necessary roles in development, although some theorists, such as those discussed in Chapter 2, stress one or the other.

Researchers ask two questions about the roles of genetic-biological and environmental aspects of development: "How?" and "How much?" The question "How?" refers to the ways in which heredity and environment combine to produce development. For example, how do **genes,** the microscopic elements that carry the blueprints of heredity, combine with environmental factors, such as nutrition, to produce growth? Answers to the question "How?" come from studies of people in general. The question "How much?" refers to the sources of differences among individuals. How much of the differences in height among people in your developmental psychology class is due to nutritional differences while the students were growing up (environmental effects) and how much to each student's different heredity (genetic effects)? Answers to the question "How much?" come from studies of the ways that individuals differ in their development. "How?" and "How much?" are both important questions.

BIOLOGICAL DETERMINANTS

Our heredity is of two kinds: the general inheritance of our species that makes us into that peculiar primate, *Homo sapiens,* and our specific inheritance from our parents and grandparents and great-grandparents that makes each of us visibly and temperamentally different from other members of our species. Both inheritances are biological determinants, and they begin working on us at the moment of

conception and continue their work until we die. Your heredity determined your gender, the color of your eyes, the fact that you have two of them and that they perceive various wavelengths of light, your growth from an infant to an adult, and your susceptibility to various diseases, such as diabetes.

Genetic Factors

Answers to questions about genetic influence on behavior and development are difficult to obtain. Researchers cannot experimentally manipulate a human being's genetic structure. Nor can they select two people, ask them to mate and produce a child, and subject their offspring to one environment or another in order to determine the kinds of behavior that might be attributed to genetic differences or to experience. How, then, do we know about the contributions of genetics to human behavior?

Genetic Studies with Animals. One way to study human genetics is to derive a set of general principles from research on lower animals, in which nearly ideal genetic research can be performed. One type of experiment involves breeding genetically related animals until pure strains are produced. A variant of this technique involves breeding animals for a selected trait. For example, one might test a group of rats on their ability to learn the path through a maze and interbreed those rats that learn quickly. If one repeats this process with the offspring, generation after generation, a group of rats will at last be born that are almost "purebreds" for superior performance in mazes. Studies applying these breeding techniques to mice and rats have shown that genetic differences can affect aggressiveness, maze-learning ability, hoarding, exploratory behavior, sex drive, alcohol preference, and a variety of other traits (McClearn, 1970).

This kind of experimentation indicates that different strains of animals do not always respond to the same life experience with the same kind of behavior. Therefore, it is impossible to predict the outcome of a particular learning experience unless one also specifies the genetic make-up of the organism.

For example, Daniel Freedman (1958) was interested in the effects that indulging or disciplining a puppy during its early weeks of life would produce on its self-control. He selected dogs from each of four different breeds: Basenji, Shetland sheepdog, wire-haired fox terrier, and beagle. The caretakers indulged some of the dogs from each breed between the third and eight weeks of their lives by encouraging them to play, to be aggressive, and to engage in rough-and-tumble activities. In contrast, the caretakers disciplined other dogs from each breed by

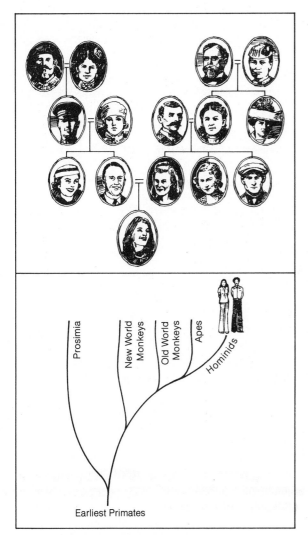

Prosimia

New World Monkeys

Old World Monkeys

Apes

Hominids

Earliest Primates

Figure 3.1 (*top*) The family tree of one human being. This tree traces the ancestry of a single individual and covers a time span of a little more than a hundred years. Inheritance on this scale accounts for the biological determination of certain characteristics that distinguish one individual from another.

(*bottom*) The evolution of *Homo sapiens*. This tree traces the ancestry of an entire species and covers a time span of tens of millions of years. Inheritance on this scale accounts for the biological determination of characteristics that all human beings have in common. (After Washburn and Moore, 1974)

restraining them, teaching them to sit, stay, come on command, and so forth. After this training, each dog was tested; when it was hungry, its caretaker took it into a room containing a bowl of meat. For three minutes the caretaker prevented the animal from eating by hitting it on the rump with a rolled newspaper and shouting "No" every time the dog approached the food. Then the handler left the room, and an experimenter recorded the length of time that elapsed before the dog began to eat the meat.

Some theories of development might lead to the conclusion that an overindulged dog will not be able to inhibit its impulse to eat in such a test. But the results of eight days of testing indicate that such a prediction is not valid for dogs. In two breeds, the terriers and the beagles, the indulged animals waited longer before approaching the food than their disciplined companions. Neither the indulged nor the disciplined Shetlands ever ate the food, and all the Basenjis dug right into the meal. Although this experiment tells us nothing about human beings, except to be cautious about sweeping predictions, it is clear that one cannot predict the effect of early indulgence versus discipline on a dog unless one first specifies its genetic make-up or breed.

Just as both the genetic make-up of an organism and its environmental circumstances affect the development of a given behavior, momentary environmental circumstances also affect the way that behavior is expressed or whether it appears at all. In many cases, organisms have hereditary behavior patterns, but they display these actions only in the presence of a releasing stimulus, as discussed in Chapter 2.

For example, Niko Tinbergen (1951) has observed that the male stickleback fish will attack a strange male stickleback only if the intruder is ready to mate, a condition revealed by a red belly. The fight that ensues looks natural and flexible, but the fish protecting its territory merely imitates the fighting characteristics of the intruder. If the intruder bites, the defender bites back; if it threatens, the defender threatens, and so on. The intruder's red belly releases the defender's attack, and each fighting thrust of the intruder releases a response that is identical to the stimulus. The result is an adaptive, natural, and flexible behavioral pattern, but its components are fixed patterns released by the specific stimuli of the intruder. Thus, genetic behavior requires the appropriate environmental stimuli in order for it to appear.

Human Genetics. How do we know about genetic effects in human beings, whose breeding cannot be manipulated? With our present knowledge, we cannot answer questions that ask *how* genes affect the development of behavior. Many genes contribute to the development of most behavioral characteristics. For example, at least 150 genes affect brain development. This estimate is on the low side and is based on the knowledge that 150 independent genes can cause different forms of mental retardation. We know that several hundred more genes are probably required to develop a normal brain, because the causes of many forms of retardation have not yet been identified. But we do not know the ways in which these hundreds of genes act together to produce a normal brain or normal intelligence.

Genes exert their influences throughout the life span. The timing of growth and aging and the sequence of development are related to gene action. Genes are "turned on" at some but not other points in development. The "turned on" genes are active in producing substances within the body that create new structures, regulate their functions, or maintain their state. Genes are carried on the **chromosomes,** which will be discussed in Chapter 4. The appearance of enlarged segments of chromosomes, called puffs, is related to genetic activity. Puffs appear on different segments of different chromosomes throughout life, suggesting that genetic activity continues to help determine how development proceeds. Lissy Jarvik and Donna Cohen (1973) have shown that breaks in chromosomes and unusual numbers of chromosomes are increasingly found in people's cells as they grow older. As will be indicated in Chapter 22, aging may somehow be related to, among other things, gradual deteriorations in the genetic code.

Questions that ask *how much* genetic differences affect the development of individual differences are easier to answer. Still, we have conclusive answers only for some abnormal traits that are caused by single genes, and in Chapter 4 you will see how such single-gene traits are transmitted from parent to child. In the case of normal traits, such as height, we get some idea of whether genetic factors are involved by comparing the trait among both related and unrelated people. The more closely these people are related and the more similar the trait, the more likely it is that genetic factors have influenced the trait. For example, appearance is obviously influenced by genetic differences, because genetically related people resemble each other more than unrelated people do, whether they grow up together or not. For example, taller parents tend to have taller children than shorter parents do.

Table 3.1   Correlations of Intelligence Test Scores

CORRELATIONS BETWEEN	MEDIAN VALUE
Unrelated persons	
Children reared apart	−.01
Children reared together	+.24
Collaterals*	
Second cousins	+.16
First cousins	+.26
Uncle (or aunt) and nephew (or niece)	+.34
Siblings, reared apart	+.47
Siblings, reared together	+.55
Fraternal twins, different sex	+.49
Fraternal twins, same sex	+.56
Identical twins, reared apart	+.75
Identical twins, reared together	+.87
Direct line	
Grandparent and grandchild	+.27
Parent (as adult) and child	+.50
Parent (as child) and child	+.56

*Descended from the same stock, but different lines.
Source: Adapted from Arthur Jensen, "How Much Can We Boost IQ and Scholastic Achievement?" *Harvard Educational Review,* 39 (1969), 49.

Parents who make high IQ scores tend to have children who score higher than the children of lower-scoring parents. This tendency shows clearly in Table 3.1, which presents the correlations between the IQ scores of pairs of individuals who bear different degrees of genetic similarity to one another.

To understand this table one must know something about **correlation coefficients.** A correlation is a numerical expression of how closely two sets of measurements correspond. A correlation of .00 represents no direct relationship at all. For example, in Table 3.1 the correlation between the IQ scores of two children who are unrelated and reared apart is −.01, essentially .00. This number implies that knowing the IQ score of one child tells you nothing about the IQ score of the unrelated child. If a correlation coefficient were +1.00, then the correspondence between pairs of individuals would be perfect. In this case, knowing that one child had the highest IQ score in his group would indicate that the other child also had the highest IQ score in his group (but not necessarily the *same* IQ score). If the correlation were −1.00, then if one person had the highest score in his group, the other had the lowest score in his group. In psychological research, correlations are rarely exactly .00 or +1.00 or −1.00. Rather, they fall at various places in between. The larger the coefficient, the more closely two measures correspond and the closer the standing of pair members within their respective groups.

As the relatedness between two people increases, the correlation between their IQ scores also increases. Notice that in Table 3.1 the correlations for siblings (brothers or sisters) are not very different from the correlations for fraternal twins (twins developed from two separate egg cells). This is to be expected, because on the average both siblings and fraternal twins share half their genes. But identical twins (twins developed from a split single female egg cell) have identical genetic make-ups, and their IQs show much higher correlations. Both the mother and the father also share half their genes with their children, so that the correlation for parents and children is about the same as for siblings and fraternal twins. Therefore, IQ scores appear to be directly related to the degree of genetic relatedness.

However, such evidence does not allow us to say that genetic make-up is the primary determinant of a person's intellectual ability. As relatedness between individuals increases, so does the similarity of the environment in which they live. Unrelated children reared apart share no common environment, and the correlation of their IQ scores is essentially .00. Brothers and sisters share some of their environment, but because they are born at different times and because each is subjected to some unique life experiences, their environments are not identical. In addition, because identical twins look alike, parents are more likely to treat them alike than if they were fraternal. As a result, it is possible to interpret the evidence presented in Table 3.1 as simply indicating that the IQ scores of two people are similar when their environments are similar (M. Schwartz and Schwartz, 1974).

Another way of trying to discover how much genetic differences affect intellectual ability is to compare the IQ scores of related individuals, some of whom live in the same environment and the rest of whom live in different environments. For example, one could look at adopted children and compare their IQ scores with the IQ scores of both their biological parents and the parents who reared them. Researchers who have studied this problem (Honzik, 1957; Scarr-Salapatek, 1975; Skodak and Skeels, 1949) have discovered that correlation coefficients between the IQ scores of adopted children and their biological parents are greater (approximately +.35) than between those same adopted children and their rearing parents (near .00). In fact, there is little difference between the correlations for adopted children and their biological parents and the correlations for children reared by their own parents (Figure 3.2). This

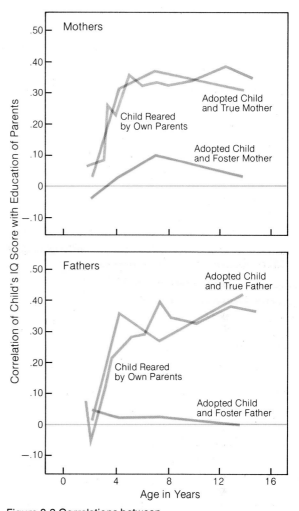

Figure 3.2 Correlations between children's IQ scores and estimated IQ scores of parents. Reddish lines are based on Skodak and Skeel's research, and the other lines are based on research by Honzik. Note that in this research parents' educational level was used as a rough estimate of their IQ score because it was not possible to administer a test to each parent. The two top lines in each graph show that there is an increase with age in the correlation between children's scores and those of their true parents. The bottom line in each graph shows that there is little or no change with age in the low correlation between adopted children's scores and those of their foster parents. (Adapted from Skodak and Skeels, 1949; after Honzik, 1957)

result presumably argues for a genetic component in intelligence.

However, when one looks at the *average* IQ score of these children, it appears that this score is closer to the average IQ score of their upper-middle-class foster mothers than to the average IQ score of their impoverished biological mothers. In one study the average IQ score of the biological mothers was 86, but the average IQ score for the children was 106, a score near the estimated IQ of the parents who reared them. This evidence argues for an environmental component of intellectual ability and suggests that the absolute value of a person's IQ score can be improved if he is placed in a rich environment.

Results like these illustrate a crucial concept for understanding genetic influences: the **reaction range.** The genetic make-up of each person has a unique range of possible responses to the environments that he may encounter. In other words, there are some limits on how each of us can respond to good and poor environmental conditions. In the case of height, good nutrition will make all of us taller than poor nutrition will, but in both kinds of environments some of us will be taller than others. Genes do not specify a particular height for anyone. They do specify a pattern of growth that varies depending on nutrition and other environmental factors. The final height we achieve depends on both genetic and environmental factors.

The development of intellectual skills that are sampled by IQ tests also has a reaction range. No matter how stimulating the environment, few people become Albert Einsteins or Leonardo da Vincis. And in other than very deprived circumstances, most people do not become mentally retarded. Each person has a range of perhaps twenty to twenty-five IQ points in which his IQ score will tend to fall, depending on his rearing conditions (Scarr-Salapatek, 1975).

Heritability

A common misunderstanding of the way researchers describe genetic influence on a given trait has also fueled the nature-nurture controversy over IQ scores. Suppose one hundred people take an IQ test. Their scores will differ, and the differences between their individual scores is called **variability.** We know that the individuals in the group have different genetic compositions as well as different life experiences. But how much of the variability in IQ test scores is associated with differences in their genetic make-up rather than differences in life experience? The relative contribution of genetics to IQ test performance is the **heritability** of IQ in this group.

But heritability is only an estimate based on a small number of cases, which may or may not represent the general population. Suppose it were possible to find a group of people with identical genetic make-up. If these individuals were randomly placed in various environments and then given an IQ test, none of the differences in their IQ scores could be attributed to differences in their genetic composition. The heritability would be .00. On the other hand, if it were possible to rear a group of individuals with totally different genetic dispositions in the same environment, then all the differences in their IQ test scores would be associated with differences in their genetic make-up. Heritability would be 1.00.

These examples demonstrate that the size of the heritability coefficient depends on the specific research sample. Many estimates of the heritability of

Figure 3.3 Different heritabilities of the same behavioral trait—excitability—in two imaginary groups. (*top*) These individuals are genetically identical, but their environments differ. Differences in excitability within this group are attributable to environmental variability. Heritability, therefore, equals .00. (*bottom*) The range of excitability in this group is exactly the same as it is in the other group, but here the individuals have identical environments and are genetically dissimilar. Differences in excitability within this group are attributable to genetic variability. Heritability equals 1.00.

IQ came from research with white, upper-middle-class groups, and such families probably do not represent the full range of genetic make-up or environments among the population of a country—or a race or a social group.

Because heritability depends on the specific characteristics of the sample, heritabilities for a given trait may change from one year to the next, especially if the factors that produce the trait change. Years ago, for example, the heritability for tuberculosis was quite high, because the bacillus for TB was present in the environment of nearly every individual. Therefore, whether one actually developed the disease was highly dependent on his inborn biochemical susceptibility to that bacillus. In contrast, the TB bacillus is now present only in the most unsanitary circumstances. Today, therefore, the major determinant of whether one succumbs to TB is exposure to the bacillus, because many people who have a biochemical susceptibility to TB never come in contact with the bacillus. Consequently, the heritability for TB is now quite low.

The cause of TB is the same today as it always was: the invasion of the TB bacillus in an individual with a biochemical susceptibility to that bacillus. But the heritability for TB has changed because whether one gets the disease is now more closely associated with where he lives than with his biochemistry. Therefore, the fact that a trait has high heritability does not mean that genes cause it, nor does low heritability mean that environmental circumstances cause a trait to appear.

There is an old expression that genes set limits on development while environments determine what actually develops. This is *not* true. Environments are equally implicated in setting limits on development by providing only certain opportunities and stimuli for a person to develop a particular trait, whereas

genes are equally responsible for determining the level of development by responding to given environments in unique ways. Individual differences among people, then, are caused by genetic differences in their reaction ranges *and* by specific differences in their environments.

ENVIRONMENTAL DETERMINANTS

Environmental determinants play a powerful role in the development of the growing child. Even the most radical of the biologically oriented theorists discussed in Chapter 2 would agree. But the term "environment" is too broad to have much scientific usefulness (Wohlwill, 1973). One must always specify which features of any environment affect the behavior in question. For example, to explain why a number of children achieve low scores on IQ tests, some environmentalists merely point to the obvious disparities between advantaged and disadvantaged homes, schools, and neighborhoods, claiming that (somehow) all of the noticeable differences determine differences in IQ scores. However, as this section will make clear, there are various ways of defining the environment and of explaining how experience influences development. None of these ways is right in all cases; none is always wrong. All can be useful, depending on the behavior that one tries to explain. At the same time, it should be understood that, when two people say that environment determines a particular behavior, they may be speaking of different kinds of influence.

Physical Determinants

Physical environments include those essential but mundane features that make life possible; more interesting physical influences, such as the mother's uterus in the prenatal period; and situations, such as growing up in a high-rise apartment or in a house. It is obvious that all organisms must have sufficient air, water, food, and light to maintain life. Without these there is biological deterioration and even death. What is not so obvious is the extent to which other features of the physical environment affect the course of development. For example, the environment of the mother's uterus is critical to the survival and development of the fetus, which requires an efficient exchange of oxygen and nutrients and the elimination of wastes. If the maternal environment is deficient in nutrients such as calcium or protein, the infant's development will be stunted. Other maternal environments are crowded: Short mothers have small and premature babies more often than tall mothers do, and

twins are often so crowded that they are born prematurely. As Chapter 4 will explain, the maternal physical environment also has other important effects on fetal development.

Physical environments at later ages encapsulate people metaphorically rather than literally, as the uterus does. Each of us develops in a physical context that has limiting and determining effects on our development. For example, life in a nomad's tent and life in an apartment have different influences on a growing child. Urie Bronfenbrenner (1973) has recently highlighted an **ecological** approach to development, one that takes into account a child's physical as well as his social setting. Earlier, Roger Barker and Herbert Wright (1951) described the interplay between one boy and his Kansas town where he could dig, jump, run, explore fields, and engage in a variety of activities in a physical environment that was very different from the concrete and asphalt surroundings of an inner-city child in Detroit.

Think of the city child who wants to dig. His parent must take him down fifteen floors in the elevator, then walk him four blocks through automobile traffic, crowds of pedestrians, noise, and a whirring visual kaleidoscope to a park. In contrast, the suburban child merely walks out into the backyard and digs by himself. Urban children, like suburban children, develop in a physical context that offers some kinds of experiences and limits others. Their social environments are equally different.

Figure 3.4 For children living in the country or in a large city, differences in environmental determinants extend to such areas as the type and nature of family and peer relationships, educational opportunities, and the understanding and utilization of different facets of the physical environment.

Social Determinants

The social environment includes all those effects that people have on one another in families, in peer groups, and in neighborhoods. It also encompasses the influences of social institutions such as schools; cultural and subcultural values, attitudes, and beliefs; and media such as newspapers and television.

Family. Most children grow up in the context of a family—father, mother, perhaps brothers and sisters. The family has been shown to influence many aspects of behavioral development: sex roles, self-concepts, and interpersonal and intellectual skills. Fathers have been shown to be important in the early years of a boy's life if he is to develop appropriate masculine sex roles. This influence showed clearly when E. Mavis Hetherington and Jan Deur (1972) studied young adolescent boys who had lost their fathers. Boys who had lost their fathers before they were five years old were less masculine in behaviors such as competitive and rough-and-tumble play. Boys who had lost their fathers later in life were no different from boys who had grown up with fathers present. But as the boys reached adolescence, the effects of a fatherless boyhood tended to decrease. On the other hand, another study (Hetherington, 1972) indicated that the early loss of a father had no apparent effects on girls until they reached puberty. Then the adolescent girls behaved inappropriately around males. This research, although limited to lower-class and lower-

middle-class girls, indicates that girls may acquire from their fathers the social skills needed to interact with the opposite sex.

The age and sex of one's siblings also helps determine sex-role development. Boys with older sisters show a weaker preference for the masculine sex role than boys with older brothers or boys who lack older siblings (H. Koch, 1966; Sutton-Smith and Rosenberg, 1970). Girls with older brothers are more masculine in sex roles than are girls with older sisters or no older siblings. Because older siblings tend to act like parents toward younger children in the family, especially if there is a large age difference, it is not surprising to find that older siblings appear to affect the sex-role development of younger children.

Families also provide a context for intellectual development. The opportunities that are available to a child and the way that the parents respond to his curiosity affect what he learns and how rapidly he learns it. If there are many children in the family, their intellectual skills tend to be less well developed than those of children in smaller families. Birth order also has an effect: First-born children and those early in birth rank tend to have higher IQ scores than children born later. The effects of family size and birth order seem to come about because parents pay less attention to any one child when there are many and to later-born children in general (Belmont and Marolla, 1973). The dilution of parental attention may also be responsible for the lower IQ scores of

twins as compared to those of single children. When there are twins to care for, the amount or quality of attention that parents can give seems to diminish.

Peers. Peers affect the behavioral development of people from early school age throughout the life span. When children go to kindergarten or first grade, they move partly out of the family world into the environment of the peer group. The peer group usually has its own values and rules of behavior, which may differ radically from those of the family.

In middle childhood and adolescence, the peer group is almost as strong as the family in providing a testing ground for becoming a person. Because one cannot go through life being "Mama's boy" or "Daddy's girl," one has to establish other identifications and goals. Adolescent peers are decidedly important in the development of a sense of identity (Erikson, 1968). Because peers share the problems of establishing independence and identity, they provide positive support in the often painful process of becoming an adult.

In later years peers continue to influence behavior. They are friends, consultants on problems, people to compete with and emulate. Although little research has been done on the effects of peer groups in adulthood, young parents often consult other young parents on questions about child rearing. Older adults share common experiences and gain support from peers in their increasingly difficult problems of adjustment to adult children, retirement, and changing physical status.

Schools. Schools socialize children in many of the same ways that families and peer groups do. The staff sets standards of conduct and values that may or may not be the same as those of the children's families and friends. Notable problems have arisen when the school represents an alien middle-class white world in the middle of a culturally different neighborhood. Some chicanos and blacks have recently demanded more control over what their children are taught in school, because they believe that the established curriculum (and perhaps the staff) is irrelevant. Most parents believe that schools have profound effects on their children's future success. They believe that getting along with teachers, earning good grades, and scoring well on standardized tests are related to opportunities for further education and to entrance into prestigious occupations.

Indeed, studies of nations where education is not available to all children suggest that schools do affect the intellectual achievements of children. At the very least, schoolchildren learn new ways to apply their cognitive skills to problems that the society says are important (and therefore puts in the school curriculum). The effects of schools are not limited to the intellectual realm. Schools also influence social skills, psychological growth, and children's feelings about the rules and regulations of society.

Media. Television and other media affect behavior, for good and for bad. Many years ago a famous radio program, "The War of the Worlds," created panic in New Jersey. Many listeners believed that Martians had landed, and they either fled or prepared to defend themselves against the aliens.

Today, it is virtually impossible for a child to grow up without being exposed to heavy doses of television. Surveys indicate that 99 percent of all families with children own television sets, and most children spend from one-fifth to one-third of their waking hours before the flickering screen (Lyle, 1972).

Recently, the effects of showing aggression on television have been hotly debated, and Chapter 15 will explore research that applies to the controversy. In general, watching violence on television does not seem to trigger aggressive behavior in most children, but some violence-prone youngsters appear to be influenced toward more aggression by watching aggressive models (Bandura, 1973).

Educational television programs like "Sesame Street" and "The Electric Company" have been

Figure 3.5 Family, siblings, peers, schools, and the various media are among the many social factors that have a profound impact on almost all aspects of development. It is primarily through these social determinants that individuals become gradually socialized into the diversity of American subcultures.

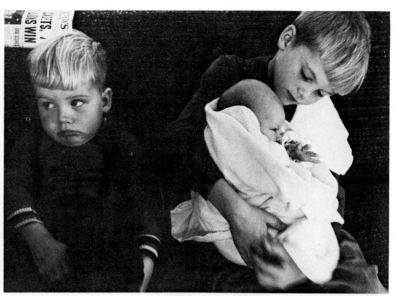

designed to teach specific number and letter skills and reading to children who would usually have difficulty acquiring these skills at school. Both programs have demonstrated success in teaching specific skills to the children who watch them: The more often the children watch, the greater the improvement in their skills (Lesser, 1974). But middle-class children also watch these programs, and they seem to benefit as much as or more than the disadvantaged children for whom the programs were designed. This means that widespread watching of educational television maintains the greater literacy of advantaged children over disadvantaged children.

It is obvious that the social environment has strong influences on the development of behavior. As has been noted, however, if one is to show what part of the environment affects some behavior, he must specify the determining aspects of the environment and describe how they affect development.

STUDYING DETERMINANTS

How does a developmental psychologist who wants to discover the determinants of a particular behavior go about identifying them? Before he can gather the information that might explain that behavior, he must first design a study. Distinctions among methods for collecting information on human development depend on how much **control** the investigator has. He may or may not have control over (1) the selection of subjects for study, (2) the experience they have in the study, and (3) the possible responses they can give to that experience. At one extreme of control is the simple, **naturalistic observation** of behavior without any interference from the investigator. At the other extreme is **experimentation,** where the experimenter can control all three aspects of his study. Between the two extremes are **clinical studies** and numerous types of **field studies,** where some but not other types of control are possible.

No one study ever proves all that it proposes. A soundly designed and executed study can, at best, change our subjective judgment that a conclusion is correct. When the research design of an investigation conforms to acceptable scientific standards, we have more confidence in its results.

In psychology, there has probably never been a truly crucial study that provided a clear basis for choosing between two opposed theories. Such investigations are rare in any science. As noted in Chapter 1, the final test is replication. A scientific finding becomes established when it has been found in several investigations (and the more, the better)

conducted by different researchers in different places but using the same basic methods.

Naturalistic Observation

Certain aspects of human behavior, particularly behavior in natural settings, are most appropriately studied through observational methods. Even naturalistic observations have rules for categorizing and recording what the observer sees. The major advantage of such observational studies is their closeness to what actually happens in everyday life. Because the observer is recording natural behavior, there are few problems in generalizing the results to "real-life" situations. The major problem is to determine which of many factors, or **variables,** that are uncontrolled in the study have important effects on the results.

For example, psychologists may wish to study the effects of racial integration on social behavior in a neighborhood. To conduct this study, they must observe the people's behavior before and after the groups have been integrated or contrast the behavior of people in integrated neighborhoods with that of people in segregated neighborhoods. These observations could be made in numerous ways. The psychologists could observe residents at predetermined intervals and count the number of people engaged in like-race and unlike-race social interaction. They could count the incidence of aggressive, dependent, and dominant types of behavior. Before any of this could be done, however, the observers must have clear definitions of the variables they are concerned with. Will they consider physical nearness to be an example of social interaction? How will they define aggression? Can two observers watching a scene at the same time get comparable results?

The critical aspect of naturalistic observation is having explicit rules for categorizing and recording what the observer sees. If such a study is conducted well, valuable information can be gained about the everyday effects of a potentially important environmental variable, such as racial integration, on human behavior. This information can be acquired only through the observational method.

Clinical Study

Clinical study often consists of in-depth interviews and observation. It may be controlled: The same methods can be applied in a standardized way to each subject, or the psychologist can vary his approach with each subject. When clinical study is designed with appropriate controls, it qualifies as a method of science and can yield interesting and important data. For example, Hetherington's studies of father loss used in-depth interviews and observation of adolescent girls and their mothers. The procedures for a controlled study must be clearly and precisely defined; the investigator is left to his own resources only in such matters as introducing the subject to the clinical situation or maintaining his cooperation, and even these actions may cause bias unless explicitly stated and controlled.

The studies of Jean Piaget (1952b) are an example of the clinial method. In his earlier studies, Piaget talked freely with a child, asking whatever questions seemed necessary to reveal the child's concepts and thinking processes. However, Piaget realized that differences in presenting the questions could affect his results. Because he was also critical of standardized tests, he chose an intermediate method. In his recent studies, he has used a more standardized procedure. By presenting the same questions to all children, Piaget has gained a stronger base for suggesting that the differences in children's responses at different ages are the result of actual changes in their cognitive activity.

Field Study

Field studies are studies of naturally occurring behavior in which the researcher controls some aspects of the situation. Such studies are often more closely controlled than simple observation or clinical studies. Because for ethical or practical reasons many developmental determinants cannot be brought under experimental control, an investigator may choose to use a field study. For example, if a researcher wishes to study the effects of prematurity on infant development or the effects of confinement to a mental hospital, he cannot randomly assign subjects to those experimental conditions. Nevertheless, a psychologist may want to study the effects of such events. He would do so by comparing premature infants to full-term babies and hospitalized persons to nonhospitalized persons.

Problems of sampling always arise in field studies, because random assignment is not possible. Premature infants, for example, may differ from full-term babies in more than their length of gestation. They are more likely to have younger, more disadvantaged mothers; they may receive less adequate maternal care. It is important, therefore, for the investigator to be aware of the ways in which his comparison groups differ. Because he can never prove that he has found all the differences between his groups, the results of

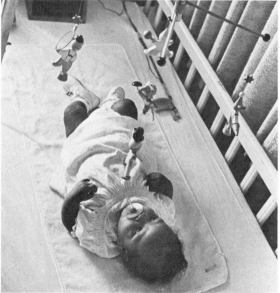

Figure 3.6 The nature and degree of control that an investigator may have depends on the phenomenon being studied and is reflected in the extreme situations pictured here. *(top)* Naturalistic observation yields data less subject to control but more generalizable to "real-life" situations. *(bottom)* Laboratory experimentation allows for the control and manipulation of many of the variables under study, sometimes at the expense of generalizability of the results.

field studies are often less certain than those of true experiments.

In field studies the investigator may not have complete control over the experience that the subject receives, nor may he have control over the possible responses the subject can give. Compromises are often necessary. In the study of prematurity, for example, the investigator might provide the mothers of both premature infants and full-termers with instructions for an infant-stimulation program. He could visit the homes regularly to educate the mothers and to observe the babies; he could supply the same educational toys and give the same tests of development to both groups at the end of the study. In these ways, he could gain partial control over the experiences of the two groups, and he could obtain the same samples of behavior at the end. In a study where standard tests are not possible, he also might not have good control over the behaviors he observed.

Ethologists often use field studies to ascertain the evolutionary significance of a behavior. For example, after a long period of natural observation of black-headed gulls, Niko Tinbergen (1972) wondered why black-headed gulls always removed eggshells from their nests as soon as the young gulls had emerged. To carry away the pieces of shell meant that the parent bird had to leave the nest when the young gulls needed warmth and protection from possible predators. After a series of studies in which nests were set out in varying conditions and the researchers concealed themselves to watch the results, Tinbergen

discovered that the white inside of the broken egg-shell attracted predators to the remaining whole eggs or to the young birds that were in the nest. The gulls' quick removal of eggshells had definite survival value for the species.

Field studies are justified by the importance of the developmental events they investigate. Often the most important phenomena are those that researchers cannot legitimately control.

Experimentation

An experiment involves the investigation of the effects of particular variables on behavior. All the precautions of objectivity, clarity, reliability, and replicability required of controlled clinical and observational study are necessary in the experimental method. However, it is often much easier to attain these goals through an experiment, primarily because the investigator is better able to control and manipulate the variables under study.

Studying behavior through the experimental method is not as unnatural as some might think, and the method has been used successfully in thousands of psychological studies. In a typical experiment, Arthur Jensen and William Rohwer (1965) designed a study to show developmental changes in children's learning. Their subjects were children from kindergarten through the twelfth grade. Jensen and Rohwer showed the children pairs of pictures of common objects. Half of the children at each age level were asked to name each picture, and the other half were

Figure 3.7 Hypothetical example illustrating apparent changes with age in IQ scores. The dots representing average scores of samples of people at different ages in a cross-sectional study show a downward trend in IQ score with age. The dots representing average scores of these same samples of people tested again ten years later as part of a longitudinal study show a similar downward trend in IQ score with age, but for each age group there also was an increase in the average score, as discussed in the text. (Adapted from Nesselroade, Schaie, and Baltes, 1972)

Figure 3.8 (*opposite*) Representation of a combined cross-sectional and longitudinal research design. As discussed in the text, first samples of children at each of four ages (two, four, six, and eight) are selected and studied. Two years later the same samples of children are studied again, and another sample of ten-year-olds is included. If differences found the first time among the samples of children of different ages are not found again, the researchers can only conclude that there may have been some difference between age groups earlier, perhaps in experience, that no longer is apparent.

asked to construct a sentence that related each pair of pictures. Afterward, all the children were presented the pairs of pictures and were asked to learn the members of each pair well enough so that when one picture was shown, they could recall the other. From the second grade, children who made sentences learned the material much faster. This experiment, therefore, illustrates the powerful effects of requiring a child to relate objects in a meaningful manner through the construction of sentences and thus adds to psychologists' knowledge of learning in children. It is doubtful that this information could have been obtained so efficiently or so convincingly had the researchers relied on naturalistic observation or clinical or field studies.

Longitudinal and Cross-Sectional Designs

Much of the information we have concerning development comes from studies that compare different age groups, called **cross-sectional studies.** Most often the researcher assumes that the differences among such groups are the result of developmental changes. If the samples of people at various ages are not selected carefully, the cross-sectional design has two major flaws: Different age groups may be affected by experiences peculiar to their **cohorts** (age-group members), and age-group changes may not represent the pattern of growth for individuals. For example, a cross-sectional study of the decline of IQ scores with age might show a curve like that in Figure 3.7. IQ scores appear to decline with increasing age.

Remember, however, that people studied at age eighty in 1975 were born in 1895, whereas those studied at age twenty in 1975 were born in 1955. Much has happened to our cultural and social environment in the time between those two groups of cohorts, and sociocultural influences affect the development and maintenance of intellectual skills. In fact, there is good evidence that, as a nation, each new generation scores higher on IQ tests, presumably because longer education and mass communications expose more people to the information required to score well on such tests (Baltes and Schaie, 1974). Younger cohorts score higher on IQ tests than older cohorts did at the same age. Thus, what appears to be a dramatic decline in IQ scores over age is in part an effect of the lower scores for older groups throughout their lives. Cross-sectional studies cannot detect cohort changes.

However, not all cross-sectional studies are flawed by cohort effects. If differences appear between closer age groups, such as three- and four-year-olds or even six- and ten-year-olds, it is improbable that cohort effects are responsible. The sociocultural environment changes too slowly to produce such effects in four years. With close age groups, it is more likely that differences are due to development.

Cross-sectional groups also may not show the actual pattern of individual change, especially for a developmental shift that occurs rapidly. At puberty the growth of any one individual accelerates and decelerates rapidly, but because different individuals

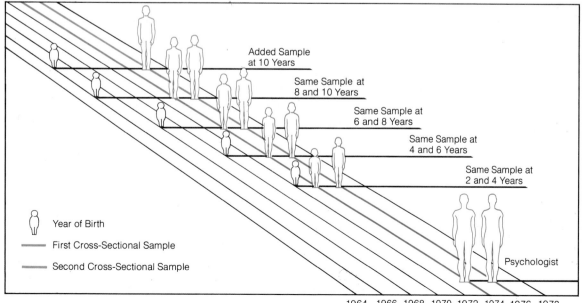

Added Sample at 10 Years

Same Sample at 8 and 10 Years

Same Sample at 6 and 8 Years

Same Sample at 4 and 6 Years

Same Sample at 2 and 4 Years

Year of Birth

First Cross-Sectional Sample

Second Cross-Sectional Sample

Psychologist

1964 1966 1968 1970 1972 1974 1976 1978

Year

Figure 3.9 Fraternal twins at ages ten and fifteen. Twin pairs, fraternal and identical, have been subject to extensive cross-sectional and longitudinal investigations in an attempt to understand the relative contributions of genetic and environmental factors to such diverse developmental phenomena as IQ, growth rates, and social relationships.

begin and end their growth at different times, graphs of group averages will show a smooth curve of growth for the entire cohort. Cross-sectional data alone would not reveal the pubescent growth spurt.

Studies that follow the same subjects over time, **longitudinal studies,** may seem to answer all problems in developmental studies. The same people can be compared to themselves at ages twenty and eighty. But there are problems here, too: The fact that the same people have been studied repeatedly over many years may have affected their development, and the long-term changes that appear in their behavior may be a response to sociocultural shifts as well as evidence of developmental changes. Life-span shifts in the sociocultural environment are obvious. Most people have lived through pre- and post-Sputnik, the assassinations of President John F. Kennedy and Martin Luther King, the Civil Rights Movement, and so forth. These shifts in our environment may have had profound effects on some aspects of our development.

Neither cross-sectional nor longitudinal studies alone can provide the basic data for developmental studies. Because of this, K. Warner Schaie (1965) has proposed that the two designs be combined to provide controls over the biases in each design. He suggests that researchers sample subjects cross-sectionally and then follow them longitudinally until the samples overlap in age. For example, initial samples drawn at ages two, four, six, and eight can be followed for two years until the two-year-olds are four, the four-year-olds are six, and so forth. A final cross-sectional sample can be drawn at age ten to compare to the longitudinal eight-year-olds who would then be ten. The effects of repeated testing, if any, will appear as differences between the starting scores for four-year-olds and the ending scores for the two-year-olds at age four. If the whole design is repeated some years later to detect shifts in the sociocultural environment, cohort effects will appear. If important environmental shifts had occurred, the scores at all ages would be higher or lower than the scores in the first study.

The desirability of using both cross-sectional and longitudinal designs becomes clear if we consider linear growth. Height measurements of a cross-sectional sample would indicate that people grow until middle adolescence and then begin to shrink. The "shrinkage" would be due to cohort effects: People born a number of years ago are shorter on the average than people born more recently, and they were always shorter. A longitudinal study of people now in their seventies would show that they grew until late adolescence and then maintained their heights until late adulthood, when they may actually have shrunk a bit. A longitudinal study of a younger cohort would find them reaching maximum growth at an earlier age; because of better nutrition, they are both taller and earlier maturing. In the case of height, it is necessary to separate the truth about development from long-term changes in the sociocultural environment. In the case of other factors, it is important to separate developmental change from the effects of repeated measurements.

The chapters in this unit have explored the concept of development, some of the theories that have evolved to explain it, the biological and environmental determinants that affect a developing organism, and some methods that researchers use to test theories and study determinants. In the rest of the book, we will change our focus from the general principles of developmental psychology to the developing individual and will trace his life from the moment of conception through childhood, adolescence, and adulthood.

SUMMARY

1. Human development is the result of multiple interacting causes operating through heredity—the person's nature—and through environment—the person's nurture. Questions arise over "how" and "how much" each contributes to development.

2. In studying the role of heredity, researchers frequently have studied animal genetics. Such studies help establish general principles and provide important information on the effects of genetic and genetic-environmental interactions. However, they cannot provide specific details about the way these interactions affect human development. The study of individuals of various degrees of relatedness has provided some insight into the way that genetic differences affect the development of human beings. An important concept in understanding research on the effects of genetic factors on human beings is the concept of reaction range, which refers to the limits set by genetic conditions on an individual's possible behavior.

3. The term heritability refers to the relative contribution of genetics to a trait or behavior. As an estimate it varies with who is studied and when. Heritability does not indicate that either genes or environment "cause" the trait or behavior. Instead, the appearance of a trait is a function of both genetic and environmental determinants.

4. Environmental determinants of human development include physical and social determinants. Physical determinants include those ecological features that maintain life—air, water, food, and light—and those features—life in a tent or apartment—that create different responses.

5. Social determinants include all those effects that people have on one another in families, peer groups, social institutions, and the media. From birth to death, these influences direct, limit, and enhance the development of the individual.

6. In studying the determinants of human development, different methods have different advantages and disadvantages in terms of their reliability, efficiency, and representativeness. Most of these advantages and disadvantages are associated with a given method's degree of control over who is studied, the setting or circumstances, and the behaviors that can occur. At one extreme is naturalistic observation and at the other is experimentation, with many types of field and clinical studies in between. Longitudinal and cross-sectional studies, in which the same or different individuals are studied at various ages, are required to provide some of the information needed to investigate different developmental determinants.

SUGGESTED READINGS

Barker, Roger G., and Herbert F. Wright. *One Boy's Day: A Specimen Record of Behavior.* New York: Harper & Row, 1951.

Dobzhansky, Theodosius. "Differences Are Not Deficits," *Psychology Today,* 7 (December 1973), 96–98+.

Doherty, Michael E., and Kenneth M. Shemberg. *Asking Questions about Behavior: An Introduction to What Psychologists Do.* Glenview, Ill.: Scott, Foresman, 1970.

Jencks, Christopher. *Inequality: A Reassessment of the Effect of Family & Schooling in America.* New York: Harper & Row, 1973.

Rosenthal, Robert. "Self-Fulfilling Prophecy," *Psychology Today,* 2 (September 1968), 44–51.

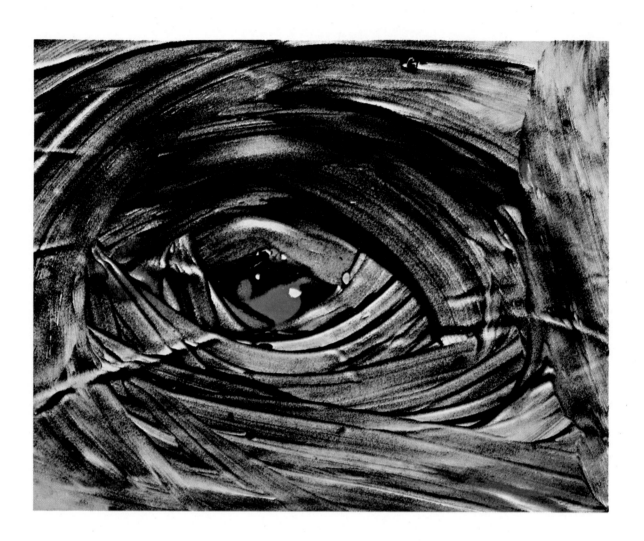

A newborn baby is both an end and a new beginning. The forty weeks of growth within the mother's body suddenly ends with birth. No other developmental period will ever end so dramatically in so short a time. Birth represents both separation and deprivation, independence and the necessity for self-reliance. No longer will the baby be able to rely on the resources of the mother's body; he must rely on his own. Much that will distinguish the child for the rest of his life has already happened. The baby's heredity, fully determined at conception, has already had its initial expression in his physical form. An active, inquiring, responsive infant enters the world equipped with a growing body and rapidly expanding motor, sensory, and mental capacities. This unit describes the baby's development within the womb and traces his first four weeks of independent life.

UNIT II
The Beginning of Life

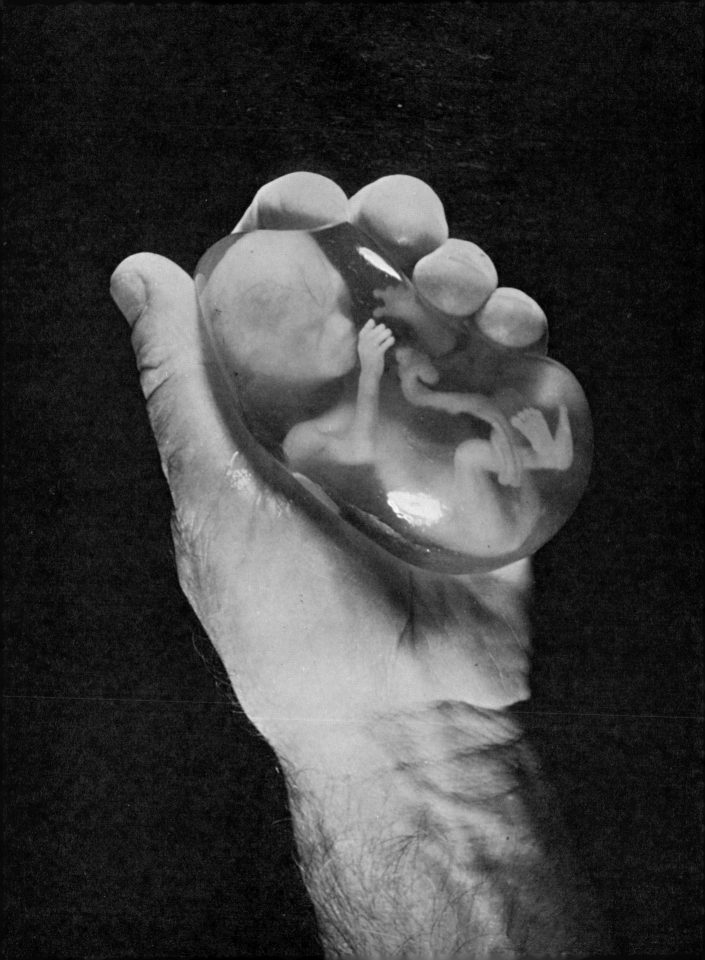

4

PRENATAL DEVELOPMENT

Life begins when two cells unite in the mother's body. At that instant, the inheritance of the new individual is established, giving him a unique physical appearance and disposing him toward certain personality characteristics and mental abilities. But this genetic composition is expressed only in an environmental context, and the two together determine how a person looks and behaves. Perhaps the oldest debate in psychology is how much influence inheritance or environment has in producing any given trait. Further, when a characteristic is "inherited," what does that fact tell us about how the trait will develop and about the possibility of changing that characteristic through life experiences?

When one considers that forty weeks after two tiny cells come together a viable and behaving human being emerges, it is clear that more growth and development takes place during the prenatal period than during any comparable segment of life history. The structures and functions that emerge during this time form the basis of the new individual's body and behavior for the rest of his life.

In this chapter we will follow the development of the fertilized egg into a healthy, normal baby who is ready for independent life outside his mother's womb. We will study the transmission of specific traits from parent to child, a subject that was introduced in Chapter 3. The behavior and capabilities of the growing fetus will become apparent, and the problems that can arise in the course of development will be spelled out. We will look at the link between the mother and her unborn child and will discover the importance of maternal health, diet, habits, and emotions.

HOW LIFE BEGINS

During the course of history, people have held a variety of beliefs and superstitions about the beginnings of a human life. Until the middle of the eighteenth century, it was commonly believed that life began with a completely formed and functioning miniature human being. During the prenatal period this miniature person simply became larger.

A major debate of this period raged over the source of this preformed fetus (Needham, 1959). Some biologists held that it was somehow contained in the mother's egg and that the father's sperm merely stimulated the growth of the already-formed baby. Other scientists claimed that the preformed infant existed in the head of the father's sperm and that the mother's womb served as an incubator in which the preformed individual grew. Anton van Leeuwenhoek, the inventor of the compound microscope, observed semen with his new instrument and in 1677 claimed that he saw in the sperm little animals of both sexes who copulated and produced new animals. Other scientists reported being able to tell the difference between the semen of donkeys and horses because the animals in the sperm of donkeys had longer ears.

In 1759 Kaspar Wolff asserted that both parents contributed equally to the beginning of life and that an embryo began as a cluster of globules. This assertion had major implications. Because it contended that the very young organism lacked the organ systems and structures that it must possess at birth, prenatal development had to consist of the appearance and growth of new cells, structures, and functions, not simply an enlargement of a preformed individual. More than fifty years later, Karl von Baer (1827) substantiated this theory when he discovered the mammalian egg cell under his microscope, and the science of embryology began.

Conception

The life of each person begins at the moment of conception, when the sperm cell, or **spermatozoon**, from the father unites with the egg, or **ovum**, of the mother. The ovum is the largest cell in the human body, and it can sometimes be seen without a microscope. The eggs mature in the female's ovaries, and one egg is released approximately every twenty-eight days during the woman's fertile years. The freed egg, which can survive approximately seventy-two hours, travels down the **Fallopian tube** toward the uterus (see Figure 4.4).

Whereas all the eggs that a woman will produce are present in immature form in the ovaries at the beginning of her fertile years, a man continually produces new spermatozoa. During normal intercourse, the male releases approximately 400 million spermatozoa, which may survive in the female genital tract for approximately seventy-two hours.

From one standpoint, it is a wonder that sperm and egg ever get together. First, the egg can be fertilized for only three of the twenty-eight days in a **menstrual**

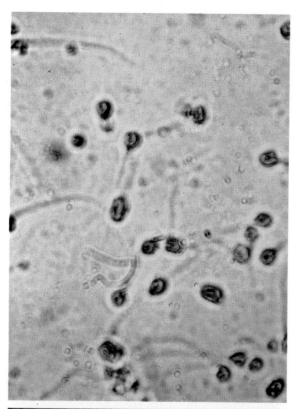

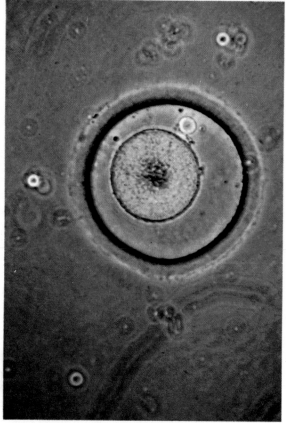

cycle. Second, only a small percentage of the sperm manage to pass through the **cervix,** the pinhead-sized opening that separates the vagina from the uterus. Third, the sperm must be sufficiently active so that its long, thin tail can move it through the uterus and up the Fallopian tube to contact the egg. Fourth, the egg must travel down the Fallopian tube fast enough to meet the sperm while both cells are alive. Such a variety of circumstances must be met before conception can take place that, some physicians estimate, one couple in ten is unable to conceive. On the other hand, it takes only one of those 400 million spermatozoa to fertilize an ovum, and some couples achieve conception after one act of sexual intercourse.

Chromosomes and Genes

The traits and dispositions that parents transmit to their offspring are coded in twenty-three pairs of chromosomes, which are present in every cell of the body (see Figure 4.2). The chromosomes are composed of beadlike strings of genes, microscopic entities containing the codes that produce inherited physical traits and behavioral dispositions. These genetic codes are apparently embodied in a complex chemical called **deoxyribonucleic acid,** or DNA. Whatever a person passes on to his offspring is contained in approximately 10,000 to 50,000 genes composed principally of DNA molecules, which somehow contain a chemical code that guides the development of bones and eyes, brain and fingernails, as well as dispose the offspring toward certain behav-

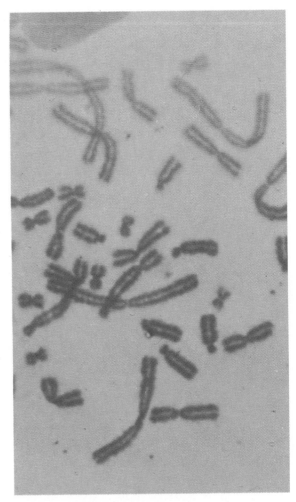

Figure 4.2 Part of the set of forty-six human chromosomes is shown magnified and stained. The chromosomes assume this form in preparation for division. (Courtesy Leonard Hayflick. Copyright © the President and Fellows of Harvard College)

Figure 4.1 (*opposite, top*) Living, active human spermatozoa, highly magnified. The waving tail propels the sperm toward the ovum, and the head of the sperm contains the nucleus, which carries the twenty-three chromosomes. (*bottom*) A living human ovum, magnified. The human egg is approximately the size of one of the periods on this page. Unlike many other vertebrate ova, the human egg lacks large amounts of yolk and instead depends on nourishment from the mother's blood via the placenta. (From Rugh and Shettles, 1971)

68

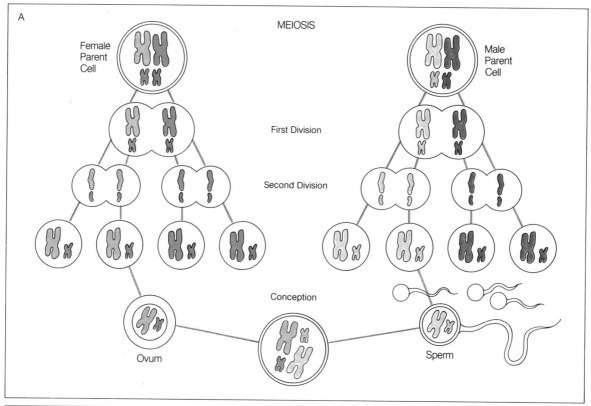

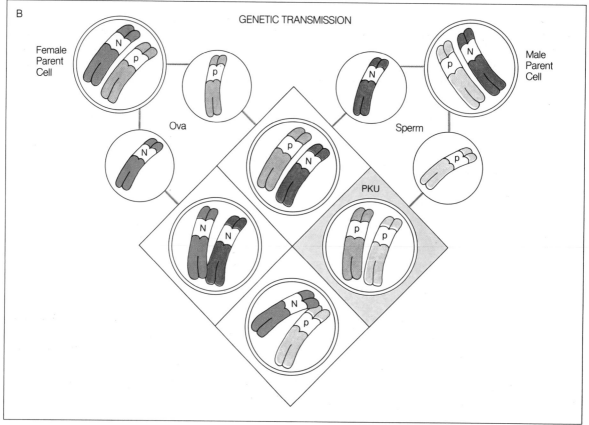

ioral patterns. All that information is contained in a fertilized cell smaller than the period on this page.

The Production of Sex Cells

Most cells of the human body contain twenty-three pairs of chromosomes, direct copies of the original twenty-three pairs with which each person begins his life. There is one major exception, however, and that occurs in the production of the ova and spermatozoa, or **gametes.** At puberty the gametes begin to form by a special kind of cell division called **meiosis.** During meiosis, a normal cell containing twenty-three pairs of chromosomes divides and divides again to produce four cells that contain one of each type of chromosome. The process begins when chromosomes of the same type start to pair up within the nucleus of a cell. The members of each chromosomal pair divide and gravitate to opposite ends of the cell, which then splits into two cells each containing twenty-three *single* chromosomes rather than twenty-three *pairs*. These cells then reproduce themselves, producing four cells each having a set of twenty-three *single* chromosomes. At conception, when a sperm unites with an egg, the result is a single cell having twenty-three pairs of chromosomes. Figure 4.3A illustrates meiosis in two pairs of chromosomes.

Genetic Transmission

Children sometimes resemble their parents in certain physical characteristics and sometimes do not. For example, a mother and father may both have brown

Figure 4.3 (*A*) The production of sex cells. Certain cells in the ovaries of the mother and in the testes of the father divide twice in a special pattern of cell division called meiosis to produce gametes—ova and sperm—that have only half the number of chromosomes of the parent cells. The chromosomes occur in the parent cells in pairs, and each chromosome is itself a double strand. For simplicity, only two of the twenty-three pairs of human chromosomes are shown here. In meiosis, first the members of each pair split up (*First Division*), and then the chromosomes themselves split in half (*Second Division*). They regenerate their missing halves in a subsequent step (*next line*). The union of the gametes in conception results in a zygote that has the full number of chromosomes, half from the mother and half from the father.

(*B*) Transmission of alleles in the inheritance of PKU. In this diagram only a single pair of chromosomes is represented. These chromosomes bear the alleles *N* and *p*. Both parents have both forms of the gene, and therefore they produce gametes with chromosomes bearing either the *N* or the *p* gene in equal numbers. Depending on which gametes happen to unite in conception, the new cell may have the alleles *NN*, *Np*, *pN*, or *pp*. Because *p* is a recessive gene, only babies with *pp* will have PKU.

hair, but one of their three children may be blond. How are physical characteristics passed on from parent to child?

Although hair color is a common and easily observed characteristic, its transmission is complicated. It is simpler to explain genetic transmission by examining a characteristic that depends on a single pair of genes. Consider **phenylketonuria,** or PKU, an inherited inability to metabolize phenylalinine, a component of some foods. If this metabolic abnormality is left untreated, the afflicted child will have fair skin and hair, a small head for his body size, eczema, agitated and restless behavior, a stiff gait, and moderate to severe mental retardation.

In order to understand how PKU occurs, let *N* symbolize the gene corresponding to normal metabolic ability and *p* represent the gene for PKU. The related genes, *N* and *p*, are called **alleles.** Now look at Figure 4.3B, which illustrates the alleles in only one pair of chromosomes. The parent cells in the figure contain the alleles of interest, labeled *N* and *p*. In this example, the mother's and father's cells have a gene for both *N* and *p*. When the parent cells divide to form gametes, half of the father's sperm cells and half of the mother's ova will contain a gene for PKU (*p*) and half will contain a gene for the normal metabolic condition (*N*). During conception, one of four possible combinations of these gametes will result. Depending on which male gamete unites with which female gamete, the new baby will have a genetic inheritance of *NN*, *Np* (which is the same as *pN*), or *pp*; these are shown in Figure 4.3B. If the selection process were perfectly random, one-fourth of the offspring of these parents would have the combination *NN*, one-fourth would have *pp*, and one-half would have *Np*.

But which of these offspring will be normal children, and which will show symptoms of PKU? In this example, the *NN* baby will be normal, and the *pp* baby will have PKU. These offspring are **homozygous,** which means that their cells have matching genes for this characteristic. But an *Np* baby is **heterozygous,** meaning that his cells have different genes for the same trait. Are these *Np* babies normal, or do they have PKU?

The answer depends on which gene is **dominant** and which is **recessive.** A dominant gene is one whose corresponding trait appears in the individual even when that gene is paired with a different gene for the trait. The paired gene whose corresponding trait fails to appear is recessive. In the case of PKU, the normal gene is dominant over the recessive PKU gene, and therefore *Np* individuals will be normal.

Notice that there is not a perfect one-to-one correspondence between the genes a person carries and the traits that appear. This lack of correspondence illustrates the difference between **genotype** and **phenotype.** The genotype is the specific combination of alleles that characterize one's genetic make-up, whereas the phenotype is the nature of the trait as it appears in the individual. The genes that produce PKU can combine to form three genotypes: *NN, Np, pp.* But there are only two phenotypes: normal and PKU. The genotypes *NN* and *Np* both produce the normal phenotype because *N* is dominant over *p.* Therefore, there are some differences between one's genetic make-up (genotype) and what one actually looks like and how he behaves (phenotype).

For a variety of reasons, genetic transmission is rarely as simple as it is in the case of PKU. First, dominance is not always all-or-none. That is, there appear to be gradations of dominance, so that one allele for a trait is not totally dominant. The result may be somewhat of an "average" of two extremes. Second, one allele may not express itself unless an allele of quite a different characteristic is also present. Consequently, it is possible for a person to carry a "dominant" gene that does not affect his phenotype. Third, most traits, especially behavioral ones, are **polygenic,** which means that several genes have an equal and cumulative effect in producing the trait. In other cases, some genes in the combination have more influence than others on the phenotype.

The more scientists study the process of human genetic transmission, the more complex it seems. One simply cannot point to a single gene that is responsible for a given behavioral trait. Later in this chapter we will discuss some of the issues and complexities of genetic transmission.

PRENATAL GROWTH

As soon as a sperm and an egg unite, development begins and progresses at a rapid rate. In approximately forty weeks, the organism goes from one tiny cell to a living, functioning, and behaving newborn baby.

The course of prenatal development falls into roughly three periods. During the first two weeks after conception, called the **germinal period,** the fertilized egg is primarily engaged in cell division. In the next six weeks, the **embryonic period,** the organism begins to take shape, and its various organ systems begin to form. Thereafter, from approximately eight weeks after conception to birth, the developing organism is called a **fetus.** The total **gestation period** usually lasts about 280 days (forty weeks or nine calendar months) calculating from the beginning of the mother's last menstruation. The **menstrual age** is the age of the fetus, when calculated in this way.

The Germinal Period

Almost immediately after fertilization, the egg begins the process of cell division that will eventually produce a human body made up of many billions of cells. Although the cells of an adult are highly differentiated according to their location and function in the body (for example, nerve cells are quite different in form and function from muscle cells), the cells at this point in development are all identical.

It is estimated that the fertilized ovum takes approximately three days to progress through the Fallopian tube to the uterus, where it floats freely for another four or five days before becoming **implanted** in the uterine wall. By the end of the first two weeks, the cells have multiplied greatly in number and have

Figure 4.4 The early development of the human embryo. Fertilization occurs at the upper end of the Fallopian tube. By the time the fertilized ovum reaches the uterus, it has already divided many times. Within seven or eight days, it is securely implanted in the uterine wall, where the process of prenatal development continues.

begun to differentiate themselves. An outer membrane (**chorion**) and an inner membrane (**amnion**) form a sac that surrounds and protects the developing organism. In addition, the microscope can distinguish the **placenta,** which transmits nourishment and wastes between the mother and the fetus, and three primary layers of cells. These layers are the **ectoderm,** which is the source of future cells composing the skin, sense organs, and nervous system; the **mesoderm,** from which the muscular, circulatory, and skeletal systems will develop; and the **endoderm,** which will give rise to some of the digestive glands in the alimentary canal.

One phenomenon that needs explanation is how cells become differentiated into nerve, muscle, fat, and blood. Some scientists have speculated that newly produced cells are essentially neutral, or undifferentiated. Somehow, these neutral cells are attracted to locations that need them, and then by some means, probably chemical, they are differentiated to serve the purpose required at that location.

For example, suppose that you cut your hand. Neutral cells are sent to the wound, where they are transformed into specialized skin cells by chemicals apparently released by layers of tissue immediately below the skin. If the wound is not too deep, the cell differentiation is almost perfect, and there is no scar. However, if the cut is deep enough to destroy the layers that produce the differentiating chemicals, the body's repair job is incomplete, and a scar forms. It is possible that the fetus develops by similarly transforming neutral cells.

By the end of the germinal period, the two-week-old organism is already anchored to the lining of the uterus, which maternal hormones have prepared for the developing egg. With both the organism and its host ready for development, life is on its way.

The Embryonic Period

Within four weeks after conception, the organism is already about one-fifth of an inch long, 10,000 times larger than the original fertilized egg. In addition, its

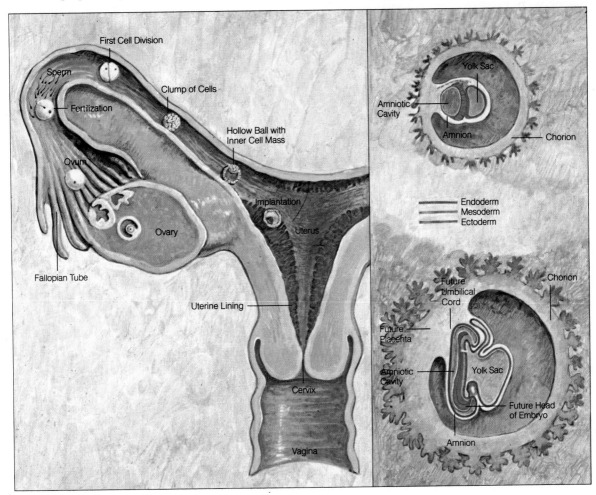

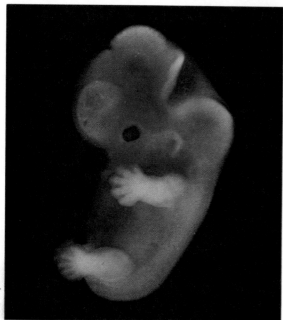

heart is beating to pump blood through microscopic veins and arteries, and there are the beginnings of a brain, kidneys, liver, and digestive tract and discernible indentations that will eventually become jaws, eyes, and ears.

Organs along the central axis of the body develop first; the extremities develop later. Thus, in the early weeks the organism is literally all head and heart. Later, the lower part of the body begins to enlarge and to assume its newborn proportion and size.

By the end of the embryonic period, the organism is almost an inch long, and it is clearly human. What look like gill slits of a fish are really rudimentary forms of structures in the neck and lower face. What seems to be a primitive tail eventually becomes the tip of the adult spine; the tail reaches its maximum length at about six weeks and then slowly recedes. The head is clearly distinct from the rounded, skin-covered body and accounts for about half the embryo's total size. The eyes have come forward from the sides of the head, and eyelids have begun to form. The face clearly contains ears, nose, lips, tongue, and even the buds of teeth. The knobs that will be arms and legs grow, and in a matter of weeks, they differentiate into hands and feet and then into fingers and toes (see Figure 4.5).

In this early period, the brain sends out impulses that coordinate the functioning of other organ systems. The heart beats sturdily, the stomach produces minute quantities of some digestive juices, the liver manufactures blood cells, and the kidneys purify the blood. One can distinguish testes or ovaries, and the

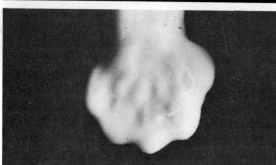

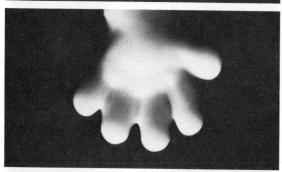

Figure 4.5 (*top*) Normal fetus at forty days. Note the formation and initial structuring of brain, eye, ear, fingers, and toes. (From Rugh and Shettles, 1971)

(*bottom*) Hand development. In the fifth week, hands are a "molding plate" with finger ridges. In the sixth week, finger buds are formed. In the seventh and eighth weeks, the fingers, thumbs, and fingerprints form; note the prominent touch pads. (Courtesy Carnegie Institution of Washington)

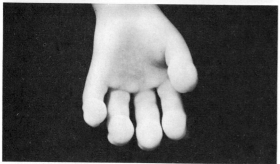

Figure 4.6 (*opposite, left*) Photograph of an x-ray of a two-month-old fetus. Note the extensive development of the skeleton. Advanced bone formations appear as darkened regions.

(*right*) Human fetus at three months, with the placenta attached. The placenta provides for physiological exchange between the developing fetus and the mother by permitting the passage of gases, nutrients, and metabolic wastes. (From Rugh and Shettles, 1971)

endocrine system has begun to produce hormones. However, all these organ systems are in a primitive form, and it will be several months before they can be considered fully functional (Falkner, 1966).

The Fetal Period

Approximately eight weeks past conception, when bone cells begin to develop, the developing organism is known as a fetus. Within twelve weeks it has begun to stretch out a little from its C-like posture, and the head is more erect. The limbs are nicely molded, and folds for fingernails and toenails are present. An external inspection could readily determine the sex of the fetus. The lips become separate from the jaws, rudimentary beginnings of teeth are apparent, the nasal passages of the nose have formed, the lungs have acquired their definitive shape, the brain has attained its general structure, the eye is organized, and the retina is becoming layered. The pancreas secretes bile, and the bone marrow has begun to produce blood. At this time the fetus weighs about an ounce and is approximately three inches long.

By sixteen weeks the fetus is approximately six to seven inches long and weighs about four ounces. Until now, its head has been enormous in relation to the rest of its body, but by sixteen weeks the lower part of the body has grown until the head is only about one-fourth of the total body size. The sixteen-week-old fetus looks like a miniature baby. Its face looks ''human,'' hair may appear on the head, bones can be distinguished throughout the body, and the sense organs approximate their final appearance. All major

internal organs have attained their typical shape and plan. Although the fetus could not survive if it were delivered at this point, its development has progressed so far that almost all basic systems and physical characteristics are present, down to hair on the head and sweat glands.

Although most basic systems are present in rudimentary form by sixteen weeks, certain functions necessary for survival outside the uterus are not yet fully developed. One of these functions is the ability to breathe. A necessary component in this process is the liquid **surfactin,** which coats the air sacs of the lungs and permits them to transmit oxygen from the air to the blood. Around the age of twenty-three weeks, the fetus develops a way to produce and maintain surfactin, but if it is born at this time, it often cannot maintain the necessary surfactin levels and may develop **respiratory distress syndrome** (formally called hyaline membrane disease of the lungs) and die. However, by about thirty-five weeks (sometimes earlier), the fetus develops a new system for maintaining surfactin, and this new method will allow it to live outside the uterus (Gluck and Kulovich, 1973).

Generally speaking, 180 days (twenty-six weeks or approximately six months) is regarded as the minimum possible age at which a fetus may survive. Babies have been born and survived from as early as 180 to as late as 334 days after conception, although the normal term of pregnancy is 266 days from conception (280 days or forty weeks from the onset of the last menstrual period). If born much before term,

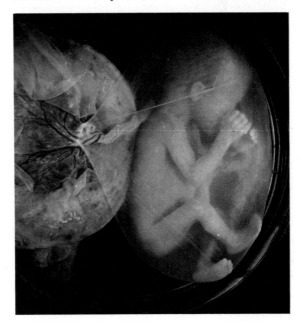

the fetus must be placed in an incubator, which helps regulate the baby's body temperature, facilitate his breathing, maintain the acidity-alkalinity balance of his blood, and so forth. Fetuses born after 252 days of gestation (thirty-six weeks) are considered to be of normal term, although unusual circumstances may still make special care necessary for the first few days or weeks of life.

During the final period of prenatal development, at a time when the fetus could survive on its own, its organs step up their activity, and its heart rate becomes quite rapid. Fat forms over its entire body, smoothing out the wrinkled skin and rounding out contours. The fetus usually gains about one-half pound a week during the last eight or nine weeks in the uterus. At birth the average full-term baby is about twenty inches long and weighs a little more than seven pounds, although weight may vary from less than five to more than twelve pounds and length may vary from less than seventeen to more than twenty-two inches.

PRENATAL BEHAVIOR

How early in its life can the fetus respond to stimuli, what kinds of responses does it make, and what kinds of spontaneous behavior does it show? The major behavior that characterizes the fetus is movement. Mothers sometimes report feeling such movement when the fetus is approximately sixteen weeks old (Feldman, 1920), although the muscles of the fetus are capable of movement at about eight weeks.

The only way to observe prenatal behavior is to watch the spontaneous behavior and reactions of embryos and fetuses that have been removed from mothers. Davenport Hooker (1952) studied embryos and fetuses delivered by Caesarean section. Those organisms too premature to be saved were placed in a chemical solution that was kept at normal body temperature. Hooker then observed the organisms' spontaneous movements and reactions to stimuli and recorded them on film for later study. His research shows that by twelve weeks the fetus can kick its legs, turn its feet, close its fingers, bend its wrists, turn its head, squint, frown, open and close its mouth, and respond to touch.

By twenty-three weeks the fetus shows much spontaneous activity, as many pregnant women report. It sleeps and wakes as a newborn does, but it also undergoes sluggish periods not found in the newborn. The fetus even has a favorite position for its naps. By twenty-four weeks it can cry, open and close its eyes, and look up, down, and sideways. By this

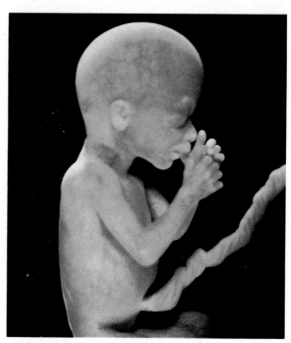

Figure 4.7 Normal fetus, at five months, apparently sucking its thumb. (From Rugh and Shettles, 1971)

Figure 4.8 (*opposite, top*) Models indicating the features and position of the fetus during preparation for passage through the birth canal. (Reproduced, with permission, from the *Birth Atlas*, published by Maternity Center Association, New York)

(*opposite, bottom*) Sequence showing some of the steps in the final stages of the normal birth process. The crown of the head appears first, and, as soon as the head emerges, the mouth and nose are cleaned (with a suction bulb) to prepare the baby for independent breathing. Soon after the baby is born, the uterus contracts and expels the placenta.

time it has also developed a grasp reflex and will soon be strong enough to support its weight with one hand. It may hiccup. During the final eight or nine weeks, the fetus is quite active, although its actions become limited by the increasingly snug fit of the womb.

Behavioral development in the prenatal organism corresponds to the development of its nervous system and of the muscles of its body. The earliest responses found in embryos appear at about seven and one-half weeks. When one strokes the area of the mouth with a fine hair, the fetus responds in a general manner, moving its upper trunk and neck. As the organism develops, more and more of its body becomes sensitive to stimulation, and the response eventually narrows to the area stimulated. Thus, when one touches the mouth, only reflexes about the mouth appear. Within the last few months before birth, the fetus behaves essentially as it does at birth, with grasping, sucking, kicking, and other typical infant reflexes.

Can a fetus learn? The answer is probably yes, depending on what you want to teach him. Lester Sontag sounded a loud noise near a pregnant woman's abdomen. At first the sound produced a large change in fetal heart rate, but after Sontag repeatedly made the noise near the woman's abdomen on successive days, the fetus no longer responded. Apparently, it had adapted to the sound—it had ''learned'' it in a sense (Sontag and Newbery, 1940). David Spelt (1948) showed that a fetus twenty-eight weeks old or more who responds to very loud noises can also learn to respond to the neutral stimulus of a vibrator applied to the maternal abdomen. Neither of these observations has ever been repeated, although both seem to suggest that a fetus is capable of a rudimentary kind of learning.

BIRTH

Near the end of a pregnancy, the fetus normally lies head down in the uterus, which resembles a large sack with its opening into the vagina constricted by the cervix (see Figure 4.8). By processes as yet unknown, labor is initiated. The upper portion of the

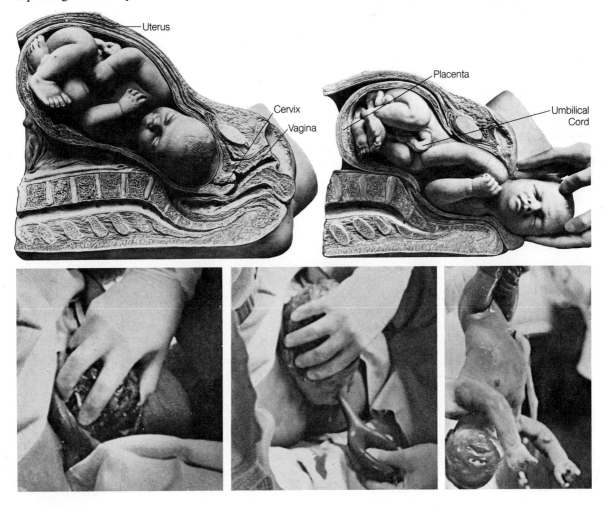

uterus contracts at regular and progressively shorter intervals while the lower part of the uterus thins out and the cervix dilates to permit the fetus to pass through the birth canal. Because the uterine contractions are often accompanied by the mother's attempt to assist in expelling the fetus, this process is called labor. For first-born infants, labor often lasts thirteen to fifteen hours, although its actual length varies greatly from mother to mother and is markedly less for later-born children.

The first stage of labor usually begins with faint contractions that grow stronger and more frequent. Once the cervix is completely dilated, the second stage of labor is reached, and the fetus passes head first through the birth canal and is born, a process that lasts approximately eighty minutes. After birth the physician cleans the baby's nose and mouth with a suction apparatus to make breathing easier and to prevent substances from entering his lungs. After the physician stimulates breathing with a sharp pat on the baby's sides or back, he ties and cuts the umbilical cord. In the final stage of labor, uterine contractions expel the **afterbirth**—the placenta, its membranes, and the rest of the umbilical cord. This process lasts approximately five to twenty minutes, and the afterbirth is immediately examined by the physician to determine whether it is complete and normal.

Not all deliveries proceed in this normal fashion. In a breech delivery, the baby's buttocks appear first, then his legs, and finally his head. Such deliveries can be dangerous because the baby may suffocate before his head emerges. Some babies must be delivered surgically, by Caesarean section, because of medical complications that would make a long labor dangerous for the life of the mother or child or because the fetus is in an abnormal position.

The newborn baby is assessed for appearance (color), heart rate, reflex irritability, activity, muscle tone, and respiratory effort to determine whether he will need further medical help. A much-used and practical scoring system for assessing these attributes is known as the **Apgar score** (Apgar and James, 1962). Each of the characteristics is rated 0, 1, or 2 (2 being best), and these scores are added to constitute the baby's Apgar score, which may vary from 0 to 10.

DEVELOPMENT AND BIRTH COMPLICATIONS

Whereas most pregnancies follow a normal course of development and most babies are normal and healthy, a genetic abnormality or an environmental factor will occasionally affect the developing fetus. Some of the resulting defects are minor, some respond to medical or surgical intervention, and others are so serious that they threaten the life of the baby.

Chromosomal Abnormalities

When a cell divides to form a gamete, the process may go wrong. During meiosis, a pair of chromosomes may fail to separate, so that one of the gametes has one chromosome too many and the other lacks a chromosome. If the missing chromosome is a sex chromosome, the fertilized egg may live to develop into a baby that suffers from **Turner's syndrome.** Such children tend to have short stature, a webbing or shortening of the neck, a broad-bridged nose, low-set ears, and short, chubby fingers. They generally lack secondary sex characteristics and have mild to moderate mental retardation.

The cell with an extra chromosome may produce a person with an abnormal number of chromosomes in all his cells. Each of the twenty-three pairs of chromosomes has been numbered by researchers. If the fertilized egg has an extra Chromosome 21 (three instead of two), the egg will develop into a baby who suffers from **Down's syndrome** (formerly called mongolism). These children tend to be short and stocky and to have a broad nose bridge, a large, protruding tongue, an open mouth, square-shaped ears, a broad, short neck with extra, loose skin over the nape, and large folds of skin above the eyes that give the child an "oriental" appearance. These children frequently have congenital heart disease and other problems and often do not live past the teens. They have moderate to severe mental retardation, although the extent of retardation varies considerably from case to case.

Down's syndrome is caused in one of two ways. In one case, Down's syndrome arises when extra material from Chromosome 21 becomes attached to another chromosome. This process is much rarer than the other, but the tendency is inherited and is not related to the mother's age. The other cause of Down's syndrome arises when an error in cell division produces an offspring with an extra chromosome, a genetic make-up unlike that of either parent. This tendency is not inherited. The likelihood of producing children with Down's syndrome through this process increases markedly as the mother ages. For some reason, Chromosome 21 is more likely to fail to separate during meiosis in older women. Some studies show that the risk of producing a child with Down's syndrome is only about 1 in 1,500 for mothers fifteen to twenty-four years of age and 1 in 1,000 for mothers twenty-five to thirty-four years of age, but the ratio rises to about 1 in 70 for mothers forty to forty-four years old and 1 in 38 for forty-five-year-old mothers (Hamerton *et al.,* 1961; Knobloch and Pasamanick, 1962). Other abnormalities also occur more frequently in children born to older mothers, which is the reason most geneticists encourage parents to have their children before the mother reaches forty.

Amniocentesis

Down's and Turner's syndromes are only two of many possible chromosomal abnormalities. In addition, as we will see in a later section, a fetus can suffer from a variety of life-threatening diseases. Obviously, it would be helpful to be able to detect a chromosomal abnormality or potentially fatal disease early in the course of pregnancy.

Fortunately, it is possible for a physician to insert a hollow needle through the maternal abdomen and draw out a sample of amniotic fluid. This process is called **amniocentesis.** Occasionally this procedure has been done as early as sixteen weeks after conception, but most physicians prefer to wait until the fetus is twenty weeks old.

The fetus sheds cells into this fluid, and if the fetal cells in the sample of amniotic fluid are grown in a culture, technicians can perform chromosomal analyses that will detect abnormalities such as Down's syndrome, Turner's syndrome, and others. In addition, the chemical composition of the amniotic fluid frequently provides clues to other diseases and reveals

whether the fetus can produce enough surfactin to avoid respiratory distress when it is born. In addition, tests can detect the blood group of the fetus. Should a potential difficulty like Rh incompatibility exist, blood compatible with that of the mother can be transferred into the abdomen of the fetus, where it can gradually be absorbed.

Prematurity

A historical problem in dealing with the subject of the premature baby is the definition of that term. Years ago, "premature" simply referred to the baby that was born before **term,** a **gestational age** of 266 days from conception. This definition proved to be inadequate, because some early babies were of normal weight and health. Moreover, some babies born late had serious weight deficiencies and reduced abilities to survive. As a result, the definition of prematurity came to be made in terms of birth weight, and newborn babies were considered premature if they weighed less than 2,500 grams (about 5-1/2 pounds) at birth, regardless of their gestational age. This criterion has also proved to be inadequate, because some newborns who weigh less than 5-1/2 pounds may be less than full term but may otherwise be perfectly normal.

The potential problem baby is the one who is underweight for his gestational age, a condition referred to as **small-for-dates.** Under such circumstances, it is likely that some aspect of development has gone awry and has inhibited fetal growth.

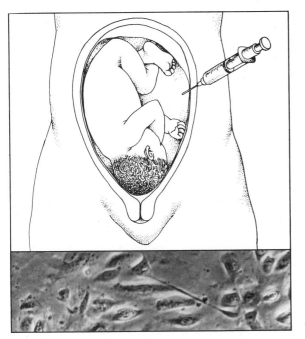

Figure 4.9 The process of amniocentesis. (*top*) Culture cells are withdrawn from the amniotic fluid and (*bottom*) then examined for any evidence of chromosomal abnormalities.

Some babies are simply born small. For example, a baby may weigh only two pounds; if this baby was born substantially before term, his young gestational age explains his small size. If he gets proper premature-infant care, he may show an accelerated "catch-up growth" once he reaches approximately five pounds. (Catch-up growth is discussed in more detail in Chapter 6.) By three years of age, he may be of average height and weight. In contrast, the small-for-dates infant of two pounds who spent the full 266 days in the womb is likely to have physical problems. Whatever circumstance kept him from gaining weight also seems to inhibit his catch-up growth. Thus, a small-for-dates infant is likely to remain somewhat shorter and lighter in weight than one would expect (Cruise, 1973).

Maternal Health

Although the environment within the womb is usually stable, it is not immune to influences that can alter or kill the developing organism. When the mother is exposed to excessive x-rays or other radiation, especially in the first few months of pregnancy, the fetus is in danger of malformation. Deficient secretion of certain hormones from the mother's endocrine glands may affect fetal development, and the incompatibility of an inherited blood substance (the Rh factor) between mother and child can, if not detected, result in miscarriage, mental retardation, or heart defects. Drugs and maternal nutrition can also affect the fetus.

Because most of the basic organ systems develop in the first third, or **trimester,** of pregnancy, problems in maternal health are likely to have a greater impact on the fetus at this time than later. Timing is apparently the crucial factor in determining whether an environmental influence will produce an abnormality in the developing fetus. If some destructive agent is introduced at the time an organ is forming, that organ may never develop fully. However, the agent may have less serious effects on organs already formed or those that are not ready to make their appearance. Such vulnerability in the fetus at different points during its development is an example of a kind of **sensitive period.** But sensitive periods are not limited to prenatal development, and some psychologists have investigated possible sensitive periods in early childhood for some behaviors (J. Scott, 1968).

Disease. If a pregnant woman contracts rubella (German measles) during the first trimester, the disease may cause such abnormalities in the develop-

ing fetus as blindness, deafness, brain damage, and heart disease. Fortunately, not all babies born to mothers who have suffered from rubella are abnormal, but the earlier the mother catches the disease, the more likely it is that her baby will be affected. A study by Richard Michaels and Gilbert Mellin (1960) indicates that 47 percent of the babies born to mothers who had rubella during the first month of pregnancy were abnormal, whereas 22 percent of babies whose mothers had the disease in the second month and 7 percent of those whose mothers contracted it in the third month were seriously affected.

Other diseases in the mother can also have unfortunate consequences for the fetus. Two that are approaching epidemic proportions in the American adult population are **syphilis** and **gonorrhea** (Metropolitan Life, 1969). Although the placenta manages to screen a good many of the organisms that cause syphilis, some make their way from the mother's blood through the placenta, transmitting the disease to

Figure 4.10 Pregnancy, for many couples, is viewed not only as an expression of love and sharing but also as presenting new and exciting challenges for the future.

the fetus. Therefore, if a pregnant woman is in only the first or second stage of syphilis, with symptoms of canker sore, rash, or fever, and if she receives treatment, her baby is likely to be born without ill effects. But if she remains untreated or if she is in a more severe stage of the disease, the baby may be born with congenital syphilis. If the mother has a mild case of the disease, her baby may have a rash, anemia, jaundice, or other mild problems, but if the mother is seriously infected, her baby may suffer a wide variety of debilitating and sometimes horrible abnormalities.

As the fetus moves down the birth canal, it can come into contact with the **gonococcus,** the bacterium that produces gonorrhea. A number of years ago, many babies became blind when their eyes were infected during the birth process. Because many women have gonorrhea without showing any symptoms, it has become common practice to place drops of silver nitrate or penicillin in the eyes of all newborn

babies. The practice has almost wiped out this kind of blindness.

Nutrition. Almost all vitamins, minerals, and nutrients are transported to the fetus through the placenta. The fetus stores none of these necessary substances against the time of its independent existence except iron, which breast milk will not supply in adequate amounts. Consequently, the nutritional state of the mother, especially during the first trimester, appears to be important for normal development.

Severely deficient maternal diets are associated with increased rates of abnormality (Robinson and Robinson, 1965). Diets deficient in calcium, phosphorus, and vitamins B, C, and D are associated with higher frequencies of malformed fetuses (Murphy, 1947). During the German occupation of the Netherlands in the 1940s, when food became extremely scarce, the rate of stillbirths and premature births increased among Dutch women, and birth weight and

birth length of their babies decreased. After the war, when food again became plentiful, these rates returned to normal (C. Smith, 1947). Additional data supporting the importance of adequate prenatal nutrition for fetal development come from depressed areas of the United States and from other countries where individuals customarily exist on relatively poor diets. In these regions, dietary supplements have been shown to reduce mortality rates and improve general health (Harrel, Woodyard, and Gates, 1955).

A review of the findings on maternal nutrition clearly shows that a poor maternal diet can be dangerous to normal prenatal development (Montagu, 1950), but it is less clear how serious and widespread the effects of malnutrition actually are on the developing fetus in industrialized societies where minor deficiencies in the mother's diet may not produce severe symptoms in either mother or baby. Some nutritionists have argued that the fetus can suffer untoward consequences even when the maternal diet is only mildly deficient and the mother shows no recognizable clinical symptoms. However, others claim that the fetus gets first call on nutrition and that the mother must live off any surplus.

Too much may be as bad as too little. There is a suggestion that an excess of calories and certain foods may be just as bad as a deficiency. In fact, overeating during pregnancy may produce an unusual number of fat cells in the fetus, leading to later obesity in the developing child (Brook, 1972; Eid, 1970).

Drugs and Smoking. A golden rule of obstetric practice has been to advise women to take as little medication during pregnancy as possible. The thalidomide tragedies of a decade ago, when many mothers who took the sedative thalidomide during the early weeks of pregnancy produced babies with grossly deformed arms and legs, vividly illustrated the terrible consequences of the use of certain drugs.

Of more recent concern are the possible effects on the developing fetus of marijuana, amphetamines, and heroin and of hallucinogenic drugs such as LSD, psilocybin, mescaline, and DMT (Fort, 1970). Initial research reports suggested that these drugs may be **mutagenic;** that is, they may alter the genetic structure of the sex cells. In contrast to maternal diet and disease, mutagenic drugs may affect fetal development even though the mother stops using them before she becomes pregnant. More recent articles have questioned whether the use of these drugs is indeed associated with genetic abnormalities (Dishotsky *et al.*, 1971; Houston, 1969). However, if the mother takes certain drugs during pregnancy, fetal malformations may be more likely than if she does not. Sometimes the newborn infant of a heroin user must go through withdrawal, because heroin can pass through the placental barrier.

Even cigarette smoking can influence the fetus. Cigarette smoking by pregnant women who normally do not smoke produces an increase in fetal heart rate. It is possible that heavy smokers do not eat properly, and the resulting dietary deficiency may have a greater impact on the fetus than the inhalation of nicotine and tar. Recent studies have shown that mothers who smoke during pregnancy give birth to babies who are, on the average, lighter and smaller (Butler and Goldstein, 1973).

Emotional Condition. It is not far-fetched to suspect that a woman who is pregnant and under considerable emotional stress is likely to produce a newborn baby that is in some way changed because of her emotional situation. Indeed, the effect of maternal emotions has been a frequent subject of folklore.

Some scientific investigations have suggested that the mother's emotional state can indeed influence her offspring. A number of researchers have demonstrated that stressful experiences in human and rat mothers during pregnancy influence the activity level, birth weight, heart rate, motor development, and emotionality of their offspring (Joffe, 1965; Thompson, 1957). In fact, there may even be a grandmother effect, in which stress in a pregnant rat mother affects the emotionality of the second generation of offspring (Denenberg and Rosenberg, 1967).

Abortion. Sometimes pregnancies are terminated, and the developing organism is expelled or removed from the uterus. If this happens spontaneously and without deliberate interference on the part of the mother or a physician, it is called a **miscarriage** when the fetus is less than twenty-eight weeks old and a **spontaneous abortion** if the fetus is older. Years ago, it was popularly thought that miscarriages and spontaneous abortions were nature's way of eliminating an abnormal fetus and that such an event, although often producing sadness and emotional upset in the mother and father, should be viewed as a blessing. Today, science provides support for this notion; examinations of spontaneously aborted fetuses indicate a much higher rate of abnormalities than are found among normal, live births.

There is some evidence that male fetuses are spontaneously aborted more often than female fetuses. Although it is difficult to make such estimates, it is believed that approximately 130 to 150 males are conceived for every 100 females, but only about 106 males are born for every 100 females (Beatty and Gluecksohn-Waelsch, 1972). Consequently, it would appear that the prenatal death rate is higher for males than for females, a proposition that squares with the fact that following birth, females resist infection better, survive the infancy period more often, and live longer than males do (Fryer and Ashford, 1972).

Since the United States Supreme Court upheld the right of abortion, legal **induced abortions** have been more frequent. Physicians prefer to abort a fetus before it is twelve weeks old. After twelve to sixteen weeks, a Caesarean-like operation is usually required, and such surgery is more complicated and a greater risk for the mother than early abortion is.

The decision to have an abortion, especially when the life or health of the mother is in no danger, often presents complicated legal, psychological, social, and moral problems. From society's point of view, one important legal question is whether a fetus has a right to be born, and if so, at what point in his development does this right begin? Another important question is whether a woman has the right to determine how many children she will bear and when she will bear them. These issues become the focus of passionate debate and personal conflict.

In spite of all the possible complications of the prenatal period set forth in this chapter, most babies come into the world as normal individuals. As each baby emerges from the dark of the uterus, he ends his most intimate human relationship. Within the womb, he was completely dependent on his mother for the automatic satisfaction of all his needs. At birth he starts his life as a separate individual. In the next chapter, we will look at the beginnings of independent life—the world of the newborn child.

SUMMARY

1. The life of each person begins at the moment of conception, when the father's sperm cell, or spermatozoon, unites with the mother's egg, or ovum. These gametes each have twenty-three single chromosomes made up of genes, which make possible the genetic transmission of traits and predispositions from parents to their offspring.

2. The complex processes of genetic combination determine the offspring's genotype, the unique combination of genes that he carries. The phenotype, or physical expression of those genes, is often different from the genotype because some genes are dominant and some are recessive. The inherited metabolic abnormality called PKU appears when two recessive genes for the trait are paired. The dominant normal gene masks the gene for PKU.

3. During a 266-day gestation period, the organism rapidly progresses from a fertilized egg engaged in cell division (germinal period) to an embryo with organ systems beginning to take shape (embryonic period) to a fetus that increasingly resembles a human being (fetal period).

4. Behavioral development corresponds to development of the fetal nervous system and muscles. At eight weeks, the fetus is capable of movement; by twelve weeks, a variety of motor activities; and by twenty-eight weeks, a rudimentary kind of learning. Twenty-six weeks is the minimum possible age at which a fetus may survive outside the womb.

5. Birth begins with labor, in which strong uterine contractions push the infant and the afterbirth through the birth canal. At birth, the physician evaluates the baby's appearance and functioning.

6. Complications occasionally occur in prenatal development and birth. Chromosomal abnormalities that occur during meiosis (detectable by a process involving amniocentesis) can result in a missing or extra chromosome, which often creates physical abnormalities. In prematurity, the small-for-dates baby, who at birth is underweight for his gestational age, is the potential problem baby.

7. Maternal health, including diseases, nutrition, use of drugs, and emotional stress, can also complicate prenatal development, depending on timing and other factors. Pregnancies are sometimes terminated through the natural processes of miscarriage and spontaneous abortion, or the mother may undergo a legal induced abortion, a focus of heated debate.

SUGGESTED READINGS

Berrill, Norman J. *The Person in the Womb.* New York: Dodd, Mead, 1968.

Liley, Helen M. I. *Modern Motherhood.* New York: Random House, 1967.

Montagu, M. F. Ashley. *Prenatal Influences.* Springfield, Ill.: Charles C Thomas, 1962.

Montagu, M. F. Ashley. *Life Before Birth.* New York: New American Library, 1964.

Rugh, Roberts, and Landrum B. Shettles. *From Conception to Birth: The Drama of Life's Beginnings.* New York: Harper & Row, 1971.

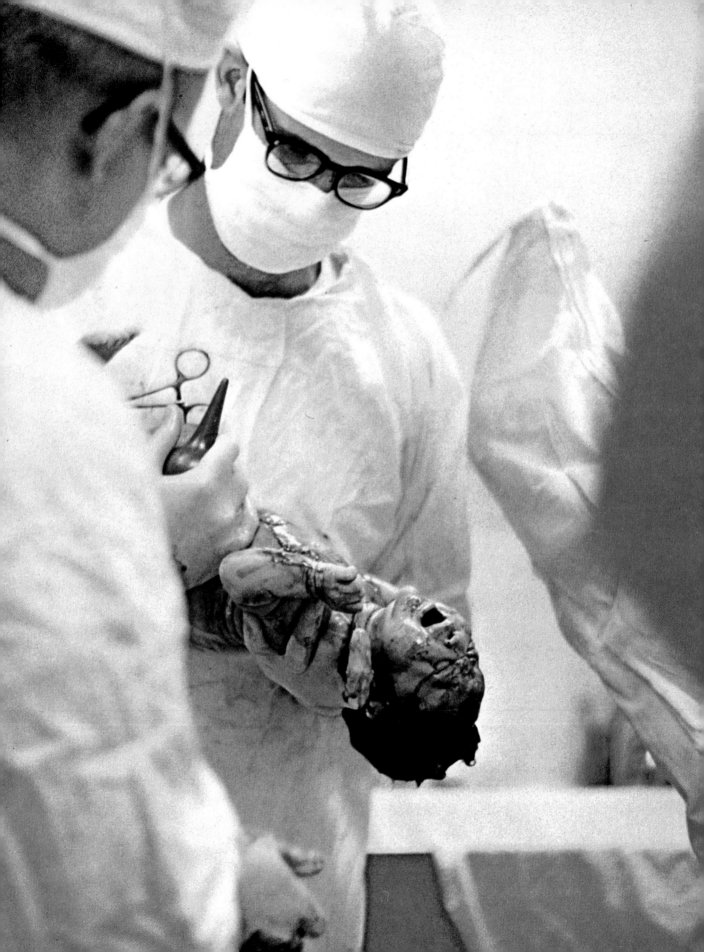

Birth marks the beginning of a new existence and the start of a rapid expansion in many aspects of adaptation and development.

5

THE WORLD
OF THE NEWBORN

A newborn baby is a curious mixture of competence and incapacity. All his vital organs are formed and functional. Unlike the newborn kitten or puppy, his eyes are open. He can see and hear and smell; he can cry and feed and move his limbs. The evolution of his species, the genetic mixture presented him by his parents, and his experiences in the womb have already begun to shape his development and behavior.

Yet until recently, other ideas have dominated thought about the human newborn. One was championed by the British philosopher John Locke (1690), who suggested that a newborn baby was akin to a blank tablet on which the finger of experience would write. Locke proposed that we all come into the world nearly devoid of behavioral dispositions and that we accumulate our mental abilities and personality through learning and experience. Many years later, the American psychologist William James (1890) supposed that the world must appear terribly chaotic to such a naive baby, "assailed by eyes, ears, nose, skin, and entrails at once, [who] feels it all as one great blooming, buzzing confusion. . . . " These scholars emphasized the helplessness of the human newborn, who possessed almost no structure or functions to deal with his new environment and who waited passively for the environment to fill his unmarked psychological notebook with the marks of social and mental experiences.

In the last decade there has been considerable scientific interest in the psychological world of the human newborn. Recent studies suggest that Locke and James were wrong. In this chapter we will see a baby named Matt enter the world with a variety of functions and skills to cope with his environment and to sample its character. As we follow Matt through the first few weeks, it will become plain that he is no passive sponge that soaks up the events taking place before him; instead, he is an active, searching, dynamic force who creates much of his own experience.

We will discover that although the newborn baby is ugly and shriveled in appearance and spends most of his time asleep, his body is remarkably prepared for life outside the womb. We will find that many of Matt's basic body functions, such as sleeping and waking, hunger and thirst, sucking, elimination, and body temperature, are kept in balance according to rhythmic biological schedules. Various studies will demonstrate his possession of a set of reflexes, many of which he will lose in a few weeks, that help him accomplish the task of feeding and coping with this strange environment. We will look at Matt's sense organs and find that most of them are functional, or soon will be, and that he uses them in an active and selective search of his environment. As we will discover, Matt is capable of learning, and he possesses the rudiments of his own personality and unique temperament. Finally, we will see how the way he looks and listens or the way he quiets when upset may provide the roots for his social development, which begins with his parents.

The technical term for a newborn baby is **neonate,** a word derived from Greek and Latin terms. Although some would limit the neonatal period to the first week of life and others would limit it to the first two weeks, most researchers agree that we can refer to a baby as a neonate until the end of his first month of independent life (Pratt, 1954).

BIRTH: THE NEWBORN

To most of us, the thought of a little baby brings to mind images of a warm, roly-poly, cuddly, cooing bundle of softness and joy. Although this characterization will be apt in a few weeks, the sight of the newborn baby sometimes disappoints, if not shocks, his parents. The American psychologist G. Stanley Hall (1891) once described the neonate as arriving with its "monotonous and dismal cry, with its red, shriveled, parboiled skin . . . , squinting, cross eyed, pot bellied, and bow legged. . . . " Others have likened his physical appearance to that of a defeated prize fighter—swollen eyelids, puffy bluish-red skin, a broad, flat nose, ears matted back at weird angles, and so forth. Of course, if one considers the wet, cramped quarters of the womb from whence he came and the violent thrusting necessary for his deliverance, his ragged appearance is not surprising.

At the moment of birth, the newborn emerges blotched with his mother's blood and covered with a white greasy material called **vernix,** which has lubricated him for passage through the birth canal. His puffy, wrinkled appearance derives in part from the presence of fluid and small pads of fat under his skin. Some newborns have fine hair, called **lanugo,** over parts of their body. When the baby emerges, the lanugo appears pasted to his skin by the greasy vernix, but after he is cleaned and dried, he may look quite furry for a few weeks until the lanugo disappears.

A newborn baby often looks somewhat battered. For example, his head may be oddly shaped or even peaked, a condition made possible by the fact that the "bones" of his skull are not yet hard and consist of overlapping pieces of cartilage. This condition allows his head to compress so that he can emerge through his mother's pelvis. As a result, his head may be

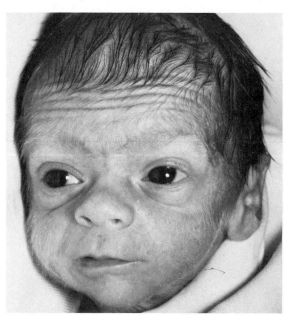

Figure 5.1 Photograph of a normal premature baby, showing distribution of lanugo hair on his face and illustrating the shape and proportion of facial features characteristic of most newborns.

lumpy: hard in some places and soft in others. In fact, the soft areas at the crown of his head that lack cartilage frequently pulsate up and down as his blood supply is pumped about his head. At the other end of his body, his legs are often bowed, and his feet may be pigeon-toed or even cocked at strange angles because his legs were tucked about him in the cramped quarters of the womb.

The newborn baby looks odd, and he may sound strange as well. In the womb, the baby was suspended in liquid, and he arrives with his nasal and oral passage filled with *amniotic fluid* and mucus. In Western hospitals, the physician cleans these passages with a suction bulb as soon as the baby's head has emerged from the womb so that the newborn does not inhale this liquid into his lungs with his first gasping breath. However, sometimes a little remains, and bursts of rapid gasps, chokes, gags, coughs, and pauses can sound like a badly operating steam engine.

After the umbilical cord is tied and cut, a nurse washes the vernix from the newborn's body with a medicated soap, drops silver nitrate or penicillin into his eyes to prevent infection, makes simple tests for certain diseases (such as PKU), and then swaddles the baby and allows him to sleep.

Although a newborn will occasionally jerk or cough up mucus, his first sleep is usually quite deep. He is difficult to arouse, and even a loud sound may fail to elicit any obvious response. During this sleep, his body is preparing to function on its own. In the womb the placenta linked his circulatory, digestive, temperature regulation, and excretory systems with those of his mother, but now his own physiological equipment must take over these necessary functions. While these systems are being balanced and tuned, a baby frequently does not eat. His stores of fats and fluids tide him over until his first nourishment, which may take place within several hours of birth or may not occur for several days. As a result of this delay in feeding, most newborns lose weight during the first few days of life.

BASIC FUNCTIONS AND RHYTHMS

Fortunately, the newborn is not thrust into the world without some mechanisms to keep his body systems in balance. A certain pattern or rhythm characterizes many of these basic body functions.

Temperature

The human being is a warm-blooded animal, which means that his body takes steps to keep its tempera-ture within a certain range. In the newborn, temperature regulation is important because the functions performed by most cells and organs are governed by enzymes that can act only within a narrow range of temperature. If the baby's temperature is much lower than the optimum, several of his body functions might slow to dangerous levels. For example, his metabolic rate might decline so much that he dies. If his temperature is too high, his physiological activity might be too rapid, triggering a mechanism that tends to shut down enzyme activity. Moreover, when a newborn is too hot, he tends to breathe more rapidly, his blood becomes too acid, and several other biochemical and physiological systems are thrown out of balance. Consequently, the baby must maintain a relatively constant temperature.

When an adult becomes overheated, his metabolic rate slows, his blood vessels dilate so that more blood can go to the body surface where heat is dissipated into the air, he sweats and loses heat through evaporation, and he pants and releases heat by exhalation. Conversely, if he is too cold, he conserves heat by shunting blood away from the surface of his body, where it would cool, and he may move around or shiver, a muscular activity that generates heat. In the adult these are surprisingly efficient systems; few people ever have difficulty regulating their body temperature.

The newborn baby has a problem that derives from the fact that for his weight he has more surface area exposed to cool air and less insulating fat than an adult. Together these factors mean that a newborn loses heat almost four times as fast as an adult does (Brück, 1961). The newborn rapidly develops mechanisms to deal with this problem. Within fifteen minutes of birth, premature and full-term babies will respond to cold by constricting surface blood vessels and increasing their heat production. Two or three hours later, the newborn baby's metabolic response to cold is nearly as good as that of the adult, relative to the baby's body weight if not to his body surface area. The newborn's problem is not that he lacks the equipment to regulate his temperature but that his task is so great.

The efficiency of the newborn's temperature control is quickly put to the test in its first encounters in the hospital environment. Whereas the womb generally remains at a constant 98.6°F., the gaseous environment that greets the newborn is invariably colder: rarely over 80°F. and sometimes as low as 60°. Because the baby is born wet and then bathed, he

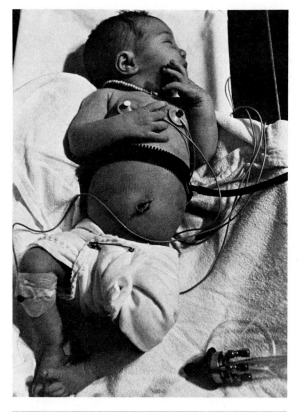

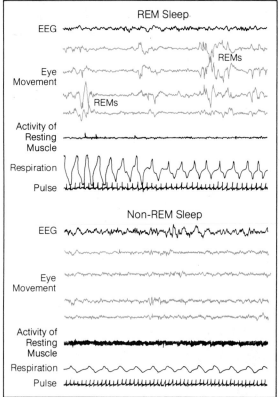

loses considerable heat through evaporation and exposure of his skin to cool air. In fact, the drop in temperature may be so steep and rapid that the baby would have to produce twice as much heat energy per unit of body weight as the adult does in order to offset these conditions (Adamsons, 1966). Although many hospitals try to minimize this shock, life in the womb remains considerably warmer than life in the delivery room or hospital nursery, and the newborn needs to be able to regulate his temperature to handle the transition. This is one reason that very small neonates often require a stay in the incubator.

Sleep

Newborn infants sleep a lot—approximately sixteen out of each twenty-four hours, which amounts to two-thirds of the day. Unfortunately for parents, the newborn packages this sleep into seven or eight naps per day, with his longest single sleep averaging about four and one-half hours. Consequently, the newborn is roughly on a four-hour sleep/wake cycle, sleeping a little less than three hours in each four. However, by six weeks of age, his naps have become longer, and he takes only two to four of them each day. Even the newborn sleeps a little more at night than he does during the day (about 60 percent of his sleeping takes place during the dark hours), and by approximately twenty-eight weeks of age most children sleep through the night without waking even once (Gesell *et al.*, 1940).

Figure 5.2 (*top*) This baby is in a stabilimeter crib, which measures his muscular activity. The belt around his abdomen measures respiration, and the electrodes on his chest produce electrocardiographic records. When electroencephalographic recordings are made, electrodes are placed at the outer corner of the eyes. Although cumbersome, this apparatus is not uncomfortable for the baby. (*bottom*) Recordings showing the differences between thirty seconds of REM sleep and non-REM sleep in a newborn. Besides the heightened eye activity during REM sleep, note the absence of muscle activity and the rapid respiratory rate and changing respiratory amplitude. (From Roffwarg, Dement, and Fisher, 1967)

Figure 5.3 (*opposite*) Proportion of REM/non-REM sleep over the life span. The graph shows that the proportion of REM sleep tends to decrease until about the age of five and then remain relatively constant. The proportion of non-REM sleep tends to increase during the first few years of life and then gradually decrease, in part because of the ongoing steady increase in waking time. The age scale used here is not proportionately true, and derived, approximate values are used for the age intervals. (After Roffwarg, Muzio, and Dement, 1966)

In addition to differences in the amount and phases of his sleep, the quality of the newborn's sleep is also different from that of the adult. Recently scientists have studied certain body activities that occur during sleep in both adults and babies. There are two general kinds of sleep, distinguished principally by whether **rapid eye movement** (REM) occurs. During REM sleep, eye movements are accompanied by more rapid and changeable respiration, less muscular activity, and a more even pattern of brain waves. In Figure 5.2, the tube around the baby's stomach expands and contracts with his breathing, the electrodes on his chest detect his heart rate, and the stabilimeter that he lies on detects his body movements. In addition, electrodes placed near his eyes detect his eye movements, and other electrodes placed on his head record his brain waves on an electroencephalograph (EEG). The minute electrical changes that accompany muscular movements are amplified and written by a polygraph on a continuously flowing sheet of paper. The figure shows a thirty-second period of REM sleep and a thirty-second period of non-REM sleep. Notice the rapid eye movements, the steadier EEG, the limited muscle activity, and the varied respiration record of REM sleep as compared to non-REM sleep.

Figure 5.3 shows both the amount of sleep and the proportions of REM and non-REM sleep for people of different ages (Roffwarg, Muzio, and Dement, 1966). The newborn spends almost half of his sixteen hours of sleep in REM sleep, and it is not until he is almost five years old that this proportion drops to approximately 20 percent, which is the adult average. Notice that the amount of non-REM sleep changes little over the childhood years, indicating that much of the newborn's extra sleep is composed of REM sleep.

What do the rapid eye movements of REM sleep signify? If an adult is awakened during REM sleep, he often reports that he has been dreaming. Consequently, some people have supposed that newborn babies (and perhaps one's pet dog) dream during REM sleep. Physiologically, the REM sleep of neonates is nearly identical to that of dreaming adults, but it is unlikely that a newborn baby experiences anything like the integrated series of clear images that most adults do, especially when one considers the limited visual capability and experience of the newborn. But one cannot say that the neurological activity of REM sleep serves no purpose or is even irrelevant to dreaming. Adults whose REM sleep is interrupted become nervous, anxious, and have trouble concentrating (Dement, 1960), and they make up for the loss of REM sleep by showing a higher percentage of it in subsequent sleep periods. Some scientists have suggested that the brain requires periodic neural activity, either from external or internal sources, and that REM sleep signifies self-generated activity in the absence of any external stimulus. Because newborns sleep so much and have less opportunity to respond to events in the world around

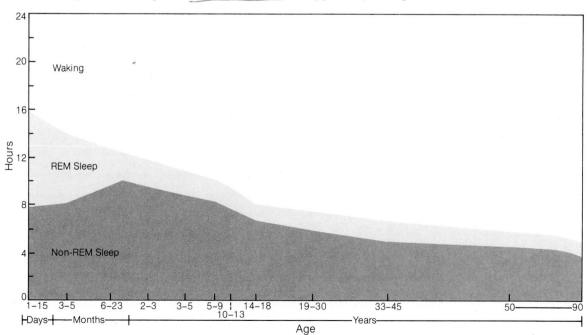

them, they therefore require more of this neurological self-stimulation. Premature babies show even higher percentages of REM sleep than full-term infants do. It is possible that such activity is necessary before birth if neurological development is to occur. Therefore, the first function of REM sleep may be as an internal stimulus to neurological development; later it will carry the visual patterns and integrated experiences that constitute the dreams of older children and adults (Roffwarg, Muzio, and Dement, 1966).

Feeding

The newborn's sleep/wake cycle is closely tied to his need for nourishment. The typical neonate sleeps, wakes up hungry and upset, eats, remains quietly alert for a short time, becomes drowsy, and then falls back to sleep. If fed every time he appears hungry, a baby may demand as many as ten to fourteen feedings each day (Trainham and Montgomery, 1946). Fortunately, within a few weeks most babies adapt to a schedule of five or six feedings a day.

Books advising parents often suggest a four-hour feeding schedule. The four-hour schedule may have emerged from a study in 1900 of three newborns who were fed a barium-milk solution and were x-rayed periodically after they swallowed it. The study showed that within four hours the stomach had emptied (Frank, 1966). Some years ago it was common practice to feed young babies on a strict schedule regardless of whether they appeared to be hungry.

Parents even waked sleeping babies to feed them. Figure 5.4 shows what kind of schedule a baby might choose if left to his own design, a regimen called **self-demand feeding.** C. Anderson Aldrich and Edith Hewitt (1947) studied one hundred babies who were allowed to establish their own feeding schedules during the first twelve months of life. At every age different babies demanded different numbers of meals. For example, during the first month of life, 60 percent of the babies ate every three hours, 26 percent ate every four hours, and approximately 10 percent demanded a feeding every two hours. Most newborns begin by putting themselves on a three-hour schedule and reach three meals a day by the time they are ten months old. Consequently, although all babies show some rhythm in their feeding patterns and all progressively require fewer daily feedings as they grow older, there are marked differences among babies with respect to the frequency of feeding. Because of studies like this, parents are now encouraged to feed their babies whenever they are hungry while working toward fewer and fewer feedings as their babies grow.

Elimination

As one might expect, because the neonate eats frequently, he also eliminates waste frequently. He may urinate up to eighteen times in a day and have a bowel movement four to seven times every twenty-four hours. However, by the time he is eight weeks old, he eliminates less often and may have only two

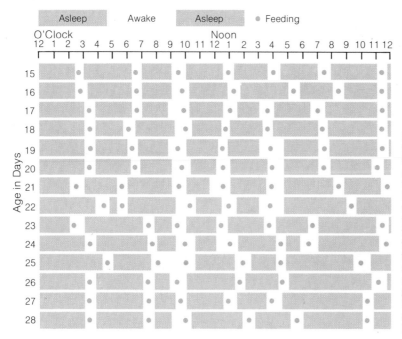

Figure 5.4 One baby's self-demand feeding schedule during her third and fourth weeks of life. Her feeding and sleeping periods during these two weeks occur fairly regularly each day. Note, however, that during the third week she takes seven feedings and that she starts to stay awake longer at the late-morning and midafternoon feeding periods. During the fourth week, she begins to take six feedings, she tends to stay awake longer at a number of feeding periods, and she sleeps for a longer continuous period before her early-morning and early-afternoon feedings. (After Gesell and Ilg, 1937)

bowel movements each day, one when he wakes up in the morning and one during or shortly after a feeding (Gesell *et al.*, 1940). The newborn's tendency to eliminate is quite involuntary and cannot be trained. The infant's voluntary control over the neuromuscular mechanisms that control urination and defecation begins to emerge during the second year of life.

Sucking

A basic rhythmical behavior that has been studied in great detail is the newborn's sucking. Being able to suck effectively is the foundation of feeding and therefore of survival. Consequently, it is one behavior that the newborn must perform competently and precisely.

The young baby sucks rhythmically, in bursts separated by pauses. On the average, a baby will put together approximately five to twenty-four sucks in a single burst, sucking at a rate of approximately one to two and one-half times each second, and then take a brief rest. Although a baby's hunger, age, health, and level of arousal influence his pattern of sucking, individual babies also have their own characteristic patterns of sucking (Kessen, Haith, and Salapatek, 1970).

The baby's sucking has two components. The first, **negative pressure,** consists of the vacuum that the baby produces in his mouth much as adults do when drinking through a straw, but this vacuum is accomplished in a different way. An adult usually creates an oral vacuum by drawing air into his lungs with his diaphragm, whereas a baby closes off the oral cavity in the back of his mouth, seals his lips about the object to be sucked, and then lowers his jaw to create a negative pressure. It is probably good that the infant does it his own way, for if he did not, he might draw milk into his lungs. In the second component of sucking, called **expression,** the baby presses the nipple against the roof of his mouth with his tongue, first applying heavy pressure at the front of his mouth and then progressively moving his tongue toward the rear. He draws milk out of the nipple more by expression than by negative pressure.

Although the neonate's feeding performance may be a little ragged during the first few days of life, he quickly develops a fairly smooth coordination between sucking, swallowing, and breathing. The fact that he can swallow almost three times faster than an adult and that he is able to suck at the same time he takes in air aids the baby in this feat. Adults who sucked in a liquid and breathed at the same time

would probably choke. The baby can manage simultaneous sucking and breathing because he extracts milk from the nipple by expression instead of by inhalation. Within a week or two of birth, a baby integrates these several response components into an efficient symphony of movement. It should be clear that the rudimentary behaviors required in sucking are well-established at birth, but the baby must learn to integrate these elements into an efficient pattern and rhythm. As we will see, much of the baby's early behavior represents inborn tendencies that become modified by experience.

REFLEXES AND SENSORY CAPABILITIES

Some years ago, many people believed that the newborn baby could not sense the physical energies in his environment. It was held that he could not see clearly, smell, or taste and could feel only pain, cold, and hunger. However, research has established that the neonate's senses, although not as precise as those of the adult, do inform him about his world. On the other hand, the reflexes of the newborn attracted the attention of neurophysiologists and pediatricians much earlier, and their studies have provided us with an extensive catalog of reflexive behavior.

Reflexes

The newborn comes equipped with a set of reflexive behaviors that are elicited by specific stimuli. Some of these reflexes are adaptive and may help the new baby feed or avoid danger. Others appear to be vestiges of the past, left over from man's nonhuman ancestors deep in his evolutionary history. Still others are simple manifestations of neurological circuitry in the baby that will later come under voluntary control or will be integrated in more useful patterns of behavior. Most of these reflexes disappear within a few weeks or months, primarily as the result of neurological development, especially in the cortex of the brain (Minkowski, 1967). There are a number of reflexes whose survival role is relatively obvious. Babies close their eyes to bright light and twist their bodies or move their limbs away from sources of pain. When a baby is hungry, he will respond to pressure on his palms by sucking.

The Rooting Reflex. The rooting reflex is the baby's tendency to turn his head and mouth in the direction of any object that gently stimulates the corner of his mouth. A baby is most likely to show this at about a week or two of age when he is quietly

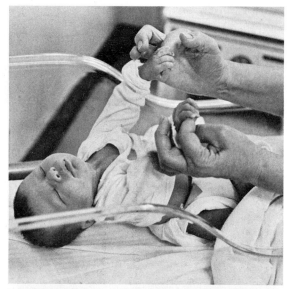

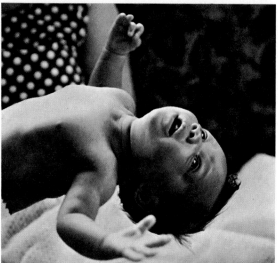

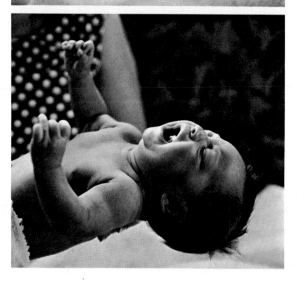

awake with his eyes open, especially if he is somewhat hungry. If one strokes the corner of the baby's mouth with an index finger, moving sideways from the mouth toward his cheek, the newborn may move his tongue, mouth, or even his whole head toward the stimulated side. At first this reflex appears even when one strokes the cheek a long way from the mouth. As the baby gets older, the reflex appears only when the stimulation is at the mouth, and only the baby's mouth will respond. This reflex has obvious adaptive significance because it helps the baby place the nipple in his mouth. Babies sometimes learn to suck their thumbs while rooting.

Grasping and the Moro Reflex.   A baby in the first few weeks of life has a strong grasping reflex. If one places a one-week-old baby on his back and inserts a finger into his hand, the baby is likely to grasp it sturdily. Sometimes a grasping newborn can literally hang by one hand.

Ernst Moro (1918) first described the **Moro reflex,** which consists of a thrusting out of the arms in an embracelike movement when the baby suddenly loses support for his neck and head. It is easily seen after the first week when the baby is alert and his eyes are open or barely closed. It can be elicited by holding a baby with one hand under his head and the other in the small of his back and then rapidly lowering one's hands, especially the hand holding his head, to an abrupt halt. A second way to obtain the Moro reflex is to lay the baby on his back with his head looking

Figure 5.5 *(top)* The grasping reflex. *(middle and bottom)* The Moro reflex.

straight up and then slap the mattress behind his head with enough force to jerk his head and neck slightly. Typically, his arms shoot out and upward and his hands curl slightly as if preparing to grab something. In fact, if your finger is in a baby's hand when somebody else provides the stimulus for the Moro, you can feel the baby suddenly tighten his grip on your finger. The Moro reflex decreases as the baby gets older; it is difficult to elicit after the baby is three months old, and it is almost always gone by five or six months.

The meaning and purpose of the grasping and Moro reflexes are not clear. It has been suggested that this behavior is an inheritance from our animal ancestors. Because monkeys carry their young on their backs or stomachs, a loss of support is less likely to produce a fall if the youngster reaches out and grasps the fur or skin of his mother's underside (Prechtl, 1965).

Walking Movements. A one- or two-week-old baby may show behavior that resembles the movements required in walking. One of these is a **stepping** motion that can be elicited by holding a baby under his arms while gently lowering him to a surface until his feet touch and his knees bend (see Figure 5.6). If one slowly bounces the baby lightly up and down, he may straighten his legs out at the knees and hip as if to stand. Then if he is moved forward, he may make stepping movements as if he were walking, although he can neither support his weight nor maintain his balance.

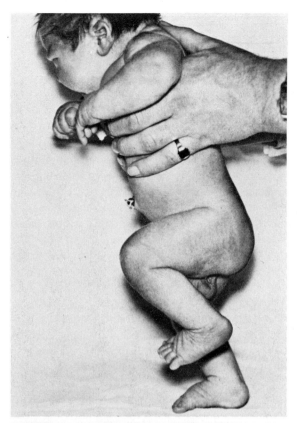

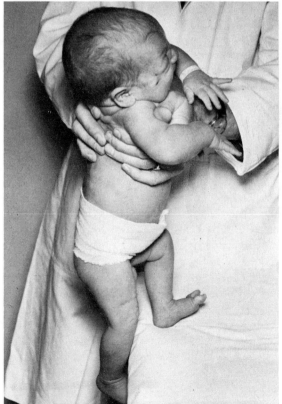

Figure 5.6 *(top)* The stepping reflex.
(bottom) The placing reflex.

The second walking motion, a **placing** response, is simply the baby's propensity to lift his feet onto a surface. If held up and moved toward a surface until the top part of his foot touches the edge, he is likely to lift up his foot and place it on the table.

These behaviors have relatively little practical utility in themselves, because the one- or two-week-old baby possesses neither the strength nor balance either to walk or to step. However, the two reflexes appear to indicate a certain inborn neurological organization that forms the basis for later standing and walking. These reflexes tend to disappear between the third and fourth month, probably because the baby's cortex has developed to a point where it inhibits them. When stepping movements next appear, they will be voluntary acts from a baby who is getting ready to rise up and walk.

Sensory Capabilities

The human being's ability to detect various stimuli provides the basis for the development of many behavioral systems. Consequently, it is important to know about some of the newborn baby's sensory capabilities. If we know what the newborn can see, hear, smell, and taste, we can discover which events in the environment might influence him.

Vision. If an adult holds one finger a few inches from his nose and another at arm's length, he can quickly alternate his focus from one to the other, an ability called **visual accommodation.** The newborn does not possess this capability. Instead, he is like a fixed-focus camera: Only objects that are about nine inches from his eyes will be in focus. Focal distance varies from baby to baby, ranging from seven to fifteen inches. By the time he is six weeks old, the baby's ability to accommodate appears to improve markedly, but he will not be as skilled as an adult until he is approximately four months of age (Haynes, White, and Held, 1965). You can begin to appreciate the staggering limits this places on the young baby's visual experience by focusing on your finger, held about nine inches from your nose, and then attempting to concentrate on other objects in the room. This limited focus is one mechanism that minimizes the baby's "blooming, buzzing confusion"; it sharply reduces the amount of distinctive visual stimulation that gets through to him.

When an adult looks at an object, he focuses both eyes on it. Each eye sees a slightly different image, and by a mechanism called **convergence,** the two images come together until he sees only a single object before him. If you hold your finger at arm's length, focus on it, and then move it toward the tip of your nose, you can feel the muscles of your eyes perform this function. The newborn does not possess this ability until he is about seven or eight weeks old. If, therefore, one holds two objects nine inches in front of the baby's face, it is possible that his right eye will literally look at the right object and his left eye will look at the left one (Wickelgren, 1967).

Visual **acuity** refers to the ability to see objects clearly and to resolve detail. If a newborn could see equally well at all distances, then the week-old baby would have approximately 20/200 vision. In terms of adult standards, this means that at a distance of twenty feet from an object, the newborn sees it about as well as you would at a distance of 200 feet. Translated into experimental terms, 20/200 vision means that the baby can discriminate a 1/8-inch stripe from a gray background at a distance of nine inches. However, his vision improves so rapidly that by the time he is three months old he can see 1/64-inch stripes at a distance of fifteen inches, and by six months, he can see as clearly as the average adult (Dayton *et al.,* 1964).

Audition. There is no question that the newborn baby hears. His ears operate four months before he is born, the basic neurology that enables him to discriminate between different tones and intensities is probably ready two months before birth, and approximately one month before birth he is prepared to direct his attention toward a sound. All normal newborns can hear, and some can hear very well. In fact, one study suggests that the faintest sound that a baby can detect is about as soft as the faintest sound heard by the average adult (Eisenberg, 1970). However, whereas the newborn can hear a sound as opposed to no sound, he has more difficulty in discriminating between one sound and another. For example, the average newborn can only detect the difference between tones of 200 and 1,000 cycles per second, which is roughly comparable to the difference between a foghorn and a clarinet (Leventhal and Lipsitt, 1964). On the other hand, some exceptional infants have responded to tones that differ as little as 60 cycles per second, which is roughly equivalent to one step on a musical scale (Bridger, 1961).

Taste and Smell. Unfortunately, scientists know little about the newborn's ability to taste or smell. It is likely that a baby has little taste sensitivity at birth. He may not be able to detect much difference between salt, sugar, lemon juice, bitter quinine, and tasteless distilled water, although he may prefer milk or sweet-tasting glucose to a salty brine (K. Jensen, 1932). The newborn does react to strong odors: He will turn his head away from the smell of ammonia or vinegar, and he can distinguish between some complex odors (Engen and Lipsitt, 1965).

PERCEPTION AND ATTENTION

If Matt were simply a passive recipient of anything that the environment presented him, then he would not attend to or respond to some stimuli and ignore others. However, this is just what he does. He looks at some things and not at others, which indicates that he is actively selecting and filtering those aspects of his world that he will notice and learn about.

Visual Attention

As we will see in Chapter 7, the two-month-old baby notices brightness, movement, and pattern. But does the neonate respond to these aspects of the world? As far as *brightness* goes, objects that are too bright or too dim will not capture his gaze. Maurice Hershenson (1964) found that a baby who is two or three days old will look longer at objects of moderate brightness than at those that are too bright or not bright enough. This research confirms the experience of parents, who often report that their newborn shuts his eyes and turns his head from bright lights, especially from sunlight.

Babies respond early to *movement.* A five-day-old newborn who is sucking on a pacifier will stop his rhythmical sucking if a light moves across his visual field (Haith, 1966). Despite the fact that his right eye and his left eye do not always look at the same thing, the newborn can pursue a moving object with his eyes if it does not move too rapidly (Dayton *et al.*, 1964). However, not until he is approximately three to six weeks old will his visual pursuit become coordinated and smooth. This suggests that if the movement is not too rapid, even newborns will be more attracted to a moving object than to a stationary one.

A great deal of research has been devoted to a baby's attention to *pattern.* As early as 1944, Fritz Stirnimann found that babies only one day old would look longer at a patterned surface than at a plain one. Robert Fantz (1965) performed some of the first modern experiments on the baby's attention to different forms. He used the apparatus pictured in Figure 5.7 to study babies between two days and six months old. Fantz placed the baby in a drawerlike carriage and slid the carriage into the looking chamber, where

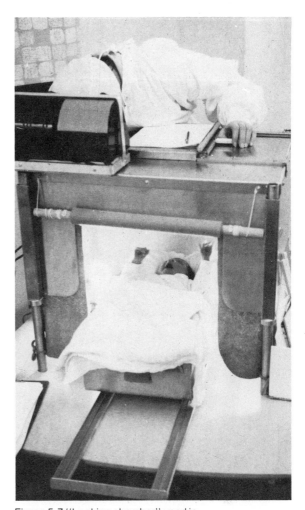

Figure 5.7 "Looking chamber" used in Fantz's studies of perceptual development in babies. The baby lies on his back looking up at two panels. Contrasting visual stimuli—for example, an outline of a human face and a half-white, half-black oval figure—are placed on the panels, and the baby's eye movements are observed and recorded to determine which of the two panels he looks at more often and for a longer period of time.

stimuli were placed directly above the baby. When Fantz used this procedure, he also found that newborns attend more to patterns than to homogeneous gray stimuli. As the babies reached two or three months, they preferred more-complex, three-dimensional stimuli and bull's-eye patterns. We will return to this experiment in Chapter 7.

Contrast. When a baby looks at a visual pattern, what aspect of it attracts his attention? In order to find out, William Kessen, Marshall Haith, and Philip Salapatek developed a device that records a baby's eye movements. The shifting gaze of six different babies can be seen in Figure 5.8. Notice that the newborn tended to look at the edges of a triangle, especially at the vertex, where black-white contrast is highest. These newborns did not systematically scan the entire shape; instead, they concentrated their attention on a corner and perhaps on the sides forming that corner (Salapatek and Kessen, 1966).

The conclusion seems to be that newborn babies do not look in a random fashion; instead, their attention is attracted to and maintained by points of high contrast. Moreover, once the neonate finds such a point of contrast, he is not likely to search the figure for another. That development must wait until he is a few weeks older.

Search Strategy. Although the newborn does not scan an object in detail, he does possess some simpler visual strategies. Suppose a newborn girl wakes up in a totally dark room. Lauren is more likely to open her eyes and scan the environment in a horizontal direction than in a vertical one. In addition, there is a certain rhythm to her scanning (approximately two scans per second) roughly the same as her sucking rate. In short, the rule appears to be: If there is no light, search systematically with a predominantly horizontal, rhythmical eye movement (Haith, 1966).

If there is light available, the baby first adopts the

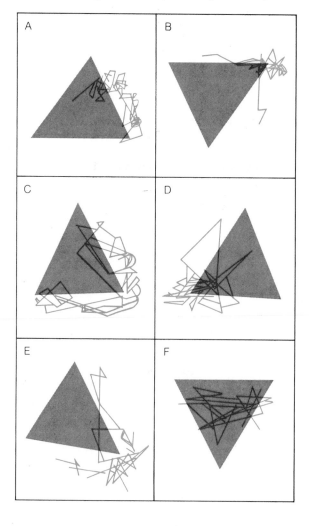

same strategy of horizontal, rhythmic search. But instead of searching for the light, Lauren searches for edges or points of high black-white contrast in her visual field. Because her scanning strategy is mostly horizontal, she is more likely to encounter a vertical line or a black-white edge than a horizontal one (Kessen, Haith, and Salapatek, 1970). Moreover, some research suggests that the brighter the contrast between the light and the dark areas of the object, the more likely the baby is to look at it. As Chapter 7 shows, the scanning strategies of the older baby are much more sophisticated.

Auditory Attention

Is the neonate a selective listener to the sounds of his world as well as a selective viewer of its sights? The answer to questions of auditory attention are difficult to obtain for two reasons. First, it is relatively easy for scientists to determine when a baby looks at something or what part of an object he focuses on by observing where his eyes are turned. It is much harder to tell whether an infant listens and even more problematical to tell what aspect of an auditory stimulus he listens to. Some information has been gained by monitoring the heart rates, respiration rates, and sucking patterns of babies when they are exposed to various sounds.

Babies do respond differently to sounds of contrasting frequencies or pitch. Low tones tend to quiet a baby who is upset, whereas high frequencies are likely to distress him and may even produce a kind of freezing reaction (Eisenberg *et al.,* 1964). Some scientists have called attention to the parallel between the newborn's response to these sounds and the tendency among adults to use sounds of different frequencies to convey feelings of distress or calm. For example, the acoustical properties of musical instruments, alarm systems, and even some words used to describe our reactions to certain events use high frequencies to alert and convey excitement or disturbance and low frequencies to communicate relative calm (Eisenberg, 1970).

There is also some indication that the newborn responds more to sounds in the frequency of the human voice (200 to 500 cycles per second) and to sounds of moderate length, approximately five to fifteen seconds in duration (Eisenberg, 1970). Chapter 8 describes how this response to the human voice plays a role in the development of language.

It should be clear from these examples of visual and auditory attention that the newborn's perceptual world is somewhat less confusing than psychologists once thought. Although the newborn's sensory systems do function, his ability to detect stimuli or to discriminate among them is seriously limited. Because his eyes focus at about nine inches, a considerable amount of the visual environment is simply not available to him. Although some babies are quite good at discriminating between one kind of sound and another, the average newborn perceives many sounds as the same that adults would detect as different. Finally, the newborn baby is selective about what stimuli will attract his attention or increase his responses: He tunes some things in and tunes other things out. As a result, the newborn neither detects nor pays attention to much of what adults perceive. The newborn's perceptual world is probably simpler and more orderly than we might guess.

ADAPTING TO THE WORLD

Given that the baby has many ways of sensing events in the outside world and given that he has certain

Figure 5.8 In this perception experiment, newborn babies were presented with a large black triangle on a white field. (*left*) Infrared marker lights were placed behind the triangle and reflected in the baby's pupil, permitting the baby's eye movements to be traced and photographed. (*right*) Besides showing that the infants looked more toward the corners of the triangle, the six tracings illustrate the wide variation in patterns of scanning that occurs among babies. (From Salapatek and Kessen, 1966)

coordinated patterns of behavior for meeting situations that might arise, what are the mechanisms by which he adapts to his environment? How does he come to know more about his world?

The neonate can learn—at least some things under some circumstances. For example, he learns to integrate sucking and breathing into an efficient feeding process, and he can learn to modify these behaviors to fit the circumstances at hand. In addition, he is able to form crude memories of certain stimuli, to remember those stimuli for five to ten seconds, and then to detect whether a subsequent stimulus is different from that memory.

Learning to Suck

You will recall that sucking has two components, negative pressure and expression, and that the baby must learn to integrate these elements with breathing in order to eat efficiently. Scientists have studied this learning potential in newborns by constructing an artificial feeding situation.

Arnold Sameroff (1968) designed the special apparatus shown in Figure 5.9. The nipple given the baby had three tubes coming from it. Tube A detected how much the baby pushed or bit at the nipple—the expression component of the suck. Tube B detected the amount of negative pressure that the baby exerted. Tube C was connected to a supply of milk and delivered 1/10 cc of milk whenever Tubes A and B reported that the baby had exerted enough negative pressure or expression to satisfy the researcher. It was

possible, for example, to set the apparatus to deliver milk only when the baby exerted a certain amount of negative pressure, regardless of how much he pushed or bit at the nipple. Under this condition, two- to six-day-old babies increased the amount of negative pressure they exerted on the nipple to whatever pressure it took to get the milk. However, if the conditions were reversed and milk was delivered only when the baby vigorously expressed the nipple, he soon began to bite and lap at the nipple with his tongue. In fact, these newborns learned to change either aspect of their sucking within a minute of the time that Sameroff changed the requirements for milk delivery. There seems to be no question that the newborn infant can quickly learn to change the way he sucks when necessary.

Memory and Perceptual Analysis

The newborn baby spends most of his hours either asleep, fussing and crying because of hunger, or feeding. In fact, the average newborn probably is quietly alert only about thirty minutes in every four hours. Many parents are fond of putting mobiles and other objects in the crib with their newborn. Is it possible that a young baby, who is alert for such short periods, can become familiar with such objects—that is, can form a memory of them, retain that memory, and recognize an old mobile as familiar or detect a new one as strange?

Steven Friedman explored this possibility with babies from one to four days old (Friedman, 1972;

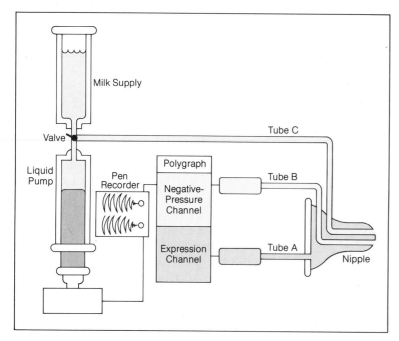

Figure 5.9 Diagram of the nipple and nutrient delivery system used by Sameroff in studying the sucking behavior of newborn babies. The experimental apparatus is designed to record both the expression and negative-pressure components of sucking and to deliver a preset amount of nutrient depending on the degree and type of sucking pressure being studied. (From Sameroff, 1965)

Friedman, Bruno, and Vietze, 1974). One of the checkerboards pictured in Figure 5.10 was shown to a baby for sixty seconds at a time. Friedman presented the stimulus again and again until on two successive occasions the baby looked a total of eight seconds less than he had looked the first two times that he had seen the object. When this happened, the infant had **habituated.** The process of habituation is roughly analogous to becoming bored with a stimulus, which implies that the baby has learned and remembered something about it. Such a decline in looking after repeated exposure may signify that the baby has formed a memory of that stimulus. On the other hand, the baby may cease to look because he is tired or fussy; perhaps he really does not remember the stimulus at all. In order to find out whether the baby was showing memory or fatigue, Friedman changed the stimulus on a later test. If the baby looked longer at the new stimulus than he did the last time he saw the familiar one, he must have had a memory for the familiar one that told him that the new stimulus was different from the old. Figure 5.10 shows the pattern of looking times for one neonate to the repeated sight of a given stimulus and to the introduction of a new one. Notice that, during the familiarization phase, this neonate looked for about the same length of time again and again until suddenly his looking time dropped sharply on two successive occasions. When Friedman introduced a new stimulus, the baby looked a long time (almost the entire sixty seconds), indicating that he detected the new stimulus as being different from his memory of the familiar event.

Given the stimuli used in this study, it was also possible to ask whether a newborn looked longer at a new stimulus that was radically different than he did at one that was only slightly different from the familiar stimulus. The results suggest that the length of time the babies looked at the novel stimulus depended on how different it was from the familiar stimulus. It appears that newborns perform a crude perceptual analysis of the difference between the new stimulus and their memory of the familiar one.

On the basis of this and other research, we can conclude that newborns can form a memory of a stimulus, retain that memory for five to ten seconds until a new stimulus is presented, retrieve that memory, and make some kind of analysis of the relationship between the familiar and novel stimuli.

Conditions for Learning

It is clear that the human newborn can learn. However, just how much he actually does learn in his natural environment is another question. Of course, he learns some things in order to survive—his integration of the components of sucking is an example. But we have also seen that the newborn works under certain handicaps and that the environment in which he finds himself may not satisfy the stringent requirements necessary before he can sense, perceive, attend, and perhaps learn.

One requirement of the learning situation appears to be *timing*. For example, if an investigator wants the

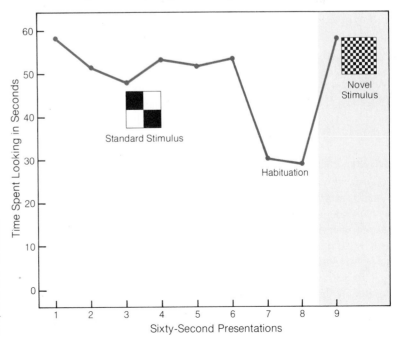

Figure 5.10 One newborn's response to familiar and unfamiliar checkerboard stimuli. After seven sixty-second exposures to the standard (familiar) stimulus, the baby became habituated. When the baby was then exposed to a novel (unfamiliar) stimulus on the ninth presentation, however, he immediately looked at it for an extended time. (After Friedman, 1972)

newborn to learn to increase negative pressure on the nipple to obtain milk, the milk must be delivered almost immediately after the baby responds with negative pressure. There can be almost no delay of reward for the newborn; he must receive his reinforcement in less than one second or he will not learn (Millar, 1972). Another requirement is *repetition;* a stimulus must be presented over and over again with only short delays between each presentation in order for the young baby to form a memory of it (Lewis, 1969). However, as a baby grows older, he is able to learn when there are greater delays between his response and the reward or between the presentation of one stimulus and another.

Moreover, whereas the scientist can construct a situation that satisfies the newborn's requirement for close timing, the baby's natural environment does not always meet that rigid standard. The delay between his actions and their effects on the people and objects around him will often be longer than a second, making learning impossible. Even when the condition of timing is met, the condition of repetition may not be. For example, a bat of the baby's hand may immediately remove a blanket that has fallen across his face, but he may not have the opportunity to push away another blanket. In a sense, then, there may be a period of "natural deprivation" (J. S. Watson, 1966) in which the baby is capable of learning but in which the conditions of his world deprive him of the circumstances he requires to do so.

PERSONALITY AND SOCIAL RELATIONS

It is difficult to talk about the personality of a newborn like Matt. Adults think of personality in terms of verbal, cognitive, and emotional behavior displayed in a social context. It is difficult for Matt to express a personality in this way. However, newborn babies do differ in their motor activity, irritability, and responsiveness, and they do engage in primitive social relations.

Activity, Irritability, Responsiveness

Some newborns are simply more *active* than others. Some frequently thrash about with their legs and arms or later bang toys and shake rattles with considerable gusto; other babies are more placid, moving more slowly and with less exaggeration. Mothers are sometimes aware of this activity difference even before their babies are born: Some fetuses kick and move about more than others, and there is some relationship between such fetal kicking and differences in behav-

ior among children for at least two years (C. E. Walters, 1965).

Newborns also differ in general *irritability*. Some cry a lot, but others do not. Certain babies are restless sleepers and tend to have fits of irritability during sleep or wakefulness (P. Wolff, 1967). There is also some evidence that irritable or fitful sleepers may have different personalities as young children from babies who do not show such restless sleep (Thomas, Chess, and Birch, 1970).

Newborn babies also differ in *responsiveness.* Some babies are cuddlers. They are soft and snuggly and seem to enjoy being cuddled, kissed, and rolled about in one's arms. In contrast, other babies resist such affectionate play by stiffening their bodies when they are handled (Schaffer, 1971). It is easy to understand how such a rudimentary social response might have a substantial impact on parents who had been looking forward to the opportunity to hug and kiss their newborn and who find themselves parents to a noncuddler. They may falsely infer that their baby dislikes them or that they are inadequate parents, forming negative attitudes that could color the way they subsequently interact with their child.

Many studies have documented these early personality differences among babies. An important early study by Margaret Fries (1954), in which she carefully observed the amount and vigor of neonate activity, led her to classify newborns into three activity types: the active, the moderately active, and the quiet. Joy Osofsky and Barbara Danzger (1974)

Figure 5.11 The general tone of a baby's personal-social interactions is often reflected in the complex and intimate interplay of his own and his mother's characteristics.

went one step further; they observed the relationship between characteristics of newborn babies and their interactions with their mothers. They found that newborns they had rated as highly responsive to sound had mothers who often talked and cooed and sang to them. They also found that newborns they had rated as highly responsive to touch had attentive mothers with highly expressive faces who touched them a lot. Although the correlation between the babies' responsiveness and the mothers' reactions to them may have had a hereditary component, it is likely that the mothers quickly learned to give their babies the kind of stimulation that the babies seemed to respond to.

Other newborn predispositions that may be important to a child's personality have been identified and described by Alexander Thomas and his colleagues (1963). These researchers decided that the intimate knowledge mothers gain in the constant care of their babies would be a source of meaningful data. Using carefully formulated interviews, they conducted an extensive study that disclosed four major behavioral characteristics that seem important for personality: the baby's activity level; his approach-withdrawal behavior, as seen in the baby's characteristic first reaction to any new stimulus; the baby's threshold of responsiveness, or the amount of stimulation required to evoke a visible or audible response from him; and his general quality of mood, such as friendly, unfriendly, joyful, or angry.

Of course, child and adult personality are much more complex than these simple categories would imply. A child's personality is a developing and evolving set of tendencies to behave in various ways. Nevertheless, it is easy to see how the general tone of social interaction within the family could be influenced by the baby's characteristic activity, irritability, and social responsiveness.

Social Relations

Obviously, social relations in the newborn are primitive by adult standards. Nevertheless, social relations require some minimal communication between individuals, and rudimentary communication of a non-verbal sort certainly exists between the newborn and his parents.

Historically, the way in which a newborn was fed was thought to have major consequences for both the child's developing social relations and his personality. Such ideas stemmed from Freudian theory, which placed great emphasis on the possible impact of events early in the child's life, and in Chapter 9, we will examine some of these important early experiences. Because the newborn spends most of his waking hours feeding, it made good sense to assume that social relations began in the feeding situation. In addition, one of the biggest differences among babies appeared to be whether they were breast- or bottle-fed. Claims for the psychological advantages of breast feeding are still made today, but there is no good evidence to show that there are any pervasive social or personality differences in later life to distin-

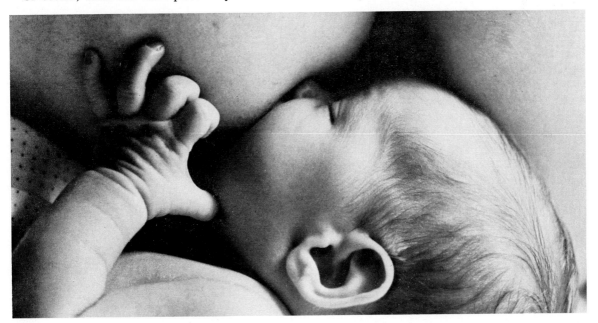

guish breast-fed from bottle-fed individuals (Caldwell, 1964).

Perhaps the most obvious method that the newborn uses to communicate with his social environment is crying. Generally speaking, a baby cries as if to say "Help me," and even quite young babies display different cries depending on whether the crying is stimulated by hunger, pain, or anger. Each cry can be distinguished by the pattern of pauses between bursts of crying, by the duration of the cry, and by its tonal characteristics. The baby's crying appears to be a wired-in, autonomous activity. If earphones are placed on the newborn's head and sounds are played to him while he cries, his crying pattern shows no interruption, even though such competing stimulation would disrupt the speech of an adult (P. Wolff, 1967).

But social communication is necessarily a two-way street, and one wonders if the differences in crying are detectable by parents or only by scientists armed with complex technical instruments. Complex instruments are superfluous. If a mother hears tape recordings of the cries of her own baby and the cries of four other babies all responding to a slight pinprick on the foot, the mother readily picks out the cry of her own baby even when he is only a few weeks old (Lind, 1971). When a mother responds to the hunger cry of her baby, it may be with more than a simple verbal statement that her child is hungry. In fact, mothers respond physiologically and prepare to breast-feed, as shown in Figure 5.12; the increased flow of blood and milk raise the surface heat of her breasts (Lind,

1971). Many a lactating mother can relate occasions when her baby has given a hunger cry and she has discovered milk gushing from her breasts in response.

Communication also occurs when a parent responds to a crying baby. There are several ways to quiet a crying baby besides feeding him. One is to stabilize his temperature and keep something in contact with his skin. Perhaps it is for this reason that babies have been swaddled for literally centuries (P. Wolff, 1969).

Movement also quiets a crying baby, but certain types of movement are better than others. One psychologist developed a rocking machine to determine how rapidly and how much rocking would quiet a baby best. The result: One rock per second, approximately 2-3/4 inches in depth, will calm a baby within fifteen seconds, and he will remain quiet even after the rocking stops (A. Ambrose, 1969).

Auditory stimulation, especially pulsating sounds, also appears to quiet an infant. In an early experiment, babies who listened to sounds roughly comparable to human heartbeats for four days cried less and gained more weight than babies who did not hear the sounds. This result prompted the researchers to conclude that the baby was conditioned while in the womb to his mother's heartbeat and that heartbeats therefore have special importance throughout human life (Salk, 1962). However, subsequent research has indicated that heartbeat sounds, the beats of a metronome, and even a lullaby are equally effective in quieting a newborn infant, and any of these is better

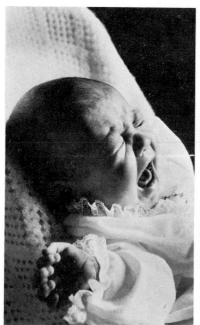
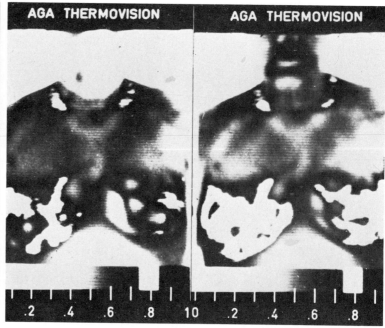

than no sound at all (Brackbill *et al.*, 1966). In fact, even continuous sounds, sights, or pitching and rocking movements have calming effects on one-month-old babies, and the more of these different stimuli that one applies at a time, the more effectively the infant's distress is reduced (Brackbill, 1971). Consequently, almost any stimulus, but especially moderately varied stimuli, will quiet a baby.

As noted earlier, a baby is especially responsive to the human voice. Recent studies indicate that babies as young as twelve hours move their bodies in rhythm with human speech (Condon and Sander, 1974). Babies responded to live or recorded speech, in either English or Chinese, but failed to respond to disconnected vowel sounds or to tapping. The investigators suggest that from the first day of life the newborn may be preparing for later speech.

SUMMARY

1. Newly arrived from complete dependence on the uterine environment, the newborn, or neonate, undergoes a period of remarkable development.

2. The newborn quickly begins to function with patterns or rhythms: body temperature becomes regulated soon after birth; sleep, composed of both REM and non-REM patterns, evolves into a four-hour sleep/wake cycle for many newborns; feeding, left to the newborn's self-demand, occurs every three to four hours for many newborns; and elimination patterns develop in accordance with feeding.

3. Sucking, a basic rhythmical behavior, is a complex behavior consisting of negative pressure, or creation of a vacuum, and expression, or drawing the milk out with the tongue.

4. From birth, the newborn is equipped with a set of reflexive behaviors that may be elicited by specific stimuli. These include the rooting reflex, the grasping reflex, the Moro reflex, and stepping and placing responses.

5. The sensory capabilities of the newborn keep him in touch with his environment. Visually, he becomes capable of accommodation, or focus; of convergence, or seeing one image with both eyes; and of acuity, or seeing detail. The newborn's auditory sense allows him to discriminate loudness and pitch, and his senses of taste and smell are functioning.

6. The newborn actively selects and filters the visual and auditory stimuli around him. He directs his visual attention to objects according to their brightness, movement, pattern, and contrast and according to certain search strategies. Auditory attention is similarly selective.

7. In adapting to the world, the neonate learns to integrate sucking and breathing into an efficient feeding process. He also can form short-term memories of certain stimuli and then compare new stimuli to them. This learning appears to depend on the timing of reward and the repetition of the stimulus.

8. Newborn babies differ in their motor activity, general irritability, and responsiveness to affection; these predispositions influence the tone of the baby's social relationships and thus may influence the evolving set of tendencies later defined as the child's personality. Feeding and responses to his crying offer the newborn his first chances for social interaction.

SUGGESTED READINGS

The Boston Children's Hospital Medical Center. *Pregnancy, Birth & the Newborn Baby.* New York: Delacorte, 1972.

Brazelton, T. Berry. *Infants and Mothers: Differences in Development.* New York: Delacorte, 1969.

Caplan, Frank (ed.). *The First Twelve Months of Life.* New York: Grosset & Dunlap, 1973.

Lipsitt, Lewis P. "Babies: They're a Lot Smarter Than They Look," *Psychology Today,* 5 (December 1971), 70–72+.

Rutherford, Frederick W. *You and Your Baby.* New York: New American Library, 1971.

Figure 5.12 In response to her baby's hunger cry, a mother physiologically prepares to breast-feed, as shown by thermographs of changes in the surface heat of her breasts, generated by the increased flow of blood and milk.

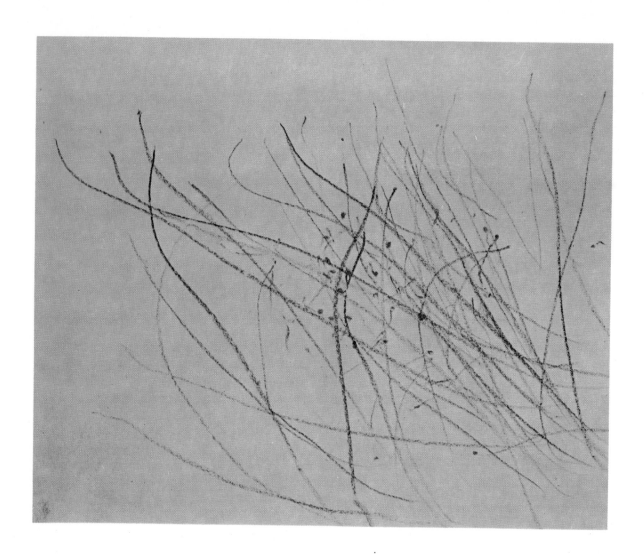

In the course of the first two years of life, a normal infant develops the ability to communicate with his parents and other people and to understand what they say to him. He gains some twenty pounds in weight and a foot or two in height. He changes from a sensory being that may only partially understand his world to a thinker who not only perceives the world in detail and acts effectively on it but also remembers his past and plots his future actions. By the time a child is two, the hand that held a rattle clutches a fat crayon and produces scribbles that appear to bring him pleasure. With the beginning of language, the child's social capabilities expand far beyond the smile and coo that he brought into the world. His early attachment to his mother expands, and the independent toddler makes friends with other children. This unit is about how and why these developmental changes take place.

UNIT III
Infancy:
The Dawn
of Awareness

Rapidly developing motor skills are one of the major highlights of physical growth during the first two years of life.

6
PHYSICAL GROWTH: FUNDAMENTALS

At birth, all normal infants can be recognized as members of the human species, but marked structural differences have existed among them since soon after conception. Newborn infants differ in such physical variables as height (length), weight, muscularity, hairiness, dental development, and a host of other measurable characteristics. As the child grows, these physical differences persist. Some, such as height and weight, may become more pronounced; others, such as hairiness, less pronounced.

The process of growth can be described as a series of interactions between the growing organism and its environment. As a by-product of this process, a baby becomes larger, the structure and function of his body become increasingly complex, and he approaches ever more closely his adult size, organic structure, and body build. In fact, the rate of physical change is greater at infancy than at any other time after birth.

One of the major reasons that psychologists study physical changes is to gain insight into the relationships between inherited factors and factors in the child's environment. If they can establish such relationships, they can begin to identify the conditions that lower a child's efficiency or hinder normal development. Once such interactions are understood, there also is some possibility of controlling unwanted deviations from normal patterns of growth.

In Chapter 4 we traced the development of the fetus from the moment of conception to the time of birth. In Chapter 5 we considered the first few weeks of the baby's life after he emerged from the mother's womb. In this chapter we will follow the baby's physical development until he reaches his second birthday. Basing our discussion on some of the basic principles that govern all physical growth, we will outline some of the ways in which psychologists have tried to summarize growth, the measures they have used, and the descriptions they have developed of the average infant. We will develop a general picture of the growth that takes place and the motor abilities that appear in the first two years of life. Because each baby's combined environment and heredity is unique, we will consider the ways in which physical development may differ from one child to the next. We will see how such differences can affect a child's personality and social behavior and how the motor changes of infancy influence the baby's intellectual and perceptual growth, broadening his world in many ways.

DIRECTIONS OF GROWTH

The systematic study of any phenomenon, whether it is growth or gravity, usually begins with a description of the way that phenomenon ordinarily occurs. Thus, the systematic study of physical development requires the observation of large numbers of infants over a considerable period of time. From such observations scientists have learned how growth appears to operate most of the time, and they have been able to formulate some basic principles of growth and to outline the general development of the average infant.

At the most general level of description, three basic principles underlie the growth and development of all body systems. These are cephalocaudal development, proximodistal development, and differentiation and hierarchic integration.

Cephalocaudal Development

The word "cephalocaudal" comes from the Greek word for "head" and the Latin word for "tail," and cephalocaudal growth in infancy refers to the direction of the body's physical growth. It is reflected in the order in which parts of the body become larger and in the order in which functions and structures become more complex. Cephalocaudal growth progresses from head to foot; a baby's head develops and grows before his torso, his arms, and his legs. This pattern of growing seems to reflect the fact that the most rapid embryological development occurs in or near those cells destined to be parts of the brain and nervous system (Debakan, 1959).

At birth a baby's head is nearer to its adult size than any other portion of his body. From birth to adulthood, a person's head doubles in size, and the trunk trebles. His arms and hands quadruple in length, and his legs and feet grow fivefold. Much of the increase in height that takes place in childhood is an increase in the length of the lower limbs. As a child grows, his head contributes proportionately less to total body length, shrinking from one-quarter of the total at birth to one-twelfth at maturity (Bayley, 1956). These changes in body proportions show in Figure 6.1.

The movement and motor ability of a baby also become more controlled and complex in progression from head to toe. The baby first gains control over the muscles of his head and neck, then his arms and

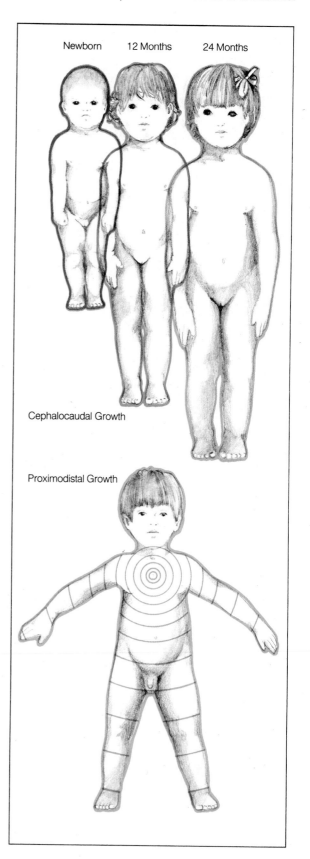

Newborn   12 Months   24 Months

Cephalocaudal Growth

Proximodistal Growth

Figure 6.2 Drinking from a cup requires the combination and integration of specific skills and actions. This year-old infant is well on her way to learning to use and adjust her grasping and sucking skills in drinking from a cup.

Figure 6.1 (opposite) Physical growth and motor abilities develop in two directions simultaneously: from top to bottom (cephalocaudal) and from center to periphery (proximodistal).

abdomen, and finally his legs. A baby learns to hold up his head before he learns to sit; he learns to sit before he can walk. He uses his hand as a unit before he can control the finer movements of his fingers. Long before he can walk or run steadily, a baby can make complicated, controlled movements of his arms and fingers, picking up even tiny specks of lint.

Proximodistal Development

Both physical growth and motor development also proceed in a proximodistal direction (Merminod, 1962). That is, growth progresses from the center of the body toward the periphery. A baby learns to control the movements of his shoulders before he can direct his arms or fingers. In general, control over movement seems to travel down a baby's arm as he becomes increasingly accurate and sophisticated in his attempts to reach for and grasp an object. In the same manner, a baby gains control over his upper leg before he can manage his lower leg or his foot.

Differentiation and Integration

A third trend of growth and development has been labeled in a number of ways. We will call it differentiation and integration. Differentiation means that an infant's abilities become increasingly distinct and specific. He gains mastery of movement after movement. For example, a baby may react to a shoe that is too tight with his whole body, wiggling, thrashing, crying, and generally creating a ruckus. As the baby grows older, his movements become more specific, so that his response to a tight shoe is to thrash about only the offending foot. Eventually he learns to make very specific responses; for example, he may ultimately say, "Foot hurt." Even at this later age, sensory stimulation from the foot is transmitted to the brain and interpreted, influencing the form of the infant's language, which is a complex behavior.

Complex responses require the infant to combine and integrate many more specific, distinct, and differentiated skills. *Hierarchic* integration is the term Heinz Werner (1948) used to describe this trend toward combining simple, differentiated skills into more complex skills. For example, after the baby has mastered the use of his arms as levers, the muscles of his abdomen as lifters of the upper body, and his neck muscles to control his head, he develops hierarchic patterns of movements that bring each separate motor capability into the service of the others in a highly organized way. At last, after each of these various simpler movements has been developed, the baby puts them all together and soon can sit up.

Consider another example, the combination and

integration of simple skills involved in learning to drink from a cup without help. Little Lauren must first be able to sit up and to fixate her eyes on an object. She must then be able to use her visual information to reach out, find the object, grasp it, and hold it upright. She then must combine visual information with kinesthetic information about the position of her own head and mouth, arms and hands, in order to bring the cup to her mouth, tilt it at the correct angle, stop tilting it before it spills, and swallow. Of course, the information described here is just a fraction of the information that Lauren uses in drinking from a cup, but she combines and integrates it all so smoothly that one seldom considers the number of simple abilities that may be involved.

NORMS

The principles of growth that we have just discussed describe growth and development at a general level. Some psychologists have compiled detailed, specific outlines of individual events in the infant's growth process. A number of investigators (for example, Bayley, 1956; Cattell, 1940; Gesell, 1925; Griffiths, 1954; Lenneberg, 1967) have analyzed the developmental sequence in which various physical characteristics and various motor, language, and social skills emerge. Investigations like these have produced outlines that describe the development of important attributes and skills and the approximate ages at which they appear in the average child. Such descriptive outlines are called **norms.**

Drawing on these norms, we can summarize the most likely patterns of infant growth and development and present a profile of the growing infant's first two years. During the first year of life, the baby shows extensive growth changes. His body length increases more than one-third, and his weight almost triples. A typical baby boy who is twenty inches long and weighs seven and one-half pounds at birth, for example, will probably be twenty-eight or twenty-nine inches long and will weigh approximately twenty-eight pounds by the time he is one year old. During these first two years, his head will grow more slowly than his trunk and limbs, so that his proportions become more adultlike. In addition, his facial skeleton will become relatively larger, so that his cranium is no longer so out of proportion with his face (see Figure 6.3).

In the first two years of life, the difference between boys and girls in growth rate and body proportion is so slight as to be of no practical significance. Even so early, however, the composition of male and female bodies differs. Baby girls have proportionately more fat and both less muscle and less water than boys (Falkner, 1966).

By carefully observing many children, scientists have described and charted literally hundreds of small but important motor developments that occur in the first two years of life. Figure 6.4 presents a simplified look at some of these norms for motor development. You should note that each of the motor milestones in the figure emerges in small steps over a period of

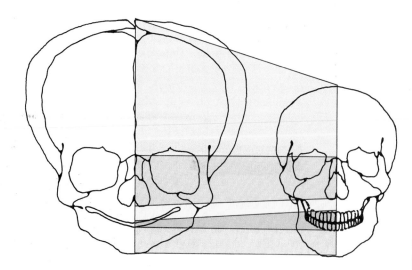

Figure 6.3 Changes in skull and facial proportions with growth. The skull outlined at the left is that of a newborn, whereas the skull at the right is that of a mature adult. (Adapted from Jackson, 1923)

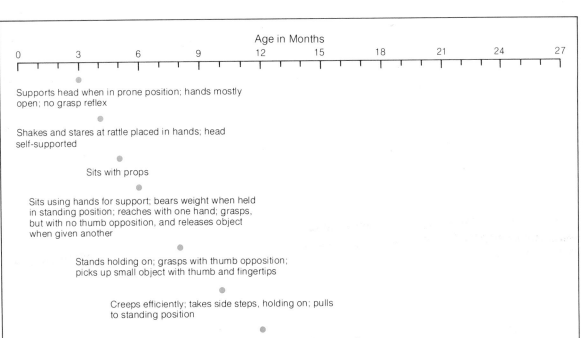

Age in Months

Supports head when in prone position; hands mostly
open; no grasp reflex

Shakes and stares at rattle placed in hands; head
self-supported

Sits with props

Sits using hands for support; bears weight when held
in standing position; reaches with one hand; grasps,
but with no thumb opposition, and releases object
when given another

Stands holding on; grasps with thumb opposition;
picks up small object with thumb and fingertips

Creeps efficiently; takes side steps, holding on; pulls
to standing position

Walks alone or when held by one hand; seats self on
floor

Walks sideways and backwards; walks upstairs and
downstairs with help; throws ball

Grasp and release fully developed; sits on child's
chair with fair aim; has difficulty building tower of
three blocks

Runs, but falls in sudden turns; quickly sits then
stands; walks up and down stairs with little or no help

Figure 6.4 Diagrammatic
representation of some of the major
milestones in motor development that
occur over the first two years of life.
Each dot indicates the approximate
average age of occurrence. Individual
infants may demonstrate these skills
somewhat earlier or later than the
average indicated. (After Lenneberg,
1967, and Bayley, 1969)

weeks or months and that it is possible to outline a number of further steps in the development of a single ability such as grasping or walking. Drawing on these detailed descriptions, we can develop portraits of the infant at different periods in the first two years of life.

In the first three months of life, the infant spends a great deal of time sleeping, eating, and crying. During these weeks, the parents see the small but steady changes in their baby's behavior and come to feel that the infant is really beginning to see and hear and notice his new world. Although the amount of time an infant spends sleeping or crying varies greatly from one child to the next, the average infant shows a noticeable decrease in these activities at about twelve weeks. By this time, he has usually given up at least one feeding. Now parents can get some sleep.

During this period, vocalizations other than crying also increase. This development partly comes about simply because the baby's lessened crying allows him more time to make other sounds. He also comes more and more to pay attention to things that go on around him. His crying may increase again during a later period; if it does, however, the causes will be different.

About the third month, the infant begins to show even more visual involvement in the world around him. He begins to respond more to repetition and to show more signs of boredom (or habituation) when the same scene or object is presented over and over again. At this time the baby's first appreciation of a three-dimensional world also appears. Once a baby like Matt can raise his head over the edge of his crib or bassinet, he can also begin to explore and interact with his environment. This physical development allows him to acquire more information about his world, and as we will see in Chapter 7, an increase in mobility is followed by an increase in knowledge.

During the period from four to seven months, many developmental changes occur. Perhaps the most important of these is improved eye-hand coordination, which allows the baby to reach for and grasp objects accurately. The first tight, reflexive grasping disappears, and in its place the baby makes eye-guided, purposeful reaches for objects. Now that he can control his hands, most of the things the infant does reach will end up in his mouth, regardless of their size, shape, or sanitary condition.

By the time he is six months old, the infant usually can roll over completely, both from back to stomach and from stomach to back. At this age he also often discovers his own feet and becomes quite fascinated by them, especially since he still has little muscular control over his feet and legs. It may seem to the infant that his feet pass quite unexpectedly in and out of his visual field. In most respects, he now seems to be a more human creature, responding warmly to people and events with the smiling, cooing, and wiggling that foreshadow those social and emotional developments that we will discuss in Chapter 9.

It is at about seven months that a baby's first teeth usually appear. He now tests those teeth, chewing on all the objects that end up in his mouth. About this same time, he may begin to sit up without help, and "drop and fetch" becomes a favorite game: The baby does the dropping; adults do the fetching. Because he seems capable of endless repetition, his parents tire of the game long before he does.

At about eight or nine months, the baby may begin to crawl. Crawling differs from creeping, which occurs about a month later. Crawling is done on the belly, often with the feet dragging along behind. Creeping is done on the hands and knees. Babies crawl in a wide variety of ways. Some scoot along either sideways or frontward on their bottoms. Some push themselves with their legs, using a leg motion rather like that used when swimming the breaststroke; some propel themselves with their arms or with just one arm. Many infants learn to move backward first. Some babies do not creep or crawl at all, but one day they simply get up on their feet and walk.

During the first half of the second year of life, the majority of infants, but by no means all, take their

Figure 6.5 Photographic depictions of the development of movement and motor coordination from the simple and basic activity of crying to such complex activities as crawling and walking.

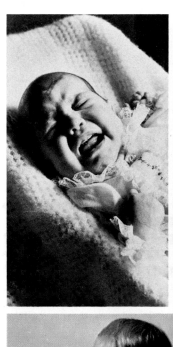
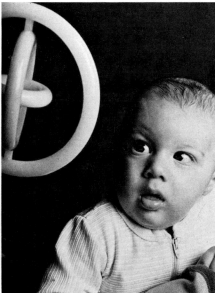
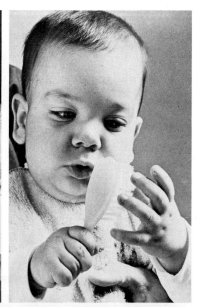

first steps (Falkner, 1966). The consequences of this development for the life of a child and his parents are incalculable. The increased opportunity that walking gives to a child and the increased danger that it can place him in only begin to suggest the importance of adultlike mobility. Fortunately for parents, a child at this stage usually begins to respond well to simple commands, and he also may be able to express some of his own desires in simple one- or two-word utterances. When his parents react positively to his simple requests, the baby often becomes fascinated with naming objects. We will discuss these language developments fully in Chapter 8. For our purposes here, interest lies in the fact that nature provides for the nearly simultaneous development of extreme mobility, adequate comprehension, and at least the rudiments of expressive language.

By eighteen months an infant can run, if somewhat clumsily, and can drag or push a toy along as he propels himself through the environment. During the next six months, there is also likely to be a dramatic increase in the child's vocabulary (Lenneberg, 1967). In fact, some children speak and move so well by the middle or end of the second year that they hardly qualify as infants. Selected norms for motor development during the infant's second year, shown in Figure 6.4, indicate that his range of physical capabilities also continues to expand during the period from eighteen months to two years.

By the time the infant is two, he will be able to walk well and to run reasonably well, if incautiously. He may be able to use 200 different words, point to the parts of his body, and play alone for short periods of time. His parents will probably stop referring to him as "the baby." The child at this point has emerged from the infant.

USING NORMS

It is important to understand the significance of norms, what they can do, and, perhaps more importantly, what they cannot do. Norms are based on simple mathematical calculations that reflect the average growth tendencies for a large number of children. Norms do not tell us what is abnormal or unacceptable. They do not explain growth or development; they merely describe it. Norms do not tell us what is ideal; they merely indicate what is most likely to appear in the development of children at particular chronological ages.

Norms can be useful in describing how most infants develop. For example, they can provide guidelines for assessing the effects of environmental

change on behavior, such as the effect of separating a child from his mother, or they can be useful in studying cross-cultural and subcultural variations. They have also been used to examine the effect of institutionalization, of sex, and of birth order on a child's development. They have been helpful in studies of prematurity and of early pathology (Kessen, Haith, and Salapatek, 1970). However, except for cases of large, obvious deviation, the value of norms as a predictor or diagnostic tool for an individual child is usually limited.

Two main problems arise when one attempts to use norms as diagnostic tools. First, the wide range of variability among normal children limits the usefulness of norms in making statements about one particular child. Second, developmental tests in infancy do not correlate with childhood measures of intelligence. This is an important point, because parents unfortunately often seem to expect norms of, say, motor-skill development to tell them something about their child's intellectual capacities. However, several authors, including Nancy Bayley (1949) and Psyche Cattell (1940), have shown that the relationship between such developmental measures in the first eighteen months of life and intelligence-test scores between five and eighteen years is, for all practical purposes, zero.

It is equally important to recognize that there is great specificity in skills. That is, Lauren's ability to catch a ball cannot be used to predict her ability at the high jump or the hundred-yard dash. After early infancy, practice also plays a large part in the level of a child's motor skills, as we will see in Chapter 10.

INDIVIDUAL VARIABILITY

As we have seen, the most common way of looking at growth is to compare a child at successive ages with the average of a large group of normal children of the same ages. The resulting individual curve of growth shows the child's growth scores relative to the average child and his relative position in a representative group of children. It should be understood, however, that despite the nearly universal sequences of growth that are described by some norms, there is great variability among children. In fact, if a rule must be established, it would emphasize deviation from the norm. Newborn infants, for example, show great individual differences in the relative proportions of various parts of their bodies. These differing proportions lend some infants a long and thin look, some a short and round one, and others every conceivable aspect in between. Also, there is greater variation in growth among boys than among girls, and individual growth patterns are more stable for girls (Tanner, 1970). A study by Howard Meredith (1963) illustrates the amazing range of individual differences in physical growth. In his study of Iowa males, the lightest boy at the age of eighteen weighed no more than the heaviest of the boys had weighed when he was eight. The boy who was lightest at age eight weighed about the same as the heaviest boy had at age two.

There is, of course, also great variability in the age at which perfectly normal children master motor skills. We have noted that some normal children never crawl or creep at all but go directly from sitting to standing and taking their first steps. The normal range for the onset of walking is itself large, perhaps from as early as eight months to as late as twenty.

Individual Time Patterns

There also are great differences in *patterns* of growth. Some normal children mature much slower or faster than the mythical average infant described by pediatricians' and psychologists' charts. Researchers have found, for example, that rates of maturation seem to be related to certain types of body build. The child who is broadly built, large, and strong is likely to be a fast grower, whereas a slender, long-legged but small, lightly muscled child is likely to grow more slowly (Bayley, 1956).

It may well be that in some areas, individual development that does not match the norm even has some distinct advantages. Paul Mussen and Mary

Cover Jones (1957) have found, for example, that male children who develop earlier than their age-mates may experience some psychological and social benefits. In a number of ways, early-maturing boys appear to be better adjusted than late-maturing boys. We will discuss the implications of such findings in Chapter 17.

One possible solution to the problems created by great differences in growth among infants is to look at an individual's growth only in relation to his own time pattern. Longitudinal data on the same child over long periods of time allow one to make statements about that child's growth relative to himself. This means that one takes the child's own status at a particular time (for example, height, weight, the closure of the bones in his hand) and uses it as the standard against which to compare his status at other times. Such time patterns for individual children can be compared to relevant norms in order to find any indications of relative precocity or slowness in patterns of growth.

Individual time patterns are more or less stable measures of growth. However, there is some evidence that severe dietary deficiencies and stress can affect these individual patterns, resulting in a temporary slowing of growth. When the condition responsible for the retarded growth is eliminated, a child often goes through a period of "catch-up" growth. J. M. Tanner (1970) calls this temporary deviation from the child's normal growth curve and the subsequent return to it the **canalization** of growth. He

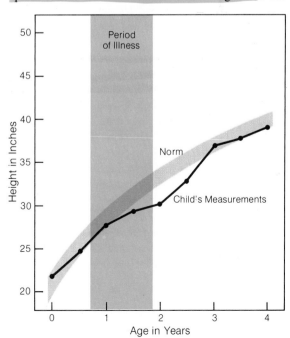

Figure 6.6 Illustration of the concept of canalization. The graph shows the effect on the growth of a young child of an illness in which his food intake was greatly reduced for approximately one year. When the illness ended and food intake was restored to normal levels, the period of catch-up growth was completed in approximately two years. (Adapted from Prader, Tanner, and von Harnack, 1963)

argues that the growth curves of individual children are genetically determined and self-stabilizing. Illness or malnutrition may temporarily deflect a child's growth from this natural curve, as a stream can be temporarily deflected from its normal course by an obstruction, but the child later catches up if his environment becomes normal.

Newborn babies also show catch-up growth in both weight and height. From birth to six months or so, smaller babies gain more weight than larger ones (Tanner, 1970). This explains the fact that small women often bear babies who become large adults. Such newborn catch-up growth is usually completed by the end of the third year. Because most babies have caught up by that time, if one knows the height and weight of a three-year-old, the chances are quite good that he can predict the child's approximate weight and height as an adult.

The Role of Nutrition

Unfortunately, dietary deficiencies are even today a common cause of abnormal growth patterns during infancy. In Chapter 4 we saw the effect of extreme dietary deficiency on the developing fetus. The importance of diet in growth and development continues after the baby is born. If, for example, one of two groups of average babies has a protein-deficient diet while the other eats protein-rich food, the deficient babies will grow to be shorter and less muscular, on the average, than the well-fed babies will. If the two groups are compared to the norms of growth, it becomes clear that it is the deficient babies who are behind in development, while the well-fed babies are growing according to the average.

Severe, prolonged protein deficiency can lead to kwashiorkor, a severe, often fatal disease found among infants in developing countries whose diets consist largely of breast milk after they are a year old (Scrimshaw, 1969; Waterlow, 1973). The symptoms of this disease include scaly skin, profound apathy, diarrhea, swollen limbs and abdomen, and liver degeneration. According to studies reported by Heinz Eichenwald and Peggy Crooke Fry (1969), when infants who are suffering from kwashiorkor eat adequate protein, they begin to grow rapidly but never catch up with normal children of their own age. This finding underlines the importance of diet as a central environmental determinant of normal physical growth.

The importance of nutrition for human growth is also reflected in growth records of infants who have been exposed to wartime famine. These children show delayed growth during such periods of malnutrition (Tanner, 1970). If the episode of malnutrition is neither too severe nor too long, children can usually overcome effects of acute malnourishment (catch-up growth). However, a child who is chronically undernourished will suffer permanent effects. Such children generally grow to be smaller adults than they would have been had they eaten an adequate diet. Nevin Scrimshaw and John Gordon (1968) have discussed the probable effects of such severe malnutrition on the human nervous system. They point out that, while head circumference shows no relationship to intelligence among normal children, it is a reasonably good indicator of brain size. They then cite the reports of researchers in Mexico, Guatemala, Peru, Uganda, and other developing countries that show that children who have had severely deficient diets from birth show smaller head circumference than children of the same ethnic group who have always been well-fed.

Severe malnutrition in laboratory animals, especially when the animals are very young, also stunts brain growth. For example, John Dobbing (1968) and others have recently shown that young pigs that suffer severe malnutrition during their first year of life never catch up with normal animals. Even after two and one-half years of normal feeding, such animals show structural changes in their nervous systems.

Although this combined evidence provides a picture of the effects of general malnutrition on physical growth, it is also known that specific deficiencies can have specific effects. For example, calcium is an essential element in the diet of infants because it is crucial to the replacement of cartilage in the skeleton with bone. A deficiency of calcium during infancy and childhood can lead to a condition known as rickets, which is characterized by softening and malformation of the bones.

Nutrition, then, plays an important role in a baby's development, both while he is in the womb and after he is thrust into the world. When dealing with middle-class infants in developed countries, it is easy to forget nutrition's part in establishing the internal environment of the child. But when looking at babies who have never received adequate diets, one finds it hard to overestimate the importance of proper food.

DEVELOPMENT OF MOTOR ABILITIES

In our discussion of norms, we sketched some of the sequences in which a child's motor abilities appear. As such motor abilities develop and become coordinated, the child undergoes correlated physiological growth. In early infancy, for example, when changes are most rapid, a baby's ability to perform motor functions correlates highly with his muscular development. The repeated observation of correlations between physical growth and motor development have led some researchers to look for internal growth that may be related to both, as in growth of the brain.

Cortical Control

Jesse Le Roy Conel's pioneer studies (1939–1963) of the postnatal development of the human cerebral cortex are among those that appear to demonstrate a possible basis in the central nervous system for the orderly development of an infant's motor and sensory functions. This and other work seem to show that certain areas of the brain control particular sensory and motor functions and that these areas develop at different rates. As soon as the specific area in the cortex develops, the corresponding functions appear in the infant's behavior.

At birth the baby's brain has already reached 25 percent of its adult weight. Although the baby's cerebral cortex is primitive, the brain itself has almost its full complement of neurons.

As you will recall from the discussion in Chapter 5, at the time the baby is born, the electrical activity of his brain shows characteristic wave patterns when he is awake or sleeping. Gradually, the wave pattern changes as the child develops, and sometime during the period between ages eleven and fourteen, the typical adult pattern emerges (S. Rose, 1973).

Postnatal development of the cortex can be followed in two directions. One is the sequence in which the functional areas of the brain develop; the second is the advancement of body functions within each of these areas (Minkowski, 1967). The early stages of development are characterized by an orderly sequence in which the primary areas of the cortex begin to function efficiently. First, the primary motor area in the precentral gyrus develops, then the primary sensory area in the postcentral gyrus (see Figure 6.7). Next the primary visual area, at the back of the head in the occipital lobe, develops, followed by the primary auditory area at the side of the head in the temporal lobe. At first, these primary areas function at a simple level. For example, the baby can control some of his basic body movements, and he can hear and see. However, the cortical association areas, which must develop before the baby can integrate and interpret the stimuli he encounters, lag behind the corresponding primary areas.

The cortical control of behavior develops sequen-

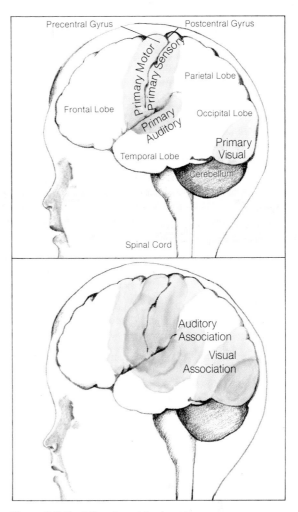

Figure 6.7 (*top*) Drawing of the human brain, showing some of its major structures and their location and indicating the location of those primary sensory and motor areas of the cerebral cortex discussed in the text. (*bottom*) Similar drawing, showing location of later-developing association areas of the cerebral cortex, as discussed in the text.

tially. Whereas most of the cerebral cortex thickens during the baby's first three months, the primary motor area develops more rapidly. Again, the cephalocaudal and proximodistal developmental patterns hold true; cortical control of the head, upper trunk, and arms appears before that of the legs, and cortical control of arm movements appears before the baby can use his hands skillfully. The other primary cortical areas develop in sequence, and the infant is capable of controlled movement and simple visual and auditory functions. At this time the cells of the motor and sensory areas rapidly develop a sheath of **myelin,** which keeps nerve impulses channeled along the neural fibers and reduces the random spread of impulses from one neuron to another (Windle, 1968).

When the baby reaches the age of six months, the primary motor and sensory areas are still the most advanced, but other areas of the cortex are beginning to catch up. There is marked growth in the cortical motor areas that control the hands, upper trunk, head, and legs. Between six and fifteen months, growth of these motor areas slows down. The infant can then control his hands and arms, but control over his legs is not nearly so well developed. In fact, some children still do not walk at fifteen months. During the period from six to fifteen months, the visual association areas of the cortex are still more advanced than the auditory association areas. By the time the child is two, however, his primary motor and sensory cortical areas are well advanced and his cortical association areas have developed further. This continued cortical development enables the two-year-old to integrate the information he gets from his environment and his own movements into more complex patterns of behavior.

The relationship between growth of particular cortical areas and the development of motor functions is *correlational.* You will recall that correlations do not tell us what is cause and what is effect. Therefore, some authors have argued that the baby's use of his body and nervous system causes the growth of appropriate brain areas, instead of brain growth leading to increased physical and mental control. Steven Rose (1973) is among those who suggest that the barrage of sensory information that assails the newborn when he emerges from the shelter of the womb leads the cortex to grow and neural connections to develop. In support of this position, one can point to studies of animals that have shown that parts of the nervous system atrophy without stimulation (Rosenzweig, Bennett, and Diamond, 1972; Wiesel and Hubel, 1963). Yet studies of premature human babies show that they reach various motor milestones

at what would be the same age, calculated from the moment of their conception rather than from the time of birth, as those born at full-term, despite the fact that premature babies receive an extra month or two of external stimulation as a result of their early birth (Douglas, 1956).

Handedness

A puzzle in the field of motor development is handedness: Only 5 percent of the world's adult population is left-handed, although a full 15 percent of preschoolers are "lefties." There is no known genetic or constitutional basis for handedness, and it is certain from the variety of clever and capable southpaws in the world that they are at no real disadvantage in a world designed for the convenience of the right-handed. The facts suggest a partially experiential basis for handedness. Rhesus monkeys, who do not encounter human society, split half and half in left- and right-handedness.

It is not at all clear why many fewer than half of the human species start out left-handed, although one possible explanation has to do with **cerebral dominance.** That is, the left side of the brain controls the voluntary muscles of the right side of the body, and the right side of the brain controls the voluntary muscles of the left side of the body. In most people, the left hemisphere becomes dominant. But whether most of us are right-handed because we are left-brained or left-brained because we are right-handed is uncertain (Hécaen and Ajuriaguerra, 1964).

Handedness begins to become evident in the latter

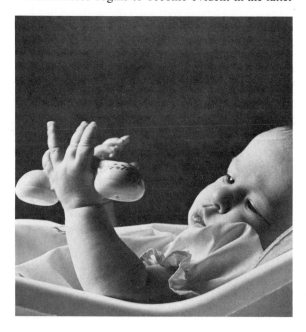

part of the first year. Almost as soon as the infant can use his two hands independently, he prefers the right. Some children persist stubbornly in their preference for the left hand despite the amazement of parents, the efforts of right-handed teachers, and the extreme difficulty of dining between two right-handed neighbors. More rare than the leftie is the ambidextrous person. It is said that Babe Ruth was one of the few truly ambidextrous people. That he chose to pitch baseball left-handed was not based on any natural advantage but on the fact that there were so few southpaws available, which is one of the few competitive advantages that fall to the left-handed minority.

Coordination of Movement

Developments in the baby's coordination of motor activities parallel the growth of the appropriate cortical areas. The orderly development of the baby's ability to grasp provides a good illustration of this increasing coordination of movement (Gesell, 1929). As we mentioned earlier, when shown an object, the newborn infant may not appear to notice it. During the first few weeks, however, the baby's visual attention continues to develop, and by sixteen weeks he fixes his eyes on the object for long periods and strains his body toward it, showing apparent attention and interest. By twenty weeks he makes crude approaches to the object with both hands. Four weeks later he uses only one hand to reach toward it and usually manages at least to scratch the object. After another four weeks, the baby flexes his whole hand while he reaches. Somewhat later he pokes at the

object with his index finger. Finally, at about forty weeks mature grasping appears, and the baby opposes his thumb and forefinger when trying to grab a toy.

The development of walking and running also illustrates the increasing complexity of the infant's brain and abilities. A normal baby's first attempts at locomotion, for example, rely heavily on the use of the arms. Thus, Lauren may drag her rump along the floor while sitting or crawl on her belly, dragging her legs along behind. Next she learns to pull herself up, using her arms for support and balance. At this point she takes her first few wobbly steps, and then more complex developments appear in rapid succession. Between fourteen and twenty-four months, for example, the baby learns to walk sideways, backward, upstairs, and downstairs and to run (Bayley, 1969). In discussing cortical control, we pointed out that the primary motor and sensory areas are quite advanced by the age of two. The increasing sophistication and integration of a child's locomotion reflect this growth. Consider the sensory information and motor skill that a child must integrate if she wishes to walk up and down stairs. She must use both visual information and kinesthetic feedback to guide her steps, as well as posture changes, weight shifts, and further visual responses. When we consider walking from this perspective, it seems a minor miracle that most babies walk so easily and well at such an early age.

ROLES OF MATURATION AND EXPERIENCE

The relative roles of maturation and experience in the development of various motor skills have been stud-

Figure 6.8 The development of grasping behavior. (*opposite*) At twenty weeks of age, infants can hold objects without firmly grasping them. (*left*) By twenty-eight weeks, they can use their palms to close in on and pick up an object. (*right*) By forty weeks, grasping, with thumb and forefinger opposition, is much like an adult's.

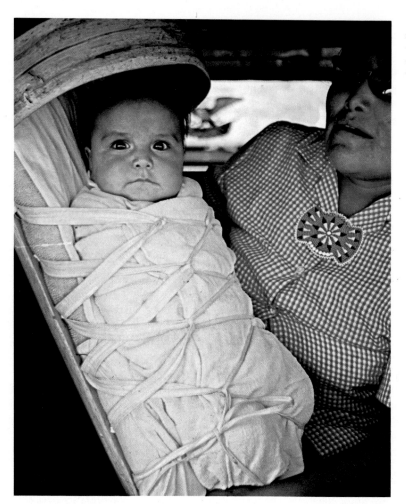

Figure 6.9 (*top*) Although Hopi infants spend much of their first year bound to cradleboards, which limit motor activity and practice, they begin to walk at about the same time as most infants in this and (*bottom*) other countries and settings. (Adapted from Hindley *et al.*, 1966)

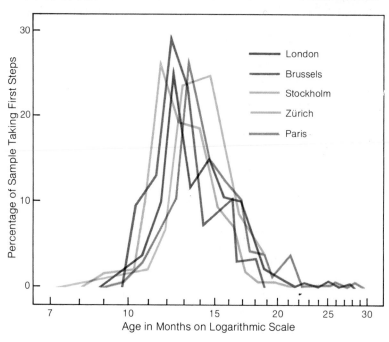

ied in a number of ways. One method is to observe the age at which infants in different cultures acquire these skills, because different cultures give babies different opportunities to practice them. For example, Hopi Indian infants spend their first year bound to cradleboards; nevertheless, they walk at about the same time as infants in other cultures who have had more practice in muscular coordination (Dennis and Dennis, 1940). Records from five of Europe's largest urban centers show that, even though child-rearing methods differ and, as a result, infants in some areas receive more encouragement to walk, most infants in the five cities take their first steps within a few months of one another (see Figure 6.9).

Another method of studying the relative contributions of maturation and experience is **co-twin control,** in which the experimenter gives one of a pair of twins some experiences believed to be important in learning a skill and withholds or delays those same experiences for the other twin. Probably the best-known co-twin–control study was done by Myrtle McGraw (1935, 1939). She gave one twin practice in crawling and standing and kept all opportunities from the other. Despite the difference in their experience, both twins crawled and walked at the same age. Practice did make a difference, however, in the way the twins developed individualistic skills, such as swimming and skating.

A third method that has been used to evaluate the relative roles of maturation and experience is to deliberately restrict a child's movement. For example, Wayne Dennis (1941) left a pair of female twins

on their backs from birth to nine months, never allowing them to sit or to stand. Yet the sitting and standing of both twins emerged fully developed, with little or no practice. It should be noted, however, that except for the experimental restriction, both girls had a fairly normal environment.

A number of years later, the same investigator conducted a series of studies designed to examine the possible effects of a poor environment on the development of motor skills (Dennis, 1960; Dennis and Najarian, 1957; Dennis and Sayegh, 1965). The studies were conducted in institutions that were, by most standards, socially and environmentally impoverished. Children were neither attended to by adults nor surrounded by a stimulating environment. The children showed retarded motor development from the time they were two months old. In one study, Wayne Dennis and Yvonne Sayegh (1965) worked with infants in The Creche, a foundling home in Lebanon. In that institution infants spent most of their first year lying on their backs in cribs. Some of the infants in their study who were more than one year old could not sit up. The infants in the experimental group were propped into a sitting position and were allowed to play with such simple attractive objects as fresh flowers, pieces of colored sponge, and colored plastic disks strung on a chain for as little as an hour each day. Despite this seemingly small amount of stimulation, the babies' developmental age jumped dramatically.

In a related study, Burton White and Richard Held (1966) investigated the effect of enriched stimulation

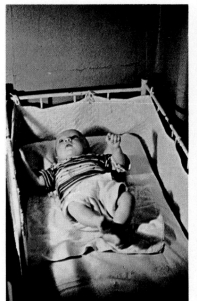 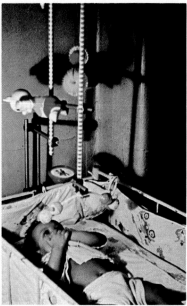

Figure 6.10 Illustration of the two extreme environmental conditions in the White and Held experiment. (*left*) In the usual institutional crib environment, there are few things to look at or touch. (*right*) In a massively enriched crib environment, there are many things to look at or touch. In comparison to these two extremes, a slightly enriched environment, involving only one object at a time to look at or touch, resulted in faster development of infants' reaching behavior.

on the development of grasping. They concluded that appropriate extra stimulation could accelerate the baby's acquisition of grasping. However, more-detailed studies have suggested (B. White, 1967, 1971) that stimulation must be appropriate to both the age of the baby and his abilities. Too much stimulation, for example, may be irritating or confusing to the baby, at least for a short time, and may fail to accelerate the development of his motor skills.

It seems clear from studies such as those of Dennis, White, and their colleagues that, even though a baby's motor development may not require any practice beyond normal freedom for spontaneous activity, some environments promote effective development, whereas others do not.

PHYSICAL AND SOCIAL CHANGES

Each new development—sitting, crawling, or walking—vastly increases the infant's perceptual, social, and emotional world, as we will see in later chapters. When Matt becomes strong enough to lift his head over the edge of a crib or cradle, he infinitely expands his ability to initiate social contact or perpetuate it, to explore the environment with his eyes, and to learn to cope with it. An infant who can sit demonstrates some control over his abdominal muscles, but, what is perhaps even more important, sitting frees his hands for exploration. Now he can experience the world tactually by grasping, poking, turning, dropping, pouring, and throwing. He can initiate physical contact with other human beings by reaching out to be picked up, grabbing a hand, poking at a face, patting an arm.

Crawling and walking give Matt a full chance to satisfy his curiosity, to go and touch, to pull and push and drag and chase, and to initiate and sustain social interactions. At last he can find someone by himself, follow that person, tug on him, and walk hand in hand. It is easy to forget that infants discover the world by banging, chewing, dismantling, and touching. Curiosity and exploratory behavior are essential to learning, language development, concept formation, and social development. Each time a child's physical abilities increase and his perceptual world widens, his potential for learning more about his social world increases. He learns what people do, how they feel, and what they like and do not like. He learns that touching brings a smile, tugging gets attention, and hitting brings a reprimand. He learns whom to seek out and whom to avoid.

It has been emphasized that children differ in their growth and development: Some are large, some

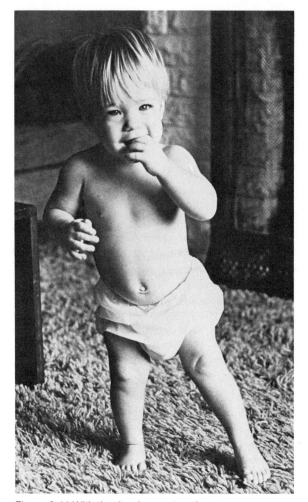

Figure 6.11 With the development and expression of greater mobility, the infant gains access to a widely expanded world of people, objects, and experiences.

small, some fast, some slow. Richard Bell (1968) reminds us that, although parents affect their children, children also stimulate their parents to behave in certain ways. For example, David Levy (1958) studied mothers and their newborn infants before they left the hospital. He found that the infant's physical state (awake, asleep, crying, and so on), not the mother's "maternal attitude," appeared to account for the way each mother handled her baby.

Although little empirical research on this subject exists, it seems clear that, for example, the child who walks early, say at nine or ten months, but who learns to respond to commands at fourteen or fifteen months is likely to require much more parental patience and physical restraint, to provoke more irritation, and generally to get into more trouble than the child who learns to walk later. On the other hand, the child who walks late may be the focus of much parental anxiety and concern. His parents may devote much time to pulling him upright, encouraging, perhaps even dragging him. Or his parents may view his relative slowness as a reflection of their own failure and therefore ignore him.

Erik Erikson (1963) points out that mastery of a skill such as walking helps to make the child a part of his culture; the child becomes "one-who-can-walk" and acquires a status different from that of "one-who-cannot-walk." The consequences of this transition are hardly trivial; in Western, industrialized, child-centered America the consequences are profound. Cultural recognition, plus the physical mastery itself, contributes not only to the child's social relations and status but also to his necessary and budding self-esteem.

SUMMARY

1. From the systematic study of physical development, scientists have formulated three basic principles that underlie the growth and development of all body systems: Cephalocaudal and proximodistal development describe directions of growth; differentiation and integration refers to increasing specificity and complexity of growth and skills.

2. Psychologists have also compiled descriptive outlines of important attributes and skills. These summary outlines are called norms and are based on simple mathematical calculations that indicate average tendencies for a large number of children. Although norms are used to describe how most infants grow and develop, they do not explain or indicate what is abnormal or ideal.

3. Despite nearly universal sequences of development described by some norms, there is great variability among children. Because a given child also shows variability, looking at his growth only in relation to his own pattern usually provides the most stable measure. Nutrition continues to play an important role, and malnutrition can result in diseases that will temporarily or permanently affect a child's growth pattern.

4. Development of an infant's motor abilities follows the course of development in the brain and central nervous system. Different areas of the brain develop at different rates, and, as a certain area develops, corresponding sensory and motor abilities appear. Handedness is a puzzle in motor development and may be due to either genetic-constitutional or experiential influences. Coordination of movement also appears to follow nervous-system development.

5. Psychologists have used several methods to study the relative roles of maturation and experience: determining the age at which infants in different cultures acquire certain skills, giving only one of a pair of twins some experience considered necessary in learning a skill, and determining the effects of certain restrictions in a child's experience. In general, it appears that, although only minimal normal practice may be necessary, some environments promote effective development whereas others do not.

6. Changes in strength, coordination, and stature are likely to have a strong impact on the infant's personal and social development. Being able to sit, crawl, or walk permits the infant to explore the world and allows him to test and understand what he can do and who he is in relation to other people.

SUGGESTED READINGS

Gesell, Arnold L., Frances L. Ilg, Louise B. Ames, and Janet L. Rodell. *Infant and Child in the Culture of Today: The Guidance of Development in Home and Nursery School.* Rev. ed. New York: Harper & Row, 1974.

McWilliams, Margaret. *Nutrition for the Growing Years.* New York: Wiley, 1967.

Rosenzweig, Mark R., Edward L. Bennett, and Marian C. Diamond. "Brain Changes in Response to Experience," *Scientific American,* 226 (February 1972), 22–29.

Spock, Benjamin M. *Baby and Child Care.* Rev. ed. New York: Pocket Books, 1968.

Tanner, J. M., and Gordon R. Taylor. *Growth.* New York: Time-Life, 1965.

During infancy, a normal baby becomes a thinker who perceives and acts effectively in the world.

7

COGNITION: FROM SENSING TO KNOWING

The adult mind is organized. Healthy adults clearly distinguish between what is within them—their thoughts, feelings, and dreams—and what is outside them—the physical world of objects and the social world of people. The things outside bear relationship to one another. Some are related by being members of the same category of things. The banana, potato, and pork chop are all foods. The hammer, knife, and saw are all tools. Some things are related in terms of action and its effects. The light switch on the wall is related to the physically dissimilar and spatially remote light on the ceiling. The pressing of a key on the typewriter is related to the letter that appears on the blank page.

Adults recognize that some things that appear to be dissimilar are in fact similar. The water that pours from the tap is the same substance that escapes as steam from the teakettle spout or that clinks as ice in a glass of lemonade. Adults accept such transformations as maintaining the identity of the object that has been transformed. They accept certain different things as equivalent to one another, such as A and a. Other transformations surprise people and demand explanation. If a friend covers something with a handkerchief and it has disappeared when he removes the handkerchief, you are puzzled. Your expectations about the behavior of the world are violated.

All these features of adults' orientation to the world seem so commonplace, so natural, that it is hard to believe that human beings do anything other than passively observe the way things are. It is hard to believe that this commonplace organization of things into categories and into cause-and-effect relationships is, in fact, the product of a long and challenging journey called cognitive development.

In Chapter 6 we watched the way that the infant's motor skills develop as he matures and interacts with his world. In this chapter we will follow the development of his **cognition** during his first two years of life. The term cognition refers to the way in which each of us comes to know about our world and to what we know about our world. It includes several processes such as sensing, perceiving, using symbols, and reasoning, and we will learn how these processes develop in the growing infant. We will discover what infant studies allow us to infer about the developing mind, and we will see how biological maturation and cumulative experience produce cognitive progress during these two years. Finally, we will consider how the infant's interactions with his environment affect his subsequent intellectual growth.

COGNITION

The lengthy story of cognitive development is the story of how the infant progresses from the limited and dissociated store of knowledge and intellectual skills that he possesses at birth, through childhood, to the concept-rich, well-ordered store of knowledge that most adults use so well.

By the time we complete our tale of the first two years, we will have seen the infant as a remarkably active organism, curious about the world and himself and eager to make sense of them both, constructing from his varied experiences new hypotheses about how its parts fit and mesh and about which of his actions are permissible and which are forbidden. We will see him as an architect of time, space, and objects and as a designer and user of symbols. Cognition is the vehicle by which the infant becomes so intellectually accomplished.

In 1949 Gilbert Ryle, an English philosopher, distinguished between at least two kinds of knowledge. The first he called *knowing that* or *knowing about* something, and the second, *knowing how* to do something. For example, after studying the grammar of a foreign language, you may be able to state quite precisely all the rules for conjugating its verbs. Yet when called on to speak the language, you may be unable to do so without many errors in your choice of verb form. You know *about* but not *how*. On the other hand, you may speak English fluently and without error, yet be unable to state the grammatical rules that describe the words you are uttering so effortlessly. You know *how* but not *about*.

As we look at the nature of the infant's knowledge, it is wise to keep in mind this distinction between knowing that such and such is the case and knowing how to do something. Because infants are incapable of using language to describe what they know about the world, we must infer what they know about it from what they do and from when and how frequently they do it. In making such inferences about the ideas and perceptions of infants, we must be careful not to assume that they perceive and conceptualize things and events the way that we do.

Basically, the environment makes its mark through the various sensory receptors that the infant possesses as a living organism. Infants are biologically constructed so as to be able to pick up certain aspects of the physical world; in other words they are capable of **sensation,** of receiving stimulation or information from the external world. It is important, however, to distinguish between sensitivity to a certain physical or chemical property of the universe and the act and experience of seeing, hearing, smelling, tasting, and touching.

A higher level of knowing about the world is reflected in the infant's **perceptions** of that world. Perceptions are built on sensation but go beyond it. What the infant does with the sensations he receives at his sense receptors determines what those perceptions will be. And what he does is affected primarily by his previous experience but also by the innate characteristics of his nervous system.

Cognition, in turn, includes more than just sensation and relatively immediate perception. We adults are much less bound in our thinking to concrete experience than young children and infants are. Most of our concepts and beliefs have been translated into symbols, such as words and pictures. This ability to represent our knowledge of the world with symbols and to use those symbols to assist us in imagining new combinations and transformations of reality that we have never experienced is one of the great cognitive achievements of the human species (Furth, 1969).

In trying to understand perception and cognition in infants, it is particularly important to realize that the infant may perceive or know certain things that he cannot easily convey to us because of his inability or unwillingness to behave in a way that would reveal this knowledge. Indeed, a considerable amount of the methodological ingenuity of infant research derives from attempts to get around this problem. Consider a concrete example. If you show a five-month-old baby girl a toy, she will reach out and pick it up. If, however, you drop a cloth over the toy before it has been picked up, the baby will sit quietly and will make no attempt to remove the cloth and get the toy. Her failure to look for the hidden toy could be due to any of several reasons. Perhaps she does not try because out of sight means out of mind to the infant, so that the vanished object no longer exists for her. Or possibly, she simply lacks the motor skills necessary to remove the cloth and get the toy. She may even have the motor skills but no longer be interested in the toy because some other interesting thing has captured her attention.

The difference between these three interpretations

is not trivial. It is important that we be able to distinguish lack of conceptual skill from lack of motor skill and both from lack of interest. The extensive use in infancy research of autonomic responses such as changes in heart rate and in galvanic skin response and of simple-to-execute motor movements such as slight head turns, eye fixations, and eye movements is a way of getting at what the infant knows without requiring that she use any difficult motor skill to inform us. The concern with taking into account the physiological state of the infant, such as when she last ate or slept, is a way of minimizing "lack of interest" factors as reasons for her failure to respond to certain tasks or situations that test her knowledge (Kessen, Haith, and Salapatek, 1970).

PERCEPTUAL FUNCTIONING

Before they can investigate the baby's cognitive processes, researchers must know how well the baby's senses function. It is through his senses that the baby transforms the raw material of stimulation into information. Matt, for instance, relies on his eyes, ears, mouth, hands, nose, and skin to extract information about the pains and pressures, the sounds and sights, and the tastes and smells in his world.

Seeing

Before the end of his first year, the baby's visual system functions like that of an adult in many respects. What he sees has very different meanings to him from what the same sight will convey several

years later (Haber and Hershenson, 1973). However, a number of studies indicate that vision is probably the most important source of information about the environment in the infant's early months of life.

A study by Thomas G. R. Bower (1966) appears to show that even a baby of six to eight weeks can judge the distance of objects. Bower trained infants to turn their heads to the side whenever a twelve-inch cube was placed about three feet away from them. After the babies had learned to discriminate between the presence and absence of the cube, he showed them a thirty-six-inch cube at a distance of about nine feet. At that distance, the large cube produced the same size image on a baby's retina as the small cube had at three feet. The only basis for discrimination was the distance of the two objects, but the babies could make the discrimination. Furthermore, they could make it even if they were allowed to use only one eye.

Other evidence indicates that during the third month of life significant changes occur in the visual world of the infant (Kessen, Haith, and Salapatek, 1970). For one thing, as the baby's ability to discriminate improves, he begins to watch strange objects in preference to familiar ones. For example, Joseph Fagan (1971) showed infants of five, seven, and ten weeks of age visual stimuli, some that were already familiar to the babies and others that were novel, and studied their responses. He found that seven-week-olds preferred the familiar stimulus, whereas the ten-week-olds preferred the novel one. Fagan, Robert Fantz, and Simon Miranda (1971)

Figure 7.1 Representation of experimental conditions used by Bower to test infants' perception of distance. Although the retinal size of the novel (test) and original stimuli were the same, infants responded less frequently to the test stimulus, indicating that they perceived the difference in distance between the two experimental conditions. (Adapted from T. G. R. Bower, "The Visual World of Infants," copyright © 1966 by Scientific American, Inc. All rights reserved)

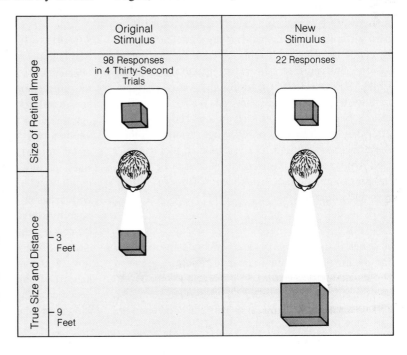

were interested in knowing whether biological maturation of the visual system played a role in these preference changes over time. They conducted the same familiar-versus-novel preference test using one group of infants born four weeks before they were due and another group born at full-term. When they compared the results, they found that eleven-week-old "preemies" did not behave like eleven-week-old full-termers. In fact, the preemies did not behave like eleven-week-old full-termers until they were fifteen weeks old. In other words, the preemies' four additional weeks of visual experience in the world did not affect their visual preference behavior. Their visual system needed to reach a certain level of biological maturation before they could respond to the familiar-novel dimension of visual information.

It is one thing to perceive the quality of relative distance, which Bower demonstrated in small babies. It appears to be quite another to use these visual cues as "warnings" about possible dangers associated with depth, such as falling off tables or chairs. In a novel experiment, Eleanor Gibson and Richard Walk (1960) studied infants' use of depth information by placing the infants on what appeared to be the edge of a cliff (see Figure 7.2). Their experiments showed that an infant who is old enough to crawl will not crawl over the deep side of a visual cliff, even to reach his mother. And when restricted to using only one eye, infants avoided the deep side of the cliff just as the infants with normal vision did, showing that binocular differences are not required to perceive the apparent danger. Because the infants in these experiments were between eight and twelve months old, it was difficult to say whether they had learned the behavior or whether it represented a maturation of vision. Subsequently, however, Sandra Scarr and Philip Salapatek (1970), using the visual-cliff apparatus designed by Gibson and Walk, found that infants begin to use depth cues to avoid edges shortly after they reach seven months of age, but only if they have begun crawling before that time. It seems, then, that some crawling experience is necessary before the infant can learn that visual cues of depth signify possible hazards.

Hearing

Another major source of environmental information for the developing infant is sound. Auditory perception is important in learning to understand and speak language and in determining the location of people or events in space. Little research has been conducted on the development of hearing in infants after they are two months old. One of the few studies was conducted by Jerome Kagan and his colleagues (1971), who wanted to determine the extent to which eight-month-old boys could recognize familiar sounds. They read four sentences to each baby in the study. Two of the sentences used such words as "smile" and "daddy" that are frequently part of parents' interactions with their babies, and the words were arranged in a meaningful way. The two other sentences were nonsensical. Kagan and his colleagues found that the babies responded in a different manner to these different combinations of sounds. The meaningful sentences with familiar words brought about a higher rate of babbling in the eight-month-old babies than did the nonsensical ones. This effect occurred even when the person who read the sentences was a male stranger, whose voice was unfamiliar.

Toward the end of his first year, the infant has progressed considerably beyond his auditory capacities of the first few months, which even then were quite impressive. At that time the infant was sensitive to such things as the frequency, duration, and intensity of sounds. By the end of the first year, however, he is also sensitive to the differences between various combinations of sounds and recognizes certain words. As was the case with the infant's development of visual perception, in auditory perception a sensitivity to the meanings attached to various inputs emerges. The infant is now on the threshold of language acquisition, which will progress rapidly during his second year.

Touching and Other Senses

Sights and sounds and smells provide the infant with considerable information about his world, whether the objects in it are close to him or far away. The senses of touch, pain, and taste tell him even more about that part of the world that he can grasp, handle, apply to his skin, or suck. Although the senses of smell, touch, and taste do not play the same primary roles in cognitive activity after a child leaves infancy (adults tend to think visually or verbally rather than with tastes or smells), their importance in the infant's cognitive development should not be underestimated. Remember that everything the child can reach enters his mouth, there to be explored with his tongue and lips. The baby is a tireless reacher, grasper, and handler of objects, which he studies not only with his eyes but with his fingers. As Jean Piaget (1954) has shown, by the latter part of his first year, the infant

Figure 7.2 Visual-cliff apparatus. A human infant of crawling age (about six to seven months) may cross the glass surface over the "shallow" side *(top left)* to reach his mother, but he is likely to refuse to venture out over an edge that visually appears to be a sudden drop *(top right)* or cross over the surface on the "deep" side *(bottom)*, even if his mother is on the other side urging him to join her.

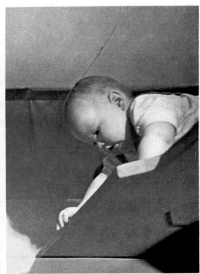

will construct notions of objects in terms of their combined touchable, tastable, smellable, hearable, seeable, graspable, and reachable characteristics.

Sensory and Sensory-Motor Coordination

The senses of the healthy infant do not function independently of one another or of the infant's motor abilities (Gibson, 1969). Rather, they work as a team, and their teamwork improves as the baby gets older. Because most events or objects provide multiple kinds of stimulation, the infant learns that stimuli from one of his senses signal that other stimuli are probably near him in space or in time. For example, if the baby hears a sound, he learns that it pays to look because he may see some interesting sight.

Very early during his first year, the baby learns to expect certain kinds of auditory-visual correlations that we take for granted and notice only when our expectations are violated. For example, you may have watched a film in which the sound track was not precisely synchronized with the picture and noticed the discrepancy between the mouth movements of the actors and their voices. You may have been disturbed because you expected a temporal correlation between what you saw and what you heard. Other relationships between sights and sounds are spatial: They often come from the same location. At what age do infants expect a definite relationship between what they see and what they hear from people talking to them? Eric Aronson and Shelley Rosenbloom (1971)

studied this expectation of a correlation between what is heard and what is seen in three-week-old infants. They used the spatial relationship between the sights and sounds of the mothers to detect the babies' expectations. Each infant sat facing his mother, who talked to him in any way she chose. (One mother recited the Gettysburg Address.) After some time, a mechanism displaced the mother's voice so that it sounded to the infant as if it came from a point three feet to the right or left of her mouth, which, of course, is not a normal circumstance. The dislocation disturbed the infants, indicating that by three weeks a baby has already detected and expected this association between the location of his mother's mouth and the sounds she makes.

When does the baby search with his eyes for the source of a sound that is outside his field of vision? Nancy Bayley (1969) found that 50 percent of the normal two-month-old infants she observed moved their eyes in apparent search when an unseen bell or rattle sounded. However, they did not necessarily look for the source in the correct direction. The more precise ear, eye, and head coordination required to turn the head and look in the correct direction for the sound source developed somewhat later in the babies that Bayley studied. Half of all four-month-old babies did this, and almost all had reached that level of intersensory and sensory-motor cooperation by the time they were six months old.

Another important coordination that develops in

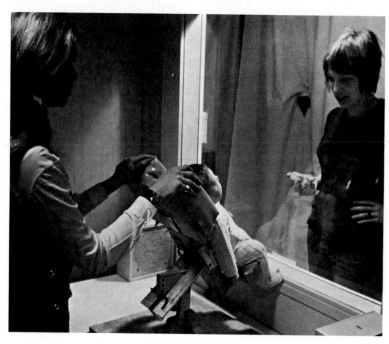

Figure 7.3 Experimental set-up in Aronson and Rosenbloom's investigation of the effects on infants of voice displacement. The mother's voice can be displaced so that it is heard coming from one of the speakers at the side, although the infant sees her speaking in front of him.

the first half year is that between the eyes and the hands (described in Chapter 6). We adults take it for granted that our hands will reach out the proper distance to touch or grasp objects that appear in our line of sight. But it is not until four and one-half months of age that half of all infants will be able to touch a cube that is placed in front of them on a table, and not until six months are virtually all infants that skilled.

The importance of this eye-hand coordination is reflected in the view of many students of infancy and early childhood that the origins of intelligence lie in the sensory-motor experiences and developments of infancy. For example, Piaget's two books (1952b, 1954) on infancy are full of vivid descriptions and perceptive interpretations of age changes in infants' sensory-motor coordination and of their link to concepts of objects, space, time, and causality.

As we indicated earlier, some of the intersensory and sensory-motor coordinations that emerge during the first year of life clearly reflect the infant's experiences. For example, he learns that he must fully extend his arm to reach a stuffed animal one foot away, because in the past he has not been able to grab a toy at that distance without reaching for it. On the other hand, maturation of the visual and motor functions in the central nervous system also may contribute to the development of the four-month-old's visually directed grab for an object. All these coordinations improve during the second year of life,

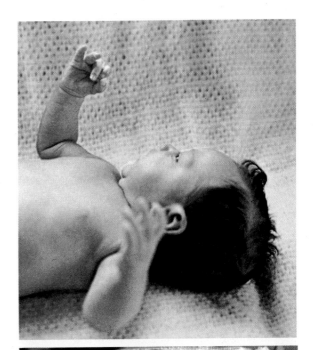

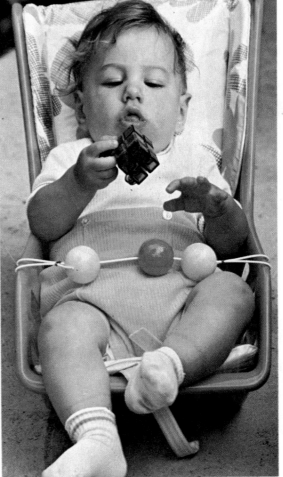

Figure 7.4 Eye-hand coordination during infancy develops from a relatively uncoordinated use of eyes and hands to a steadily smoother and more complex pattern of coordination that allows elaborate exploration of objects.

because the infant has greater opportunity to use them on the diversity of objects and events he encounters.

ATTENTION

People do not and cannot attend to all the stimuli in their environment. This selective attention begins almost at birth, and a number of factors determine why a baby will attend to one thing rather than to another. For example, certain absolute features of stimuli may determine attention. Robert Fantz (1961) exposed infants ranging in age from one to six months to a set of six flat disks. Three of the disks were patterned, and the other three had no patterns but were brightly colored. At all age levels, the infants preferred to look longer at the patterns than at the brightly colored but unpatterned disks. Fantz hypothesized that the ability to recognize a pattern, particularly that of the human face, has played a more significant role in infant survival over the course of human evolution than color recognition has. If so, it suggests that the human infant is constructed so that when patterns and colors are presented simultaneously, the patterns are more likely to attract his attention.

As the infant gets older, the relationship between a given stimulus and his previous experiences with related stimuli plays a greater role in determining what will attract his attention. He is said to build up an **expectancy** for certain stimuli, and violations of this expectancy make him attend. In general it has been found that stimuli that are moderately discrepant from those the baby has previously encountered will be particularly attractive (J.Kagan, 1972). For example, Charles Super and his colleagues (1972) exposed infants to mobiles at home every day for three weeks. These mobiles differed in varying degrees from a standard mobile. The researchers then showed the infants the standard mobile. They found that the infants whose original mobile was of medium similarity to the standard one attended most to the standard mobile. But babies whose original mobile was closely similar to the standard and those whose mobile was extremely different showed less interest when presented with the standard.

A concept closely related to deviations from expectancy is **novelty**. A stimulus can be novel without being discrepant from some previous expectancy; therefore, novelty and discrepancy are not identical, although it is not always easy to separate the two. Hildy Ross, Harriet Rheingold, and Carol Eckerman (1972) studied the attractiveness of novel objects to one-year-old infants. They presented infants with an opportunity to explore one of two rooms and to play

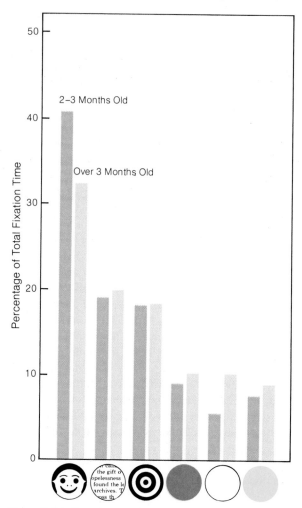

Figure 7.5 In Fantz's experiment, disks were shown to infants in a looking chamber. Fixation-time percentages indicate that, whether the infants were younger or older than three months, pattern is looked at longer than color or brightness. (Adapted from Robert L. Fantz, "The Origin of Form Perception," copyright © 1961 by Scientific American, Inc. All rights reserved)

with one of two toys that differed in their novelty. The infants chose to explore the more novel of the rooms and to play with the more novel of the toys. Another study by Meyer Parry (1972) suggests that the strength of the attentional "pull" of novelty may be reduced if the setting in which a baby encounters a novel situation or object is itself an unfamiliar one.

Often the infant's selective attention is a result of the "payoff" he receives for attending to one aspect or feature rather than to another. If, for example, Lauren, who initially prefers looking at form rather than at color, is rewarded with a smile, a tickle, or some other pleasant consequence for looking at color and gets no reward for looking at form, she may learn to shift her attention to color, the feature she originally preferred less. This is an example of learning to attend rather than of spontaneous attention, and learning to attend plays an increasingly important role in intellectual development as the child grows past infancy. However, such learning can and does occur even in the baby's earliest weeks.

Another concept related to attention is that of habituation, which, you will recall, refers to the decrease of responsiveness to a stimulus with repeated exposure to it. Stimuli that attract the attention of the infant come to bore him after a while, and he will shift his attention to another stimulus or even fall asleep. Habituation and the response to novel stimuli are basic to the infant's ability to learn. Unless the infant can remember a stimulus, there can be no conditioning, no adaptation, no learning of any sort (McCall, 1971).

Infants habituate to some stimuli more rapidly than to others. Leslie Cohen (1972) has attempted to distinguish between the physical properties of stimuli that attract the attention of infants and those that sustain their attention once it has been attracted. Using a specially designed checkerboard pattern, he found that the overall size of the checkerboard played a more important role in catching the attention of the infants, as measured by the time it took them to turn toward the checkerboard, than did the number of squares in the design. On the other hand, once the checkerboard had grabbed their attention, the number of squares that the board contained was more important than its overall size in determining how long the infants looked at it.

Attention is important because of the intellectual processing that goes along with it. As we mentioned before, sensation underlies perception, which in turn underlies cognition. To investigate the cognitive aspects of attention, some researchers have studied the baby's response to a human face (Ahrens, 1954; Haaf and Bell, 1967). A young infant sees much less in a face than an adult does. Babies under one month showed no preference for any of those faces shown in Figure 7.6. These infants will smile at any nodding object that is approximately the size of the human head. Eyes, nose, and mouth are irrelevant; only motion is important. By the time a baby is six weeks

Figure 7.6 Illustration of the facial features and expressions required to elicit smiling responses in infants of various ages, as discussed in the text. (Adapted from Ahrens, 1954)

Under 6 Weeks   10 Weeks   12 Weeks

20 Weeks   24 Weeks   30 Weeks

old, eyes have begun to attract his attention, but any two blobs will also produce a smile. When he is ten weeks old, eyebrows evoke the best smile, although at this stage even crude representations of eyes and brows provoke the infant's response.

After the baby is three months old, the eyes must be realistic to elicit a smile. Until this time, the infant reacts independently to eyes, the outline of a head, and motion. That is, the eyes need not be within a face; the head outline need not have eyes; and the motion need not be that of a head. Once he is past the age of twenty weeks, however, only the three features together will release his smile.

When the baby is twenty weeks old, a face without a mouth will cause him to withdraw instead of smile. And by the time he is twenty-four weeks old, he will smile more to a broadly smiling face than to a pursed mouth, and angry and wrinkled brows start to make him withdraw. At twenty-eight weeks he will attend and babble more to a female face than to a male face, which suggests that he clearly discriminates between males and females. Around the age of thirty weeks, he begins to differentiate familiar from unfamiliar faces, and, by the time he is eight months old, he easily tells the difference between a living face and the model of one.

It cannot be stressed too often that those features of the world to which the infant selectively attends will ultimately form that baby's perceptions of and ideas about the world. Events that attract or hold his attention, or that he actively seeks out, form the bases of his construction of reality. Those that, although physically present ''out there,'' fail to attract or to hold his attention or that he deliberately chooses to ignore do not.

CONCEPTS AND SYMBOLS

You believe that objects remain the same, even though they may move from one place to another or undergo other transformations that do not affect their basic identity. On the other hand, if at the same time you see two objects with identical features, you assume that they are separate objects. And if you see an object on Tuesday and an object with identical features on Wednesday afternoon, you assume that you have either seen the same object twice or two separate objects at two different times. To make certain, you may try to find out what has happened to the object since you first saw it. Even if you find out that you have seen two separate objects, you usually believe that the first object still exists somewhere, even though it is now out of sight.

These interrelated ideas about the identity and permanence of objects and about their potentials for moving from one place to another or for disappearing from view and reappearing are not present at birth. A baby devotes a good part of his first two years to building this intricate conceptual network of objects, movement, time, space, and causality. The infant acquires these ideas as a result of his sensory, perceptual, and motor interactions with the environment. As we mentioned earlier, understanding of the infant's gradual acquisition of beliefs about reality comes in part from Piaget's (1952b, 1954) observations of his own three children and from subsequent studies inspired by his reports.

Piaget noted that, if an object a baby of less than four months is watching disappears from view, the baby will tend to act as if the object had never been there or perhaps will keep looking at the spot where he last saw it. Typically, he will not initiate an active search for it. It is as though the object exists only when it is being immediately perceived.

During the next four months or so, however, the baby often initiates a search for an object that he sees disappearing from view. For example, if his cup falls from his high chair while he is looking at it, he may lean toward the floor to see where it went instead of just staring at the spot where it was. Even though the cup is out of sight, he now acts as though he expects it to be somewhere else. But this occurs only when he sees it starting to move away. If the cup were suddenly covered by a towel or a napkin, he would

Figure 7.7 Representation of an experiment, like that of Bower, investigating the development of object identity in young infants. When infants younger than about sixteen weeks see a moving object emerge from behind a screen and then come to a stop, they are likely to continue to track its path of movement. This suggests that they do not realize that the moving and stationary objects are one and the same.

not try to pick up the covering to get it, even though he is physically quite able to do so. At this point in the development of his object concept, the object seems to exist for him only to the extent that he can continue an activity he was already performing on the object, such as looking at it.

This failure of the infant to dissociate the objects of the world from his own actions on them is an example of the infant's inability to differentiate the self from the world and is sometimes called **egocentricity.** In the sense that egocentricity is used here, it does not mean selfishness but the failure to realize that other people do not see things from his perspective.

Object Identity

Several experimenters have supplemented Piaget's early observations with more precise analyses of the responses of young infants to different types of movements, disappearances, and features of objects. For example, Alastair Mundy-Castle and Jeremy Anglin (1969) conducted an experiment in which an object appeared on the infant's right and rose vertically out of sight; then an identical object dropped down on the infant's left and subsequently fell vertically out of sight, while the one on the right rose into view again. After viewing a number of such cycles, infants of less than sixteen weeks simply looked from side to side in order to see the objects. However, sixteen-week-olds assumed a circular trajectory of a single object; their eyes followed a circular path that corresponded to the possible trajectory of the object.

Thus, after a baby is four months old, the moving object continues to exist for him, even though it is temporarily out of view. Mundy-Castle and Anglin also found that, if the object that vanished on the right did not reappear on the left, sixteen- to eighteen-week-olds, unlike twelve- to fourteen-week-olds, looked back to the right. From such behavior we can infer that a four-month-old infant realizes that an object can change direction.

In another study, Bower (1970) investigated infants' reactions to a moving object that emerged from behind a screen and came to a stop. The older infants stopped following it with their eyes, whereas the younger ones, strangely enough, continued to track its path of movement, even though it had stopped moving. It was as if the stationary object now in front of them was different from the one they had just seen moving. They did not seem to realize that moving objects may stop and yet be the same. On the other hand, it seems that the older infants realized that movement does not affect basic object identity.

Undoubtedly the most important object for the infant is his mother. When does the infant realize that, although he may see his mother at different times in different places, she is one and the same person? Using special optical devices, Bower (1971) exposed four- and six-month-old infants to simultaneous multiple images of their mother. The younger infants responded to each of the images with delight. The older infants showed signs of distress. Bower inferred from these findings that the younger baby

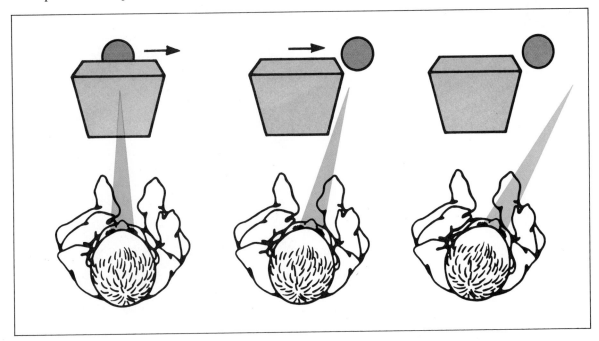

does not realize he has only one mother, so he experiences no incongruity when he sees several. In fact, the more, the merrier. However, the older infants already realize that they have only one mother who, although she may be seen on many different occasions, is never seen more than once at a single time. Simultaneous multiple images violate their understanding, and they become upset.

Object Permanence

If the young infant does not assume that his mother exists when he is not looking at her, then her sudden disappearance without a trace should not surprise him. Because for the infant she no longer exists, the absence of any clue about her new location does not contradict any of his notions about her, and he should not wonder "Where did she go?" Bower (1971) tested this deduction, using mirrors and special lighting to show babies an image of their mother. Then he made the image gradually dissolve into nothingness. Infants under twenty-four weeks watched their mothers fade away and disappear with no evidence of upset. However, infants older than twenty-four weeks reacted to the dissolution of their mothers with considerable upset and appeared to search for them. This behavior of the older baby indicates a conceptual advance, a belief that, regardless of what he has just seen, mother must exist somewhere.

The baby soon extends this belief in the permanence of his mother to other human beings and indeed to other objects. However, the extension of the belief

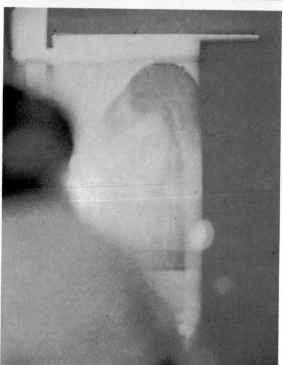

Figure 7.8 Experimental set-up showing how a mother's disappearance is effected and how it presumably looks to the infant.

does not facilitate the search, which can only be expedited when the baby acquires specific knowledge about objects. One of the first things that the infant more than six months old learns is that some objects are self-mobile. People, for example, move of their own volition. Other objects are inanimate and must be moved. The inexplicable disappearance of an inanimate object is thus likely to upset the baby, whereas the similar disappearance of an animate object will produce searching. The baby's search is guided by growing knowledge of the characteristics and abilities of the object in question.

In observations of his own children, Piaget (1952b, 1954) found that, during the last four months of their first year, his children searched for objects that they saw him place behind a screen. Although this search represents a definite advance in the child's understanding of what happens to objects that are removed from his view, his notion of object permanence is not yet like ours. Consider the following: Piaget moved a toy behind a screen while his child was observing. The child retrieved it. Piaget made his move in this game again, and the child again responded appropriately. This was repeated several more times. Then Piaget, with his child attending to his actions, modified the game by hiding the toy behind a screen located in a different place. As surprising as it may seem, the child insisted on searching for the toy in the original location. He relied on his history of successful search at Point A rather than on the evidence of his eyes that the object had moved to Point B. A recent study by William Landers (1971) showed that babies with less experience in successful searches for the object at A shift their search to B more readily than those with more such experience do.

When Piaget followed up his observations of his children during the first half of their second year, he found that they would search at Point B, but only when they had observed him move the toy behind the screen at Point B.

During the second half of the second year, Piaget's children were able to infer not only a single invisible displacement of objects but several. When Piaget successively hid the object enclosed in his hand first at Point A, then at B, then C, and so forth, the children systematically searched his hand and all these locations. They inferred that the object had to be somewhere that Piaget had been, even though they did not actually see him move it. Thus, by the end of the second year children have basically the same understanding as adults about the permanence of objects and about their existence independent of the child's own activity with respect to them.

Piaget believes that all infants acquire their final concepts of the permanence of objects by going through the same sequence of stages that he observed in his own children, although various children will move through the stages at varying rates. Recent studies of larger samples of infants tend in general to corroborate Piaget's view (Gouin-Décarie, 1965).

Most theorists agree that the infant acquires his concepts of object identity and permanence and his

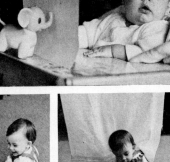

Figure 7.9 (top) This infant of about six months has not yet developed a concept of object permanence. (left) She looks intently at a toy elephant that is in front of her, (right) but when the elephant is blocked from view, she gives no indication that she understands the toy is still there.

(bottom) This older infant realizes that the disappearance of an object does not necessarily mean that it is no longer there. (left) When the object he sees (middle) is shielded from his view by a towel, he searches for it, (right) crawling under the towel to find the object.

knowledge of the distinctive features of objects by his active involvement in the world of objects. By looking at, listening to, smelling, tasting, grasping, sucking, throwing, and moving all kinds of things frequently and repeatedly, he learns which objects are small or large, rough or smooth, squeezable or hard, and bitter or sweet and which produce loud or soft noises when struck. As he gets older, he notices specific features of objects, and his definition of an object becomes more differentiated. As we saw earlier, infants come to recognize more and different features of the human face as they get older (Ahrens, 1954). Similarly, the infant's ideas about space, time, and physical causality derive from his observation and manipulation of people, things, and events.

Representational Skills

How well does the infant remember the past? How adept is he at using mental images and names to stand for things that are not present? Toward the end of his first year and throughout the second, the infant begins to create and use symbols. Imitation, language, and imaginary play are particularly important ways in which the infant can represent absent people or objects. These representational activities appear in rudimentary form in infancy and develop rapidly during the preschool years, as we will see in Chapter 11. Although at first the infant may only imitate behaviors he has just observed others perform, later he is able to defer his imitations for several hours. His own imitative movements stand for those that he saw before in another individual. When he is thirsty or hungry he will say "milk, milk." The word is a symbol for the thing. Later he realizes that some pictures or photographs correspond to people or objects and begins to acquire the notion of graphic representation of objects. His inclination to search in several different places for objects that have been hidden also suggests a use of mental imagery.

These representational skills, which become increasingly important cognitive acquisitions and tools during the child's second year of life, are related to his memory capacities. Unfortunately, we still have no clear picture of the development of memory in infancy. We can, however, divide memory itself into several component processes, such as the ability to code and store information and the ability to retrieve it by recognizing or recalling it.

The infant's ability to store information is important for his ability to recognize discrepancies. If he does not remember a previously seen pattern, he cannot realize that a later pattern is different. Fagan (1971), whose studies of visual preference in younger babies were mentioned earlier, also studied the recognition memory of older infants. He found that five-month-olds preferred novel stimuli to familiar ones when both were presented seven minutes after the babies first saw the familiar stimuli. This indicates that the five-month-old can recognize certain visual stimuli at least seven minutes after having seen them.

Memory is also an important factor in the acquisition of the concept of object permanence. We saw that when an infant of two months is looking at an object that is covered by a screen, he seems to lose interest in it, suggesting that it no longer exists for him when out of sight. However, an experiment by Bower (1971) indicates that it may be necessary to qualify this statement. After covering an object with a screen, Bower surreptitiously removed the object. He then took away the screen, immediately with some two-month-old infants and after ten seconds with others. As we would expect from Piaget's observations, those infants for whom the objects had been out of sight for ten seconds showed no surprise at not seeing it again. If the object no longer existed, there was no reason why it should reappear when the screen was removed. However, those for whom it had been out of sight only momentarily were surprised that the object had disappeared. They seemed to have a fleeting belief in the existence of the disappearing object. But this belief was not sustained when the babies had to rely on their memory of the object for at least ten seconds.

Another limitation on infants' cognition that may result from their relatively short-term memory is illustrated by the effects of delayed reinforcement on learning. For example, a study by Craig Ramey and L. Lynn Ourth (1971) showed that, if a reward is to reinforce a baby's behavior, the reward must come immediately after the baby acts. When there is a delay of even three seconds, the infant does not learn to connect the reward with his own behavior. This suggests that, by the time he gets the reward, he has forgotten what he did. On the other hand, older children have little trouble learning to associate such delayed rewards with their behavior (Brackbill, Wagner, and Wilson, 1964).

INFANT-ENVIRONMENT INTERACTION

The perceptual and cognitive developments that we have examined are products of the child's interactions with his environment. Each influences the other, and

Figure 7.10 Interest in certain objects
or activities depends on a number of
representational cognitive abilities. For
example, this older infant finds that a
jack-in-the-box is fun, partly because
she is able to reproduce an
expectation. In addition, she opens
and closes the box repeatedly, in part
because surprise is a reward but also
because she sees that she is right—
Jack is still there.

there are several ways that these effects occur. Furthermore, students of infancy sometimes view these interactions from different perspectives.

Learning

The term "environmentally induced developmental change" corresponds roughly to what most psychologists call learning. The baby will learn and his behavior will be modified by either classical or operant conditioning processes, which we described in Chapter 2.

One of the most important and powerful unconditioned reflexes is the baby's sucking reflex, which is elicited by the presence of the mother's nipple in the baby's mouth. Shortly after birth, the sight, smell, sound, and feel of mother as she prepares to nurse the baby will be enough to elicit sucking. These previously neutral stimuli become associated with the unconditioned stimulus "nipple-in-the-mouth," thereby acquiring the ability to influence the infant's sucking behavior. Researchers have classically conditioned numerous other reflexes of the infant and have conditioned them to a wide variety of previously neutral stimuli (Brackbill, 1967). But, as Hanuš Papoušek (1967) has shown, stable classical conditioning occurs more readily in older infants than in younger ones, and it appears that biological maturation is an important factor in the changing capacity of the infant to respond to classical conditioning.

However, as early as the first week of life, and forever thereafter, infant behavior is subject to operant conditioning. In one study by Harriet Rheingold, Jacob Gewirtz, and Helen Ross (1959), four-month-old infants who were tickled and smiled at when they babbled tended to increase their rate of babbling. Researchers have operantly conditioned sucking, smiling, crying, head turning, looking, and many other behaviors by arranging for some reward to occur only if the behavior occurs. The rewards that have proved effective are quite varied, and one of the more interesting is the privilege to see a sharply focused pattern. Einar Siqueland and Clement Delucia (1969) designed a special pacifier that controlled the focus of a pattern on a television screen. When the infant sucked the pacifier vigorously, the pattern remained in focus. But if his sucking slowed, the picture blurred. The baby tended to suck more energetically when this consequence was linked to his behavior.

By experimenting with the behaviors he can perform, the infant learns which ones are most effective in getting the world to do his bidding and when, or in what particular circumstances, the desired results are

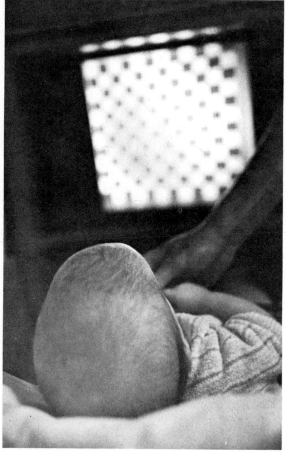

produced. John S. Watson (1971) has suggested that the responsiveness of the environment is of primary importance to the development of a baby's behavior and perhaps plays a greater role than the amount of stimulation the child receives. He placed automated mobiles over the cribs of two-month-old infants for ten minutes a day over a period of two weeks. The babies who were able to control the mobile, switching it off and on with a turn of the head, benefited more from this experience, as measured by a learning test given six weeks later, than did babies who simply watched the moving mobile but could not control it.

Because the child's perceptions and cognitions come from his experiences, it also appears that the infant reared in a bland, restricted, and nonresponsive environment is less likely to be intellectually competent than one brought up in a diversified, responsive world. A child cannot know about places and things if he has not dealt with them, and the more varied and frequent his dealings with them, the more he comes to know. A concept of a ball based exclusively on having seen one is "poorer" than a concept of a ball derived from learning how it feels and what happens to it when you bend or bite or roll it. And, as we will see in Chapter 9, the broader and more responsive the social environment, the more the infant will understand about how different people think, act, and feel.

Exploring

Although many of the sensations from which perceptions are formed impinge on the infant no matter what

Figure 7.11 (*opposite*) Siqueland and Delucia's experiment on learning in young infants. This four-month-old infant is being shown a pattern on a televisionlike screen. (*top*) He can keep the pattern in sharp focus by sucking on a pacifier hooked up to the projector. For a while, he will suck with great energy and interest to keep the picture in sharp focus. (*bottom*) Eventually, however, he is likely to become somewhat bored, decrease his sucking, and the picture fades. Typically, when a different picture is then made available, the energy the infant puts into sucking once again increases.

he does, the infant is far from a docile organism. As we pointed out in Chapter 6, from the earliest weeks of life, infants actively explore the world during their waking hours. They stare at and fixate segments of their visual field. They scan it with their eyes; they chase after moving light and moving objects. If all that their world offers is repetitive exposure to the same things, they become bored and search with their eyes for novel sources of stimulation.

Although his eyes are the most important sense organs for exploring the world, an infant investigates with other parts of his body as well. As you recall, the lips, tongue, and teeth, the hands and fingers, and the ears are all tools of the infant explorer. As a baby, Matt, for example, will grasp objects and try to suck them, not just for the pleasure of sucking but for the information about the form, texture, hardness, and taste of the object that he gets from the touch and taste receptors of his mouth and its parts. Or when Matt is not sucking objects, he may run his nimble fingers over the surfaces of objects and through their crevices. If objects are squeezable, they will be squeezed; if crushable, crushed; and if throwable, thrown. The baby will drop objects to produce bangs and thuds and other noises and will coo and cry and listen to his own improvisations in sound. All of these activities of the infant generate stimulation that never would have occurred if a baby were nothing more than a passive spectator observing the world that chances to go by.

Another aspect of the infant as explorer is demonstrated in a study by Hanuš Papoušek (1967), who

Figure 7.12 In exploring his world, the young child applies skills acquired earlier to novel situations and experiences. In applying his skills to the novel situation of a latch on a gate, he may not only learn how to open it but also develop an understanding of the cause-and-effect relationships that are involved.

found that even in the first months of life infants will master complex learning tasks purely for the joy of solving a problem. He reinforced babies when they turned their heads twice to the right, three times to the left, and once to the right again. His reinforcement was a seconds-long burst of white light. But the babies barely glanced at the light; they apparently used it only to prove to themselves that they had solved the problem. These six-month-old infants enjoyed the challenge of a puzzle.

Older infants often deliberately set difficult tasks for themselves. They work on these tasks for long periods, often showing signs of frustration yet persisting for days until they solve the problems. A clear example of this striving for competence in the environment arose in Bower's longitudinal study of the development of the concept of object permanence. In this laboratory experiment, the infants were often confronted with various hidden objects as in the object-permanence experiments described earlier. Later, according to their mothers, they spent hours at home hiding objects and retrieving them. At a later stage, when the problem in the laboratory was to find an object that had gone out of sight while moving on a complex trajectory (for example, ricocheting off the wall), the babies when at home would roll objects under tables, under beds, and off walls and would crawl after them until, at the end, they could readily retrieve a vanished object. The point is that these infants developed a concept of object permanence about nine months earlier than the average baby. This acceleration was not the direct result of any intervention by the experimenters. In this case, the experimenters simply introduced the infants to a problem, and then the infants actively explored and developed their own cognitive understanding.

Adapting

Life is full of challenges for the infant. His knowledge about the world and his knowledge of how to deal with it that was effective yesterday may be less effective today as he encounters new objects, people, and events. Consider an infant who has been exclusively breast-fed for several months and who uses his mouth very competently to suck. Now he is given a cup or a spoonful of solid food. At first he tries to incorporate, or *assimilate,* the cup or food to his mouth-using skills by sucking at them just as he sucks the nipple. Because this is not successful, he has to modify, or *accommodate,* his mouth-using skills to these new elements of his environment. By the time he successfully adapts, he has simultaneously assimilated new objects to his prior mouth-using skills and changed these skills so that they can be effective with the new elements. This explanation of the infant's adaptation is closely associated with Piaget's (1952b, 1954) theory of cognitive development (discussed in Chapter 2).

Consider another example, an infant who uses his fingers and hand to hold and squeeze rubber balls or rattles. He knows that a certain pressure on these objects will produce an entertaining squeak. Now

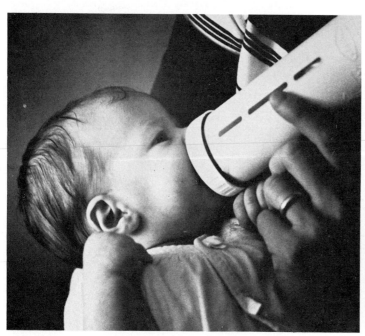

give him a luscious red tomato. Although the tomato feels somewhat different from a ball or rattle, he may try to squeeze it—he tries to assimilate or fit the new object into his squeezing skills. Unfortunately, its texture does not fit his hand-using skills, and tomato juice runs down his arm. Quickly he learns that tomatoes can indeed be held but only if they are held with less pressure than he applies to rubber balls; he modifies his hand-using skills. This adaptive response includes both assimilation and accommodation. Of course, some infants are not so perturbed by the effects of squeezing tomatoes as their mothers are. If this is the case, the infant's challenge becomes that of accommodating to his mother rather than to the tomato. As the infant grows, he will continue to use old responses on new objects and to modify his old responses, assimilating and accommodating his skills as he learns to adapt to his widening world.

SUMMARY

1. The human infant is active and is curious about his world. During his first two years, he organizes and reorganizes his understanding of the world and the people, objects, and events that fill it. His increasing cognitive understanding builds on his sensations and perceptions of the physical and social world, but his ability to think is not restricted to concrete experience alone.

2. By the end of his first year, the infant can judge distance, discriminate familiar from unfamiliar ob-

jects, and use visual cues as warnings. His hearing becomes sensitive to combinations of sounds, so that he recognizes certain words and attaches meanings to them. Most important, all the infant's senses working together, and combined with his motor skills, provide him with extensive knowledge of his environment.

3. Selective attention to certain stimuli continues from the moment of birth. Previous experience as well as certain physical features of objects appear to determine what infants usually will attend to. Stimuli that violate an expectancy or that are novel are often most likely to attract the infant's attention, and human faces may hold a unique fascination for the infant, partly because of his growing cognitive competence.

4. Much of an infant's first two years appears to be spent building a conceptual network of interrelated ideas about objects and events. Gradually, he comes to recognize that objects remain the same and are permanent even when certain changes may make it appear that this is not the case. The infant's play and his ability to imitate and to remember all contribute to his ideas about objects and events, and, from infancy on, these cognitive skills aid his abilities to imagine, symbolize, and recall.

5. In general, the cognitive development of the infant can be seen as a complex product of his interactions with his environment, which involves his learning, exploring, and adapting. He learns how to respond to the world and how it responds to him; he actively explores, generating new stimulation and information; and he adapts to the world either by assimilating objects to fit his skills or by accommodating his skills to the demands of the situation.

SUGGESTED READINGS

Bower, Thomas G. R. "The Object in the World of the Infant," *Scientific American,* 225 (October 1971), 30–38.

Church, Joseph (ed.). *Three Babies: Biographies of Cognitive Development.* New York: Random House, 1966.

Gibson, Eleanor J., and Richard D. Walk, "The 'Visual Cliff,'" *Scientific American,* 202 (April 1960), 64–71.

Ginsburg, Herbert, and Sylvia Opper. *Piaget's Theory of Intellectual Development: An Introduction.* Englewood Cliffs, N.J.: Prentice-Hall, 1969.

Kagan, Jerome. "Do Infants Think?" *Scientific American,* 226 (March 1972), 74–83.

Figure 7.13 Throughout infancy, physical and cognitive skills are interdependent and changing. At first, some characteristics of objects in the world are only discovered and understood by chewing or grasping, but later others come to be known by mere touching or looking.

The development of language is a
cognitive and social accomplishment
that, in many ways, begins during
infancy.

8

LANGUAGE: BEGINNINGS

Little Lauren is one year old and her mother is playing with her, making various cooing noises. Among the noises comes something like "givemommyakisssweetie . . . givemommyakiss." At the same time, Mommy expectantly puts her cheek near Lauren's lips. Lauren does not know much about language, but she senses that she is supposed to do something. She also senses that this particular set of noises that her mother is making sounds somehow different from the cooing, and the specially accented noise "kiss" reverberates in her ears. Another time Daddy says "lookatthedoggy" when a small furry animal comes into sight. Lauren is ready to learn to talk. What does she have to do? What does she have to know?

If you had never learned to understand speech and to talk, it would have been difficult to live in your family and to grow up in this (or any) human society. You could learn only what you saw others do. There would be some things, of course, that you could learn or figure out by yourself; not all thinking is verbal. For example, musicians, engineers, and artists make use of aural and visual images and spatial relationships. But imagine trying to learn what you now know of history or of how our society works without being able to understand or speak a language.

The word "infant" comes from the Latin word for "without language," and if one does not possess a language until he has command of its *structure*, then the immature human being is an infant throughout most of his second year. For although a baby may communicate, until he begins to put words together, he is not truly dealing with the structure of his native language.

In this chapter we will discuss some of the early achievements of the child in deciphering his native language. We will examine some of the ways in which the very young baby responds to speech sounds, the first sounds that the baby makes himself, and the distinction between babbling and talking. We will set forth the level of cognitive development and the human attempts to communicate that must precede the baby's first words and the form those first words will take. We will learn how the infant overextends and then shrinks the meaning of his early words so that "bow-wow," for example, changes in meaning from "dog" to "animal" and back to "dog" again. We will discover the significance of the infant's progress from one- to two-word utterances and the way that he masters the basic grammatical machinery of his language. In the first two years, as we will see, the infant tunes up his cognitive and linguistic abilities until he becomes a speaking human being. This tuning is the result of a complex interplay of cognitive and linguistic development, paced by neurological maturation.

HUMAN LANGUAGE

How does the language of human beings differ from the language of animals? After all, a worker bee can dance on the floor of the hive to tell her fellow workers where to find nectar (Von Frisch, 1967). A father quail can warn his foraging family of approaching danger, and your dog can use a combination of whines, barks, and body movements to tell you when he wants his dinner, when he wants to play ball, and when he wants to go outside.

Roger Brown (1973) has suggested that human language, whether English, Russian, Chinese, or Urdu, possesses three important properties. First is **semanticity,** or meaningfulness. By semanticity, Brown means that the symbols of human language represent an enormous variety of people, objects, events, and ideas. Although animals such as the honey bee with her dance or chimpanzees with their calls and grunts can communicate limited meanings, the number of things that they can "talk" about is quite small.

Brown's second property of language is **productivity,** the ability to combine individual words into an unlimited number of sentences. As Noam Chomsky (1972) has pointed out, except for common clichés such as "How are you?" or "Have a nice day," almost every sentence we hear or speak is brand new. According to one estimate, if you were to utter all the possible twenty-word sentences in English, you would be talking for 10,000,000,000,000 years (Farb, 1974).

The last essential property of language, according to Brown, is **displacement,** the ability to communicate information about objects in another place or another time, such as the book in the next room or the pot roast you ate last Sunday. Displacement is the property that allows us to transmit information from one generation to another so that we do not have to rediscover all knowledge every thirty years or so.

At every linguistic stage, the child's cognitive understanding of the world about him lays the basis for the development of his own ability to understand and to speak a language. The development of language cannot begin until the baby can recognize objects and events in his world (see Chapter 7) and can relate his perceptions to each other in memory. Once maturation brings him to the point where he can form and store internal representations of objects and events, he is ready to hook the system that he uses to communicate his emotions into his cognitive understanding. The first words emerge and, with them, the fundamental basis of human verbal interaction. By two or two and one-half years, the rudiments of word combination and grammar are present and, with them, the roots of complex communication.

The infant's development of language depends on two important notions: *structure* and *figuring out.* Speech relates to meanings, or ideas, in precise ways.

The words "kiss" and "this" have different meanings in English simply because they begin with different sounds. "Mommy kisses baby" and "Baby kisses Mommy" have different meanings in English just because the order of the words is different in the two utterances. These are *structural principles* of English that the child must discover, because such principles differ from language to language. Linguists call these structural principles the **grammar** or **syntax** of a language.

Each language has its own collection of speech sounds, which are used to build words in that particular language. And each language has its own ways of combining words into sentences. For example, in Russian the equivalent of "Mommy kisses baby," with the three words in that order, could mean either that Mommy gets kissed or that baby gets kissed, depending on whether the word for "Mommy" or the word for "baby" has a particular sound on the end of it. "Mama tseluyet malyutkU" means "Mommy kisses baby," but "MamU tseluyet malyutka" means "Baby kisses Mommy." So, if you were a Russian one-year-old, you would have to learn to pay special attention to the sounds that come at the ends of words, but if you were an American one-year-old, you would have to learn to pay special attention to the order of words.

In either case, the baby must be able to pay attention to the ways in which speech is structured or organized. If he is to communicate meanings and understand what people are saying, he must actively *figure out* the ways in which speech is organized in his native language. No baby knows, to begin with, what particular native language he is destined to acquire, yet all children manage to acquire their native language with amazing ease and rapidity. This leads us to believe that human beings are in some way endowed with specialized information-processing abilities that make it possible for them to figure out the structure of their own language, just as they are able to figure out the structures of the other sights and sounds and smells and feelings that are necessary in order to function as thinking and feeling human beings in society.

But the infant who is figuring out his own language cannot depend on isolated words; he must learn enough about meanings in the nonlinguistic world to discover how the two systems are related. He can and sometimes does learn all these things before he begins to speak. In fact, some children who cannot speak at all because of physical handicaps show that they completely understand the function of language and its intricacies. Eric Lenneberg (1962) studied one such child and tested him in several ways for language comprehension. The child, who was then eight, was told a short story and questioned in complex grammatical constructions about its contents. From his responses, there was no doubt that he had learned to understand his native language, English. Such experiments make it clear that having knowledge of a language is not identical with speak-

ing. Because knowledge of a language may be established in people who lack the ability to speak, knowledge must be fundamental, and the ability to speak, accessory.

PRESPEECH DEVELOPMENT

Before a baby is ready to say "dada" or "mama" or "milk" or "bow-wow," he has a long road of development and learning to travel. He takes his first steps along that road in the very first month of life, almost before his parents are aware that he is interested in anything more than a full stomach and a dry bottom. Earl Butterfield (1968) studied newborn babies in the hospital and found that they already attended to sound, which is a basic step in attending to and developing language. When the babies were only twenty-four hours old, he gave them a chance to hear music. By sucking a pacifier, the babies could turn on tape-recorded classical, popular, or vocal music. The babies clearly sucked to get the musical reinforcement. Although these babies were not learning a language, they were attending to the sounds in their environment and actively controlling them.

Attention to Speech

Long before he can actually speak, a baby pays special attention to the speech he hears around him. Within the first month of life, his response to the sound of the human voice will be different from his response to other sorts of auditory stimuli (Menyuk, 1971). At first the sounds that he notices might be

Figure 8.1 Units in human speech (patterns of sounds) correspond to other objects (such as people) and are, therefore, meaningful. The possibility of using these units to refer to things that are, for example, hidden from view illustrates the property of displacement. A limited number of these units can be used in different combinations to communicate an unlimited number of new meanings.

only those words that receive the heaviest emphasis and that often occur at the ends of utterances. Very soon, these differences in adult intonation can influence a baby's emotional states and his behavior. Long before he develops actual language comprehension, the baby can sense when an adult is playful or angry, attempting to initiate or terminate behavior, and so on, merely on the basis of cues such as the rate, volume, and melody of adult speech.

More significant for language development than his response to general intonation is recent evidence that a tiny baby can make fine distinctions between speech sounds. Peter Eimas and his colleagues (1971) have shown that one-month-old babies can hear the difference between the sounds "ba" and "pa," a very subtle distinction. These investigators used an intriguing method to make their discovery. They knew that a baby will suck on a nipple at a constant rate as long as nothing new or startling strikes his senses but that a sudden change in stimulation will cause him to suck at a more rapid rate. By giving a baby a pacifier attached to electronic recording equipment, Eimas and his colleagues were able to monitor the baby's rate and intensity of sucking. They repeatedly presented the sound "ba" to the baby until his sucking reached a stable rate; that is, until he habituated to that stimulus. Then they switched to the sound "pa"; babies as young as one month immediately increased their rate of sucking, indicating their ability to distinguish between these two very closely related sounds.

This study suggests that a baby comes into the world with the ability to make precisely those perceptual discriminations that are necessary if he is to acquire human language.

Babies obviously derive pleasure from sound input, too: Even as young as nine months, they will listen to nursery rhymes, songs, or stories, although the words themselves are beyond their understanding. Even some adults find themselves lulled by sound and never think to seek the meaning of words in Mother Goose rhymes: What is the *tuffet* that little Miss Muffet sat on? And what exactly are *curds* and *whey?* For several years, in fact, it is the surface of sound, in both what children hear and what they say, that attracts them. When children begin to use words, they continue the playful use of language in combinations of nonsense words and in rhyming games. For them, language is a sensory-motor delight rather than the route to prosaic meaning that it often is for adults.

Prespeech Sounds

Despite the infant's sharp discrimination and enjoyment of certain speech stimuli, it usually takes at least a year before he is able to produce sounds that can be identified as words. It is much more difficult for him to acquire motor control over the various muscles and organs involved in producing speech than it is for him to perceive auditory distinctions (McCarthy, 1954). The progress from crying to babbling to speech usually follows the same sequence in most infants,

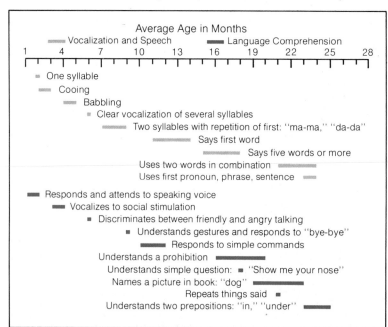

Figure 8.2 Some highlights of language development during the first two years of life. Some infants may not show or pass through all the linguistic developments indicated. Note also that the average ages shown are approximations and that the length of the bars reflects the range in average ages that different researchers have reported for a particular linguistic development. (Adapted from Lenneberg, 1967; McCarthy, 1954; and Bayley, 1969)

Figure 8.3 *(opposite)* Early babbling appears to be a type of motor play and experimentation.

but some, of course, pass through the various linguistic developments shown in Figure 8.2 earlier or later than the suggested ages.

The first sound a baby makes is a cry, and within days, if not hours, he is able to use his cries to communicate gross messages to his parents. When Peter Wolff (1969) studied infant vocalization, he found that even in the first weeks of life a baby has three patterns of crying, as mentioned in Chapter 5: the basic rhythmical pattern (often erroneously called the hunger cry); the anger cry; and the pain cry. By playing a tape recording of a baby's cries on different occasions when the mother was out of the room, Wolff discovered that a mother recognizes the differences in the cries of her own baby and responds dramatically. Whenever Wolff played the pain cry, for example, the baby's mother immediately rushed into the room with a worried expression on her face.

After three weeks of age, the baby's vocalizations gradually increase in frequency and variety. Some sounds, of course, are physical and digestive mouthings and gurglings, but by the second month he invents new noises, from squeals to Bronx cheers, and repeats them in a circular fashion (P.Wolff, 1969). Sounds of joy, called cooing, also may begin to occur at this time, usually when babies appear to be happy: after eating, while watching a smiling face, when listening to singing, and while looking at or handling objects.

After three months adults can increase the frequency of the baby's sounds by responding to them. From the very start, sounds and gestures develop as communicative acts because of the way that others react. The baby's crying and cooing and attempts to make contact with other human beings prepare him for the ability to speak. Infants in institutions with few adults around make fewer spontaneous noises and may not even cry much, because crying is a part of the child's social interaction (Brodbeck and Irwin, 1946). If no one comes to answer a cry, crying becomes a useless vocalization. For example, in a series of experiments, Harriet Rheingold, Jacob Gewirtz, and Helen Ross (1959) used simultaneous smiles, sounds, and light touches to the abdomen to condition institutionalized babies' vocal responses. They did not reinforce coughs, whistles, squeaks, snorts, fusses, or cries of protest. The reinforcement, which closely resembled a common variety of adult-infant play, quickly doubled the babies' vocalizations.

By the time he is four or five months of age, the baby produces sequences of alternating vowels and consonants, such as "bababababa." Such sound sequences, called **babbling,** give the impression that the baby is uttering a string of syllables. The capacity to keep saying the same sequences over and over again, as in repeating syllables, indicates that the baby has achieved a great extension of motor control.

The primary function of babbling is probably to develop motor control over the speech musculature

and to coordinate the production of sounds with the perception of sounds. That is, when the baby feels certain patterns of motor activity involving the muscles of his throat, tongue, and lips, he associates those movements with the sounds that he hears himself making. Babbling may thus be a form of motor practice that facilitates later speech development.

But babbling may not be directly related to the acquisition of any particular native language (McNeill, 1970a). The speech sounds of children from different language communities cannot be distinguished from one another until near the end of the first year, when intonational variations begin to appear in the child's vocalizations. Charles Osgood (1953) once recorded all the babbling produced by one baby in his first year and discovered that the taped babbles appeared to include all sounds used in known languages. As this study indicates, babbling includes many sounds that an adult cannot make and that the baby himself may not be able to say a year later. Much babbling also appears to be sheer motor play, in which the baby produces many accidental sounds that have nothing to do with communication.

Even deaf babies babble, which suggests that at first this sort of vocalization is indeed motor play. Because the babbling of normal six-month-old babies shows a greater diversity of sound than the babbling of deaf infants, we can suppose that hearing speech sounds stimulates the baby. Soon after six months, deaf infants stop babbling, and hearing infants go on to greater diversity and experimentation in their speech play (Lenneberg, 1967).

Near the end of the first year, the infant's *intonation*, or the rising and falling pitch of his utterances, becomes more and more like adult speech. At this time the infant may produce long, complex sequences of meaningless sounds with the pitch contour of adult sentences. These charming sequences may appear when the child is pretending to read or to talk to a doll when no one else is present. By the time such sequences are present, a listener can distinguish the intonation differences among language communities. Once the infant begins to consistently use certain "words" that adults can recognize and interpret, he has entered the final prespeech stage.

Cognitive Precursors to First Words

As we pointed out in Chapter 7, a child cannot use words meaningfully until he has some notion that there is a world of enduring objects and people and that people can act on objects. These notions of object permanence, object identity, and causality are partly

the result of the baby's sensory-motor development during his first year of life. By the time he celebrates his first birthday, the infant has begun to imitate events well after they have occurred, which is convincing evidence of his ability to *represent* objects and events to himself. Jean Piaget (1951) has described and analyzed various facets of the development of this important ability.

Piaget watched the development of his own three children closely and made detailed observations. He reports many instances of the one-year-old's ability to imitate what he has experienced. For example, when his daughter Jacqueline was sixteen months old, she was impressed by an eighteen-month-old boy's tantrum. As Piaget describes it:

He screamed as he tried to get out of a play-pen and pushed it backwards, stamping his feet. J. stood watching him in amazement, never having witnessed such a scene before. The next day, she herself screamed in her play-pen and tried to move it, stamping her foot lightly several times in succession. (page 63)

Piaget points out that, because Jacqueline did not imitate the boy's behavior until the following day, she must have been able to store some representation of the event in her mind, acting it out in imitation much later. This cognitive development is, of course, an essential prerequisite for language.

An infant at the same stage of development also tries to use his own motor acts and sounds to represent events to himself. For example, Piaget reports how a year-old infant tried to keep track of the demonstrated manipulation of a matchbox:

T. was looking at a box of matches which I was holding on its end and alternately opening and closing. Showing great delight, he watched with great attention, and imitated the box in three ways. (1) He opened and closed his right hand, keeping his eyes on the box. (2) He said *"tff, tff"* to reproduce the sound the box made. (3) He reacted . . . by opening and closing his mouth. (page 66)

The ability to talk about things rests on the ability to picture them to oneself. About the time that the infant is able to do this, he begins to imitate the words that he hears. Before he can use these words in his own speech, he must remember them along with his memories of what was happening at the time that he heard them. Just as the one-year-old is able to imitate events some time after he has experienced them, he is able to use words some time after he has heard them. So the abilities to imitate and to store internal images of sights and sounds are necessary prerequisites for the development of language.

By the time an infant like Lauren is one year old,

she will begin to remember and imitate sound sequences such as "kiss" and "doggy." But this is not enough, because language is not only a collection of words: It is a collection that makes sense. Unless Lauren has begun to make sense of the world, she will have no way of relating words to their meanings. So Lauren must notice that, when Mommy says "Give me a kiss," she waits for Lauren to touch Mommy's cheek with her lips, and when Daddy says "Look at the doggy," there is some recognizable thing in the perceptual world of sight and sound and touch that will come to be known as a "doggy."

However, words are only one means that the infant uses to symbolize his ideas. His first words emerge at the same time that he begins to use symbolic gestures and to engage in make-believe play. The little boy who opened and closed his hand and his mouth after watching Piaget open and close the matchbox was using a symbolic gesture. At another time, such an infant may push a little stone along the table, pretending that it is a car, or he may rub his hands saying "soap," pretending that he is washing. Spoken language emerges as one of a complex of symbolic behaviors that help the infant to remember and play with what he has experienced. Words, gestures, and make-believe play all reflect the level of an infant's understanding of the world. And as the infant engages in these symbolic behaviors, they assist him in refining and organizing his cognitions and feelings.

Communicative Precursors to First Words

At the same time that the baby is busily exploring the world of objects and events around him, he is also trying to communicate with other people in his world. He makes contact by smiling and babbling. He makes demands by reaching, calling, and crying. And even when he is simply exploring objects, he indicates his involvement by vocalizing at the same time that he examines a toy or tugs at the cat's tail. Long before his first words appear, the baby has been communicating by the use of gesture and vocal sounds. The baby's vocal sounds have characteristic intonation patterns that others can interpret as communicating such things as desires, frustration, satisfaction, or rejection. As you will remember, he could communicate his general condition when he was less than a week old.

R. V. Tonkova-Yampol'skaya (1973), a Soviet investigator, studied the development of intonation patterns in the prespeech vocalizations of Russian children. She found that such patterns stabilize before infants develop words and that babies in the first year

Figure 8.4 The peek-a-boo game engenders an early form of language use and comprehension in which gesture and speech are intricately tied.

of life are able to learn intonations signaling happiness as well as commands, requests, and questions. Infants' intonation patterns for several kinds of communication correspond closely to typical adult patterns, as Figure 8.5 shows. For example, babies at seven to ten months of age express commands with the same sharply rising then falling pitch that adults use. About the beginning of the second year, infants first use the intonation that signifies a question. This pattern is easily distinguished from others by the sharp rise in pitch at the end. Because pitch and emphasis can affect utterances profoundly, sometimes even reversing the meaning of a remark, this early learning of intonation plays an important part in the continuing development of language ability.

FIRST WORDS

Although some babies begin to use a variety of single words toward the end of their first year, most will pass their first birthdays before their vocabulary has

more than three words, according to Orvis Irwin (1949). Although Irwin reports no sex differences in language ability until about eighteen months, some studies have shown a clear but slight edge for girls, and some investigators have found that, in newborns, girls vocalize more than boys (McCarthy, 1954).

Functions of First Words

It is natural that an infant's first words will carry on the patterns of behavior and intent that he has developed during the prespeech period. He has already been using speechlike sounds, intonation patterns, and gestures to express several basic functions of communication, and his first words will function in the same way. They will *refer* to objects and events, *express* mood states, and *command* adults to carry out actions that the infant desires. These functions show clearly in Table 8.1, which gives the first seven words of a child whose language development was studied in detail by her linguist father, Werner Leopold

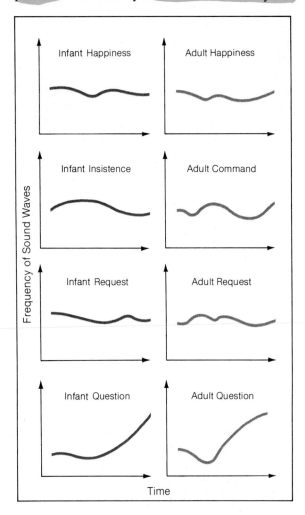

Figure 8.5 Comparison of several kinds of intonation patterns of infants and adults. The sample illustrations for infants are based on data for infants from seven to twenty-four months of age. Each graph represents a change in pitch of the voice (frequency) over time (seconds). (Adapted from Tonkova-Yampol'skaya, 1973)

Figure 8.6 (*opposite*) Three intonation patterns for the word "door" spoken by an infant at the one-word stage. (After Menyuk, 1971)

(1949). Some of her first words, such as "dididi," primarily express emotion, and Leopold believes that language begins to develop when a baby attaches some emotional meaning to one of her babbles. You can see that early words like "uh?" perform several functions at once for the little girl. For example, when she said "uh" and pointed to a toy that had fallen, she was simultaneously referring to the toy, expressing her concern that it had fallen, and requesting that it be given back to her. The single word thus functions to refer, express, and command in an undifferentiated utterance. As we will see, once the child is able to combine *several* words in one utterance, these functions will become differentiated in her speech. For example, the statement "Dollie fell," which refers to an event, is clearly different from the command "Give dollie." But all of the functions are already implicit at this early linguistic stage when the infant can say only "dollie," "fell," or "give."

The period in which the infant can utter only one

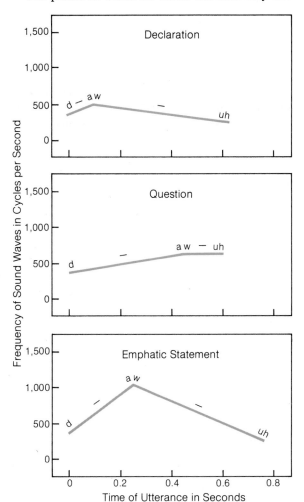

Table 8.1   The First Seven "Words" in One Child's Linguistic Development

UTTERANCE	AGE IN MONTHS	MEANINGS
uh?	8	An interjection. Also demonstrative, "addressed" to persons, distant objects, and "escaped toys."
dididi	9	Disapproval (loud). Comfort (soft).
mama	10	Refers vaguely to food. Also means "tastes good" and "hungry."
nenene	10	Scolding.
tt!	10	Used to call squirrels.
piti	10	Always used with a gesture, and always whispered. Seems to mean "interest(-ed), (-ing)."
deh	10	An interjection. Also demonstrative. Used with the same gesture as above.

Source: Adapted from David McNeill, *The Acquisition of Language: The Study of Developmental Psycholinguistics* (New York: Harper & Row, 1970), p. 22; based on material from Werner F. Leopold, *Grammar and General Problems in the First Two Years*, Speech Development of a Bilingual Child: A Linguist's Record, Vol. 3 (Evanston, Ill.: Northwestern University Press, 1949), p. 6.

word at a time often lasts until he is nearly two. As Paula Menyuk and Nancy Bernholtz (1969) have shown, during this period the infant often relies on intonation to communicate the intention of a single word. For example, in Figure 8.6 you see intonation patterns of the word "door" as spoken by an infant on three different occasions. Menyuk and Bernholtz tape-recorded these utterances and played them to listeners, who agreed when the child's use of "door" was a declaration, a question, or an emphatic statement. It was clear that the child was not simply using the word "door" to name an object. When the child used a falling pitch (frequency contour), listeners judged the utterance as having a naming, or referential, function. But when the same word was uttered with a rising intonation, listeners interpreted it as a question. And when the intonation rose sharply and then fell, it was heard as an emphatic assertion or demand. Thus the single word "door" could mean: "That's a door" or "Is that a door?" or "Are you going to open the door?" or "Open the door!" or "Close the door!" and so forth.

However, such simple utterances—early one-word utterances and later two- and three-word utterances—can be fully understood only in *context*. On hearing a recording of the word "door" spoken with an emphatic intonation, you may not be able to decide whether the child wanted the door opened or closed or merely wanted the listener to pay attention to the door. But if you are watching a toddler stand in front of a closed door and you know that on the other side of the door her father is repairing a light switch, you would know immediately that the emphatic utterance ''door'' means that you have been asked to open it. Communication succeeds at these early stages because adults are good at guessing the child's intentions. The child gives a partial clue to his intentions in his speech, intonation, and gesture. The importance of intonation and gesture will not decline as the child matures. Even adults rely on these cues when communicating with their peers. For example, Albert Mehrabian (1971) has estimated that only 7 percent of the information we give to others comes from our words; the rest comes from our intonation, our gestures, our facial expressions, and the way we hold our bodies. Because the child's communicative needs are always embedded in an ongoing context of activity, it is generally possible for adults to figure out what he is trying to say. As his vocabulary and grammar develop, he will be able to talk about objects and people that are not present, about things he did yesterday or wants to do tomorrow. Context will no longer be so necessary; his language will have the property of displacement, and true conversation will become possible.

Form of First Words

Early words, unlike babbling, do not sample a wide range of sounds. Indeed, when a baby first begins to speak, he may be unable to imitate sounds that he made earlier in playful babbling. His first words tend to be short, of one or two syllables, and each syllable generally consists of a consonant followed by a vowel. The first words will probably consist of a front consonant like ''b'' or ''p'' and a back vowel like ''a.'' This is true no matter what language the infant is to speak. Roman Jakobson (1968) reports that an infant who is to learn English says ''tut'' before ''cut''; one who will speak Japanese says ''ta'' before ''ka''; and an infant growing up in Sweden says ''tata'' before ''kata.''

Suppose the baby's first word is something like ''ba'' for ''ball.'' An observer with a tape recorder who is lucky enough to get many examples of a baby using this word will find that its pronunciation varies from ''bee'' to ''bow'' and that the consonant also varies: It is sometimes *pa, va, da,* or *tha.* It is because the listener expects to hear and thinks of the word ''ball'' that he believes the baby has a stable pronunciation of it. In fact, although the baby is able to perceive the differences among sounds in the adult speech that he hears, he devotes a great deal of effort to figuring out how to produce the whole complex of sounds that correspond to adult words.

Arlene Moskowitz (1970) believes that the first units the child organizes in his speech may be syllables rather than separate vowels or consonants. The first syllable may be produced when the infant simply releases his lips while vocalizing, producing a

sound such as "ma" or "ba." The first distinction between consonants that an infant makes is often between a sound such as "ma," which he produces by releasing air through the nose with his lips together and then opening his mouth, and "ba," which he produces by suddenly letting the air out between his lips. Once he has reached this point, he may be able to say "mama" and "ba" as distinct words.

Because the infant has few consonants at his command during his second year, his store of syllables is small and he often repeats them. For example, David may say "pa-pa" or "bi-bi" or "car-car." He may also utter two different words with different meanings, and they will sound the same because his small collection of syllables offers few possibilities for different word forms. For example, David may say "ba" to imitate the words "ball," "bird," and "flower." The first time he says "ba," his mother or father will probably say "ball" when a ball is nearby or "bird" when a bird flies by. Such auditory reinforcement helps the infant to shape his "ba" until at last he does say both "ball" and "bird" (McCarthy, 1954).

The child continues to work at differentiating among speech sounds and then at producing the appropriate ones, often well into his second and third years when he enters the stage of grammatical speech. By the time he is four, he has learned some amazingly complicated aspects of word construction, but he may still have motor difficulties in articulating one or two

Figure 8.7 Illustration of representative sounds and meanings in infants' first words.

sounds. These difficulties do not stand in the way of his basic grand achievement, the understanding and production of sentences, which begins to develop about six months to a year after he first uses meaningful words. Many young children spontaneously outgrow any problems of articulation. If such speech difficulties persist into later childhood and cause a child to be socially stigmatized, however, they may play a significant role in his social and psychological development.

Meanings of First Words

By the time the infant can use single words, he has acquired the object permanence and object identity discussed in Chapter 7. Now that he is beginning to speak, his words make it possible to infer quite a bit about his development of concepts. Among the communicative functions performed by his first words, that of reference reveals the way that he perceives and arranges his world. An infant's first words are usually very different in their apparent range of meaning from the conventional meaning that adults attribute to the sounds. For example, one little girl used a single word to refer to a dress, a coat, a white hat, and the carriage she rode in and to ask to take a walk or to report that she had taken one. It is easy to see how the mother's use of a word while dressing the girl to go out may have led the girl to include in its meaning all the related events and experiences for which she had no separate names. In another case, a little boy used a single word to refer to breast, biscuit, a red button on a dress, a bare elbow, an eye in a portrait, and his mother's photograph. The perceptual basis for these generalizations is obvious.

Eve Clark (1973) has studied such **overextensions** of early word meanings in detail. She has examined many of the nineteenth- and twentieth-century diary studies kept in various languages by linguist and psychologist parents and has concluded that, when an infant extends a word to include a number of dissimilar objects or events, it is usually possible to find some perceived similarity among the objects or events. These overextensions of meaning give us a glimpse of the similarities that very young children notice. Clark gives six examples of major categories that various young children have used to sort out their worlds:

Movement. An infant first used "sh" to refer to the sound of a train and then extended "sh" to refer to all moving machines.

Shape. This is a common basis for overextensions. A category of small round objects appears in many of the studies. For example, one infant first used "mooi" to refer to the moon and then successively extended this word to cakes, round marks on a window, writing on windows and in books, round shapes in books, tooling on leather book covers, round postmarks, and the letter O. Another infant said "kotibaiz" first in reference to the bars of his cot and then to a large toy abacus, a toast rack with parallel bars, and a picture of a building with columns.

Size. "Fly" began, for one infant, as the name for a specific insect and then generalized to specks of dirt, dust, all small insects, the infant's own toes, crumbs of bread, and a toad.

Sound. "Koko," for one Yugoslav infant, first referred to the crowing of a cockerel. Subsequently the child used it to refer to tunes played on the violin, tunes played on the piano, tunes on an accordion, tunes on a phonograph, and finally to all music and even to a merry-go-round.

Taste. This category appears infrequently in the diary studies. One example is the word "candy," which an infant extended first to mean cherries and then to refer to anything sweet.

Texture. An infant extended the meaning of "bow-wow" from a real dog to a toy dog, then to a fur piece with an animal head, and finally to other fur pieces without heads.

As new words enter the child's vocabulary and as new experiences refine his concepts, he restructures and reorganizes these early word meanings. His new discriminations allow him to reverse the process, gradually refining his grand generalizations. This development becomes clear when it is charted for a single word (see Figure 8.8). Clark shows how an infant could first overextend and then restructure the meaning of "bow-wow" and how that restructuring relates to the child's acquisition of other animal names. At first, the infant might learn "bow-wow" from his mother, who uses it when they see a dog. Soon after, however, he uses the same word to refer to a variety of animals—dogs, cows, horses, sheep, and cats—presumably setting up a conceptual category on the basis of shape and movement. Then he learns the word "moo" for cows and is able to distinguish cows from other animals. At this step his animal vocabulary contains two words: "moo," referring to cows, and "bow-wow," referring to all other animals. As he learns more animal names, he

keeps subdividing his initial general class, so that eventually he has separate names for dogs, cows, horses, sheep, and cats.

Clark points out that at each step the available animal names take on more precise meaning, based on those perceptual features that the infant uses to distinguish animals. For example, at Step IV, the category "bow-wow" may include the feature of small size, because "bow-wow" refers only to fairly small animals like dogs, cats, and sheep, whereas the words for horse and cow may include among their features the meaning of large size. This demonstrates the process by which the global meanings of an infant's first words narrow as he learns new words and begins to attend to new features of objects and events. Each time the infant learns to notice and apply a new feature to his world, such as small, living, soft, and so forth, he may restructure the meaning of a number of words (McNeill, 1970a).

The earliest words of infants vary markedly among different families and even among children in the same family, according to the interests of a young child and of those around him. But the first words usually express the same basic notions (K.Nelson, 1973). The early vocabulary generally includes words for common things the child tries to handle, such as "cup" or "ball"; people he wants to name, such as "Mama" or "Dada"; actions he performs, such as "up" and "off"; names of locations; terms for changes and quantities, such as "all-done," "no," and "more"; and terms for values and feelings, such as "want," "mad," and "good." Once the infant has acquired these basic vocabulary tools, he is ready

Figure 8.8 A hypothetical example of how an infant overextends and restructures the meaning of the word "bow-wow," as discussed in the text. (Adapted from E. Clark, 1973)

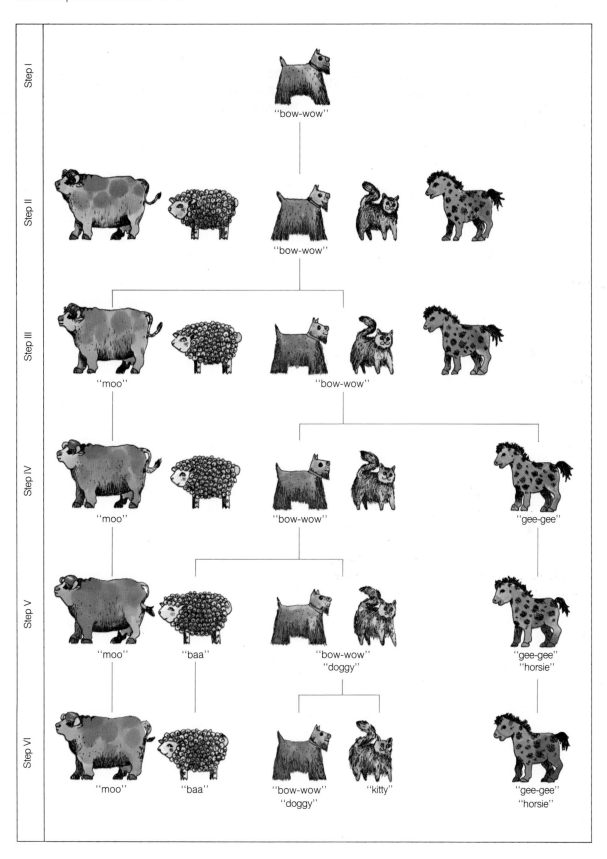

for the momentous step of combining words into longer utterances. But just as his first steps on his own two feet had to wait for a certain level of motor control, so the emergence of *grammar* must wait for a certain level of neurological maturation. And just as crawling prepared the infant to walk, one-word utterances prepare him to speak in a truly human way.

FIRST SENTENCES

An infant knows more than he can say. Even when he can speak only one word at a time, he appears to understand the longer utterances of his parents and his older brothers and sisters. He can also mean more than he can say, as a number of researchers have pointed out (McNeill, 1970a).

Meaning at the Two-Word Stage

Toward the end of the one-word period, the infant makes sequences of separate one-word utterances that seem to relate to a larger meaning, even though he speaks each word separately, with its own falling intonation. For example, Lois Bloom (1973) has described a one-year-old girl who struggled to put a button into her pocket while she sat on the pocket. She said "button" and then "pocket," but she was not able to join the two words together into a single utterance. A month or two later the same girl was able to say "button pocket" with no long pause between the two words and with a falling intonation that spread over the whole utterance. The emergence of the two-word stage seems to be the result of some increase in neurological capacity that allows the young child to plan and to produce a two-word utterance before running out of immediate memory. Thus, the new development at this stage is an increase in the amount of information that the child can fit into one utterance. It is important to note, however, that the words and concepts that the young child expresses with two words were already present in his one-word utterances. Although the ability to speak a two-word sentence represents a clear advance in the young child's expressive capacity, it does not represent a new level in his thinking (Slobin, 1973). He can use his language only to express concepts and relationships that he already understands at least in part. The two-word stage is significant because it represents a striking advance in the young child's ability to code his understanding in linguistic terms and to begin to project his ideas more fully into the world of human social and intellectual interaction.

The meanings expressed in two-word sentences reflect the level of understanding of a child of about two years of age. Early language development has now been studied in many different cultures, and everywhere the picture is the same. Somewhere around his second birthday, the child starts to put two words together to express the same universal range of basic concepts. These concepts form the core of all human language. Indeed, a large part of later language development is simply a matter of elaborating and refining the basic notions that are already present at this beginning stage.

Figure 8.9 Illustration of infants' representative first sentences and grammar.

Cataloging the Two-Year-Old Mind

A number of psycholinguists have been gathering child language data from around the world (R. Brown, 1973; Slobin, 1972, 1973). The following list of basic meanings expressed during the two-word stage comes from data collected among children who speak English, German, Russian, Finnish, Turkish, Samoan, and Luo (spoken in Kenya). But it would probably be possible to compile the entire list from two-year-old speakers of any single language. It is, essentially, a catalog of the two-year-old mind.

Identification. Such utterances as "See doggy" are extensions of the simple pointing responses that the baby makes during the prespeech period and the same responses, accompanied by the object's name, that he makes during the one-word stage.

Location. Along with pointing, the infant can signal the location of an object with such words as "here" and "there," as in "Book there." If he wishes to indicate the relationship of being in, on, or under something else, he uses a fixed juxtaposition of words with no preposition: "Baby chair," "Baby car," "Dollie down."

Recurrence. Presence, absence, and repetition seem to be aspects of things and actions that infants take into account very early. Such utterances as "More write," "Another bang," and "Book again" are among the first sentences that he speaks.

Nonexistence. An infant who observes the repetition of an experience also notices the disappearance of an object or the cessation of an activity. His early sentences express nonexistence in such forms as "All-gone ball" and "Milk all-done."

Negation. An infant uses a negative construction to *contradict* an adult utterance or to avoid a possible misunderstanding. For example, he may point to a picture of a dog and say "Not cat." He can use a similar form to *reject* the imposition of an adult desire, as when he says "No water" when offered a drink.

Possession. An infant at the one-word period who says only "Daddy" when he sees Daddy's coat or chair later may say "Daddy coat" or "Daddy chair."

Agent, action, and *object.* Although the infant obviously understands that agents act on objects, at the two-word stage he can express only two terms of this three-term relation in a single sentence. So he can say "Daddy throw" (agent-action), "Throw ball" (action-object), and "Daddy ball" (agent-object), though he cannot yet say "Daddy throw ball."

Action-location. The infant can talk about an action and at the same time specify where the action takes place, provided he does not want to say anything else about the situation. His utterances are ruled by the same two-word limit that left him unable to say "Daddy throw ball." Thus, if he wants his mother to sit in the rocking chair, he can say either "Sit chair" (action-location) or "Mama sit" or "Mama chair" but not "Mama sit chair" or "Mama sit on chair." When these longer utterances finally

emerge, they will once again reflect understanding that the infant already possessed at the two-word stage.

Action-recipient. The infant can talk about who is to benefit from various actions, saying such things as "Give papa," meaning that something should be given to his father, or "Cookie me," leaving no doubt in the listener's mind that he is demanding a cookie, although the imperative verb that makes the command is unspoken.

Action-instrument. The infant who uses utterances such as "Cut knife," as distinguished from "Cut bread," indicates that he has some notion of the use of instruments to carry out actions.

Attribution. The infant begins to modify nouns with attributes, saying "Red truck" and "Big ball," slightly later than he learns to state other basic relationships. Sometimes the range of such alternatives available to him is very limited.

Questions. The infant can transform all the preceding sentence types into simple questions merely by saying them (in most languages) with a rising intonation. At this early period he generally also possesses several question words, especially "where," which he uses simply with nouns ("Where ball?") or verbs ("Where go?") in two-word combinations.

The universality and comprehensiveness of the list of meanings found at the two-word stage is impressive. The child is clearly communicating a wide range of ideas. In fact, it is hard to think of basic notions to add to the list in order to describe adult speech. What do these simple utterances lack besides length?

FROM TWO WORDS TO GRAMMAR

The crucial feature that develops in the next several years is what the linguists refer to as *grammar,* and it is a feature hinted at on the first pages of this chapter. Grammar does not mean the schoolbook rules of how to speak "properly" but rather the rules that all of us know implicitly and use to organize our words into sentences. You recall that most of the two-word utterances found among children who speak various languages are difficult to interpret outside of *context,* that is, outside the situations in which they were uttered. If David says "Baby chair," for example, does he mean "This is the baby's chair" or "The baby is in the chair" or "Put the baby in the chair" or "This is a little chair"? The list of possible interpretations could go on and on, because there is not enough *grammatical* information in the simple two-word combination "Baby chair." It is grammar that

makes it possible for you to understand all the possible interpretations in the previous sentence, although you are not now in an actual situation containing babies and chairs. For example, you understand the difference between "the baby's chair" and "baby in the chair" because you know the grammatical functions of the possessive *'s* and the locational "in the" as they are expressed in English. Knowledge of the role of inflections, prepositions, word order, and so on makes it possible for you to produce and understand sentences outside any immediate, relevant physical context. It is the development of this grammatical knowledge that will actively occupy the child's mind from two to five, and we will further explore this development in Chapter 12.

When linguists first began to analyze the speech of children at the two-word stage, they concentrated on the formal grammatical rules that govern the distribution of word classes, such as nouns and verbs, in the child's sentences. Lois Bloom (1970) argues that such an analysis is of little use because it treats a sentence like "Baby chair" the same no matter how it is used. And if David says "Baby chair" at lunchtime to mean "Baby Lauren is sitting in her highchair," he may say "Baby chair" to mean "That is Baby Lauren's highchair" when visiting Lauren's house. In both cases, David uses two nouns, but on one occasion he indicates Lauren's location, and on the other, her possession of the chair.

The rudiments of grammar appear in the child's speech toward the end of the two-word stage. These first grammatical devices are the basic formal tools of human language; they are intonation, word order, and inflection.

Intonation

We have already discussed the important role that intonation plays in earlier periods of language development, when a baby can indicate a request with a rising tone or a demand with a loud, insistent tone. But toward the end of the two-word stage, another device, a contrastive stress, becomes available. In the example of "Baby chair," an English-speaking child may emphasize the first word, saying "BABY chair" to indicate possession ("That is baby's chair"), or emphasize the second word, saying "Baby CHAIR" to indicate location ("Baby is in chair") or destination ("Put baby in chair"). Of course, you recall that intonation may also be used to differentiate a statement from a question. For example, "Daddy book" spoken without a rising tone may mean "This is Daddy's book," whereas "Daddy book?" with the

Figure 8.10 The development of language during infancy is marked by a steady increase in communication skills in interacting with the animate and social world.

rising tone means "Is this Daddy's book?" or "Will Daddy read a book?"

Word Order

In English and in many other languages, the order in which the words are spoken partly determines the meaning of word combinations. English sentences typically follow a subject-verb-object sequence, and children learn the rules early. In the example presented earlier, "Daddy throw ball," children use some two-word combinations ("Daddy throw," "Daddy ball," "Throw ball") but not others ("ball Daddy," "ball throw," "throw Daddy"). As soon as a child has a sense of this basic word-order rule of English, he can distinguish between the meanings, for example, of "Tickle Daddy" and "Daddy tickle." In other words, as Roger Brown (1973) and other psycholinguists have pointed out, the child does not produce a random collection of words, using the two words that are his limit in any order. Instead, he uses his knowledge of word order grammatically to distinguish the meanings of the word combinations that he produces. And linguists, parents, and other children can use their own knowledge of word order to decipher the speech of a child in the two-word stage.

Inflection

Grammatical markers, such as the possessive 's and the past tense -ed, that are added to words to change their meanings are called inflections. English uses few inflections compared to some other languages, and the child learns such English inflections as the plural and the possessive quite early, making it possible to mark, for example, the possessive meaning of "Baby's chair" and the plural "Baby chairs." Some languages provide different word endings (inflections) to express a large number of contrasts in meaning, such as the Russian example of "Mommy kisses baby" that appeared earlier in this chapter. Children who learn highly inflected languages are quick to acquire the word endings that express those notions implicit in speech at the two-word stage, such as direct and indirect object and locations. The direct-object inflection (as in the Russian example) is one of the first endings that children pick up in learning such languages as Russian, Serbo-Croatian, Latvian, Hungarian, Finnish, and Turkish (Slobin, 1973).

From this discussion, it should be clear that by the time he reaches the end of the two-word stage, the young child has mastered much of the basic grammatical machinery that he needs in order to acquire his particular native language: words that can be combined in order and modified by intonation and inflection. These rules occur, in varying degrees, in all the languages of the world. As a result, all languages are about equally easy for children to learn, and all children are ready to master the grammatical subtleties of their particular native language by the time they are about two and one-half years old. In Chapter 12 we will discuss the further course of language development and will explore some of the possible reasons that all children master the complexity of grammar with such apparent ease and rapidity.

SUMMARY

1. Human language possesses three important properties: semanticity, productivity, and displacement. During his first two years, the infant becomes a speaking human being by discovering the structural principles of his language—its grammar—and by actively figuring out how speech is organized.

2. From the first month of life, the baby pays special attention to the speech that he hears around him. Despite his ability to discriminate between sounds, it usually takes at least a year for him to acquire sufficient motor control to be able to produce identifiable words. He acquires this muscular control first through crying and later through babbling. Given the close interplay between the infant's increasing cognitive understanding and his linguistic development, his spoken language emerges as one of a complex set of symbolic behaviors that help him to remember and use what he has experienced. By the end of his first year, the infant's intonation patterns usually communicate commands, requests, and questions, as well as involvement.

3. The infant's first words usually function to refer, express, and command. Most often, such one- and two-syllable utterances can be understood only in context. First words are likely to be repeated syllables made up of a consonant and a vowel, which will eventually be shaped into actual words. These early words often have an overextended range of meanings based on perceived similarities such as movement or shape. These global meanings become more precise as the infant restructures them and makes sharper discriminations.

4. The infant often knows and means more than he can say. Thus, although two-word sentences may communicate more information, they do not represent a new level of thinking. By about two years of age, however, the infant can usually put several words together and can express and understand an impressive range of basic universal concepts involving objects, actions, and events.

5. A rudimentary grammar appears in the infant's language toward the end of the two-word stage and includes the basic tools of human language: intonation, word order, and inflection. With these first grammatical devices, the child is ready to master the further subtleties of his native language and to produce and understand sentences outside an immediate context.

SUGGESTED READINGS

Bloom, Lois. *One Word at a Time: The Use of Single Word Utterances Before Syntax.* The Hague: Mouton, 1973.

Cazden, Courtney B. *Child Language and Education.* New York: Holt, Rinehart and Winston, 1972.

Mehrabian, Albert. "Communication Without Words," *Psychology Today,* 2 (September 1968), 52–55.

Slobin, Dan I. "Children and Language: They Learn the Same Way All Around the World," *Psychology Today,* 6 (July 1972), 71–74+.

Weir, Ruth H. *Language in the Crib.* The Hague: Mouton, 1962.

With increased competence in movement, thought, and communication, an infant also becomes a unique person in his social world.

9

PERSONALITY: FROM ATTACHMENT TO SOCIABILITY

"She's not a playmate—she can't do nothin'," Matt pouted, regarding the new baby with disgust. The baby's eyes opened, seemed to wander uncoordinated, and then came to rest on the happy-face button that Matt was wearing. "Hey, she's looking at my button!" cried Matt, snatching it off his shirt and moving it back and forth in front of baby Susan's eyes. His sister briefly followed the button with slow jerky movements of her eyes; she even turned her head to follow it to one side. A fleeting upturn of the corners of her mouth evoked a response from her brother: "She's smiling, look, she's smiling!" In his excitement, Matt slipped and fell heavily against the bassinet. The baby startled and reacted with her whole body: flailing arms and legs, screwed-up red face, and imperative screams. Matt ran to get his father. After his father rocked Susan and soothed her, he placed her back in the bassinet. Matt, who had been observing quietly, headed outdoors to play. As he walked out of the room, he looked back and said, "She's nothin' but a cryer and a wetter."

From these unpromising beginnings, Matt's new sister will develop into a complex, social, unique individual. Susan will pursue numerous goals in life; relate to people in a variety of ways; be angered, frightened, and elated; and have beliefs, attitudes, and values that in part reflect her upbringing and in part are unique to her.

This chapter traces the beginnings of that development. In it we will see how early experiences, which begin at the moment of birth, contribute to a baby's developing personality. We will find wide agreement with the supposition that these early experiences affect later development but little agreement as to how and why these effects come about. We will look at a baby's first social bond with her primary caretakers and discover that this attachment plays an important role in the baby's developing trust in the world and in her growing sense of self. Even her early play will affect the development of her personality. By the end of the chapter, we will have examined the ways in which the important lessons of the infant's first two years of life lay the groundwork for the person that the baby will eventually become.

PERSONALITY DEVELOPMENT

It is easy to see that an infant learns to walk, to eat with a spoon, or to say his name. However, people often think of personality as given, as something that one is born with. Although each baby comes into the world with certain temperamental predispositions that tend to shape the course of his personality development, most psychologists are convinced that what we think of as personality is largely the product of learning. How people feel about themselves, whether they are assertive or demure, whether they are anxious in social situations, how they enact their roles as females or males are all learned patterns of behavior.

Personality development refers to the growth of the individual as a social being, a person who carries on the important activities of life in interaction with other people. For example, Susan's sense of herself as a separate being will be closely connected with her sense of other people as continuing, existing beings. The behavior of important people in her life will contribute to Susan's consistent definition of them. Thus, their attitudes and actions will powerfully affect her sense of personal identity, of the continuity and sameness of "me" over time and across situations. How other people respond to her will affect even the way that she incorporates such "facts" of her existence as sex and race into her sense of gender and ethnic identity. And the specifics of her self-concept, her thoughts and feelings about the kind of person she is, will first form when she adopts the attitudes toward herself held by important others in her life.

Another way of looking at the development of such enduring dispositions as self-concept is to say that various aspects of social interaction become internalized. At first Susan will be regulated by her parents, but later she will be able to regulate herself in their absence. She will eventually be able to criticize herself, pat herself on the back, and carry on private conversations with herself. A sense of separateness, a sense of the continuity of one's existence, a sense of one's qualities and value, and the continuing dynamics of one's relationship with oneself are all central aspects of personality functioning, and all are developmental achievements. Each of these aspects of "self" emerges out of social interaction, each has great import for feelings and emotions, and each has a basis in cognitive structure.

Of course, self-concept is only one developmental achievement. Although most theorists agree that it is one of immense importance, they tend to lay different stress on other aspects of personality development.

One way to understand these divergent approaches to early personality development is to compare them directly, as done in Figure 9.1. As you can see, there is variation in what is considered to constitute the most important features of early personality development. On the other hand, all agree that early experience is of primary importance in establishing the enduring dispositions we call personality.

EARLY EXPERIENCE

The notion that early experience is of primary importance for later life was popularized by Sigmund Freud (1917). His idea that certain experiences during infancy are crucial for personality development has been adopted by many developmental psychologists with very different theoretical outlooks.

Types of Effects

Much of the evidence demonstrating the effects of early experience comes from studies of nonhuman species. Severe restriction or deprivation of experience in early infancy causes a variety of striking behaviors in animals, and many of these behaviors seem to persist into adulthood. These deprived animals are often quite different from normal animals in both social and emotional development. For example, puppies who spent their first few months in isolation from other puppies and from human beings showed "bizarre postures and a tendency to be unresponsive to playthings, people, and other puppies" (J. Scott, 1967). A puppy less extremely deprived will behave more normally but may have an intense fear of

Figure 9.1 Summary descriptions of some major theoretical viewpoints on personality development during infancy.

Sigmund Freud, the founder of psychoanalysis, emphasizes the sensual nature of the infant's early interactions with his world. In Freud's view, the infant's attachment to his parents is based on his desire for sensual gratification. He suggests that infants go through psychosexual phases of development—oral, anal, and phallic—during which they derive sensual pleasure from stimulation of the corresponding area of their body. Parents affect the child's personality development by either gratifying or frustrating these desires.

Erik Erikson is a psychodynamic theorist who proposes that the infant learns early to distinguish between himself and those who satisfy his biological needs. In his theory of psychosocial stages of development, the interactions between the infant and his parents give him an ego identity, or a self-concept, and pleasant interactions create an attachment and a trust for his parents. In this view, if the infant learns to trust his parents because they meet his needs successfully, he will develop a more coherent self-concept and a sense of self-esteem.

Alfred Adler is a psychodynamic theorist who bases his theory on the infant's striving to overcome feelings of helplessness and incompetence in a world of people larger and stronger than himself. Adler proposes that the desire to conquer these feelings of inferiority motivates the infant to seek help and attention from his parents. The family can either support and encourage or hinder the infant's struggle to attain superiority—that is, to release himself from his feelings of inferiority. In this view, striving for social superiority is a stronger motivation than seeking gratification of sensual desires.

Erich Fromm, a psychodynamic theorist, considers birth as creating in the infant anxiety-provoking feelings of separateness from his mother, in contrast to his former (prenatal) physiological dependence on her. Fromm perceives the infant as oriented from birth toward a relationship with his parents as a result of his innate need for rootedness. In this view, if the parents respond to the infant with warmth and love, they will communicate a love of life and create in him a desire for productivity. On the other hand, if the parents make inappropriate demands that are difficult or impossible for the infant to fulfill, he will be prevented from realizing his potential and develop a dependent personality.

Harry Stack Sullivan is a psychodynamic theorist who sees the infant's need for a sense of security and satisfaction as the prime motivation. According to Sullivan, the infant derives his sense of self from his parents' approval or disapproval of his behavior. From his perception of his parents' positive or negative attitudes toward him, the child develops a sense of either security or insecurity, and within this context he can modify his behavior and see himself in relation to others. In this view, the insecurity that comes with disapproval is a powerful motivator of ''good behavior.''

Walter Mischel is a social-learning theorist who emphasizes the role of social experience in the infant's personality development. Mischel evaluates early experience in relation to what it teaches the infant and according to whether it aids or impedes his social development. In this view, the infant's attachment to his mother or parents is a learned behavior that develops from the association of his parents with the gratification of his needs and the reduction of discomfort. Parents shape behavior and learning according to how they respond to the infant's actions in particular situations. And the infant learns to exert control over his environment to reduce his discomfort and to gain satisfaction of his needs.

strange people and strange situations. Chimpanzees reared in a restricted environment also are more timid, especially in novel situations (Menzel, Davenport, and Rogers, 1963).

If impoverishment of the early environment can have such strong effects, we might expect that enrichment of the early environment will also have a major impact on infant animals. A variety of evidence suggests that this is so. Although restriction often produces animals that are more fearful than normal, extra stimulation at an early age often produces less fearful animals (Denenberg, 1966), even when the extra stimulation consists of mild electric shocks. Animals raised in enriched early environments also tend to be bold and curious in new situations (Forgus, 1954). Such evidence seems to indicate that, at least for some species or strains of animals, early experiences have important and enduring effects on developing patterns of response to the world.

Limits on Effects

Although early learning can have pervasive and enduring effects on later development, other research suggests that such a formulation is too simplified. For one thing, there is good reason why dispositions cannot be stamped in at an early age. A brief look at some investigations of imprinting and of fear and laughter, for example, suggests that there are strong constraints on early experience.

Sensitive Periods. Research with animals has led many investigators to conclude that only during a certain period of its life can an animal form a particular kind of strong, long-lasting social attachment. In certain species of birds, this attachment, called **imprinting,** occurs when a baby bird, fresh from the shell, sees a certain type of moving object, which it then follows. In the normal course of events, the young bird becomes imprinted to its mother, but a human being, a rubber ball, or any other moving object may also produce imprinting. The bird will overcome substantial obstacles in order to continue to follow this moving object (or others like it) and will show great distress when the object is out of sight (E. Hess, 1964). Such an attachment can be highly resistant to change. A young bird will try to feed the object to which it is imprinted and may even use it as a model for a suitable mate (an effect that introduces complications into the lives of certain ethologists). Imprinting occurs *only* during a certain critical or sensitive period of an animal's infancy (see Chapter 4 for more about sensitive periods).

Figure 9.2 Imprinting. A few hours after they were hatched, these baby geese saw ethologist Dr. Konrad Lorenz instead of a mother goose. The goslings thereafter followed Dr. Lorenz around as if he were their mother.

Some theorists have suggested that, just as normal young birds or goats or sheep become imprinted to their animal mothers, so human babies become attached to their mothers. This concept oversimplifies the process in human beings, but it does not contradict the theories of Freud and other personality theorists. The imprinting phenomenon is important, for it suggests that a human being is open to certain types of experience during certain developmental periods. If the proper learning does not occur during these periods, it may not occur at all.

Other Constraints. Although strong emotions may affect human learning, some learning is necessary for emotion to develop. Consider, for example, some of the complex relationships that are involved in the emotional aspect of personality development referred to as fear. When Matt stumbled against the bassinet and Susan responded with wails and other signs of distress, she was not truly afraid. Although sudden loud noises, unexpected events, and physical pain may produce crying, distress, and avoidance reactions in newborns and very young babies, their responses are not fear in the sense that adults mean when they say that someone is afraid.

True fear requires a rather sophisticated level of cognitive development, and several studies have demonstrated the cognitive underpinnings of the emotion of fear. To be afraid, the baby must be able to hold the feared object or situation in his memory, and the appearance of the object must call up the percep-

tual and emotional experiences that were with it in the past. Later, the mere men object will be enough to evoke fear.

The changes in the nature of child reported in early studies by Arthur Jersild and Frances Holmes (1935) clearly indicate the increasing importance of cognitive development (see Figure 9.3). For example, no children below the age of two years were afraid of bodily harm and few were afraid of the dark, being alone in the dark, or imaginary creatures, whereas a significant percentage of four- to six-year-olds feared these things. These fears, in contrast to "fear" of sudden loud noises, require imaginative constructions based on the generalization of past experience.

In a more recent study, Sandra Scarr and Philip Salapatek (1970) found similar developmental trends. They reported that, between the ages of five and eighteen months, there was an increase in infants' fear responses to strangers, to a grotesque mask, and to heights (as measured by the visual-cliff technique described in Chapter 7). These fears could develop only after the infants learned about the familiar and safe aspects of their environments. During the same period, there was no increase in infants' fear of loud noises or of a suddenly appearing jack-in-the-box.

Suppose that when Susan was six months old Matt suddenly thrust his head over the side of her crib and made a grotesque face. Would she scream with fear? She might laugh at Matt's face but scream at the same behavior in a stranger. Laughter and fear both seem to

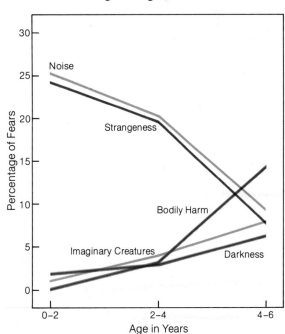

Figure 9.3 Developmental changes in the nature of children's fears as indicated by their responses to a few different objects and situations. (Adapted from Jersild and Holmes, 1935)

occur in response to a stimulus that is unfamiliar or incongruous in comparison with a familiar standard of reference.

For example, L. Alan Sroufe and Jane Wunsch (1972) studied the development of laughter from its appearance at around four months through the first year and found that babies laughed when confronted with a mask instead of becoming fearful as the infants in the Scarr and Salapatek study did. There were important differences between the two studies: The mask that elicited laughter in the Sroufe and Wunsch study was human-looking and was worn by the baby's mother; the mask that elicited fear in the Scarr and Salapatek study was nonhuman and was worn by the experimenter. Sroufe and Wunsch speculated that an incongruous event arouses tension that, depending on the circumstances, will either lead to crying and avoidance or will be released in laughter.

Findings such as these on fear and laughter suggest additional limitations to the notion that early learning experiences automatically establish enduring personality dispositions. They indicate, just as the imprinting data do, that an infant or a child is not always open to the same learning experiences. In addition, the same learning experience may produce opposite effects, depending on the maturational state of the infant, his cognitive growth, his past experiences, and his surroundings.

ATTACHMENT

A human baby arrives on the social scene prepared by millions of years of primate evolution to respond to the sights and sounds of people and to behave in a way that elicits responses from them. These built-in biases are the building blocks for complex systems of social behavior, which begin in the family. In most cultures, the closest relationship of all is between mother and infant. They are involved for a time in a close symbiotic relationship in which the child is almost an extension of the mother's being.

In this light, it is no surprise that investigators have taken a keen interest in the development of the special bond between an infant and its caretaker called **attachment.** A look at attachment helps answer some questions already raised: How does early learning shape basic personality? How do parents and others influence children? How do predispositions help to determine personality development?

As Figure 9.4 shows, some theorists call these systems of social behavior "instinctual," but that does not mean that the systems are rigidly determined. Instead, these social behaviors, as they devel-

op through the infant's interactions with others, serve functions that have always been related to survival in the evolutionary past. The final organization of such human ways of relating to others as smiling and crying is complex and flexible; such behaviors are predispositions that the long course of socialization in a particular human society shapes and elaborates.

Susan, for example, came into the world with the predispositions common to all human infants; she also possesses her own bundle of individual characteristics, such as her activity level and her general irritability. In the first two years of life, she will develop patterns of interactions with adults and children that are inseparably linked with the rest of her personality development. Through this social interaction, she will develop a sense of self, of a "me" who is distinct from parents and peers. In turn, this emerging sense of self will change the pattern of her social interaction.

The patterns of this social commerce coordinate with Susan's other developmental achievements. Her early behavior on the social level reflects the development that occurs on the cognitive level. For example, her level of cognitive understanding sets limits on the kinds of social behavior that can be expected at various stages of development. Before Susan can move out to interact with her peers, she must establish a primary social bond, and the nature and function of that primary attachment is the focus of much psychological investigation.

Attachment in Monkeys

As with studies of early experience, research on attachment is heavily indebted to work with animals. As Figure 9.4 shows, early views on attachment, both psychoanalytic and behavioral, have assumed the importance of the feeding process. As J. P. Scott (1962) has noted, this assumption can lead to an unromantic conclusion: Infants love us only because we feed them. However, data from the primate laboratories of Harry and Margaret Harlow and other researchers have demonstrated convincingly that there is more to attachment than being fed, even for infant monkeys (Harlow, 1958). In one ingenious series of studies by the Harlows (1966, 1969), infant monkeys were raised in cages with two surrogate mothers: One mother substitute was covered with soft terry cloth; the other was of hard wire mesh and was equipped with a feeding mechanism. If feeding were the only or the most important factor in attachment, the little monkeys would have spent more time expressing their attachment to the wire "mother,"

Figure 9.4 Summary descriptions of some major theoretical viewpoints on the development of attachment behavior during infancy.

Sigmund Freud bases his theory of attachment on instinctual drives. In this view, attachment is a particular kind of object choice: The infant initially goes through a stage of complete self-preoccupation, termed narcissism, but later recognizes people as instrumental in satisfying his drives and becomes attached to those who feed, care for, and protect him.

René Spitz is a neoanalytic theorist who considers need-gratification essential in forming an attachment and who uses naturally occurring infant behavior to demarcate different stages. In Spitz's view, the smiling response to human faces identifies the beginning of a transition stage, whereas the appearance of an anxiety reaction to strangers heralds the stage of true object relations. According to Spitz, the anxiety response to strangers is the earliest indication that the infant can discriminate the loved one from other people, a distinction necessary for a real love relationship.

John Bowlby is a British child psychiatrist in the neoanalytic tradition who proposes an ethological theory of attachment based on the interaction between adaptive predispositions in the infant as well as in the adult caretaker. Bowlby suggests that definite types of stimulation (a human face, a human voice, a strange object) elicit particular behavior in the infant (smiling, alertness and scanning, crying). The infant's behavior, in turn, is considered to elicit complementary behavior in the adult. Thus, an infant's smile may trigger a smile in the adult and perhaps also a strong attraction to the infant. In addition, an infant's cry may cause the adult to approach and soothe the infant, thus ending the crying.

Mary Ainsworth is a developmental theorist with an ethological view of attachment who emphasizes how the constant feedback between the caretaker and the infant continually modifies the instinctual predispositions of each. In this view, each infant-adult pair evolves a unique pattern of interaction. As an infant becomes more experienced, he fears fewer things, and he also develops more elaborate communication systems. According to Ainsworth, these advances may cause a decline in both the frequency and the intensity of attachment behavior.

Robert Sears is a developmental-learning theorist who views attachment, or dependence, as a secondary drive derived from other drives. In this view, many primary drives, such as hunger, thirst, pain, and discomfort, are satisfied by the caretaker. Consequently, caretakers acquire a positive value to the extent that they reduce the intensity of drive states. Thus, a secondary drive for the caretaker's presence develops, resulting in the infant's becoming attached to the caretaker.

Jacob Gewirtz is a behavioral-learning theorist who proposes that attachment is a function of reinforcement. In this view, the interaction between an infant and his environment, especially with the caretaker, is mutually reinforcing. Thus, adult and child come to exert control over each other's behavior, and the two develop a specific pattern of response—attachment.

Lawrence Kohlberg is a cognitive-developmental theorist who sees the motivation for interpersonal competence—that is, for producing mutual stimulation and for sharing interesting activities—as underlying the formation of human attachments. In this view, genuine social attachments are formed only to another social self. Thus, Kohlberg suggests that, until the infant acquires the concept of object permanence at around nine months and with it a notion of "selves," such responses as smiling at familiar faces and showing anxiety when confronted with strange faces are not specifically social but merely reflect the child's general cognitive responses to the familiar and the unfamiliar. According to this view, a specific infant-caretaker attachment during the first year is not critical to later capacities for social attachment. Therefore, if mutually stimulating interaction motivates true attachment, then interaction with a variety of persons, including peers, should promote attachment at any age.

which fed them. But the monkeys spent much more time clinging to the cloth mother, which gave them no nourishment at all.

The monkeys seemed genuinely attached to the cloth mother; when these monkeys were given a choice of things to observe in the Harlows' "love machine," which allowed them visual access to various objects, they chose to look at the cloth mother much more often than they chose the wire mother. Infant monkeys raised under normal conditions showed no preference for either artificial mother and rarely chose to look at them. Monkeys raised under experimental conditions also used the cloth mother, but not the wire mother, as a security base when they were put in a strange place or when a fearful object was placed near them. In such a situation, the infant monkeys at first appeared to be terrified, but when they could cling to the cloth mother, they soon ceased showing signs of distress. Eventually, they began to use the cloth mother as a base for exploration, leaving to manipulate some of the novel objects but returning frequently to cling to their soft, snuggly mother, as monkeys raised with real mothers do. The wire mothers were never used in this way.

Clinging is a behavior that young monkeys normally display at birth; it seems to be as natural to them as scanning and vocalizing are to human infants. It should not be surprising, then, that clinging has proved to be so important to the monkey's development of attachment. The attachment also is lasting: A monkey raised with a terry cloth mother will, after a year's separation, run to embrace its soft form and cling to it passionately. But monkeys raised with wire mothers show no "love" at all after any appreciable separation, providing evidence that contact is important to the formation of attachment in monkeys.

Attachment in Human Beings

Unlike the immediate imprinting that occurs in lower animals, the development of attachment in human beings takes months to appear, requires a complex intermeshing of infant and caretaker behaviors, and is subject to much variation. Whereas attachment in human beings and in monkeys follows a similar pattern, the response of the human baby to its mother develops more slowly than the monkey baby's attachment to its mother.

Attachment in human babies refers to the early love relationship between baby and caretaker (usually a parent), and developmental psychologists study it by examining specific kinds of behaviors associated with such a relationship. These behaviors first show that an attachment exists and later show how the relationship develops and changes. The signs of attachment include positive behaviors such as smiling and joyous greeting and negative behaviors such as crying when the caretaker leaves. One of the most important aspects of attachment behaviors is that they are directed toward some people and not toward others, an aspect that is perhaps the crucial element in identifying attachment relationships.

A baby's earliest responses to people are rather indiscriminate and do not reflect a true attachment to specific people. Any person is likely to cause him to smile or vocalize in the early months of life. However, some evidence indicates that both smiling and vocalizing develop whether or not the baby experiences the sight and sound of other human beings.

You will recall that deaf babies babble and coo during the first six months. In a related finding, Irenäus Eibl-Eibesfeldt (1970) has reported that blind children begin to cry, smile, and laugh at the same time that sighted children do. Of course, these children do not smile in response to a human face but in response to their parents' voices or to social play (Freedman, 1964). The early appearance of smiling and vocalizing in all children regardless of their perceptual abilities suggests that the initial appearance of these emotional behaviors is controlled primarily by maturational processes. Apparently, the baby elaborates them in response to social stimuli and incorporates them into a system of attachment behavior that has had adaptive value over the centuries.

Discrimination in response to specific people begins to emerge around five months. The frequency of social smiling to familiar faces remains constant or increases (J. Ambrose, 1961), but the frequency of smiling to strange faces that was so prevalent at about two or three months drops off or even disappears. Harriet Rheingold (1969) has suggested that the talking, smiling human face, with its changing expressions and movements, interests and attracts the young baby. Gradually, through a variety of learning experiences, the face of the principal caretaker elicits and reinforces a variety of positive emotional and social responses in the baby. Although these learning experiences include situations in which the baby associates the parent or caretaker with the cuddles and food that satisfy his primary needs or drives, the interactions are not limited to such basic situations.

This change in social smiling is one of the earliest indications that the baby is differentiating the world into the familiar and the unfamiliar and is evidence of the baby's developing memory. Clearly, the baby must be able to recognize familiar faces in order to be able to give them his special smile. The attachments to specific people that he develops about this time increase in intensity until just before his first birthday and then seem to level off (see Figure 9.6).

It is likely that specific attachments are related to the baby's development of object permanence, which is discussed in Chapter 7. Silvia Bell (1970) has found that most babies are aware of their mothers as objects who continue to exist when out of sight

Figure 9.5 (*opposite*) Infant monkeys in the Harlow experiments. (*top*) When a large and frightening toy bear was placed near a baby monkey, (*middle*) it ran to the cloth-covered surrogate mother for comfort, then later (not shown) ventured out to explore the bear. The monkey remained fearful of the bear if it had only a wire mother (*bottom left*) and no cloth mother (*bottom right*) to cling to.

Figure 9.6 During the early weeks of life, most infants prefer not to be separated from the person they are with regardless of who that person is. Such "indiscriminate attachments" begin to decline at about the same time that the infant starts to show preferences for specific persons, such as his mother. (Adapted from Schaffer and Emerson, 1964)

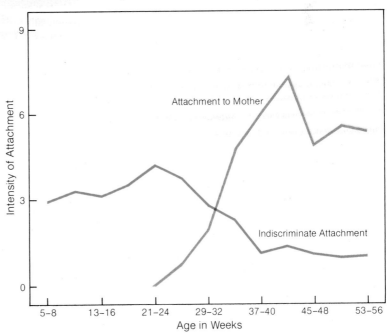

slightly before they demonstrate such an awareness with physical objects. Because the comings and goings of the human caretaker are related to the satisfaction of the baby's needs, it may be that the baby pays special attention to the location of this very important "object." Bell also found that babies who had developed secure and stable attachments to their mothers were aware of their mothers as permanent objects earlier than babies with less stable attachments. Furthermore, babies who acquired the concept of person permanence early also developed the concept of physical object permanence earlier, suggesting that understanding in the social realm has positive effects on understanding in the physical realm.

PARENT RESPONSIVENESS

Although the infant learns attachment to a caretaker, the emotions involved in the parent-child relationship run both ways. The love of the mother, father, or other caretaker for the baby and the baby's love for his parents each affect the development of the other's emotion and the fears or anxieties that may complicate it. One way to make this circular relationship clear is to look at it from each side.

Parental Styles

Even in the same culture, no two sets of parents have precisely the same attitude toward their children, nor do they rear them in exactly the same way. Some parents limit their caretaking to the essentials of feeding, cleaning, and sheltering their babies; others interact extensively with cuddling and games. H. Rudolph Schaffer and Peggy Emerson (1964a) found that, whether the mother-infant interaction consists primarily of caretaking activity or of social play, the attachment that develops seems equally strong. It appears that the crucial factor in the relationship is the baby's development of a cognitive representation of his mother as a distinct person, a step facilitated by increased exposure to his mother. As noted in Chapter 7, this occurs at about the time (twenty-two to twenty-four weeks of age) that a baby begins to show surprise when he sees what appear to be several copies of his mother.

The notion that experience with the caretaker speeds the development of attachment finds support in the work of Mary Salter Ainsworth (1967). She has noted that Ugandan infants, whose mothers generally interact more extensively with them than Western mothers do, form specific attachments somewhat earlier than the Scottish babies studied by Schaffer and Emerson. Among the Ugandan babies, attached

infants received more care from caretakers than nonattached infants did.

The behavior of parents also appears to affect a baby's social initiative and his ability to cope with frustration and stress. For example, Leon Yarrow (1963) found that the sensitivity of parents to their baby's signals (such as distressed crying or sociable cooing) and how appropriately, consistently, and flexibly they respond are more important than the amount of physical contact they give. Such flexibility requires that the parent adapt to the baby's individual characteristics and rhythms. The importance of this kind of parental responsiveness is also demonstrated by Silvia Bell and Mary Ainsworth's (1972) finding that a mother's prompt response to her crying infant with close, comforting physical contact is associated with fewer and shorter bouts of crying in the baby's first year and not the reverse, as some people think.

Class and Cultural Differences

Because adults in different societies or in different socioeconomic classes in the same society react to infants in different ways, class and culture also affect personality development. Jerome Kagan and Steven Tulkin (1971, 1972) have studied the influence of social class on maternal attitudes and behavior. Their observations of ten-month-old babies showed that, whereas both middle- and lower-class mothers hold, tickle, kiss, and bounce their babies, many other maternal behaviors are likely to differ between these social classes. A middle-class mother was more likely than a lower-class mother to vocalize within two feet of her baby, imitate his sounds, engage in prolonged "positive interaction," give verbal rewards, and encourage her baby to walk. About two-thirds of the lower-class mothers in the study used food to soothe their irritable babies, whereas less than one-third of the middle-class mothers solved problems with food.

When Kagan and Tulkin tested these babies in the laboratory, they found no class differences in the babies' levels of reactivity to meaningful and meaningless speech. However, middle-class babies quieted more dramatically to highly meaningful speech with a high degree of inflection than to other stimuli, and they were more likely to look at a stranger after hearing such speech than the lower-class children were. Middle-class infants also quieted more to their mothers' voices than to strangers' voices, and they vocalized more than lower-class infants did after listening to recordings of their mothers' voices.

Parent-infant relationships also vary across societies. Urie Bronfenbrenner (1970) has described some

Figure 9.7 Two of the many different styles of mother-infant interaction reflecting and affecting the development of attachment. Some parents may interact extensively with their infant, whereas others may limit their caretaking to basics.

of the differences between the Soviet Union and the United States in the parent-infant relationship and the socialization of children. These differences can be traced to the contrast between a family-centered and a collective-centered system of child rearing.

The Russian baby receives significantly more physical handling than his American counterpart does. Breast feeding is virtually universal in Russia, and babies are held most of the time, even when not being fed. The Russian baby gets much more hugging, kissing, and cuddling than the American baby does, but at the same time he is held much more tightly and is allowed little freedom of movement. The Russian mother is generally much more solicitous and protective, and her efforts to protect her baby from discomfort, illness, or injury curtail his mobility and initiative. Such differences in child rearing across cultures can have subtle but deep effects on personality development.

INFANT RESPONSIVENESS

Although the effects of parents on infants have been heavily investigated, the effects of the infant's characteristics on his caretakers have been largely overlooked. To see the importance of the infant's reactions, contrast the satisfaction of the mother of a highly active, irritable, uncuddly baby with the satisfaction of the mother of a peaceful, snuggly infant. You will recall from Chapter 5 that research has established the presence among infants of various activity or temperament types that affect the emotional quality of the mother-infant interaction. A study by H. Rudolph Schaffer and Peggy Emerson (1964b) indicates that babies who actively resist cuddling tend to develop attachments later than cuddlers do. "For some infants," say Schaffer and Emerson, "it appears, contact is not comforting." Cuddlers have a more intense attachment to their caretakers throughout the first year of life than noncuddlers do, but this difference seems to disappear during the second year, apparently as a result of the infant and mother adapting to each other's style. In Schaffer and Emerson's study, a baby who actively resisted contact did not always prevent social interaction between himself and his parents. Instead, the baby and his parents gradually evolved a system of social interaction that did not depend on physical contact. The intensity of these attachments bore no relation to feeding, weaning, or toilet-training practices. Once again, maternal responsiveness and the amount of mother-child interaction were related to attachment. Babies were more strongly attached to mothers who responded rapidly to their needs and who spent more time interacting with them.

As the baby develops the primary attachment to his mother or other caretakers, other emotional responses occur. These responses include the positive features of trust and security, but they also include the baby's fear of strangers and of losing contact with his mother. Once a baby can appreciate the joys of trusting and feeling security, he is also capable of fearing the loss of contact with his mother and capable of fearing strangers.

Separation Anxiety

A baby's distinctly negative reaction to separation from his attachment figure and his attempts to regain contact with that figure are called separation anxiety. This attempt to regain contact may first appear in the baby's crying and reaching out when he is separated from his mother. Later he may crawl or walk in pursuit of her.

Separation anxiety seems to be based on a fear of unusual situations, a fear that the presence of an attachment figure appears to reduce. The attachment figure becomes a security base for the baby. For example, Mary Salter Ainsworth and Barbara Witting (1969) have demonstrated that a baby, when placed in a strange situation, will first establish contact with a caretaker. Somewhat later he will venture out on short forays into the strange environment, exploring bits of it, but he always returns to his caretaker between expeditions.

For example, when a parent brings his infant or toddler on a first visit to a friend's home, the young child clings to (indeed, hides behind) the parent. Only after he becomes accustomed to the new setting is the child likely to relinquish his grasp on his parent's leg. You may recall that both the Harlows' cloth-surrogate-reared and normally reared young monkeys showed a similar reaction in a strange environment.

On the other hand, Harriet Rheingold and Carol Eckerman (1970) saw no anxiety in a similar separation-and-return pattern among infants placed in a novel situation. The infants they studied seemed to be sharing their joy and excitement with attachment figures. It is undoubtedly true that the baby uses attachment figures both to reduce fear and to share in the pleasures of life, and it seems that the same general pattern of behavior serves both purposes.

Brian Coates, Elizabeth Anderson, and Willard Hartup (1972) have observed babies before, during, and after a brief separation from an attachment figure. They found that a baby cried more while he was separated and touched more when his attachment figure returned. They also found that babies who spent more time touching their mothers before they were separated cried more while their mothers were gone and that babies who cried more during the separation spent more time touching their mothers after they returned. Apparently, certain babies are less able to cope with strange situations, and that inability to cope shows itself in different ways.

Stranger Anxiety

When this fear of the unusual is provoked by a person, it is called stranger anxiety. Stranger anxiety usually develops a month or two after specific attachments begin. A baby appears to go through four phases in his reaction to strangers (see Figure 9.8). At first he does not discriminate between strange and familiar persons. Later he responds positively to strangers, although less positively than to familiar people. Then he goes through a period of reacting to strangers with fear if an attachment figure is present, looking back and forth between the stranger and his caretaker as though comparing the strange person with the familiar one. At this time, he merely becomes sober and stares at the stranger. It is not until he is around eight months old that he responds to strangers with fear and withdrawal, and this reaction is particularly intense when his attachment figure is absent (Ainsworth, 1967).

George Morgan and Henry Ricciuti (1969) investigated both the developmental timing of stranger

Figure 9.8 For many infants, the reluctance to be separated from their mother after a specific attachment has been formed is related to a fear of new situations and people. It has also been suggested that a baby's reactions to strangers develop and change over the first year of life. The illustrations presented here depict one sequence of phases in the development of stranger anxiety, as discussed in the text.

anxiety and the calming effect of a caretaker's presence. They found that at eight, ten, and especially twelve months a baby responds more positively to the approach of a stranger if he is seated on his mother's lap than if he is four feet away from her. At four or six months, however, a separation of four feet makes little or no difference: the baby responds positively to the stranger in either case.

However, separation and stranger anxiety are less likely to develop if a baby develops a secure attachment to his caretaker. For example, Ainsworth and Witting (1969) found that a year-old infant with a secure attachment to his mother uses her as a base from which to explore a strange situation and that he is not distressed by the presence of strangers. Such an infant orients toward his mother's whereabouts when she leaves and greets her emphatically when she returns. Infants who appear to have developed insecure attachments do little exploring and are upset by the appearance of a stranger. An insecure infant shows distress when his mother leaves but does not orient toward her location, and he may not greet her when she returns. Securely attached infants also spend much more time exploring at home, but insecurely attached babies tend to be inactive and fussy.

These studies are in harmony with Erik Erikson's (1963) theory of personality development. The child's first task is to solve the conflict between trust and mistrust in interpersonal situations. The baby who has developed secure attachments will show evidence of basic trust. Trust is usually assumed to be something that a person possesses, an inner attitude. Yet trust reflects a system of interaction with the social world. A rudimentary sense of personal identity emerges in the infant, which depends on his recognition that his memories and anticipated sensations and images are firmly correlated with the familiar and predictable things and people of his world. This relatively comfortable, nonanxious certainty about the world and one's place in it allows a baby to venture into new realms of experience. These forays bring new challenges and anxieties.

Multiple Caretaking

Problems of separation raise the problem of the maternally deprived infant and the possibility that multiple caretakers may assume child-rearing tasks. In today's world, multiple caretaking is a frequent form of infant care even among babies who are not in institutions. Does the lack of a central caretaker mean that a baby will suffer from discontinuous or inadequate interaction? Research by Michael Rutter (1971)

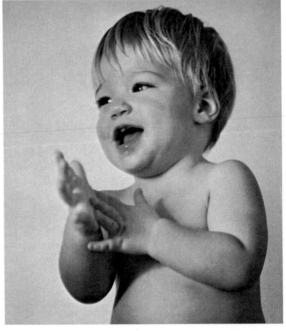

indicates that when the main attachment figure shares caretaking with other people, as when mothers work or when the baby is part of an extended family, children will thrive as long as the other caretakers provide stable relationships.

Additional research indicates that children reared in Israeli kibbutzim show normal social and emotional development (for example, Gewirtz, 1965). In a kibbutz, infants are reared communally in residential nurseries by several caretakers and see their parents only for a few hours a day or on weekends. In such arrangements, the kibbutz caretaker sees to the daily needs and training of the child, and the parents primarily provide emotional gratification (Thompson and Grusec, 1970). Again the conclusion emerges that parents may be absent for significant amounts of time without radically influencing attachment patterns, as long as someone who cares is present.

A more serious challenge to an infant's well-being is a loss or lack of mothering. Michael Rutter (1971) has reviewed the research on **maternal deprivation** and suggests that the concept is really a catchall term for a variety of early experiences. It is necessary to specify the nature of the caretaking arrangements and the kinds of stimulation that babies receive in order to investigate long-term emotional effects.

Thus, researchers have not proven that the primary caretaker is absolutely essential for normal development. Although early studies of children reared in institutions found devastating effects on their social and intellectual development, it is now clear that these unfortunate children suffered from a general lack of the stimulation necessary to social and cognitive growth as well as from the absence of a single stable caretaker. The babies in Lebanese institutions that you read about in Chapter 6 showed gains in cognitive growth as well as in physical development when interesting objects were introduced into their lives for only a few minutes each day.

Research with monkeys also indicates that development can follow a relatively normal course in the absence of a parental relationship. Monkeys raised without mothers or mother surrogates but with other baby monkeys for company were more normal in their adult social and sexual behavior than were monkeys raised with a surrogate mother but without peer contact. These findings support Lawrence Kohlberg's (1969) suggestion that it is the opportunity for pleasurable social interaction that is important to the infant's social-emotional development, not a specific tie to a caretaking person.

Not all infants who suffer maternal deprivation are able to cope with their loss. An infant who finds his attachment to his primary caretaker ruptured may develop depression, or an extreme sadness. The British child psychiatrist John Bowlby (1953) has observed what he regards as depression in fifteen- to thirty-month-old healthy infants after they had been separated from their families and placed in a hospital or other resident institution. After an initial phase of active protest and crying, such an infant falls into a phase of despair or depression. He becomes with-

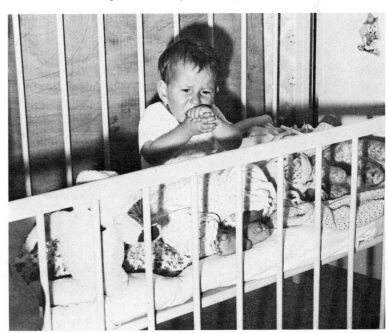

Figure 9.9 (*opposite*) The trust that develops with secure attachment to a caretaker or caretakers engenders a sense of eagerness and security in the infant.

(*right*) For some infants, the lack or disruption of a secure relationship with a primary caretaker can have strong and long-lasting negative effects on social and emotional development.

drawn and inactive, makes no demands of the environment, cries intermittently though without specific cause, and seems to show feelings of increasing hopelessness and sadness. Later, the depressed infant gradually moves out of this phase into one of increased emotional distance. He begins to interact in a pleasant but shallow manner with his institutional caretakers, and when his parents visit him, he responds in an aloof and detached way.

THE DEVELOPMENT OF SOCIABILITY

Although attachment to parents is of primary significance in the life of the infant, the spectrum of significant relationships soon broadens. Susan will have to contend with Matt as a potential threat or aid to her well-being, just as she will have to contend with Matt's playmates, her playpen peers, and possibly her younger siblings. It is within the first two years of life that we find the rudimentary development of personality usually termed sociability. As we have seen, the early experiences of infants and young children dispose them in varying degrees to regard and to approach other human beings with warmth, positive expectations, and trust.

Interactions with Parents

The baby's early sociability is largely a product of interactions with his parents. And, as emphasized before, the process of socialization is always a mutual affair, affecting the behavior of participants on each side of the interaction.

As the baby begins to venture away from his mother, he can explore a wider and wider world. Carol Eckerman and Harriet Rheingold (1974) investigated ten-month-old infants' exploratory responses to toys and people. They placed the babies in an unfamiliar environment and gave each the opportunity to approach and touch an unfamiliar person or toy. The babies promptly approached the toys and played with them. They rarely made physical contact with the strangers; instead they looked at the strangers and smiled. These results suggest that looking and smiling at persons serves an exploratory function similar to touching and manipulating toys.

Some investigators have noticed sex differences among year-old infants in response to separation from their mothers. Susan Goldberg and Michael Lewis (1969) watched the behavior of mothers and their infants and discovered that boys played more roughly with toys than girls did, that they manipulated light switches and doorknobs instead of playing only with toys, and that, when separated from their mothers by

a picket fence, they tried to get around it. Girls played quietly with toys, stayed near their mothers, and, when separated from them by a fence, cried.

But Goldberg and Lewis believe that they failed to document any biological sex differences. They noted that mothers treated boy and girl infants differently. Mothers discouraged their sons from touching them and suggested that their sons play with toys that lay across the room. Mothers of girls, on the other hand, allowed their daughters to play near them and to touch them. It may be that mothers deliberately encourage boys to be independent from a very early age. Western society has long expected males to be more independent than females.

Studies by Rheingold and Eckerman (1970) also suggest that early behavior does not depend on gender. They recorded children's forays from their mothers, placing forty-eight children between one and five years old in an L-shaped yard behind a house, which allowed a child to leave his mother's field of vision. Age, not sex, was the critical factor in whether the child left his mother's sight. Therefore, although there were wide individual differences among children who were two or older, one could predict how far the boy or girl would travel from his or her mother if one knew only the age of the child.

Striving for Competence. A baby may not act sociably merely to secure reward and avoid punishment from others. He may also find intrinsic satisfaction in acting on, exploring, and getting to know the social world. For example, Rheingold and Eckerman (1970) point out that, although an infant shows anxiety at being left by his parents, he shows no anxiety when he leaves his attachment figure to explore. They suggest that a separate motivational system, which they have termed **detachment**, coexists with the attachment system and interacts with it. The infant's movement toward detachment in the second year of life is motivated by the desire to be competent, to know the social and object world: to touch, take apart, put together, figure out toys and other objects and to evoke responses (smiling or attention) from new people. Novelty, complexity, and change—interesting new stimulation—draw infants away from the comfortable familiarity of attachment figures.

But detachment is not the opposite of attachment, nor does it signal the end of attachment. The desire to be close to familiar and loved people and the desire to try out new experiences and expand one's competence appear to coexist throughout the life of the

individual. An infant who is secure in his attachments feels safe to explore and to develop his sense of self as an independent agent or a causer of effects in the world. From his explorations, an infant brings back new knowledge and abilities that he may incorporate into increasingly differentiated and interesting interactions with familiar and cherished others. The concepts dependence and independence have often been used to describe these two movements, but these concepts are usually thought of in either-or terms, without an awareness of their reciprocal relationship.

Autonomy. Toward the end of the second year, the infant enters a period of social development that parents everywhere have observed and decried: the two-year-old's "negativistic crisis." This apparent reluctance on the part of the infant to agree with anything his parents suggest and his consistent response to all questions or commands with "No" represent a push toward autonomy in its first concentrated form.

With the advent of language and the mental activity that accompanies it, the infant becomes aware of a distinction between self and other that is not only physical but mental, a distinction between his own will, or intentions, and the will of other people, most notably his parents. Prior to this time, the infant depends on parents and caretakers for the satisfaction of most of his needs. David Ausubel (1958) has called this an executive dependence: The parent acts as an executive arm, instrumental to the infant's needs. As

Figure 9.10 As the infant's competence in handling his expanding world increases, he becomes more aware of, and expressive of, his intentions, needs, and desires and less directly dependent on others for their fulfillment.

an infant becomes more aware of his effect on the world, however, he strives for executive independence, or autonomy: He wants to do things for himself. But, more fundamentally, the negativistic infant is experimenting to discover the substance and limits of the center of activity and initiative that he is constructing: the self. Parents frequently note that the clash of wills seems to be conflict for conflict's sake; the infant is concerned not with an issue but with the principle. In terms of the infant's developing social cognition of self and other, that is a wise observation.

Interactions with Peers

Although most of Susan's social relationships during her first two years are with adults, she also has some social contact with her peers. The earliest data concerning the importance of infant peer relations come from some observations of institutionalized babies. Katharine Bauham Bridges (1933) reported that by the age of two months, institutionalized babies would orient toward the movements of a baby in an adjoining crib. She found that a baby rarely responded to the cries of other babies until the tenth month. From this time, there was a marked increase in peer interaction.

Another study describes peer interaction from six to twenty-five months. Maria Maudry and Maria Nekula (1939) used a "baby party" technique. They found that babies between the ages of six and eight months ignored about half the overtures of other babies. The interactions that took place were little more than exploratory looking and grasping, the same sort of interactions that they conducted with their toys. Fighting between babies, mainly over toys, peaked between nine and thirteen months and then decreased.

It is often toward the end of the first year that an infant begins to see peers as sources of enjoyment. The one-year-old will often pass a toy to a peer and display obvious pleasure when the other child receives it. That same object can quickly become the target of a tug-of-war, however, and the loser in the battle will scream in distress. One-year-olds also stimulate each other to begin play sequences. For example, one infant starts banging on a table or taking toys out of the toy box, and the others join in. As each new treasure is pulled from the box, mutual smiles break out. Real enjoyment seems to come from this mutual play.

Both the Bridges study and that of Maudry and Nekula found that, toward the middle of the second year, infants attend positively to peers once they have resolved their conflicts over play materials. In other words, toys serve as vehicles for both positive and negative social contact. For the nineteen- to twenty-five-month-old, play objects and playmates are more successfully integrated, and social interactions begin to predominate. An infant of this age now modifies his behavior to adjust to his playmate's activity.

Peer interaction is one example of the great social expansion that takes place in the second year of life. During this year, almost all infants are mobile, and many become quite adept at speech. Peer interaction

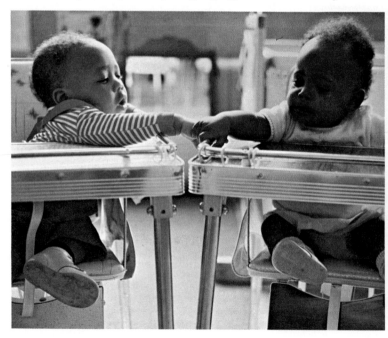

allows a young child to try his skills and to explore his differentiating sense of self. Children may begin to have truly reciprocal relationships, learn to take turns, and enjoy each other's actions. Some understanding of others' feelings can usually be seen at this time. Many children will start to form real attachments with specific peers and squeal with delight on spying them. An infant of one and one-half to two years may appear to comfort a peer in distress, or at least to observe him with concern.

The Significance of Play

Given the importance of peer play in the development of sociability, as well as the universality of early play, many investigators have been drawn into deeper study of play. The baby's developing cognitive structure, his evolving emotions, and his broadening view of self and others are all involved in play. It is through play that the baby finds out much about the world of people and things in relation to himself. Lest this statement make it sound as if games are all work and no play, it should be noted that, although play serves all these functions, the baby may play just for the fun of it. As Brian Sutton-Smith (1971) has pointed out, "The pleasure in play is the pleasure of mastery; the functional becomes fun."

The baby's fun begins as soon as he becomes familiar with his environment, can attend to events around him, and has control over the parts of his body used in the game (Call, 1970). John S. Watson (1972) has analyzed early social games between the two- and three-month-old baby and another person as a special instance of the way that a baby can experience clear control over some part of his world. In social play, the response of the other person shows the baby his power. Each time the baby does something, such as make a sound, the other person responds by doing something, such as making another sound. Or perhaps the baby blinks, and the other person touches the baby's nose; or the baby squirms, and the other person blows on his tummy. Watson's research indicates that such play leads the baby to smile and coo, which delights the other person and makes the game likely to continue for some time. This entire sequence, in which the baby registers a connection between his action and its clear effect in the world and the intrinsic pleasure that it brings him, serves as a prototype for later, more complex forms of play.

The question arises, of course, as to the importance of parents or peers in such games. The development of sociability through games may simply be a by-product of the infant's basic desire for control or mastery of the environment. Consistent with this view, Watson found that a mobile turning above a crib in response to a baby's movements will release the same kind of smiling and cooing as play with another person. Apparently it is the relationship between the baby's behavior and its clear effect in the world that is critical in early social play, not the interpersonal relationship with a person who produces the effect. Nevertheless, Justin Call (1970), who agrees that early games show the baby the first signs

Figure 9.11 Peer interactions change considerably over the first two years of development, from minimal interactions during the first nine months, through a period sometimes characterized by competition and fighting for toys, to the reciprocal play patterns that require cooperative efforts and provide mutual satisfaction and enjoyment.

of regularity in the universe and his power over the world, reminds us that these games are also one of the first forms of communication between the baby and his mother.

The intellectual aspects of play have been particularly stressed by Jean Piaget (1951), who feels that play serves critical functions in the development of the child. It is consistent with Piaget's point of view, as set forth in Chapters 2 and 7, that he sees play as developing in qualitatively different stages. Piaget identifies three levels of play activity: **practice play, symbolic play,** and **cooperative** (or **reciprocal) play.** At each level, play fulfills an essential function for the child's intellectual and emotional growth.

According to this theory, during the sensorimotor period, which ends with development of language, play is primarily assimilatory, incorporating the environment into the child's understanding. By this Piaget means that the baby at play tries out an old scheme on new objects, practicing and exercising it. For example, if the infant already knows how to reach for an object with a stick (he has a scheme for this action), he will tend to use that same pattern to reach for other objects or just to move the stick for its own sake. Infants seem to feel real pleasure and satisfaction when they repeat behaviors that they already know. The infant "repeats his behavior not in any further effort to learn or to investigate, but for the mere joy of mastering it and of showing off to himself his own power of subduing reality" (Piaget, 1951).

Thus the baby's first type of play is practice play. He bangs the side of the crib, shakes a rattle continuously, or swings his arms back and forth in front of his face. This early practice play is thoughtless, devoid of any social reference, and intrinsically pleasing. Indeed, it is quite egocentric. However, as the infant enters the second year of life, play comes to reflect his growing social conceptions. As mentioned in the previous section, children start adjusting their play to the behavior and desires of their peers. Play begins to become cooperative. Finally, as the child acquires a mastery of language, his play will become increasingly symbolic and complex; Chapter 13 will discuss how symbolic and reciprocal play increase during early childhood.

SUMMARY

1. Most psychologists are convinced that personality—how people feel about themselves and how they respond to others—is largely a product of learning and that, from the moment of birth, learning affects the infant's developing personality.

2. Although early experience can have pervasive and enduring effects on later development, investigations of different kinds of early learning and behavior suggest that there are strong constraints on the effects

of early experience. These constraints may involve sensitive periods in development as well as maturational state, cognitive growth, and previous experience.

3. In studying personality development, psychologists have paid special attention to the primary attachment bond between an infant and his caretaker. Studies of both monkey and human infants have illustrated the complex nature of this relationship. In human babies, this early love relationship takes months to develop, requires extensive intermeshing of infant and caretaker behaviors, and is subject to much variation.

4. Differences in parent and infant styles of responding are shown in the mutual and reciprocal nature of the attachment. In general, differences in parental styles do not seem to affect the strength of attachment. However, parental sensitivity and flexibility of response to the baby's needs do seem to affect such personality characteristics of the baby as his initiative and reactions to stress.

5. As the infant develops a primary attachment, separation and stranger anxiety may appear. These emotional behaviors seem to depend on the strength of the infant's attachment to his caretaker and on his reactions to novel situations. In cases where caretaking is shared or temporarily absent, research suggests that its effects on the infant are likely to vary with the infant's reaction and the amount and kind of caretaking stimulation that is presented, removed, or replaced.

6. Although the infant's early personality and sociability are largely a product of interaction with his parents, peer interaction usually becomes increasingly important during the second year of life. Motivated by a desire for competence, the infant is likely to begin to show detachment from his parents and increased autonomy. Peers and play appear in turn not only to become sources of enjoyment but to provide essential stimulation for the infant-child's intellectual and personality development.

SUGGESTED READINGS

Anderson, Robert Henry, and Harold G. Shane (eds.). *As the Twig Is Bent: Readings in Early Childhood Education.* Boston: Houghton Mifflin, 1971.

Bronfenbrenner, Urie. *Two Worlds of Childhood: U.S. and U.S.S.R.* New York: Simon and Schuster, 1972.

Call, Justin D. "Games Babies Play," *Psychology Today,* 3 (January 1970), 34–37+.

Harlow, Harry F. *Learning to Love.* San Francisco: Albion, 1971.

Lewis, Michael. "Culture and Gender Roles: There's No Unisex in the Nursery," *Psychology Today,* 5 (May 1972), 54–57.

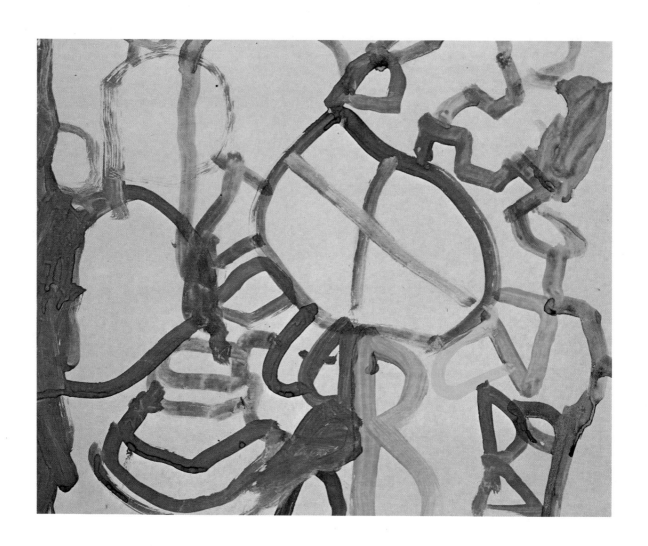

Between the ages of two and six, the toddler becomes a child. His chubby body begins to slim, and his sometimes awkward attempts at the games of childhood become smooth and skilled. As he uses more sophisticated techniques to explore the environment, his increased experiences and rapidly developing understanding allow the young child to enter a wider world. Although his parents retain the.strongest influence on his development, other children and adults begin to play an increasingly important role. Society further strengthens its influence on the growing child by transmitting cultural values and by holding him to what it considers appropriate behavior for one of his sex. When you finish this unit, you will see that there are many ways in which the continuous interaction of child and society affect development.

UNIT IV
Early Childhood: The Formative Years

Increases in size, strength, speed, and coordination enable the young child to engage in more demanding and complex activities.

10
PHYSICAL CHANGE: GROWTH AND SKILLS

Although the facts of physical development are interesting in themselves, their major psychological impact lies in the fact that sheer changes in physical size radically change the fundamental aspects of the child's world. As Lauren gets bigger, she can do more with her increased physical and behavioral potential, and she can interact in different ways with her physical and human environment. Lauren as a baby could neither move nor reach effectively. The toddler is limited to climbing on low objects and pulling down things that are in reach. Although she has discovered how to use tools—she can get the dishes off the table by pulling the tablecloth—as she grows taller, she can interact directly with the objects on the table. And as her body and muscles develop, she acquires the ability to do things more skillfully. There is also no question that parents and others treat a larger, older, more capable child differently. Her increased abilities allow the young child to interact with others in a greater variety of ways.

As you recall, Chapter 6 described the physical growth and development of the infant and pointed out that, as infants begin to gain control over their bodies and their environment, their opportunities for exploration increase sharply. In tracing an infant through those first two years, we noticed the uses and limits of norms and the wide individual differences among infants.

In this chapter we will follow the young child until he is six, looking at normative development during those years and again stressing individual differences. We will continue to examine the influence of the environment on the growing child and notice that diet, illness, socioeconomic status, and maternal care and emotional stress can affect physical growth. We will trace the continuing development of motor abilities, especially strength, speed, and coordination. We will see that the acquisition of individualized skills depends in part on appropriate practice and instruction. We will explore differences between boys and girls in motor and physical growth. Finally, we will consider some of the ways that physical changes during early childhood influence a child's personal development and affect his behavior in social settings.

GROWTH CHARACTERISTICS

Growth in early childhood is not as dramatic as it was during infancy. The rate of growth, in both height and weight, decelerates markedly during infancy and, about the time a child is three or four, settles into a steady rate. Figure 10.2, which charts the average child's annual height increase, shows a velocity curve that flattens and remains about the same until just before the child enters puberty (Falkner, 1966). Growth, however, continues to be relatively rapid, and the average child grows two and one-half inches in height and gains five to seven pounds each year.

As this period of growth starts, there is often a sudden, marked change in a child's appetite. He eats less, and his parents often become alarmed. This decrease in appetite is normal and comes from the smaller energy needs of a child in the steady period of growth (E. Watson and Lawrey, 1967).

There is little difference between the size of boys and of girls throughout the childhood years, although girls tend to be a little shorter and lighter. The size of a baby at birth and his adult size show little correlation. But by the time he is three, a child has settled into his own growth curve on the way to his destined adult size. Thus, as we noted in Chapter 6, stature during early childhood correlates highly (+.70) with adult size, making predictions of adult stature practical (Bayley, 1956).

Most body tissue, with a few exceptions, follows this general curve of growth. Fat, which increased rapidly during the baby's first nine months and then remained steady, begins to lessen. Most children undergo a true loss of body fat during early childhood (Espenschade and Eckert, 1967). This is sometimes referred to as loss of "baby fat."

Another important exception to the growth curve is the skull, and of course skull size correlates highly with brain mass. There is such a rapid growth of skull and brain mass that, by the time the child is two or three, this mass has reached about 80 percent of its adult size. By this time the child has emerged from the sensitive period of brain growth, when adequate nutrition is essential to normal brain development (Dobbing, 1974). Although most of the myelination (which was discussed in Chapter 6) is complete around eighteen months, some myelin sheaths continue to develop, and the number and size of nerve endings within and between cortical areas continue to grow at least until adolescence (Yakovlev and Lecours, 1967). When a child is about four, the fibers that connect his cerebellum to his cerebral cortex are mature. The cerebellum, as shown in Figure 10.1, is part of the brain stem, and the connecting fibers are necessary to the fine control of voluntary movement involved in such skills as writing. The reticular formation, tissue within the brain made up of both myelinated and unmyelinated fibers, continues to mature throughout childhood (Tanner, 1970). It is probably essential to the maintenance of arousal and attention.

In addition to these increases in size and changes in organ structure, a child undergoes other physical

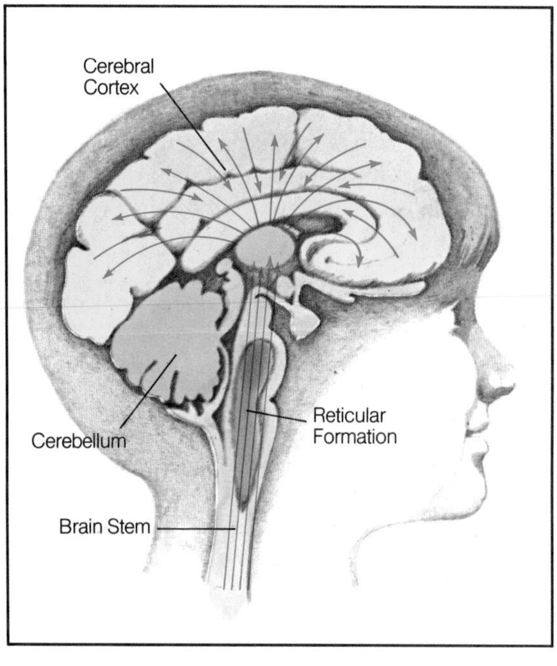

Figure 10.1 Illustration of brain development and activity of the reticular formation. Neural impulses traveling up from the spinal cord and down from various cortical areas pass through the reticular formation, causing it to send diffuse messages to the rest of the brain, arousing and activating it.

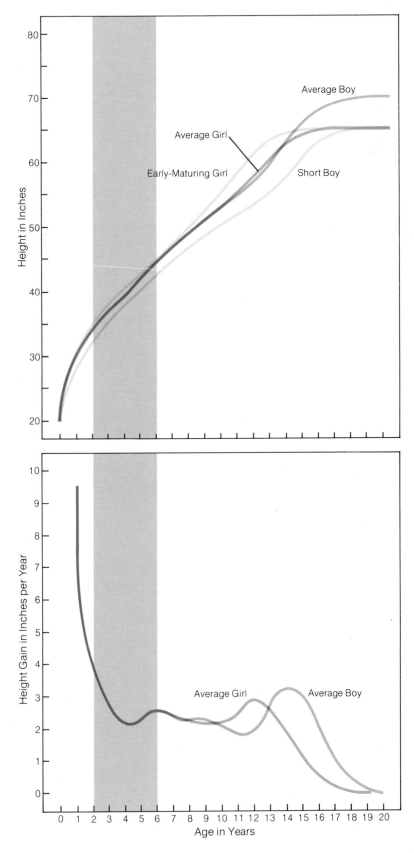

Figure 10.2 Sample growth curves for children two to six years of age (shaded area). (*top*) The growth curves of an early-maturing girl and a short boy are compared to similar curves depicting the rates of growth for an average boy and girl. (*bottom*) Averaged and smoothed curves for boys and girls show inches gained in height per year. After the initial growth spurt of infancy, the rate of growth (velocity) first declines and then remains relatively stable (until puberty). (Adapted from Bayley, 1956)

changes as he develops. His head and upper body approach their adult proportions; his limbs grow rapidly and his trunk, appreciably, so that by the time he is five or six, a child's physical proportions are far closer to those of an adult than to those of the large-headed, round-bodied infant.

A child's pelvis and shoulders do not broaden substantially during these years. The boy's body lacks the V-shape of the adult man, and the girl's lacks the curves of a woman. At this time body proportions of boys and girls are similar: straight and flat.

A five-year-old's heart rate is slower and more stable than that of an infant. The young child's respiration also steadily becomes slower and deeper, and his blood pressure shows progressive increases. These maturational processes enhance the child's capacity for continuous and strenuous effort.

In discussing these general trends in growth, one should remember the importance of individual differences. Recall the studies of "normal" children in Chapter 6 in which the lightest eight-year-old boy was no heavier than the heaviest eight-year-old had been at the age of two. Figure 10.2 presents a few of the many possible growth curves that appear in a large sample of normal children.

Because genetic influence plays such a large part in determining growth patterns, it is always important to compare a child to his parents and siblings before comparing him to a standard for a large population. This is especially necessary when the child may appear to diverge greatly from such standards. Growth standards based on mean parent size, now being developed, will be a great help to pediatricians and developmental psychologists.

ENVIRONMENTAL INFLUENCES ON GROWTH

A variety of environmental factors can greatly affect a young child's growth. These factors, which include diet, general health, and other socioeconomic determinants, can either support or impede normal growth and development.

No one is entirely sure how or why environmental factors influence growth during early childhood. J. M. Tanner (1970) has discussed some of the possible hormonal and chemical factors that may be part of the internal mechanism that regulates growth. Nutrition, illness, and stress may affect the composition and production of these chemicals.

Socioeconomic background, illness, and stress may influence growth at least in part through their indirect effect on nutrition. Children who are ill or extremely upset may not eat as much or as well as

healthy, contented children. Children from lower socioeconomic classes may have parents who cannot afford to provide proper nutrition and medical care or who do not understand how to provide sufficient proteins, vitamins, and minerals on limited budgets by using inexpensive but unfamiliar high-protein food such as soybean flour.

Diet

As Chapter 6 made clear, children must have an adequate diet if they are to grow and develop normally. High-quality protein provides most of the material for growth, and carbohydrates provide the enormous amounts of energy that the two- to five-year-old expends. Finally, the proper amounts of fat, minerals, vitamins, and water allow the growing child to develop properly and to utilize other nutritional elements.

Students of childhood growth have made numerous studies of the effects of malnutrition on the young child. Georg Wolff's (1935) study of Berlin children during World War I demonstrated that malnutrition at age five retards the development of height and weight. However, once these children had a normal diet, they began to overcome the adverse effects and by adolescence had caught up with their well-fed contemporaries. (The phenomenon of catch-up growth was described in detail in Chapter 6.) Studies of war children in Russia, Spain, France, Belgium, and Japan have shown the same general results as those in Berlin (Acheson, 1960).

Figure 10.3 Socioeconomic status and physical development. Disturbances in physical development due to inadequate nutrition can result from unavailability of necessary dietary elements, prohibitive costs, lack of knowledge regarding daily requirements and proper eating habits, and other factors associated with lower socioeconomic status.

Ironically, dietary excesses can also upset normal growth patterns. I. P. Bronstein and his colleagues (1942), Hilde Bruch (1957), and other researchers have found that obesity in children most often results from overfeeding; malfunctioning glands are only rarely responsible. In affluent Western nations such as the United States, the opportunities for excessive feeding are great, and it has been demonstrated that an excess of even the healthiest of foods produces, instead of ever-larger, healthier children, children who may become unhappy and socially maladjusted. Recent studies (Dwyer and Mayer, 1973) have suggested that it is possible that overnutrition in infancy (often caused by a mother determined to have a large, healthy baby) may lead to a multiplication of extra-large fat cells. Such a baby is susceptible to obesity and may easily become a fat child or adult. Parents may also produce obese children by forcing food on a two- or three-year-old whose growth rate has settled into the childhood plateau described earlier.

Illness

A child who escapes serious illness will have a more regular and satisfactory pattern of growth than one who is very ill for any length of time, because severe illness tends to slow certain growth patterns. Studies of child health and development show that children from two to six years old catch the greatest number of communicable diseases (Stuart and Prugh, 1960). Some of these diseases involve the respiratory or intestinal tracts, but few, if any, have important effects on growth in most children. Although a child's growth rate may slow slightly during an extended bout with illness, catch-up growth normally compensates for such slowing. For example, Roy Acheson (1960) found that one year of severe, confining illness resulted in a height loss of only about one-fourth inch.

In general, if a child is ill for a short period, as most children are, he will have no difficulty overcoming the growth deficit arising out of the illness. But if a child has serious and protracted illnesses, he may be permanently underdeveloped, not merely from the effects of the sickness but because he has lost the periods of reasonably steady growth needed for adequate development.

Socioeconomic Status

The setbacks to growth caused by illness are most readily seen among children of the lower socioeconomic classes. As pointed out in Chapter 6, inadequate medical care and poor diet combine to make the children in developing nations and impoverished children in wealthy nations the most likely victims of growth abnormalities produced by insufficient diet and long illness.

Inadequate nutrition can have less dramatic but more insidious results than actual starvation. The low energy levels that come from malnutrition can produce a sluggish child whose interest is hard to arouse. Undernourished children are more vulnerable to all infections, but especially to disease of the eyes, skin, and respiratory and gastrointestinal tracts. Because

these children are unlikely to have regular medical care, they may also suffer from nagging ailments, including badly decayed teeth.

In England, the 1958 National Child Health Survey demonstrated that the more skilled the father's occupation, the more rapidly the children grew. The differences between the children of highly skilled and less skilled fathers grew steadily larger among children between the ages of two and four and one-half. Studies conducted in Scotland support the results of the English survey (E. Scott, Illsby, and Thomson, 1956). Children of higher socioeconomic backgrounds tend to be larger at all ages. Part of the differences in stature among socioeconomic groups is probably a result of the fact that children of the wealthier classes grow and develop earlier. However, as the slowly developing children mature, they do not make up all the height difference, which means that there is a socioeconomic difference in adult height.

Differences in nutrition and availability of medical care are no doubt partially responsible for these socioeconomic differences. Children from poor homes suffer more illnesses, are more vulnerable to accidents and disaster, and undergo more physical trauma than middle-class children do (R. Hess, 1970). Some have suggested that class differences in habits of sleep, exercise, and general home life may also contribute to the effect.

Maternal Care and Emotional Stress

In another set of English studies (Acheson, 1960), maternal care was related to children's height. A group of social workers rated the "efficiency" of the mothers, a measure that included how organized the mother seemed to be at meeting her child's basic needs. The more efficient the mother, the taller the children. When inefficiency was combined with poor socioeconomic conditions, the effect on growth was even more striking.

In these same studies, birth order also appeared to correlate with height. First-born children tended to be taller. This height advantage could be, at least in part, a result of greater maternal efficiency. It may be that the more children in a family, the more difficult it is to provide organized, efficient care.

Some investigators also believe that severe psychological distress can retard growth. E. M. Widdowson (1951) found that children in an orphanage under the regime of a punitive and unfair house-sister grew more slowly than orphanage children whose diet had 20 percent fewer calories. An extreme form of physical retardation called "deprivation dwarfism"

also seems to be associated with severe emotional distress in young children (G. Powell, Brasel, and Blizzard, 1967). If these children are removed from their disturbed environments, they show catch-up growth. But only very severe psychological or physical stress can affect a child's growth; the everyday stresses and illnesses of a child's life have little impact.

DEVELOPMENT OF MOTOR ABILITIES

The young child participates in a much more demanding and complex world than he encountered as an infant. He steadily acquires new skills and abilities that allow him to take part in new activities, and his experiences at play and in nursery school elaborate and refine these abilities. Running, jumping, manipulating objects, competing with peers in games, and learning to dress himself all contribute to his new efficiency. During these years, many of his new abilities develop through maturation. Although no research has been done on the effects of cortical control and hormonal influence during this period, it is reasonable to assume that both play a regulatory role in the child's increasing competence. As he grows, he becomes stronger, faster, and more coordinated. However, individual skills that depend on instruction and practice also become important.

Strength, Speed, and Coordination

How each child responds to new physical demands depends on a number of physiological factors. His ability to exert force is limited by the strength of his body's muscles. The speed with which he can move is influenced by the mass of that part of his body being moved. And his reactions depend on the type of stimuli, the nerves' transmission of the impulses, the relative complexity of the movement, and his general physical and psychological condition. These motor abilities—strength, speed, and coordination—are components not only of childhood play but ultimately of all mature activity.

As size and weight, particularly of muscle tissue, increase, *strength* is enhanced. A child's strength doubles between the ages of three and eleven. Three-to six-year-old boys and girls exhibit similar degrees of strength, but after age six the boys start to gain strength more quickly than girls do, although this difference is not great until adolescence is reached.

Speed is a sensory-motor function that starts to be important in the more demanding play of young children. A major factor in speed is **reaction time,** the interval of time that elapses between the instant a stimulus is presented and the individual's reaction to

Figure 10.4 Throughout early childhood, motor abilities continue to develop and mature. With increases in size, strength, speed, and coordination, the child delights in practicing and refining new motor skills.

Table 10.1   Gutteridge Scale of Motor Skills

PHASE	SCALE	DEGREE OF MOTOR SKILL
No attempt made	1	Withdraws or retreats when opportunity is given
	2	Makes no approach or attempt but does not withdraw
Skill in process of formation	3	Attempts activity but seeks help or support
	4	Tries even when not helped or supported but is inept
	5	Is progressing but still uses unnecessary movements
	6	Is practicing basic movements
	7	In process of refining movements
Basic movements achieved	8	Coordinates movements
	9	Performs easily with display of satisfaction
	10	Shows evidence of accuracy, poise, and grace
Skillful execution with variations in use	A	Tests skill by adding difficulties or taking chances
	B	Combines activity with other skill or skills
	C	Speeds, races, or competes with self or others
	D	Uses skill in larger projects such as dramatic play

Source: Adapted from M. V. Gutteridge, "A Study of Motor Achievements of Young Children," *Archives of Psychology* (1939) No. 244. Copyright © 1939 by the American Psychological Association and reproduced by permission.

it. Speed also can be a measure of the absolute time it takes a child to perform a given task. During these years, children learn to use their speed in games that require fast reactions from their minds and bodies, as well as in simple tasks such as running across a playground.

Coordination refers to many aspects of motor performance, including accuracy of movement, poise, smoothness, rhythm, and ease. Coordination involves far more than strength or speed alone and is therefore a better index for determining which child is more able and agile. A child acquires coordination more slowly than he acquires strength and speed, because coordination requires the interplay of sensory and motor skills that often depend on the maturation of the small muscles and on practice. Children themselves are extremely conscious of their own and their playmates' degree of coordination; thus, a child's relative mastery of tasks requiring coordination can influence his self-sufficiency and self-confidence.

Many skills depend on increased coordination. For example, a child begins throwing a ball by jerking his arms from his sides, standing with his feet planted firmly in one place and his body facing the target. When he is two, a child can manage to execute this pattern using a small ball such as a tennis ball. By the time he is four, he has developed a relatively smooth, easy pattern that includes throwing overhand, shifting his body weight, and rotating his body away from the target and then toward it as he throws the ball (Sinclair, 1973).

Skills

The expansion of a child's physical activity fascinates his parents; it is also important to his pattern of social development and maturation. There are, of course, large individual differences in the ages at which various children are able to do different things, as well as differences in the degree of their skill and coordination in each activity.

Although maturation of muscles and bones plays a large part in the emergence of such skills as running, jumping, and skipping, the opportunity to practice and the encouragement of others help to guarantee smooth, speedy, confident mastery and refinement of such abilities. As a child masters a particular motor skill, he must carry it through several stages of proficiency. M. V. Gutteridge (1939), after conducting research on more than 2,000 preschool children, produced a scale of motor-skill development. This scale is reproduced in Table 10.1; it can be employed to measure the specific skills of any child.

The Gutteridge scale is particularly useful because it provides four general phases of motor development; within each phase are varying degrees of skill. The first ten degrees of skill mark the progressive acquisition of the ability; the final four degrees (A–D) measure the child's elaboration and use of the ability after he has achieved complete competence.

The work of Gutteridge and others helps to outline the child's developing abilities between ages three and six. For example, Lauren, like most other three-year-olds, has mastered the basic human walk. She takes steps that are uniform in height, length, and

Figure 10.5 The normal play activities
of early childhood depend on skills
involving the child's developing control
over his body's actions.

width, alternates her feet when going upstairs, and can jump from the bottom stair with both feet. She also has tricycle riding down to an art.

Lauren also displays a fair amount of control over her arms and hands. She can catch even a small ball if it is well thrown, even though she keeps her arms straight out in front of her, and she can hold a crayon with her fingers and can copy a circle. Lauren is faster at everything than when she was two, and she is also stronger. She is just beginning to develop the balance so vital to many skills and sports. She can stand with both feet on a walking board that is elevated slightly above the floor, and she can alternate her feet part way down the board.

All these new skills are reflected in Lauren's personal and social development. She feeds herself proficiently, puts on her own shoes, and unbuttons almost anything. Her highchair has disappeared, and Lauren joins the family circle, functioning independently and even enlivening the conversation from time to time with a tale from nursery school or a searching question.

David, a typical four-year-old, is now a well-coordinated, versatile person, and he manages everything better than Lauren does. He walks downstairs, alternating feet, and climbs a ladder like an adult. His walk is easy, swinging, and graceful, sometimes revealing his own special swagger or grace. His running has so improved that he runs and kicks soccer-style with a consistent, smooth apposition of his arms and legs. David's arm and hand control has

become increasingly refined. He can draw a man that is unmistakably human, if somewhat oversimplified. He can also throw a ball overhand, shifting his weight and rotating his body from side to front in relation to a target.

David puts his new skills to use in the personal and social realms as well as on the playground. He is an independent person. He gets up by himself in the morning, can tell the front of his T-shirt and blue jeans from their back (an immense help if you dress yourself), and puts them on. He can wash his face and hands and brush his teeth without help, pour a bowl of cereal and douse it with milk, grab a spoon, turn on "Sesame Street," and pull up a chair. Because David lives in a relatively safe neighborhood with no busy streets to cross, he can run down to the corner and mail a letter by himself.

Matt, who is five, can do everything David can do with greater ease and grace and less intense study. He runs so well that he uses running as a tool in games; he has complete control over starting, stopping, and turning, can walk or run while be bounces a ball, and can even stand on one foot with his eyes closed. Matt can execute a beautiful somersault with his head tucked and his back rounded, and he criticizes his own performance.

Matt's new physical skills affect his personal and social development; they also make it possible for him to enter the world of formal schooling. He can use a knife and fork like a professional, dress and undress himself, count up to ten objects, and print a

few letters. He can draw a man complete with head, body, arms, and legs, and occasionally he even puts in teeth and eyebrows.

Practice and Instruction

The emergence of many of the skills just discussed is to some extent a matter of growth and maturation, but a child needs the opportunity, the place, and the encouragement to engage in them. Caroline Sinclair (1973) points out that instruction and coaching are not really necessary for simple movement patterns and suggests that a child needs only the time, space, equipment, and encouragement.

There are, however, more complicated motor skills that children learn only with formal instruction and equipment. These include such sports as swimming, skating, skiing, tennis, and so forth. Many children receive their first exposure to these skills during early childhood. Early exposure to and practice of these complicated skills appears to give children an advantage in their performance. For example, in Myrtle McGraw's (1935) co-twin study, discussed in Chapter 6, although one twin seemed to gain little from training in such skills as walking and stair climbing, early training in swimming had some advantages. Researchers began training one twin to swim at eight months, and, when he was seventeen months old, he could swim up to fifteen feet without help. McGraw also had success in teaching diving and skating. Other studies have demonstrated that observation and verbal instruction increase a child's skill at throwing and

catching, and, of course, fine motor skills like writing and drawing improve with certain kinds of instruction. Children's drawings, for example, have been improved by such techniques as redirecting their eye movements (Abercrombie, 1970).

Bryant Cratty (1967) has developed a set of guidelines for teaching skilled performance to children. He suggests that any skilled performance can be divided into three phases—pretask, task, and posttask—and that the best instruction varies with each phase. For example, pretask instructions should be kept to a minimum, describe the basic mechanical principles of the skill, and present information about the task's extent, intensity, duration, and difficulty. During the task, instructions should not interfere with the child's performance. At this time, a child finds visual demonstrations or minimal manual guidance helpful. Posttask instructions should give the child immediate and clear feedback about his success or failure.

Generally, directions should always emphasize what the child is to do instead of cautioning him about possible errors, and, if speed is important, it should be emphasized early. Cratty believes that repeatedly slowing down a child's performance on a task that requires speed may ultimately be detrimental.

GIRLS AND BOYS

As noted in the section on growth characteristics, until puberty the differences in appearance between girls and boys are slight. During early childhood, the developmental differences between the sexes are

Figure 10.6 Many newly emerging skills, some simple, others more complicated, require time and opportunity for instruction and practice if the child is to learn them or to become proficient.

198

relatively minor, and discerning them requires fine measurement. For example, boys are about 80 percent as mature as girls of the same age on measures of skeletal maturity, until adolescence (Tanner, Whitehouse, and Healy, 1962). Although the average boy is slightly taller than the average girl, girls are usually ahead of boys in motor development.

Adolescent girls and women have greater amounts of subcutaneous fat than adolescent boys and men, and this sex difference is apparent from birth. Young girls also lose their fatty infant tissue at a far slower rate than their male contemporaries do (Stolz and Stolz, 1951).

Although boys grow faster than girls during the first few months of life, girls outstrip boys from seven months until they are four years old. Between four and puberty, there are no apparent differences in the velocity of growth.

There is an old rule that states that a child reaches half of his adult height by the end of his second year. However, differences discovered in the growth patterns of boys and girls make this old rule unreliable. Most girls grow up faster than most boys, and therefore girls reach the halfway mark sooner: between the ages of one and one-half and two. At the rate most boys grow, they reach the halfway point in height at about two and one-half (Acheson, 1966).

Until they are four, girls have a slight advantage in the development of motor skills. Around the age of three, males become more proficient than girls at tasks that require strength, such as throwing (Sinclair, 1973). By age seven, girls demonstrate about 10 percent less muscular strength than boys. Louis Govatos (1959) tested ten-year-old children and found no sex differences on tasks as diverse as jumping, reaching, the standing broad-jump, the twenty-five yard dash, or throwing a ball for accuracy. Boys were more proficient than girls in tasks that require superior strength in the arms and legs, such as soccer-style kicking or throwing a ball for distance.

Physical sex differences occur in some involuntary functions as well (one such difference is shown in Figure 10.7). In a measure of **vital capacity** (lung capacity), girls, when asked to inhale as much air as they could and then to expel it, demonstrated 7 percent less vital capacity than boys (Sherman, 1973). Vital capacity can be an important factor in tasks that require sustained energy output. Females exhibit lower **basal metabolism** rates than males; that is, they require less energy while resting to maintain the same amount of body tissue. Boys develop larger hearts and lungs than girls. In addition, boys have a lower heart rate than girls (Hutt, 1972).

There are also indications that the brain develops differently in boys than in girls. Jesse Le Roy Conel (1963) found some evidence that, at about the age of four, neural tissue grows and matures earlier in the brain's left hemisphere for girls and in the right hemisphere for boys. Another study (Taylor, 1969) suggests that the female brain matures more rapidly

Figure 10.7 Graph depicting basal metabolism rates for boys and girls. The basal metabolic rate of boys is higher than that of girls, indicating that boys convert food and oxygen to various forms of energy faster than girls do. The difference is slight throughout childhood but increases somewhat during adolescence. (Adapted from Lewis, Duval, and Iliff, 1943)

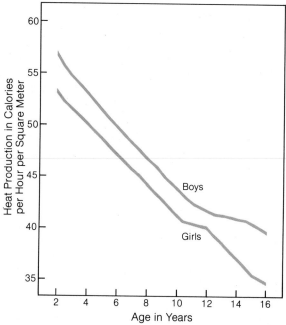

and that one hemisphere becomes dominant earlier (a process known as **lateralization**) than it does in the male brain.

Chapter 6 discussed cerebral dominance and pointed out that the left side of the brain, which eventually becomes dominant in most people, is believed to be more active in the development and organization of language abilities than the right side. A number of researchers (Buffery and Gray, 1972; Ornstein, 1973) have suggested that the right hemisphere dominates in nonverbal functions such as imagery, spatial perception, drawing, and dance. Corinne Hutt (1972) is among those who have tried to show that the earlier dominance of the left hemisphere in girls can explain their superior verbal abilities. There is also speculation that boys demonstrate superior spatial abilities because the left hemisphere becomes more dominant later and less completely in males than in females.

During early childhood, motor abilities and physical growth play an important part in the developing self-image of both boys and girls, as the next section will demonstrate. When children are asked what they like and do not like about themselves, physical characteristics, appearance, and motor abilities play an important part in their answers (Jersild, 1952). However, boys are more likely than girls to make a direct social test of their physical abilities (Herron and Sutton-Smith, 1971). As later discussions of personality development will show, the "social hierarchies," or patterns of dominance and submission, for groups of boys more often seem to rest on who is bigger, faster, and tougher than girls' hierarchies do. Children's social hierarchies, of course, reflect their parents' values. Studies of sex-role behavior clearly show that adults value strength and athletic abilities more in males than in females (Sherman, 1973).

PHYSICAL AND SOCIAL CHANGES

Crawling and walking, as Chapter 6 stressed, widen the infant's social and emotional world. Physical growth and motor development continue to affect the young child's social and emotional behavior. A boy who is much smaller than his peers or one who is clumsy and throws a ball poorly will find his size or lack of skill an important factor in his relationships with his peers. Investigators have, therefore, addressed themselves to a number of childhood skills and physical development patterns in order to understand their relationship to social behavior.

During early childhood, children can begin to determine for themselves whether they are physically

the equal of their classmates. Running, climbing, jumping, and tumbling have been the subjects of research because they are easy to measure and present almost limitless opportunities for young children to compete with one another. Boys, especially, seem to spend a good deal of time establishing social hierarchies on the basis of physical strength and skill. Questions like "Who is the toughest?" and "Who is the biggest?" and "Who can run the fastest, climb the highest, or jump the farthest?" seem to have great social significance for the young boy (Herron and Sutton-Smith, 1971). In Chapter 13, we will look again at the possible effects of skills and strengths on personality development.

As long as forty years ago, L. M. Jack (1934) established that the child who has achieved proficiency in some motor ability is more likely to be chosen as a leader in athletic and social activities. Children who fail to establish leadership become less sure of their talent and experience stress and unhappiness. In order to demonstrate how this kind of situation can be influenced, Jack taught certain skills to five nursery-school children. The children were all low in social interactions with their peers. When the children had mastered the special skills, they were paired with others in situations that would allow them to use the new abilities. In every case, the children showed significant changes in behavior: They asserted themselves, gave directions to the children who lacked their special ability, and in general showed social ascendancy. The change was not complete; it applied only to activities in which they could display their specific talents. But children who at first had been unable to lead or to assert themselves demonstrated that, with the appropriate experience, they could effectively take an assertive role.

Although physical prowess does not seem to play as important a part in the social hierarchies of girls, motor skills and outdoor play are still related to female social development. Their importance showed clearly in the case of Polly, a three-year-old girl who demonstrated problems in both motor skills and social development. Joan Buell and her colleagues (1968) instituted a program in which Polly was rewarded whenever she used outdoor play equipment. As long as Polly stayed on the equipment, a teacher remained close, smiling and talking to her. As a result, Polly's use of outdoor play equipment increased substantially, and so did a number of play and social behaviors that the researchers had not directly rewarded. Polly began to touch and talk to other children more frequently, to use their names, and to engage more

often in cooperative play. Buell and her colleagues concluded that outdoor play is intimately related to a child's social relationships. Children of both sexes who enjoy and participate in these activities experience increased social contact and develop advanced patterns of play and social interaction.

In addition to the effect that motor skills may have on a child's social behavior, physical shape itself (how tall, short, broad, or muscular a child becomes) can influence social and personality development. For thousands of years, people interested in human behavior have tried to classify patterns of physical growth into "body types." The early Greeks hoped to use body type to predict the diseases a person might develop. In more recent times, psychologists like William Sheldon and his colleagues (1940, 1954) have tried to predict behavior from body type. However, this approach remains inconclusive. About all that can be said at present is that, for example, a boy with a muscular body is likely to be better at motor skills and elicit admiration and approval from parents, teachers, and peers. In turn, he may be inclined to become more self-confident and ambitious in his athletic activities and social relationships.

The different aspects of physical development combine to contribute to the social integration and personal integrity of the child. They make children appear more adultlike, which enhances society's tendency to treat them as such. Erik Erikson's (1963) explanation of the relationship between physical and

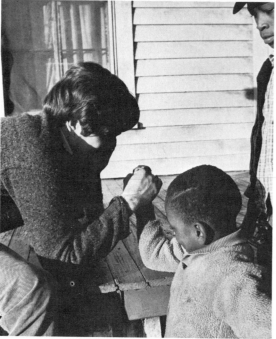

Figure 10.8 A young child's self-image, social relationships, and emotional development are all based in part on his physical stature, appearance, and skills.

social-emotional development, which was discussed in Chapter 6, builds on his idea of walking as the first step toward making the child a part of his culture. The child strives to imitate and to become adult, and his increasing physical resemblance to adults and increasing ability to act like them facilitates this goal. The little boy who has the strength and stamina to imitate Daddy in play automatically becomes more like Daddy both in his own eyes and in those of onlookers. As the child becomes more like an adult, his self-esteem is enhanced, and this process continues into later childhood. Cultural integration and acceptance play their role, as do the moment-to-moment approval and encouragement of parents. But probably the greatest boost to self-esteem comes from the child's own internally generated satisfaction when he demonstrates his physical competence. Competence is a real, approved, and apparent indication that a child is growing up.

SUMMARY

1. The rate of growth in both height and weight decelerates markedly during infancy and settles into a steady rate by the time a child is three or four. However, growth continues to be relatively rapid. During early childhood, there is a loss of "baby fat"; in contrast, skull size and brain mass, including nerve endings and connections between brain areas, continue to grow and mature; and the child's body begins to approach adult proportions.

2. As at other times in development, a variety of environmental influences can either support or impede the child's physical growth. These influences include such features as diet, general health, and type and quality of maternal care. In general, proper nutrition and good health are likely to result in more rapid and fuller physical growth and development.

3. Increases in strength, speed, and coordination enable the young child to participate in more demanding and complex activities. He steadily acquires new physical skills and abilities such as those involved in jumping and dressing himself. Although maturation and practice are basic to the child's development of skills, encouragement and some formal instruction in more complicated skills are often required if the child is to acquire or become proficient in them.

4. During early childhood, physical growth and developmental differences between the sexes are relatively slight: The average boy is a little taller than the average girl, whereas girls are a little more advanced in some areas of motor development. Differences between the sexes have been found in vital capacity and metabolic rate, and there is some evidence to suggest that differences in cerebral dominance of boys and girls may be associated with different kinds of abilities.

5. Motor skill and physical growth continue to affect the development of the young child's social and emotional behavior. Research suggests, for example, that a child's self-image and social status are likely to vary with how skilled he is in certain games and activities. In addition to his physical prowess, a child's personal and social acceptability may vary with the way that he and other children and adults evaluate his body appearance.

SUGGESTED READINGS

Cratty, Bryant J. *Perceptual and Motor Development in Infants and Children.* New York: Macmillan, 1970.

Grollman, Sigmund. *The Human Body: Its Structure and Physiology.* 2nd ed. New York: Macmillan, 1969.

Hutt, Corrine. *Males & Females.* Baltimore: Penguin, 1972.

Sinclair, Caroline B. *Movement of the Young Child: Ages Two to Six.* Columbus, Ohio: Merrill, 1973.

Tanner, J. M., and Gordon R. Taylor. *Growth.* New York: Time-Life, 1965.

Changes in children's thinking during early childhood are reflected in their understanding of perceived relationships among objects and events in the world.

11
COGNITION: CHANGES IN THINKING

David and his father were having a heart-to-heart talk. With all the seriousness of his four and one-half years, David began to speak about getting married when he grew up. "I'll move into a different house," he said, "then I won't be your son anymore." One of the attributes that defined David's concept of "son" was living in the same house as his father. He had heard the word "son" used in various situations and had even used it himself. Because in David's experience the father of the child referred to as "son" had either been present or clearly known to be living at home, David's understanding of the concept was not illogical. However, although young sons usually do live in the same house with their fathers, such a definition does not correspond to the culturally accepted one, and David's definition will have to be modified to remove the notion that residence is a defining attribute of the concept "son." In order to communicate effectively, he must transform his early definition of "son" into a new one that more closely fits society's understanding.

Redefinition of concepts is one of the intellectual tasks that face the young child. In this chapter we will look at the cognitive changes that occur during early childhood and will find that they are considerable. We will discover that what the child's senses pick up and what he gives his attention to will determine his concepts of the world. We will see that the young child uses self-generated as well as culturally transmitted symbols, that he accumulates knowledge about the objective world, and that he continually refines his concepts in the direction of their adult use. We will examine the pervasive role of private and social play in the child's daily encounters with the world. The way that his burgeoning linguistic capabilities mesh with his intellectual skills will become clear, and we will discover that the young child's interaction with adults and other children results in both emotional and intellectual benefits. But throughout these early years, one characteristic remains fairly constant: the child's basic curiosity about his environment and his quest for meaning.

PERCEPTUAL ADVANCES

As the perceptual skills of the young child develop, he isolates and abstracts more of the distinctive features of his environment. As we saw in Chapter 7, the one-year-old could only discriminate the features of the human face; by the time they are six, many children are adept readers, differentiating the features of the alphabet that distinguish one letter from the other letters.

Perceiving Distinctive Features

A two-year-old is aware of certain parts of the human body. As an infant he probably spent considerable time observing his own hands and fingers. He has seen numerous people from different angles and has watched them move their faces, torsos, and limbs in a variety of ways. However, there are many levels of awareness of objects. Knowing that the human hand has fingers on it is not as differentiated an awareness as knowing that it has five fingers, each a unique size and shape and each occupying a particular position with respect to the others and to the rest of the hand. As children get older and have more experience with objects and events, they tend to isolate more of the distinctive features and to relate these features in a comprehensive manner.

The child's changing perception of the human body during this period illustrates his continual differentiation of features and their integration into the whole. For example, David requested a paper and pencil and began drawing a picture of a man. Suddenly he stopped and asked, "Daddy, is the neck attached to the head?" Although the child had seen heads and necks on many people and on himself in the mirror, he was unsure of the precise spatial relationship and wanted another opinion before proceeding with his picture. This incident provides a glimpse at a perception in the midst of a shift.

In a more controlled situation, Beverly Celotta (1973) studied the development of children's ability to differentiate the parts of the human body and to perceive the spatial relationships between them. She devised a Mannikin Construction Test and used it with three-, five-, and seven-year-olds. Each child was given sixty pieces of felt representing legs, arms, neck, clothing, and so forth. In front of the child was a red felt board on which the investigator placed a part representing a human head. She instructed the child to complete the figure, using any of the sixty pieces spread out before him that he wished. Celotta found that seven-year-olds did better than five-year-olds in building mannikins and that five-year-olds did better than three-year-olds, both in number of body parts used and in the appropriate placement of the parts. This improved performance with age shows how a sophisticated perception of the human body develops gradually during early childhood.

Sensory Coordination

How well do the young child's different senses communicate? For example, does a youngster who learns about an object by feeling it recognize the object when he is later permitted only to look at it? There is considerable evidence that the young child's ability at tasks of intersensory recognition improves dramatically between the ages of three and six (Abravanel, 1968; Blank and Bridger, 1964; Zaporozhets, 1965).

In one study V. P. Zinshensko and A. G. Ruzskaya (see Zaporozhets, 1965) presented children of three, four, five, and six with abstract forms that they were permitted to explore by touch but could not see. These researchers then tested the children to check their visual recognition of the objects that they had explored with their fingers. At about age five, there was a sharp improvement in performance. Three- and four-year-olds failed to visually recognize about 45 percent of the objects that they had touched, whereas five- and six-year-olds erred only about 25 percent of the time. This increase in intersensory coordination probably develops because the mental images of the five- or six-year-old are more detailed and precise than those of the three- or four-year-old, which is a result of the older child's longer exposure to objects and his more sophisticated methods of exploration.

Another kind of intersensory coordination, in this case the relationship between visual and auditory perception, has been investigated by Alice Vlietstra and John Wright (1971), who taught young children to discriminate between intensities of sounds. They wondered if learning how to tell differences between intensities of sounds makes it easier for youngsters to learn how to tell differences between intensities of visual stimuli. If a young child comes to understand that the quality "stimulus intensity" can be perceived by any of his sense organs, then his experience with intensity in one sense, such as hearing, should transfer to a different sense, such as vision. However, if experience with intensity does not transfer from one sense to another, the child would find his experience with the intensity of sound of no help when he tried to discriminate between the intensity of two visual stimuli, such as two lights of varying brightness. When Vlietstra and Wright tested children who had

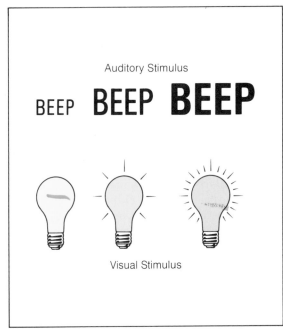

Auditory Stimulus

BEEP **BEEP** **BEEP**

Visual Stimulus

Figure 11.1 After learning to discriminate among different intensities of an auditory stimulus, young children found it easier to discriminate among comparable differences in intensities of a visual stimulus, indicating transfer of experience from one sense to another, as discussed in the text.

learned to discriminate the intensity of sounds, they found that there was indeed a transfer to another sense; the children found it easier to discriminate differences in visual intensity provided that the same general levels of intensity were considered correct in both tasks. The existence of such transfer indicates that children can coordinate the information they gather through their separate senses into an increasingly complex perception of the world.

EDUCATING ATTENTION

The child's concepts of the world depend on which characteristics of it get his attention. During early childhood, the child's ability to shift his attention increases, particularly in response to the verbal instructions of others.

Attention Preferences

In Chapter 7 we learned that the infant prefers to attend to some features of stimuli rather than to others. Such preferences are also found in the young child, and they play an important role in his learning to discriminate among objects and events. For example, most, though not all, children between the ages of four and six tend to pay greater attention to the form of objects than to their color, whereas those between two and three generally prefer color to form (Stevenson, 1972). If young children are required to sort objects of various colors according to their shapes, those children who initially attend to shape will find this task easier, whereas those who first attend to color will find the task more difficult.

Joan Gusinow and Louis Price (1972) attempted to discover how resistant to change the color and form preferences of four- to six-year-olds are. They first determined whether children preferred form to color by asking them to match blocks. Then the children were allowed to earn toys by matching the blocks on the basis of the unpreferred dimension. That is, children who matched blocks by shape had to match by color to get a toy and vice versa. When these children were later given another matching test, many of the children voluntarily switched preferences; many of those who had originally preferred color matched by shape, and many of those who had originally preferred shape matched by color. Gusinow and Price also found that children who were also required to name their unpreferred dimension (color or shape) to earn toys were more likely to switch their preferences on later tests than children who were not required to name the dimension. This study goes beyond demonstrating that four- to six-year-olds have dimensional preferences. It shows that not all young children prefer the same dimensions and that appropriate rewards can alter the child's preferences. Finally, it shows that the appropriate use of language can add to the effectiveness of material rewards in altering children's dimensional preferences.

Focused Attention

One may hear a frustrated parent or nursery-school teacher complain that a young child cannot concentrate on a task. There is both truth and falsehood in this assertion. Is the child who rapidly switches his attention from one toy or activity to another "easily distractible" or "curious and exploratory"?

It is true, for example, that, when confronted with a problem that requires sustained attention to one or two properties or dimensions and deliberate ignoring of other, irrelevant information, the four- or six-year-old is usually less effective than the eight-year-old in solving the problem (Osler and Kofsky, 1965). The younger child tends to respond to irrelevant cues more frequently, which of course hinders his performance. He also has greater difficulty in classifying information into categories that are relevant to the task.

This developmental difficulty showed clearly in an experiment by Sheldon White (1966). Young children were compared with nine- and ten-year-olds on three discrimination-learning tasks. In each task White presented the child with pairs of bird pictures. When the child selected the correct picture, he was given a marble or a piece of candy; when he selected the incorrect picture, he got nothing. The correct, rewarded stimulus was the positive cue, and the incorrect stimulus, the negative cue. In White's first task, both the positive and the negative cue remained the same for all trials; the children saw the same pair of bird pictures on each trial, but the position of the birds changed. In his second task, the positive cue was always the same, and the negative one changed from trial to trial. In his third task, the negative cue remained the same throughout, but the positive cue was different on each trial. Eight- and nine-year-olds learned all three of these discriminations at the same speed. But young children were hampered by White's procedure of varying the cues on the second and third tasks. They learned which cue was correct much faster in the first discrimination problem. However, although younger children had greater difficulty than older children did, they were still able to solve the problems.

The young child's less efficient attending does not mean that he has a "short attention span." Many youngsters spend long periods of time exploring objects that interest them. Their dedicated perseverance at a task may even bewilder their parents. For example, after the fourth or fifth reading of a picture book, the young child may say, "Daddy, read it to me again," although by that time his father may be quite bored and inattentive to the simple plot with its limited vocabulary and sentence structure. Whose attention span is longer, the child's or the father's? Obviously, attention spans depend as much on the

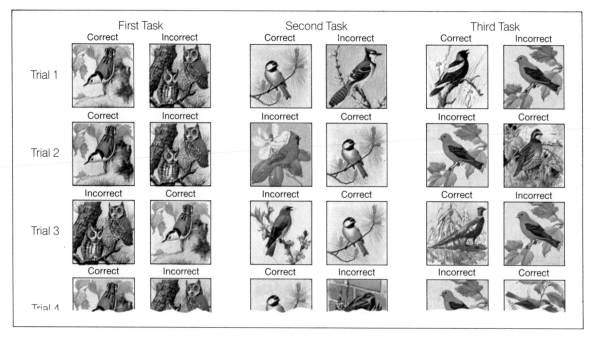

nature of the material being attended to as on the intellectual level of the person whose attention span is being measured.

CHILDREN'S THINKING

The young child's mind, like his body, is in perpetual motion. In Chapter 7 we saw how the processes of assimilation and accommodation operate in the intellectual life of the infant. It is possible to interpret many of the young child's cognitive activities in a similar way. As he fits newly observed phenomena into his patterns of understanding, he constantly modifies his concepts of the world. Sometimes this modification consists simply of adding new members to a category that he already knows. For example, most five-year-olds know the difference between the concepts of color and shape. If you give them a red circle and a blue square and ask them to name the color of the items, most will say "Red and blue." Similarly, if you ask them to name the shape, they will say "Circle and square" (or some other words that they use to refer to shape, such as "wheel" or "tire" for a circle). However, because of limited experience, a child may not be aware of the existence of such colors as beige, violet, or maroon or such shapes as diamonds or parallelograms. When he is exposed to these new instances, he modifies his concepts by extending the range of items included in them. Sometimes, however, the modification requires a drastic revision instead of an extension.

Jean Piaget has studied the thought of young children extensively (Piaget and Inhelder, 1969). In his view there are certain general features that characterize early ways of thinking about many aspects of the physical and social world. One of the most characteristic of these is the young child's tendency to base many of his ideas about things on their most conspicuous perceptual features. He will defend these "incorrect" perceptually influenced ideas about objects, even though some transformation of their perceptual features would easily prove him wrong. Indeed, the four- or five-year-old sometimes does not imagine transformations at all. In other instances he does, but his immediate perceptual experience is more convincing to him than is his awareness that the objects' appearances would differ after some hypothetical transformation.

Conservation

This aspect of the young child's thinking shows clearly in his lack of the notion of conservation of quantity. This particular concept has probably been the most extensively studied of the four- or five-year-old child's basic concepts relating to the nature of physical substances, and, as we noted in Chapter 1, is an example of the *modification* of earlier skills. The young child's confusion over apparent volume shows clearly in a simple experiment. The researcher fills two glasses of the same size and shape to an equal level with colored water. A child is asked whether the two glasses contain the same amount of water. When the child asserts that the amounts are the same, the researcher pours the water from one glass into a shorter, broader glass, so that the levels of colored water in the two glasses differ. A four-year-old, when asked whether each glass now contains the same amount of water, usually will say, "No! This one has more water in it because it is higher." When the water is poured back into its original glass, the child usually will again say that the two glasses have the same amount of water in them. When he is asked, "How do you know?" he answers, "Because I can *see* that they do."

Other changes in the external appearance of identical objects may also convince the young child that the total quantity of one has been altered. For example, place in front of a four- or five-year-old two rows of seven checkers each, as demonstrated in Figure 11.3. Then ask the child if one row has more, less, or the same amount of checkers as the other. The child may correctly answer that the two rows have the same amount of checkers. Next bunch the checkers in Row 1 together. Ask the child if Row 2 has more, less, or

Figure 11.2 These pictures are similar to those used in the three tasks of White's experiment on the discrimination learning of younger and older children. (Adapted from S. White, 1965)

Figure 11.3 A conservation experiment. The child is shown two rows of seven checkers, evenly spaced, and asked which has more. Most children reply that they are the same. When one row is rearranged so that the checkers are bunched together, as shown, children four or five years of age usually say that the original row contains more.

the same amount of checkers as Row 1. To the surprise and chagrin of many parents who have tried to prove Piaget wrong by administering this test to their own clever children, most four- or five-year-olds respond quite emphatically that there are more checkers in Row 2 than in Row 1. They may even retain this view despite their realization that, if the checkers in Row 1 are returned to their original position, the two rows will once again have the same number of checkers (Piaget, 1952a). These young children believe that the number of checkers varies with the dominating perceptual feature of the row, in this case length or spread. However, by the time the child is seven, he responds to the posttransformation question with an emphatic "Of course they are the same, you didn't add any or take any away, you just put them closer together." He may even respond in a tone of surprise mixed with disdain at an experimenter who could ask such a silly question; the seven-year-old has forgotten that only two or three years earlier he had argued otherwise and no less emphatically about the transformation.

Can a four- or five-year-old who fails to conserve quantity be taught the concept? Some researchers have successfully taught conservation of quantity to nonconservers. As we reported in Chapter 1, Rochel Gelman (1969) trained five-year-olds who had failed the conservation-of-number test to attend to the number of objects and to ignore irrelevant transformations in size, color, and spatial arrangement. The training enabled them to conserve quantity on a later test. Her experiment shows that attention plays an important role in this type of concept learning. However, researchers using other procedures to teach conservation to young nonconservers have been much less successful (Flavell, 1963). Thus, the concept of conservation of quantity, which is obvious to the seven-year-old, is not easily taught to four-year-olds.

As Gelman's experiment demonstrates, one should be cautious about asserting that a child is unable to learn or to understand certain discriminations or concepts. Often all that is really meant is that the child has greater difficulty than other children in mastering these concepts or that an appropriate method of teaching him has not yet been formulated. Of course, some concepts or tasks may indeed be beyond some children's ken regardless of the ingenuity of any parent, teacher, or psychologist. However, the literature on intellectual development provides many instances where what was once thought to be beyond a child's level of comprehension has been shown to be teachable by newly developed modes of instruction

(for example, Anderson, 1965; Schimmel, 1971; Schnall et al., 1972).

Other general concepts of the physical world that Piaget and others have studied in children are weight, volume, and area and their relationships; time, movement, and speed and their interrelatedness; and spatial properties of two- and three-dimensional objects. As already pointed out in this chapter, the general picture emerging from these studies is that the young child's concepts differ from those of the adult in many respects. Furthermore, as we also saw in Chapters 2 and 7, Piaget believes that each of these adult concepts is the final product of an orderly progression through several versions and revisions of earlier forms of the concept. He further believes that the order in which people acquire these various versions and revisions is unalterable and universal, although different children may progress through each sequence of concept development at different rates, and some people may never even attain the most advanced form of the concept. Although many researchers agree with Piaget's views about necessary stages in the formation of concepts, many others do not (for example, Staats, Brewer, and Gross, 1970), and the question remains open.

Types of Concepts

Specific physical properties such as volume, weight, and so forth are not the only concepts children must learn if they are to function effectively in their environments. As we have just seen, on a relatively simple level children learn about visible properties of specific objects. They know, for example, that the trucks called fire engines are red and have long hoses and sirens and that animals known as elephants are massive and have long trunks and tusks.

Many concepts are defined by the conjunction, or combination, of several attributes or properties. In conjunctive concepts all the attributes of a category must be present in a specific object in order for the object to be included in the category. For example, among the defining attributes of "dog," at least at the level of the average person's usage, are four legs, furriness, and a bark. The three-year-old who sees a cat and hears it meow and yet calls it a dog probably has a concept of "dog" that includes four legs and furriness but not the attribute of having a bark rather than a meow. This type of error in concept acquisition is frequent and understandable in the preschooler (Saltz, 1971); it is similar to that overgeneralization demonstrated by the infant in Chapter 8 who called all four-legged animals "bow-wow." A child usually

requires repeated exposure to learn which attributes define concepts and which do not.

A second type of concept that is even more difficult to learn is the **disjunctive concept.** In this type of "either/or" concept, a member of the category may possess some, but need not possess all, of several different attributes. For example, a citizen of the United States is someone who *either* was born in the United States *or* has been naturalized in this country (Saltz, 1971).

In many instances, attributes that relate to the use or *function* of an object define common concepts. These attributes are not apparent on inspection, and members of the same class may look very different. For example, if young Susan's parents do not tell her explicitly that "food" refers to all edible things, she may err in using the term until she discovers for herself the common attribute of fruits, vegetables, fish, meat, and poultry: edibility. Although Susan may correctly apply the term "food" to a wide variety of objects, she may do so strictly on the basis of specific word-thing associations for each kind of food. Until Susan has abstracted the property of edibility, she may also refer to some nonfoods as food, and she may fail to include in the category some of the things she eats that she has never heard others call food. Because adults tend to provide young children with fewer verbal definitions of concepts than they give to school-aged children, the younger child has to rely extensively on his own powers of discovery and abstraction in figuring out adult con-

Figure 11.4 (*top*) Illustration of a conjunctive concept, showing that, in this case, all three attributes—"flies," "small," and "feathers"—are required to classify and call something a "bird." (*bottom*) Illustration of a disjunctive concept, showing that, in this case, either the situation of "bedtime" or "when it's dark" can be a defining attribute of "night."

Figure 11.5 (*opposite, left*) A young child is likely to have difficulty reasoning about the relation of a part or parts to a whole, and, if shown a collection of lemon drops and licorice drops, he is likely to reply that he has more lemon drops than candy when asked which one he has more of.

Figure 11.6 (*opposite, right*) Example of a transitivity problem, which requires the joining together of two instances of the relational concept "longer than."

cepts. These powers may not always be equal to the challenge (Ausubel, 1968). In fact, one important function of formal schooling is to remove some of the guesswork in concept learning. Teachers and books supplement the child's self-discovery method with systematically presented verbal and nonverbal definitions or examples of concepts.

Many concepts are challenging to learn because they involve fairly complex *relations* between things and events. Jean Piaget (1952a) has also studied several of these complex concepts and has discovered that they are difficult for the average youngster to master. A four- or five-year-old child who happens to have eight lemon drops and five licorice drops is likely to admit that (1) lemon drops are candy and (2) licorice drops are also candy but still insist that (3) he has more lemon drops than candy. However, he knows that he has more lemon drops than licorice drops. The problem arises because he does not seem to realize that if A includes both B and C, as in Figure 11.5, then A *must* be greater than B alone or C alone. An adult takes it for granted than an entire class is greater than any of its parts. Many young children do not.

Another relational concept that is self-evident to adults is the concept of **transitivity.** If Matt is older than David and David is older than Susan, then obviously Matt is older than Susan. Yet many four-year-olds have difficulty making this deduction, which requires the joining together of two instances of the relational concept "older than." By the time the child is seven, he usually has a much better grasp of these and other relational concepts, and he comes to understand many of these concepts without the aid of formal instruction. Several factors are involved in this general conceptual advance, including a greater use of language, more efficient attending, and a superior capacity for generating and testing ideas about information received from the environment.

Egocentrism

A pervasive feature of the young child's thought is his egocentrism, which influences many of his ideas. You will recall that, in our discussion of perceptual and intellectual development in infancy in Chapter 7, we said that, according to Piaget, the baby first "defines" or knows objects in terms of his activity upon them. Somewhat later he differentiates himself from the objects of the world. This differentiation is not, however, complete in early childhood. Although at the sensory-motor and the perceptual level a very young child distinguishes himself from the rest of the world as an object in space and time, he is still egocentric in some ways. He tends to think that other people see things the way he sees them and that they experience his own behavior, thought, and feelings about things. He even ascribes thoughts, feelings, and life itself to some inanimate objects.

This egocentric aspect of the young child's thinking is reflected in many of his primitive notions about the causes, purposes, and activities of such things as dreams, night and day, the sun, moon, and clouds,

A
Candies

B
Lemon Drops

C
Licorice Drops

Are there more lemon drops or more candies?

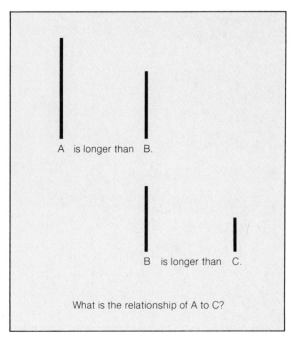

A is longer than B.

B is longer than C.

What is the relationship of A to C?

and mountains and rivers. A young child tends to interpret the objective world from a subjective perspective. Because the sun and moon appear to follow the young child around, he believes that they do. And because he thinks that other people see things the way he does, he believes that others also perceive the sun and moon as following him around. The young child also believes, because he is restricted to this subjective perspective, that the "purpose" of mountains and other worldly objects is their utility to him and to the world he knows. Thus, although at one level the young child is not egocentric when he recognizes the mountains as distinct physical objects, he is egocentric when it comes to ascribing meaning to objects in his world.

This level of thought affects the young child's view of reality. For example, Monique Laurendeau and Adrien Pinard (1962) used an interview procedure to investigate the ideas that four- to twelve-year-old children had about dreams. Among the kinds of questions they asked children were:

Where does a dream come from?
Who makes the dreams come?
While you are dreaming, where is your dream? Where does it go? In what place is it?
What is a dream made of? Can you touch your dreams? Why not?
Are dreams true?

These questions were meant to find out how well the children distinguished dreams from reality. Laurendeau and Pinard found a clear difference in the kinds

Figure 11.7 An egocentric aspect of young children's thinking is shown in their ideas about the nature and purpose of dreams and in their frequent willingness to assume that other people experience their dreams too.

of answers given by four- and five-year-olds on the one hand and seven-year-olds on the other. About half of the four-year-old children believed that dreams originate from a source external to the dreamer and that they take place in front of him, on the wall or on the pillow. Quite "logically," they often believed that their eyes were open while they dreamed, because one could not see a dream with one's eyes closed. But almost none of the seven-year-olds "reified," or made "real," their dreams. Their overwhelming response was that dreams both originate and occur inside the individual and cannot be seen by anyone else. Thus, in general, the four-year-olds failed to differentiate clearly separate levels of experience, the *truly* external and objective things that they see when awake from the *apparently* external but subjective visions they see in their dreams, whereas seven-year-olds easily made this distinction by *substituting* a new realistic understanding for an old belief, as pointed out in Chapter 1. Some of the children, particularly six-year-olds, were in a transitional stage. Their explanations included both internal and external viewpoints about their dreams, even though at a strictly logical level the two explanations were contradictory.

Just as the six-year-olds may be at ease with contradictory explanations of dreams, most young children appear to take a relatively nonchalant attitude to logical contradictions. On the other hand, it has been demonstrated that proper exploitation of the logical contradictions in a child's thinking can spur his intellectual development (Smedslund, 1961). Several investigators have even hypothesized that logical inconsistencies are fundamental to cognitive growth. Presumably, contradictions involve cognitive conflict that motivates the child to seek new information and to reorganize the old, thereby clarifying his understanding of the world and reducing the tension (Berlyne, 1960; Piaget, 1967; Smedslund, 1961). That this sometimes occurs is clear, even in infants who demonstrate heightened attention to stimuli that are moderately different from their expectations, as the babies in Chapter 7 who watched mobiles did.

REPRESENTATIONAL SKILLS

During the second year of life, the infant begins to use symbols, and this frees him somewhat from the constraints of the immediate world of experience. As noted in Chapter 7, among these symbols are language, imagery, imitation, and play. During the next few years, the young child uses these symbols to represent an ever-widening range of objects and events. But imitation, language, play, and imagery are more than ways to represent previous experiences. These symbols function as tools for the young child's understanding and intellectual mastery of his world. They become closely linked to his learning, reasoning, and acquisition of concepts. By the time he is six, language in particular begins to play an increasingly important role in some types of the child's concept learning.

Although symbol use develops extensively during this period, the young child continues to be an active explorer of the concrete, real world. His use of symbols to represent reality does not replace his natural curiosity about and exploration of the physical universe but supplements it. In fact, precisely because many of the concepts that young children acquire about people, events, and objects derive from their actual experiences, the concepts are often imperfect when measured by adult definitions. This imperfection arises because the child's experiences are limited and, therefore, insufficient for him to discover the more sophisticated ideas of the older child or the adult (Ausubel, 1968).

Imitation

Imitative skills, which are among the first forms of symbolic behavior, play an important cognitive role during early childhood. As we saw in Chapter 7, the infant's ability to imitate what he sees and hears advances markedly at the beginning of his second year. These imitations are symbols themselves, and they are also evidence for the existence of other symbols, in picture or in sound, within the child's mind. These mental symbols, of course, cannot be observed, but adults can infer their presence from the child's actions.

When a four-year-old watches his father read a book and himself takes up a book, turns the pages, and pretends to read, his imitative behavior represents the actions of another. They stand for or symbolize something. This kind of direct and immediate imitation of an action is a primitive symbol.

However, if the child picks up a book the next day and imitates his father reading, then in addition to viewing his imitative behaviors as symbols of reading at the level of action, we can infer that the child has created a mental image of his father in the act of reading. This memory is a condensed, internal imitation, in thought rather than in action, and it allows the child to imitate some behavior in action long after the event. This deferred imitation is frequently observed among young children.

Figure 11.8 Imitative behavior represents the actions and activities of people and objects. Young children steadily develop their imitative skills, demonstrating competence in both immediate and deferred imitation and in both real and make-believe situations.

Drawing, which is discussed later in this chapter, is another form of imitation. In this case, the imitation is reduced to a graphic, schematic representation. The child depicts only certain features of a scene, and the drawing's resemblance to the original scene of father reading is less a "copy" than his physical imitation of the act was. Children do not usually begin to draw objects until they are past two, and drawing remains a significant activity during early childhood. In general, the symbolic nature of imitation makes it a milestone in intellectual development, because it forms the basis for human civilization: for language, mathematics, science, and the arts (Piaget, 1951).

Language

Language is the representational skill par excellence, and the relationship between language and thinking is close. If you had a tank with fifty octopuses and removed ten of them to give to a friend for her birthday, how many octopuses would remain in your tank? Correct—forty.

Notice that you solved the octopus problem in a second or two and without getting your hands wet. You use verbal symbols for things and actions to help you reason rapidly and efficiently. If you had a tank of octopuses and the time to move them, you could solve the problem by manipulating your octopuses, although the verbal solution remains easier and quicker. However, we use language to refer not only to concrete entities and simple actions performed on them, but to complex events and intangible relationships as well. It is only because we possess well-developed symbol systems that we are able to consider and reason about things at complex and abstract levels. In fact, we can even reason about unicorns and time travel, about purely imaginary or hypothetical situations that never have occurred and probably never will.

Investigators have used a variety of approaches to look at the developmental relationship between language and thought in children. John Flavell, David Beach, and Jack Chinsky (1966) were interested in finding whether five-year-olds spontaneously use language to help them solve a simple memory problem. They showed children pictures of familiar objects, pointing to some of them, and later asked the children to point to the same pictures in the same order. The five-year-olds performed less well than the eight-year-olds. It appears that the children's difference in performance on this task related to differences in their use of language. A majority of the eight-year-old children repeated the names of the pictures that they

had to remember. However, almost none of the five-year-olds spoke the names aloud. The younger children did not spontaneously use their knowledge of the words to help them remember the pictured objects. Thus, although the young child understands language and communicates with it, he does not automatically use it in all cases where it would be helpful.

Some investigators (Kendler, 1972) believe that language is critical to concept formation, and Marion Blank and Wagner Bridger (1964) have found at least one instance in which it is essential. They discovered that young children could not discriminate between one and two flashes of light unless they could attach verbal labels to them. When the experimenters told a child to "pick the one that goes like this," and pointed to the light flashing once, but "don't pick the one that goes like this," and pointed to the light flashing twice, a young child could not master the task. But a child of the same age who was told to pick the light that flashes one time but not the light that flashes two times easily learned to follow the experimenters' instructions.

Although a five-year-old may not use language on his own as an aid to memory, he does use it extensively to guide his behavior and to help him plan his actions. For example, young children often talk to themselves as they play. Indeed, a child may actually engage in a dialogue with himself as he draws a picture or builds a tower of blocks: "First I'll put this block over here and it will be the fence . . . no, put it there. OK . . . now this one goes here . . . and this one on top. Oh-oh, it's going to fall down . . . so put it next to the fence where it won't fall." In this case, the child's language is "thinking out loud." Thus, according to Lev Vygotsky (1962), in infancy language first develops separately from thought, and thought develops separately from language, but after the two intersect during early childhood, they influence each other considerably.

The relationship between language and cognitive development has also been studied by Hans Furth, who has spent many years conducting research on the intellectual abilities of deaf children. Most children who are born deaf or who become deaf in infancy learn to speak their native language haltingly, if at all. However, intellectual development proceeds even among those who never learn a spoken language. According to Furth (1964, 1969), the thinking processes of deaf, linguistically deficient, elementary-school-aged children are generally similar to those of children who hear and are linguistically competent.

On some types of cognitive tests, young deaf children perform less well than young hearing children, but Furth attributes this difference to the restricted experience and training of the very young deaf child, which becomes a less important factor when he enters school. Based on research with the deaf, Furth (1969) agrees with Piaget (1967) that intellectual development is considerably less dependent on linguistic ability than most people assume.

Although it may be possible to think, reason, and solve problems without a spoken language, some kind of symbol system is necessary for many activities. But language is only one of several symbol systems used by man. The deaf themselves frequently use sign language, and human beings also use visual imagery, pictorial representation, and written notational systems (such as the symbols of music or complex electronic circuits) to depict the world. People often think with these tools. However, some intelligent behavior can be acquired without any symbol system at all. Indeed, the infant himself acquires a substantial set of intelligent behaviors before he begins to use verbal symbols. It is probably safe to say, however, that language development and cognitive development go hand in hand, that they continually interact, and that both are primary tools for bringing order to the world.

No one formally tutors the young child in the intricacies of either language or cognitive development. It is as if he gradually discovers their subtle features and comes to use them without being able to explain what he is doing. Many of his developmental tasks consist of acting upon the world to find out how it works and how it responds to his actions. Often, as we will see, this activity takes the form of play.

Play

During the ages of two through seven, a substantial part of the child's waking hours are devoted to imaginative and other kinds of play (Herron and Sutton-Smith, 1971; Singer, 1973). In symbolic or make-believe play, a child spends many hours engaging in monologue or dialogue with imaginary playmates and playing games of pretense with them or with his flesh-and-blood friends. He uses his own internal imagery to create things that stand for something else. A child can become so involved in his world of make-believe that he may even react with fear to an imaginary character that has been assigned a threatening or terrifying role. One perceptive moralist stated that insensitively grabbing a toy boat from the young child who is its imaginary captain is an offense to the child comparable to depriving an adult admiral of the command of his ship.

Young children also play games with rules that specify constraints on permissible activity (for example, games of marbles). In addition, they also engage in mastery play, which focuses on dealing competently with challenging materials, such as in putting together the pieces of a puzzle or in riding a tricycle without losing one's balance (Singer, 1973).

Figure 11.9 The close interplay between language and cognitive development is shown in the coordination of the thinking and talking involved in counting out loud and pointing to objects.

Figure 11.10 (*opposite*) Play helps the young child to understand the world and his or other people's places in it. The play may be make-believe and involve trying out roles, involve a game that is played in a prescribed way, or consist of challenging and testing one's skills.

The active play behavior of the young child appears closely related to his cognitive development, and the child often uses play to help him assimilate new information from the environment into his existing modes of understanding (Piaget, 1951; Schachtel, 1959). In the world of make-believe, children can repeat and reflect upon statements or comments that they have heard adults make and that they do not initially understand. By repeating, reflecting, and transforming this information during make-believe, they integrate it into what they find to be a satisfying framework of understanding. For example, Jerome L. Singer (1973) tells of a three-and-one-half-year-old boy pretending to drive an ice-cream truck. He made the usual ding-a-ling noises and commented about the different kinds of ice cream he had for sale. When Singer asked him about this game, the boy replied, "I'm playing college." The boy, it seems, had heard his father tell about his work as an ice-cream truck driver while attending college. For this three-and-one-half-year-old, "father being in college" was a novel and incomprehensible piece of information. In his attempt to process it so that it would fit into his level of knowing, he put together his understandings of ice cream, driving, trucks, and selling and repeatedly played his game, which was somehow related to "being in college." After a while, he probably felt that he better understood "being in college."

Play indeed helps the child to understand the world, but it has other functions as well. In Chapter 13, for example, we will discuss the social and emotional functions of play and how it helps prepare the child to assume various roles.

Memory

The young child's memory develops steadily from babyhood. At about four months, you will recall, the baby realizes that a moving object continues to exist when it is out of sight; at about six months, he realizes that he has only one mother; and at about eight months, he will search for an object that has been placed behind a screen. And, of course, his acquisition of language is even further proof of his growing memory.

Three- and four-year-old children frequently recognize and even recall events or objects after the lapse of several months or a year in which no reference to the event or object was made by others. Often the child recollects some aspect of the original scene, such as the color of a hat worn by a guest, that the parent hardly noticed. Furthermore, the young child's vocabulary increases at a rapid pace. He remembers which words are associated with which objects, an ability that demands a considerable memory for specifics. In general, then, the young child remembers those things that he attends to, that he considers interesting, and that occur in the natural experiences of daily living.

There is evidence that the young child's memory for information also is enhanced when information is presented in a meaningful context. For example, Soviet psychologists L. V. Zankov and D. M.

Figure 11.11 Two examples of the scoring criteria used by Golomb to assess children's cognitive competence in producing a human figure using different media. (From Golomb, 1973)

Mayants (1940) studied the memory of objects in five- to seven-year-olds and found that the method of presentation affected the child's memory. When objects were presented separately, the children remembered least. When objects were presented in pairs, they did better. But when the pairs were arranged so that the children could make a meaningful connection between the two objects, they remembered best of all, indicating again that the cognitive ability of young children is often better than their casual performance would indicate.

Using Graphic Symbols

During these early years, the young child also begins to use artistic media, representing objects, animals, and people with crayons, pencils, paints, and clay. Many investigators have noted a three-step sequence in young children's drawings of a person. At first the child tends to make a circular figure with few or no differentiating parts, such as the various organs and limbs. Somewhat later the drawings assume the shape of a tadpole: The head and limbs are attached directly, but the body has no trunk. Finally, the child draws a complete person with head, trunk, and attached limbs. This developmental sequence appears to illustrate the concept of *addition* of skills, as discussed in Chapter 1.

Recently Claire Golomb (1973) attempted to discover whether a child's early imperfect drawings reflected a lack of cognitive competence or the explorations of a graphic medium by an inexperienced artist trying to create adequate symbols. Golomb reasoned that, if the child's early drawings reflect a deficient analysis and synthesis of the human figure, this deficiency should appear uniformly across a wide variety of media, even when the child receives explicit instructions. On the other hand, if the youngster is experimenting with ways to represent a body that he perceives adequately, he will produce variations in the number and choice of parts and in the organization of the figure, according to the medium he is given. To test these opposing hypotheses, Golomb presented 105 children ranging in age from about three and one-half to seven and one-half years with representational tasks using a variety of media. Older children produced more differentiated and better-organized figures than younger children did, but the overall pattern of results showed that the media and the investigator's instructions had a definite effect on the nature of the symbol that children constructed. Golomb interpreted these findings as supporting the view that the young child is an inventor of symbols rather than a confused and incompetent copier of what he sees, and she believes that the inferior performance of younger children may be due in part to the younger child's inexperience in using artistic media and his more playful attitude toward the symbols he creates.

SOCIAL INTERACTION AND COGNITION

A young child's inability to take another's viewpoint often results in apparently selfish behavior. But as his

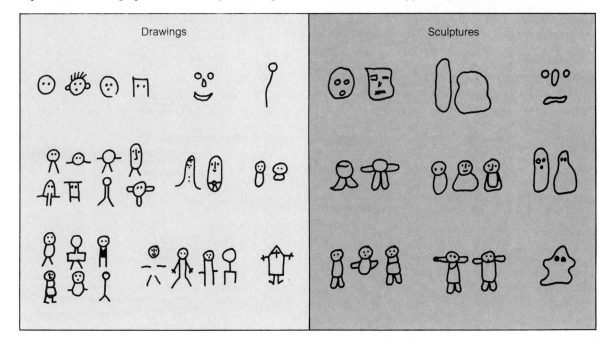

Drawings | Sculptures

interactions with his family and his friends expose him to different outlooks, his experiences will affect his intellectual development. Indeed, one aspect of intelligent thinking is being able to consider an idea from more than one perspective. Often a person learns that he has misunderstood a concept when others correct him by refusing to accept his view. Young children often engage in vehement debates as each pits his understandings against those of his peers. Such debates spur reflection and, through cognitive conflict, ultimately modify a child's understanding.

For example, two five-year-olds argued over whether cave men are real. The young believer said, "My father's father's father's father's father was a cave man." The other remained skeptical. The believer retorted, "You go home and ask your mother if cave men are real. She will tell you to go ask your father, and he will tell you that they are real!" In view of the seriousness and vehemence attending the dispute, the skeptic probably asked his father and either modified or clarified his understanding. Were it not for the social interaction, the child may never have questioned his belief that cave men are imaginary. But his argument probably led to a more differentiated concept: Cave men were real long ago, but they are no longer real today.

Social interaction also appears to affect a young child's comprehension of the rules that govern chil-

dren's games. Some time ago, Piaget (1932) found that young children tended to believe that the rules of a marble game were fixed and absolute rather than conventions for play that could be changed by mutual consent of the players. The children in this study lived in homes where the parent-child relationship was one-sided and authoritarian. Children were not asked for their views, nor did they receive explanations when they were told how to behave. As they got older, the children interacted more with peers and less with parents, and they played the game according to more flexible rules. As they interacted more with other children, they had greater opportunities to assert their own points of view, to have them challenged, and to hear diverse opinions. The younger children's rigid interpretation of rules may have been due, in part, to the limited and one-sided nature of their social interaction, whereas the more flexible and realistic rule comprehension of the older children may have been affected by the cooperative nature of their social interactions. Thus many kinds of social interactions have increasingly important effects on the child's developing cognition.

SUMMARY

1. As the young child's perceptual skills develop, he isolates and relates more distinctive features of the objects and events in his world. His ability to coordinate the information that he receives through his

separate senses also improves dramatically as a result of greater experience, more sophisticated ways of exploring, and changes in cognitive understanding.

2. The child's concepts of the world continue to depend on which aspects of it get his attention. As in infancy, previous experience as well as certain physical features of objects and events are most likely to determine what a given child will attend to. Focusing and shifting attention are likely to vary with the complexity of a task, its rewards, and the effectiveness of instruction.

3. During early childhood, the child continues to fit newly observed phenomena into his understanding and to modify his concepts of the world. He may have difficulty recognizing or imagining that certain perceptual changes do not actually alter given aspects of the physical world, as in a conservation task; but his thinking gradually changes as he adds new examples of concepts that he already knows, discovers which attributes define a concept and which do not, learns that an example of a concept may possess some but not all of several attributes, and finds that some concepts are based on different and complex kinds of relationships. In general, the young child's thinking often tends to reflect his egocentrism—his view that others see, think, and experience things the same way that he does.

4. The cognitive skills involved in imitation, language, play, and memory continue to fulfill a major role in the child's construction of a conceptual network of interrelated ideas about objects and events. Symbolizing and imagining supplement rather than replace his natural curiosity and exploration of the real world. Increasingly, advances in these skills become closely linked to advances in a child's ability to learn, reason, and acquire concepts.

5. During early childhood, as well as later, social interactions appear to have a strong effect on a child's cognitive development. Through his interactions with family members and age-mates, the child is exposed to different viewpoints that may change his own understanding. Such interactions are likely to gradually decrease a child's egocentrism.

SUGGESTED READINGS

Piaget, Jean. *Play, Dreams and Imitation in Childhood.* C. Gattegne and F. M. Hodgson (trs.). New York: Norton, 1962.

Risley, Todd. "Learning and Lollipops (Jenny Lee)," *Psychology Today,* 1 (January 1968), 28–31+.

Saltz, Eli. *The Cognitive Bases of Human Learning.* Homewood, Ill.: Dorsey Press, 1971.

Singer, Dorothy G. "Piglet, Pooh & Piaget," *Psychology Today,* 6 (June 1972), 71–74+.

Sutton-Smith, Brian. "Child's Play—Very Serious Business," *Psychology Today,* 5 (December 1971), 66–69+.

Figure 11.12 Cognitive development involves a changing and active ability to know, do, and understand, and each of these aspects is likely to show the influence, in one form or another, of friends and playmates.

Above and beyond all else, it is language that makes us human.

12

LANGUAGE: UNDERSTANDING AND USING

Between the ages of one and one-half and four years, normal children all over the world master the basic grammar of one or more of the world's thousands of different languages. This ability of a small child to learn the complex structure of a language is remarkable. Moreover, each child is exposed to a different sample of the language; that is, children like Lauren and Matt hear a personally unique set of sentences from the adults and children that they interact with in their early years. Yet all children exposed to one language or dialect of that language learn to understand other speakers of that language and end up using the same pronunciation, grammar, and vocabulary as the other members of their speech community. This means that each child in a speech community arrives at the same basic linguistic rules. As stated in Chapter 8, this process appears to be a result of the child's ability to figure out the underlying structure of human language.

When young children and their parents move to a country where a different language is spoken, the children learn to understand and speak the new language with an ease and rapidity that their parents cannot hope to equal. With time, the young immigrant or visitor to a foreign land will sound like a native speaker of the new language, but his parents rarely, if ever, achieve perfect mastery of the same new language. The saying "so simple a child can do it" is thus turned around. How does the child do it?

In Chapter 8 we brought the child to the threshold of grammatical development. We left him at the point where he could make simple two-word sentences, using the universal linguistic devices of intonation, inflection, and word order to convey basic meanings through combinations of words. In this chapter we will examine some of his information-processing abilities in greater detail. You will discover that young children tend to impose regularities on language beyond those that exist. We will look at the methods that psycholinguists and developmental psychologists use to test a child's awareness of the rules of his language. The role of learning in language acquisition and the dependence of language on cognitive development will be discussed, and we will examine the influence of socioeconomic and ethnic differences on language development. When you finish this chapter, you should have a general understanding of how the child who could speak only in two-word utterances becomes a competent master of his complicated language during the childhood years.

PROPERTIES OF LANGUAGE

All languages have a large but finite vocabulary of words whose meanings must be learned. You will recall that semanticity, or meaningfulness, is an important property of language. In Chapter 8 we suggested that the child learns the features of meaning for each word in his vocabulary, gradually refining his meanings as his experiences broaden. One cannot ordinarily guess the meaning of a word from its sound, and even after the child adds a word to his vocabulary, its use cannot be divorced from context. Some words have more than one meaning: "meet" can be used in "The swimming meet has been postponed" and "We meet on Saturday"; "light," in "This is a light color" and "This suitcase is light when empty" and "Turn on the light." Some aspects of word formation are productive; for example, by using affixes, one can compose new meanings from words he already knows: "sad," "sadness"; "begin," "beginning"; "operate," "operation."

It is the *syntax* of a language—the underlying rules that determine the form of sentences—that provides for the richest expression of creativity. As noted earlier, syntax makes it possible to combine individual words into an unlimited number of sentences. People do not understand sentences by recognizing the precise sequence of words. Rather, they understand sentences because they know the rules of combination that make up the syntax of a language. Because people cannot possibly memorize all possible sentences of their language (the number is potentially infinite), each must learn in childhood the basic rules for making and understanding sentences.

At first it may seem surprising that the number and variety of possible sentences in a language is unlimited. But consider, for a moment, the sentences in this book. Although they are not difficult to understand, probably only a few are exact repetitions of sentences that you have seen or heard before. Each is a novel event. You will not find the last sentence, "Each is a novel event," anywhere else in this book; and the same is true of almost every sentence you ever speak or hear.

This fact of linguistic creativity, or *productivity,* makes special demands on a psychological explanation of how language is learned (Chomsky, 1972). Although a child hears sentence after sentence, he ends up knowing not a list of sentences but the rules for making sentences. Because these rules are not visible or audible in the speech he hears, he cannot imitate them or directly copy them. In fact, not even the most skillful linguist can state all the rules for the English language and certainly no parent ever tries to teach his three-year-old the rules of English language production. Because linguistic structures cannot be given to the child from outside, he must construct them in his own head, applying his basic linguistic capacities to the sounds and sights and experiences of his world (Bever, 1970; Slobin, 1973). Psychologists and psycholinguists are just beginning to understand how this complex cognitive feat is possible.

The third essential property of language set forth in Chapter 8, *displacement,* has been present in the child's language ever since he could ask for a cookie that was in the kitchen or for his father who was at the office (R. Brown, 1973). As the child matures, his language will include increasingly remote elements, and he will speak of events that occurred hundreds of years before and of such abstractions as the elements of formal logic.

THE CHILD'S AWARENESS OF GRAMMAR

Psychologists studying language development discover the facts of early language acquisition by *observing* the child's natural speech and by studying his attempts to systematize, or simplify, language.

Observation

When observing young children, psycholinguists use indirect evidence to infer a child's knowledge of rules. Children sometimes correct their own speech; for example, Lauren catching a glimpse of herself in a mirror might say, "I see me in the mirror . . . I see myself in the mirror" or, on another occasion, "I seed . . . saw it." Each time a child corrects his own language errors, he shows that he believes certain combinations of words are incorrect, thereby revealing that he has a formal system of grammar (W. Miller and Ervin, 1970). But such instances, though revealing, are relatively rare and give information on only a few scattered aspects of language. To discover children's knowledge of language regularities, one must examine the evidence from large samples of children's speech, noting the sets of well-formed utterances, the types of omissions and errors, and, most important, the sets of utterances children produce that they probably have not heard.

Roger Brown, Courtney Cazden, and Ursula Bellugi-Klima (1968) have studied the speech development of three children, whom they call Adam, Eve, and Sarah. At the start of their study, Adam and Sarah were twenty-seven months old, and Eve, eighteen months. Adam and Sarah were studied until they were five years old; Eve was studied for nine months (at which time she moved away). In those nine months, however, Eve had already passed far beyond the stage of development that Adam and Sarah had reached at the beginning of the study (see Figure 12.1), demonstrating that there is considerable difference among children in the ages at which they begin to combine words and in their rate of progress through the levels of linguistic development.

Brown and his colleagues selected these children because they were just beginning to combine words into two-word utterances and because their speech was clear and easy to understand. The researchers visited Adam and Eve at two- or three-week intervals, spending two hours each time; they visited Sarah every week for a half hour. During these visits, they recorded everything each child said and everything that was said to him, and they kept notes on the objects and actions that accompanied speech. A full record of the contexts in which each child spoke was necessary because a child often relies on the nonlinguistic context of his utterance to convey part of his message.

Between visits, Brown and his co-workers met in a research seminar to discuss the state of the children's development and to suggest experiments. For example, at one point Adam would sometimes pluralize nouns and sometimes not. Someone suggested that he be tested to see whether he could distinguish a correct form from an incorrect form. On the next visit, a researcher asked, "Adam, which is right, 'two shoes' or 'two shoe'?" His answer, produced with enthusiasm, was "Pop go the weasel!" This response, which is known among psycholinguists as the "pop-goes-the-weasel phenomenon," demonstrates that the two-year-old child is not a model experimental subject. Only special techniques can reveal the details of what he knows about his language.

But Brown's recordings over this crucial period in language acquisition produced valuable information, and the techniques of observation and analysis developed by researchers such as Brown and his colleagues, Lois Bloom (1970), Susan Ervin-Tripp (1970), and others have become the standard first phase of investigation in studies of languages other than English (Ferguson and Slobin, 1973). The following dialogue between Eve and her mother, when Eve was about two, gives some idea of what natural conversation can show about the nature of early childhood speech:

Eve: Have that?
Mother: No, you may not have it.
Eve: Mom, where my tapioca?
Mother: It's getting cool. You'll have it in just a minute.
                      . . .

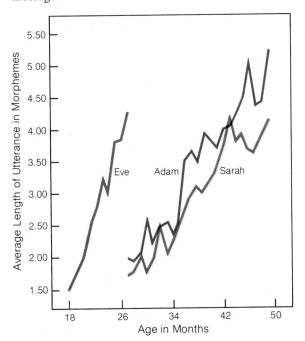

Figure 12.1 Graph showing the increases with age in the average length of utterances for Eve, Adam, and Sarah. Morphemes are small linguistic units of speech that have definable meanings. (Adapted from Brown, 1973)

Eve: You gonna watch me eat my lunch?
Mother: Yeah, I'm gonna watch you eat your lunch.
Eve: I eating it.
Mother: I know you are.
Eve: It time Sarah take a nap.
Mother: It's time for Sarah to have some milk, yeah. And then she's gonna take a nap and you're gonna take a nap.
Eve: And you?
Mother: And me too, yeah. (Bellugi, 1970, page 33)

Notice that both participants in the dialogue make statements, requests, and negative sentences and ask questions. However, interesting differences appear between the speech of the adult and the child. Certain elements that are characteristically and systematically missing from Eve's speech are present in her mother's sentences. Eve's mother uses auxiliary verbs (forms of *to be, to do,* and so forth) wherever English syntax requires them. These grammatical elements are not present in the child's speech. Eve, for example, says "It time," whereas her mother says "It's time." The child's speech, although understandable, lacks the required auxiliary verb.

Within three months, Eve's language showed a dramatic change. Compare her sentence structures in the previous dialogue with sentences in this dialogue:

Mother: Shut the door, we won't hear her then.
Eve: Then Fraser won't hear her too. Where he's going?
. . .
Eve: Could I get some other piece of paper?
Mother: You ask Fraser.
Eve: Could I use this one?
Mother: I suppose so.
Eve: Is Fraser goin' take his pencil home when he goes?
Mother: Yes, he is.
Eve: Then we don't see him.
Mother: Nope, probably not. He'll share the paper with you while he's here.
. . .
Eve: Now let me draw you a lady. I can't. I not know . . . make one.
Mother: You don't know how to make one? You look at Fraser's lady and see if you can make one.
Eve: I can't. I think I have tear one and I think I can write one. (pages 33–34)

Now Eve uses auxiliary verbs in negatives, questions, and statements. Her sentences are also longer and more complex. She can join simple sentences together with words like "when" and "and." She still makes errors, of course, and some of these errors reveal that she is beginning to figure out the rules of English. For example, she says, "Then Fraser won't hear her too," whereas an adult would say, "Then Fraser won't hear her either." There is an odd rule in English that changes "too" to "either" in negative sentences (it is correct to say "Fraser will hear her too"). Eve has not figured out this rule for negative statements, but her use of "too" indicates that she understands the general function carried out by both "too" and "either," even though she does not use "either" in negative statements.

Overregularization

Developmental psychologists and psycholinguists are especially interested in a child's speech errors, because grammatical errors reveal the extent to which a child has control of certain language rules. Many errors that children make can be looked on as their attempts to make the language more regular or systematic than it actually is. For example, Eve's use of "too" in both positive and negative utterances is a regularization of adult English, which requires one to use "too" in positive sentences and "either" in negative. You will recall that, as the child builds his vocabulary, he gradually moves from a generalization such as "bow-wow" for all animals to a separate word for each species. His syntax also suffers from overgeneralization, because he forces each utterance to follow the rules that he has figured out. The child's errors in his use of the past tense of verbs and the plural forms of nouns most clearly reveal overregularization in English.

English verbs, in most cases, change form from present to simple past tense: "I *walk* to school; I *walked* to school." Although a few verbs do not change their form to express the past ("hit," "hit"), the regular way to form the past for English verbs is to add *-ed:* "walk," "walked"; "ask," "asked." However, many common verbs form their past tense in an irregular manner: "go," "went"; "come," "came"; "drive," "drove"; "break," "broke." Investigators in the field of child language have found that some children learn a number of these irregular past forms as separate words at an early age and produce correct sentences: "It broke"; "Daddy went out"; "I fell." Often they use these correct past tense forms for many months. After a while, however, the child discovers the rule for forming regular past tenses, and the irregular forms that he had correctly produced may disappear from his speech, to be replaced by overregularized forms. The child now may say: "It breaked"; "Daddy goed out"; "I falled." Indeed, these overregularizations persist into the elementary-school years, and it is hard to believe that a six-year-old who persistently says "It breaked" said "It broke" when he was two.

What looks like regression is actually a sign of progress in the child's analysis of his language. Clearly, children have not heard the overregularized forms from their parents, and such forms occur even in the speech of first-born children, who have no older siblings to learn the incorrect forms from. The child constructs such overregularized verbs to conform with the regularities that he has noticed in the speech of others. And so a change from "went" to "goed" is not evidence that the child is regressing; on the contrary, it indicates that he has, on his own, discovered a regular pattern in the language and is using it in his speech.

During these periods of overregularization, the child's speech sometimes seems remarkably impervious to gentle efforts at correction. The following conversation, reported by Jean Berko Gleason (1967), may serve as an example:

Child: My teacher holded the baby rabbits and we patted them.
Mother: Did you say your teacher held the baby rabbits?
Child: Yes.
Mother: What did you say she did?
Child: She holded the baby rabbits and we patted them.
Mother: Did you say she held them tightly?
Child: No, she holded them loosely.

Although his mother substitutes the correct verb form twice in this short dialogue, the child persists in repeating "held" as "holded," tenaciously clinging to his own linguistic structures. Apparently, regularity heavily outranks previous practice, reinforce-

Figure 12.2 Illustration of rule use in young children's speech. Note overregularization of the past tense of verbs and the plural form of nouns and of the formation of negative sentences.

ment, and immediate imitation of adult forms in its influence on children. The child seeks regularity and is deaf to exceptions (Bellugi, 1970).

The power of apparent regularities shows up repeatedly in the children's speech of every language that has been studied (Slobin, 1972). For example, when a Russian noun appears as the object of a sentence ("He liked the *story*"), the speaker must add an appropriate ending to "story" that will mark the noun as a direct object. However, the precise suffix chosen depends on the gender and the concluding sounds of the particular noun. The Russian child, of course, does not learn to put all these rules into effect at once. Rather, he continues to reorganize his system in successive sweeps of overregularizations. Just as the English-speaking child is content, for a while, to express the notion of past tense (and he does not notice whether the form should be "holded" or "held"), the Russian-speaking child is content to communicate which noun in a sentence is the direct object without worrying whether the suffix he chooses also tells whether that particular noun is formally masculine, feminine, or neuter.

The formation of plurals is another area in which children tend to overregularize. For example, the English language has several ways to indicate whether a speaker is talking about one or more objects. If you pay close attention to the way that you pronounce the plural, you will find that there are three regular plural sounds in English: *s* (as in "roots," "books"), *z* (as in "barns," "bees"), and *ez* (as in "horses," "matches"). A child must learn the rules for using these three plural endings, depending on the final sound of each word. English also has some irregular plural forms, many of them common words: "foot," "feet"; "mouse," "mice"; "man," "men"; "child," "children." These irregular forms, like irregular verb past-tense forms, must be learned as separate vocabulary items.

The linguistic context in English does not always indicate whether the speaker is considering one object or more than one. If someone says, "Point to the sheep," it would be as correct to point to one sheep as to many. Based on this fact, Jean Berko (1958) constructed a way to test the child's knowledge of the rules for forming plurals from several singular nouns.

For the test, an investigator shows a child some object for which there is no name. (Large stuffed toys of unfamiliar shape, like the pictures used in one test, are shown in Figure 12.3.) The investigator names these objects with possible but nonexistent English words. She presents the child with one object and

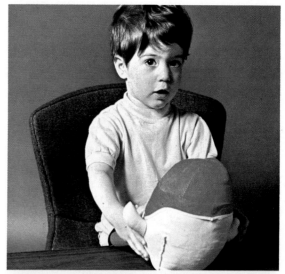

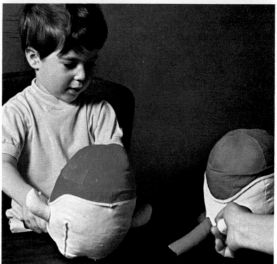

says, for example, "Here is a wug." Then she puts down another, similar object next to it and says, "Now there is another wug. There are two _____ ?" The child obligingly fills in the nonexistent but regular item, "wugs," pronouncing it *wugz* if he knows the appropriate rule for forming plurals in English.

From these tests and from observations of free speech, researchers have found that the child who has been correctly using some irregular plural forms ("feet," "men," "mice") may, for a time, overgeneralize his newly discovered rules of formation and say "foots," "mans," "mouses," another example of the kind of overregularization that appears in the child's use of verbs. Thus a child may learn the irregular form but apply the plural rule anyway, saying "feets," "mens," "mices."

TESTING COMPREHENSION OF GRAMMAR

The ways in which a child comprehends speech give the psycholinguist additional evidence of the child's understanding of syntax. When a child responds correctly to a command or question, his parents often believe that he understands all or most of the language that they address to him. Susan's mother may say to her small child, who can speak only two or three words at a time, "Go over to that chair and bring me my knitting." When Susan does so, her mother may be impressed by Susan's apparent understanding of a lengthy command. However, Susan needs to understand only a word or two of the adult sentence

("knitting" and perhaps "chair") to be able to comply. In addition, it is likely that her mother looked in the direction of the chair on which the knitting was prominently displayed; she may have pointed to it and then held out her hand. The linguistic and environmental context of speech addressed to the child is usually rich with cues that aid in understanding, just as the contextual cues of one-word utterances permit adults to interpret the speech of toddlers, as pointed out in Chapter 8.

To test adequately for a child's comprehension of some grammatical rule, it is necessary to eliminate all cues of intonation, gesture, or facial expression. In the preceding situation, for example, a tester, with hands folded in her lap, might look at Susan (not at the object she wants her to bring) and might ask her first, "Bring my knitting to me." Then, after returning the knitting to its original position, she would ask Susan, "Bring me to my knitting." Perhaps she would try other variations as well: "Me to knitting my bring" and just "Knitting, please." The point is to establish carefully controlled conditions that test the child's knowledge of grammatical rules.

Careful testing of this sort reveals that children often develop their own simple rules for figuring out the meanings of sentences, although these strategies sometimes lead the child into misinterpreting some kinds of sentences. A good example comes from studies of children's comprehension of *active* and *passive* sentences. Children hear many examples of simple declarative sentences, each containing an actor, an action, and the object of that action: "Mommy is eating soup"; "Jane feeds her doll"; "Alfred loves Suzette." In each of these sentences the relationship between the actor ("Alfred"), action ("loves"), and object of the action ("Suzette") is expressed by word order.

Colin Fraser, Ursula Bellugi, and Roger Brown (1963) have developed some tests that reveal a child's comprehension of grammar. In one of their tests, the child sees several pictures and must point to the one described by the sentence he hears. For example, he is given a pair of pictures, one in which a dog chases a cat and another in which a cat chases a dog. The child is asked to point to the picture that shows "The cat chases the dog" or "The dog chases the cat." Another technique, developed by Janellen Huttenlocher, Karen Eisenberg, and Susan Strauss (1968) and by Thomas Bever (1970), asks the child to act out sentences such as "The car follows the truck" when given a toy truck and a toy car to manipulate (see Figure 12.4). Most children of about three perform

Figure 12.3 Illustration of singular-plural test. (*top*) The child is handed an object for which he has no name and is told, "Here is a wug." (*middle*) Then another is put down, and the child is asked to finish the sentence "Now there are two _____. (*bottom*) If the child knows the rule for forming plurals, he can respond with "wugs."

well on these tests, and they also use the correct word order in their own speech. But tests of simple active sentences alone do not make clear what sort of sentence-interpretation rule the child follows.

Not all English sentences place the actor before the verb and the object of the action after the verb. In *passive* sentences, for example, these relationships are reversed. Compare "The truck was broken by John" and "John broke the truck." The two sentences have the same meaning, but the order of major elements is different. In both sentences, it is clear that John is the actor and the truck the object, because toy trucks cannot break boys. But in sentences such as "The car follows the truck" and "The truck is followed by the car," you must know more than simple word order if you are to figure out what is doing the following and what is being followed.

When a four-year-old's understanding of passive sentences is tested by showing him pictures or by asking him to demonstrate, for example, "The truck is followed by the car," he is seldom correct. In fact, most four-year-olds point to the wrong picture or carry out the opposite action each time.

Thomas Bever (1970) has studied the development of children's interpretive strategies for such active and passive sentences and has shown that children go through several strategies before they arrive at the complex rules of adult English grammar. For example, he gave children between the ages of two and four a toy horse and a toy cow and asked them to act out sentences such as the following:

1. The *cow kisses* the horse.
2. It's the *cow* that *kisses* the horse.
3. It's the horse that the *cow kisses*.
4. The horse *is kissed by* the *cow*. (pages 303–308)

Surprisingly, two-year-olds act out the first three sentence types correctly, but their performance is random on the fourth (passive) sentence. They are as likely to have the horse kiss the cow as to have the cow kiss the horse.

Bever suggests that, if a two-year-old hears a noun and a verb in a row, he will assume that the noun is the actor. This noun-verb sequence is "a kind of primitive *gestalt*"—a perceptual unit that is heard as meaning "actor-action." But if another word or words interrupt this simple sequence, as in the passive Sentence 4, the child's strategy fails, and he makes a random choice of actor.

Four-year-olds, according to Bever, have developed a different strategy, in which they hear the first noun in a sentence as the actor and the noun following

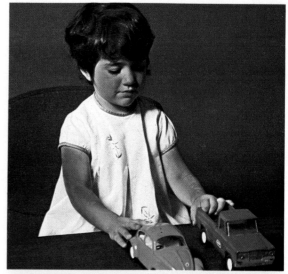

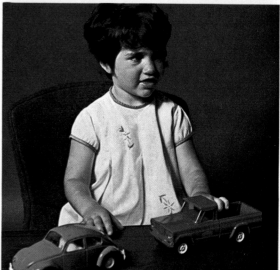

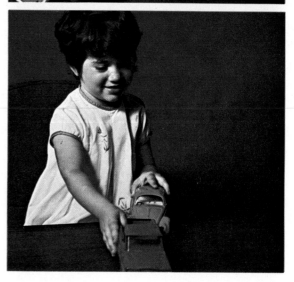

the verb as the object of action. This strategy leads them astray on sentences like ''It's the horse that the cow kisses,'' and they tend to pick the horse as the actor. In addition, following such an interpretation rule, they process a passive sentence as if it were an active sentence with some extra, uninterpretable parts. Thus they consistently reverse the interpretation of passives and act out Sentence 4 by having the horse kiss the cow.

Bever's demonstration of children's strategies for interpreting sentences indicates that the child does not progress directly toward adult grammar but rather constructs and discards a variety of provisional grammars as he goes along. As a result of these changing strategies, sentences that are correctly interpreted at one age (for example, the two-year-olds' correct understanding of ''It's the horse that the cow kisses'') may be misinterpreted at a later age.

RULES AND PERFORMANCE LIMITATIONS

In Chapter 8 it was noted that children who are just beginning to speak seem to operate under severe performance limitations and can produce only one- or two-word utterances. Recall Lois Bloom's example of the one-year-old girl who, when trying to get a button out of her pocket, said ''button'' and ''pocket'' as two separate one-word utterances but could not put them together into a two-word utterance. And a child at the two-word stage could say ''Daddy throw,'' ''Throw ball,'' and ''Daddy ball,'' yet could not say ''Daddy throw ball'' in a single utterance. At these

very early phases of language development, the limitations on a child's performance seem to be simply a matter of the number of words. Later, however, the limitations seem to be a matter of the number of rules or grammatical operations that a child can carry out when producing a single sentence. Performance limitations at these stages can therefore give additional indirect evidence of the child's grasp of linguistic rules.

A study by Ursula Bellugi (1968) provides a good illustration of how a child's ability to form questions is limited by his facility with particular linguistic rules. In English, in order to ask a question that can be answered Yes or No, the order of the subject of the sentence and the auxiliary verb is inverted. For example, you may say ''He can swim'' but ask ''Can he swim?'' If you want to ask a specific kind of question (for example, a question about place or time or manner or cause of swimming), you must insert a specific question word at the beginning of the sentence and then invert the order of subject and auxiliary. For example, you ask ''Where can he swim?'' ''When can he swim?'' and so forth.

Children, however, frequently ask questions such as ''Where he can swim?'' ''What he can ride in?'' ''Why he's doing it?'' and the like. In such questions, the child has correctly placed the question word at the beginning of the sentence but has failed to invert subject and auxiliary. However, the same child is able to invert subject and auxiliary in a simple yes-or-no question. For example, the child who asks ''What he

Figure 12.4 (*opposite*) To test a young child's comprehension of active/passive sentences, (*top*) a car and truck are placed before her on a table. (*middle*) When told, ''Show me the truck follows the car,'' she responds correctly to this active sentence. (*bottom*) After the vehicles are placed before her again, she is told, ''Show me the car is followed by the truck.'' This time she responds incorrectly, carrying out the action opposite to that asked for in this passive sentence.

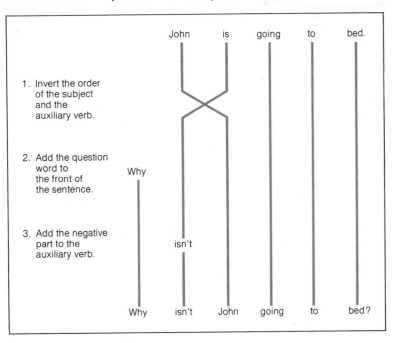

Figure 12.5 Diagrammatic analysis showing a basic sentence at the top and the series of transformations involved in forming questions, as discussed in the text.

can ride in?'' can also ask, correctly, "Can he ride in a truck?" Apparently he can either insert the specific question word or invert subject and auxiliary, but he cannot carry out both operations in the same sentence.

At the next level of development, the child can handle two operations simultaneously and will correctly produce questions such as "What can he ride in?" The performance limitation, however, still blocks the application of a third rule to sentence production. For example, if the question is negative, the child appropriately attaches the negative element to the auxiliary in simple yes-or-no questions, producing forms such as "Can't he go out?" He can also invert subject and auxiliary, asking questions such as "Why can he go out?"

But the child can handle only limited complexity at this point. Combining negation, inversion, and a question-word in the same sentence appears to be too much for him to handle, as illustrated in the following example:

Adult: Adam, ask the Old Lady where she can find some toys.
Child: Old Lady, where can you find some toys?
Adult: Adam, ask the Old Lady why she can't run.
Child: Old Lady, why you can't run? (Bellugi, 1968, page 40)

Clearly then, the child regularly applies each of these three grammatical operations—insertion of the question word, inversion of the subject and auxiliary, and negation—to his speech production, but at a certain level of development he can apply no more than two of these operations in the same utterance.

By the time he is about four years old, a normal child has mastered most of the grammar of his language, although he will continue to add to his knowledge of complex syntactical structures (Palermo and Molfese, 1972). This seems to be true regardless of the language that he is learning and regardless of the setting in which he has been exposed to the language (Slobin, in press). He spends the school years in learning details, such as irregular endings, complex vocabulary items, and involved sentence constructions, as the rest of this chapter will show. But the basic rules of word order and of forming proper endings are well stabilized by kindergarten age, as are the rules for question formation and for negation.

LANGUAGE AND COGNITIVE DEVELOPMENT

Asking whether language is the result of learning or of neural maturation is like asking whether a person's intelligence is the result of environment or heredity.

As noted in Chapter 3, both nature and nurture are important. Donald Hebb, Wallace Lambert, and G. R. Tucker (1971) have pointed out that posing such a question is like wondering whether the length or the width of a field contributes most to its area. Before a child can handle his native language, he must have certain nearly universal human experiences, and he first must reach the appropriate level of cognitive development.

Learning and Parental Teaching

Of course, an American child learns the rules of English, a Russian child learns those of Russian, and so on; a child can learn only the particular language that he is exposed to. Although some psychologists stress the role of imitation and reinforcement, by word and by deed, in the child's learning of language rules (Staats, 1971), many psycholinguists stress instead the creativity or productivity of syntax. They point out that the child develops rules that allow him to produce and interpret an endless variety of novel sentences. A child cannot imitate rules, they say, because he hears only sentences.

A child's sentences are often different from adult sentences. When a child like Matt says "All-gone sticky" after washing his hands or asks "What he can ride in?" or says "I seed two mouses," he is not imitating precise forms that he has heard others use. Instead he is generalizing, applying his grammatical rules to his store of words. Indeed, children seem unable to comprehend speech except in terms of their own level of grammar. Recall the child who persisted in saying "holded," even though the experimenter repeatedly said "held." David McNeill (1966) gives another example of a child's tendency to imitate only in terms of his own grammatical rules:

Child: Nobody don't like me.
Mother: No, say "nobody likes me."
Child: Nobody don't like me.
[Eight repetitions of this dialogue follow.]
Mother: No, now listen carefully; say "*nobody likes me.*"
Child: Oh! Nobody don't likes me. (page 69)

If it is so hard for a child to hear an adult utterance as different from his own version, even in the face of such insistent counterevidence, it is hard to imagine how a child could learn new linguistic forms solely through imitation. Of course, the child must pick up the elements of the language from the speech he hears, but he must reassemble the elements each time he speaks.

A great deal of learning about the nature and use of language occurs during its development, and a young child may practice different combinations of words, actively testing the language. Ruth Weir (1962) set up a tape recorder near her son's bed and for several nights recorded the solitary talk of her two-year-old at bedtime. The transcript reveals the boy working at the language, trying out different nouns, pronouns, adjectives, and verbs:

On the blanket—Under the blanket. . . . Berries—Not berries. . . . Too hot—Not too hot.

. . .

Can bite—Bite—Have a bite. . . . Broke the vacuum—The broke—Get some broke—Alice broke the baby fruit. (page 19)

Some concepts can be learned only in terms of other words. Neither a child's sensory-motor responses to the questions of others, such as touching a pair of boots when someone asks him "Why is the boy wearing boots?" (Ervin-Tripp, 1970), nor his own pointing and gesturing will express concepts like "how" and "why." As Marion Blank (1974) makes clear, it may be that the young child learns the meanings of "why" and "how" only by producing the terms before he understands them and by using the words over and over in numerous situations. Once the child learns to ask "why" and "how" questions, however, he has automatically forced the adults around him into the role of teachers.

Although in the nobody-likes-me dialogue a mother is actively trying to correct her child's speech, attempts at formal language teaching like these are rare. Most of the time, parents are too busy interacting with

a child to pay much attention to his grammar. If three-year-old Lauren asks, "Why cause horses can't fly?" her parent will answer the question instead of pointing out that her grammar is faulty. Indeed, communication can be carried on remarkably well regardless of the child's grammar level, as the conversations in this chapter have shown.

Roger Brown, Courtney Cazden, and Ursula Bellugi-Klima (1968) examined a large body of tape-recorded interactions between adults and children and found no evidence that conscious teaching on the part of parents plays any serious role in grammatical development. They noted that parents often corrected gross errors in a child's choice of words, and, once in a while, the parents corrected a pronunciation error. But most often it was the truth of an utterance that determined a parent's approval. When Eve wanted to say that her mother was a girl and produced "He a girl," her mother replied, "That's right." But when Sarah said, with perfect grammar, "There's the animal in the farmhouse," her mother corrected her, because the building was a lighthouse; and when Adam stated, "Walt Disney comes on on Tuesday," he met with disapproval, because the Disney television program appears on Sunday. Truth, not correct grammar, is more likely to evoke verbal reinforcement from parents. But words are not the only reinforcement that parents give. Whenever a child successfully communicates and his language gets him a cookie, an open door, a glass of water, or some other thing he wants, his verbal behavior is rein-

Figure 12.6 Young children quickly learn about the uses of spoken language—partly because it is to their advantage to be able to do some such thing as ask their mother for a cookie.

234

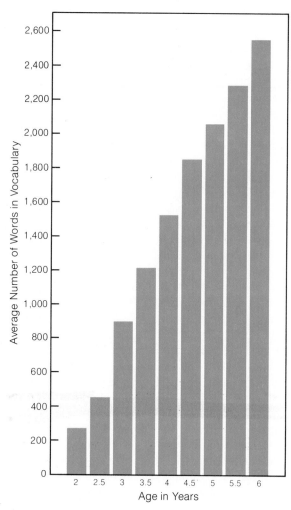

Figure 12.7 Graph showing the increase with age in average size of vocabulary. Although the learning of new words does not necessarily indicate the learning of new concepts or meanings, both are likely to develop together. (Adapted from Lenneberg, 1967)

forced. The requirement for reinforcement, however, is still intelligibility, not grammatical precision.

Semantics and Social Cognition

Although a child has mastered the major syntactical rules of his language by the time he is four or five, he still has a long way to go before he reaches an adult level in semantic development and in the ability to adapt his language to the situation. Psycholinguists have generally been more interested in the syntax than in the meaning of a language, but some syntactical studies (such as the studies of a child's mastery of the passive construction discussed earlier) indicate that form and meaning can become closely intertwined.

In Chapter 8, the way that young children first overgeneralize and then restructure the meanings of words was discussed. For example, children often attach meanings to words that are different from those that adults give them. Thus, words such as "bright," "hard," and "sweet" have both a physical ("The light is bright") and a psychological ("She is a bright child") meaning to adults. Solomon Asch and Harriet Nerlove (1960) showed that three- and four-year-olds first learn the physical meaning of these words and often deny that such concepts as "bright" or "sweet" can be applied to people. Seven- and eight-year-olds are aware of both meanings, but see no relationship between a bright light and a bright child. A few nine-year-olds relate the two meanings, but not until a child is eleven or twelve is he likely to have a firm grasp of the dual functions of words. Apparently a child learns the two meanings separately and only much later unifies them. David Palermo and Dennis Molfese's (1972) survey of semantic studies turned up many such examples of the child's gradual semantic development.

In the absence of other people, of course, none of us would develop language. Our utterances are meant to communicate meanings to others, and we learn to use language socially in many different ways for many different purposes: to express emotions, to describe objects or events, to ask questions, to give commands, to tell stories, and to speculate.

John Flavell (1970) has studied the way that the child's ability to adapt his language to his audience and his situation develops. On one occasion, for example, Flavell gave children the task of explaining to two adults how to play a game. One of the adults was blindfolded; the other was not. Older children gave the blindfolded adult much longer and more detailed instructions than they gave to the adult who could see the game. Younger children tended to give the same message to each, and some of the younger children even talked to the blindfolded person as if he could see, directing the adult to "This one" and "Over there." When Flavell set up a different situation, in which one listener was an adult and the other a child, older children again gave different instructions to each person, whereas younger children were less able to allow for differences between their listeners.

In a survey of research, McNeill (1970b) also noted that children have difficulty in instructing other children, that their verbal descriptions are shorter than those of adults, and that the descriptions they give are often highly idiosyncratic. That is, a child will describe an object as resembling "mother's dress," which conveys information only to people who have seen mother's full, gathered skirt. An adult is likely to describe the same object as looking like an "upside down cup." As Sam Glucksberg, Robert Krauss, and Robert Weisberg (1966) have pointed out, children are better at decoding messages than at encoding them. When they hear descriptions formulated by adults, their understanding soars. Even so, they behave as if they understand all messages, accepting noncommunicative messages passively and without asking for new or fuller descriptions.

LANGUAGE FUNCTIONING AND ENVIRONMENT

All children learn to handle their native languages, but the language a young child hears from his parents will help shape the style of his developing speech. The attitudes of his parents toward language, the richness of their vocabularies, their response to his attempts at speech, and the amount and kind of conversation that takes place in his home are likely to affect his own attitude toward speech, vocabulary size, fluency, and language style, as well as to influence his degree of success in formal education.

Social-Class Differences

One might expect to find differences in the way that children from different social classes use language. Studies that compare language use of children from different social backgrounds indicate that children from the more advantaged sections of society do score higher on tests of pronunciation, vocabulary, and sentence structure than children of families from lower socioeconomic groups do (R. Hess, 1970). However, there is no conclusive evidence to show that middle-class children use superior sentence structure or grammatical patterns.

Children from different social classes, on the other hand, do show differences in their expressive language. For example, Daniel Miller and Guy Swanson (1966) have pointed out that individuals in lower socioeconomic groups more often tend to express themselves with gestures, whereas those in higher socioeconomic groups tend to express themselves with words. A series of studies by Basil Bernstein (1962, 1966) also seem to indicate these kinds of

Figure 12.8 Learning to read, write, and understand one's language requires not only cognitive development but also a history of appropriate experiences.

Figure 12.9 Variations in the experiences of children from different socioeconomic backgrounds are reflected in their choice of words, gestures, style, and other aspects of expressive language.

expressive language differences. Bernstein analyzed the speech of sixteen-year-old boys from the lower and middle classes who were matched for intelligence. He discovered that the middle-class boys used more elaborate descriptions of experience, showed a wider vocabulary, used more nouns, and spoke fluently, with short pauses in their utterances. The boys from the lower socioeconomic class made fewer distinctions, used more common words, tended to use more pronouns, and seemed to make longer pauses in their speech.

Given the usual high correlation between the language of parents and that of their children in vocabulary, style, and choice of particular forms, socioeconomic differences in such aspects of child speech probably are to be expected. The linguistic environment of middle- and lower-class homes is likely to differ in many ways. Esther Milner (1951) and Suzanne Keller (1963), for example, found that middle-class families are likely to eat together, using the mealtime for whole-family conversations, whereas children from lower-class families tend to eat alone or with siblings, thereby missing such opportunities for verbal interaction with adults.

However, peers also influence speech. William Stewart (1964) observed that, among black families who have lived in Washington, D.C. for two or three generations, it is common for children to speak a variety of English much closer to the speech of newer immigrants from the South than to their parents' Standard English. It may be, therefore, that children from lower socioeconomic families lag behind on some measures of language development merely because they talk less with adults and talk more with their peers.

Special Schooling
In the last few years, several language-training programs have been organized to develop a number of language skills in so-called disadvantaged, but otherwise normal, children. Some of these programs have used various learning-based procedures, involving specific objectives, specific sequences of instructions, adult modeling, social approval, and other rewards. The results of such efforts indicate that the programs can increase a child's rate of spontaneous speech, the correctness of his speech, the appropriate timing of his talking, his story-telling skills, and his descriptions of his own behavior. But note that these programs focus on specific language skills and not on the basic structure of a language.

Much of the thinking behind compensatory education programs for lower-class minority children in the United States supposes that "cultural deprivation," or poverty, results in various kinds of language deficits and that these various aspects of deficient language delay or block full cognitive development (Bereiter and Engelmann, 1966). However, most studies indicate that all children learn basic rules of language equally well, according to universal patterns of development. In this sense there is no such thing as a "language deficit" in child development. There is, as other studies have shown, a "language difference." Social environments certainly differ in regard to how well they match the school environment. Clearly, children who have acquired the motivations, habits, speech forms, and vocabulary and pronunciation skills demanded by the school system will perform better in that system than children whose social backgrounds have led them to acquire different motivations, habits, speech forms, and vocabulary and pronunciation skills. It should be clear, then, that the mismatch between home environment and school that has been observed in various social groups in this country and others is not based on purely linguistic factors.

A recent study by Marida Hollos and Philip Cowan (1973) presents clear experimental evidence that supports such a position. They studied in detail the cognitive development of children in several different social settings. Consider their description of one setting:

Children spend most of their time in solitary play or in observation of others. Since there are few commercial toys and games, solitary play involves manipulation or observation of objects that occur naturally in the environment. . . . Most frequent interaction takes place with the mother; the father spends much of the day away from the house. . . . The amount of verbal interaction between mother and child is limited. Mothers do not prompt or encourage children to talk, ask questions, or suggest activities. There are no periods of storytelling or of discussions. . . . Interaction and communication between adult members of the family is limited to mealtimes and evenings. The major part of the evening is devoted to watching television . . . (pages 632–633)

This sounds like the "culturally deprived" situation that has been described as typical of lower-class blacks in our city slums. It is, however, a description of life on an isolated Norwegian farm, a setting that has for many an aura of "wholesomeness" far removed from the atmosphere of the inner-city slum. Hollos and Cowan compared these isolated Norwegian farm children with children of families of similar size and educational background in a small village and in a medium-sized town in Norway. The village and town children spent much of their time playing with other children and encountering many adults in a variety of social settings and returned in the evenings to more talkative family situations than the isolated farm children did. Yet basic language development was similar in all three groups, even though the village and town children had many more opportunities for verbal interaction.

What might we expect of the cognitive development of these children? A psychologist who stresses the role of verbal interaction and contact with the viewpoints of other people would predict more advanced cognitive development in the village and town children. A psychologist who minimizes the role of language in cognitive development would predict no important differences among the three groups. In fact, the actual results are more varied and more interesting than either of these simplified positions would lead one to believe.

The children took a number of different tests of cognitive ability. The first set of tasks tapped the child's ability to think logically about physical properties of objects and their relationships. Another collection of tasks dealt with the child's ability to take a viewpoint other than his own, which of course the egocentric child cannot do. Hollos and Cowan found that the isolated farm children were relatively advanced on the first set of cognitive tasks and that the village and town children were relatively more advanced on the second set of tasks.

This finding paints a complex picture of the roles played in early cognitive development by language and verbal interaction. Apparently, the manipulation of objects and close observation of physical changes helps a child to acquire the ability to think logically about the physical properties of objects and their relationships. Verbal interaction with different persons helps a child to develop the cognitive abilities necessary to take a point of view other than his own. Both abilities are important for schooling and necessary for development. And, indeed, all children eventually reach acceptable levels of development on both sets of abilities. Because the verbal environment affects only some aspects of cognitive development, the role of verbal training as a preparation for schooling must be looked at in a less simplistic manner (Hollos, 1974).

The problem of schooling, therefore, is neither one of teaching the child to think nor of teaching him to speak. Instead, after making the child feel at home in the school environment, psychologists and educators

should find out which aspects of cognition need stimulation for a particular child or group of children and then devise the appropriate means (not necessarily verbal) to foster that particular facet of cognitive growth.

Dialects and Language Development

Much of the impetus in compensatory-education programs has been devoted to getting American black children to speak standard middle-class (non-Southern) American English (generally referred to by teachers as "correct English"). Although it is certainly the case that a person's chances of social and economic progress in our society are enhanced if he speaks the dominant dialect, there is no basis for relating a particular dialect to special success in normal mental development.

In linguistic terms, Black and Standard English are minor variants of the same English language; and in developmental terms, the acquisition of the two dialects follows similar patterns. For example, studies of black children in the Oakland ghetto, carried out by Dan Slobin and Claudia Mitchell-Kernan (Slobin, in press), show no serious differences between the basic pattern of language development in ghetto children and in the middle-class Harvard children studied by Roger Brown. The Oakland children spend most of their time learning language from older siblings and playmates, who watch over them during much of the day. This situation, however, is common in cultures around the world and seems to have no effect on the

Table 12.1   Dialect Differences in Negative Utterances of Preschool-Age Children

OAKLAND CHILDREN	HARVARD CHILDREN
That's not no bathroom.	It wasn't no chicken.
I'm not doing nothing.	I wasn't doing nothing.
I don't get no whipping.	I don't want no milk.
Nobody wasn't scared.	But nobody wasn't gonna know it.
Why bears can't talk?	Why I can't put them on?
But Renée or nobody wouldn't peel me no kinda orange.	Nobody won't recognize me.
Why she won't sit up?	Why we didn't? Why it's not working?
Nobody wouldn't help me.	No one didn't took it.
I don't have no suitcase.	It don't have no wings.
Never I don't get no whipping.	I never won't get it.

Source: The Oakland examples are drawn from unpublished data of Claudia Mitchell-Kernan, and the Harvard examples, from unpublished data of Roger Brown.

basic rate of a child's acquisition of syntax. The two dialects are especially close at the preschool period, as shown in the examples in Table 12.1. They are roughly equivalent on functional and grammatical grounds, although their social consequences in the contemporary American social system are vastly different.

During later childhood, the dialects diverge. But even at the adult level, the dialects differ only superficially, as linguist William Labov (1973) has pointed out. For example, school teachers often criticize Black English because it apparently lacks the verb *to be*. Labov (1969) has shown, however, that the verb occurs in many places in Black English. Speakers of Standard English often contract *to be* to a simple *'s* in the present tense ("He's big" rather than "He is big"). Wherever Standard English can contract, Black English can, but does not always, omit the verb ("He big"). But omission in such instances is not an indication that Black English lacks an important part of English grammar. As you can see in Table 12.2, wherever it is impossible to contract *to be* in Standard English, it is impossible to delete *to be* in Black English. For example, in order to emphasize a statement, Standard English puts heavy stress on the verb ("He IS big"). In this situation, "is" also appears in Black English, and the Black form is the same as the Standard.

Given differences as subtle and superficial as these, it is difficult to believe that the acquisition or use of Black English has major consequences for cognitive development. However, the vocabulary, pronunciation, and style of Black English label the child

Figure 12.10 The enrichment program shown here is called Project SEED. It was designed to teach high-level mathematics to "disadvantaged" elementary-school students. It has been successful in raising the students' self-concept as well as their conceptual-reasoning skills and general intellectual performance.

240

Table 12.2 Examples of *be* in Two Dialects of American English

BLACK ENGLISH	STANDARD ENGLISH
Deletion	*Contraction*
She the first one.	She's the first one.
But he wild.	But he's wild.
You out of the game.	You're out of the game.
We on tape.	We're on tape.
He always complainin'.	He's always complaining.
He gon' try to get up.	He's gonna try to get up.
Nondeletion	*Nondeletion*
I was small.	I was small.
You got to be good.	You've got to be good.
Be cool, brothers!	Be cool, brothers!
He *is* a expert.	He *is* an expert.
Is he dead?	Is he dead?
Are you down?	Are you down?
Is that a shock or is it not?	Is that a shock or is it not?
I don't care what you are.	I don't care what you are.
Do you see where that person is?	Do you see where that person is?

Source: Adapted from William Labov, "Contraction, Deletion, and Inherent Variability of the English Copula," *Language,* 45 (1969), 715–762. The Black English examples are drawn from Labov (with some abbreviation), and the Standard English equivalents have been supplied for the purposes of this comparative table.

speaker in the eyes of the middle-class speaker of Standard English. Sometimes communication even breaks down. If a black child tells his teacher "Dey ain't like dat," the teacher assumes that the child has said "They aren't like that." Instead, the message that the child intended was "They didn't like that." When communication continues to break down, the teacher decides that, because the child's speech is unintelligible, he is unintelligent. A vicious circle is

Figure 12.11 Peers exert a strong and often decisive influence on both the development and maintenance of language and dialect differences.

set up. Because the teacher expects the child to do poorly, he fulfills her expectation and fails (Rosenthal and Jacobson, 1968).

One way to break the circle is to instruct teachers in Black English so that they can understand their students. (This suggestion, of course, applies equally well to middle-class teachers of Chicano or Puerto Rican students or any students who speak a different language or dialect in their homes.) However, speaking Black English does have major consequences on success in American society. Eventually these children will have to come to terms with the Standard dialect, because it is a necessary tool for social and economic advancement.

SUMMARY

1. During childhood, a youngster becomes essentially competent in understanding and using his complicated language. He continues to learn and to refine the meaning of words (semanticity), to master basic rules for making and understanding sentences (productivity), and to extend his ability to talk about things that are not present (displacement).

2. By observing young children's natural speech and by examining the types of omissions, errors, and well-formed utterances that they make, psycholinguists have found that a child attempts to simplify language by making it more systematic or regular than it actually is. In English, for example, this is likely to be shown when a child overregularizes the past tense of verbs ("breaked") and the plural forms of nouns ("foots").

3. The ways in which a child comprehends speech also indicates an increased knowledge of grammatical rules. Thus, over time, he appears to construct and discard a variety of provisional rules, and he may correctly interpret a certain kind of sentence, such as a passive one, at one age but not at another.

4. Children's ability to use an increasing number of rules or grammatical operations gives additional evidence of their grasp of linguistic structure. For example, a child's ability to form questions in English appears to move from using only one operation to using two or more.

5. Throughout childhood (and later), a child continues to actively test and expand his use and understanding of his native language. He structures and restructures the meanings of old and new words that are learned and continues to learn to use and to adjust his language socially for expressing emotions, telling stories, describing objects or actions, asking questions, and so forth.

6. The developmental effects of variations in linguistic environments on language skills are indicated by research on social class, special schooling, and variations in American dialects. Although such studies reveal no major differences among children in their acquisition of the basic grammar of their native language, observed social-class and ethnic differences in pronunciation, vocabulary, fluency, and other kinds of skills have often been mistakenly interpreted as indicating language "deficits" rather than language differences.

SUGGESTED READINGS

Bellugi, Ursula. "Learning the Language," *Psychology Today,* 4 (December 1970), 32–35+.

Brown, Roger W. *Words & Things.* New York: Free Press, 1958.

Fleming, Joyce D. "The State of the Apes: Field Report," *Psychology Today,* 3 (January 1974), 31–38+.

Hebb, D. O., W. E. Lambert, and G. Richard Tucker. "A DMZ in the Language War," *Psychology Today,* 6 (April 1973), 54–62.

Moore, Timothy E. (ed.). *Cognitive Development and the Acquisition of Language.* New York: Academic Press, 1973.

The early childhood years are typically a time of venturing forth to explore the social world and of forming new relationships.

13

PERSONALITY: ESTABLISHING SOCIAL INTERACTIONS

The years from two to six are the magic years of childhood. Probably at no other time do children experience so much that is new, exciting, and pleasurable. And at no other time in their lives do they confront so many challenges, conflicts, anxieties, and fears. During these formative years, children turn away from caretakers and expand their world to include other children, other adults, and an ever-widening environment.

Like all children, as they grow up, Matt and Susan become more and more like adults. By learning from their parents what is correct and valued, from imitating the acceptable behavior of their brothers and sisters, from observing other adults in person and on television, all children absorb a way of behaving that is similar to the behavior of those around them.

Because the people in one child's world are different from the people in another child's, each child has a different way of behaving. Sometimes the differences are great, as exist between a child raised in a primitive native culture in New Guinea and one raised in an urban American family. Sometimes the differences are relatively small, as between an American child raised by parents of French heritage and one raised by parents of English heritage in the same small town. But the differences can run deep and can extend to such modes of thinking as approaches to solving problems, the tendency to plan, and basic value systems.

In this chapter, as in Chapter 9, we will consider the development of the child's personality as a function of socialization. We will see how the child's contact with his parents, his peers, and his culture affects his personality. After discussing the general process of socialization, we will look at the process of identification, a major mechanism of socialization. We will examine sex-role development as both a significant aspect of personality development and an excellent example of the consequence of identification. Finally, we will consider the various sources of socialization—parents, peers, play, and culture—paying special attention to sex-role development and to various methods of socialization: reinforcement, punishment, and modeling.

THE PROCESS OF SOCIALIZATION

The process of psychologically growing into a society is called socialization. Socialization forces a person to become part of his society and to share in its culture. Socialization requires the individual to behave in culturally approved ways and to pay at least lip service to the dominant values, ideals, and motivations of the numerous groups of which he must become a part. The socialization process prescribes acceptable behavior for each role. It also discourages behavior that it deems undesirable. The outcome of socialization depends on one's cultural, familial, and physical environment.

Although what constitutes socialization differs across cultures, many psychologists believe that the same individual and social mechanisms operate in all children in all cultures. The four basic mechanisms are (1) the desire to obtain affection, regard, acceptance, and recognition; (2) the wish to avoid the unpleasant feelings that follow rejection or punishment; (3) the tendency to imitate the actions of others; and (4) the desire to be like specific people whom the child has grown to respect, admire, or love, a process called **identification.** By focusing on identification in the development of sex roles, the next section will demonstrate the methods by which each of the major mechanisms affects the growing child. Later in the chapter, discussions of parent, peer, and cultural influence will illustrate the other aspects of childhood socialization.

Much of a child's socialization comes about when he takes on the characteristics and matches the behavior of people that he admires. Sigmund Freud (1917) called this process identification and saw it as particularly important, especially in the development of moral standards, sex roles, and social attitudes.

Although identification has a central role in social-learning and cognitive approaches to personality development as well as in Freudian theory, each group ascribes a different role and function to the process. Freud believed that identification evolves from the child's psychosexual conflict with, and attachment to, his parents. As described in Figure 13.2, the child identifies with the parent of the same sex, thus undergoing structural changes in personality. The social-learning view presented by Walter Mischel (1968) sees identification as part of the general process of learning and, therefore, important if the child is to acquire complex behavior. Lawrence Kohlberg (1963), who along with Jean Piaget (1951) represents a cognitive-developmental perspective, presents identification as an aspect of a particular phase of cognitive development and considers it a way for the child to enhance his competence by sharing the skills of others.

Despite these differences in their views of the origin and functioning of identification, all three groups hold in common: (1) the central place of identification in the socialization process; (2) the child's development of new, complex behavior by

Figure 13.1 Children's storybooks frequently reinforce or teach adherence to social rules. For example, Tootle the Engine's attempts to "go off the beaten path" are greeted with disapproval, as signified by the red flags. Eventually he succumbs to social pressure and returns to the track. The message of the story is clear: Conform to certain prescribed social standards, and avoid doing that which runs counter to others' wishes.

Figure 13.2 *(opposite)* Summary descriptions of some major theoretical viewpoints on personality development during early childhood.

Sigmund Freud emphasizes the notion that early childhood is critical in the socialization of the individual. In his view of psychosexual stages of development, during early childhood, the child's sensual pleasure is focused on the genitals, and the child's fantasies about gratifying these desires results in sexual conflict with the parent of the opposite sex. According to Freud, the conflict is resolved when the child comes to identify with the parent of the same sex, which forms the basis for appropriate sex-role development. Whether the parent responds with warmth and affection to the child at this time, thereby indirectly satisfying the child's desires, affects his personality development. In addition, the same-sexed parent with whom the child has come to identify is the model for the values that will be part of the child's adult personality.

Alfred Adler, like Freud, places great importance on the early-childhood socialization of the child. According to Adler, if the family supports and encourages the child's striving to achieve competence (to overcome his feelings of inferiority), he will become able to reciprocate his parents' love and to enter into cooperative relationships with his peers. In this view, the child's concept of his sex role develops early, and, by implication, if the child receives disapproval from his parents instead of their support for his attempts to achieve independence, his personality development will be adversely affected.

Harry Stack Sullivan, unlike Freud and Adler, does not place special emphasis on the socialization process in early childhood. Instead, he emphasizes how parental reactions to the child's behavior influence the child's sense of self. Sullivan holds that the child's behavior patterns are modified by the demands of his environment. In this view, the most important factors in shaping the child's personality and self-concept are the responses of his peers and parents to his efforts to acquire appropriate sex-role behavior.

Erik Erikson concurs with Sullivan's view that peer and parental responses are important factors in socialization during early childhood. The development of appropriate sex-role behavior results from the child's identification with his same-sexed parent and assimilation of his parent's behavior into his own personal identity. In Erikson's theory, peer-group and parental support and encouragement of the child's initial attempts to acquire appropriate sex-role behavior can help the child achieve a positive self-image and a strong personal identity.

Erich Fromm, similar to Sullivan, sees the process of socialization as continuing throughout childhood and as consisting of society's shaping of the individual's character. As Fromm sees it, society's goal, as communicated through the parents, is presumably to make the child want to conform to the existing social system. Thus, sex-role development is shaped by the interplay between the child's innate potential and external social pressures. According to Fromm, the child will move toward self-fulfillment to the extent that society permits self-expression.

Walter Mischel, like Fromm and Sullivan, sees the process of socialization as continuous from infancy throughout childhood. From his interactions with his environment, the child learns increasingly complex behaviors as well as the consequences related to the performance of those behaviors. Thus, in Mischel's view, sex-role development involves the learning of particular behaviors as they are modified by the consequences of performing them. In general, parents and, later, peers are influential in shaping the child's behavior by providing the consequences for it.

matching the behavior of his parents; and (3) the particular significance of this mechanism in the development of sex roles.

SEX-ROLE DEVELOPMENT

Matt and Susan were not born male and female—psychologically. They became so. At a time when sex-role behavior is receiving close social attention, it is appropriate to discuss it as an example of socialization. Sex-role development is a complex process, with far-reaching implications for personality functioning. The development of sex differences also highlights important questions about the interaction of biological and social experience in the determination of behavior.

Freud thought that, around the age of five, a child becomes psychologically feminine or masculine by incorporating, through identification, the traits of the same-sexed parent. Recent research indicates, however, that children include their gender in their basic self-concept as soon as they begin to acquire language, around the age of two, and that this self-labeling occurs before there is any real understanding of the various traits and behaviors associated with being male or female (Money and Ehrhardt, 1972). Parents and others, of course, communicate to the child in a variety of ways that he is a boy or she is a girl. Lois Gould (1972) writes humorously about the consternation caused by a set of parents who would reveal only that their child was an X. How, others fretted, was this X to be treated?

An important personality task in early and middle childhood consists of learning the behaviors and qualities that society considers appropriate and desirable for a person of his or her gender. Cultures make many distinctions, both large and small, between the social roles of the sexes, and these **sex roles** encompass behaviors that have little to do with the reproductive and erotic differences dictated by biological equipment.

In their precise meanings, the terms *gender identity* and *sex role* are not entirely synonymous. However, for the purposes of this text, they will be used more or less interchangeably. One distinction that developmental psychologists can make is that there is wide variation in the degree to which a person who clearly identifies with his or her gender manifests stereotypically masculine or feminine traits. For example, a child may identify with a same-sexed parent who shows characteristics more traditionally associated with the other sex, such as a nurturant father or an achieving mother. Presumably, such a child still would have an unambivalent gender identity, but in addition his or her sex-role behavior would be less conventional than usual.

Children whose behavior deviates widely from their socially defined sex roles suffer rejection from adults and peers and, therefore, tend to encounter difficulties in personality development (Mussen, 1969). This problem more often arises with boys (who dread the epithet "sissy") than with girls (who usually regard "tomboy" as acceptable). Boys appear to have a greater need than girls to differentiate themselves from the opposite sex in order to gain a secure sense of gender identity, possibly because of their heavy contact with an important female (mother) during their formative years (Chodorow, 1971).

Sex-role behavior has typically received more attention than gender identity because of the importance society places on a child's behaving in socially appropriate ways, as defined by sex roles. Because cultural conceptions of what is masculine and what is feminine have important influences on the kind of person that a child will become, the next section will look more closely at the cultural bases of sex-role development.

Cultural Bases

Before a child even learns that there are two sexes, parents begin a training program (pink for girls, blue for boys) devoted to having her or him acquire the proper gender identity and learn the behaviors, attitudes, and feelings that fit the social role of her or his sex. Every culture establishes acceptable and unac-

Figure 13.3 Learning "appropriate" sex-role behavior begins almost at birth. The ways others respond to children, the toys they are given, the expectations held of them, the models they pattern their behavior after, and the instructions, rewards, and punishments they receive for acceptable sex-role behavior all contribute to this learning process.

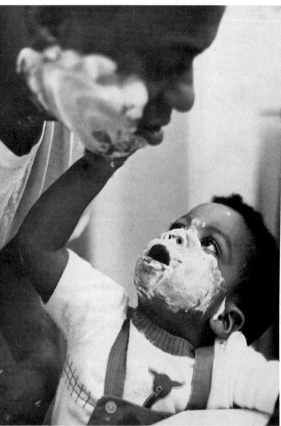

ceptable patterns of behavior and psychological standards for the sexes, and these sex-role standards are imposed at an early age (Schell and Silber, 1968).

Sex roles are inevitably interwoven with the status that society attaches to each role. Male dominance was one of the earliest bases of discrimination among human beings, presumably because survival among hunting and gathering tribes depended on physical strength and the ability to move about unencumbered by childbearing and nursing. Male children have always been valued, and many cultures regularly practiced infanticide on excess female babies (de Mause, 1974). The superiority of the male sex role has been perpetuated by incorporating it into the customs, laws, and socialization practices of successive generations.

A cross-cultural survey of primitive societies by Herbert Barry, Margaret Bacon, and Irvin Child (1957) disclosed that the more its economy requires physical strength, the more strongly a society emphasizes sex differences in socialization. In most societies, whether ancient, primitive, or modern, the prestige of the task determines whether it is assigned to males or to females. Women have generally been treated as if they were members of a minority group, and there are many parallels between traditional treatment of women and the treatment of blacks in American society.

Children learn these status differences early. While they are growing up, both sexes generally prefer the male role with its freedom, authority, and power (J. Kagan, 1964). Studies have shown that children in our society think men are very important and able to do whatever they like. Men are the bosses, they have the most money, they get the most comfortable chairs, and they get angry a lot. Children also describe men as being more fun than mothers and as having better ideas.

As we will see in more detail in discussing adolescence, as a boy grows, he discovers that society has defined his vocational role as primary and his role as spouse and parent as secondary; the reverse is true for a girl. To fulfill these social roles, boys are likely to be reared to achieve and girls are likely to be reared to conform. Thus, as soon as children enter early childhood, almost all societies foster achievement and self-reliance in boys and obedience, nurturance, and responsibility in girls (D'Andrade, 1966). One boy, asked by Ruth Hartley (1960) what boys have to know and should be able to do, answered:

They should know what girls don't know—how to climb, how to make a fire, how to carry things; they should have

more ability than girls; they need to know how to stay out of trouble; they need to know arithmetic and spelling more than girls do.

The difference between male and female roles goes beyond actual sex-role behavior; it extends into sex-role stereotypes—simplified, fixed concepts about the behaviors and traits typical of each sex. Learning their society's stereotypes is a major developmental task for young children. Lawrence Kohlberg (1966) has found that, by the time they are five or six, children have clearly sex-typed the virtues. A girl comes to perceive feminine competence and status as based on being attractive and nice rather than on being powerful, aggressive, or fearless. In a similar way, Jerome Kagan (1964) has described the social stereotypes of males and females in contemporary American culture:

In sum, females are supposed to inhibit aggression and open display of sexual urges, to be passive with men, to be nurturant to others, to cultivate attractiveness, and to

Figure 13.4 Environmental circumstances and age and sex of the participants are three of the factors that often influence an observer's labeling of a particular behavior as either assertive or aggressive.

maintain an affective, socially poised, and friendly posture with others. Males are urged to be aggressive in face of attack, independent in problem situations, sexually aggressive, in control of regressive urges, and suppressive of strong emotions, especially anxiety. (page 143)

In studying these sex-role stereotypes, psychologists have taken a particular interest in the development of two sex-related traits—aggression and dependence.

Assertion and Aggression

Children around the world bicker, toss epithets, shove, kick, hit, fight, and break things. All cultures have rules for socializing aggressive behavior, for teaching youngsters the dos and don'ts of managing their feelings of hostility and anger. These feelings arise in situations that pose a personal threat by appearing either to jeopardize an individual's physical well-being or to interfere with values and goals that he believes are important. The immediate emotional response is anger at the threatening person or object;

the adaptive response involves taking effective action to avert the threat.

Unfortunately, the concepts of assertiveness and aggressiveness become tangled in our thinking. This is particularly true with respect to competition and strivings for success. A person tends to describe behavior in himself as assertive that he would label aggressive in anyone else. And because this culture values gentleness in women, an assertive girl is likely to be called aggressive; her behavior violates the female sex-role stereotype. One way to avoid this subjective dilemma is to define **assertiveness** as verbal or physical behavior that is appropriate and that injures no one and **aggressiveness** as verbal or physical behavior that is inappropriate or harms someone. The confusion between the terms can have disastrous consequences. An environment that seeks to stamp out all aggressive behavior in children may also inhibit legitimate self-assertion. In the healthy socialization of aggression, the child learns effective

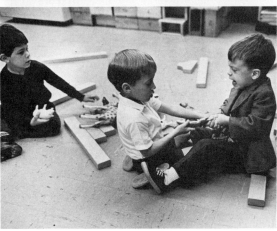

ways to "stand up" for himself without injuring others.

As a child grows and becomes more independent, he is likely to find that his new assertive behavior meets increased parental demands and restrictions. This situation leads many developmental psychologists to agree that the development of assertiveness needs serious study. However, past research has been devoted to understanding aggression. This emphasis is in part the result of the social consequences of aggression and in part the result of Freud's early concern with it. Whereas the rest of this section will focus on male and female differences in aggression, the importance of assertiveness should be kept firmly in mind.

There is a good deal of evidence that in this society it is difficult for females to be either assertive or aggressive. Several studies (Buss and Brock, 1963; Cosentino and Heilbrun, 1964) have found more anxiety and conflict about aggression in females than in males. Women who feel angry tend to feel guilty about it and tend to cope in ineffectual ways, with indirect displays of hostility, with sudden hostile outbursts, or simply by avoiding the situation.

Data gathered by developmental psychologists are consistent with the stereotyping of aggressive behavior as appropriate only for boys (Maccoby and Jacklin, 1975). In a study that followed eighty-nine children from early childhood to young adulthood, Jerome Kagan and Howard Moss (1962) found that the amount of aggressive behavior in males remained stable over the years but that aggressive behavior declined in females. Our society tolerates aggressive behavior in boys, so the aggression they show in early childhood is not likely to be the target of systematic efforts toward change.

Other investigators have found that boys as young as two are more physically aggressive and more negativistic than girls. In addition, when children and adults are asked to describe their fantasies and dreams or to rate their own behavior, boys and men report more physical aggressiveness than girls and women do (Mischel, 1968).

The consistency of the finding that males are, on the average, more physically aggressive than females suggests possible biological contributions to such behavior. By now, however, it should be clear that the developing child's behavior is a product of continuous interaction between constitutional factors and the child's own social environment. The question is whether any constitutional factors that are linked with sex might predispose boys toward physical aggressiveness. Seymour Feshbach (1970) has suggested that males may not be predisposed to aggressiveness but that their greater physical strength and more vigorous motor impulses may lead to different social experiences. For example, boys have greater success than girls in getting what they want by hitting. Also, parents more often frustrate a boy's impulsive acts, thereby stimulating his aggressive reactions.

Regardless of any predisposing constitutional factors there may be toward acquiring aggressive behavior, the social environment can overwhelmingly influence aggressiveness in one direction or the other. Whereas physical aggressiveness is the hallmark of masculinity in many cultures (for example, in the warrior), patterns of aggression for each sex vary widely from one culture to another (B. Whiting, 1963). The problem comes down to the relative ease with which children of each sex can learn whatever sex-role behavior their culture values and considers appropriate. Thus, facilitating or inhibiting aggression to the desired level, as well as channeling it into the desired forms, may require socializing agents that devote more effort to children of one sex than to the other.

As Feshbach (1970) and others have indicated, the form of aggression, which is influenced by society, is important in considering the differences in aggressive behavior between males and females. A variety of studies have demonstrated that, from nursery school on, boys are likely to express aggression in physical ways, whereas girls are likely to scold or argue or to use indirect forms of aggression, such as gossip, a concerted resistance to demands, and subtle forms of rejection. Girls who are overtly aggressive tend to be rejected by their peers (E. Green, 1933) and disliked by their teachers (Levitin and Chananie, 1972). Boys are not less likely than girls to meet disapproval for such overt aggression, but, because they are stronger and more active, their aggressive attempts are more likely to be successful.

Dependence and Independence

As you will recall, Chapter 9 described the process of attachment in infancy, pointing out that an infant attaches himself to one or more persons and that he attends to them, seeks attention from them, derives pleasure from interacting with them, shows distress when separated from them, and seeks physical contact with them in strange or threatening situations. Such manifestations of attachment undergo drastic changes as the young child ventures into the world of

playmates and other adults. By the time he is three or four, his attachment has evolved into the somewhat similar but less intense behavior that psychologists have described as **dependence.**

Most developmental psychologists distinguish between two kinds of dependence: emotional, referring to the child's relations with people; and instrumental, referring to the child's relations with the environment. In **emotional dependence,** the child's aims are affection and support; he finds people rewarding and satisfying in themselves. In **instrumental dependence,** a child seeks help and comfort as a means to other ends, as when he asks an adult to help him perform a task or to aid him in a conflict with a playmate.

Several factors influence the type and degree of dependence shown by a young child. When he finds himself in a situation that evokes anxiety or stress, he is likely to show increased emotional dependence. And when a child is deprived of social contact, particularly with adults, he is also likely to behave in ways that indicate increased emotional dependence (Hartup, 1964b).

In early childhood, there is a high correlation between emotional and instrumental dependence, but as the child gets older they become less related. Thus, a four- or five-year-old who shows extreme instrumental dependence may show little emotional dependence (Emmerich, 1966).

By the time boys and girls are six or seven, they show relatively stable and well-defined differences in

Figure 13.5 Increased expression of independent behavior often results in situations in which (*top*) the child needs affection and support from adults (emotional dependence) or (*bottom*) needs their help in accomplishing a task (instrumental dependence).

dependence (Mischel, 1970). During this period, boys tend to check with their mothers less often and to become more independent, exploratory, and assertive. Girls, on the other hand, generally continue to check more frequently with their mothers, to be less assertive and more dependent, and to stay in secure surroundings. The stable pattern of dependence in girls generally continues into adulthood, probably because the cultural sex-role stereotype supports such behavior in women.

However, sex-role stereotypes are undergoing continued change in contemporary American society. Traditional conceptions of masculine and feminine behavior are becoming more fluid, and more and more husbands and wives share career, housekeeping, and child-care roles. Such parents are less likely than conventional parents to exhibit rigid sex-role differences and are less likely to expect them from their children.

PARENT-CHILD RELATIONS

The goals, values, and life style of parents have a great effect on the growing child, whether that effect be admiration and imitation or alienation and rejection. As the earliest and most durable source of socialization, a child's parents are the first people with whom he identifies, and they remain the strongest influence in his sex-role development. This overwhelming importance has led developmental psychologists to take an intense interest in parent-child interactions.

Traditionally, parent-child interactions have been studied in terms of child-rearing practices. This has involved measuring certain aspects of parental behavior (such as permissiveness or hostility) and certain aspects of child behavior (such as aggression or dependence) and then seeing if any of those aspects of parent and child behavior are correlated. Some studies indicate that highly permissive parents have extremely independent children (Winder and Rau, 1962). Restrictive parents, on the other hand, tend to have highly dependent children.

Frequently, however, it appears that various aspects of child rearing interact in other ways. Parental permissiveness, for example, may lead to high levels of aggression in a hostile family situation but to low levels of aggression in a warm, nurturant home environment (Sears, 1961). The same kind of parental behavior also appears to have different effects on boys and girls. Thus, parental rejection or hostility appears to increase dependence in boys (H. Smith, 1958), but maternal hostility is associated with increased independence in girls (J. Kagan and Moss, 1962).

Over the years, and partly as a result of these mixed findings, most developmental psychologists have become increasingly skeptical about studying parent-child interactions through child-rearing practices. Among other difficulties, it is apparent that the particular results from a study of child-rearing practices depend on what group of families is studied, how the investigators define factors such as aggression or dependence, and how they measure them. In addition, other research indicates that the behavior of parents is likely to change over the years (J. Kagan and Moss, 1962). That is, a parent who is permissive with a three-year-old may be restrictive by the time that the child begins school. And a parent who is aloof and cold to a young child may be warm and nurturant when that same child reaches adolescence.

Because developmental psychologists want to identify more precisely the ways that parents serve as influential agents in the growing child's socialization, more detailed approaches to studying parent-child interactions have centered on such factors as the significant role of parents in reinforcing and punishing a child's behavior (Patterson, 1972). For example, if Matt is highly aggressive, an examination is made of the situations in which his aggression takes place (such as when playing with his sister Susan or at the dinner table) and what happens after he takes the aggressive action (such as Matt gets to play his favorite game, or he does not have to eat spinach, or he is sent to his room).

Based on the findings of such studies of particular interactions between parents and children, and between adults and children in general, it is clear that the way that an adult responds to a child's behavior can have a potent effect. For example, Paul Brown and Rogers Elliott (1965) found that, when nursery-school teachers ignored boys' physical and verbal aggression and at the same time paid attention to and praised their cooperative acts, the boys' aggression dramatically decreased. Then the teachers stopped reinforcing cooperative acts. Verbal aggression among the boys remained low, but physical aggression increased. However, as soon as the teachers went back to ignoring aggression and praising cooperation, physical aggression again decreased.

As might be expected, similar analyses of sex-role development indicate that boys and girls are likely to be reinforced or punished differently for the same kind of behavior. For example, boys are likely to be reinforced for aggressive acts and punished for indications of dependence. Girls, in contrast, are likely to be punished for aggressive acts but reinforced for showing dependence.

Although punishment will be discussed further in Chapter 16, the topic requires general comment here as well. The easiest and most common way of getting a child not to think or act in certain ways is to punish him. As most parents find, punishment works and is often effective in controlling a child's behavior. However, punishment also produces undesirable results, particularly when the punishment is physical. When parents use physical punishment on a child, the child is likely to respond with fear or more anger, negative feelings that he may come to associate with his parents or the situation. In addition, the parent who hits his child is serving as a model of physical aggression. He demonstrates to the child that, when one disapproves of another person's behavior, the appropriate way to react is to hit him.

PEER INFLUENCE

As Chapter 9 followed Susan through her first two years, it was pointed out that an infant interacts primarily with members of her own family. As Susan grows and can move about more easily, other people, especially other children, begin to enter her life. She begins to play outdoors more often, and she encounters other children in her neighborhood. She may go to a nursery school or a day-care center, where she meets children from other neighborhoods. All these trends change Susan's world from one that is populated almost entirely by giants to one in which an ever greater number of people are near her own size and share her interests. During these early childhood years, the child first has a real peer group, and the importance of that group steadily increases.

Much of what young children learn about their world they learn from other children, and most of what they learn, from whatever source, they practice and rehearse within the peer group. Thus, the peer group is the place where children perfect the roles that they will play in later years. During early childhood, a child's dependence on adults often decreases while dependence on peers (such as in seeking approval or asking for help) often increases. In fact, well-adjusted youngsters tend to have a comfortable reliance on their peers (Emmerich, 1966).

Peer Influence in Monkeys

The role of peers as agents of socialization is not uniquely human. Students of primate behavior are generally convinced, both from laboratory studies and from studies conducted in the wild, that early contact with peers is necessary for the normal development of mammals. In fact, it is almost impossible to conceive of socialization among rhesus monkeys or chimpanzees in the absence of peer interaction. Because of this similarity across species, primate social interaction can provide insights that help clarify the role of peers in the socialization of the human child.

In many primate species, young animals spend much of their time in a play group consisting of other infants and juveniles (K. Hall, 1968; Kummer, 1968). Within this group, young primates practice the

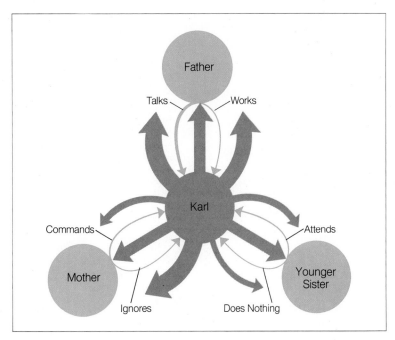

Figure 13.6 A representation of some key interactions between a child exhibiting a high frequency of aggressive behaviors and other members of his family. The arrows between individuals represent behavioral interactions that are likely to follow each other, with more frequently occurring behaviors represented by thicker arrows. Karl whines, yells, and disapproves quite frequently, whereas the responses of various family members differ both in nature and frequency. The illustration also shows that some responses increase Karl's aggressive behaviors more than others. (Adapted from Patterson, 1971)

behaviors that they will be expected to perform as adults. It is here that primates perfect the intricate patterns of facial gestures and social threat. And it is here, by approach and mounting during play, that young primates learn adult sexual behavior. Rough-and-tumble play within the peer group also develops the aggressiveness that primates use both to maintain status and to defend the group against predators.

Harry and Margaret Harlow (1969) reviewed a series of laboratory studies documenting the importance of peers as socialization forces in primates. As described in Chapter 9, the Harlows and their associates raised some infant monkeys with surrogate mothers; other infants were raised in total isolation from other members of their species. These young monkeys never learned to play the usual monkey games; they never had the opportunity to acquire the social roles that they would need in later life. After six to twelve months of such isolation, these monkeys found it almost impossible to fit within a group when, as adolescents, they were introduced to others of their kind. They tended to remain isolated from the rest of the group; they rarely engaged in social play; and when they did, it was with other isolates. Even individual play was infrequent among the twelve-month isolates.

Such isolated monkeys encountered great difficulties when they became sexually mature. Males did not know how to approach young females (or even that it was females that they should approach), and the females did not know how to entice and yield to the males. Both males and females showed episodes of abnormal aggression. For example, they attacked and bit young monkeys, which normally reared animals almost never do. They also launched attacks against the largest and most dominant adult males, an extraordinarily maladaptive action for an adolescent.

Clearly, these monkeys had severe social problems. To try to pinpoint the cause of these problems, researchers raised more monkeys, but each group was raised in a different manner. Some monkeys spent the first few months of their lives with their mothers but had no contact with any other monkeys. Another group of monkeys spent the first few months of life with other monkey infants. The infants raised with only their mothers behaved in a far less abnormal manner than did the monkeys raised in isolation. They were, however, less affectionate with peers and more aggressive than monkeys raised in a normal manner. Furthermore, the longer the baby monkeys were isolated with their mothers, the more abnormal their behavior.

Researchers had suspected that the peer-raised animals would show severe social problems, and for the first several days it appeared that their suspicions were correct. The infants simply clung together in a "choo-choo" pattern, as shown in Figure 13.7. This pattern soon broke up, however, and the monkeys established normal play with strange monkeys. The later development of peer-raised monkeys seemed almost completely normal. They showed affection and played normally, and they demonstrated only

normal aggression. There was a tendency for these monkeys to show closer ties with their early companions than with other monkeys, but even this difference was slight.

In view of the importance usually assigned to parents (see Chapter 9) in the rearing of monkey and human infants, these results are surprising. They seem to indicate that, at least among rhesus monkeys, parents may be less important in some respects than the peer group as a socializing agent.

Peer Reinforcement

One important way in which children influence each other is through actions that support or encourage behavior. That is, if one child supports another child's behavior, his approval will make it more likely that the first child's behavior will occur again. Approval, affection, and attention usually are encouraging social behaviors. But such behavior does not always reinforce an action, and many other social acts also have reinforcing effects. In addition, the kinds of events that reinforce an activity such as aggression differ from those that reinforce an activity such as sharing. And because of differences in his past experience, one child may respond to behavior that has little or no effect on another child. Nevertheless, many actions, such as praise and affection, act as encouragement for nearly everyone in a wide variety of situations.

These social reinforcers seem to be strongly related to popularity within the peer group. Popular young-

sters approach others in a friendly manner and are generous with praise and approval. For example, Rosalind Charlesworth and Willard Hartup (1967) found that young children who frequently were supportive of other children tended to distribute their approval among nearly all their peers. This study also found a strong positive correlation between the amount of reinforcement a child gave and the amount he received.

On the other hand, in another study Hartup (1964a) found that young children performed better at simple tasks when they disliked another child than when they liked him. Hartup used a marble-dropping task to assess reinforcement among four- and five-year-old children. A child picked up marbles one at a time from a bin and dropped them through holes into a container. Periodically, either the child's best friend or another child that he disliked expressed approval. During the short session, a child dropped marbles faster when the disliked child approved his performance than when his friend approved.

The effectiveness of approval from a disliked child may have something to do with expectations. Joanne Floyd (1965) found that children who received unexpectedly large or small rewards in a sharing task changed their patterns of sharing more radically than children who got shared rewards that they had more or less expected. Thus, it may be that children expect their friends to approve their actions, so that a friend's behavior merely meets the expectation. However, a child may expect disliked children to disapprove of

Figure 13.7 (opposite) The role of peer influences in socialization is depicted in the play behavior of normal young children and monkeys. However, the Harlows found in their studies that, if monkeys are raised from birth only with peers and are isolated from adult interaction, some strange, if only temporary, patterns of behavior may occur, such as (right) the "choo-choo" train relationship shown here.

his actions, so that approval from such children exceeds expectations and has a more powerful influence.

A child's playmates can also affect his aggressiveness. Gerald Patterson, Richard Littman, and William Bricker (1967) describe just how this process works in a nursery school. These investigators observed children and recorded their reactions to aggression. When attacked, 97 percent of the children either became passive, cried, assumed a defensive posture, told the teacher, retrieved their property, or retaliated with an aggressive act of their own. In other words, after nearly every instance of aggressive attack, a child reacted in a way that was either potentially reinforcing or punishing. When a physical attack was followed by passiveness, crying, or defensiveness, the young attacker soon tended to act aggressively against his original victim. Counteraggression, on the other hand, was often followed by changes in the attacker's behavior. He was likely either to act in a

changed manner toward his former victim, to pick a different victim, or both.

Other studies of how children encourage one another's behavior have shown that direct manipulation can change the way that children interact in the schoolroom. For example, Robert Wahler (1967) observed a group of nursery-school children and selected five whose behavior was related in some way to encouragement from their peers. He then enlisted the aid of the children's friends. Wahler asked the friends of children whose behavior was tied closely to peer reinforcement to decrease the attention that they paid their friend when he acted in a certain way. He asked the friends of the children whose behavior was less closely linked to other children's support to increase their attention and approval. Within a few days, the selected behavior dropped among the first group of children and increased among the second group. When Wahler told the children's friends to resume their usual treatment, the five children went

Figure 13.8 Peers provide one another with numerous opportunities for comparison and for learning through observation and imitation.

Figure 13.9 (*opposite*) Modeling and imitation of aggression. Frames in the top row are from experiments in which Bandura and his associates showed children a film of adult models being aggressive toward a Bobo doll. The frames in the bottom two rows show examples of the behavior of two children who watched the film and were then given a chance to play with the same toys. Children generally imitated the behavior they had observed and were even more likely to do so if the adult in the original film was rewarded for her aggressive acts.

back to behaving just as they had before the experiment began. Studies such as this one indicate that, by remaining alert to established patterns of peer reinforcement, parents and teachers can often use the peer group to help solve its own problems.

Peer Modeling

Reinforcement is not the only way in which children influence one another's behavior; **modeling** is also powerful. Seeing another child behave in a certain way can affect a child's behavior for at least three different reasons (Bandura, 1969b). First, the watching child may learn how to do something new that he previously either could not do (such as working a puzzle) or would not have thought of doing (such as riding a bicycle with "no hands"). Second, a child may learn what happens when one acts in a certain way. He may note that aggression gets other children into trouble or that disobeying does not always bring punishment. As a result of this knowledge, his own behavior may change. Third, a model may suggest how a child can behave in a strange situation. For example, a child may stand around nervously at a birthday party until another child begins throwing cake. Immediately, he and the other children join in the new tribal ritual.

Experiments by Albert Bandura, Dorothea Ross, and Sheila Ross (1963) and by David Hicks (1965) provide a good illustration of modeling. In these experiments (as illustrated in Figure 13.9), they showed a group of young children a film in which a model struck a large rubber doll with a mallet, sat on the doll, and screamed at it. When the children who had seen the film were given the same kind of doll and a mallet, they proceeded to act aggressively toward the doll, copying a number of the filmed model's actions.

A model can also establish a situation in which his peers are likely to behave in a certain way. For example, Thomas Wolf (1972) told young boys that

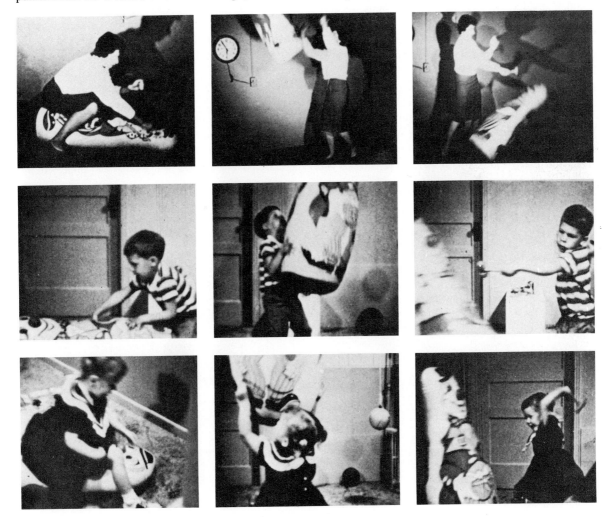

they were not to play with a particularly attractive toy in the experimental room. Later, some boys heard another boy say that he expected most children would obey and would not play with the toy. Other boys heard a peer say that most children would disobey. The children who heard the model say that he expected disobedience disobeyed more often. Apparently, the model's statement made the attractive option of playing with the toy seem the appropriate thing to do.

Additional research has shown that the pleasant or unpleasant consequences received by a model affect the watching child as if he had received those consequences himself. If the model is reinforced, the child is more likely to imitate his behavior (B. Clark, 1965), whereas when the model is punished, the child is less likely to imitate him (R. Walters, Parke, and Cane, 1965). Suppose that one child sees another grab a third child's toy. If the aggressive child gets to keep his booty, the watching child is likely to grab another child's property. If, however, the grabber is punished and made to return the toy, the watching child is unlikely to imitate his action.

Peer models can influence positive behavior as well as aggression and disobedience. For example, Willard Hartup and Brian Coates (1967) asked four- and five-year-old children to watch one of their classmates complete a series of ten maze-drawing problems. Between problems, the model received a number of tiny plastic trinkets, which he divided between himself and a mythical child from another class. The model was actually the experimenter's confederate and had been coached to give away most of his trinkets to the "other child." Thus, the model appeared to be highly altruistic. After the model had left the room, the experimenter asked the other children to complete the same maze-drawing task. They also received trinkets and were given an opportunity to divide them with the "other child." A control group of children, who had not seen the model, were also given the same task, trinkets, and instructions. As Figure 13.10 shows, the children who had watched the altruistic model gave away many more trinkets than children in the control group did. This study provides straightforward evidence that, by the time a child is four or five, peer models can influence a socially approved activity such as sharing.

Just as peer encouragement is not always effective, so the effectiveness of a peer model varies. The Hartup and Coates study of altruism shows that two factors seem to bear upon the effectiveness of a model. In that study, a child's tendency to copy a model was related to the nature of his previous interaction with the model and the nature of his interactions with the entire peer group. For example, popular children more often imitated a child who had previously reinforced them than a child who had never given them attention or approval. On the other hand, unpopular children seemed readier to imitate a child who had never paid them any attention than a child who had reinforced them. Recall that popular children are generous with praise and approval and

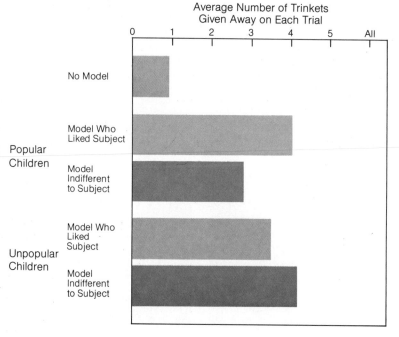

Figure 13.10 The results of Hartup and Coates' study of children's altruistic behavior. Children had six trinkets that they could give away in each trial. In all four of the experimental conditions, children saw an altruistic model, and in each case they shared more trinkets in comparison to the children in the control group, who saw no model. In addition, popular children gave away more trinkets when the model they saw was a child who usually reinforced them, whereas unpopular children tended to give away more trinkets when the model they saw was a child who had never before shown them attention or approval. (After Hartup and Coates, 1967)

get a good deal of it themselves, whereas unpopular children are rarely reinforced.

Using slightly older children, Hicks (1971) demonstrated that the kind of behavior modeled also affects the likelihood of imitation. Young girls watched a model and judged a number of behaviors as either "awful" or "nice." Two months later the girls imitated those behaviors that they had rated "nice" much more frequently than those that they had rated "awful." Earlier, it was pointed out that modeling can act as a signal of the appropriateness of a response. Although it seems evident that modeling does establish the appropriateness of an action when a child is unsure about what others expect, Hicks's results indicate that children continue to regard some behavior as inappropriate despite seeing a peer model it and that they are unlikely to imitate such behavior. It also appears that imitation is most likely to occur when the modeled actions are so distinctive that children are unlikely to confuse them with other behavior.

Thus far, we have seen that both adults and peers can serve as models, which might lead one to wonder which model a child is likely to follow. Hartup (1964b) has noted that children who imitate models tend to do so whether the model is an adult or another child. However, Hicks (1965) has noted that peer models are more effective than adult models in showing new kinds of aggressive acts to young children. In any case, models do exert a powerful effect on young children and can change their behavior in many ways.

FUNCTIONS OF PLAY

As was shown in Chapter 9, the child's play, in addition to being fun, serves a variety of functions: exploring the world, trying alternative roles, and testing of new skills. As children enter the third year, their play takes on a more reciprocal quality (see Figure 13.11), in which the child is more attuned to the feelings and responses of others. It also incorporates the child's increasing ability to symbolize and imagine, so that play may include elements that are not present ("Pretend like we have horses") or material that is not factual ("You be the mommy").

Jean Piaget (1951) describes symbolic, imaginative play as essentially egocentric and as transforming the real into the desired. He writes:

In most cases, indeed, the doll only serves as an opportunity for the child to re-live symbolically her own life in order to assimilate more easily its various aspects as well as to resolve daily conflicts and realise unsatisfied desires. (page 107)

Using his increasing role-taking ability, the young child engages in a great deal of fantasy play that intermingles elements from the roles children see enacted around them ("I'm Daddy getting the baby dressed for bed"), from television ("We're on a ship, and there are sharks all around us"), and from seemingly pure fantasy ("This is the time I learned how to fly"). Any available prop seems to generate a string of associations, which the child weaves into play that is sometimes infinitely flexible ("We can all walk on water") and sometimes extremely rigid

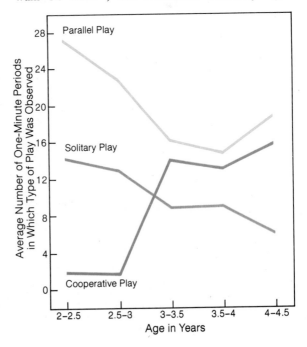

Figure 13.11 With increasing age and continued cognitive-social development, there are related changes in types of play. For example, solitary and parallel play decrease while cooperative play increases. (Adapted from Parten, 1932–1933)

("You can't be a fireman because you don't have a hat on").

The play of young children builds on all the elements found in the toddler's play. As children practice a variety of roles and deal with the inevitable conflicts that arise, their egocentrism decreases and their skill in role-taking increases. A child begins to understand the effects of his actions on others and to see his playmates as individuals, not just as objects of play. Because of this new ability to differentiate among people, a child's specific attachments increase during early childhood. He forms friendships that may be remarkably durable. At nursery school, a child often seeks out his preferred playmates as soon as he arrives and remains near them all day.

For example, Catherine Garvey and Robert Hogan (1973) compared the play of toddlers and young children. They found that young children are mutually responsive and adapt their words and actions to those of their playmates. On the other hand, toddlers engage in parallel play and make little effort to adapt to their playmates (see Figure 13.11). Such an advance is a clear indication of the young child's socialization.

The same influences in socialization—reinforcement, punishment, and modeling—that operate in relations with parents and peers affect the young child's play. But play differs in that here the child has the opportunity to create situations in which these socializing influences can operate.

Through play, the child often tests different behavior without actually experiencing the dangers that the real action might hold, and he directly or indirectly enjoys its positive results. He can assume various roles and discover what happens to a person who engages in that behavior. For example, Matt can play the "bad guy" without being punished, or he can play the "good guy" and enjoy the pleasure of helping someone. A child can test skills in play that life might not allow him to test in reality. Thus,

driving a car, riding a horse, and cooking a meal can all be practiced by a child of three or four.

During social play, a child also can try out various kinds of peer interactions by creating rules for games or by developing a way to cooperate or share. This interaction gives him the opportunity to experience the results of certain social behavior within a limited setting. Finally, a child can find out how certain consequences "feel" by administering to himself the consequences of his behavior. For example, a young child may slap his own hand and tell himself "no-no" when he spills his mud pie.

Modeling is incorporated into play in much the same way as reinforcement and punishment. An imaginary superhero can provide a model of generosity and helping. A child can learn new skills, such as building a self-supporting arch with blocks, by watching a more skillful playmate. Watching other children cooperate at play through sharing a set of cooking pots and pans may teach a child these

Figure 13.12 As a valuable component of socialization, play provides young children with opportunities for testing and further developing a wide variety of physical, social, and cognitive skills.

positive skills. Finally, play with dolls can provide self-generated modeling. As he plays, the child creates and then observes parent-child interactions. When he has the daddy doll spank the child doll for getting out of bed, a child provides himself with a form of modeling, even though he himself manipulated the doll's behavior.

SUBCULTURES AND PERSONALITY

The values adhered to by a child's parents vary depending on the particular culture that they belong to. The United States is not a homogeneous population with one set of values and standards but rather a variety of subcultures, which often vary greatly in structure and values. These subcultures may result from regional, religious, racial, ethnic, or economic differences. As we will also see in our discussion of adolescence, the way in which important personality and social behaviors such as aggression, sex-role development, dependence, and competitiveness are handled varies greatly within different groups (R. Hess, 1970).

The socialization of different values and personality characteristics may come about in two ways. First, different values are adhered to in separate cultures, so that the child is reinforced for different behavior. Thus, a black urban family may reinforce assertiveness more than a rural Chicano family does. Structural differences in the socializing unit may also influence socialization. Thus, a child whose father is absent learns different things from what the child whose father is present learns. A variety of structural considerations may vary across subcultures: Lower-middle-class mothers are more likely to work than extremely wealthy mothers; families in lower socioeconomic groups spend more time watching television; rural families are more likely than urban families to have grandparents, aunts, or uncles in the household; Catholic families are likely to have more children than Jewish families. Whereas subcultures may subscribe equally to independence or helpfulness, their structural differences may lead them to treat such behavior differently.

The values, child-rearing methods, and life styles of families in various subcultures differ as does their access to various resources and financial security. As Melvin Kohn (1963) puts it:

Members of different social classes, by virtue of enjoying (or suffering) different conditions of life, come to see the world differently—to develop different conceptions of social reality, different aspirations and hopes and fears, different conceptions of the desirable. (page 471)

What adults consider desirable, probable, and possible in life will determine the qualities that they instill in their children. Parents in one social class will emphasize one quality in their children while neglecting another, and the reverse may be true in another social class. For example, as we will see in more detail in discussing adolescence, lower socioeconomic class parents may value their child's overt conformity to the prescriptions and proscriptions of society, whereas middle-class parents may stress the development of self-direction in their child. In one social class, these lessons may be taught casually and with little pressure, but another social class may teach them intensely and under close guard (R. Hess, 1970).

Socioeconomic status has also been found to affect a number of social behaviors. For example, most parents of lower socioeconomic status are more likely than parents of middle-class status to use physical punishment and ridicule with their children (Bayley and Schaefer, 1960). On the other hand, middle-class parents are more likely than lower-class parents to emphasize independence in early childhood, expect excellence in school performance, and believe in the possibility of success (Rosen, 1956).

Ethnic differences may also lead to the stressing of different values. Spencer Kagan and Millard Madsen (1971) studied children from Mexican, Mexican-American, and Anglo-American backgrounds to determine the extent to which each group socialized cooperation and competition. Pairs of children played a game that offered a choice of cooperation or competition. Kagan and Madsen found two important differences: Four- and five-year-olds were more cooperative than seven-, eight-, or nine-year-olds; and rural Mexican children were most likely to cooperate in order to win a game, Mexican-Americans were next most cooperative, and urban Anglo-Americans, most competitive. Kagan and Madsen interpreted these results as showing that different subcultures have different norms of behavior and that the predominant Anglo-American orientation is competition.

Another important difference that has been found among subcultures regards **locus of control.** A person with an internal locus of control has a general expectation that he is in control of his own life and that he controls his own fate. A person with an external locus of control has a general expectation that his fate is controlled by forces outside him. Mark

Figure 13.13 Subcultural differences in socialization result in wide and enduring differences in most aspects of children's development.

Stephens and Pamela Delys (1973) found that, by the time children entered nursery school, differences in locus of control appeared between socioeconomic classes. Middle-class children were more likely to feel internally controlled, whereas lower-class children were more likely to feel externally controlled.

Thus, differences in the behavior of children may be the result of both adherence to a subcultural norm and structural factors, such as access to various culturally enriching situations that make the likelihood of success higher. Whereas personality and social behavior are largely learned, the course of that learning and, therefore, the development of personality and behavior patterns may be radically different from family to family.

SUMMARY

1. The process of psychologically growing into a society is called socialization. A major mechanism in socialization and personality development is identification, through which a child takes on characteristics, values, and attitudes of people he admires.

2. Sex-role learning provides an excellent illustration of socialization and identification. Learning the behavior and qualities that society considers appropriate and desirable for a person of his or her gender is an important personality task. Sex-role stereotypes—simplified, fixed concepts about the behaviors and traits typical of each sex—are established early, and, by the time they are five or six, children are strongly influenced by such sex-typed virtues as aggressiveness and independence for boys and attractiveness and dependence for girls.

3. As the earliest and most durable source of socialization, a child's parents remain the strongest influence in his personal and social development. Thus, the way that parents reward and punish their children's behavior has a potent effect on the development of such characteristics as aggressiveness and on sex roles in general.

4. The role of peers as agents of socialization usually becomes more intense and pervasive during early childhood. A child increasingly learns attitudes and behaviors involved in various roles from other children. He actively practices within his peer group the role behaviors that he has learned and that he will perform in later years. As with his parents, much of what the child learns to do from interacting with his peers depends on what he has observed them doing (modeling) and whether it is encouraged or discouraged (rewarded or punished).

5. Play may also involve such socialization influences as reward or punishment and modeling. Through play the child can test different behaviors by assuming various roles and discovering what happens to a person who engages in those behaviors. As in infancy, play continues to serve a variety of functions: fun, exploring the world, testing new skills, and learning how other children see and do things.

6. Because children are raised in different subcultures, they are likely to show personality and other types of behavior patterns that differ. Thus, from family to family, the development of different views, values, and behavior may be encouraged and strengthened.

SUGGESTED READINGS

Ginott, Haim G. *Between Parent and Child: New Solutions to Old Problems.* New York: Macmillan, 1965.

Green, Richard. "Children's Quest for Sexual Identity," *Psychology Today,* 7 (February 1974), 44–51.

Harlow, Harry F., and Margaret K. Harlow. "Social Deprivation in Monkeys," *Scientific American,* 207 (November 1962), 136–146.

Lynn, David B. *The Father: His Role in Child Development.* Belmont, Calif.: Brooks/Cole, 1974.

Patterson, Gerald R., and M. Elizabeth Gullion. *Living With Children: New Methods for Parents & Teachers.* Champaign, Ill.: Research Press, 1968.

In later childhood, the developing boy or girl comes under further direct control of society in the form of school, which has the official task of presenting formal education. The child's cognitive structure evolves and stabilizes; he develops new and more realistic ways to categorize his world, to operate in it competently, and to perceive its parts and the logical and causal relationships among them. At the same time, through his games and social experiences, he develops social skills that help him to understand how others think and feel. During this period, the differences between appropriate male and female behavior sharpen, and each child tends to play primarily with peers of his or her own sex. Now he lays down friendships and patterns of social behavior that may last throughout his life. A sense of right and wrong continues to evolve; the child who began life as an amoral infant becomes a being with a sense of guilt that plagues him when he violates his own moral code. As a reminder that development is cumulative and continuous, this unit looks at the development of morality over the life span.

UNIT V
Later Childhood:
Growing Up

During later childhood, marked developmental changes take place in the ability to create, learn, and understand.

14

COGNITION: ADVANCES IN THINKING

When David was four, he unwrapped his red and blue Superman costume with great excitement. He put on the suit, waited impatiently for his mother to tie the red cape around his neck, crouched down, tensed his muscles—and tried to fly. He was surprised and disappointed that his feet remained on the ground. The innocence and gullibility of young children like David is a frequent theme in literature. Just as many children are sure that a man in a red suit drives a team of reindeer through the sky to bring them presents, many do not realize that the claims presented in television advertisements for breakfast cereals may not be true. The young child may think of truth as relevant to only statements that he makes and perhaps to those of a few immediate friends, his family, and neighbors.

Now that David is ten, he readily understands truth as also applying to the statements of people he meets and to the media, and he may use the concept to evaluate books that he reads. Most developmental psychologists would agree that the ten-year-old's understanding of concepts tends to be more general and inclusive than the young child's. However, the ten-year-old probably does not think of truth as a general concept that he can apply to any statement ever made about any subject by any person at any time in history. By the time he is fifteen, David's concept of truth will probably be in accord with the abstract and general definition "something that is the case," and he will be able to apply it to an infinite number of events or statements.

In this chapter, we will see that the growing child becomes more capable of abstract thought and less dependent on concrete, real-life examples in learning new concepts. The strategies that he uses to solve problems will become more systematic, more thorough, and more often based on deductions. We will find that, during the years from six to twelve, a child learns to attend more selectively. We will examine his understanding of natural phenomena and see him acquire the ability to comprehend and to deal with relational concepts. It will become apparent that his increased sensitivity to language reflects this intellectual advance.

As his word definitions become more abstract, he uses metaphor more effectively and appreciates the ambiguities of meaning. We will discover that the child gains new ability to envision the viewpoint of another and that this decrease of egocentrism appears in the language he uses when asked to teach a less competent child. We will also discuss recent insights into the cognitive roles that play serves during these years. Finally, we will look at the use and abuse of psychological tests that have been constructed to measure intelligence and intellectual development.

SELECTIVE ATTENTION

You will recall from Chapter 7 that babies are selective attenders and from Chapter 11 that this preference for one stimulus over another plays a role in the young child's learning. As a child grows, his attention becomes more reliable and sustained, and he tends to focus on what he judges to be the important aspects of a situation.

Children, especially in school, are constantly presented with tasks that require them to pay sustained and formal attention to relevant parts of material to be learned and to ignore irrelevant parts. For example, in learning to read, children must pay close attention to the shapes of letters and to their sequential order. However, the shading of the print or the size of the letters is usually irrelevant. A **P** is a **p** is a *p,* but a "rose" is not a "sore" is not an "eros," nor is an *o* identical to a *q* or a *c*. It may be that developmental differences exist in children's ability to determine which aspects of a situation are relevant to a learning task and which are not and to deploy their attention accordingly. Chapter 11 included evidence that the four- to six-year-old is more likely than the eight-year-old to respond to irrelevant cues or distracters in a task.

John Hagen and Gordon Hale (1973) studied changes in selective attention among children between the ages of seven and thirteen by using a simple learning task. The children were told that they would have to remember the *location* of some pictures that they would see. Then each child was shown a row of picture cards. On each card were two pictures, one of a common household object, such as a television set or a lamp, and one of an animal, such as a camel or a cat. The experimenter then turned the cards face down and showed the child a "cue card" with one of the animals or one of the objects on it. The child was then asked to point to the one card in the set face down in front of him that pictured the same animal or object. The number of correct matches over a series

of these trials was the measure of the child's *central learning*. After the child was tested on picture location, which was the task given to him, he was asked if he remembered which objects had been paired with which animals in the set of cards. His correct recall of the pairings measured his *incidental learning*.

A child who scored high on incidental learning must have paid attention to features that were irrelevant to the task described to him. Conversely, a child who scored low on incidental learning must have paid little attention to the irrelevant aspects. It is reasonable to infer, therefore, that a child who scored high on central learning and low on incidental learning is more selective in his attention. As instructed, he concentrated exclusively on location and hence learned little or nothing about the pairings.

As Figure 14.1 shows, children's performances on the central-learning task improved with age in a very straightforward way (even though in this case the learning task also involved a possible distraction consisting of tape-recorded piano notes). The older the child, the higher his memory-for-position score. On the other hand, Figure 14 .1 shows no significant change in incidental-learning scores for children from ages seven through eleven. All scored lower on incidental-learning than on central-learning tasks. However, the incidental-learning scores of twelve- and thirteen-year-olds dropped.

From these findings, it appears that even the youngest children are capable of directing their attention to the central aspect of a task and that this capacity continually improves with age. Because incidental learning does not increase with age, it seems that, as a child like Lauren grows older, she becomes more competent at selective attention, focusing on only the relevant features of a clearly defined task. In other words, the older child learns more about what he understands to be important. However, at about the age of twelve, the child's selective attention seems to become so powerful that he appears to exclude irrelevant material from consciousness, learning less than he would have several years earlier about incidental features.

There are, of course, many situations in which a person does not know in advance which features are relevant and which are irrelevant, as the bitter experience of studying the "wrong" things for an examination testifies. In an ambiguous learning situation, therefore, it is often a wise policy to use broad and nonselective attention at first in order to find out by sampling from the range of possibilities and by searching memory which components are relevant and which are not. There is some evidence that eight-year-old children are superior to five-year-olds in using this sample-and-search strategy and are even as competent as twelve-year-olds (Hale and Morgan, 1973). Thus, as a person matures, his past experiences lead him to concentrate on what he expects will be the relevant aspects of a situation. As the rest of the chapter will show, attention, perception, and cognition become increasingly intertwined.

ADVANCES IN CHILDREN'S THINKING

The thinking of older children continues to advance in its use of symbols. From about the age of seven, when what Jean Piaget (Inhelder and Piaget, 1958) calls the *concrete-operational* stage begins (see Chapter 2), the child's use of logical operations to represent physical reality grows.

Concepts

The growing child shows a continually increasing sophistication in his ability to deal with concepts and rules. A concept represents a characteristic common to a number of different events or objects. For example, a "fruit" is no single thing, but it is many more or less sweet, edible portions of plants that we generally group together for convenience. Like all human beings, the child uses concepts such as "fruit," "sweet," "friend," "star," "round," or "red" to organize the world about him. By applying these and a myriad of other concepts, the child simplifies his world, reducing the barrage of complex sensation to manageable proportions and, once he knows that an object or event belongs in a certain category, using what he knows about the category to tell him more about the object (Flavell, 1970). From Chapter 1 you may recall that using earlier skills to develop later skills is an example of *mediation*. In this section we will see how mediation is involved in the understanding of relational concepts and how the rules of conservation develop in later childhood.

Relational Concepts. In Chapter 11 we saw that the young child often finds it difficult to understand concepts that involve relations between two or more things or events. He often errs when he reasons about the notion of conservation of quantity (rearranging a row of objects does not affect their number), about transitivity (if A is larger than B and B is larger than C, then A is larger than C), and about the relationship between the whole and its parts (if A = B + C, then A is more than B alone or C alone). During later childhood, the ability to handle some of these concepts appears to undergo developmental changes.

For example, Gerald Winer (1974) found measurable advances in reasoning about relational concepts among seven-, eight-, and nine-year-old children. He asked them six questions, such as "If I had four apples and three pears, would I have more apples or more things to eat?" and "If I had two butterflies and six birds, would I have more birds or more things that fly?" The nine-year-old children answered the ques-

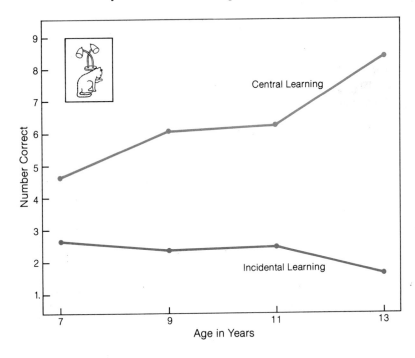

Figure 14.1 Graph summarizing the results of Hagen and Hale's study of children's attention and learning. A sample illustration of the cards used in the study is shown at the top left. The central-learning line shows an increase with age in the average number of pictures correctly identified on the basis of their location. The incidental-learning line shows no change in the average number of pictured pairings of animals and objects recalled until it drops at the end (age thirteen). The difference in correct performance at each age indicates consistently higher success on the central-learning task. (Adapted from Hagen, 1967)

tions correctly more often than the seven- or eight-year-olds did. And when Winer showed a child a picture of, for example, two butterflies and six birds along with the question, the child's reasoning did not change. Apparently, the ability to comprehend the relationship between a class of objects and its parts, like some other cognitive skills, develops gradually and at different times for different children. Thus, many children in primary school lack the understanding and still maintain, as did the young child in Chapter 11, that they have more lemon drops than candy. By the age of nine, however, a child usually knows that he has more candy.

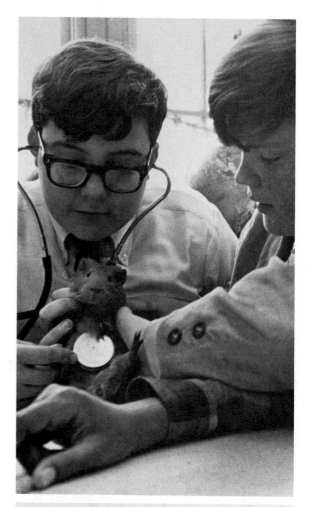

Conservation. In our earlier discussion of relational concepts, we noted that young children have difficulty understanding that transformations of perceptual features do not necessarily change other properties of physical substances. For example, by the time a child is six or seven years old, he usually acquires the concept of the conservation of quantity. This means, for example, that his parents could no longer placate him when he begs for jelly beans (if they ever could) by simply spreading out the ones that he already has, nor would pouring orangeade from a squat glass into a tall, narrow one convince him that his amount of orangeade has doubled. About this time he also usually realizes that if he pours the orangeade back into the squat glass, the level will be just where it was before. Thus, he has acquired another concrete operation: **reversibility.** Having acquired reversibility, the child is able to prove to himself that the amount of orangeade has remained the same by mentally returning the liquid to its previous state, or by reversing the procedure in his mind.

In addition to number and quantity, other properties of physical substances remain constant, even though they appear to have undergone dramatic transformations. The Eiffel Tower would weigh the same as it does now if it were compressed into a solid square of metal. A short, thick chunk of clay stretched into a long, thin, spaghettilike string would displace the same amount of water.

Piaget's experiments (Piaget and Inhelder, 1969) on children's notions of conservation reveal an interesting phenomenon. Although seven-year-olds realize that the mass of an object such as a piece of clay does not change when the clay is stretched or compressed, they fail to realize that its weight and volume also remain unchanged. Furthermore, Piaget found that children always acquire the various kinds of conservation in the same order. First the child under-

Figure 14.2 During later childhood, reasoning about objects, events, and concepts is likely to be less affected by perceptual changes that appear to alter relationships in the physical world. In dealing with conservation and other tasks, for example, children more often attempt to analyze, evaluate, and explain things on the basis of objective procedures and principles. In doing so, they sample and search and test hunches in a more systematic manner.

stands conservation of quantity, then, at about the age of nine or ten, he grasps the notion of conservation of weight, and finally, at about ten or eleven, he realizes that there is also conservation of volume, in the sense that the amount of water displaced by an object is not affected if its shape is changed (Piaget and Inhelder, 1941). Other researchers have confirmed Piaget's basic findings about the sequence of these acquisitions (Sigel and Mermelstein, 1966; Uzgiris, 1964).

Although a child of about nine realizes that changing the shape of an object does not affect its weight, he does not transfer this realization to other kinds of changes. For example, K. Lovell and E. Ogilvie (1961) found that children who "passed" the weight-conservation test when an object's shape was altered still thought that butter loses weight as it melts and that water becomes heavier as it freezes.

Developmental psychologists are still far from understanding exactly how a child acquires these conservation concepts or why he seems to acquire them in a particular order. A child can learn that weight is unaffected by certain transformations by being told and shown that this is so, and no doubt some children do learn the concept in this direct manner. However, even without formal schooling, we constantly experience the heaviness or lightness of objects that we lift, push, or pull. We "know" from our handling of objects, although we may not realize that we know, that things do not get heavier or lighter if we change their shape or their color. Many children may conserve weight in the sense of knowing to maintain constant muscular pressure in lifting a ball of clay that has just been elongated, even though, if asked, they would state that its weight had changed. Thus, using the distinction made in Chapter 7, they may *know how* but not *know that* or *know about*.

Causal Reasoning

As we saw in Chapter 11, the young child has many incorrect ideas about certain common natural phenomena such as dreams. His understanding is **precausal**; he maintains that some events are either completely or partly caused by psychological, subjective factors. For example, he may believe that good dreams come to him because the dreams want to entertain him and that nightmares come because they want to punish him.

There are several kinds of precausal thinking, and the child does not shift from precausal to causal thought in all areas at the same time. As noted in Chapter 11, by the time a child is six or seven, he no longer believes that dreams are external to himself,

Figure 14.3 The way that children order and understand the physical world typically becomes less egocentric, magical, and precausal during the later childhood years. These excerpts are from an illustrated children's book by Etienne Delessert, *How the Mouse Was Hit on the Head by a Stone and So Discovered the World,* produced with the assistance of Piaget, which describes the world through the eyes of five- and six-year-old children. The book tells of a mouse who never left his home beneath the ground until the day he discovered the world while digging a tunnel. (*top left*) The mouse discovers the sky and clouds. (*bottom left*) He talks to the moon.

and he realizes that others can neither see nor touch his dreams.

One kind of precausal thinking that continues to play a role in the beliefs of children is **artificialism**, which refers to explanations that involve either God or man as the artisan of all natural things. We should not confuse the child's belief in God as creator with the belief of the religious adult in a Creator. The child's God is more like a giant or a magician, as this discussion with a nine-year-old child on the origin of night makes clear:

Adult: Tell me, what is night?
Child: It's dark.
Adult: Why is it dark at night?
Child: The clouds make it dark.
Adult: Where does the dark come from at night?
Child: From the sky.
Adult: Where do these clouds come from?
Child: From the sky.
Adult: How does the sky make these clouds, with what does it make them?
Child: It's good Jesus. He makes them and hangs them in the sky. He makes them alone, with nothing. (Laurendeau and Pinard, 1962, page 174)

This child pictures Jesus as if He were cutting clouds out of cotton and then hanging them up in the sky to produce night. If the child had meant this as a poetic description, Monique Laurendeau and Adrien Pinard (1962) would not have considered it a precausal, artificialistic explanation. However, the child first tried to offer an explanation based on physical elements (the clouds), then shifted to the artificialistic one, presumably because he considered it to be more intellectually sound.

A twelve-year-old deals with these same questions about the origin of night in an entirely different manner. Consider the following discussion, which Laurendeau and Pinard classify as an example of causal thinking:

Adult: Tell me, what is the night?
Child: It's when the sun goes down. It's dark.
Adult: Why is it dark at night?
Child: Because the sun is down and it's the sun which projects light during the day.
Adult: Where does the dark come from at night? What makes it night?
Child: It comes from nowhere, it's the color of the sky. In the daytime, it's the sun which makes it blue, and when the sun is gone it becomes dark.
. . .
Adult: Where does the sun go at night?
Child: Behind the clouds. (page 178)

Although this twelve-year-old's explanations are not at all scientifically "correct," he does base his

reasons on concepts of physical causality. The sun does not really go behind the clouds, but the older child knows that, if a source of light is blocked by another object, then the light will not shine. Thus, it is not the correctness of the child's reasoning but its formal properties that determine whether it is causal or precausal.

Laurendeau and Pinard found that the transition in thinking from artificialism to notions of strict physical causality takes place gradually during the years from six to twelve. Some children still offer artificialistic explanations for the origins of night when they are eleven or twelve. However, the percentage of times that older children use this kind of reasoning usually declines sharply. Of the seven-year-olds that Laurendeau and Pinard studied, 74 percent attempted to explain the night by at least a partial appeal to either human or divine creation but, among the twelve-year-olds, only 10 percent resorted to this sort of reasoning. By the time they reach adolescence, children have frequently abandoned artificialism in many respects for other kinds of thinking.

Problem Solving

As a child gets older, he more often tends to define common objects in terms of the abstract category to which they belong (an orange is a fruit) rather than in terms of their specific use (an orange is for eating) or their particular perceptual features (an orange is round). Thus, as David grows from the four-year-old who believed he could fly to the relatively sophisticated ten-year-old, his concepts become more general. But he is still a long way from the adolescent, who easily manipulates hypothetical situations.

However, the fact that children like David have many concepts that are less general or abstract than those of adolescents does not mean that children are incapable of learning and using abstract concepts in a meaningful way. Children between the ages of seven and eleven can learn new abstract concepts if they are provided with concrete examples, physical or verbal, of the new concept. They do find it extremely difficult, however, to learn an abstract concept simply from a general definition that mentions the abstracted attributes of the concept but fails to specify a concrete instance. For example, ten-year-old David would probably find the concept of "government" incomprehensible if he were told nothing more than "Government is the group of persons that makes and administers the policies of a political unit or organization." In general, it is not until he is twelve or so that the child is likely to think more abstractly and to need fewer specific examples to help his understanding.

The increasing capacity for abstract thinking that develops in early adolescence is closely related to the strategies that are used in solving problems whose solution requires one to consider several factors. The adolescent in Piaget's formal-operational period (see Chapters 2 and 18) is more orderly, thorough, hypothetical, and logical than the younger child when called on to identify the factor or factors that are responsible for an event.

A look at the pendulum-problem experiment, which was conducted by Bärbel Inhelder and Jean Piaget (1958), illustrates differences that often appear among younger children, older children, and adolescents. These two Swiss psychologists presented elementary- and high-school students with strings of different lengths and objects of different weights, which the children could attach to a rod so that they swung like pendulums. Inhelder and Piaget pointed out to the children that each of the various possible pendulums would swing through its arc at a different speed. The problem before each child was to determine the factor or factors that account for the speed with which a pendulum traverses its arc. The four intuitively plausible causes are (1) the weight of the object, (2) the length of the string, (3) the height from which the object is released, and (4) the force of the initial push.

Inhelder and Piaget were primarily interested in the thought processes of the children as they tried to solve the pendulum problem. Of the four possible factors, only the length of the string affects the speed of the pendulum. A child can discover this solution either by methodically trying all possible combinations of the four factors (varying a single factor with each trial) or by imagining trials of all possible combinations of factors.

The youngest children, six and seven, almost always concluded that the force of their own initial push determined the pendulum's speed. They did not approach the problem methodically; they failed to set up an experiment in which they varied each of the factors separately. It was hard for these children, who were in the preoperational stage, to imagine that the motion of the pendulum *may* be independent of their own thrusting.

Children between eight and thirteen were somewhat more systematic, but not enough so to solve the problem. At first they varied some but not all of the factors, having particular difficulty with weight. They also accurately judged the differences in the pendulum's movements. But not until the experimenter showed the way could they isolate the effect of one factor from the effect of others. They could not generate on their own a set of procedures that specified all possible combinations of the four factors. As a result of these limitations, they concluded that length of the string is one determining factor but not that it is the only relevant one. They found it particularly difficult to exclude factors.

Only the fourteen- or fifteen-year-old anticipated all possible combinations, tested them experimentally,

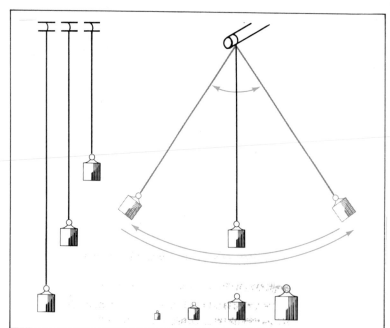

Figure 14.4 Illustration of a pendulum problem. The child is given a set of weights (pictured at bottom) and a string that can be shortened or lengthened (as pictured at left). His task is to determine which factor or factors account for the speed with which a pendulum traverses its arc. (After Inhelder and Piaget, 1958)

and deduced not only what affects a pendulum's speed but also what factors are irrelevant. On the basis of this and other experiments, Inhelder and Piaget concluded that adolescent thought is characterized by the ability to hypothesize and to deduce.

Although Inhelder and Piaget found that eleven- and twelve-year-olds usually fail to solve the pendulum problem, Robert Siegler, Diane Liebert, and Robert Liebert (1973) have recently developed a training procedure that successfully taught even ten-year-olds the skills that enabled them to solve it. They conclude that Piaget is correct in stating that ten- and eleven-year-olds do not usually solve such problems on their own but that this does not mean that such problems are beyond children's intellectual grasp. As Chapter 11 indicated, a child's inability to solve a problem does not mean that he is unable to grasp the concept involved. Just as four-year-olds can be taught to understand conservation, a ten-year-old can learn to perform some of the mental activities that often do not develop until adolescence.

CHANGES IN REPRESENTATIONAL SKILLS

During the years from six to twelve, the growing human being becomes an even more skillful user of symbols. His cognitive advances in later childhood are characterized by more sophisticated representational skills that take several forms.

Imitation

Imitation takes various forms in the young child, as you will recall from Chapter 11. Imitation can be external action or internal image, and it can vary in the degree to which it corresponds with that which is imitated. During later childhood, imitation continues to contribute to cognitive acquisition.

For years, research on the relationship between imitation and intellectual development seldom went beyond the preschool years. Recently, however, psychologists have become interested in the connection between imitation and cognition during later development. It is common knowledge that, in learning to perform complex actions, it is often useful to watch another person and then try to imitate his behavior. Lynn McLaughlin and Joseph Brinley (1973) set up an experiment to find out if children could also learn to solve problems more efficiently by first observing a model solve them.

They devised two sorting tasks, one with fifteen blocks, the other with fifteen animal pictures. The blocks could be sorted into four separate groups according to either their *shape,* their *color,* or their

proportions. The pictures could be sorted into groups according to either the *kind of animal,* the *number of animals* on each card, or the *presence or absence of faces and/or cage bars.* Children from seven through twelve were asked to sort the blocks into four groups. McLaughlin and Brinley told each child that, although there were several possible ways to sort, only one would be considered correct. The correct solution was to classify the material on the basis of multiple attributes.

McLaughlin and Brinley found that, regardless of age, children who watched the model and children who had a chance to practice sorted blocks better than children who neither saw the model nor practiced. However, only eleven- and twelve-year-olds were able to abstract the general principle that guided the solution and transfer it from blocks to animal pictures. Thus, it seems that children as young as seven can imitate the problem-solving performance of a model as long as the task is identical to the one that they watch. Even more promising, this study and others like it (Denney, Denney, and Ziobrowski, 1973; T. Rosenthal and Zimmerman, 1973) imply that using filmed, televised, and live models can be practical ways to teach older children problem-solving and abstraction skills.

Language

Chapter 12 stressed the fact that, by the time a child is four or five, he has mastered a good part of the complex structure of his native language, and the chapter went on to show that linguistic development extends into adolescence. Much of this linguistic development seems intimately related to the child's cognitive development. Children cannot really understand the increasingly complex meanings of sentences that they hear if the concepts expressed in those sentences are beyond their intellectual grasp. After all, in order for a symbol to be meaningful, the symbol user must first comprehend the object, event, or relationship for which it stands. Furthermore, as our earlier discussion of language made clear, the child's ability to understand how meaning changes as the order of identical words changes—as in the sentences "The boy was hit by the girl" and "The girl was hit by the boy"—is itself a cognitive feat of significance. The child's developing ability to understand depends on the *inclusion* of earlier language skills, as noted in Chapter 1. Advanced language use and comprehension probably depends more on cognition than cognition depends on language, although language is undoubtedly important for certain kinds of intellectual skills and makes concept learning easier and concept use more flexible.

On the other hand, Piaget (1972) has argued that, during childhood, a child learns new concepts and rules best by working extensively with concrete materials. According to Piaget, concepts and rules can be derived more readily from active play, exploration, and investigation than from listening to or reading about them. He believes that verbal formulations tend to bore or frustrate the child. Although Piaget's emphasis on the fundamental importance of concrete over verbal experience is not universally accepted (Ausubel, 1968), he does focus on the role of language in formal concept learning, in everyday reasoning, and in a systematic approach to solving complex problems.

Chapters 8 and 12 explained that, from infancy on, language and thought become closely intertwined but also that certain aspects of cognitive development appear to be relatively independent of language (Hollos and Cowan, 1973). In this section you will read about several studies that have a direct bearing on the language-thought issue.

Words and Metaphors. The growing child's increasing tendency to deal with abstractions shows clearly in developmental changes in his capacity to use metaphor, which depends on the ability to perceive relationships between different objects or qualities. In one study of metaphor, Howard Gardner (1974) asked children to match items such as those shown in Column B in Figure 14.5 with the appropriate adjectives from Column A. Most adults would maintain that the first adjective of each pair in Column A is the most appropriate metaphor for the first item of each pair in Column B and that the second adjective is the most appropriate metaphor for the second item.

When Gardner presented students ranging in age from three and one-half to nineteen years with examples of such items as those shown in Column B, he found that even the youngest children were able to make numerous metaphorical matches. However, seven-year-olds outperformed the younger children, and eleven-and-one-half-year-olds outperformed the seven-year-olds. But there the improvement stopped: Eleven-and-one-half-year-olds did as well as college students.

It is apparent, therefore, that children are intellectually capable of appreciating poetic metaphor—they may even create poetry on their own (K. Koch, 1970)—and that this capability increases during the elementary-school years. Gardner's study also indicates that a child's ability to perceive relationships between objects that differ in appearance improves steadily until about age eleven, when it reaches adult levels, and that this perception of relationships is expressed with language.

Jokes and Riddles. The appreciation of jokes and riddles is also tied to language and cognitive development. Many riddles and jokes are based on the fact

Column A	Column B
Sad—Happy	Hearing the phrase "A cloudy afternoon"— Hearing the phrase "A bright morning"
Warm—Cold	Seeing the color red— Seeing the color blue
Hard—Soft	Seeing a photograph of a frowning face— Seeing a photograph of a smiling face
Loud—Quiet	Seeing thick line drawings— Seeing thin line drawings
Dark—Light	Touching a piece of abrasive sandpaper— Touching a piece of mild sandpaper

Figure 14.5 Representation of some adjective pairs (Column A) and related item pairs (Column B) like those used by Gardner in his study of the development of appreciation of metaphor, as discussed in the text. (After Gardner, 1974)

that words and phrases have more than one meaning. In order to appreciate the humor, David and Lauren must be aware of the multiple meanings of the word or phrase and see how an unanticipated meaning resolves the incongruity.

Sigmund Freud (1960) suggested that there is a developmental sequence in the appreciation of humor. At first the child enjoys mere nonsense, which is a form of unresolvable incongruity. Later he is amused by jokes that have meaning—their incongruity can be resolved.

Thomas Shultz (1974), who has studied children's appreciation of both riddles and jokes, views a riddle as a question followed by an incongruous answer. The listener must figure out how the incongruity makes sense; his pleasure comes when he succeeds in resolving the problem by explaining the incongruous answer. A similar analysis applies to jokes.

In his study of riddles, Shultz tested Freud's hypothesis by systematically studying children's appreciation of jokes and riddles at the ages of six, eight, ten, and twelve. The children heard a series of riddles, each having three possible answers. For example:

Why did the farmer name his hog Ink?
1. Because he kept running out of the pen.
2. Because he kept getting away.
3. Because he was black. (page 101)

As you can see, in Variation 3 the incongruity is removed: The hog was named Ink because he was black. In Variation 2 the incongruity remains but is not resolved: It is pure nonsense for a farmer to name his hog Ink because he keeps getting away. In Variation 1, however, the incongruity can be resolved.

In a similar study of jokes, Thomas Shultz and Frances Horibe (1974) used an identical technique, presenting a series of three possible jokes:

1. Order! Order in the court!
   Ham and cheese on rye, please, Your Honor.
2. Silence! Silence in the court!
   Ham and cheese on rye, please, Your Honor.
3. Order! Order in the court!
   I only want the truth to be told, Your Honor. (page 14)

An adult would probably consider only Variation 1 of the hog riddle and 1 of the court joke to be funny. The other selections strike one as either straightforward or as nonsense.

In both studies a clearly discernible change in the child's appreciation of humor appeared between the ages of six and eight. Six-year-olds did not appreciate jokes or riddles whose humor depended on resolving a linguistic ambiguity, whereas children of eight and older did. The six-year-olds found simple, unresolved incongruity humorous. The eight-year-olds found both the incongruity and its resolution humorous. With age there was also an increase in comprehension of the dual meanings of key words and phrases in the jokes and riddles.

Apparently, a six-year-old's mastery of language is not developed enough for him to enjoy the linguistic

Figure 14.6 Poems written by nine- and eleven-year-old girls. Unconstrained by many adult preconceptions and rules, children often see and represent common phenomena in novel ways.

Fire
Flickering flames of gold and red
Creeping forward like a cautious thief
Devouring greedily the old, dry twigs;
Wisps of light gray smoke
Floating higher and higher
In the damp air of the dawn.

Thunder
I hear
the drummers
strike
the sky.

The Scared Clouds
The clouds are stuck and scared to move
For fear the trees might pinch them.

subtleties involved. He is, as Freud suggested, limited to the enjoyment of nonsense. As the child matures and his vocabulary expands, he becomes aware of multiple meanings and appreciates the resolution of incongruity.

Play

The function of children's play has been stressed many places in this book, and you will recall from the discussion in Chapter 13 that some investigators believe play helps the young child assimilate new information from the environment into his existing modes of understanding.

Jerome L. Singer (1973), who has studied fantasy and make-believe in children for many years, feels that children between the ages of nine and thirteen have a considerable interest in make-believe activities and fantasy games but that this interest is largely suppressed. Because our culture tends to discourage what it views as nonutilitarian thought, it may be that parents and teachers, without realizing it, signal disapproval of children's fantasy games (Pulaski, 1974).

Studies by Singer and a number of his students indicate that fantasy is associated with verbal fluency, increased concentration, originality, and imagination (Singer, 1973). Although there may be hereditary differences in the ability of individuals to fantasize spontaneously (Wallach, 1970), children can be taught to develop their imaginative capacities.

For example, Sybil Gottlieb (1973) has developed promising techniques with children under twelve. After classifying children as high or low on the ability to fantasize, she showed abstract films to groups of children and interpreted the films realistically to one group and imaginatively to the other. Then she showed another abstract film and asked the children for written interpretations. Those children in the group who had heard a fanciful interpretation of the first film showed a sharp increase in the amount of fantasy they used—even children who had originally been classified as low fantasizers. But her attempts to use the same techniques with children over twelve failed. One cannot conclude, on the basis of this study, that older children are unable to learn to use fantasy. But it appears that younger children are much more receptive to Gottlieb's techniques.

Memory

The child's memory continues to develop in the years from six to twelve. It was pointed out in our prior discussion of cognitive development that three- and

four-year-olds can recall events that happened as much as a year before and that a meaningful context helps the young child to remember information. Older children tend to group material that must be remembered into categories, which enhances their ability to recall it.

During later childhood, the child's developing cognitive skills interact with his memory in a manner that has surprising results. If you, for example, were asked to recall an event that you had observed two weeks ago, you would expect to remember it reasonably well. But if you were asked to recall it after six months, you would expect your memory to have faded somewhat. You certainly would not expect your memory of the event to improve with the passage of six months.

However, the interaction of the child's memory and cognition makes it appear that, in certain cases, his memory does improve with time. For example, Piaget and Inhelder (1968) showed children a group of ten sticks of various lengths and asked them to draw the arrangement from memory. After six months, the same children, asked to redraw the sticks, produced a copy that was closer to the original display than the first drawing they had produced. Apparently, the child's memory for objects is not simply an internal copy of his original perception. It appears that, as a child's comprehension of what he has once seen develops, his memory changes to conform to his new understanding.

In a similar study, Hans Furth, Bruce Ross, and James Youniss (1974) showed children ranging in age from five through nine years a picture of a glass tilted from the horizontal base to a 45° angle, as in Choice A of Figure 14.7. The children were told: "This is a glass with cola in it. It is tilted and on a table. Now draw this picture on your paper, just the way you see it here."

Many children in elementary school do not realize that the level of the liquid remains horizontal with respect to the table even though the glass is tilted. They have not yet acquired this particular understanding of spatial transformations, even though they have seen numerous tilted glasses of milk, water, orange juice, and so forth.

The same children again drew the tilted glass at varying intervals. Furth found that the oldest children reproduced the drawing more accurately on all these occasions. However, 20 out of the 116 children drew more accurate pictures in sessions that were held after six months than they had drawn earlier. Although this represents only 17 percent of the total sample, the finding is of interest because it goes against the intuitive expectation that recollections will remain the same or deteriorate over time. Furth maintains that, during the six-month interval, these children had acquired a more sophisticated understanding of what happens to the level of contained liquids in general and that this knowledge affected the way that they remembered the picture. Thus, the child's memory of a perception is not simply a static photograph but the product of an active process in which advances in cognitive maturity modify the information that the child stored earlier.

SOCIAL INTERACTION AND COGNITION

Role-taking and communication skills also are bound up with cognitive development. As earlier chapters noted, the young child is egocentric; often he assumes that other people see things just as he does, and he is even unaware that other perspectives exist. This egocentrism often interferes with his attempts to communicate with language. For example, Chapter 12 reported that children under six will give instructions to a blindfolded person as if he could see. Similarly, when recounting an episode to a friend or a parent, a young child may leave out essential details, making the story almost meaningless to the listener.

In an attempt to find out how long this tendency persists, John Flavell (1966) conducted a series of studies that examined role-taking and communication tasks. In one study, Flavell showed children from seven to sixteen a set of seven pictures that, like a

comic strip, illustrated a story when "read" in the proper order.

For example, one set of pictures might tell the following story:

1. Boy is walking.
2. Boy sees dog.
3. Dog chases boy.
4. Boy sees apple tree.
5. Boy climbs apple tree to escape from dog.
6. Boy watches dog depart.
7. Boy eats apple.

The child narrates the story as he looks at the pictures. Afterward, the experimenter removes three of the pictures, leaving only four, which tell quite a different story:

1. Boy is walking.
4. Boy sees apple tree.
6. Boy sits in apple tree with dogs in background.
7. Boy eats apple.

At this point, a second person enters the room, and the child is told that this person will see the four pictures for the first time. The child's task is to predict the story that the new person would tell after seeing the four pictures.

Flavell found that many of the seven- and eight-year-olds found it difficult to separate their predictions about the story that the newcomer would tell from their own prior narrations. Either they restated the seven-picture story or else they initially predicted a "pure" four-picture story but, upon questioning, reverted back to the information about the dog that

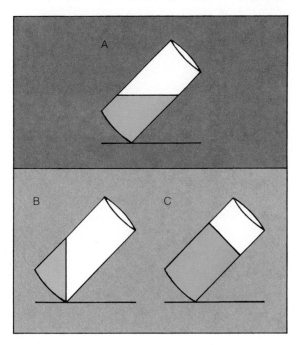

Figure 14.7 Representation of a tilted-glass experiment like that of Furth, Ross, and Youniss. (A) Depiction of the actual angle of the level of liquid in a tilted glass. (B and C) Depiction of the angle reproduced by two children. (Adapted from Furth, Ross, and Youniss, 1974)

only they had seen. One dialogue resulted in this exchange:

Child: He's singing, and then he runs—he sees a tree. He climbs up it and he's eating an apple.
Adult: Fine. Why does Mr. X think that the boy wanted to climb the tree?
Child: So the dog don't get him—bite him. (1966, page 170)

On the other hand, children who were nine or older had little difficulty in separating what they said from what Mr. X saw.

THE CONCEPT OF INTELLIGENCE

The discussions in the chapters on intellectual and linguistic development have focused on the changing abilities of children as they progress toward biological and social maturity. They have looked at the changing ways in which the typical child knows his world. In this final section, we will examine a related aspect of intellectual development: intelligence tests and the concept of IQ that grew out of attempts to assess a child's intellectual abilities.

Changing Viewpoints About IQ

Early developmentalists concerned themselves with plotting changes in mental age as chronological age increased. Put simply, the standard, or normal, mental age for a child would be that which is typical or usual for most other children of his age. In order to determine whether a given child deviated from the typical and if so, by how much, investigators used

Figure 14.8 The pictures and procedure used in Flavell's study of the development of children's story-telling skills. (*top*) The set of seven pictures tells the story discussed in the text. (*bottom*) After three pictures are removed, the four remaining pictures tell a quite different story, as discussed in the text. (Courtesy of John Flavell)

standard testing procedures to devise behavioral norms for each age. In order to assess intelligence, they developed the convention of IQ—a quotient that represents a child's performance relative to the performance of numerous other children who have previously been tested under the same conditions. Fundamentally, therefore, given the way that intelligence tests are constructed and standardized, the IQ score provides no more than a descriptive statistic relating a child's present performance to that of other children of his chronological age.

Unfortunately, the early association of the psychological measurement of intellectual ability with a program of various physical measurements caused many people to suppose that tests of intelligence produced scores that are as accurate and immutable as physical measurements. People often assumed that IQ is largely determined by heredity and that experience has only minimal effects on the measure. Today psychologists know that environmental circumstances can produce considerable variability in IQ scores. They have also grown suspicious, on the basis of long-term repetitive measurements of intelligence, of the alleged stability of intelligence.

IQ scores often fluctuate; the scores of approximately 20 percent of American children change by at least fifteen IQ points between the ages of six and ten, and some children's scores, although not many, change by as many as fifty points. External influences at the time of the examination, including the manner of the examiner and the attitude of the child, can affect a child's performance. Thus, Matt, who may have made average scores on standardized tests of intelligence at age six, could score considerably higher several years later. Many factors determine a child's intellectual performance, among them biological change, general education, life experience, motivation, and personality. Therefore, one should be wary of making important decisions about the future of an individual based on only one or even just a few assessments of his intellectual abilities (McCall, Appelbaum, and Hogarty, 1973).

For many years psychologists also thought that an IQ score measured practically everything of importance in cognitive development. Performance on an IQ test was taken as an index of creative abilities, productive thinking, and problem-solving abilities. Along with this faith in the IQ test went a belief that it was not possible to train mental capacities.

On the basis of new evidence and experience, these ideas about IQ have been modified, and the concept of what IQ really measures is being redefined. Today psychologists know that a person's IQ score can be deceptive. They realize that intelligence is not a single, unitary entity. Rather, it refers to a wide range of abilities and skills, some of which are related to one another, and some of which are not; some of which are measured by IQ tests, and some of which are not measured by them.

What IQ Does and Does Not Measure

Most psychologists agree that intelligence is based on the ability to benefit from experience and the ease with which a child can learn a new idea or a new set of behaviors. It is generally assumed that each person has a ceiling, a point above which he will not be able to profit from experience in a particular activity, and that this ceiling is governed by environmental and hereditary factors. Chapter 3 discusses some of the data regarding hereditary influence on intellectual ability.

However, the debate about the genetic contribution to tested IQ performance continues to rage. Arthur Jensen (1969) fathered the modern controversy by arguing that 80 percent of the differences among the IQ scores of individuals can be traced to differences in their genetic backgrounds, whereas others have suggested that a close examination of these data reveals so many problems in untangling genetic and environmental influences that there is little evidence for a genetic component to IQ (Kamin, 1973; M. Schwartz and Schwartz, 1974).

It is instructive to try to interpret Jensen's claim that the heritability for IQ is .80, in light of our previous discussion in Chapter 3. First, the statement implies that in a group of individuals, approximately 80 percent of the difference in their scores is associated with differences in their genetic make-up. This does not mean that 80 percent of an individual's IQ score is "determined" by genetics and 20 percent by environment, as if eighty of the one hundred points of an average child's IQ score were contributed by his genes. A complex and interdependent set of genetic and environmental circumstances that scientists are only beginning to understand causes the child's test performance.

Second, as we noted in Chapter 3, the heritability of .80 depends on the nature of the samples used to calculate it. Heritability may not be the same among blacks as among whites, among upper-middle-class individuals as among the poor, among individuals tested in the 1930s as among those tested in the 1970s or 1980s.

Third, because of the way genetic research must be

done with human beings, often involving variation in both hereditary and environmental influences, the accuracy of that estimate of .80 heritability, even in the specific samples tested, is questionable.

Fourth, even if human heritability for IQ were .80, this finding does not suggest that all attempts to stimulate or improve intellectual functioning would be fruitless. It may be difficult to change intellectual ability or it may not, depending on whether we can discover which experiences are most important for its development.

It is also particularly important to remember that an intelligence test does not include many questions that require a child to learn anything. The majority of the questions measure a skill or a segment of knowledge that the child already possesses rather than his ability to learn something new. Thus, the IQ test does not measure the basic processes that most people acknowledge as contributing heavily to intelligence.

The intelligence test is a good measure of what a child knows how to do and what he has taken from his culture. It is also a reasonably good predictor of the child's grades in school. If the child has a strong motivation to improve the quality of his intellectual skills and has high standards for intellectual mastery, he is likely to have a higher IQ score than a child who is not highly motivated or who has low standards. Because middle-class children are more consistently encouraged than lower-class children are to learn to read, spell, add, and write, a child's IQ, social class, and school grades all should be positively related to each other. This is generally the case. In addition, the personality attributes of children who do well in school (persistence, lack of aggression, and responsible behavior) are similar to the characteristics of children from middle-class homes.

The IQ score, when properly used, can be regarded, then, as an efficient and accurate way of summarizing the degree to which a child has learned the concepts and rules of middle-class Western society. The IQ score is useful because it predicts fairly well how easily a child of eleven like Matt will master the elements of calculus or history when he enters college. However, the specific questions that are asked on an intelligence test have been chosen to make this prediction possible. The child is asked to define "shilling" rather than "peso." He is asked to state the similarity between a fly and a tree rather than the similarity between "fuzz" and "Uncle Tom." He is asked to copy a design rather than to defend himself against the neighborhood bully.

There is no reason to discard present IQ tests

merely because they are biased toward measuring skills that upper- and middle-class white Americans value and teach. But the parent and teacher should appreciate the arbitrary content of the test. If one's primary objective is to predict the child's success in school subjects, then the IQ test is the best instrument psychologists have devised so far. After the child is three or four years old, the test does a creditable job of predicting who will obtain good grades in elementary school, high school, and college. (For skills such as music or art, there are special tests that are more appropriate.)

Psychologists need more exact knowledge about the separate cognitive functions and how they are combined in thought, and everyone must come to realize that the actual, overt behavior of a child in a test situation depends as much on his motives, fears, and expectations as it does on the richness and quality of his mental structures.

SUMMARY

1. During the years from six to twelve, a child's attention continues to become more reliable, sustained, and selective. Thus a child is likely to learn more about those aspects of a task that he and others understand to be important and meaningful and, in an ambiguous situation, to sample the range of possibilities in an attempt to decide which features are relevant.

2. Typically, a child's attending and thinking also show advances in other ways. For example, he is likely to show a continually increasing sophistication in his ability to understand and use concepts such as those involved in a conservation task, and he may be able to imagine a reverse operation that proves he understands the physical relationships involved. Precausal thinking may also become less apparent during this period as the child more often attempts to understand, examine, and explain things in causal terms. Similarly, problem solving is likely to become more complex and efficient as the child develops a fuller understanding of how to solve problems involving several factors.

3. Advances in the child's imitation, language, play, and memory both reflect and produce, in an interactive way, marked developmental changes in his ability to learn, reason, and acquire concepts. Thus, complementary changes in the child's language skills and cognitive development are reflected in his understanding and use of words and metaphors and in his appreciation of the multiple meanings and linguistic subtleties of jokes and riddles.

4. Social interactions continue to have a strong influence on cognitive development. Through interacting with others and advancing in role-taking and conceptual skills, the child is likely to show a decreasing egocentrism in communicating with others and in considering a situation from their perspective.

5. Although the concept of intelligence and the use of intelligence tests are often assumed to be adequate ways of measuring, describing, or explaining differences in cognitive development, there are serious limitations to such views. Basically, intelligence tests and IQ scores indicate a child's performance relative to the performance of other children. They do not measure or reflect many important cognitive skills or abilities, and they do not show or demonstrate that a child's performance is stable or that it cannot be changed by training or education.

SUGGESTED READINGS

Berlyne, Daniel E. *Structure and Direction in Thinking*. New York: Wiley, 1965.

Bruner, Jerome S. *The Relevance of Education*. New York: Norton, 1971.

Ginsburg, Herbert, and Sylvia Opper. *Piaget's Theory of Intellectual Development: An Introduction*. Englewood Cliffs, N.J.: Prentice-Hall, 1969.

Piaget, Jean. *The Science of Education and the Psychology of the Child*. New York: Viking, 1971.

Pulaski, Mary Ann Spencer. "The Rich Rewards of Make-Believe," *Psychology Today*, 7 (January 1974), 68–74.

Later childhood continues to be not only a time of expanding social relationships and testing of new roles but also a time during which the primary forces in socialization continue to exert major influences on personality development.

15

PERSONALITY: EXPANDING SOCIAL INTERACTIONS

Eleven-year-old Matt watched the other boys jump off the end of the pier, bob to the top, and swim away. He took a hesitant step forward, then stopped and stared into the deep water. His friends began calling to him: "Come on!" "Jump!" Matt could swim, but not well, and the ten feet between him and the water seemed like a hundred. "What's the matter," yelled another boy, "are you afraid?" The demands of his friends overcame his fear. Matt shut his eyes and jumped into the cold water.

During the years from six to twelve, the influence of a child's peer group can be extremely important in shaping his development. When the six-year-old first skips off to school, the process of role identification slips into high gear. During the later years of childhood, each child learns what the adult society expects of him. He learns to meet a few of these expectations in the classroom itself, from books and pictures and teachers who tell him what is good and what is bad, what he must do and what he cannot do. However, most of what a child learns at school takes place on the playground. Thus, Matt may learn from playing basketball with his peers that cheating is not tolerated, or he may learn from typical playground intrigues that one should stand up for his close friends.

In this chapter, we will examine some of the changes in the child's world as his personality develops throughout later childhood. We will focus on aspects of personality, such as sex roles and aggression, that were discussed in Chapter 13 and will broaden our discussion to consider other roles that the child plays as well as additional kinds of behavior. We will examine the development of generosity and helpfulness as examples of positive qualities and will look at the effects of popularity and leadership. We will also stress the relative decline in parental influence on the growing child, along with the relative increase of peer influence. We will see that play assumes additional functions in later childhood and that a child's ability to assume different roles also influences his personality development. Finally, we will consider the growing impact of society on the child, particularly in the important areas of television, drug use, and education.

Sigmund Freud considers later childhood to be a period of sexual latency in contrast to early childhood, when, in his view, the child's sexual fantasies resulted in a conflict between the child and his parents. According to Freud, the repression, or exclusion from conscious thought, of the child's sexuality during this period permits him to form peer relationships with children of the same sex and allows him to assume the role of either leader or follower. According to Freud, the child's peers and authority figures such as parents and teachers continue to have a great influence, particularly in strengthening the child's self-image or causing him to further repress his sexual urges.

Alfred Adler stresses the continuing importance during later childhood of the child's struggle to overcome his feelings of inferiority, although the child's efforts are now directed toward his relationships with his peers (whereas they had previously been directed toward his parents). According to this view, the child's striving for superiority can be expressed in such socially approved behaviors as generosity and giving aid—both of which help the child to establish control over his environment in positive ways. Adler holds that the child who successfully learns to control his environment (at school and in competition with his age-mates) becomes popular with his peers and may achieve leadership status, thus increasing his feelings of competence.

Harry Stack Sullivan also emphasizes the continued importance of peer and parental responses to the child's developing personality. According to Sullivan, the child learns to adjust his behavior in positive and negative ways to meet the demands of his environment through his relationships with peers. In this view, as the child learns to adjust to the requirements of others, he begins to engage in mutual, reciprocal human relationships. In addition, authority figures other than parents and peers teach the child a practical sense of social subordination. In Sullivan's view, then, the child eventually learns to respond selectively to his social environment and comes to act in accordance with an increasingly consistent self-concept.

Erik Erikson, like Sullivan, places great emphasis on the influence of others in the child's role development during later childhood. Erikson suggests that the child's popularity and potential for leadership are a function of his relative success in learning to exert control over his environment, which thereby enables him to make positive contributions to those around him. According to Erikson, the child's learning takes place in the context of school and society. Thus, in this view, the child acquires a positive self-concept from the ability to be productive, self-directing, and accepted.

Erich Fromm, like Erikson, stresses the significance to the child's personality development of the feeling of being productive. In Fromm's terms, as the child makes more contact with a widening range of peers and adults, he is constantly faced with the choice between productive self-realization (or independence) and returning to his family for support. In this view, growth—in the form of new freedom from dependence on family and peers—comes in the choice of productive self-realization. According to Fromm, peers and adults, as the transmitters of society, play a central role in shaping the child's self-concept by encouraging or restricting his efforts, and the child will achieve self-fulfillment to the degree that he is able to create loving, trusting relationships with his peers.

Walter Mischel sees peer-group pressure and the impact of the school as two significant forces shaping the child's behavior. From observation and participation, according to Mischel, the child learns to conform to the demands and expectations of peers as well as parents and other adults and, in the process, learns both positive and negative behaviors. In addition, from observing which behaviors meet with social approval and which are punished, the child can acquire the behaviors necessary to become popular or to assume a position of leadership. In Mischel's view, then, the child develops a clearer and more complete self-concept through interacting with his expanded environment and through assessing his behavior in relation to the consequences provided by both peers and adults.

ACQUISITION OF ROLES

As we will see in this chapter, children often learn more from their peers than they do from adults. But parents, peers, play, and society all have a major part in the socialization process (see Figure 15.1), and, as the child grows into his sex role, the interplay of these forces becomes clear.

Sex Roles

Around the age of five or six, children tend to segregate into same-sex friendship and play groups, and these segregated groups endure until the romantic interests of adolescence draw children out of them. Each sex professes a contempt for the other. Girls talk about "yukky boys," and boys refer freely to "dumb girls." Girls practice their girlness by playing house and rehearsing the romantic fantasy of being a bride, and boys assert their boyness by sports, rough-housing, and adventuring. The romantic chant used for years by girls to accompany jumping rope—

Down in the valley where the green grass grows
There sat Helen as sweet as a rose.
She sang and she sang and she sang so sweet,
Along came her fellow and kissed her on the cheek

—is unlikely to be represented in boys' play. Boys and girls are aware of this division of interests, and Figure 15.2 shows the kinds of activities that children between the ages of eight and eleven see as being the domain of one sex or the other (Hartley and Hardesty, 1964). There is a good deal of continuity between girls' play activities and traditional adult female roles (home maintenance and child care) but much less continuity between boys' play and adult male roles. Boys seem to have a great need to assert their masculinity—perhaps to distinguish themselves from the primarily female influence at home. As Chapter 13 stated, calling a boy "sissy" is a strong weapon of behavioral control. Girls are likely to engage in activities stereotyped for boys, whereas boys are reluctant to take part in girls' activities.

As the continuity between girls' play and female roles would suggest, the games that children play provide an important context for acquiring sex roles. Watch three seven-year-old girls playing house. The oldest (or the most dominant) will assign the roles at her pleasure, switching them around from time to time to add interest to the game. "Let's play like I'm the daddy," she may say. In almost every culture, children "play like" adults in their free time. Grown-ups may take this imitation as flattery, but the activity serves the same useful socialization process as more formal learning does. In playing house, a girl picks up some of the essentials of her adult role and, perhaps of greater importance, learns how to shift readily from one role to another.

If the little girl who is playing the mother wishes to go to the office and work and leave the father at home to care for the baby, the other children soon put her straight. In sex-role stereotypes, mothers just do not leave fathers at home to do dishes and wash dia-

Figure 15.1 Summary descriptions of some major theoretical viewpoints regarding personality development during later childhood.

pers. Such cultural standards of appropriate sex roles exert far-reaching effects on children's personalities. Behavior that accords with traditional sex-role standards—aggressiveness and sexuality for boys, passivity and dependence for girls—tends to remain stable through adulthood (J. Kagan and Moss, 1962), whereas sex-inappropriate behavior is more likely to be modified.

This channeling of children's proclivities and capacities along lines defined by society as sex-appropriate can restrict a child's potential. Aletha Stein, Sheila Pohly, and Edward Mueller (1971) studied boys and girls in the sixth grade to see if labeling a neutral task as masculine or feminine or both led to a change in children's performance. They found that achievement on the tests was related to the label. Boys did best on ''masculine'' tasks, worst on ''feminine'' tasks, and in between on tasks labeled as appropriate for both sexes. Girls did as well on ''both'' tasks as they did on ''feminine'' tasks but performed worst on tasks labeled ''masculine.''

The emotional components of sex-role identification become so strongly ingrained during childhood that many would reject as abnormal anyone who tried to reverse his or her sex-role behavior. The emotional conditioning associated with sex and gender roles so pervades the child's social environment that it is practically invisible to later, rational inspection. Because individuals cannot consciously recover the experiences that conditioned their attitudes toward sex roles, they often tend to believe that their own

Figure 15.2 Chart illustrating the effects of sex-role stereotypes on the way that boys and girls classify childhood activities. As the chart shows, there is a high degree of agreement between boys and girls about the activities that are seen as the province of one sex or the other. For example, all boys and girls felt that playing with doll carriages is a girl's activity, and almost all saw playing with trucks as a boy's activity. (After Hartley and Hardesty, 1964)

 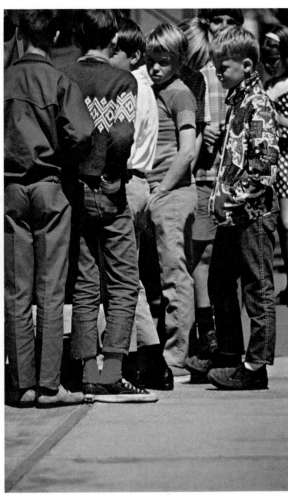

Figure 15.3 Segregation in same-sex
friendship and play groups is a
hallmark of later childhood. Within
these sex-segregated groups,
socialization continues to influence
personal-social development by
providing opportunities for trying out
sex-appropriate behaviors.

attitudes are genetic constants that accompany particular sex organs rather than an accumulation of years of learning.

Peer Roles

A child comes to have definite reactions to and expectations of other children (and of himself, depending on how other children respond to him). Organization creeps into children's relationships, and two kinds of patterns characteristically develop during this period. The first is the elaboration of an ingroup-outgroup sense of belonging that is supported by special group activities and rituals and the exclusion of outsiders. A child learns to define his special qualities and ways of behaving in relation to how his group acts and, frequently, in contrast to how outsiders act. Fortunately, group organization is not rigid during these years, and many such cliques break up and reform, so that temporarily and arbitrarily excluded children may later slip into the fold. A second pattern of group interaction that soon emerges is the development of hierarchies. Any child in a fifth-grade classroom can rattle off an ordered list of the smartest, the most athletic, and the most popular, and childen show a surprising consensus. The roles and positions that a child takes in peer-group play provide his training for assuming adult social roles later.

Chapters 9 and 13 emphasized that the child's developing personality grows out of an interaction between what he brings to social situations and the ways that other people treat him. Perhaps nowhere is this so clear as in the child's popularity. The child who emerges from secure and rewarding relationships at home with his parents and siblings tends to be trusting, confident, and interested in and capable of both initiating rewarding interactions and receiving overtures from others. These characteristics correlate with a child's popularity as measured by **sociometric analysis,** a method that charts how often a child is chosen by his peers as a preferred friend or companion (Campbell and Yarrow, 1961).

However, children's behavior, the responses of others to them, and their expectations form an interlocking web, each feeding into the other, so that it is difficult to say which comes first. For example, research has shown that a child's physique is likely to influence his popularity, indicating that the child's own behavior is not the only factor that determines his role in the group. J. Robert Staffieri (1967) investigated the relationship between the popularity and the physique of boys from six to ten years old and found that muscular boys are more popular than boys who

are skinny or plump. Most of the boys that he studied wished for a muscular build in accord with the masculine stereotype.

Although popular children tend to assume leadership roles in their peer group, children tend to be discriminating in their assignment of leadership roles. When children are organizing a baseball game, they generally listen to an athletically skilled child; when they are staging a play, they turn to an imaginative child. Thus, in a study of leadership among a large number of six- to eleven-year-old children, C. Wade Harrison, James Rawls, and Donna Rawls (1971) found that, whereas the leaders tended to be more intelligent, active, aggressive, achieving, and socially adept than children who rarely led, they tended also to be more competent in a specific area of development.

It is apparent from this discussion, then, that children play many roles in these years before puberty and that the roles they assume can have major implications for their personality development. A look at some examples of positive and negative behavior will show more clearly how this happens.

PERSONAL-SOCIAL DEVELOPMENT

As the growing child tests himself in a variety of roles, he discovers much about himself, about others, and about the world at large. The neonate who was unaware of the existence of other people becomes a child who must work with those people and allow for their needs as well as his own. Behavior that forwards such consideration is regarded as positive; behavior

that interrupts such consideration of others is regarded as negative. This section will focus on generosity and assisting others as examples of positive behavior and on aggression as an example of negative behavior.

Positive Behavior

Although there is some evidence that helping others is an adaptive action that has been selected for in the course of evolution (Trivers, 1971), it does not spring forth fully developed at birth. Whether due to learning, to cognitive development, or to other factors, helping behavior definitely changes with age (F. Green and Schneider, 1974). The term "altruism" covers a great variety of specific helping actions, ranging from the simple sharing of candy or toys to springing to the aid of a child at the mercy of a bully.

Generosity is a form of positive behavior greatly valued by society and is a characteristic that is likely to increase with the child's age. Thus, older children usually are more willing than youngsters to share with others, whether they are sharing candy, toys, or money. This appears to come about for several reasons. First, older children often find it easier to part with possessions simply because they do not seem especially valuable. For example, Lauren, at the age of three, regarded a nickel as a huge sum that would bring her the pleasures of bubble gum, candy, or some trinket. Consequently, she would have been reluctant to part with it. In contrast, David, who is ten, sees a nickel as such an inconsequential amount that it can easily be given to help others.

Second, older children simply have had more opportunities to learn that people are supposed to help others. They may have seen their parents donate to charities or do volunteer work in hospitals. They may have rung doorbells on Halloween to collect money for UNICEF. They may have heard people say that "A friend in need is a friend indeed" and that "It is better to give than to receive." Such experiences generally make it clear to children that their society places a premium on helping other people.

Third, as Chapter 14 indicated, older children are also less likely to be egocentric. They are learning to take the perspective of others and to empathize with people who need help. Kenneth Rubin and Frank Schneider (1973), for example, measured the egocentrism of their seven-year-old subjects and then gave them an opportunity to donate candy to poor children and to help a younger child complete a task. The children who were better able to see things from another's viewpoint were more likely both to donate candy and to assist the younger child.

Various sorts of experiences may lead children to become generous. Obviously, anything that causes children to become less egocentric will be likely to increase generosity, but seeing another act in a generous manner will have the same effect. For example, Joan Grusec and Sandra Skubiski (1970) found that children who watched an adult donate to charity were more generous in their own donations. However, when the adult simply said that the children should share their money with the charity, donations

Figure 15.4 Leadership in clubs, on teams, and in other group activities of later childhood is usually determined on the basis of overall popularity and skill in specific areas of activity.

were markedly smaller. Verbal expresssions had strong effects on children's giving only among girls who had previously had a warm relationship with the adult who urged generosity.

James Bryan and Nancy Walbek (1970) have noted that, although exhortations do not affect children's behavior, they do increase children's statements that people should be altruistic. The lesson from these studies seems clear. If you want children to talk altruistically, just talk altruistically yourself. However, if you want them to behave altruistically, you should act in an altruistic manner (see Chapter 16). Children can learn hypocrisy just as they can learn altruism.

As indicated, a warm relationship did induce generosity in the girls who heard exhortations to donate in Grusec and Skubiski's study. Apparently, such adult nurturance also increases the effectiveness of other methods. For example, in a study of young children, Marian Yarrow, Phyllis Scott, and Carolyn Waxler (1973) found that, whereas any adult model

could affect children's immediate behavior, children who saw a warm, nurturant model were still generous two weeks after they watched the generous adult. It seems that the models who have strong, lasting effects on children are likely to be those who have close, rewarding relationships with the children—such as parents. Without such a relationship, examples are likely to have only a fleeting effect.

Although giving aid is a second kind of altruism, it is quite a different form of positive behavior from generosity. While generosity is usually clearly defined, the circumstances in which aid may be appropriate are usually confusing and unclear. It may not be obvious to the child that an emergency exists, that responsibility for help rests on him, or even that he is competent to help. As one might expect, this kind of altruistic behavior follows a different developmental course from that taken by generosity.

Ervin Staub (1970) has studied children's tendency to help in an emergency. He left children alone in a room for a few minutes, and, during this time, each

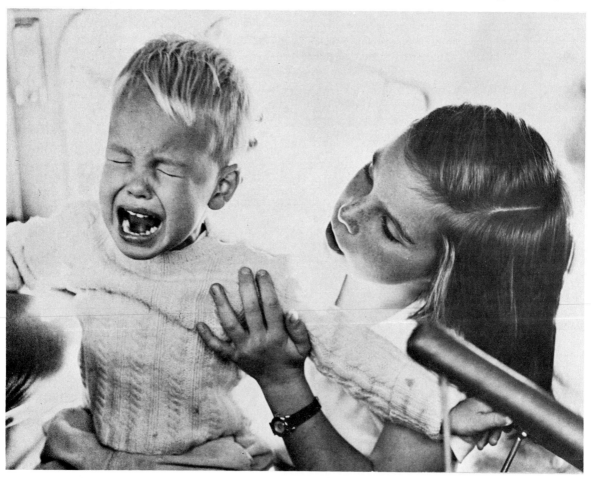

child heard a crash and the sound of another child crying in an adjacent room. Staub noted whether the child either entered the room, presumably to give assistance, or offered unsolicited information to the experimenter about the sounds of distress he had heard. In contrast to the finding that older children are more likely to share, Staub found that children's tendency to assist a crying child first increased with age and then decreased. Staub suggests that the reason that few young children assist a child in distress is because they are unable to empathize with others. As children get older, they are able to put themselves in another's position, and so they are more likely to help. In later childhood, however, children also begin to be sensitive to criticism and disapproval. Older children, therefore, are reluctant to help for fear of incurring an adult's disapproval.

In a subsequent investigation, Staub (1971) strengthened the case for believing that fear of disapproval affects a child's tendency to give aid when he studied the influence of modeling and nurturance on

such helping. In a situation like that used in his earlier study, he found that children who had a warm relationship with the adult investigator were more likely to help than those who lacked this relationship. He suggests that, because children believe that a warm, nurturant adult is unlikely to criticize them, the principal barrier that keeps older children from giving aid is removed.

In this study, Staub also found that an adult example increases helping and speculated that this effect occurs because it demonstrates that the child will not be criticized if he leaves the room to help. In generosity, you will recall, other reasons appeared to account for the influence of an adult model. Presumably, the adult model showed the child that generous behavior was correct, but even young children are likely to know without adult guidance that they should help someone who is hurt.

If altruism is the kind of behavior that helps people, other behavior can be potentially destructive to human relationships. A further look at the way aggression can be increased or decreased, along the lines indicated in Chapter 13, will show how negative behavior often develops in the growing child.

Negative Behavior

Although theoretical debate over whether human beings have an inherent drive toward aggression continues to rage, there is no question that children do frequently respond to frustration or thwarting with aggression. For instance, one of the earliest forms of peer interaction is one child shoving another to obtain a desirable toy. However, a child is expected to learn to control his expression of aggression very early. As soon as he begins to throw tantrums, to hit, and to throw his toys about, his parents try to control his actions. On the other hand, as the child continues to experience restraints at home, he also increasingly comes to see that controlled aggression, such as that on the football field or in the fight ring, is highly valued. The child, therefore, must learn when, where, and how to express aggressiveness in order to maximize his gain and minimize his punishment.

In this development, as the child gets older, he appears to shift the way in which he expresses aggression. As he increasingly encounters punishment for his aggressive acts, he becomes more discreet about when and where he commits them. Therefore, the development of aggression is not uniform. A child who gets away with aggression toward his siblings or his neighborhood playmates

Figure 15.5 With the expansion of certain social roles and responsibilities during later childhood, situations are likely to arise in which children are expected to help or provide assistance and to share valuable possessions with others. However, the extent to which such altruistic behaviors are expressed by a given child depends on the kinds of developmental experiences he has with other children and adults, both within and outside his family.

may be a model of decorum in the classroom and a ferocious fighter on the playground. Another child, whose parents punish him severely for aggressive acts, may be docile at home and a terror at school.

Several studies have examined the manner in which aggressive expression changes as children grow older. Willard Hartup (1974), who has studied this development, distinguishes between **hostile aggression** and **instrumental aggression.** Hostile aggression aims at hurting another person, whereas instrumental aggression aims at retrieving or acquiring an object, territory, or privilege.

In two early studies (Dawe, 1934; Goodenough, 1931) it was found that young children were more likely to engage in instrumental aggression and that the proportion of hostile acts increased with age. More specifically, Dawe found that 78 percent of the interpersonal conflicts among eighteen-month-old infants centered on possession of toys or other objects but that children about five or six years old quarreled over possessions only about 38 percent of the time.

As these results imply, the way that children express aggression appears to change with their cognitive development. Thus, as indicated in earlier discussions, children under six have difficulty in imagining another viewpoint or in making inferences about other people (Flavell *et al.*, 1968). If hostile aggression depends on the child's attributing negative intentions to the person who frustrates him, then younger children should be less likely than older children to show this kind of aggression.

Using this rationale, Hartup (1974) recently attempted to test and extend the earlier findings of Goodenough and Dawe. He observed children at play over a ten-week period and found that older children (from six to eight years) showed less total aggression than younger children (four to six years). This difference in total aggression was due primarily to the preponderance of instrumental aggression among younger children. As he had expected, older children showed a higher proportion of hostile aggression. Hartup also found, as had Goodenough, that children shifted from physical to verbal aggression as they got older, confirming a change in both the form and amount of aggression as children develop. Thus, as children get older and their acts of physical aggression are punished, they also become more subtle in the way that they express such behavior.

The same socializing influences that are important in teaching a child to behave in generous or helpful ways also operate in teaching a child to behave in aggressive ways. You will recall from Chapter 13, for

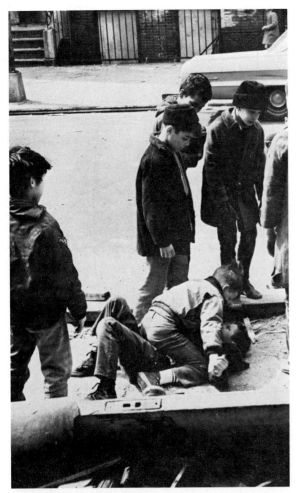

Figure 15.6 Examples of hostile and instrumental aggression. With advances in social skill and cognitive development, physical forms of hostile or instrumental aggression are likely to decrease in frequency. Because older children are more likely to be punished for physical acts of aggression, hostile verbalizations, subtle or not, often come to replace physical expressions.

example, that watching someone behave in a violent or aggressive manner has a great deal of influence in eliciting aggressive behavior. And, as the later section on television will show, witnessing a model may affect aggressive action in a variety of ways.

However, as noted before, witnessing others act aggressively does not always lead the observer to imitate the aggressor. For example, Marian Martin, Donna Gelfand, and Donald Hartmann (1971) allowed one hundred children to observe a model go through a unique sequence of aggressive behavior. The children then played either alone, in the presence of a male or female adult, or in the presence of a boy or girl of their own age. The investigators found that the children were most aggressive when a peer of the same sex was present. When an adult was present, a child initially showed little aggression. But if the adult showed no disapproval of the child's aggressive acts, the child became more and more aggressive. Apparently, the mere presence of an adult tends to inhibit aggression, but as the child becomes aware that his aggressive acts are either acceptable or neutral in the adult's eyes, his inhibitions disappear.

As the child grows and comes into contact with an increasing number of people, he is exposed to a widening variety of models who can influence him toward positive or negative behavior. He is no longer so much the product of his family. However, a look at the family circle shows that it remains a potent force on the child's developing personality.

PARENT INFLUENCE

In later childhood, a child's parents continue to control many aspects of his life and to exert a strong influence on his socialization. A child still depends on his parents for his material wants: food, clothing, shelter, and other physical necessities. He also depends on them for attention, affection, physical contact, and play. Because the manner in which his parents fulfill his physical and psychological needs affects the child's behavior, the degree of parental control remains strong. As noted in Chapter 13, sex-role behavior continues to be heavily influenced by parents, and positive social behavior such as generosity or helpfulness is largely the result of parental responses to the child's actions (Rosenhan, 1970).

On the other hand, parents' strong control over a child's needs also gives them the power to withhold physical and psychological resources. Parents often punish an infant or a young child by withholding their affection or by spanking. Whether by withholding

approval, affection, and rewards or by following a
child's acts with unpleasant consequences, parents
can and do continue to punish older children.

As the discussion of negative behavior has indicated, a child may behave in a number of inappropriate
or even antisocial ways. His acquisition of roles
comes about as much through his attempts to avoid
unpleasant consequences as through his responses to
praise or reward. These factors, together with the
child's increased sensitivity to harsh words, censure,
and criticism, create innumerable situations in which
his parents are likely to resort to punishment.

But parents do more than punish. They continue to
serve their children as models of both appropriate and
inappropriate behavior. The absence of one of these
powerful models can be a potentially major force in a
child's life. Single-parent homes may differ in many
ways from homes in which both parents are present.
As the discussion of sex roles noted, most psychological study of such homes has focused on the effects
of father absence, especially on boys.

For example, E. Mavis Hetherington (1966) has
found that boys without fathers tend to be less
aggressive and more dependent on the peer group
than boys whose fathers are present. Boys without
fathers in the home also participate in fewer games
that involve physical contact. Father absence seems to
affect even academic skills; when boys without fathers enter college, they tend to show the typical
feminine pattern of higher verbal than mathematical
scores on entrance tests (Carlsmith, 1964).

Most developmental psychologists attribute these
differences to the lack of a masculine model rather
than to such factors as the disturbance of an attachment relationship, and there is substantial evidence to
back up this belief. First, these differences are most
common in males and seem to center on such sex-
typed behavior as aggression and dependence. Second, children whose fathers are absent are much more
active than children whose fathers are present in
vying for the attention of older males, which suggests
that the children feel a real need for a relationship
with an adult male.

Finally, it appears that other male role models
reduce the differences in behavior attributed to the
absence of a father. As noted earlier, fatherless boys
who have an older brother are more aggressive and
less dependent than those without an older brother
(Wohlford *et al.*, 1971). Furthermore, the presence of
an older sister does not reduce the influence of the
older brother. Apparently, the mere presence of a
male role model, rather than a balance between males

and females in a family, is important. Of course, an older brother does not completely replace a father (Biller, 1968), even though he does seem to reduce the usual effects associated with the absence of a father.

A limited sort of father absence (and mother absence) may also be changing the way that American children are socialized. Urie Bronfenbrenner (1967) notes that the increasingly common white-collar job and community service of both parents means that they are likely to spend less time in the home interacting with their children than was true among earlier generations. The children are, in essence, pushed out of the family and into the peer group. Bronfenbrenner speculates that, as a result of such changes, American children may come more and more to look to the peer group as a model not only of peer relations but also of the values and ideals traditionally handed down from parents to children.

PEER INFLUENCE

With the beginning of the school years, the peer group increases in size and in importance. A child finds a large number of schoolmates of his own age as well as many others of slightly different ages. This new peer group includes children from different neighborhoods, children who would remain strangers without the school setting. A wider group of acquaintances, however, does not necessarily lead to an increase in the number of close friends. Whereas during early childhood the child became close to an

increasing number of other children, during later childhood, friendships increase in intensity rather than in number. An older child spends more time with his friends. Occasionally he plays after school at a friend's house or spends the night with his friend. Along with this increased intensity comes stronger influence.

The strong influence that peers can have on a child's behavior was clearly demonstrated in a study by Philip Costanzo and Marvin Shaw (1966). These investigators asked children to compare the lengths of a pair of lines. One line was obviously longer than the other, but all except one of the children were confederates of the investigators, and they chose the incorrect line. When the child who was not a confederate denied the evidence of his senses and agreed with the obviously incorrect judgment of the group, he had altered his own judgment to conform to that of his peers. As Figure 15.8 shows, a child's susceptibility to this form of peer influence increased with age, reached its peak during the preadolescent years, and then gradually declined. Such results as these indicate that peers can be especially important as guides to appropriate behavior during later childhood.

Hartup's (1970) descriptions of peer influence may help to explain this rise and subsequent decline of peer influence. As Hartup has suggested, peer influence may initially rise as the growing child's egocentrism decreases. He also speculates that the later decline can be explained by the child's ability to reinforce himself. By self-reinforcement, Hartup

Figure 15.7 (*opposite*) As primary agents in the socialization of appropriate and inappropriate behavior and as the chief dispensers of many forms of rewards and punishments, parents continue to exert major influences on personal-social development during later childhood.

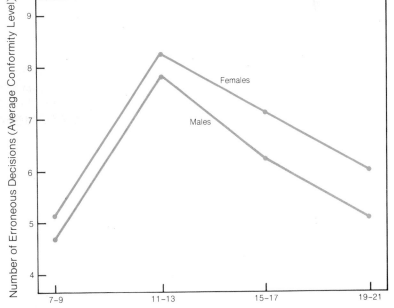

Figure 15.8 Graph summarizing the results of children's conformity to the judgments of a peer group. The results for both females and males show that susceptibility to peer influence increases with age until early adolescence and then gradually declines. Such data are but one indicator of the importance of peer influences in later childhood. (After Costanzo and Shaw, 1966)

means that, as the child interacts with his peers, he begins to internalize the statements they make about his behavior as well as the effects of their responses to him. Through this process of internalizing the judgments of others, the child develops the ability to evaluate his own actions.

His self-evaluation can be either negative or positive. Social punishment by peers—in the form of ostracism, ridicule, or finding a scapegoat—and physical punishment, such as fighting, are tremendously powerful forms of control. The child also learns to internalize these negative reactions and expressions of his peers, and gradually his behavior comes under the control of his own self-criticism and punishment. Thus, in a variety of ways, peers can exert a good deal of influence during later childhood.

In addition to coming under the increasing influence of his friends and acquaintances, the child begins to encounter more often a unique form of peer influence: the *group*, a formal, structured collection of peers. Thus, it is most often during later childhood that the formation of groups such as youth gangs increases.

The tendency of children to form structured groups has been inspected in a number of studies by Muzafer and Carolyn Sherif (1953, 1964). They divided boys into two groups and observed the group functioning closely. Inevitably, a hierarchical structure formed among the boys in each group. As would be expected from the previous discussion of leadership in this chapter, the most popular boys did not automatically become leaders, nor were leaders always the most talented or the toughest.

Functioning independently of the status of individual group members, group cohesiveness exercises a great deal of influence on a child's behavior. Competition within a group may decrease cohesiveness (Stendler, Damrin, and Haines, 1951), but the Sherifs have found that evenly balanced competition between groups results in greater cohesiveness within each group. Although occasional rancor may appear just after a competitive defeat, group members generally become much closer to one another in competitive situations. Because competition between groups produces a cooperative atmosphere within an individual group, it is not surprising that it should promote group solidarity. However, in a study of unbalanced competition, when one group consistently lost, the losing group threatened to collapse in disharmony (Sherif and Sherif, 1953). Apparently, when the unpleasantness generated by defeat becomes con-

stant, it simply overcomes any tendency within the group for members to cooperate.

Whether competition was balanced or unbalanced, it produced a considerable amount of friction between groups. The boys looked down on members of the other group, and the situation eventually exploded into open hostility. This intergroup hostility further strengthened group cohesiveness and increased the influence of the group over the behavior of its members. Further, boys who were not normally hostile participated in intensely aggressive acts for the sake of the group. In such a case, it seems that the structured group has the ability to overpower any tendency the child has developed toward self-judgment and to lead him to engage in behavior that he would normally avoid.

FUNCTIONS OF PLAY

Play socializes the growing child, as the discussion in Chapter 13 noted. In early childhood, play is characterized by dramatic fantasy and the use of symbols and imagery. The older child, however, is more socialized, more attuned and accommodated to social reality. Play during later childhood, therefore, consists more and more of games regulated by rules that everybody accepts. Although dramatic play continues in a formal, structured way (as in plays put on for parents and friends or neighborhood games of cops and robbers), the spontaneous activity of playfully transforming reality in order to act out personal desires and conflicts seems increasingly to become interior dialogue, fantasy, and daydreams (Klinger, 1969).

The socializing function of play shows clearly in a study of children's games by Iona and Peter Opie (1969). The Opies found two main functions in all child-organized play. First, games provide a structure for children's relationships. Second, games allow a child to experience adult life in easy bits and nonthreatening pieces.

Rules and Practice

Rules provide the structure of games. Children spend a great deal of time making rules for the games they play, and it is usually important to them that those rules, no matter how silly they may appear, be followed without deviation. Whereas younger children consider their rules to be absolutely binding, as they grow toward adolescence, children come to understand rules as conventions, agreed upon for specific purposes and therefore open to modification

Figure 15.9 Throughout later childhood, play continues to serve a variety of functions. Rules and regulations become more prominent and come to govern not only the games but also the social relationships that may develop as a part of those activities. Achieving competence in games that require practice and the development of new skills further contributes to the development of a positive self-concept. In addition, certain types of ''make-believe'' play provide children with opportunities to experience various real and fantasied roles in life.

by common consent. As noted earlier, Jean Piaget (1932) considers this change in attitude to be part of the child's development of mutual respect and cooperation.

Although a leader may break a rule, a child with low group status finds himself under tremendous pressure to conform to the established rules. If he fails to do so, he is often expelled from the group and is not allowed to come back until he promises to keep the faith. This slavish attention to detail probably serves the child in many ways. He learns that social commerce must be regulated in order to sustain interactions for any length of time. (At a younger age, children merely drift away from their peers if they do not like the rules). He learns that, once a more or less formal structure has been set up, he can relax and enjoy himself within its confines without having to worry about being rejected. And rules provide a means by which a new arrival to the group may rapidly find his place.

Play also continues to serve the second function: as the training ground for personality characteristics and social behaviors that will be important in adulthood. Brian Sutton-Smith and John Roberts (1964) have characterized the world of play as a sort of buffer zone where pressures for successful social behavior are managed on a miniature scale. Children's games allow them to succeed in various ways: by decision-making ability in games of strategy such as checkers and chess; by speed and power in games of physical skill such as relays and baseball; and by luck in games of chance such as cards. Children learn to compete, but within a safe world that minimizes the penalties associated with losing or failing. Children often attach little significance to who wins or loses; they do not worry about prizes and show little concern if a game is not finished. Even when competition is strong and the desire to win high, children like games that restart almost automatically so that everyone gets a new chance. In contrast to adults, they often get most of their enjoyment from experiencing, not from winning.

Whereas games allow less symbolic elaboration than the younger child's dramatic play does, many themes that run through children's games reflect experiences from the real world that are frightening or seem beyond the child's comprehension or control. For example, Fritz Redl (1959) cites such recurrent themes as racing, chasing, attacking, seducing, capturing, harrassing, searching, and rescuing. Within the world of the game, children experience excitement

and tension. Playing hide-and-seek in the dark, the child feels the terror of waiting to be pounced on. The fun of such scary games seems to depend on their safeness: They provide quick reversals of tension within a limited and structured time period.

Children differ in the amount of playing they do (J. L. Singer, 1973). Highly anxious children tend to show little imagination or free involvement in play. Aggressive, highly impulsive children have trouble abiding by the rules of the game; the excitement becomes so great that the game structure dissolves into fighting and wild behavior. After studying the social behavior of aggressive boys, Redl (1959) concluded that games both arouse emotions and keep them in bounds, so that following rules provides important training in impulse control and self-regulation.

During later childhood, a child not only learns from games to relate to other children but he also discovers further his own capacities and worth, thereby elaborating his self-concept. Many games of prowess allow a child to test his physical abilities both against his own standards and in comparison with the abilities of others. Many games seem designed to let a child explore the capabilities of his own body for his own satisfaction. Follow-the-leader, skating, riding bicycles, tag, and even hopscotch are as much self-competitive as they are peer-competitive. A child issues his own physical challenge just to see if he can make his body do what he wants it to do. The older child who sets out on an expedition to nowhere-in-particular may climb a fence, walk along a narrow board over a ditch, swing on a rope, jump a gulley, crawl through a drainpipe, and jump off a high ledge—all simply to exercise his physical powers.

Social Cognition

Games also further the child's cognitive development. This shows plainly when the child learns to play a game with rules, such as checkers or tic-tac-toe. In competitive games that require strategy, a child must be able to take his opponent's point of view if he is to figure out his enemy's strategy and adapt his own moves to it. M. Papst (1966) compared the behavior of six- and seven-year-old children at strategic games and found that the youngest children were slow to learn the moves that would assure them of winning and also had more difficulty articulating the strategy of their opponent and its implications. The changes in social cognition that arise out of child's play require further discussion.

Suppose that Susan is an egocentric seven-year-old and has just learned to play checkers. She is likely to have much more difficulty teaching the game to a friend than eleven-year-old Matt would. She will probably have trouble explaining the rules of the game in a systematic way that takes into account the point of view of her naive pupil. She may start out talking about kings before telling about jumping and the goal of capturing the opponent's checkers. Both Susan and her friend may become confused and frustrated. As Chapter 12 makes clear, young children cannot adapt their instructions even if they know that their pupils cannot see.

The problem, of course, is that Susan does not know how to put herself in another's shoes. Piaget (1928) has suggested that the development of role taking comes about as children play games and that it leads to a decline in egocentrism. Role taking enables a child to understand how another person feels, perceives, or thinks. The child learns to make inferences about the internal psychological states of another person. As Chapter 13 states, the play of very young children is characterized by overtly taking the role of others, but one may also play another's role in imagination, as adults do all the time. Such imaginative role taking facilitates smooth social interaction.

A storytelling method for assessing role-taking ability makes use of the cognitive processes that a child needs to understand a complex social situation (Feffer, 1959). In this method, the child makes up a story involving at least three figures in a picture, and then he retells the story from the point of view of each of the actors, taking a different role for each retelling. As the child shifts roles, he must take into account each new person's experience of the action and the knowledge brought to the situation by that person. This requires the child not only to take each character's point of view but also to make sure that each new perspective fits the others. Using this procedure, Melvin Feffer and Vivian Gourevitch (1960) found a significant increase in role-taking ability among children from six to thirteen years old, with the strongest gains occurring between the ages of eight and ten.

The same social-cognitive skills that characterize role taking are necessary in persuasion. John Flavell and his colleagues (1966, 1968) have shown that the ability to persuade another person to do something increases during later childhood. Effective persuasion requires that the child identify the listener's particular needs and attitudes so that he can construct a "sales pitch." Such a sensitivity to the attributes of another reflects role-taking ability. Flavell asked children to pretend that they were trying to talk their father into buying them a television set for their room. Both the number and variety of children's arguments increased sharply between the third and seventh grade.

A third grader may argue: "Come on. I want a television for my own room. Come on. Please. Daddy, come on. Buy me a television. I want one for my room. Come on. Come on, Daddy. I want you to.

Figure 15.10 By giving older children a chance to help younger children, schools also provide an opportunity for the older child to try out new roles requiring cognitive and social skills. In this situation, the older child often begins to see the communication process from an entirely new perspective—that of teacher.

There!'' A seventh grader is likely to make shrewd arguments, anticipating reasons that his father might find convincing, from the ''everybody's getting one'' argument to the educational uses of television.

Many of the child's daily social encounters are directed toward convincing others to do something. And during these years children become much more adept at maneuvering in their social world. The accumulating research evidence pointing to marked improvement in role-taking ability during childhood has led Flavell to speculate that later childhood may be the time for developing basic role-taking skills.

TODAY'S CHILD AND TOMORROW'S

The child's subculture continues to be significant as an agent of socialization throughout childhood and, as the scope of his contact with society broadens, becomes even more important. But cultures change with time. Thus, differences in the same culture at two different times may be as dramatic as differences between two subcultures at the same time. Consequently, in a rapidly changing society, the experiences of today's children may vary dramatically from those of yesterday's and tomorrow's children.

Until the last decade or so, children had little freedom or money, and only two decades ago even eight- to ten-year-olds were expected to have some kind of part-time job (delivering papers, cutting grass, helping clean house) to supplement their meager allowance. Household chores were commonplace, as were large homework assignments for even very young children, so time was often at a premium. And lacking the instant entree into the adult world that television now offers so pervasively, yesterday's children knew considerably less about the world than today's children do.

Television

Parents are still the single most important determiner of the normal child's attitudes toward the world around him. Next in importance are his siblings and his peers during later childhood; then close relatives, schoolteachers, and religious leaders; and finally the heroes and heroines that the child reads about, hears about, or watches on television. For any given child, one may be able to find exceptions to this rank ordering, but it is a fairly accurate rating of influence. In past generations, parents blamed their offspring's misbehavior on radio, comic books, pulp magazines, and, at the turn of the century, dime novels. These days, television bears the brunt of the blame.

Recently there has been a great deal of concern about the possible effects of television violence. As the section on the development of aggression states, models may be powerful transmitters of new behavior and for many children may also reduce inhibitions on existing behavior. Television, then, with its vivid depiction of an amazing variety of aggressive acts, has increasingly become an object of concern.

A variety of studies have been conducted to assess the effects of television on children. Early studies by Albert Bandura (1973) and his associates showed that children could learn new ways to express aggression from television and similar media. D. Keith Osborn and Richard Endsley (1971) went further and investigated children's emotional reactions to various sorts of television programs. Children saw four films depicting either human violence, cartoon violence, human nonviolence, or cartoon nonviolence. Children told what they liked best and what was the scariest. The two violent films produced the most emotional reactions; the children remembered details of the violent films the best; they found the human violence the scariest; and they preferred the nonviolent cartoon. This study shows that watching television violence evokes emotional responses in children and influences them to remember the details of depicted violence.

Moving closer to the central question of whether television violence affects the way that children behave, the Office of the Surgeon General (1972) commissioned an exhaustive study of the effects of television violence but failed to reach any definitive conclusions. However, existing investigations give some clues as to how television may affect behavior.

For example, Robert Liebert and Robert Baron (1972) investigated whether watching television aggression would make children more willing to hurt another child. Liebert and Baron showed brief excerpts taken directly from regular television shows to boys and girls from five to nine years old. The excerpts were either violent and aggressive (a fist fight or a shooting) or exciting but nonaggressive (a sporting event). After they saw one of these programs, the children were given a series of opportunities either to hurt or to help another child by pushing a button. Each child was told that pushing one button would help another child (who was not actually present) to win a prize but that pushing the other button would hurt the child. They were also told that the longer they pressed either button, the more the other child would be helped or hurt.

Despite their brief exposure to these television shows, children who had observed the violent television sequence chose to hurt the other child for a significantly longer period of time than those who had watched the nonaggressive scenes. Obviously, this study uses a specialized definition of aggression, but it demonstrates that watching one kind of aggression may lead to aggression of a very different sort. It suggests that television programs depicting aggression may remove or reduce some children's inhibitions against committing violence. Additional studies support this position (Leifer and Roberts, 1972).

Television violence showed up in the classroom in a study by Monroe Lefkowitz and his colleagues (1972). They found a significant relationship between the amount of television violence that third-grade boys watched and their classroom aggression as rated by their peers. Even more impressive is their finding of a relationship between the amount of television violence that boys watched in the third grade and their aggression at age nineteen. Moreover, they concluded that it was not merely that children who commit aggressive acts watch more television violence but that children first watch television violence and then are rated as aggressive.

Although, as stressed earlier, the factors controlling expression of aggression are exceedingly complex, these and other studies appear to indicate that television violence may both teach new forms of aggressive behavior (such as the recent growth of interest in kung-fu) and relax inhibitions against aggressive expression.

The effects of television on children range beyond the effects of violent programing. Children at play often enact social roles that they have taken from television. As many feminists have pointed out, television has served as a rigidly conventional socializing influence in portraying women's roles as essentially home- and children-centered. As one author has asked, "What sort of self-concept do you develop when the role models you see on television are primarily devoted to finding the optimal coffee blend for their husbands or vanquishing kitchen odors?"

Television opens children to vast worlds of experience that were previously unavailable. It educates and illustrates things that remained abstractions to preceding generations. The generation of children who have never lived without television is now entering adulthood, so it is impossible at present to assess the long-range effects of television. But the electronic miracle affects a child's knowledge of the world, his activities, heroes, time spent with his peers, and a variety of other factors. Tomorrow's child is going to be a product of that experience.

Drugs

If television was the parental scapegoat of the 1960s, it seems likely that drugs will bear the blame for juvenile misbehavior in the 1970s. For years, drug use remained the province of the urban ghetto dweller or the musician, but today a wide variety of drugs are available in virtually every community. The marked and rapid change in availability and use of drugs has produced a new facet to the so-called generation gap. Although many parents may disapprove of alcohol use by the young, at least they understand the practice from their own experience. However, many adults grew up believing that drugs produced either insanity or incurable addiction. Thus, many of today's children know more about drugs and their properties than their parents do.

Strictly speaking, it is not adequate to speak of "drugs" without specifying the kind, because the various available drugs differ dramatically in composition and effect. But among the young, the most commonly used drug is marijuana. One random sample of 1,104 men and women in a large American city showed that almost half of those adults between the ages of eighteen and twenty-four had used marijuana at least once, whereas only some 5 percent of those adults thirty-five years of age and older reported ever trying the drug (Manheimer, Mellinger, and Balter, 1969). Although there are no reliable data on marijuana use among children from six to twelve, a recent survey of Michigan high-school students indicated that more than 50 percent of them had tried marijuana at least once and that about 25 percent smoked it regularly. A better example of a "generation gap" could hardly be found.

The long-term effects of the use of marijuana are as yet unknown (as are the long-term effects of viewing violence on television) and can only be guessed at; the social effects of the generation gap are probably more predictable. Parents with problem children will tend to blame the erratic and antisocial behavior of their sons and daughters on pot rather than realize that marijuana probably does little more than heighten already existing problems.

Education

After a child reaches the age of six, the school becomes an increasingly major force in his socialization. Today's schools are strongly influenced by a movement toward broadening the definition of education. The new definition supplements the traditional emphasis on scholastic material with a concern for personal growth (Minuchin et al., 1969). The proponents of this movement believe that a child's social and emotional development should be given as much attention as his intellectual growth. As John Holt (1964), one of the major critics of traditional schooling, has put it:

The alternative—I can see no other—is to have schools and classrooms in which each child in his own way can satisfy his curiosity, develop his abilities and talents, pursue his interests, and from the adults and older children around him get a glimpse of the great variety and richness of life. In short, the school should be a great smörgasbord of intellectual, artistic, creative, and athletic activities, from which each child could take whatever he wanted, and as much as he wanted, or as little. (page 180)

Obviously, Holt envisions an educational process that goes beyond reading and arithmetic. He and other educational reformers have taken the schools in new directions: open classrooms, schools without walls, self-paced instruction, body-movement exercises, community-involvement projects, and so forth. Inherent in each of these practices is the supposition that schooling must address itself to a broader conception of what a child should learn.

Another manifestation of the changing role of the school is the rise of sex-education programs in elementary schools. The transfer of this sensitive area to the classroom indicates people's increased awareness of the school's role as socializing agent.

Although Freud claimed that sexual development is latent during later childhood, his work was based on observations of the children of Victorian Europe. Today sexual information and misinformation are widely available, and every child meets a barrage of sexual stimuli that only adults would have encountered in other eras. In addition, as Chapter 17 indicates, children are now maturing several years earlier than Freud's young patients did. Sexual activity also is likely to begin earlier today than in the past, so that interest in sexuality is often quite high even among young children. And early experiences with sexual information may have important and lasting effects on sexual attitudes.

Until recently, most children learned the facts of procreation from their peers, from older siblings or friends, from sex manuals thrust into their hands by blushing parents, from looking up "dirty" words in the dictionary, from searching the dusty recesses of public libraries, from pornography purloined from a parent's private collection, and from graffiti scrawled on restroom walls.

Although many middle-class American parents seem reluctant to discuss reproduction, they readily communicate their sexual attitudes to their children. The very fact that this subject is seldom discussed openly and factually in most family settings leads a child to a double understanding: Sex is both evil and desirable.

With the advent of sex-education classes in the schools, much of the delicious (if neurotic) wickedness associated with the topic seems to be disappearing. In many schools, instruction in human reproduction begins in the first grade, to be repeated at regular intervals throughout the rest of the child's schooling. Most instructional materials emphasize the biological aspects of conception and birth; more delicate questions, involving moral and social aspects of sexuality, are generally left to the teacher's discretion. This latter aspect of sex education disturbs some parents, who insist that a teacher may instill a too liberal or immoral sexual attitude in their children. Although critics of sex education in the schools have been successful in having programs removed from some schools, it seems that these critics constitute a minority. In several recent surveys made in northern and eastern states, more than 70 percent of the parents polled were in favor of continuing and strengthening existing sex-education programs.

Although parents are likely to continue to be the primary instillers of attitudes and standards of behavior, the importance of television and the school as socializing agents is likely to increase. In addition, as children come to acquire many of their values and attitudes outside the family, it seems likely that the socializing influence of child on parent will also increase. In the future, children are more likely, then, to acquire more ideas and values outside their family and to transmit these to their parents, even if such ideas and values are not always accepted.

SUMMARY

1. During later childhood, the interplay of parents, peers, play, and society in socialization continues to be reflected in the personality development of the child and in the different roles that he assumes. Friendships and play usually are restricted to those of the same sex, and peer roles involving popularity and leadership become more important as more organization enters peer relationships.

2. As the child develops and tests himself in a variety of roles, he learns that behaviors such as generosity and assisting others are likely to be regarded as positive, whereas behaviors such as aggression are likely to be regarded as negative. However, most children learn both positive and negative kinds of behavior, and whether one or both types occur regularly depends on their social and situational effects, on modeling influences, and on other factors.

3. Parents continue to exert a strong influence on their developing child. They selectively guide the continuing development of their child's positive or negative behaviors by giving or withholding their attention, affection, and material resources and by providing models of appropriate or inappropriate sex-role behavior, generosity, aggression, and other behaviors.

4. During later childhood, the peer group usually increases in size and relative influence. Contacts with friends and acquaintances and participation in structured peer groups are likely to become more frequent and intense. These peer influences, in turn, provide various models of appropriate and inappropriate behavior and selectively reward and punish prescribed behaviors.

5. Through child-organized play and games, increasingly regulated by rules that everybody accepts, the child experiences a structure for relationships with his peers and acquires behaviors that will be important in adulthood. In addition, he learns more about his own abilities and worth (self-concept) and develops social-cognitive skills required in role taking and persuasion.

6. Just as different subcultures result in different views, values, and behavior among people, differences also occur over time within subcultures. Consideration of the impact of television, drug use, and sex education on children suggests that such changes in experience may result in drastically different views, values, and behavior from one generation to another.

SUGGESTED READINGS

Bronfenbrenner, Urie. "The Split-Level American Family," *Saturday Review*, 50 (October 7, 1967), 60–66.

Erikson, Erik. *Childhood and Society.* New York: Norton, 1963.

Eron, Leonard D., Leopold O. Walder, and Monroe M. Lefkowitz. *Learning of Aggression in Children.* Boston: Little, Brown, 1971.

Herron, R. E., and Brian Sutton-Smith. *Child's Play.* New York: Wiley, 1971.

Pomeroy, Wardell B. *Your Child and Sex: A Guide for Parents.* New York: Delacorte, 1974.

Figure 15.11 Sex education is a prime example of the school's increasing influence on the personal-social development of children.

Moral conduct is a product of the interaction of socialization and a complex set of developmental changes.

16

MORALITY: FROM RULES TO CONDUCT

On August 9, 1974, Richard M. Nixon resigned as President of the United States. His resignation, made when it had become virtually certain that he would be impeached and probably removed from office, was the culmination of a striking example of public immorality, the loosely connected events gathered together under the label of Watergate. When the transcripts of presidential conversations had been made public, philosophers, ministers, journalists, judges, and average citizens asked how supposedly moral men could have participated in immoral acts.

Perhaps the most tempting, and certainly the easiest, explanation of people's moral conduct is simply that some people are scrupulously moral, whereas others are less so. Observers of the national scene have consistently applied this type of explanation to the men involved in the Watergate affair. Yet most of these men were described by their neighbors as warm and helpful human beings, pillars of their communities. Many had strong religious convictions. How could their daily behavior have appeared so impeccably moral to friends and neighbors while they were involved in political immorality, and illegality, of such astonishing magnitude? This question should arouse our suspicions of easy explanations of morality. Therefore, an examination of contemporary findings on the way that moral conduct develops should help to explain how apparently moral men can behave in immoral ways.

Previous chapters in this book have concentrated on a single aspect of behavior or development during a particular phase of life. But human behavior is complicated, and intellectual, social, and emotional factors generally combine to influence any act. In this chapter, we take a particular kind of conduct, moral conduct; we consider how it involves intellectual, social, and emotional factors; and we focus on its development from early childhood to adolescence.

We will look at the way moral thought, feeling, and action can vary from one situation to another. We will trace developmental changes in thinking about moral problems and see that opportunities to take the roles of others may change the way that a child perceives and thinks about moral issues. We will discover that the way an individual child or adolescent feels when he remembers or anticipates a transgression will affect the way that he regulates his own behavior. After discussing the effect of discipline, we will examine the influence of modeling on moral development and moral conduct. Finally, we will discuss the complexities of judging the behavior of other persons.

THE COURSE OF MORAL DEVELOPMENT

For many generations, morality was the central category for defining social relationships and development, and the social sciences were called "the moral sciences." In the last few decades, morality has slipped in and out of focus as a central interest in developmental psychology. The important work of Hugh Hartshorne and Mark May in the late 1920s on children's moral conduct and that of Jean Piaget in the 1930s on moral judgment were followed by two decades of relative inactivity. In the 1930s and 1940s, thought about moral character concentrated on discussions of social adjustment, and specific concerns about moral development focused on discussions of socialization processes.

Recently, however, thoughtful psychologists and laymen have become acutely aware of the inadequacies of dealing with moral issues in terms of mental health or group adjustment. The mental-health labels are not scientific; they simply make value judgments about people in terms of social norms. And neither mental-health nor social-adjustment terms define the norms and values that represent basic ideals for people. The atrocities of the socially conforming members of the Nazi system and the crimes committed by politicians have made people acutely aware of the fact that adjustment to the group is no substitute for moral maturity.

In order to understand the moral conduct of groups, however, it is necessary to understand the development of moral conduct in the individual. Moral conduct, like any complex behavior, is determined by the interplay of many factors. When an adult such as ex-President Nixon or a preadolescent like Matt is faced with a problem that involves morality, his conduct does not take place in a vacuum. His past experiences affect his present actions, and moral conduct changes greatly between infancy and adulthood. It is generally agreed that (1) babies come into the world as amoral beings; (2) they are active

learners; (3) they acquire their first personal moral values and standards from their parents; (4) early moral edicts are tied to specific situations; (5) a child's early moral concepts and understandings differ from those of adults; and (6) a person's moral concepts and understanding change with increasing cognitive sophistication and social experience.

By the time they start school, most children still have literal conceptions of right and wrong. They are likely to show consistency between their thoughts, feelings, and actions to the degree that they have learned to do so at home. But soon they are also likely to show some discrepancy in the way that they think, act, and feel as they interact with new schoolmates. Some quickly learn by example and direct experience to be more devious in what they say and do. Others may become more consistent as they follow the precepts and ideas of peers, teachers, and others.

As children develop toward adolescence, they are likely to think and act in ways that are different from their earlier behavior. For example, the older child and the adolescent show more sophisticated ways of thinking, can move from a specific situation to a more general ethical rule, and are more likely to consider the needs and views of others. As we will see, these changes, along with increased self-regulation and wider learning experiences, usually result in a more complex form of moral conduct.

INCONSISTENCY IN MORAL CONDUCT

Although people continue to talk about moral conduct as a class of reactions that go together and that are governed by some central controlling process such as conscience, it is plain that most people display inconsistent moral conduct. After surveying the research, Douglas Graham (1972) concluded that a person is likely to show highly consistent moral conduct only when the range of situations that confront him are restricted or when a high level of abstract thinking allows him to apply general principles over many varied situations.

Over forty-five years ago, Hartshorne and May (1928) conducted a landmark study of consistency in moral conduct and disappointed all those who would like to divide the world into moral and immoral people. In the course of their research, Hartshorne and May tested literally thousands of children for many types of moral conduct (such as cheating, lying, and stealing) in different contexts (such as tests, games, and contests) in widely varied settings (such as home, church, and playground). They found that children's moral opinions and judgments as expressed on a questionnaire remained consistent, provided that the two questionnaires were administered in the same setting. When the setting was moved, for example, from a church to a clubhouse, the correlations between the scores on the two tests dropped drastically, making it appear that even the children's basic moral codes changed when the situation changed.

The children's moral behavior was even less consistent than their statements about morality. Hartshorne and May found that almost all children cheat some of the time and that knowing a child has cheated in one situation does not make it possible to predict that he will (or will not) cheat in another. Expediency appeared to determine a child's decision to cheat. When it seemed safe and easy to cheat or when it appeared that other children cheated or approved of cheating, a child was himself more likely to cheat. In some classrooms, for example, many children cheated, whereas in others, almost no one cheated. It also appeared that the child who cheats in the classroom is not necessarily the same child who tells lies there, nor is the child who lies to the teacher the same child who is likely to lie to his peers. Finally, the relationship between children's statements about morality and their actual behavior was virtually nonexistent. Their results convinced Hartshorne and May that it was foolish to try to categorize children or adults as moral or immoral. The crucial question was not whether an individual would behave morally or immorally but rather when he would do so.

Subsequent work has not challenged the basic conclusions reached by Hartshorne and May. For example, Robert Sears, Lucy Rau, and Richard Alpert (1965) compared six different tests of children's resistence to temptation in play settings. Almost all the resulting correlations were positive, but none indicated a very great degree of consistency, even though all were administered in the context of a play situation. A similar study of moral consistency led Wesley Allinsmith (1960) to conclude that a person with a truly generalized conscience is a statistical rarity.

Even when researchers have found a relationship between moral reasoning and moral behavior, it has generally been of the modest variety reported earlier by Hartshorne and May. Walter and Harriet Mischel (in press) surveyed the existing research and concluded that it is difficult to justify claims of strong links between moral reasoning and individual action. They suggest that knowing people's moral reasoning allows one to predict only 10 percent of the variation in their behavior in different situations. In such cases,

Figure 16.1 At one point or another, most children learn and believe for a time in the power of certain gestures or rituals to undo or negate what they think, say, or do.

it appears that it is often possible to predict moral behavior just as accurately from a person's need for achievement or his need for affiliation as from his level of moral reasoning (S. Schwartz *et al.*, 1969).

Overall, inconsistency in moral conduct should not be surprising. Moral situations involve strong and conflicting pressures, and only a slight change in these pressures may shift the proposed situation from moral to immoral in a person's judgment. Different circumstances may also influence different people. For one person, the chances of getting caught may determine his behavior. For another, the magnitude of the payoff may be the determining factor, whereas a third person's behavior may depend on the amount of effort involved. Moral conduct also appears to be governed by a variety of factors that make adherence to social moral standards more or less likely. Although moral reasoning may become increasingly unified and consistent as a person develops, his behavior often depends on situational constraints. Moreover, resistance to temptation is a kind of behavior pattern different from the donation of money to a charity. Both may be examples of moral behavior, but they are not necessarily governed by the same processes nor do they necessarily manifest themselves in a consistent fashion across individuals.

MORAL REASONING

The various ways in which people come to think, act, and feel morally depend partly on developmental changes in their cognitive understanding. That is, the development of moral reasoning can be seen as a specific case of general cognitive development. Thus, we would expect the same factors that are important in general cognitive development to be important in moral development.

Variation in Moral Reasoning

There are many ways to study developmental changes in moral thinking, but one of the most provocative and appealing has been proposed by Lawrence Kohlberg (1963, 1969). In this approach, a child or adult is asked to respond to a number of moral dilemmas such as the following:

In Europe, a woman was near death from cancer. One drug might save her, a form of radium that a druggist in the same town had recently discovered. The druggist was charging $2,000, ten times what the drug cost him to make. The sick woman's husband, Heinz, went to everyone he knew to borrow the money, but he could only get together about half of what it cost. He told the druggist that his wife was dying and asked him to sell it cheaper or let him pay later. But the druggist said, "No." The husband got desperate and broke into the man's store to steal the drug for his wife. Should the husband have done that? Why? (1969, page 379)

Using a person's responses to such dilemmas, as well as interviews that probe the thinking or reasoning behind them, investigators attempt to ascertain the nature and extent of his moral reasoning and its development. The assumption is that moral judgments are largely the result of moral thought in contact with a moral dilemma like the one faced by Heinz—to do or not to do good or bad under certain circumstances. By definition, no moral dilemma is easy to resolve; none of the possible outcomes is ideal. In fact, most people would prefer to avoid such dilemmas altogether. But in a moral dilemma, even doing nothing leads to a certain outcome. Thus, in many dilemmas, no matter what professed action a person takes or fails to take, he must break at least one moral rule. However, the important thing in studying a person's proposed action in the face of such a dilemma is not whether he would steal the drug but his reasons for deciding on a probable course of action.

Drawing on the results of studies that have used this method to examine the moral reasoning of children and adults, Kohlberg has suggested that there is a progressive series of six developmental stages of moral reasoning, as illustrated in Figure 16.2. Notice that the stages differ in the reasons that a person is likely to give for making a decision and in the type of concerns that he indicates for himself, authority, and/or society. The figure also illustrates

Figure 16.2 Illustration of Kohlberg's proposed order of progression in the development of moral reasoning. Descriptions of the reasoning characterizing each stage and level are presented, and each is illustrated by examples showing pro and con responses to Heinz's dilemma. (After Kohlberg, 1963)

Principled	**Stage 6**	This is a stage of fully internalized principles that the person holds as universally valid. He believes them personally and has not adopted them just because they have been laid down by authority. For example, the only soldier who refused to obey orders at the My Lai massacre during the Vietnam War had reached this stage. A person at Stage 6 believes that an act is right if it follows from self-chosen principles, principles that may even demand deviating from rules. The universal ethical principles of Stage 6 are based on a deeply balanced sense of the relationship among human beings and emphasize mutual trust and respect. A person at the highest level might say, "Do unto others as you would have them do unto you." **Pro** If you don't steal the drug and let your wife die, you'd always condemn yourself for it afterward. You wouldn't be blamed and you would have lived up to the outside rule of the law but you wouldn't have lived up to your own standards of conscience. **Con** If you stole the drug, you wouldn't be blamed by other people but you'd condemn yourself because you wouldn't have lived up to your own conscience and standards of honesty.
	Stage 5	The person at this stage recognizes that, for the sake of agreement, rules or expectations must contain an arbitrary element. Rules are social contracts made for a purpose, and specific social purposes can change. The essential obligation is the contract, not the content of a specific rule, and majority will and welfare are extremely important. This stage represents a loosening of commitment to the expectations of others and the conventional order and an emphasis on personal standards of social responsibility. The Stage 5 person recognizes these standards as valid even when special circumstances might justify deviation. A person at this stage might say, "The end doesn't justify the means." **Pro** You'd lose other people's respect, not gain it, if you don't steal. If you let your wife die, it would be out of fear, not out of reasoning it out. So you'd just lose self-respect and probably the respect of others too. **Con** You would lose your standing and respect in the community and violate the law. You'd lose respect for yourself if you're carried away by emotion and forget the long-range point of view.
Conventional	**Stage 4**	Sometimes people call this the law-and-order stage because a person at this stage bases his thinking on the dictates of established authority. Examples of this stage are numerous, because many people never get beyond it. Confronted with moral choices, a person in Stage 4 is likely to say, "Because he is the President" or "Because the Bible says so" or "A rule is a rule." He sees value in rules and obligations because he sees them as necessary for a stable society ("What would happen if everybody . . . ?"). The Stage 4 person does his duty and shows respect for authority. **Pro** If you have any sense of honor, you won't let your wife die because you're afraid to do the only thing that will save her. You'll always feel guilty that you caused her death if you don't do your duty to her. **Con** You're desperate and you may not know you're doing wrong when you steal the drug. But you'll know you did wrong after you're punished and sent to jail. You'll always feel guilty for your dishonesty and law breaking.
	Stage 3	A person at this stage internalizes the values of others. He makes up his mind about a moral dilemma on the basis of how he believes his parents or his peer group would behave or want him to behave in the situation. He wants to please and help others, thereby gaining their approval. He believes that behavior should conform to stereotypical images of appropriateness. A person at this stage might say, "It's better to give than to receive." **Pro** No one will think you're bad if you steal the drug but your family will think you're an inhuman husband if you don't. If you let your wife die, you'll never be able to look anybody in the face again. **Con** It isn't just the druggist who will think you're a criminal, everyone else will too. After you steal it, you'll feel bad thinking how you've brought dishonor on your family and yourself; you won't be able to face anyone again.
Premoral	**Stage 2**	The overriding concern is satisfying a person's own needs, and he is keenly sensitive to the consequences of any action. The Stage 2 person thinks acts are good whose outcomes are to his own advantage. He is inclined to exchange favors—"I'll do this for you, if you'll do that for me"—but he is satisfying his own desires. He does not share the perspective of others. **Pro** If you do happen to get caught you could give the drug back and you wouldn't get much of a sentence. It wouldn't bother you much to serve a little jail term, if you have your wife when you get out. **Con** He may not get much of a jail term if he steals the drug, but his wife will probably die before he gets out so it won't do him much good. If his wife dies, he shouldn't blame himself, it wasn't his fault she has cancer.
	Stage 1	Children or adults tend to decide on the basis of personal fear and the avoidance of punishment. The physical dimensions of an act or its consequences loom large as the basis for judging its degree of badness. The Stage 1 person avoids trouble by obeying powerful authorities. For him, "Might makes right." **Pro** If you let your wife die, you will get in trouble. You'll be blamed for not spending the money to save her and there'll be an investigation of you and the druggist for your wife's death. **Con** You shouldn't steal the drug because you'll be caught and sent to jail if you do. If you do get away, your conscience would bother you thinking how the police will catch up with you at any minute.

t each stage might reason in deciding
hould steal the drug. As can be seen,
ision to steal or not to steal but the
ition for his proposed actions that
n's stage of reasoning. A person at
ₐₐₐₑ may decide either way in a given situation.
Each succeeding stage is assumed to consist of a
more complex and balanced way of looking at the
moral-social world. A child or adult presumably
advances through the stages in sequence; he must
understand the reasoning typical of one stage before
he can learn to understand the greater complexities of
the next. It is also assumed that, as an individual
moves to a new stage of understanding, he must
reorganize his thoughts and feelings and not just add
new ones. Thus, as a child advances through the
stages, old moral-social relationships between the
child and other people, and between people in general, acquire a new look.

As Figure 16.2 shows, the proposed six stages
form three basic developmental levels of moral reasoning, distinguished by what defines right or moral
action. The first two stages form what is called the
premoral level, because value is placed not in
persons or social standards but in physical acts and
needs. The next two stages form the **conventional**
level, with value placed in maintaining the conventional social order and the expectations of others. The
final two stages form the **principled** level, where
value resides in self-chosen principles and standards

that have a universal logical validity and that therefore can be shared. Because the distinctness of each
stage remains uncertain (Kurtines and Greif, 1974),
we will focus on levels of moral reasoning.

Developmental Changes

There is at least suggestive evidence that, as a
developmental sequence, the levels do appear related
to age. For example, Figure 16.3 shows that, among
children from seven to sixteen, older children tend to
be at more advanced levels. Moral statements that
reflect the premoral level decrease with age. Those at
the conventional level appear to increase until about
age thirteen and then stabilize; statements that reflect
the principled level appear to increase slowly after
age thirteen, although they still constitute only a
limited proportion of the judgments among sixteen-
year-olds.

In general, the speed with which children move
from one level to the next also appears to vary with
their intellectual ability. Higher-level moral concepts
and attitudes are acquired only in late childhood or in
adolescence; apparently they require an extensive
foundation of cognitive growth and social experience.
On the other hand, although a certain level of
intellectual ability seems to be necessary for a given
level of moral reasoning, intellectual ability in itself
does not guarantee the development of higher levels
of moral reasoning. Thus, children who are above
average in intellectual ability are as likely as other

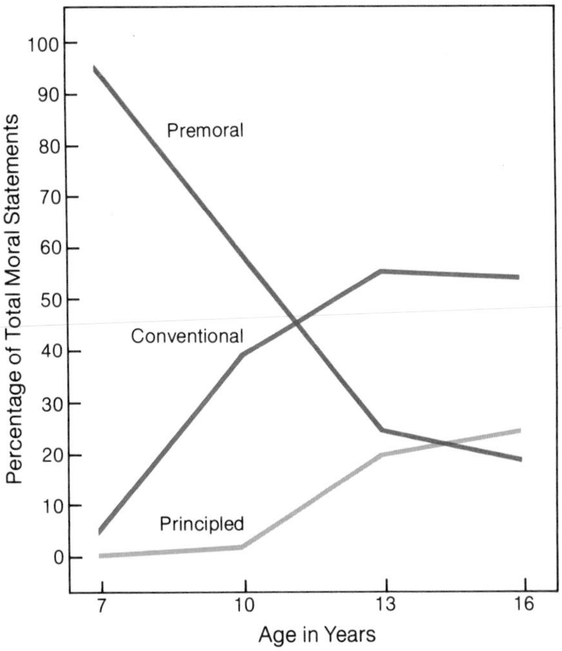

Figure 16.3 Graph showing variations
with age in the relative proportions of
different levels of moral reasoning
in a sample of American boys.
(After Kohlberg, 1963)

(*opposite*) Graph showing variations
with age in the relative proportions of
different levels of moral reasoning in
three cultures: the United States,
Taiwan, and Mexico. The samples in
each culture consist of middle-class
urban boys. Levels I, II, and III
indicate, respectively, premoral,
conventional, and principled levels.
(After Kohlberg, 1968)

children to show a lower or higher level of moral reasoning. However, a child's relative brightness and his level of moral reasoning do combine to affect what he does. In a study by Richard Krebs (1968), for example, it was found that, among children who were at an opportunistic, premoral level of reasoning, those who were bright and attentive enough to see that they could cheat jumped at the chance. Among those children who were at a rule-oriented, conventional level of moral reasoning, however, the ones who cheated seemed to be those who were not bright or attentive enough to succeed by understanding and following the rules.

Although there are still too few studies using Kohlberg's moral dilemmas to tell just how valid or reliable different results are, there is at least tentative evidence concerning several other aspects of the development of moral reasoning. It appears, for example, that under natural conditions people do not skip a level when advancing to a higher level of reasoning (Kohlberg and Kramer, 1969). In addition, children and adolescents appear to rate moral reasoning that is below their own level as inferior and that above their own level as better. However, they recall moral reasoning that is below their own level more accurately than they recall reasoning above their level (Rest, 1973; Rest, Turiel, and Kohlberg, 1969). In terms of peoples' verbal reasoning about moral dilemmas, it further appears, as Figure 16.3 suggests, that levels of moral reasoning may develop in a

similar way in all cultures (Kohlberg, 1969). Finally, studies have shown no major differences in the development of moral thinking as a result of religious affiliation (Kohlberg, 1969).

ROLE TAKING AND SOCIAL INTERACTION

The active social-cognitive process of role taking appears to play a critical part in moral development generally and in moral reasoning in particular. During childhood, for example, an individual actively participates in many social situations and practices taking the role of others. Thus, in the process of acquiring moral values, a child increasingly becomes able to take (that is, to internalize) the position or role of another person. This ability enables him to restructure the way that he perceives and thinks about moral-social issues.

This development means that young Lauren first sees standards of morality as something given and external to herself. During the premoral level of reasoning, she is too egocentric to be able to take the role or to adopt the viewpoint of others; she simply perceives moral matters in terms of consequences—whether her actions are rewarded or punished. If she reaches the conventional level of reasoning, her moral standards will begin to be more general and somewhat internal, although they are largely based on conformity to what others say: She considers the roles of others in order to do what will please them. Should Lauren reach the principled

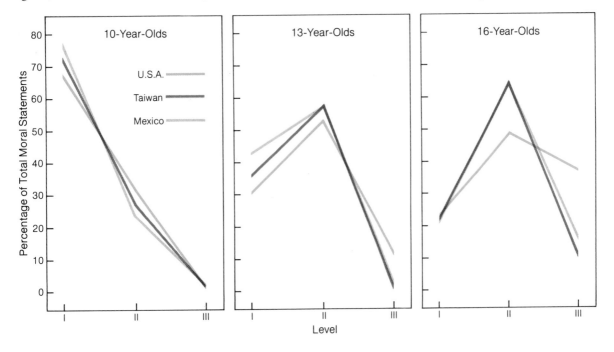

level, her moral standards will become even more general and largely internal: Before acting she will consider the viewpoints and needs of other people and of society in general.

As children develop their moral reasoning, social interactions with peers, which stimulate role-taking abilities, seem to be particularly important. For example, Charles Keasey (1971) studied fifth- and sixth-grade children and found that children who took an active part in social interaction were more likely than children who did not to show a conventional level of moral reasoning. Apparently, the ability to see that one's own actions can affect the way that another person reacts is also necessary if a child is to reach a conventional level of moral reasoning. This connection was illustrated in a study by Robert Selman (1971), who found a significant relationship between the ability to take the role of another and the attainment of conventional moral reasoning among eight-, nine-, and ten-year-olds. In addition, among

the children who were deficient in role-taking skills, some later learned role-taking skills without developing conventional reasoning, but none developed conventional reasoning without also developing proficiency in role taking.

Families, of course, also influence the development of moral reasoning by providing opportunities to take another's role. For example, Robert Peck and Robert Havighurst (1960) found that a child's moral understanding was related to participation in family activities, sharing of confidences, sharing in family decisions, and being trusted with responsibility. More recently, Constance Holstein (1972) found that parents who take their child's opinions on moral issues seriously and discuss them (thereby providing a role-taking model as well as opportunities for the child to practice role taking) are more likely to have children who reason at a conventional than at a premoral level. In addition, she found that mothers who show a principled level of moral reasoning are

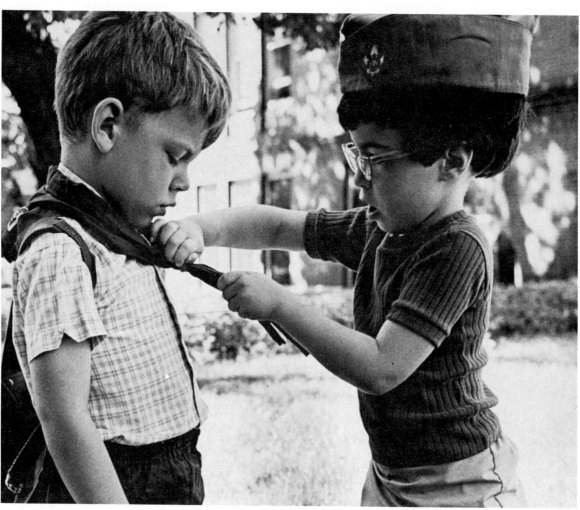

more likely than those who show a conventional level of reasoning to have children who show a higher, conventional level of moral reasoning. This finding suggests that mothers at the principled level are more likely to be skilled in role taking, to value opportunities for role taking, and to provide them for their children.

Given their superior role-taking skills, parents also are likely to adjust their own moral reasoning and action to fit their child's present level of moral understanding. For example, with small children they are likely to key their words to direct rewards or punishment, whereas with older children they are likely to talk about abstract social consequences. Thus, parents are unlikely to speak to a three-year-old in terms of property rights or justice. Instead, they are likely to admonish the child in concrete terms: "Don't touch that, it'll break" or "Don't do that, or you'll get spanked." Parents of an older child, in contrast, are likely to emphasize social consequences and personal intentions and, as the child nears puberty, to begin to justify moral action in terms of more abstract principles. An eight-year-old is likely to be told, "The lady only broke the law to help somebody else," whereas a fifteen-year-old may be told, "Laws discriminating against women are unjust."

Socioeconomic status also appears to influence the development of moral reasoning (Kohlberg and Kramer, 1969). As Figure 16.5 indicates, middle-class and working-class adolescents and young adults seem to go through the same levels of moral reason-ing, but the middle-class subjects appear to advance faster and further. This finding suggests that middle-class adolescents and young adults experience a wider range of opportunities and stimulation for role taking and social participation and that they become able to see themselves and others from more general, organized, and flexible perspectives.

In a related way, differences in level of moral reasoning between a university professor and a pre-adolescent gang member, for example, can also be seen as stemming in part from differences in role-taking skills, social-learning factors, and cognitive ability. The professor's peer group is likely to approve and reward the use of abstract principles in reasoning, whereas the preadolescent's peer group is likely to approve and reward on a more concrete basis. Such differences in group orientation reflect the primary interests of each group and are likely to have a strong influence on the moral reasoning of the group's members.

GUILT AND SELF-REGULATION

The language of morality is full of terms that relate to feelings, and most people regard the emotions of guilt, shame, anxiety, and indignation as important influences on their behavior. In fact, without resorting to the notion that it would make them "feel bad," it is difficult to understand why people do not more often engage in immoral thoughts and actions. When a person speaks of conscience, he usually speaks not of a voice that quotes the Golden Rule or of the

Figure 16.4 (*opposite*) Social interactions with peers, whether they occur in the context of a formal and organized group or everyday play, teach and reinforce cognitive and social skills that are basic to moral development.

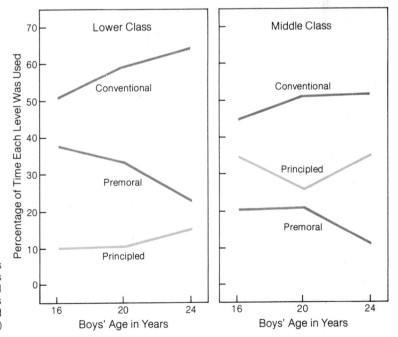

Figure 16.5 Graph showing variations with age in the relative proportions of different levels of moral reasoning in samples of boys from two social classes. (Adapted from Kohlberg, 1968)

possible consequences of his actions. Instead, he thinks of his feelings when he remembers or anticipates some transgression. As this section makes clear, how one comes to feel about his actions can be a critical factor in the development of moral conduct.

When most people talk about the moral conduct of a child and its development, they refer to the child's ability to inhibit a desire (he does not take a toy from another child) or to his resistance to temptation (he does not cheat on a test or take a piece of pie that his sister was saving). Therefore, a good deal of the research on moral development has looked at the factors that affect the development of guilt and self-regulation.

Establishing Guilt and Self-regulation

Although there have been many different theories of how guilt and self-regulation are established, they generally converge on the idea that through conditioning a person gradually develops a sense of guilt and also comes to regulate his own conduct. Thus, the young child begins by trying to do and say things that his parents approve of and by trying not to do or say things that they consider wrong. He discovers that when he does or says things his parents approve of they give him their affection, and through conditioning this affection becomes coupled with his feelings of self-approval. He also discovers, however, that when he does or says things his parents disapprove of they are likely to withdraw their affection or punish him in some other way, and through conditioning this becomes coupled with his feelings of guilt and self-reproof. As a result of this kind of learning, the child eventually may behave morally even though his parents or other people are not present. Gradually, his own internal thoughts and feelings replace external rewards and punishments administered by others, and he comes to regulate his own moral conduct. Moreover, as we will see later in this section, the child is likely to continue to learn a variety of ways of reacting to his guilt over actual or contemplated wrongdoings.

Studies have shown that the nature of the parental relationship, the explanation of the reasons for discipline, and the timing of punishment are all important factors in the establishment of guilt and self-regulation in moral conduct.

Love and Reasoning. One of the clearest ways in which parents and others promote the development of guilt and self-regulation in moral conduct is by disciplining a child for disapproved acts. Discipline goes beyond spanking or hitting a child and includes the withdrawal of affection, verbal reprimands, and social isolation. Punishing a child by withdrawing love appears to establish guilt and self-regulation much more efficiently than spanking does (Aronfreed, 1968). A child can always avoid the brief unpleasantness of physical punishment merely by avoiding the punisher. On the other hand, if a normally loving parent withdraws his or her love, the punishment lasts until the love is restored. As it also turns out, children disciplined by severe and unexplained punishment are unlikely to develop an effective sense of guilt or self-regulation and instead learn only to behave so that they will not get caught.

It was first thought that withdrawing love might be the most important factor in establishing guilt feelings and self-control. For example, Robert Sears, Eleanor Maccoby, and Harry Levin (1957) found that children who are disciplined by physical punishment develop less self-control and are less susceptible to self-critical feelings of guilt than children who are disciplined by the withdrawal of love and by reasoning. However, later studies by Martin Hoffman and Herbert Saltzstein (1967), Justin Aronfreed (1969), and others suggest that reasoning with the child is equally or more important. Specifically, verbal explanation or reasoning with the child does two things: It encourages a child to take the role of others, and it helps a child to internalize moral standards by providing him with thoughts to associate with reward or punishment. Thus, in terms of positive self-regulation, as Susan comes to adopt the moral thoughts and attitudes of her parents, she soon responds with self-approval to what are now her own correct thoughts and actions. She learns to use self-instruction and self-praise. And when faced with a temptation, such as a dazzling display of dials and push buttons on a color television set, Susan may regulate her conduct by telling herself, ''No. Don't touch it. That's a good girl. I'm a good girl for not touching it.''

Timing of Discipline. Whether physical punishment or other techniques are more effective in promoting self-adherence to moral standards is still a matter of debate (LaVoie, 1974). However, the timing of discipline appears to be especially important in the development of guilt and self-regulation. Its effectiveness depends on when it takes place. For example, in studies by Richard Walters, Ross Parke, and Valerie Cane (1965), a child was punished either just as he was about to play with a forbidden object or after he had begun to play with it. Afterward, the

Figure 16.6 Because most parents, especially middle-class parents, are likely to combine punishment with explanation, guilt and self-regulation almost always are established and developed to some degree in children. When children enter school, this aspect of moral conduct is usually also encouraged, supported, and otherwise reinforced by teachers.

child was placed in a situation in which the same forbidden object tempted him. Generally, children who were punished early showed greater resistance than children who were punished later.

The explanation for such results is that, when children are punished early, the form of anxiety that we call guilt becomes associated with the anticipation of doing something wrong. However, when children are punished *after* they have disobeyed, doing something forbidden is followed by the fear that is generated when one is caught and punished. This distinction is often characterized as the difference between guilt and shame: **Guilt** stems from deviation from one's own internalized moral standards, but **shame** is a reaction to the disapproval of others. Thus some young children may regulate themselves by saying "No, No!" while looking at and not playing with a forbidden object; others may go ahead and play with the forbidden object and then get disciplined. Similarly, one five-year-old may feel guilt when she contemplates pulling her sister's hair and resists the act, whereas another five-year-old may pull her sister's hair and then feel afraid because her father may catch her.

It is often impossible to punish a child just before or just as he begins to do something that is forbidden. However, psychologists have also found, as have many parents before them, that delayed punishment can be effective if the situation that led to a transgression is re-created as fully as possible by talking with the child and describing the forbidden action at the time the child is disciplined (Aronfreed, 1968). By

using this sort of approach, for example, Donald Meichenbaum and Joseph Goodman (1971) have been able to teach impulsive children with a history of getting into trouble to talk to themselves when they are tempted to do something forbidden. Using this kind of self-regulation, they end up modifying their own behavior.

Reasoning and Guilt

The importance of cognitive understanding and reasoning in the development of guilt and self-regulation is also shown in a number of other ways. For example, the basic feelings that a person attaches to his moral actions may be the same throughout development, but his *interpretation* of these feelings appears to change with cognitive development (Kohlberg, 1969). Thus, anxiety over deviating from moral standards may register in the pit of the stomach for children and adults alike. But a young child is likely to perceive the physical sensation as a dread of external punishment. He resists the impulse to take a quarter from his mother's purse because he thinks that his parents are watching or that God will punish him. Older children and adults, on the other hand, are likely to perceive the same physical sensation as dread of their own self-judgment and to want to avoid feeling guilty or violating a principle.

Reasoning, feeling, and self-regulation are also interrelated in other ways in moral conduct; a violation of what a child or adult considers just or moral often elicits strong feelings, such as a sense of indignation or even moral outrage. For example,

Figure 16.7 Delayed punishment for a transgression is a frequent form of discipline in real life. Its effectiveness depends on how well the situation involving the transgression is re-created and on how well the explanations given for the discipline are tied to what went on and are made to fit the individual's own understanding.

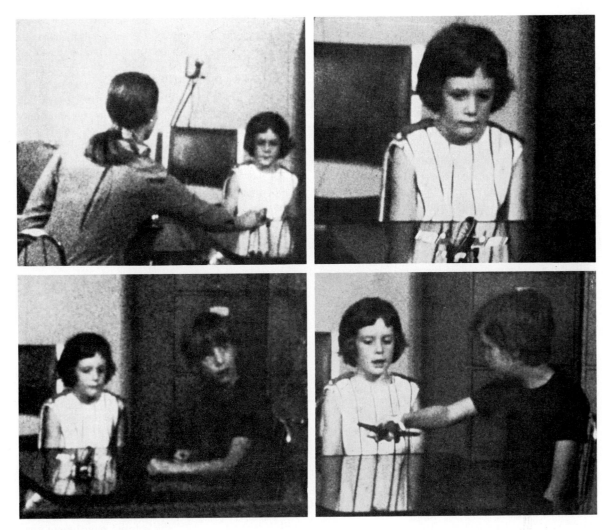

Figure 16.8 Illustration of one type of temptation experiment used in studying moral development in children. (*top left*) The girl is first told not to play with the toy. (*top right*) She is then left alone for a bit, and, as shown, she looks at but does not play with the toy. (*bottom left*) Soon another child enters the room, and (*bottom right*) when he picks up the toy, the girl tells him he is not supposed to play with it. The girl's verbal and nonverbal actions reflect her developing morality.

Kohlberg describes his son's first expression of moral reaction, which occurred at age four. At that time his son joined the pacifist and vegetarian movement and refused to eat meat because, as the child said, "It's bad to kill animals." In spite of lengthy parental arguments about the differences between justified and unjustified killing, the boy remained a vegetarian for six months. However, his principles recognized occasions of just or legitimate killing. Kohlberg recounts how, one night when he was reading aloud a book of Eskimo life that described a seal-killing expedition, his son got angry and said, "You know, there is one kind of meat I would eat, Eskimo meat. It's bad to kill animals so it's all right to eat *them*." It seems likely that the boy's attitude toward killing was not an internalization of the cultural rule "Thou shalt not kill" but a response based on his immediate empathy for other living beings and that his punitiveness was based on the primitive principle by which one bad act deserves another.

Reactions to Guilt

Because guilt is unpleasant, children generally learn how to avoid or reduce it, and this learning is likely to take many forms during the course of their socialization and the development of their moral conduct. As a child's ability to understand and to think increases and as he gains additional social experience, he learns new ways to manage his guilt. And, although individual differences in this aspect of moral development are large, most children appear to develop somewhat similar ways of managing their guilt (McMichael and Grinder, 1966).

One of the most obvious ways to avoid guilt, as we have seen, is through self-control. For example, a child can resist temptation and refuse to do something that is forbidden. If, however, he believes that he will succumb to temptation, he may learn to avoid guilt by not even thinking about forbidden things, because the thoughts themselves provoke guilt feelings.

As their cognitive sophistication increases, however, most children learn even more elegant ways of avoiding the guilt produced by what they may do or think. For example, if Matt hurts another person, he may define his actions in benevolent terms, saying, "I just did it for his own good." Or he may learn to avoid guilt and self-condemnation by telling himself that the other person is a "tattletale" or a "cheater." Other learned ways of reducing the unpleasantness of guilt appear equally effective. Matt may instead learn to confess his transgressions or to apologize for what

he says or does. Or he may learn to reduce his guilt by saying that his misbehavior was only half as bad as it could have been or as what others have done.

MORAL CONDUCT AND MODELING

Like any complex set of human behaviors, the development of moral conduct is determined by the interplay of many factors. Thus far, we have seen that role taking and empathy require experience and cognitive understanding, and we have considered some of the ways that reasoning and guilt and self-regulation in moral conduct develop and interact. But modeling also affects the development of moral conduct. As the child watches others, he learns new ways of behaving, gets information about the possible consequences of an action, and learns whether certain behavior is acceptable.

You will recall from our discussion of modeling in Chapter 15 that a child watching altruistic actions is likely to copy those actions and that what happens to the model affects the probability of the child's performing those same acts. Thus, by watching a model, the child learns how to do whatever the model is doing, whether the model is generous or selfish, aggressive or helpful, honest or hypocritical. However, once a child has learned to do or say something, he does not necessarily behave that way. As the discussion in Chapter 13 indicated, if the model is warm, powerful, and competent, the child may well copy his behavior, and especially in early childhood, that is just the way his parents are likely to seem to him. But, as we also saw in earlier discussions, the child's expectations of reward and punishment also affect the likelihood of his imitating a model. For example, if the model is rewarded, the child is likely to expect a reward for behaving in the same way. If the model is punished, however, the child is not likely to behave that way because he would expect to be punished himself.

Changes in Consequences

One of the most important findings to come out of research on the influence of observational learning on moral conduct is that an unpunished transgression appears to have the same effect on the watching child as a transgression followed by rewards. Thus, an early study found that children who see peers playing with forbidden toys are more likely to play with the toys than children who see no such transgressions (Grosser, Polansky, and Lippitt, 1951). This finding suggests that, when a child sees other children breaking a prohibition and getting away with it, the consequences anticipated by the child for violating that prohibition change.

A later experiment by Richard Walters and Ross Parke (1964) indeed indicated that, when punishment is expected, its very absence may act as a reward. They showed films of a model playing with forbidden toys to several groups of children. Some of the children saw the model rewarded, some saw him punished, others saw that nothing—either good or bad—happened to the model. These children, along with another group who saw no film, were later tested in a situation like that depicted in the film. Both the children who had seen the transgression rewarded and those who had seen it go unpunished were more likely to play with forbidden toys than children who saw the model's actions punished or those who saw no film.

However, when the experimenter indicated that no one would be punished for playing with the forbidden toys, children who saw any of the films were more likely to play with the toys than children who did not see the film. Apparently all the children who saw the film learned the model's behavior; those who did not copy it were trying to avoid expected punishment.

Subsequently, Walters, Parke, and Cane (1965) also found that, in certain conditions, only the prospect of punishment may keep a child from transgressing. Once again, they showed children films of a model playing with forbidden toys, but this time the toys were so enticing that even many of the control children who saw no film at all succumbed to temptation and played with them. In a situation of such great temptation, punishing the model was the only consequence that affected children's transgressions; children who saw the model rewarded, those who saw nothing happen to the model, and those who saw no film at all failed to resist the tempting toys.

Such studies indicate that, when children watch a model go unpunished, two things happen. First, the punishment-free transgression suggests to them that for some reason a usually negative sanction does not apply in this situation, and they modify their own thinking accordingly. Second, the children then copy the unpunished model's violations because it is apparently all right to transgress and because playing with the forbidden toys is rewarding. Another research result helps to complete the picture of how consequences to a model can affect the observational learning of moral conduct. When children see a model go unrewarded for moral behavior, such as altruism, they will also fail to copy him. Thus, in a paradoxical sort of way, seeing moral behavior go unrewarded may decrease the rate at which it occurs, just as if it were immoral behavior and punished.

Verbal and Nonverbal Modeling

As we saw in our earlier discussion, other people, notably parents and peers, strongly influence the development of a child's moral reasoning. It was emphasized, for example, that parents promote the development of moral reasoning by providing a child with role-taking models. Although there are many gaps in our knowledge about how moral reasoning and conduct develop, it seems clear that the verbal modeling of parents and others does have a strong instructional influence during the course of a child's moral development.

There is at least suggestive evidence that one of the ways that parents and others influence a child's moral reasoning is by changing the factors that he takes into consideration in arriving at his moral judgments. For example, Albert Bandura and Frederick McDonald (1963) found that, by having an adult consider personal intentions or fail to consider them in making moral judgments about stories in the presence of a child, they could get children to shift their reasoning in either direction.

Moshe Blatt (1969), using a method similar to the methods that parents use in reasoning with their offspring, also found it possible to change children's moral reasoning. As children discussed moral dilemmas in the classroom, teachers supported and clarified arguments that indicated a conventional level of moral reasoning but challenged those based on premoral reasoning. This procedure not only eventually led to changes in the children's levels of reasoning, but the differences between these children and others who had not heard premoral arguments challenged appeared to still exist a year later.

Although it seems clear that verbal modeling produces changes in children's moral reasoning, there is no evidence to indicate that these changes will automatically appear in their moral behavior as well. In fact, as many parents and others have found, children tend to model what is done rather than what is said. Thus, as we saw in Chapter 15, a parent who spanks a child for hitting his sister is modeling the use of physical aggression. The child learns not that it is wrong to hit but that hitting is proper under certain (unknown) conditions. A study by James Bryan and Nancy Walbek (1970) tested the idea that actions influence children more strongly than words. A model played a game and won gift certificates, which he either selfishly kept or generously donated to a charity. At the same time, the model either said that people should be generous or selfish or made neutral statements. Later, children who had watched the model played the game and had their own opportunity to donate winnings to charity. Those children who had watched a generous model made more donations than those children who had watched a selfish model. Most important, however, no matter what the model had said, his words had no significant effect on the children's generosity.

For many people, the course of moral development results in moral reasoning and behavior, as well as guilt and self-regulation, coming together in a relatively cohesive way and at a rather high level of morality. For example, children with nurturant parents, who have seen their parents react with helpfulness in situations of both love and distress, are themselves likely to be more helpful and consistently altruistic in later situations (M. Yarrow, Scott, and Waxler, 1973). In a similar demonstration, which also illustrates lasting parental influence, David Rosenhan (1970) points out that people who engage in dramatic social action, such as those who went to the South to work in the Civil Rights Movement, are more likely to have parents who do not merely advocate positive social action but who engage in it themselves.

CONSISTENCY IN MORAL DEVELOPMENT

Just thirty days after President Ford took office, he pardoned ex-President Nixon for any crimes he may have committed while President. After all the explanations are in, it seems likely that they will cover every imaginable pro and con argument at every conceivable level of moral reasoning. No matter what his reasons, it also seems likely that different people will continue to see President Ford's moral conduct as more or less consistent, in terms of his own life history as well as in terms of some particular standard of morality. From the developmental perspective taken in this chapter, however, it should be clear that there are no easy or certain answers to many of the questions that will be raised about the moral conduct of either President Ford or ex-President Nixon. When applied to an individual case, such questions become particularly problematical, because the kind of reliable and relevant developmental information needed to help answer them usually is unobtainable.

As this chapter has indicated, a person is likely to be more or less consistent in his moral conduct, depending on how and to what extent intellectual, social, and emotional factors combine during the course of his moral development. At present, there is no way to predict to what extent any individual or group of individuals will show consistency in moral thought, feelings, and action.

Among children, adolescents, or adults of a given chronological age, there is likely to be large variation in their moral development and in their conduct from one situation to another. An individual can and does show variation in his moral conduct in different situations. As discussed earlier, such variation may stem from developmental changes in moral reasoning, different experiences in role-taking skill, differences in learning and modeling influences, and so forth. Thus, how inconsistent or consistent a child or adolescent becomes in what he thinks, says, or does is complexly and multiply determined.

In general, it seems likely that children and adolescents who show comparatively more consistent moral conduct usually are less influenced by immediate situational pressures, show greater internal guidance in their moral reasoning, and demonstrate a more mature sense of guilt and self-regulation across more situations. Their greater relative consistency in turn appears likely to result from relatively greater cognitive sophistication and more varied role-taking experiences and from various verbal and nonverbal learning influences that emphasize consistency in both word and deed.

SUMMARY

1. During the course of moral development, the thoughts, feelings, and actions that make up moral

conduct usually become less specific and literal and more complex in form and relationship.

2. Although moral conduct is often viewed as a group of related reactions governed by some central process such as conscience, research indicates that people are inconsistent in what they say, do, and feel.

3. One of the most provocative methods used to study developmental changes in moral reasoning involves people's reactions to posed moral dilemmas. Based on this approach, it has been suggested that there may be a progressive series of stages forming three basic developmental levels of moral reasoning: premoral, conventional, and principled.

4. The active social-cognitive process of role taking seems to be crucial to facilitating moral development in general and to moral reasoning in particular. In addition, research suggests that social interaction not only stimulates the development of role-taking skills but also influences the level of moral understanding that is reached.

5. Guilt and self-regulation in moral conduct are likely to develop gradually and to become more general in their effects. However, studies indicate that their establishment and development depend on such considerations as the nature of the parental relationship, the explanation of the reasons for discipline, and the timing of punishment. As a result of greater cognitive development, a child also may come to experience strong moral feelings produced by his own reasoning and may incre cated ways of avoiding gu

6. What parents, peers, and as models think, feel, and do on moral development. For ex watches others, he learns new finds out what is acceptable, and le quences. However, whereas verbal n ers is likely to influence the developme ...'s moral reasoning, this does not necessa. result in changes in moral behavior.

7. Although prediction of consistency in moral conduct is not possible, relatively greater consistency in moral development depends on an individual's cognitive sophistication, his role-taking experience, and the extent to which various verbal and nonverbal learning influences emphasize consistency in word and deed.

SUGGESTED READINGS

Aronfreed, Justin. *Conduct and Conscience*. New York: Academic Press, 1968.

Kohlberg, Lawrence. "Moral Education in the Schools: A Developmental View," *School Review*, 74 (1966), 1–30.

Lickona, A. Thomas. *Man and Morality*. New York: Holt, Rinehart and Winston, 1976.

Tapp, June L. "A Child's Garden of Law and Order," *Psychology Today*, 4 (December 1970), 29–31+.

Wilson, John, Norman Williams, and Barry Sugarman. *Introduction to Moral Education*. Baltimore: Penguin, 1967.

Figure 16.9 Alfred Kohn's thought, feeling, and action in deciding to refuse an American Legion award indicate a high and consistent level of moral development.

MIAMI BEACH—A Miami Beach ninth grader has turned down the American Legion's service award because he finds the philosophy of the organization "personally abhorrent."

"I thanked the faculty responsible for nominating me," Alfred said later, "but I told them on the basis of conscience I could not accept the award because of the conservative political stance of the American Legion which is personally abhorrent."

The honor student particularly criticized the Legion's support of the Vietnam War and its essay contests, which he said reflect "A paranoic fear of communism that approaches the fervor of a Birchite."

"True patriotism is wanting to correct your country when it is wrong," Alfred said. "It is not waving flags in blind support of whatever policy that happens to be in effect at the moment."

"The fact that the American Legion is composed of war veterans is not sufficient justification for their continued support of our immoral presence in Indochina."

The major physical changes of adolescence turn the child into the adult man or woman. Sexual development obviously has wide psychological and social consequences. When the adolescent attempts to find sexual gratification and to discover love and security outside the home, the personality that developed and established itself in late childhood faces an inevitable test: Biological maturation forces sexual opportunities; the disappearance of the childhood home requires the construction of another. Life's joys as well as its pains arise from this confrontation between a still-developing personality and the rigor of biological and psychological development. Out of the confrontation comes the adolescent's sense of identity and self-esteem. This unit shows how boys and girls react to the transformations of adolescence and how cultural changes affect the range of choices that society presents to them.

UNIT VI Adolescence: Building an Identity

The physical-sexual changes of puberty usher in a new kind of self-awareness.

17
PHYSICAL AND SEXUAL MATURATION

As Lauren and David go through the transition from childhood to adolescence, the changes and interactions that characterize their development will be more pronounced than at any time since infancy. There will be large qualitative and quantitative changes in their bodies, primarily involving their sex organs and the secondary sex characteristics that differentiate man from woman. It is during adolescence that the adult emerges from the child.

One of the reasons that adolescence is seen as such an important phase of development is that, for the first time, the individual is truly aware of the physical changes that occur. Neither Lauren nor David can remain oblivious to the significance of the many events taking place in their bodies. The teen-ager sees, feels, and experiences body changes that are quite different from the sensations of childhood. An adolescent may experience these changes, especially those involving sexual maturity, as exciting, gratifying, embarrassing, wonderful, or even frightening.

In this chapter we will discuss the physical and maturational changes that characterize adolescence and the impact of these changes on both Lauren's and David's psychological and social development. We will look first at the adolescent growth spurt, then at sexual maturity and its impact on other areas of development. We will examine the predictability of adolescent growth and the trends toward earlier maturation and larger people over the last century. We will discuss how the individual reacts to the physical developments of adolescence and will focus on those changes that arouse the most concern in each sex. Finally, we will consider sexual behavior among adolescents and how it has changed in this century.

GROWTH CHARACTERISTICS

In the beginning, adolescence is a biological phenomenon, and sexual maturation is its central theme. Long before emotional considerations and social conflicts become important in the course of adolescent growth, hormonal changes begin to work their effects on the body. The main biological event is **puberty,** which is characterized by the attainment of biological sexual maturity. During puberty the reproductive glands first release sperm and ova. These glands are the **testicles** in boys and the **ovaries** in girls. With the release of sperm or ova, the individual is, for the first time, capable of reproduction.

In a girl, the first menstruation provides an obvious milestone in puberty. In a boy, the signs are less sharply defined: Pubic hair appears, sex organs grow, and nocturnal emissions occur. Gradually, a girl takes on the figure of a mature woman, and a boy develops the physique of a man.

Both boys and girls produce male hormones (**androgens**) as well as female hormones (**estrogens**) in relatively equal amounts throughout their childhood. As Chapter 6 noted, hormones help to regulate growth at all ages, but it is only when a child reaches puberty that the hypothalamus of the brain signals the pituitary gland to begin the hormonal production found in adult men and women. The pituitary gland stimulates other endocrine glands, the adrenals, ovaries, and testes (shown in Figure 17.1), to secrete hormones directly into the bloodstream, creating a balance that includes more androgens in boys and more estrogens in girls. These hormonal changes lead directly to the physical developments that emerge during puberty (Tanner, 1962).

During puberty, the ovaries and testes produce enough hormones to cause accelerated growth of the genitals and the appearance of secondary sex characteristics. In girls, a cyclic excretion of estrogens anticipates the rhythm of the menstrual cycle well before **menarche,** or the first incidence of menstruation (Meredith, 1967).

Physical Growth

Velocity growth curves, which were discussed in Chapter 10, take on great significance during adolescence. The plateau period of childhood growth ends, and the adolescent growth spurt begins. Adolescence is virtually the only time in a person's life that this curve accelerates. Once the adolescent reaches the maximum point of growth velocity (in the case of stature, "peak height velocity"), deceleration again occurs until the annual growth increment is zero and growth for that factor ceases (see Figure 17.2).

The dramatic character of an adolescent's physical growth curve immediately provokes the question of where the energy to maintain such intense growth comes from. The answer is, of course, from calories. Some vigorous adolescent males at peak height velocity need a daily caloric intake comparable to that of a large adult doing heavy manual work, about 6,000 calories a day. (Little wonder that some adolescents always seem to be hungry and to spend time at the local hamburger stand indulging in carbohydrate orgies.) After an adolescent reaches peak height velocity, the extra energy needed for growth declines until the individual reaches the daily caloric intake that adult maintenance requires.

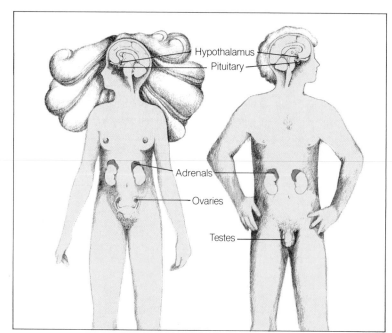

Figure 17.1 Illustrations of the endocrine system, showing only the major glands involved in pubertal changes. The hypothalamus (a part of the brain with neural and endocrine functions) signals the pituitary gland, which in turn stimulates hormonal secretions from other endocrine glands, resulting in many of the changes typifying adolescent physical and pubertal development.

Figure 17.2 Sample growth curves for adolescents eleven to twenty years of age (shaded area). (*top*) Notice that the early-maturing girl's rate of growth levels off by thirteen years of age, whereas the short boy continues to grow until approximately seventeen years of age. Individual variability is also reflected in the fact that the early-maturing girl reaches the average height for females, although the boy will be shorter than average. (*bottom*) Averaged and smoothed growth curves for boys and girls, showing inches gained in height per year. After the relatively stable period of gain in height during later childhood, the adolescent growth spurt starts, with its onset and end occurring earlier for girls than for boys. (Adapted from Bayley, 1956)

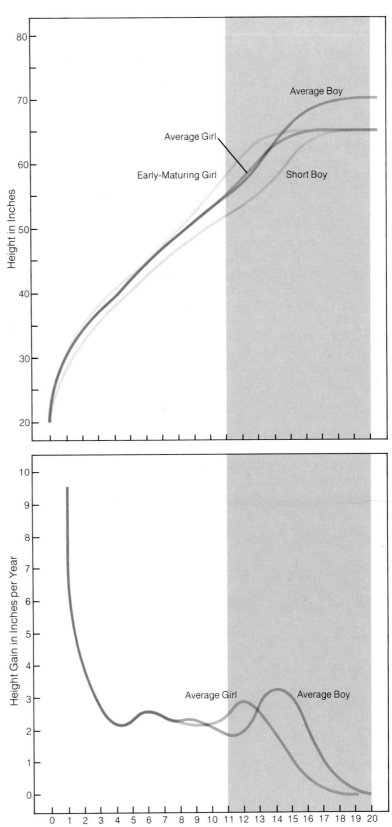

Although boys begin the pubertal growth spurt later than girls, their growth spurt lasts about three or four years longer than that of girls. For this reason, girls between the ages of twelve and fifteen tend to be taller than boys, but the boys catch up as they enter puberty and end their growth spurt significantly taller, on the average, than girls.

In general, bone and muscle tissue take part in the adolescent growth spurt, but the increase in muscle size is greater in boys than in girls; hence the adolescent male is stronger than the adolescent female. The average male also develops a larger heart and lungs, a greater capacity for absorbing oxygen in the blood and for eliminating the biochemical products of exercise, and wider shoulders, whereas the female develops a wider pelvis.

Only fat tissue develops oddly in adolescence. There is indeed an adolescent growth spurt in fat tissue, but it usually occurs before the main body begins its growth spurt. Thus, especially in some males, before the whole body spurts rapidly in size, "puppy fat" appears and often makes a healthy early pubescent male appear obese. As his body frame enlarges rapidly, this "puppy fat" is stretched and used up (presumably for the extra energy required by the growth spurt), and so the "string bean" phenomenon often replaces this early fat phase. The female adolescent does not lose fat; instead, she adds fat, and the average adult female has a good deal more fat than the male.

Both sexes experience a growth characteristic called **asynchrony.** Asynchrony refers to the fact that different body parts mature at different rates. This means that, at any given time during adolescent growth, certain body parts may be disproportionately large or small in relation to the rest of the body. This disproportion becomes most pronounced with puberty (Dwyer and Mayer, 1968–1969). For example, Lauren may complain that her hands and feet are too big, and David may object that his nose seems large or that his jaw is too prominent. As growth progresses, body proportions usually become more harmonious.

Sexual Maturation in Girls

The female growth spurt typically begins at around age ten, peaks at twelve, and continues until about fifteen. A number of events signal the onset of puberty in girls. For example, the "breast bud" develops (Douvan and Gold, 1966), and pigmented pubic hair appears. Breast enlargement begins some time around the middle of the tenth year and continues for approximately three years until full size is reached. As the entire breast enlarges, other changes in its shape and appearance occur. The areas around the nipples grow larger, more conical in form, and darker in color. At the same time that her breasts develop, a girl's voice lowers somewhat, and her vagina and uterus also begin to mature.

Pubic hair usually appears when a girl is about eleven (Hauck, 1970), but averages mean little in talking about an individual adolescent. Puberty varies so widely in its onset that such developments can

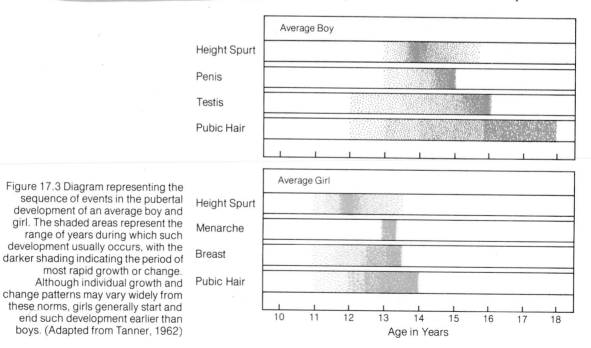

Figure 17.3 Diagram representing the sequence of events in the pubertal development of an average boy and girl. The shaded areas represent the range of years during which such development usually occurs, with the darker shading indicating the period of most rapid growth or change. Although individual growth and change patterns may vary widely from these norms, girls generally start and end such development earlier than boys. (Adapted from Tanner, 1962)

occur at any time between the ages of eight and thirteen (Tanner, 1972).

Parents and adolescents often regard menarche as the true indicator of puberty, but this event occurs relatively late in the pubertal sequence. Nevertheless, because menarche is easily identified, it is often used as a basis for making normative comparisons of sexual maturity among girls. The norms for adolescent development suggest that the average American girl is likely to have her first menstrual period between the ages of ten and seventeen (Tanner, 1972). It is rare for a girl whose glands function normally to experience menarche before she is nine or after she is eighteen. Most girls have their first period when they are about thirteen.

The relationship of menstruation to fertility is not well understood. One popular misconception is that menarche signals the attainment of full reproductive functioning. However, although menarche signals an advanced stage of uterine growth, the adolescent girl often, but not always, remains infertile for as long as twelve to eighteen months after menarche (Tanner, 1961). This period of infertility is shorter if a girl's first menstruation occurs later than average. Even four to six years after menarche, a girl is less likely to conceive than at a later time in life. Full sexual maturity and fertility is generally reached sometime in the early or middle twenties.

Sexual Maturation in Boys

The adolescent growth spurt generally occurs about two years later in boys than in girls and peaks at about the age of fourteen. The onset of puberty typically occurs at about twelve among boys, and, as is the case for girls, puberty includes more than one event. The appearance of live spermatozoa in the urine marks the onset of puberty, but because this event can be detected only by clinical tests, more observable changes are often used. These include accelerated growth of the testes and scrotum and the pubertal height spurt. Pubic hair may also appear at the beginning of puberty or within the following year.

The penis and scrotum usually begin their accelerated growth when a boy is around twelve, but there are wide individual variations, and the growth may begin as early as ten and one-half or as late as fourteen and one-half. Maturation and development of the penis continue for about five years, and the scrotum reaches maturity in about seven years (Meredith, 1967). Although the external genitalia of girls change little, in boys the changes in the penis, testes, and scrotum are substantial. The shaft of the penis length-

ens, and its head enlarges; the scrotum and testes grow larger and become pendulous. A boy is able to ejaculate semen about one and one-half years after accelerated penis growth begins (Tanner, 1972).

During adolescence, the larynx enlarges, and the vocal cords lengthen. This change leads to the gradual deepening of the male voice and sometimes to the embarrassing cracking of the adolescent boy's voice into a squeaky falsetto.

The appearance of facial hair is a final and significant event for the adolescent male. The downy hair on his upper lip, especially at the corners, becomes longer, coarser, and darker. Next, long down appears at the sides of his face in front of the ears. Later, coarse hair appears on his chin and lower cheeks. However, the ultimate symbol of masculinity, a hairy chest, does not develop until a male reaches late adolescence or even his early twenties.

PREDICTING PHYSICAL DEVELOPMENT

The uncertain timing of the various stages of maturation perplexes most boys and girls and disturbs many. A later maturer may wonder when he will stop looking like a child in the midst of his earlier-maturing peers. Similarly, an early maturer may feel somewhat embarrassed at her precocious sexual development and may wonder where things will end. A physical growth specialist, using specialized equipment, can predict the timing of sexual maturity and ultimate stature with some degree of certainty, but unfortunately such information is not available to most young people. These measures are usually taken only when significant deviance from the norm merits close medical scrutiny. The vast majority of teenagers must simply wait and hope for the best.

The need for more precise measures of development and maturation than chronological age is obvious. Merely saying that Lauren is thirteen years old tells relatively little about her. We can predict only within a wide range how tall she might become or how physically mature she is. Individual variability in height is particularly large. For example, if Lauren is tall for her age, she may be maturing at an average rate and eventually become a tall woman. On the other hand, she may be growing at an accelerated rate, finish maturing at an early age, and become a medium-height woman.

The adolescent growth spurt in height is often spectacular and, to the boy or girl concerned, may seem completely erratic. Yet it occurs within certain boundaries, some of which are more stable than others. According to measurements of boys by Don-

ald Broverman and his colleagues (1964), the beginning of pubertal growth is more variable than the end. Thus, the boy who has the earliest start in pubertal growth has a potentially longer period of growth than one with a late start.

Although individual height varies widely, a person's size at the beginning of adolescence predicts a great deal about his size at the end. Herbert and Lois Stolz (1951) found a correlation of more than +.80 between height at the onset and at the end of the pubertal period (not based on chronological age). Shifts in relative height do occur, but a boy who is taller than others at the beginning of his pubertal growth cycle is more likely to be taller at the end.

SIZE AND MATURATIONAL TRENDS

Where records have been kept, they have indicated a trend toward earlier onset of puberty for more than a century. In 1840 the average girl's first menstruation occurred at the age of seventeen; each decade since, menarche has tended to occur about four months earlier. In 1960 the average age of menarche in the United States was thirteen, and by 1970 the average age had dropped to slightly less than thirteen (Muuss, 1970).

Data about the onset of puberty in boys are not as complete as those for girls, but there has also been a trend toward earlier male maturation, at least since the beginning of this century. In addition to maturing earlier sexually, boys and girls today are also taller and heavier before, during, and at the end of adoles-

Figure 17.4 With trends clearly indicating earlier onset of puberty and overall increases in physical size, it is understandable that physical skills also change dramatically and that many adolescents are able to develop a high level of competence in an athletic skill at a somewhat early age.

cence than they were some generations ago. For example, Howard Meredith (1963) points out that in 1955 American boys were five and one-quarter inches taller than boys of their same age in 1870. Over the same period, the average weight for fifteen-year-old boys increased by thirty-three pounds.

Both sexes now reach their final adult height at an earlier age than they did a century ago. The average boy now reaches his adult height at eighteen instead of at twenty-three, twenty-four, or twenty-five, as he would have in 1880. Similarly, the average girl now reaches her full height at about sixteen instead of at eighteen or nineteen.

Such changes are not unique to the United States; many countries around the world report similar trends. If the present trend continues, girls born this year can expect to be one-half inch to one inch taller and about two pounds heavier than their mothers and to reach menarche earlier. The trend toward taller adults also shows up in their feet; the size of the average American foot is increasing about one-half inch each generation (Muuss, 1970), which means that the average shoe size is increasing one size per generation.

Presumably these trends over the centuries depend on the interplay of environmental and genetic factors, in which better nutrition and other environmental factors presently allow human size to approach the maximum of the possible genetic range discussed in Chapter 3. If the trend were purely a linear progression, one would assume that in the Middle Ages females could not bear children before they were about twenty-five and that in a few centuries they would do so before they were eight. Further, a linear trend would mean that adults in the future would be giants. None of these assumptions, of course, is either likely or biologically sensible. First, size and maturation trends form an undulating curve over time. Second, although today adults are getting larger and larger, they are also maturing earlier and earlier, and hence their growth ends at an earlier age.

There are signs that the trend toward earlier menarche has stopped among the upper socioeconomic classes in Norway, the United States, and the United Kingdom. In the two latter countries, the trend toward greater height also seems to have stopped in the upper social classes.

It was emphasized in Chapters 6 and 10 that a person's diet plays a crucial role in development and maturation and that children from upper- and middle-class backgrounds become taller and heavier and reach puberty earlier than their lower-class peers do.

Another factor is increased availability and sophistication of medical care. Today's children experience fewer of the severely debilitating diseases discussed in Chapter 10, and modern procedures prevent many diseases from exerting a negative influence. Finally, modern mobility affects the breeding patterns of the population. In earlier times, people lived in small towns or villages and lacked the transportation to move far from their homes. A person tended to marry within his own community. With the advent of better transportation, it became easier for a person to marry outside the community, thus allowing genetic factors to operate more freely.

Other factors also influence the onset of puberty within any given generation. For example, geographic and climatic variations affect the average age of menarche. A girl living at sea level is likely to have her first menstrual period several months before a girl of the same age living at a much higher altitude. In spite of traditional beliefs and a few early studies, it also appears that girls who live in hot, humid climates are likely to reach menarche later than girls who live in cooler climates.

The three-year decrease in the average age of the onset of puberty represents a radical change in the timetable of development. Childhood is shortened, and the social demands and urges associated with sexual maturity occur sooner. Unfortunately, the social and cultural climate has not adjusted to the trend toward earlier maturation. As Chapter 1 pointed out, today's adolescent still finds himself treated, in many respects, as an overgrown child.

REACTIONS TO PHYSICAL CHANGE

Understandably, physical changes of the magnitude experienced by an adolescent have a significant effect on how he feels about himself. As Chapter 15 noted, peer and social attitudes will influence an individual's reactions to these changes. One important influence is that of the mythical **body ideal,** the body type defined by the culture as "attractive" and sex-appropriate. The individual learns these ideal characteristics from peer and family expectations and from the mass media. William Schonfeld (1963) has pointed out that movies, television, advertising, and the worship of sports heroes perpetuate the reverence for the ideal body and encourage the disparagement of those whose bodies do not conform to the ideal.

Cultural body standards may also influence a person's image of his own body. Stanley Schonbuch and Robert Schell (1967) asked male college students to select photographs that most nearly resembled themselves from a group of ten pictures. Males who were fifteen or more pounds overweight tended to overestimate their size, selecting photographs that portrayed fatter men. Schonbuch and Schell speculated that the negative comments and reactions of others may lead fat adolescents to regard their body differences as greater than they actually are.

Body image appears to determine to a large extent how an adolescent feels about himself. For example,

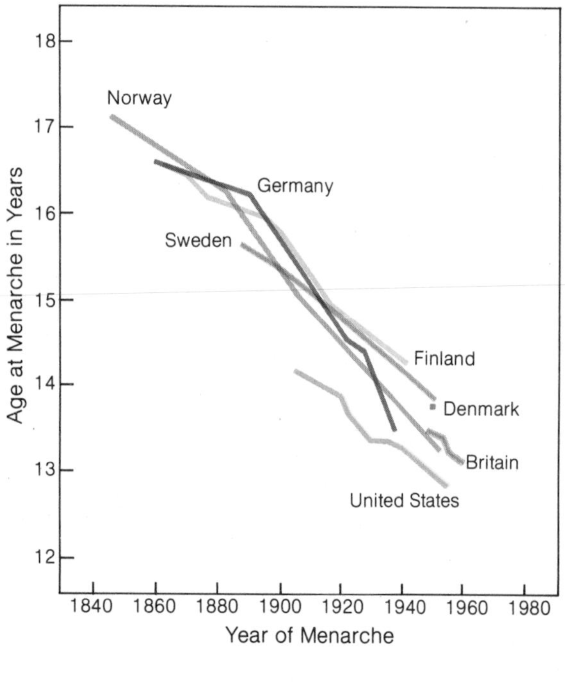

Figure 17.5 Graph illustrating the decline in the average age of menarche (onset of menstruation) in the United States and in various European countries over the last century. (After Tanner, 1962)

Boyd McCandless (1960) found a strong correlation between the way that college-aged students view their bodies (body concept) and the way that they judge themselves as people (self-concept). According to McCandless, girls, even more than boys, tend to be influenced by body image. This research suggests that a girl is more concerned about and places more personal emphasis on her physical appearance than a boy does. This is understandable when one considers the extent to which our society focuses on the beautiful woman with the perfect body, shiny hair, flawless complexion, gleaming teeth, and seductive eyes. The importance of a woman's appearance is reflected in the pervasive advertising of cosmetics, hair products, clothing, and fad diets. Although an athletic physique often is important for a boy, some alternatives exist, and boys are not as constantly confronted by the ideal physical stereotype as girls are. A man can look masculine by sporting a mustache or by flaunting chest hair. At present, men are probably less pressured by society to worry about their appearance than women are, although changing sex-role stereotypes may soon affect this difference in pressure.

Other investigators have also found that girls are more concerned than boys with the failure of their developing bodies to match the culture's body ideal. Girls perceive that boys prefer slender figures, long legs, and well-developed breasts, and they worry when their own bodies do not measure up to this ideal (Wiggins, Wiggins, and Conger, 1968). They worry about their social acceptability, and most girls tend to view their physical appearance as directly affecting their future prospects for courtship and marriage (Walster et al., 1966).

Adolescents of both sexes are especially sensitive to any body characteristic that might be interpreted as sex-inappropriate. From childhood, boys and girls learn which physical attributes are feminine and which are masculine, and they show deep concern over any deviations from those stereotypes (Schonfeld, 1964). Adolescent boys are particularly concerned about such characteristics as a circle of fat around the hips and thighs, underdeveloped external genitalia, or the development of subcutaneous tissue in the breast region. Although such developments as fatty hips and breast growth are normal and usually soon disappear, they are often a source of great embarrassment to a boy.

Herbert and Lois Stolz (1951) have identified certain physical characteristics that adolescent girls consider unfeminine. These include large hands and feet, a figure that is much too full or too thin, pigmented facial hair, and a large body. Thus, many of the normal temporary changes of adolescence may seem "unfeminine" to a girl. She grows body hair, her voice becomes lower, her hands and feet grow, and so forth. Eventually, however, a girl may be comforted by the fact that her friends are experiencing the same changes.

Some cross-cultural data suggest that adolescents in other societies may not share the American adolescent's concern with body image. For example, David Friesen (1968) has shown that Canadian high-school students seem to place more value on academic performance and less on athletic prowess, popularity, and good looks than their American age-mates do.

Breast Development

Because breast development is an obvious indicator of sexual maturity in women, it is often the focus of attention from others and of concern to the individual. The development of a girl's breasts, including size and contour, plays an important role in her evaluation of herself as a female. The emphasis of the popular media (in advertisements for brassieres and the dimensions of the playmate of the month) and the behavior of many American men add to her concern.

Most adolescent girls are likely to have ambivalent feelings about their developing breasts. For example, Lauren may be proud of her new femininity yet be embarrassed by the sudden attention that she receives from boys. She may worry that tight blouses or sweaters are too revealing and may try to hide her new bustline by wearing loose-fitting clothes or by hunching slightly. Many girls complain that their breasts are too large or too small. Extremely large breasts can embarrass a girl because they draw attention to her and cause her to feel different from her peers. Extremely small breasts can make a girl worry whether she will ever reach sexual maturity or will be attractive to men. However, in most cases, as a girl reaches her adult body proportions, breasts that seemed too large or too small during adolescence begin to appear more appropriate to her stature.

Male Genitals

The size of his genital organs, especially the penis, can have profound significance for an adolescent. Unlike girls, whose external genitalia change very little, boys' genitalia change in both size and contour. Because David can compare his genitals with those of his peers, they can become a primary source of concern. Men's rooms, showers, and gymnasiums

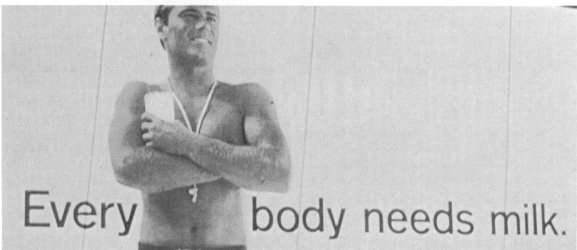

Figure 17.6 With the marked nature and degree of the physical changes occurring during adolescence, most adolescents become concerned with their own bodies and how they appear to others. Such concerns are often compounded if there is a real or imagined deviation in appearance from the ideal body images and types that are presented in the media.

provide ample opportunity for David to judge his development against that of other boys and men.

A boy with a small penis may feel particularly distressed. He may be a victim of widely held beliefs that the size of a man's penis is related to his physical strength, his virility, and his ability to sexually satisfy a woman. Sometimes a boy may consider his penis to be particularly small because he is ignorant about the wide range of penis size among normal men. He can take comfort, however, from measurements that show a great variation in penis size at all ages.

The belief that a large penis is related to masculinity and virility showed up in a study by John Verinis and Samuel Roll (1970). They found that men and women aged eighteen to twenty rated such traits as a large penis and hairy arms and chest as indications of virility and masculinity. There is, however, no empirical support for the belief that the size of a man's genitals is related to his masculinity and strength. William Masters and Virginia Johnson (1966) found that penis size is less consistently related to general physical development than any other organ of the body is. They found that the largest penis (5.5 inches in the flaccid state) in a sampling of 312 men was displayed by a man who was 5 feet 7 inches tall, whereas the smallest (2.36 inches) belonged to a man 5 feet 11 inches tall. Masters and Johnson also noted that a small penis, when fully erect, shows a relatively greater increase in size than a large penis.

Masters and Johnson and others have also reported that the ability to provide sexual gratification for a female partner during intercourse does not seem to depend on the size of the erect penis. The vagina is flexible and elastic: It accommodates to the insertion of small objects by contracting, and it distends sufficiently during the birth process to allow the passage of a baby. The vagina of a normally responsive woman therefore readily adjusts to a wide range of variation in penis size. Thus, penis size is usually a minor factor in sexual stimulation of the female; sexual technique makes the difference.

Obesity

About 10 percent of the children in the United States have been classified as obese (a judgment based on measures of weight relative to height), and in most samples the percentages become larger during the adolescent years. For example, Milicent Hathaway and Dorothy Sargent (1962) report that as many as 30 to 35 percent of adolescents are overweight.

Simply measuring the external dimensions of the body does not accurately determine obesity. Fat, muscle, bones, and skeletal shape all help determine body contours, and the contribution of each factor varies with individuals. For example, a girl with a wide bone structure may appear to have fat hips, although she may have a thinner layer of fat than a girl with narrow bone structure who looks slimmer.

Reactions to being overweight vary with sex. Girls are much more disturbed than boys by fatness (Shapiro, Hampton, and Huenemann, 1967), and girls are inclined to label excess weight as "fat," whereas boys are likely to view it as desirable bone and muscle.

Figure 17.7 Good eating habits and proper nutrition can provide the energy necessary for the physical changes and activities that typify adolescent physical development and can help to prevent such problems as obesity, with its negative effects on self-concept and social relationships.

Several factors can contribute to obesity in the adolescent. For instance, an increasing amount of evidence indicates that overfeeding babies (a common practice in the United States) causes a permanent increase in the number and size of fat cells (Mayer, 1968). Even if an overfed baby goes through childhood at a normal weight for his size, these extra fat cells remain in his body, leaving him susceptible to obesity during adolescence and adulthood. Glandular dysfunctions (for example, improper functioning of the hypothalamus or the thyroid gland) are rarely a cause of adolescent obesity. More often, teen-agers choose poor diets, eating too much starch and fat and not enough proteins, vitamins, and minerals. The young adolescent dashes off without breakfast, only to settle down later in the day to a lunch of hamburgers, French fries, a candy bar, and a malt, and then he tops off dinner with an extra piece of cake before going to bed. The tendency to eat high-calorie foods late in the day and evening can contribute significantly to obesity (Piscopo, 1970). Individuals who have such an eating pattern can be overweight and undernourished at the same time.

Whatever the reasons for obesity, the overweight adolescent is at a personal and social disadvantage. Because our culture associates obesity with such undesirable characteristics as gluttony, laziness, lack of will power, sloppiness, and general unattractiveness, the overweight adolescent often becomes the target of negative evaluations and cruel remarks. In addition, the obese adolescent may become biologically and sexually mature earlier than his age-mates and may find that his physical unattractiveness to the opposite sex only compounds his problems.

PHYSICAL-SEXUAL AND SOCIAL CHANGE

Sexual development obviously has wide psychological and social ramifications. The developing adolescent whose body conforms to the cultural ideal has a social advantage. But extremely tall, skinny adolescents and extremely short, fat ones are likely to evoke negative reactions from their peers. For example, J. Robert Staffieri (1967) found that classmates more often chose well-muscled and thin adolescents as friends than fat ones. Evaluations by others generally have a strong influence on an adolescent's social relations and behavior.

Early and Late Maturing

Developmental psychologists Mary Cover Jones and Nancy Bayley (1950) and their colleagues have followed groups of early- and late-maturing boys from early adolescence through the fourth decade of life. The boys differed markedly in social and physical characteristics during the years from thirteen to fifteen. At the same chronological age, the early maturers were taller, stronger, more attractive, and better coordinated than the later maturers, and they tended to have well-muscled bodies. The late maturers tended to be thin and were more talkative, active, busy, and uninhibited, yet they also tended to be tenser and bossier than the early maturers. These findings suggest that late maturers possess less social maturity and that they use negative behavior to get attention, thereby compensating for their physical disadvantages. Additional studies support this interpretation. Late maturers also show a greater need for social acceptance, greater anticipation of rejection, heightened dependence, and negative self-concepts (Mussen and Jones, 1957).

Schonfeld (1964) points out that many of the physical characteristics of late-maturing boys, which the boys themselves may regard as evidence of inadequate masculinity, fall within the normal range of development. When such is the case, a late-maturing boy need only wait until he catches up with his peers. But in the meantime, the values placed on athletic prowess and manly appearance (by boys and girls alike) may make him feel inferior to those who mature early.

The early maturer is more active in athletics and student government and has greater visibility in the school social system. The social advantages of early maturity also appear to continue into adulthood, when differences in physique no longer exist. In their thirties, early maturers tended to have higher occupational status, were more likely to work in supervisory or managerial positions, and reported more active social lives in clubs, organizations, and business (M. Jones, 1957). The differences that appeared when the groups were in their late thirties suggest that early maturers achieve in a conforming way, whereas later maturers' achievements are more likely to be idiosyncratic. The early maturer is likely to be conventional in both thought and attitude; he continues to have social poise and to show responsibility. The late maturer appears to be more flexible and adaptive; he tolerates ambiguity better than the early maturer (M. Jones, 1965). Thus, as Harvey Peskin (1967) suggests, it appears that the greater social advantage of the early maturer may lead him to fix on his identity early in life, thereby producing conventionality.

Studies of early- and late-maturing girls suggest that the early-maturing girl has less prestige in early

Figure 17.8 Because of expectations generally associated with more adultlike body development, early maturers often have a distinct advantage over their later-maturing counterparts.

adolescence but that, as the growth process continues, she comes to enjoy the social advantages of the early-maturing boy (Faust, 1960). At first, the early-maturing girl is somewhat conspicuous and is likely to be far out of step developmentally with boys of her own age. However, early maturity may be a source of satisfaction if a girl's favorite companions are also early maturers. At seventeen, girls who have matured early may have a more favorable view of themselves and may rate higher in popularity than they rated earlier in their teens. However, studies that follow early- and late-maturing girls into adulthood have not been especially revealing, presumably because in the past a woman's social life, status, and opportunities for achievement have depended on the status of her husband (Eichorn, 1963).

Sexual Behavior

Because the higher brain centers also govern sex in human beings, human sexual behavior is pliable and shows great variation. Interest in sex is not so tied to the reproductive cycle as it is in most mammals. A wide variety of symbols, including pictures, movies, books, and even thoughts, can arouse human beings. A woman can continue to have orgasm after menopause or after her ovaries are removed, and a castrated man may be able to have an orgasm even though he cannot ejaculate. As this section makes clear, changes over time in social conditioning have led to great differences in sexual attitudes and behavior.

The Kinsey Reports.   Before 1915, 75 percent of all first-time brides were virgins; by 1920 the figure had dropped to 50 percent. The years after 1920 to the late 1960s can be seen as largely a period of changing attitudes that incorporated earlier changes in sexual behavior (Reiss, 1973).

The Kinsey reports (Kinsey, Pomeroy, and Martin, 1948; Kinsey *et al.*, 1953) on the incidence and variety of sexual outlets were a milestone in the decades since 1920 of increasingly open exchange of information about sexual behavior. Although Alfred Kinsey's sample included too many college students among his upper socioeconomic group and too many prison inmates among the lower group, the Kinsey reports continue to be the best sources of information about sexual behavior in the United States during the late 1940s.

According to most studies, practically all boys and probably a great many girls have some kind of sexual experience before adolescence. For example, Glenn Ramsey (1943) found that, by the age of twelve, about 75 percent of all boys had masturbated and that, by the age of fifteen, nearly all reported such experience. Moreover, by the age of thirteen, about 40 percent of all boys had been involved in homosexual play. By contrast, not until late adolescence had 40 percent of the girls masturbated.

By the end of their teens, practically all boys and girls had had some heterosexual contact, ranging from holding hands to petting genitals. Kinsey's data indicated that by age twenty over 50 percent of girls had experienced orgasm, whereas nearly all boys had done so by twenty. For 65 percent of the boys, orgasm was first attained through masturbation, whereas 50 percent of the girls first reached orgasm through petting or intercourse. About 25 percent of the girls and 45 percent of the boys reported premarital intercourse before age twenty.

Social-class differences markedly affected the behavior of both sexes: 50 percent of male adolescents with grade-school educations had had intercourse by the time they were fifteen in contrast to only 10 percent of youths who subsequently went to college. For females, the corresponding figures were 18 percent and 1 percent. Although Kinsey and his colleagues chose to explain these sex differences, in biological terms, as the result of a more urgent male sex drive, a more balanced view suggests that these differences are the result of a complex interaction among neurological, hormonal, and sociopsychological factors.

The Changing Sixties. Had this section been written ten years ago, one could still have said that sexual behavior in the United States had changed little since 1920. It was not until the late 1960s that a second major change appeared in sexual behavior in this century. Prior to Kinsey's reports, a wide variety of sexual behavior was not considered fit for public view or discussion. Today, most of this behavior is presented freely by radio, movies, television, books, magazines, and newspapers. As a result, the social climate in which young people experience menarche or first ejaculation has changed considerably over the past years, but the new attitudes and behavior are the product of an evolutionary and not a revolutionary process.

Recent surveys show that Kinsey's figures now are out of date. For example, sexual intercourse among female college sophomores has risen from 20 percent (Kinsey *et al.*, 1953) to between 30 and 40 percent (R. R. Bell and Chaskes, 1970). A more recent survey of 4,600 girls between fifteen and nineteen indicates

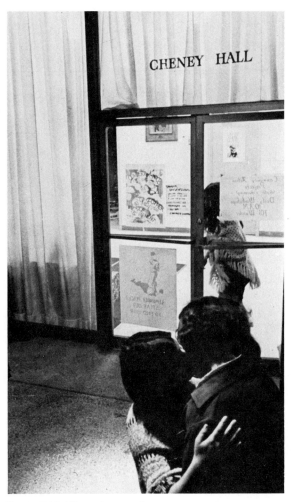

Figure 17.9 Although sex-role stereotypes continue to abound, changes over time in social conditioning have led to great changes in sexual behavior and attitudes. At present, although adolescents are generally more aware and expressive of such attitudes and behaviors, few escape the social pressures that dictate appropriate sexual attitudes and behavior for each gender.

that, among all female adolescents, 46 percent have had intercourse by the time they are nineteen (Zelnik and Kantner, 1972). These are substantial increases in premarital intercourse in a relatively short period of time, especially when the almost fifty-year plateau of unchanged behavior is considered.

Although the incidence of premarital intercourse has risen sharply in the United States, American college students appear to be no more experienced than students in other countries and tend to look inhibited alongside English college students (Luckey and Nass, 1969). Tables 17.1 and 17.2 present the results of surveys among college men and women in five countries. However, this survey, which reports sexual intercourse among 58 percent of American college men, gives the lowest figure to come out of recent studies. One recent study indicates that 82 percent of American college men have engaged in intercourse. Whichever figure is accurate, there has been a sharp increase since Kinsey reported that 49 percent of college-educated males had had premarital intercourse before they were twenty-one.

Along with a rise in sexual experience has come a drop in the proportion of males who visit prostitutes. As Table 17.2 shows, only 4.2 percent of American college men have been involved with prostitutes, whereas earlier studies had reported that 20 to 25 percent had been so involved (Kinsey, Pomeroy, and Martin, 1948).

Whereas Kinsey reported large-scale social-class differences in sexual behavior among males, the absence of information on today's noncollege men and women makes precise comparison impossible. However, it is clear that the major increase in premarital experience has occurred in the middle and upper-middle classes.

Sex Differences and Sex Roles. As all studies have shown, there are many differences in sexual behavior between the sexes. Boys reach the peak of their sexual powers earlier than girls, even though girls reach menarche earlier than boys reach a corresponding level of development. Boys desire orgasm more often than girls; they resort more than girls to sexual fantasies; they are more responsive to symbols of sex; they reach a sexual climax in dreams more often; they require less constant physical stimulation to remain aroused; they more often have had sexual relations with more than one partner; they do not tend to insist, as many girls do, that there should be a feeling of affection between sexual partners; and they prefer to go steady less often than girls.

Table 17.1 College Women's Sexual Experience

TYPE	UNITED STATES	CANADA	ENGLAND	GERMANY	NORWAY
Light embracing or fond holding of hands	97.5%	96.5%	91.9%	94.8%	89.3%
Casual goodnight kissing	96.8	91.8	93.0	74.0	75.0
Deep kissing	96.5	91.8	93.0	90.6	89.3
Horizontal embrace with some petting but not undressed	83.3	81.2	79.1	77.1	75.0
Petting of breast area from outside woman's clothing	78.3	78.8	82.6	76.0	64.3
Petting of breast area without clothes intervening	67.8	64.7	70.9	66.7	58.9
Petting below the waist under woman's clothing	61.2	64.7	70.9	63.5	53.6
Petting below the waist of both man and woman, under clothing	57.8	50.6	61.6	56.3	42.9
Nude embrace	49.6	47.6	64.0	62.1	51.8
Coitus	43.2	35.3	62.8	59.4	53.6
One-night affair involving coitus; did not date person again	7.2	5.9	33.7	4.2	12.5
Whipping or spanking before petting or other intimacy	4.5	5.9	17.4	1.0	7.1

Source: Adapted from Eleanore Luckey and Gilbert Nass, "A Comparison of Sexual Attitudes and Behavior in an International Sample," *Journal of Marriage and the Family,* 31 (1969), p. 375.

These differences in male and female sexual behaviors are, of course, influenced by sex-role stereotypes, just as many other behaviors are. According to traditional American standards, the girl should play a passive role in her sexual relations. The boy should take the initiative in petting, and he usually does. The girl accedes, and, if the approach threatens to go beyond the limits she allows, she is expected to serve as a calming conscience for both. In courtship, it is the man who is supposed to propose. Although our culture's sex-role stereotypes are gradually changing, few adolescents have escaped the social pressures that dictate appropriate sexual behavior for each gender. In the next chapter, we will look at the psychological aspects of sexual intercourse and examine adolescents' attitudes toward sexuality and appropriate sexual conduct.

SUMMARY

1. Adolescence begins as a biological phenomenon, and sexual maturation is its central theme. The first incidence of menstruation in girls and the appearance of pubic hair, nocturnal emissions, and enlarging sex organs in boys are among the signs most often used to mark the attainment of physical-sexual maturity. With the later release of sperm and ova during puberty, adolescents achieve the capability of biological reproduction. The physical and maturational changes that indicate increased hormone production are dramatically reflected in the adolescent growth spurt.

2. To the dismay of many adolescents, growth during this period is often asynchronous, with different body parts maturing at different times and rates. Because of this, and because the extent of growth varies widely, predictions of physical development often remain uncertain. However, despite individual variability, maturation usually can be expected to occur within certain more-or-less stable boundaries.

3. Size and maturational trends over the decades indicate an earlier onset of puberty, increases in size and weight, and the earlier attainment of final adult

Table 17.2 College Men's Sexual Experience

TYPE	UNITED STATES	CANADA	ENGLAND	GERMANY	NORWAY
Light embracing or fond holding of hands	98.6%	98.9%	93.5%	93.8%	93.7%
Casual goodnight kissing	96.7	97.7	93.5	78.6	86.1
Deep kissing	96.0	97.7	91.9	91.1	96.2
Horizontal embrace with some petting but not undressed	89.9	92.0	85.4	68.8	93.6
Petting of woman's breast area from outside her clothing	89.9	93.2	87.0	80.4	83.5
Petting of woman's breast area without clothes intervening	83.4	92.0	82.8	69.6	83.5
Petting below the waist of the woman under her clothing	81.1	85.2	84.6	70.5	83.5
Petting below the waist of both man and woman, under clothing	62.9	64.8	68.3	52.7	55.1
Nude embrace	65.6	69.3	70.5	50.0	69.6
Coitus	58.2	56.8	74.8	54.5	66.7
One-night affair involving coitus; did not date person again	29.9	21.6	43.1	17.0	32.9
Whipping or spanking before petting or other intimacy	8.2	5.7	17.1	0.9	5.1
Sex on pay-as-you-go basis	4.2	4.5	13.8	9.8	2.5

Source: Adapted from Eleanore Luckey and Gilbert Nass, "A Comparison of Sexual Attitudes and Behavior in an International Sample," *Journal of Marriage and the Family,* 31 (1969), p. 374.

height. Improved nutrition, more sophisticated medical care, and climatic variations are some of the environmental factors that appear to explain these changes within and across generations.

4. In this age of mass media, individuals are constantly exposed to, and quickly learn, the mythical standards that make up the culture's ideal body type. Deviations from this body ideal—whether in height or weight, the timing of maturation, or the size and contour of body parts—are likely to have profound influences on the developing adolescent's self-concept and peer relationships.

5. Physical-sexual development typically has wide psychological and social ramifications. For example, early-maturing boys are likely to be taller, stronger, more attractive and poised, and better coordinated than later-maturing boys. However, apart from variations in rates at which they mature physically or sexually, it is also clear that more adolescents today engage in a greater variety of sexual behavior at an

earlier age. Although sexual attitudes and behavior have generally become more open and some changes in sex-role stereotypes have occurred, few adolescents escape the social pressures that dictate appropriate sexual attitudes and behavior for each gender.

SUGGESTED READINGS

Kagan, Jerome, and Robert Coles (eds.). *Twelve to Sixteen: Early Adolescence.* New York: Norton, 1972.

Masters, William, and Virginia Johnson. *Human Sexual Response.* Boston: Little, Brown, 1966.

Schachter, Stanley. "Eat, Eat," *Psychology Today,* 4 (April 1971), 44–47+.

Sorensen, Robert C. *Adolescent Sexuality in Contemporary America: Personal Values and Sexual Behavior Ages Thirteen to Sixteen.* New York: World Press, 1973.

Tanner, J. M. "Growing Up," *Scientific American,* 229 (September 1973), 34–43.

The formation of one's identity as a
distinct and unique person is a
complex process, and the
developmental changes and
experiences of adolescence play a
large part in determining the outcome.

18

IDENTITY AND EXPERIENCE

Put the personality of a child in the body of an adult, furnish a need to be loved and a desire to be independent, allow a need to be self-directing but leave out any idea of what direction to take, add love but also the fear that it may not be accepted or returned, and give physical and sexual powers without any knowledge of or experience in how to use them. Then place the person you have constructed into a complex society whose values and achievements are hard to understand and harder to attain. You will have only begun to scratch the surface of an adolescent.

As Chapter 1 pointed out, adolescence is a relatively new invention in Western societies. Many other societies recognize a change in status around the age of puberty. This sometimes overnight change drastically redefines the individual's rights and responsibilities. At the same time, it constitutes an important force for behavioral development and change. The longer transition period of adolescence in the West is no less important in influencing the development of the individual. The view that adolescence is only a recapitulation and working out of the themes of childhood does scant justice to its possibilities. To be sure, the preadolescent years are important in defining where Susan and Matt begin, how much they have to work with, and what they must work on. Human development is cumulative and layered. Adolescence is built on the early phases of life but at the same time has its own tasks. Whether the adolescent accomplishes these tasks depends not only on his past but on his present, on what he is offered and on what he can make of it.

It is impossible to discuss adolescent behavior and development without taking note of the wide variety of life styles and commitments that exist in our society, and the discussions in this and the following chapter will emphasize this point. In a pluralistic society, adolescence takes many forms. In contrast to the common stereotype, adolescents share the diverse values, beliefs, and attitudes characteristic of their elders.

In this chapter we will discuss the adolescent's search for a sense of identity. We will look at self-esteem and the role it plays in developing a secure sense of identity. We will see how the cognitive changes of adolescence and the development of formal thought affect a person's self-concept and moral reasoning. We will discover that the changes in sexual behavior discussed in the last chapter have been accompanied by large changes in sexual attitudes and by a trend toward mutually satisfying, equalitarian sexual relationships. Finally, we will look at the adolescent's choice of a career, and we will explore the ways that socialization can shape that important choice.

IDENTITY: SELF AND SOCIETY

Although matters of self-definition and self-esteem are important throughout the life cycle, it is during adolescence that these matters become paramount. Developmental change often brings about a developmental crisis, a disruption of the concept of self. As Erik Erikson (1968) has pointed out, at this time of life the adolescent's body goes through marked physical changes and is flooded with sexual impulses; the young person confronts both imminent intimacy with the other sex and an immediate future filled with conflicting possibilities and choices.

Before adolescents can regain a sense of unity with themselves and with the world about them, they must incorporate their new physical and sexual attributes and the opportunities they present into a new self-concept. A society that universally recognizes these changes and attaches meaning to them makes reworking self-concepts a relatively uncomplicated task. However, in a pluralistic society like our own, the prolongation of adolescence and its bewildering variety of choices can mean greater difficulty. In either case, Erikson has postulated a "developmental crisis," a moment when development must move one way or the other.

Erikson's concept of identity has two facets: It refers to a person's feeling about himself, or self-esteem, and to the relationship between his self-concept and descriptions of him by significant others in his life (see Figure 18.1). The most important descriptions involve those behaviors that society considers basic to a person's functioning, and these descriptions are organized into subgroupings that are usually called roles. Being a male or a female is one such fundamental role. As we have seen in earlier chapters, roles provide significant connections between self and society; a person's roles both link him meaningfully to the social order and define him as an individual.

The child enters adolescence with experience in three kinds of social groups: the family, the peer group, and larger organizations such as the school. He plays at least one role in each of these groups, and for each of his roles there is a set of role-definers—people with whom the individual interacts and who define his role by indicating appropriate behavior and by supporting and rewarding him when he displays it. In a similar manner, the teen-ager comes to judge himself—his appearance, his academic achievement, his social capacities—by the standards of those who define the roles in his social groups. Among these role-definers, parents, peers, and teachers continue to be a dominant influence.

Defining the Self

The childhood self is largely defined by parents and a few other key persons, including family members, certain peers, ministers, and teachers. It reflects in a relatively uncomplicated way the immediate world of persons crucial to the child and is based on relatively simple identification with these people, as was shown in Chapters 13 and 15. The adolescent must often reexamine and reintegrate this self-concept so that it is consistent with his new capacity for rationality, his moral values, and his possibilities for work, love, and play in modern society. This process requires him to integrate emerging cognitive and behavioral abilities and to integrate new values and purposes. Above all, an adolescent's sense of self involves a movement

Figure 18.1 Summary descriptions of some major theoretical viewpoints regarding personality development during adolescence.

Sigmund Freud considers adolescence to represent the last identifiable stage of psychosexual development: the genital stage. During this stage, the individual's identity takes its final form, and, in place of narcissistic self-love, love for others and altruistic behavior develop. Although the influence of peers and parents is not considered to be as strong as it was during earlier stages, peers and parents still play an important role in providing love and realistic direction for the individual.

Erik Erikson holds self-definition and self-esteem as central concerns for the individual during adolescence. As a result of marked physical changes, powerful sexual impulses, imminent conflicting choices and possibilities, and confusion in the roles expected of him by parents and peers, the adolescent is confronted with an identity crisis. He must incorporate his new physical and sexual attributes into a new self-concept. He also must generate an orientation and a goal that will give him a sense of unity and purpose in order to make a vocational choice that will best match his view of himself. Finally, he must integrate into his self-understanding the expectations and perceptions that others have of him.

Alfred Adler emphasizes that the individual's style of life, or identity, established during early childhood, determines how the adolescent will express his strivings for competence. According to Adler, the adolescent's identity is expressed in the decisions that he must make about his sexuality and his vocation and also in his responses to his parents and his peers. In this view, the adolescent ideally will come to respond to his world with altruism, creativity, and awareness; he will express his sexuality through love and concern for others; his vocational choice will be guided by humanitarian desires; and his responses to parents and peers will be based on cooperation and compassion.

Erich Fromm sees the adolescent's struggle to establish his identity as a continuation of his dilemma since birth. In this view, the adolescent is seen as having a desire to be unique and distinctive as well as a conflicting desire to be related to and united with others. The adolescent's emerging sexuality creates for him new possibilities for expressing tenderness, love, and compassion. According to Fromm, although pressures for vocational choice can result in feelings of isolation, vocational choice is an important step in achieving productive creativity and fulfillment.

Harry Stack Sullivan suggests that adolescence involves a final stabilizing of one's self-concept, first through chumships and later through heterosexual experiences. Thus, in the intimacy of a chumship, the adolescent presumably is able to examine and change any neglected aspects of his self-concept. According to Sullivan, the emergence of a true sexual interest moves the adolescent toward heterosexual relationships. If the adolescent has little difficulty in his heterosexual relationships, he is able to enter into relatively stable and satisfying relationships with members of both sexes. In this view, along with his developing ability to engage in a full complement of interpersonal relationships, the adolescent is also expected to acquire the vocational knowledge and abilities that will enable him to make a contribution to society.

Walter Mischel takes the view that the adolescent encounters a multiplicity of adult roles and expectations as he moves out of childhood and that each of these requires him to learn new discriminations and to make new responses to his environment. Physical and hormonal changes require the adolescent to learn patterns of socially appropriate sexual behaviors. Social expectations and consequences also change during this time, forcing the adolescent to confront the responsibility of choosing a career. As agents of socialization, parents and peers continue to exert a strong influence, controlling many of the consequences of the adolescent's behavior.

away from a simple mirrorlike view of himself—in which he sees himself as a reflection of parents, peers, and teachers—to a more autonomous and more individual sense of identity, integrating independence and uniqueness with interdependence and solidarity with other people.

There are wide individual differences in the methods that an adolescent may use to attain his new self-concept. One youthful solution involves a determined attempt to change the society so as to bring it into line with the adolescent's principles and needs. Another solution is a systematic attempt to change one's self so as to fit into the existing system with less anxiety or discomfort. A third approach is the effort to carve out some special niche within society where the qualities of one's self can be preserved, enhanced, or acted on.

However, some developmental changes can threaten the adolescent's integration of his childhood self-concept and lead to what Erikson (1968) called **totalism,** an organization of one's self-concept that has rigid, absolute, and arbitrary boundaries. Totalism makes adolescents particularly susceptible to totalitarian movements and to ideologies of the left and the right. According to Erikson, if adolescents feel their emerging identities severely threatened by historical or technological development, they become ready to support doctrines that allow them to immerse themselves in a synthetic identity, such as extreme nationalism, racism, or class consciousness, and to condemn the stereotyped enemy of their new identites. This tendency toward total immersion in a synthetic identity can take other forms, and it characterized the participation of many American adolescents in the Civil Rights Movement of the 1960s, the 1968 crusade to nominate Eugene McCarthy for President, and the campaign to end the war in Vietnam.

A similar immersion into the peer group can play a major role in regulating feelings and in emancipating the adolescent from childhood dependence. What Peter Blos (1962) has called **uniformism,** or immersion into the peer group and acceptance of its norms as infallible and regulatory, may assist an adolescent in moving away from dependence on his family at a time when he still needs some external source of control. However, sometimes an adolescent clings to this source of control long after the need for it has passed, and conformity to peer-group norms merely replaces conformity to parental norms. When this happens, development is foreclosed before the ado-

lescent can achieve real self-regulation and in-dependence.

Self-esteem

Erikson (1968) has suggested that, at its best, identity is experienced as a sense of well-being. A person with a secure identity feels at home in his body, knows where he is going, and feels assured of recognition from people who count.

In general, people with low self-esteem have a relatively unstable self-concept, which means that they lack a consistent frame of reference within which to assimilate their experiences of self and others. Such a situation provokes anxiety, a state intensified by the strain of putting on a front. Persons with low self-esteem are more likely than others to be lonely. They are also more vulnerable. They are likely to be sensitive to criticism; they are bothered if others have a poor opinion of them, are deeply disturbed if they do poorly at some task, and are upset when they become aware of a personal fault or inadequacy. Others may describe them as touchy or easily hurt.

This internal distress is matched by the dismal picture of the adolescent with low self-esteem. He is awkward with others, assumes that they do not like him, has low faith in human nature, is submissive and nonassertive, and gets little respect. He infrequently participates in extracurricular activities and is rarely selected for leadership positions. He tends to be unpopular and avoids participating in class discus-sions and informal conversations. Caught up in this pattern, the adolescent with extremely low self-esteem becomes locked into a trap in which his very real isolation from others keeps him from developing a positive view of himself. His anxiety and vulner-ability often keep him from entering into any social situations that might raise his self-esteem, thereby opening the trap.

The interdependence of attitudes toward self and others, which is a feature of most personality theories (see Figure 18.1), showed up clearly in a survey that Morris Rosenberg (1965) made of 5,000 adolescents in New York State. He found that adolescents from upper socioeconomic groups were more likely than other adolescents to accept themselves, the difference being greater for boys than for girls. Adolescents from some sociocultural groups also showed greater self-esteem than others. However, Rosenberg found that the general prestige of an adolescent's social group was not the major influence on his self-esteem. Instead, self-esteem had more to do with the adoles-cent's experiences in his family and peer groups. The social-class effect seems linked to the fact that many fathers in upper socioeconomic groups tend to support their sons strongly.

Rosenberg found the lowest self-esteem among minorities within a single neighborhood. That is, being a Catholic in a predominantly Catholic neigh-borhood leads to higher self-esteem than being a Catholic in a predominantly Protestant neighborhood. This result perhaps helps to explain the self-esteem of black adolescents from predominantly black neigh-borhoods, who generally do not have the low self-esteem that one might anticipate on the basis of their group's prestige in society. Cases of low self-esteem among black adolescents appear to relate more to their experiences in family, peer, and neighborhood groups than to their group's general level of prestige.

COGNITIVE CHANGE

It is not accidental that adolescence is the first phase of life in which a person begins to think carefully about himself, his role in life, his plans, and the validity and integrity of his beliefs. Unlike the child in the stage of concrete operations, who deals largely with the present, the adolescent often is concerned with the hypothetical, the future, the remote. An adolescent remarked, "I found myself thinking about my future and then I began to think about why I was thinking about my future, and then I began to think about why I was thinking about why I was thinking

Figure 18.2 Immersion in a peer group may involve the suspension of one identity and the adoption of another, and conformity to one group may be replaced by conformity to another.

about my future.'' This preoccupation with thinking is characteristic of formal thought.

Formal Thought

The adolescent like Susan who develops formal thought can achieve a new range and flexibility of mental processes. If encouraged and supported by her environment, Susan can develop her cognitive abilities in constructive and rational ways, developing an increased capacity for planning, for the mental rehearsal of alternate plans of action, and for guiding her behavior according to long-range purposes.

Formal thought is a generalized orientation toward problem solving that involves isolating elements of a problem and systematically exploring all the possible solutions. You will recall that Jean Piaget (1952b) calls this ability to deal with logical possibilities the stage of *formal operations* (see Chapter 1). When Bärbel Inhelder and Piaget (1958) studied a group of Swiss college-preparatory students, they found that elements of formal thought first appeared among eleven- and twelve-year-olds and that fourteen- and fifteen-year-olds were consistently reasoning from hypotheses. As was noted in Chapter 14, when children are asked to determine what factors account for the speed with which a pendulum travels, only fourteen- and fifteen-year-olds usually are able to solve the problem successfully. These adolescents can anticipate all possible combinations of the four plausible factors involved, test them systematically, and then deduce which factors affect the pendulum's swing and which are irrelevant.

Figure 18.3 The marked differences in adolescents' self-concepts and levels of self-esteem, within as well as between social classes, indicate that a given adolescent's view of himself depends largely on his previous and current experiences in his family and in peer and neighborhood groups.

Figure 18.4 Depiction of formal-operational thought. (*top*) This adolescent has yet to develop a formal-operational level of thought. Her thinking is tied to the real, the here and now, the known-to-be-possible. Her thinking is rational and occurs in logical steps: She can put things in order, describe relationships between things, and count things. (*bottom*) This adolescent's thinking does show a formal-operational level of thought. In his thinking he treats the real as just a part of the possible. He can use logic in complex ways, combining many steps at once, and can generate many new possibilities, using his language skills to help him.

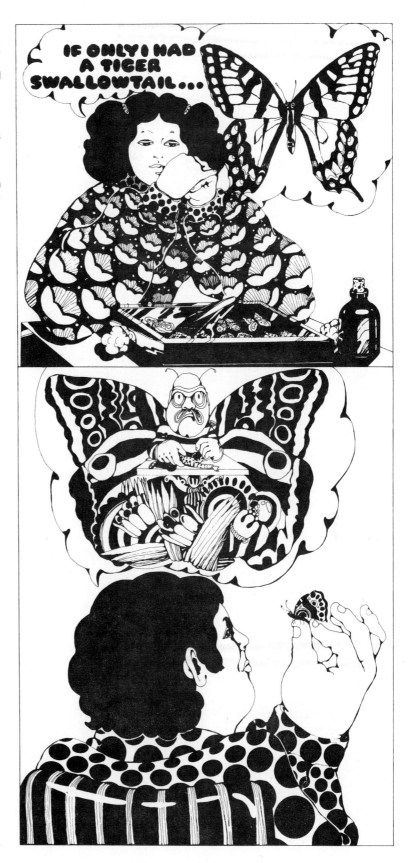

As this example indicates, the central feature of formal thought is the conception of possibilities that lie outside the immediate environment. However, some studies suggest that formal thought is neither as inevitable nor as universal a step in development as is the concrete thought of childhood. Cross-cultural studies have shown that in some societies apparently few people develop this ability to reason from hypotheses. For example, in Turkey formal thought appears in city dwellers but not in residents of primitive villages (Kohlberg and Gilligan, 1971).

Patricia Greenfield and Jerome Bruner (1966) have stressed the association between the prevalence of formal schools and the typical level of cognitive operations in a society. They attribute the greater evidence of formal thought in societies with schools to the fact that schooling provides training in written language. Writing forces a child to separate thought from objects and thus may encourage the child to let his symbolic processes run ahead of concrete fact, allowing him to develop the capacity to think in terms of possibility rather than actuality. In modern societies with widespread school systems, more middle- and upper-middle-class adolescents show formal thought than adolescents from working- and lower-class backgrounds, and adolescents in the upper socioeconomic classes develop this thought earlier (Dulit, 1972; Peel, 1971).

Although formal thought is by no means a universal characteristic of adolescence, its development constitutes a change of primary importance for the individual. Because an adolescent may see the world and the people in it, including himself, in such a different way, speculating about what might be instead of accepting what is, it naturally follows that profound changes can occur in his identity and in his social relations.

Concepts of Self and Others

Erikson identifies formal thought as instrumental in the development of the identity crisis discussed earlier. Presumably, formal thought can predispose a person to the crisis as well as help him to resolve it. There is evidence that the adolescent can take a far less simplistic view of himself than he did before (Livesley and Bromley, 1973) and that the ability to consider possibilities enables him to consider himself more in terms of what might be. Indeed, Inhelder and Piaget (1958) point out that formal thought makes it possible for a person to appreciate abstract ideals (such as honesty, courage, and love) and consequently to attach value to them. Thus, as he proceeds to

form an identity, an adolescent must consider his own impressions of self and the impressions of others about him, and he must use formal thought in order to integrate his self-concept.

To do this effectively, an adolescent must monitor his own mental activity; he must think about his thought. Such reflective thought appeared among adolescents in the study by W. J. Livesley and D. B. Bromley (1973) of developmental changes in the descriptions that children and adolescents give of other persons. They provided 320 children ranging in age from seven to fifteen with the opportunity to write free descriptions of themselves and of liked and disliked persons of both sexes. Their findings suggest a qualitative change around the age of thirteen or fourteen.

Adolescents used descriptive terms more flexibly and precisely than younger children did, often adding subtle qualifying and connecting terms. They showed a greater ability to analyze and interpret another's behavior and an increased concern with making their descriptions convincing. That is, in describing another person, only adolescents would report an impression of another person and hastily add a qualifier to dissuade the listener from drawing an inaccurate conclusion. For example, a fifteen-year-old might say of a friend, "He is shy—but not anxious." In order to make such a statement, the speaker had to consider other people's possible misinterpretations of his descriptions, thereby engaging in reflective thought.

Most impressive in the descriptions written by adolescents is the change in organization. Adolescents selected and organized their ideas in a coherent and complex fashion, whereas younger children's impressions were like beads on a string. A nine-year-old boy describes himself:

I have dark brown hair, brown eyes and a fair face. I am a quick worker but am often lazy. I am good but often cheeky and naughty. My character is sometimes funny and sometimes serious. My behavior is sometimes silly and stupid and often good it is often funny my daddy thinks. (Livesley and Bromley, 1973, page 338)

The adolescent no longer strings the elements of his impressions together but integrates them through the use of qualifying terms, distinctions between real and apparent qualities, and the verification and amplification of internal consistency. He tends to refer more often to ambitions, aspirations, wants, needs, expectations, fears, wishes, self-reproaches, beliefs, attitudes, values, and comparisons with others. Adolescents also use these categories far more in describing the self than in describing others. This change

Figure 18.5 Adolescents' impressions of themselves often involve an active comparison of how they think about themselves now in relation to certain important experiences earlier in their lives, and their current self-impressions usually continue to become more inclusive, descriptive, and organized in nature.

reflects both the adolescent's greater competence at formal thought and the privileged information a person has about himself but not about others. Some of these attributes clearly appear in a fourteen-year-old girl's self-description:

I am a very temperamental person, sometimes, well *most* of the time, I am happy. Then now and again I just go moody for no reason at all. I enjoy being different from everybody else, and like to think of myself as being fairly modern. Up till I was about 11, I was a pretty regular churchgoer (R.C.) but since then I have been thinking about religion and sometimes I do not believe in God. When I am nervous I talk a lot, and this gives some important new acquaintances a bad impression, when I am trying to make a good one. I worry a lot about getting married and having a family, because I am frightened that I will make a mess of it. (pages 239–240)

MORAL REASONING

As the discussions here and in Chapter 16 indicate, the intensity with which some adolescents espouse moral attitudes and values may or may not bear much relation to what they feel or do in the specific situations that they face. After all, adolescents are subject to the same kinds of powerful social influences as other people. In addition, they often are especially aware of the radical discrepancies between what others tell them to do and what others actually do. However, they, like others, are likely to model their conduct on what others do and not on what they say. In addition, it appears that modeling influences can bring about changes in the moral reasoning of adolescents (Prentice, 1972) as well as in their self-regulation and actual moral conduct (Thoresen and Mahoney, 1974).

You will recall from Chapter 16 that an individual's moral development does not necessarily follow a consistent, age-graded pattern. Thus, adolescents can range from the lowest to the highest levels of moral reasoning. In fact, research suggests that, in the United States, only 10 percent of middle-class adolescents and adults, and even fewer of lower socioeconomic status, are likely to develop the kind of moral autonomy that would indicate a high level of moral reasoning.

Although it remains uncertain why so few people develop a high level of moral reasoning, there is some evidence to suggest that it may result in part from a lack of development of formal thought. Thus, Lawrence Kohlberg and Carol Gilligan (1971) found that a majority (60 percent) of the people above sixteen showed advanced formal thought but that only a small proportion (10 percent) of them also showed a principled level of moral reasoning. On the other hand, every individual who showed principled reasoning was also capable of formal thought. Such results suggest that, although the development of formal thought is a necessary condition for principled moral reasoning, formal thought does not ensure the development of such reasoning.

Among adolescents who do reach a principled level of moral reasoning, a major shift in thinking apparently takes place. Thus, the adolescent who appears to be preoccupied with exposing the clay feet of his former idols may also be using his capacity for reflective thought to reexamine his own internal values and codes of conduct. His attempt to establish moral autonomy in his conduct may be the natural accompaniment to his struggle for independence in other areas of his life.

In general, research also indicates that adolescents who have developed formal thought and a principled level of moral reasoning are most likely to show a higher degree of both morality and consistency in what they think and do. For example, significantly fewer college students at a principled level of moral reasoning cheated in situations that required them to resist temptation than did those at a conventional or premoral level (Kohlberg, 1969). The adolescents at a principled level seemed to define the tempting situations as ones that involved an implicit contract based on trust, whereas those at lower levels seemed to respond to the looseness and permissiveness of unsupervised situations.

College students at a principled level of moral reasoning also appear to have shown a higher, more consistent level of moral conduct than other students in an experiment conducted by Stanley Milgram (1963). In this study, undergraduates were ordered to administer what they thought were increasingly severe electric shocks to a stooge victim. The pretense was that the victim was a subject in a learning experiment. Only thinking characteristic of a principled level of reasoning clearly defines the situation as one in which the experimenter has no moral right to ask someone to inflict pain on another person. Accordingly, 75 percent of the students who had been judged to be at a principled level refused to shock the victim, but only 13 percent of those judged to be at lower levels refused to administer the shock. (Kohlberg, 1965).

Finally, a study by Norma Haan, M. Brewster Smith, and Jeanne Block (1968) examined the possible relationship between moral reasoning and civil disobedience. They studied University of California students who did and did not participate in the original Free Speech Movement sit-in. Of the students studied, 80 percent of those who were at a principled level sat in as compared to only 10 percent of those who were at a conventional level. A clear majority of those students who were at a premoral level also sat in. However, the premoral students reported different reasons for their actions from those given by the principled students. Consistent with their level of moral reasoning, the principled students reported concern with the basic issues of civil liberties and

rights and of the relationship of students as citizens within the university community, whereas the premoral students focused on the issue of their individual rights in a conflict with power. As the actions of both premoral and principled students show, however, similar moral conduct can result from widely varied moral reasoning, at least in some situations.

SEXUALITY AND INTIMACY

The twentieth-century evolution of sexual beliefs and attitudes has included a new openness about sexual matters, a tendency to see sexual behavior as a matter of personal choice rather than of law or morality, and an emphasis on interpersonal norms and values. As noted in Chapter 17, the mass media reflect society's increasing openness about sexuality. For example, music and films directed at young people frequently center on frankly sexual themes:

. . . lower-class youth assimilated by middle-class culture joined with middle-class rebels against middle-class culture to alter the tone of American popular music. To the lower class, sex was nothing to moan over or sing pretty little sad poems about. To the crusading middle-class student rebels it was something which must be handled robustly, erotically, honestly, rather than emphasized or sublimated out of all recognition as their parents had frequently done. Middle-class rebel and lower-class swinger, hippy and minority groups had a common distaste for pretty songs. (Mooney, 1972, page 183)

This new openness also shows in the proliferation of sex-education programs in the public schools. However, as was noted in Chapter 15, most such programs tend to concentrate on the physiology of sex. A recent survey of 1,500 girls, ages thirteen to twenty, showed that the programs they participated in provided instruction about the reproductive system, menstruation, and venereal disease but were less informative about the psychological and value aspects of sexuality (Hunt, 1970). Of the girls in this study, 98 percent believed the schools should provide sex education.

Personal Choice

At a more personal level, Robert Sorensen (1973) found that 72 percent of the boys and 70 percent of the girls between thirteen and nineteen reported that they and their parents still do not talk freely about sex. Many adolescents said that conversation about sex was general and not specifically directed toward the boy's or girl's own behavior or problems. Only 18 percent reported talking with parents about masturbation or birth control; 24 percent had talked about venereal disease. Many of the thirteen- to nineteen-year-olds suggested that parents delude themselves about their children's sexual behavior by refusing to acknowledge their adolescents' sexual nature or by simply ignoring blatant violations of their own sexual standards. Sorensen found that 51 percent of the boys and 44 percent of the girls agreed with the statement "I wish my parents could overcome their own early training so that they could realize that sex is natural and beautiful." Traditional parental evasiveness in the face of new public openness about sex no doubt contributes to adolescent charges of parental hypocrisy. Only 28 percent of the boys and 44 percent of the girls believed that their own sexual attitudes are the same as those of their parents.

Among adolescent girls, 60 percent claimed that they do not talk with parents about their sex lives because they consider sex to be a personal subject that is nobody's business but their own. Sorensen found that 39 percent of all adolescents agreed that sexual intercourse is immoral unless it is between two people who like each other and who have something in common, and 69 percent agreed with the assertion that "Anything two people want to do sexually is moral, as long as they both want to do it and it doesn't hurt either one of them." There is no difference between younger and older adolescents on this point.

It appears that even young adolescents are aware of alternatives and value personal choice in sexual matters. For example, both high-school and college students see kissing, petting, and coitus as most acceptable when a couple is engaged and least acceptable outside an affectionate relationship (Reiss, 1967). Like most adults, most adolescents do not

Figure 18.6 Although some adolescents who participate in demonstrations of civil disobedience do so on the basis of a highly developed sense of morality, others are likely to do so on the basis of considerations having less to do with moral issues and more to do with disagreement over roles and expectations.

If your son is old enough to shave, he's old enough to get syphilis.

You know that wide-eyed, clean cut kid of yours. The one who's tops in his class and plays basketball on Saturdays.

The last thing on earth you'd expect him to get, is syphilis.

Well, what makes your son so special?

What makes him any different from the hundreds of nice kids who are coming down with syphilis and gonorrhea every week?

The fact is: New York City is in the midst of a V.D. epidemic. And no matter what kind of a home your son comes from, he's not immune.

In the last ten years the number of V.D. cases has gone up 500%.

But, what's more unbelievable is that over half of these victims are teenagers.

WINS felt the way to fight this growing problem was by telling people just what was going on.

We told that, in New York City schools, almost every child is taught what causes beri-beri, rickets and malaria. But rarely, V.D. And that's found much closer to home.

We told how V.D. can cause blindness, make you sterile, and even kill. How, ironically enough, if it's spotted in its early stages, V.D. may be cured with a few shots of penicillin. And how, at any one of the twelve New York City Public Health Centers, these injections are free.

In every broadcast WINS made this point: V.D. isn't a dirty word. It's a disease, and should be treated like one.

In every editorial we made our position clear: The answer is education. Our children must be made aware of the dangers, even before they become teenagers.

Since WINS brought this problem out into the open, twice as many people have requested information and educational material from City Public Health Centers.

Many people requesting a V.D. examination from local health clinics, gave the WINS V.D. campaign as their reason.

But our broadcasts go beyond New York City.

A member of the Connecticut Assembly, after hearing our campaign, introduced a bill to make treatment more easily available to teenagers who've contracted venereal disease.

WINS feels it's important to take action on problems that affect the health and well being of the community.

But, we feel it's even more important to get the community to take action for itself. When that happens, we know we've done our job. **WINS RADIO 1010 GROUP W** WESTINGHOUSE BROADCASTING COMPANY

Figure 18.7 The frank and explicit portrayal of sexual themes in the mass media reflects an increased openness about sexual matters. Although their parents continue to worry and adolescents emphasize personal choice in sexual behavior, most adolescents do not engage in or condone promiscuity.

condone promiscuity. Unlike the average adult, however, the average adolescent evaluates a specific sexual behavior within the framework of the relationship of which it is a part. Whereas adolescents believe that premarital intercourse between loving partners is more acceptable than petting without affection, adults are more likely to condemn premarital intercourse and accept petting without affection.

In general, studies give evidence of an apparent difference between the generations concerning both premarital sexuality and the affectionate relationship in which behavior occurs. However, this apparent generational difference regarding sexual permissiveness is not as great as it may seem. Adults also are becoming more permissive, and single adults are likely to approve of premarital intercourse. Ira Reiss (1973) reports that, in 1963, 44 percent of single adults were highly permissive of premarital intercourse but that only 18 percent of married adults were permissive. By 1973 the figures had risen to 74 percent and 50 percent. Thus, differences in marital status are at least as important as generational differences in attitudes toward premarital sexuality.

It also appears that assuming the role of a parent affects a person's attitudes toward sexual behavior, generally leading to a decrease in permissiveness. For example, childless couples are more permissive than couples with adolescent children. Sexual stereotypes, or the fear of a daughter's pregnancy, also appear to affect a parent's attitudes. The more sons a parent has, the more likely he or she is to be permissive, but the more daughters a parent has, the more likely he or she is to condemn premarital intercourse (Reiss, 1970). It also appears that the number of adults who approve of premarital intercourse is considerably smaller than the number who themselves have engaged in premarital intercourse (Conger, 1973).

Promiscuity

It would be a mistake to interpret the data reported in Chapter 17 on sexual activity or the data reported in this chapter on changing sexual attitudes as evidence of widespread promiscuity. In the most recent national survey of female sexual behavior among college students, 60 percent of the girls who reported premarital intercourse had had only one partner, and half indicated that they planned to marry him (Zelnik and Kantner, 1972). In the Sorensen (1973) study of thirteen- to nineteen-year-olds, 84 percent of the girls' first experiences with intercourse were with boys whom they knew well, liked a lot, went steady with, or were "engaged to be engaged to." Among boys,

56 percent of the first coital experiences were with partners whom they described in the same way. Among these adolescents, whereas 24 percent of those who had coital experience had had more than six partners before they were nineteen, 47 percent had had only one partner.

From the evidence gathered in the last decade, we can conclude that, particularly among females, there has been a change in the direction of earlier premarital sexuality but that the frequency has not increased much. It also appears that attitudes have changed so that more people judge sexual behavior as acceptable or unacceptable on the basis of the affection in the relationship. And, as we will see, this person-centered sexuality has traditionally been emphasized for females.

Gender and Equalitarianism

Traditional childhood and early adolescent socialization generally provides girls with a greater degree of competence than boys in interpersonal relationships. For most girls, sexual behavior involves incorporating sexuality into a social role and an identity that already included capacities for tenderness and sensitivity. For most boys, on the other hand, the pathway to mature heterosexual behavior involves sexuality first, and only secondarily does the capacity for concerned, tender, and loving sexual relationships develop. Thus, cultural stereotypes and parental and peer socialization emphasize, to use Reiss's (1973) terms, "body-centered" sexuality for the male and "person-centered" sexuality for the female.

The connection between this formulation and the pattern of sex differences cataloged in Chapter 17 should not go unnoticed. A girl's first intense sexual experience usually occurs in a heterosexual context; a boy's first experience is likely to occur when he is alone. Among their peers, groups of girls are likely to support and encourage one another for interpersonal competence and romantic interests, whereas groups of boys are likely to support and encourage one another for erotic interests, responsiveness to erotic stimuli, and proclaimed erotic activity. As noted in Chapter 17, adolescent peer groups also are likely to reward popularity with the opposite sex with status (J. Coleman, 1961; G. Schwartz and Merten, 1967). Thus, during adolescence, both boys and girls learn to incorporate sexual behavior into their gender roles, but the experiences each brings to his or her relationships are likely to be quite different. Further, as William Simon and John Gagnon (1969) suggest, adolescent dating and courtship can be seen as a training process in which boys train girls and girls train boys in the meaning and context of each sex's commitment to the heterosexual relationship.

The evolutionary changes in American sexual behavior and attitudes can be seen as part of a more general movement toward equalitarianism and, therefore, may affect traditional gender roles. For example, after surveying these changes, Reiss (1973) concludes that the human sexual relationship is changing from an occasion for male satisfaction of body-centered sexuality to an equalitarian relationship that involves more than physical attraction. He notes that, although people will continue to pursue sexuality for pleasure, the pleasure is more likely to be mutual and equalitarian.

Much of the increase in premarital sexuality seems to have occurred among students (particularly females) from the most affluent, elite, and liberal schools (Conger, 1973). It is, of course, precisely the same kinds of schools that gave birth to the activist movements of the 1960s and that may have created the conditions that sparked the Women's Liberation Movement. In the liberal, questioning environment of these schools, young people apparently consolidated many of the attitudinal changes of the preceding fifty years, setting in motion this century's second major change in sexual behavior.

A similar equalitarian movement appears to be taking place in other aspects of behavior related to gender roles. For example, Sandra Bem (1974) has looked at sex roles in a different way and has discovered that adolescents and adults may see themselves as either masculine or feminine or as embracing both qualities. Bem calls the latter people **androgynous** in their sex-role self-concept because they are capable of being both masculine and feminine, both assertive and yielding, depending on the appropriateness of that behavior to the particular situation. Because healthy interpersonal relationships depend on both competent assertiveness and secure sensitivity to other people, it would seem that incorporating both traditionally masculine and feminine positive attributes might lead to fuller human functioning. Thus, the finding that highly creative males and females tend to incorporate attributes of the other sex as well as those of their own (Hammer, 1964; Helson, 1966) can be seen as support for both the possibility and value of androgynous sex-role development.

VOCATIONAL IDENTITY

During adolescence, gender-role concepts, self-concepts, and the concept of future occupational

Figure 18.9 The cultural trend toward equality of the sexes at any age supports the development of androgynous sex roles, as seen among some adolescents. The concept of androgyny does not rest on superficial similarities in dress or appearance but rather on a blending of behaviors, attitudes, feelings, and modes of thinking traditionally considered masculine or feminine.

Figure 18.8 (opposite) With adolescent sexuality, the development of a deeper capacity for tenderness and understanding is made possible. Although more likely in the case of adolescent girls, falling in love for the first time is frequently a revelation of a new world of caring, warmth, and happiness for adolescent boys as well as girls.

possibilities combine to narrow a person's vocational alternatives and orientations. For the male in our society, competence in a vocational role is as fundamental a dimension of his identity as is his masculinity in the sex role. For the majority of females, at least at present, it is marriage that continues to play a crucial role in identity formation and achievement.

Society holds the male to a sharply defined criterion. The position of the late-adolescent middle-class boy, in particular, is more complex and drastic than most people realize. Like most middle-class boys, Matt is in transition from the supporting influences of family, high school, and peer groups to the still distant adult world. He clings to an unrealistic, childhood-determined vocational goal, and the college curriculum is unlikely to tell him whether he will like his projected field of work or do well in it. Yet by the end of his sophomore year, the registrar will demand that Matt commit himself to a department and to an implied career, a commitment that he has neither the experience nor the facts to make. He can only guess.

Matt's ultimate vocational choice will be a compromise between his interests, aptitudes, and values and economic considerations. Theoretically and developmentally, such a choice involves the integration of internal and external factors. First, Matt will explore possible occupations through courses, summer work, and part-time jobs; next, he will crystallize his explorations into a tentative choice of vocations; and finally, he will specify his chosen career, overtly committing himself to an occupation (Ginzberg et al., 1951; D. Super, 1963).

Cognition and Vocational Choice

An adolescent's capacity to generate possibilities and to reason from them means that his vocational thinking need not be restricted by his personal exposure to the world of work and the people in it and that he can do a better job of matching his personal attributes to future vocational possibilities. One factor that affects the adolescent's choice of an occupation is the prestige that he attributes to it.

Developmental studies of occupations and preferences provide an excellent example of the effects of cognitive organizational ability on career choice. Before a child is eleven, his thinking about a vocation appears to be primarily subjective. His preferences are based on occupational stereotypes and are unrelated to any assessment of his aptitude or other personal characteristics. He also seems unaware of the opportunities that he has or the barriers that may stand in the way of his goals (Gunn, 1964; R. Nelson, 1963).

However, as the adolescent confronts vocational choice, his ability to use formal thought, combined with his increased experiences, appears to enable him to assess various career possibilities more realistically. Thus, in a twelve-year longitudinal study of occupational preference, Leona Tyler (1964) reported that most adolescents begin to crystallize their occupational choices when they are about thirteen or fourteen. But even fourteen-year-olds know little about the choices that they soon must face, about the decision pathways any alternative might lead to, or about the irreversibility of some choices. By the time they are sixteen, however, adolescents show a more realistic appraisal of the preparation required for their chosen occupations (Douvan and Adelson, 1966). The sixteen-year-old can offer more explanations for his choices than the fourteen-year-old, and his explanations are better organized. By sixteen, when an adolescent is asked to specify an occupational choice, he is more precise: He will say that he wants to be an ornithologist instead of saying that he wants to be a scientist. An individual's appreciation of the role played by his personal opportunities and by harsh economic realities in vocational choice may continue to grow throughout adolescence. As Donald Hall (1963) has shown, high-school seniors are more likely than younger adolescents to describe themselves as understanding the necessity for choosing an occupation, and they are also more able to consider relevant factors when making that choice.

There is little doubt that increasing stability of occupational choice is also a characteristic of adolescence. Among adolescents in the ninth grade, the occupation named by a student one day or week or month is likely to change the next time he is asked about his chosen career (Super and Overstreet, 1960). More stable career choices emerge later: In one study only 17 percent of the boys and 26 percent of the girls had the same vocational plans one year after graduation that they had had in the ninth grade (Project Talent, 1966). Among boys, science careers appear to be an exception; future scientists begin to crystallize their choices between the ages of ten and fourteen (Tyler, 1964). There is also little question that there are great individual differences in stability of occupational choice; as many as half of college students change their career choices (Davis, 1963). However, many of these changes remain within the same general family of occupations, because the process of career choice soon becomes nearly irreversible. As adolescents make choices, they increasingly limit

their range of remaining choices and absolutely preclude some careers.

Gender Differences

The developmental picture of occupational choice just presented is more characteristic of males and of middle- and upper-middle-class young people than of females and working-class youth. This reflects the ways in which gender identity tends to limit occupational choice and the fact that choice itself is granted more often to the advantaged than to members of the working class.

Careers are still presented to most girls as way stations on the road to marriage and motherhood. This means that the continued development of interpersonal skills, of a capacity for intimacy, remains the major task of adolescence for many girls. Because the ultimate self-definition of a traditionally socialized girl like Susan depends on the marital role, her identity is likely to remain diffuse and misty. Her adolescent fantasies and prior gender-role learning usually have pointed her directly toward marriage. Her dependence on the marital role may also have taught Susan to derive her sense of esteem from her relationship to loved ones and from their achievements rather than from her own. It is this kind of socialization that has led Judith Bardwick (1971) to suggest that fear of the loss of love is a major motive for most women in our society and that such fear tends to result in emotional dependence among women who fail to develop any sense of vocational

identity beyond that of wife and mother. Among males, on the other hand, identity is a far more active issue in adolescence and tends to center around the interrelated themes of autonomy, achievement, and vocational choice.

These kinds of gender differences appeared when Elizabeth Douvan and Joseph Adelson (1966) asked fourteen- to eighteen-year-olds a number of open-ended questions about their plans and daydreams for the future. The boys were oriented toward the future primarily in terms of an occupational identity. Their plans were concrete even if subject to change in detail. Boys were actively concerned with the future implications of their present strivings. Their aspirations for achievement were matched by their realistic assessment of the world of work and their own assets and limitations. The fantasy concerns of boys also focused on future occupational achievement and on preparation for it.

On the other hand, the future plans of most girls differed markedly. Although their direct plans also focused on work and schooling, few girls were committed to either. Their plans for implementing their avowed goals were often unrealistic. They stressed individual achievement and its rewards less than boys did. Of the girls' occupational choices, 95 percent fell into five categories, each representing an extension of traditional female roles. The girls tended to plan for jobs as nurses, social workers, teachers, secretaries, or stewardesses. When asked about their daydreams, girls shifted dramatically away from jobs and education, and the strong strivings for achievement that would support their vocational plans were entirely absent.

As yet, no data contradict the assertion that most girls continue to be socialized in the traditional feminine gender role and that many of them prefer it. However, some investigators (Bardwick, 1971) are beginning to see the emergence of a new feminine pattern in which the achievement ethic becomes as important as interpersonal success and traditional feminine behavior. At present, these girls come largely from upwardly mobile middle- and upper-middle-class families. Such a pattern supports the findings of Douvan and Adelson (1966), who discovered a small group of *personally mobile* girls. That is, their aspirations of social mobility were directed toward their own achievements rather than dependent on the status of their future husbands. These personally mobile girls were more likely than traditional girls to be socially mature and active in leisure activities, in dating, and in seeking heterosex-

Figure 18.10 Concepts of self, gender role, and future occupational alternatives come together and narrow vocational choices and preparation during adolescence.

Figure 18.11 Changes in the social and vocational roles considered appropriate for males and females are shown in many of the social-political movements supported by adolescents as well as by their own different life styles.

ual friendships. They indicated a greater interest in assuming adult roles and responsibilities, and their time perspective extended further into the future. Girls in this group were also more self-confident and more self-accepting, and they appeared to think in a more organized fashion and to be more objective about themselves. They more often dreamed of individual achievement than traditional girls did, and they tended to judge prospective jobs by success criteria.

The number of girls who show this kind of feminine pattern will probably grow as society provides greater and more visible support for dual family and career roles and as girls who choose careers and reject motherhood less frequently become stigmatized. However, at present it appears that traditionally socialized girls are still in the majority.

SUMMARY

1. Although an individual's self-concept and self-esteem are important throughout his life, a reexamination and reintegration of one's identity is often a major developmental task of adolescence. Given new physical and sexual status and redefined rights and responsibilities, the task is to formulate a satisfactory identity in which the adolescent experiences a sense of well-being and self-esteem.

2. Most often, adolescence is the first phase in which a person begins to think carefully about himself. The adolescent who develops formal thought is now able to conceptualize possibilities outside immediate reality, to plan, and to rehearse long-range purposes. As a result, and central to his self-concept and identity, the adolescent also is likely to reconsider, in less simplistic terms than before, his own impressions of himself and others' impressions of him.

3. Adolescents are subject to the same kinds of powerful social influences that other people are. Thus, there may or may not be much of an intercorre-

lation among their espoused moral values and attitudes and what they feel and do. It also appears that, whereas higher levels of moral reasoning require formal thinking, such thinking does not always result in a higher level of moral reasoning.

4. In their sexuality and intimacy, adolescents reflect society's new openness about sexual matters. For example, adolescents are inclined to see sexual behavior as a matter of personal choice rather than of law or morality. Despite this greater openness, there has been no general increase in the frequency of promiscuity. In addition, emphasis on interpersonal norms and values has resulted in a movement away from traditional sex-typed roles and toward more equalitarian and androgynous sex-role relationships.

5. During adolescence, concepts of self, gender role, and possible future occupations are likely to combine and to narrow an individual's vocational choices. In our society, vocational roles and sex roles interact, making different demands on males and females. For the adolescent male, competence in a vocational role is likely to be as fundamental a dimension of his identity as is his masculinity in the sex role. But for the majority of adolescent females, marriage is still likely to form a basic dimension of identity and achievement.

SUGGESTED READINGS

Conger, John J. *Adolescence and Youth: Psychological Development in a Changing World.* New York: Harper & Row, 1973.

Erikson, Erik. *Identity: Youth and Crisis.* New York: Norton, 1968.

Fromm, Erich. *The Art of Loving.* New York: Harper & Row, 1956.

Goethals, George W., and Dennis S. Klos. *Experiencing Youth: First Person Accounts.* Boston: Little, Brown, 1970.

Holland, John L. *The Psychology of Vocational Choice.* Waltham, Mass.: Blaisdell, 1966.

During adolescence, as at other times in life, styles of dress, appearance, language, and recreation reflect the influence of one's social relationships.

19

SOCIAL RELATIONS AND INFLUENCE

Like many of his friends, Matt has adopted some aspects of the counterculture, even though he does not fully comprehend or share many of its values. During his adolescent identity crisis, he has found an alternative identity in the counterculture's highly visible dress, hair style, and customs. However, the fit with Matt's own history, temperament, and future is a questionable one and, in spite of his parents' concerns, his countercultural experience is not likely to last long.

In the previous chapter we emphasized the wide variety of life styles in our society and the adolescent's effort to establish his identity. The fact is, most of us spend our social lives interacting with people who are like us in important ways. We grow up in neighborhoods, which are clusters of households headed by persons with jobs of roughly similar status, with similar educational histories, and therefore with similar ways of perceiving, thinking, and behaving. We usually go to neighborhood schools until we finish high school and so interact outside the family with people much like ourselves. And when the school is composed of several social classes, chances are that the informal peer groups that arise will also reflect social-class lines. Our parents and our friends' parents usually have about the same amount of money to spend on goods and services and often spend that money in the same way. Education, income, job prestige, social interaction, and patterns of consumption all correlate highly, and they constitute the criteria that psychologists, sociologists, and laymen use to define social status.

During our examination of social influences on the adolescent in this chapter, we will return to some of the topics discussed in Chapter 18, shifting our emphasis from identity to society. We will trace the social development of the adolescent and see how his socioeconomic class affects his attitudes toward life and work. We will examine the family's influences on the adolescent's choice of occupation and on the growth of his autonomy. We will discuss the function of the peer group in adolescence and how the high-school social system affects social development. After a look at the generation gap, we will discuss the part that developmental commitments play in adolescence and early adulthood. Finally, we will turn to the concept of youth, testing it as a possible new phase of human development.

SOCIAL-CLASS DIFFERENCES

Patterns of values and beliefs stay alive as one generation transmits them to the next. Because patterns of value and belief and possessions constitute aspects of culture, we can say that each of us grows up in a particular subculture like those discussed in Chapters 13 and 15.

Social-class subcultures differ from one another in many ways (R. Coleman and Neugarten, 1971), and a major difference, as far as social development is concerned, is the subculture's attitude toward achievement. The values and beliefs that a subculture attaches to achievement can have an important influence on a person's future in our society. Bernard Rosen (1959) has identified three sets of beliefs that can affect motivation in achievement situations: *activism* (the belief that a person can manipulate the physical and social environment to his own advantage) versus *passivity*; *individualism* (the belief that a person need not subordinate his own needs to the family group) versus *collectivism*; and *future orientation* (the belief that a person should forego short-term rewards in the interest of long-term gains) versus *present orientation*. Studies have repeatedly found a subcultural difference in these beliefs; individualistic, activistic, and future-oriented values are more likely to characterize higher socioeconomic groups in our society, whereas passivity, collectivism, and present orientation are more likely to be found in lower socioeconomic groups.

Adolescents from upper-middle-class families (professional and managerial occupations) and from lower-middle-class families (semiprofessional, semimanagerial, white-collar, and skilled-crafts occupations) are more likely to have learned as children that their lives are under their own control and that they can achieve occupational status and other external symbols of success through their personal efforts (Battle and Rotter, 1963). Beginning in infancy and childhood, the experiences of the upper-middle-class adolescent are more likely to prepare him for having a career, and he grows up believing in the importance of delaying gratification in the interest of future success (Mischel, 1966). By and large, the upper-middle-class adolescent is likely to value his cognitive competencies, because the kind of future role he is

being socialized for involves using the head more than the hands (R. Hess, 1970).

For the most part, the lower-middle-class adolescent's experiences will make him look forward to a *job*, not a career (Kahl, 1961). He will value individualism and take an activistic stance toward the world and his future in it. However, the lower-middle-class adolescent and his parents are likely to see that future in terms of the security, stability, and respectability that a job brings rather than as an opportunity for development, intrinsic satisfaction, or self-actualization. In addition, most middle-class young people, whether from professional or white-collar families, share attitudes and beliefs that correspond to those demanded by schools and colleges (Douvan, 1956). Thus, the idea of prolonged schooling also is more likely to make sense to upper- and lower-middle-class adolescents than it does to youths from other social strata.

Asking him to go to college, thereby delaying immediate gratification in the interest of future success, is not likely to make much sense to the adolescent from a working-class family (semiskilled or unskilled blue-collar workers) or from a lower-class family that depends on irregular employment in marginal work roles or on welfare funds. Although fathers of working-class families take pride in their regular employment, they rarely move up; the tasks that they perform are simple, specialized, circum-

Figure 19.1 The experiences and outcomes of adolescence depend on how a person has been brought up, what kind of community he lives in, and what his society expects from him. The cumulative effects of environmental differences are well illustrated by subcultural variations associated with social class.

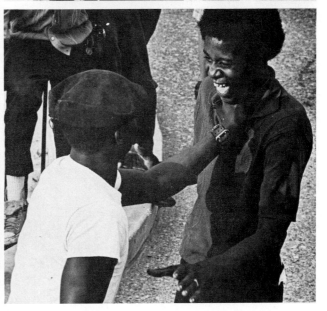

scribed, and repetitive. If they work in a factory, the pace and rhythm of work is imposed from above by supervisors and technicians. The worker on an assembly line is rewarded for following orders and coordinating his work with the rest of the line, not for showing self-direction, individuality, or innovative techniques (Blau, 1972). It is not difficult to see how conforming to authority becomes an important aspect of working-class life, and this conformity is reflected in the socialization of working-class children and adolescents. Activism and a future orientation do not prevail in this kind of environment.

Among many working-class families, employment is valued primarily as a means of providing goods and services that lead to satisfaction in the extended family. A collectivistic orientation is likely to prevail, so that loyalty to the family may stand in the way of the decisions that would permit an adolescent to move out of the working class. Actions that are taken for granted by middle-class adolescents, such as moving away, going to school in another city or state, and taking advantage of opportunities that may weaken bonds with family members, are usually less possible for working-class youth.

A passive, even fatalistic, attitude is likely to characterize the adolescent from a lower-class background. "Luck" is a frequent explanation for accomplishments and setbacks. As Lee Rainwater (1966) put it:

> In the white and particularly in the Negro slum worlds little in the experience that individuals have as they grow up sustains a belief in a rewarding world. The strategies that seem appropriate are not those of a good, family-based life or of a career, but rather *strategies for survival*. (page 206)

In a survival-oriented economy, gratifications of the present are important. The child or adolescent has few opportunities to learn that active individual effort might pay off in the interest of some long-term goal, whether that effort means studying now for a good report card or earning money to save for a car.

FAMILY RELATIONS AND INFLUENCE

The chief interpersonal theme in early adolescence is the gradual move from childhood dependence toward ever greater involvement with the wider world. For some young people, this process is fraught with visible tension and conflict, but others move away from their families with only minor internal turmoil. In early adolescence most young people feel some ambivalence about their relative dependence or independence. The fact that Susan's parents increasing-

ly permit her more freedom may bear little relation to her inner conflict between a desire for independence and her usually less conscious wishes to remain a child, to be cared for, and to avoid the potential problems and deprivations that she sees in adult life. The provocativeness of adolescents toward parents who may offer little occasion for rebellion can often be understood in the context of the adolescent's own profound ambivalence. Indeed, it is by alternating between provocative self-assertion and childlike requests for help that many adolescents gradually become able to emerge from their families.

But if the adolescent is capable of irrationality toward the adult world, adults often prove no less unreasonable. Parents may unwittingly project their unfulfilled dreams and suppressed desires onto their children, subtly encouraging them to live in a way that the parents cannot and condemning their children whether they do or do not. Thus, in many cases, charges of youthful promiscuity, irresponsibility, drug abuse, violence, and hedonism may be as much the adults' expression of their own wishes as their ideas about the perversity of adolescents.

Jobs Versus Careers

Despite the ambivalent family relations that often characterize adolescence, parents and the home environment have lasting influences on such basic decisions as the adolescent's choice of occupation. For example, investigators have repeatedly discovered that adolescents from low-status families select high-status occupations less often than might be expected, whereas adolescents from high-status families select high-status occupations more often than chance would suggest (Borow, 1966; Elder, 1968). J. Kenneth Little (1967) found that the trend held good among all graduates of Wisconsin public and private high schools in the mid-1960s. Little examined both the aspirations of high-school students and their actual later attainments. Graduates from families in the upper third in socioeconomic status held 47 percent of the high-prestige occupations, whereas the lower-third held only 20 percent of such positions. Some developmentalists have suggested that the difference comes about because higher- and lower-status families ascribe different levels of prestige to various occupations. However, other studies suggest that the difference more likely reflects the different perceptions of status groups as to the accessibility of occupations (Caro and Pihlblad, 1965; Stephenson, 1957). When August Hollingshead (1949) earlier found social-class effects on young

Figure 19.2 One of the developmental
themes in adolescence is to work out
one's psychological relationships with
people, particularly with those who
share one's daily life, such as parents,
friends, and relatives.

people's vocational choices, he suggested that lower-class adolescents tend to adjust their job desires to what they think they may hope to achieve. A number of factors can bring about such adjustment, most having to do with the way that parents in different social classes tend to influence their children's vocational development.

Parents and other neighborhood and community adults model characteristics relevant to various vocations, and they also reinforce them when the characteristics show up in adolescents. As shown in Chapter 18, gender identity serves as a kind of filter for occupational choice, leading an adolescent to eliminate certain possible vocations. John Crites (1962) examined vocational interests among male college students in relation to how they perceived their similarity to their parents. He reported that males who identified strongly with their fathers had masculine interests, males who identified strongly with both parents showed a combination of masculine and feminine interests, and males who identified strongly with their mothers showed feminine interests, as did those who identified weakly with both parents. The common finding that working- and lower-class boys generally make higher masculinity scores than middle-class boys suggests an even finer gender-identity filtering of occupations at lower status levels.

Parents and neighborhood adults also influence the development of vocationally relevant attributes that bear no relation to gender role. Insofar as middle-class parents influence the development of fear of failure and hope of success, they have an impact not only on their children's success or failure in achievement situations but on their occupational choices as well. Young people with high hopes of success more often choose high-status occupations than their peers who have a high fear of failure (Burnstein, 1963; Elder, 1968).

Adolescents whose parents have fostered a high level of self-esteem look forward to the world of work with high aspirations and confidence; adolescents with low self-esteem place the same importance on occupational success but believe that they are unlikely to attain it (Rosenberg, 1965). And, of course, parents model and reinforce attitudes and values about work in general and about particular kinds of jobs. They also may provide support when their children show high levels of educational and occupational aspiration.

Adolescents' vocational choices vary from class to class in part because parental resources also vary. A high income means more out-of-school lessons, more

books at home, more travel, and residence in a neighborhood with an excellent school. The lower-class youngster has seen, heard, read about, and experienced less, and so he has less information about occupational alternatives. Should he discover some of the possibilities that exist, his parents can provide less money and other assistance to help him attain them.

Independence and Self-control

As earlier chapters on personality and moral development have shown, the typical middle-class parent uses love, approval, attention, and praise, and their withdrawal, to encourage independent action and personal responsibility in a growing child (Douvan and Adelson, 1966). When David misbehaves, he is likely to be asked why he did so and what consequences happen to other people who behave similarly; if he is to be punished, his parents are likely to explain why. By reasoning, David's parents teach him that he can and should control his own behavior on the basis of an internalized set of standards. The parents' object, often conscious, is the development of self-control.

As the middle-class child grows into adolescence, he increasingly participates in decisions that affect him. By late adolescence, he will make decisions about peers, jobs, and money, either by himself or in consultation with his parents (Psathas, 1957). Most of the time, when David indicates that he is learning to cope with his day-to-day problems, his parents will reward him, as they have always done. Middle-class parents train children for the sort of autonomy that most can later exercise in a job or career. If David's parents fail to train him for autonomy, they are likely to regret it. As Edward Devereux (1970) has shown, when parents are totally permissive or when they control all decisions and give their child no opportunity to make decisions, adolescence is likely to be a time of stormy parent-child relations and excessive peer conformity.

Working-class parents seem to begin later than middle-class parents to train their children for independence, and they are less likely to permit their offspring to help establish the rules for appropriate behavior (Douvan and Adelson, 1966). They are likely to value obedience instead of self-control and may often teach their children conformity to authority. On the other hand, working-class parents are less likely than middle-class parents to monitor an adolescent's activities outside the family circle (Blau, 1972). Although working-class adolescents are, therefore, freer than middle-class adolescents from parental supervision, when questions of obedience do arise, the working-class parent-child conflict is likely to be greater.

Adolescent Drinking Patterns

Two words often mentioned in discussions of adolescence are rebelliousness and conformity. Some accounts of adolescent development assume that, as a child reaches adolescence, conformity to parents' wishes decreases and conformity to peer wishes increases. Other discussions assume that conflict between peer and parental standards inevitably accompanies adolescence. However, no available evidence demonstrates that the onset of adolescence necessarily means any decrease in conformity to parental demands. Studies reviewed by Willard Hartup (1970) suggest only that conforming to peer wishes increases in childhood, reaches its maximum around puberty, and then decreases in later adolescence.

Studies of adolescent drinking behavior illustrate this point. In most states, drinking is illegal for adolescents of high-school age. According to Margaret Bacon and Mary Brush Jones (1968), the number of adolescents who drink on at least some occasions varies from 86 percent in Nassau County, New York, to 44 percent in rural Kansas. However, in most communities widespread illegal drinking remains underground until an automobile accident or some other incident associated with drinking makes newspaper headlines. In the public rumblings that follow, worried parents often act on the implicit assumption that all teen-age drinking involves drunkenness and uncontrolled behavior. They cite psychological disorder, rebelliousness, and the lack of "wholesome things to do" as possible causes of adolescent use of alcohol.

Actually, every study of alcohol use has found that the drinking patterns of teen-agers directly reflect those of their parents and the community in which they live. About two-thirds of all adults in the United States drink on occasion, and drinking is more prevalent among persons of higher social status than among those of lower status. Bacon and Jones found that most adolescents who drink tend to drink moderately, to begin drinking at home with their parents, and to follow the rules of alcohol consumption that their parents set. Other studies show that teen-age drinking patterns imitate adult drinking patterns: Boys drink more than girls; city adolescents drink more than country adolescents; middle- and upper-middle-class adolescents drink more than working- or lower-class adolescents.

Because adolescents have learned from their parents and other adults to perceive drinking as an explicitly social affair, peer-group norms for acceptable drinking behavior tend to keep such behavior in line. Thus, when adolescents drink in the secrecy of the peer group, social control remains present.

Adolescent drinking also shows how behavior that poses problems for adults often is tied to the values and customs of the larger society. The adolescent has had more than a decade of exposure to adults whose behavior, legal and illegal, has been a model for his own experimentation and for the control of group behavior. But adults tend to ignore these connections; they generally consider any problem behavior as a purely adolescent problem and to label the adolescents involved as problems.

PEER RELATIONS AND INFLUENCE

The peer group can be a major influence in resolving the identity crisis (Erikson, 1968). For instance, in assuming the badges of clique membership, the fads of dress and appearance, Matt is borrowing a stereotypic identity as a temporary defense against the loss of his own identity. This sort of behavior is an example of the adolescent uniformism discussed in Chapter 18. By his clannishness, intolerance, and cruelty toward outsiders or those who are different, the adolescent can temporarily clarify who he is by affirming who he is not. But the peer group also offers positive opportunities and rewards that are crucial to identity formation. With his peers, Matt can try on new roles and use the reactions of others to judge how well the roles fit his self-concept. Identification with the heroes of the crowd may also give the adolescent a temporary sense of coherence. Even early instances of falling in love may have far less to do with sexuality than with a mutual opportunity to clarify one's self-concept through a close relationship with another person. As peer relationships are transformed during adolescence, friendship also changes, moving from the congenial sharing of activities to psychological sharing and intimacy.

Friendship

Assume that you are asked to list twelve persons who fit certain role descriptions (for example, mother, father, lover, best friend, favorite teacher, disliked male, self) and then to list for each possible combination of three people a characteristic that two of them share and that the third does not (G. Kelly, 1955). This method of eliciting the categories that individuals use to classify others can distinguish pairs of friends from random pairs of strangers. And, as Stephen Duck's (1973) studies of college students have shown, the nature of the similarity changes during the course of the friendship. In the beginning of the relationship, friends tend to apply such categories as physical characteristics or people's roles or activities to assess others. If the friendship lasts, they tend to use psychological categories such as "sly" or "tries hard"; that is, they share a way of perceiving and thinking about the unobvious attributes of self and others.

Investigators have found that similar personal characteristics are the major determinant of whether two people form a friendship (Byrne *et al.*, 1969). These studies suggest that obvious similarities are more important in the early stages of friendship but that a friendship is not likely to last unless the persons involved go on to discover that they see the world of psychological intentions, motives, causes, and characteristics in the same way.

Intimate friendships are not likely to develop in the relative absence of compatible psychological constructs. For example, Duck (1973) found that only 5 percent of the twelve-year-olds he studied used psychological constructs to describe others and that the number rose to 25 percent among fourteen- and fifteen-year-olds. Among college students, 63 percent described others in terms of psychological characteristics.

The developmental course of friendship does not contradict such a view. Friendships among girls

appear to progress from the activity-centered pairs of late childhood and preadolescence to the interdependent, emotional, and conflict-resolving relationships of middle adolescence, finally becoming relationships that are less emotional, less an instrument for reducing conflict, and more a sharing of personalities, talents, and interests (Douvan and Adelson, 1966). It is the emotional friendship that Harry Stack Sullivan (1953) had in mind when he described *chumship* and indicated that such a same-sex relationship was necessary to the later development of heterosexual intimacy and mature sexuality.

Although male friends in college use similar psychological constructs, junior-high and high-school boys appear to be less concerned with the personal relationship involved in friendship. Their friendships are more like those found among preadolescent girls and involve a congenial companion with whom one shares the same reality-oriented activities (Douvan and Adelson, 1966). As was shown in Chapter 18, this gender difference is part of a larger pattern of gender-role differences that make interpersonal relationships in this society a major factor in the formation of female identity. Males are also more likely than females to spend their adolescent social lives in cliques and gangs instead of in pairs.

Cliques and Crowds

Children who are popular with their peers are likely to be popular adolescents as well; indeed, popularity rankings from year to year throughout childhood and

Traits Important in Dates

——— According to Boys ——— According to Girls

Percentage

0 10 20 30 40 50 60 70 80 90 100

Is physically attractive

Is popular with others

Shows affection

Takes pride in appearance and manners

Is considerate of others

Is dependable and trustworthy

Has pleasant disposition

Shows maturity of behavior

Desires normal family life with children

Manages money well

Has a job

Knows how to cook and keep house

Figure 19.4 Chart showing traits that adolescent boys and girls consider important in ''dates'' that they might later marry. Sex-typing in behavior is reflected in the difference in importance assigned to certain behaviors for one sex or another by both boys and girls. (Adapted from Purdue Opinion Poll, 1961)

Figure 19.3 (*opposite*) Close friendships serve as sources for increased self-knowledge and help develop patterns of trust, intimacy, and sharing that will continue to be important in future same-sex and opposite-sex relationships.

adolescence generally remain stable (Roff, Sells, and Golden, 1972). Popularity is highly related to conformity to peer-group norms, customs, and fads. During adolescence, as in childhood, the characteristics having most to do with peer acceptance are those that define appropriate sex-typed behavior in our society (Hartup, 1970). Athletic participation and skill, standing up for one's rights, sexual prowess, and sometimes drinking prowess are valued in the adolescent boy. The popular girl is one who is fun to be with and who has interpersonal skills. Because these characteristics bring with them the positive consequences of peer acceptance, they are in turn strengthened. Thus, participation in peer activities reinforces the childhood sex-role learning discussed in Chapters 13 and 15. This continuity in socialization may be largely responsible for the general stability of popularity rankings.

Structure Changes in Peer Groups. As we saw in Chapter 15, social acceptance and its consequences are likely to occur in structured, role-related interactions among age-mates. However, adolescents bring a new element to peer relations: sexual maturation and heterosexual behavior. The structure of peer groups changes to accommodate these developments. At first the peer group is similar to the preadolescent gang; it is a clique of adolescents of the same sex. As Dexter Dunphy suggests (1963):

In order to achieve and maintain membership in this group, the individual must show his readiness to conform to the group's authority. This is made easier through his identification with the clique leader who embodies many of the social skills and personality traits admired in the group. The clique establishes and reinforces the individual's drive to achieve heterosexuality, since it is, or becomes, a subsystem of the crowd; the crowd in its turn is only a subsystem of a hierarchy of crowds. . . . About middle adolescence there is a major transformation of the clique system which has persisted in a relatively stable form. A new clique system evolves . . . Groups become heterosexual, members having established a significant relationship with a member of the opposite sex. The crowd persists long enough to ensure that the basic role characteristics underlying this relationship are thoroughly acquired. It then breaks up into cliques of loosely associated couples as members move toward marriage. (pages 245–246)

Dunphy and other observers have found also that group members generally deny the existence of a status hierarchy within the group. Nevertheless, status hierarchies do exist, and the formation of such hierarchies has been studied in detail, as the discussion of preadolescent groups in Chapter 15 indicated. The adolescent group leader gains high status by

Figure 19.5 Popularity and status rankings in high-school groups often reflect deeply held beliefs about sex roles in American society. The highly popular girl is likely to be one who has a fresh, wholesome appearance and is charming and soft-spoken. The highly popular boy is one who is athletic, aggressive, ambitious, and poised.

Figure 19.6 (*opposite*) Interactions in larger groups may result in increased self-knowledge and social knowledge and in the learning of many types of norms and values. Both formal and informal groups develop shared expectations of behavior, and adherence to these expectations is likely to lead to group acceptance, whereas deviation is likely to lead to disapproval.

virtue of some combination of personal attributes and material resources that the group finds useful. In male cliques, high status generally goes to the assertive, actively sociable, and intellectually able boy (Hartup, 1970). However, in some groups an adolescent may win status by virtue of his unique social or athletic skills or by the possession of a car or money or access to a suitable place for the group's activities. Changes in group goals are likely to lead to fluctuations in the hierarchy; as activities change, the resources of different members may become important (Sherif and Sherif, 1964). Thus, status rankings over the months and years are less stable than popularity ratings.

The High-School Social System. During high school, cliques become subsystems of crowds, and the crowds themselves may be ranked according to status. Members of the leading crowd generally embody the characteristics that bring young people to the forefront of their cliques or that made them popular with childhood classmates. The number of middle-class students in the leading crowds is likely to be out of proportion to their numbers in the student body as a whole. Because crowds are composed of cliques and because cliques are largely neighborhood affairs, crowd members tend to have the same social-class backgrounds (J. Coleman *et al.*, 1966; Hartup, 1970; Hollingshead, 1949).

Racial and ethnic backgrounds can also act as barriers to an individual's attempts to move up in the hierarchy of crowds. Social systems in large high schools, in which there is a mixture of racial or ethnic groups, are often almost totally segregated. Gifted athletes from minority groups frequently cross the line and are accepted into crowds composed of students in the majority, but few, if any, other accomplishments permit such changes. Indeed, girls, who cannot use the power of athletic success to surmount social-class barriers, are less likely than boys to attain membership in high-school cliques and crowds of high prestige (J. Coleman, 1961).

In addition to influencing the prestige of crowds, socioeconomic status affects aspirations. The average socioeconomic status of the student body tends to affect the social and vocational aspirations of individual students (Boyle, 1966). Thus, when students of lower social status attend high schools composed primarily of middle-class students, they tend to have higher aspirations than they do when they attend predominantly working-class schools. Similarly, when middle-class students are a minority, they have lower aspirations than when they are a majority. The greater aspirations of working-class boys who associate with middle-class boys showed clearly in a study by Richard Simpson (1962), who found that their patterns of participation in extracurricular activities resembled those of ambitious middle-class boys.

Gender and Achievement

Peers also affect the ways that adolescent girls like Lauren and boys like David approach situations involving achievement. In addition, factors that are

unrelated to the task itself are more likely to affect Lauren's motivations than David's. For example, James Coleman (1961) asked high-school students how they would prefer to be remembered when they left high school. Fewer girls than boys wanted to be remembered as brilliant students. Adolescents who were identified by their peers as "best scholars" were no more likely than average students to want to be remembered as brilliant. The differences that Coleman found between boys and girls appeared to develop during the high-school years. Roughly the same percentages of freshman boys and girls wanted to be remembered as brilliant scholars; then the sexes diverged dramatically, with fewer and fewer girls and more and more boys wanting to be remembered in this way.

This study tells us something about the images of self and others that adolescents find acceptable, and it also tells us about actual achievement. In every high school studied, the average achievement of the girls was greater than that of the boys. However, a single girl's grades showed less variation than a typical boy's grades did, and, through the high-school years, such variations increased more among boys than among girls. The girls named as best scholars were not the brightest girls, whereas the boys named as best scholars were likely to be the brightest boys. Finally, in those schools where academic achievement brought social rewards, the brightest students were more likely to be the actual high achievers.

These findings illustrate the potentially powerful influence that the peer culture can have on adolescent achievement. Girls apparently become increasingly subject to the norm "Good girls get good grades—but not too good." Such a norm can account for the lower amount of variation in a girl's grades, the lower amount of increase in such variation through the high-school years, and the lower relationship between intellectual ability and achievement among girls. In relation to socioeconomic factors, these kinds of findings are strongest in predominantly middle-class high schools. Girls in working-class schools are more likely than those in middle-class schools to feel that grades are important in their popularity with boys. And boys in middle-class schools appear to prefer girls who are leaders in activities to girls who are academic achievers.

This class difference led Coleman (1961) to suggest that, as society becomes more predominantly white collar and as the working class shrinks, high-school girls will strive less for academic achievement than to succeed as an activities girl, the teen-age

replica of the adult clubwoman. However, since Coleman examined adolescent society, the personally mobile girl discussed in Chapter 18 has begun to emerge. Should her numbers increase, academic achievement is likely to become more desirable for many girls.

Some of these motives that lead girls to avoid good grades appear to have been captured by Matina Horner (1969) in her notion of "fear of success." She theorizes that, if we are to understand achievement in most women, we must understand the role played by a learned motive to fear success. When women discover that aversive social consequences follow when they expend effort, persist in the face of obstacles, or compete and actually succeed, they may learn to avoid and withdraw from achievement situations. They withdraw not because they are afraid of failing but because they are afraid of succeeding.

Because of the way that most adolescent girls are still socialized, adolescence can be a critical period in the development of a female fear of success. As Judith Bardwick and Elizabeth Douvan (1971) have suggested:

Marriage and maternity are held out as wonderful goals, not necessarily as inhibiting dead ends. Although girls are rewarded for conformity, dependence, passivity, and competence, they are not clearly punished for the reverse. Until adolescence the idea of equal capacity, opportunity, and life style is held out to them. But sometime in adolescence the message becomes clear that one had better not do too well, that competition is aggressive and unfeminine, that deviating threatens the heterosexual relationship. (page 152)

Figure 19.7 The effects of traditional socialization practices regarding sex-appropriate behavior can be seen in the "hero" athlete stereotype and in the mixed reaction that may greet those whose conduct challenges traditional standards of sex-role conduct.

THE GENERATION GAP

Stereotypes that ignore the pluralism of American society have been created about both adults ("the silent majority") and adolescents ("hippies"). The activism of a few students (who generally have acted in accord with their parents' values) and of the sensationalized counterculture that developed in the country's elite colleges and universities have often been taken to represent the views and actions of all young people. Adult opposition to the counterculture has also been taken for granted. As these chapters on adolescence have indicated, the generation gap has been both overstated and oversold by the mass media, by bewildered parents, and by the community.

Manifestations of rebelliousness are by no means universal among the young, and adolescence is frequently a more peaceful and less conflict-filled period than it is often held to be. Recent exaggerations of the generation gap usually go back to earlier studies, such as those that produced the findings discussed in the last section. After demonstrating that peer standards tended to have negative impacts on school achievement and on the self-esteem of high achievers, some of these studies concluded not only that an adolescent society existed, one that increasingly affected the aspirations and behavior of young people, but that adolescents' families progressively lost any ability to influence them.

Since that time, many studies of adolescents have documented the existence of an adolescent society, yet they have always found its connections to adult society to be far more robust than earlier conclusions would lead one to believe. For example, Clay Brittain's (1963) results suggest that adolescents conform to peers in matters pertaining to choice of friends, language fads, and clothes but conform to parental values in matters pertaining to achievement, such as academic performance and job or career aspirations.

Recent studies by Denise Kandel and Gerald Lesser (1972) compared adolescents and their parents in the United States and in Denmark. They also found that in both countries parental influence is much stronger than peer influence on an adolescent's life goals. Although they confirmed earlier findings that adolescents rarely reward intellectual achievement in their peers, they also found that peers have less influence than parents on adolescents' future educational goals. As Douvan and Adelson (1966) have reported, close and harmonious relationships with parents are the rule, even among young people who are full participants in the adolescent society. In neither society is there evidence for a generation gap.

Kandel and Lesser concluded that interactions with peers often support parental values and that the adolescent subculture is coordinated with the culture of the larger society. They suggest, as does the research on drinking patterns discussed earlier, that the specter of the generation gap may arise because the young openly express the divisions that exist within society. When they can attribute social problems to a generation gap, adults may find differences that come from race, class, or conflict of interest less threatening.

Of course, adolescent social behavior varies widely from situation to situation. As Chapters 13 and 15 indicated, children learn very early, from parental reinforcement of their behavior, how to behave at different times and places. By adolescence they have become expert discrimination learners and respond on the basis of the cues built into each situation. Thus, differences in the adolescent's behavior within the family and in the peer group should be expected.

As long as the adolescent lives at home, his parents continue to exert a major influence on his behavior. As they have done for years, parents grant, withdraw, and reinstate privileges; provide and withdraw attention, approval, affection, and money; and even use coercive techniques. Thus, much adolescent behavior that is either prized or detested by parents is maintained by the consequences that the parents themselves provide.

However, the primary changes of adolescence result in a radically changed organism, and parents who do not realize this may fail to appreciate greater

Figure 19.8 Parents influence all facets of development, and they largely determine the person that the adolescent is becoming. Many parents and their adolescent son or daughter also discover and develop a relationship in which they become good friends and tolerate, if not enjoy, their differences as well as similarities.

autonomy in their son or daughter. It is tempting to speculate that what is so commonly reported as adolescent negativism may be the son's or daughter's reaction to the parents' failure to modify expectations in relation to the adolescent's new capabilities and sexual maturity.

MOVING INTO ADULTHOOD

Adolescence is a phase of life that encompasses profound transformations. A challenging, responsive, and confirming environment can enable Matt to move into a reasonable and satisfying maturity. He has the opportunity to become many things and, if he is properly encouraged, can emerge as an independent, self-directing, tolerant, humane, and ethical adult.

However, recent studies suggest that the number of adolescents who develop a clear idea of who they are and a strong sense of self-esteem may be diminishing. Many adolescents find it easier simply to allow themselves to be socialized rather than to undertake the more painful task of actively working toward adult autonomy. For example, Elizabeth Douvan and Joseph Adelson (1966) found that a serious testing of values and ideology occurs in only a minority of adolescents. They found that many adolescents tend to use the peer group only to learn and display social skills and that for many the peer group ends up being a structure that hinders further personal growth.

Commitment

From a developmental point of view, adolescence is a formative time of life. Adolescents who use these years to examine and test their values have a better chance to develop their possibilities in satisfying ways. One of the possibilities that develops during adolescence is the capacity for commitment—the capacity for loyalty to a set of imagined possibilities, to values and ideals, and to enduring relationships. The ability and willingness to make commitments is a characteristic of the psychological adult.

Underlying all other commitments is a *commitment to one's self*, not to the selfish pursuit of personal pleasure but to one's values, founded on a realistic understanding of one's capacities, potential usefulness, and real and possible achievements. This proper sense of self-understanding involves a willingness to be one's self, an effort to become more truly what one is, and a conviction that in the end one is worth being.

Such commitment to one's self is made possible by the kinds of family and social experiences we have discussed and by opportunities that enable the adolescent to test and define his strengths and weaknesses.

Forces that convince the individual of his inadequacy or that deprive him of avenues for accomplishment and respect can undermine this commitment to self.

As adolescence ends, the discrepancy in many adolescents' thinking between grandiose fantasy and slight accomplishment narrows, and the young adult turns to the accomplishment of specific tasks. In an achievement-oriented society like modern America, a central aspect of commitment is *commitment to a task.* The meaning of the task will vary from man to man and from woman to woman—the maintenance of a home and the rearing of healthy children, the reform of society, competent performance of a job, the achievement of a life's work, the writing of a poem, or the manufacture of goods. Making this commitment requires an adolescent to establish his vocational identity, a process discussed in Chapter 18. However the task is defined, the young adult ideally will turn from wondering what to do with his life to actually doing it. In this work he will strive for competence, whether he defines competence in personal terms or in terms of the traditional roles and rewards of society.

Interpersonal commitment requires that the individual have a capacity for mutuality; that is, for an intimate reciprocal relationship in which the needs and characteristics of each person are important to the other. Because, as was noted in Chapter 18, such relationships usually develop in a sexual context, most young people will realize this capacity in marriage, where each partner identifies with the other and with the creation of a new family. Others will realize this same capacity for mutuality in friendship, in work, or in shared play.

This concept of interpersonal commitment entails in addition a concern for the welfare of the community and for the care of the next generation. A young person first feels himself part of the community in adolescence; in adulthood, he translates this feeling into activities that facilitate the development of others. Most will express commitment to the community and to those who embody its future through their willingness to bear and rear children.

Finally, in a striving society that rewards and praises work, it is important to stress that one of the attainments of adolescence should be the *capacity for invigorating play.* The American legacy of puritanism makes us tend to forget that one of the tasks of adolescence is the development of the capacity to live zestfully as well as purposefully, to be capable of free and spontaneous pleasure. Adults who fail to develop a commitment to play might be moral, virtuous, and

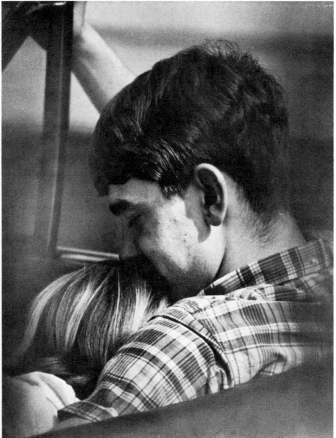

responsible, but they are also likely to be driven, compulsive, and grim.

Emergence of Youth

In the past decade, a constellation of factors has created a concept of "youth" as a possible phase of life and has created a consciousness of it similar to that associated with the concept of adolescence more than a century ago. The consciousness of youth has grown since it came to pass that at least two-thirds of all young people in this country finish high school and that over one-fourth of those between twenty-one and twenty-five are still in school. This means that substantial portions of young people are segregated into concentrated settlements with their peers, mostly in universities and colleges but also, as Richard Flacks (1971) has pointed out, in urban, often black, ghettos inhabited by those whom the educational system has not prepared for jobs. Such segregation no longer is restricted to members of the male upper-middle-class who are being educated for elite roles; today most young people live separately from their families. This means that conditions exist that encourage the transformation of an *age grade* into an *age group*, and the mass media and business have encouraged this growth of self-consciousness of youth.

Defining Characteristics. Most commonly, youth is seen as beginning with the end of secondary education. There is general agreement that youth ends when the individual assumes an adult occupational

Figure 19.9 A variety of developmental experiences enable an adolescent to know what commitments he might be willing to make or whether he can live up to commitments that he does make.

role. Those who leave school at sixteen or when they finish high school are far more likely to work and to marry sooner than those who stay in school. Youth, then, appears to be primarily a creature of social definition.

Kenneth Keniston (1968), who has popularized the notion of a period of youth, defines the concept in restrictive social-psychological terms. He sees the defining characteristics of youth as the testing of the connection between self and society, a relative disengagement from that society, and the adoption of youth-specific identities that are not expected to outlast this period of life. The involvements of youth differ from the shallower, more fluctuating enthusiasms of adolescence in that they often last many years, inspire deep loyalty, and generally provide a vantage point outside the system. As soon as a young person makes a definitive engagement with society, youth is over, whether this engagement takes the form of commitment to revolution and social change, an acceptance of the existing society, or an intermediate position.

Those whom Keniston defined in his study as youth had accomplished the traditional tasks of adolescence. They were emancipated from the family; were relatively tranquil concerning sexuality; had formed a stable and relatively integrated self-concept; showed a capacity for commitment, intimacy, and play; displayed synthesis in the moral and ethical areas; and had passed through and beyond any adolescent rebellion. Despite their accomplishments, these young men and women continued to emphasize remaining open, fluid, and in motion, not foreclosing their development in any way, and not being prematurely integrated into the established society.

Social Change. In the face of rapid social change, young people reexamine and redefine their personal relationships to the past, including the cultural past, before they are ready to move ahead in the task of creating their own future. This reexamination of the cultural tradition by perceptive young people frequently has had important and desirable consequences for society. It means that the obsolete is continually being winnowed from the enduring, that the problems and future directions of society are continually being scrutinized, and that society is assured a critical commentary on its own functioning.

Put more generally, the opening of a period of youth to larger numbers of young men and women may turn out to be part of the essential dynamic of social change and reform in modern societies. Within

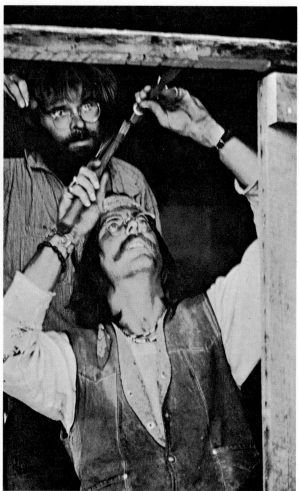

Figure 19.10 As a way of further developing their self-awareness, some individuals commit themselves for an indefinite time to a life style in which they pursue certain goals and activities that enable them to make decisions about themselves and their future.

the past decade, youth have played a major role in social change in this country. They have exposed the disgraceful legacy of slavery and segregation in American society; they were the catalysts for the agonized reappraisal of American foreign policy, especially with regard to the war in Vietnam; and they have precipitated a wave of university reforms that recognized students' maturity and civil rights.

However, in view of the low incidence of principled morality, the foreclosure of identity, and the gender-related difficulties in integrating sexuality and intimacy among many adolescents, it must be apparent that Keniston's definition of youth probably applies to only a small and privileged minority. Indeed, it must be noted that interest in youth grew out of the study of youthful dissent of the 1960s, in itself a phenomenon of the upper-middle class.

It is not certain whether youth as a separate phase of life will find its way firmly into public consciousness or formal developmental theory. At present, when the term is defined in social-psychological terms, the incidence of youth is quite low. Given the decline in dissent, the social definition of the period may decrease in the future.

Finally, it is misleading to separate adolescence drastically from early adulthood, for in most men and women these two phases of life merge and blur. Adolescence does not end; it fades away, either into youth or into early adulthood. This fading away of adolescence marks not the end of psychological development but the beginning of a lifetime of future development, as we will see in the next chapters.

SUMMARY

1. The personality characteristics and social development of adolescents are complexly determined by their prior socialization. Social-class differences in social relations and influences illustrate subcultural variations in socialization that affect almost all areas of development.

2. A chief interpersonal theme in early adolescence is the gradual move from childhood dependence. In this and other respects, parents and the home environment have a lasting influence. Among other things, parents affect their adolescent son's or daughter's basic decisions about an occupation and the amount of independence and self-control that he or she is likely to show.

3. Peer relationships also change during adolescence, and their influence on an adolescent's identity formation may be crucial. Friendships often move from the congenial sharing of activities to psychological sharing and intimacy. Early chumships often evolve into later intimate and mature heterosexual companionships. Although popularity and peer acceptance may be stable from childhood to adolescence, sexual maturation and heterosexual behavior provide a new influence that affects clique and group composition as well as an adolescent's status within a group.

4. Despite the troubled interpersonal relationships that sometimes characterize adolescence, the "generation gap" between adolescents and adults is an exaggeration. In general, research indicates a high degree of adolescent peer support of parental values and views as well as a coordination of the adolescent subculture with that of the larger society.

5. A challenging, responsive, and confirming environment can enable an adolescent to move into a reasonable and satisfying adulthood. A major potential consequence of this formative period of life is the development of the capacity for commitment, first to one's self but also to a task, to interpersonal relationships, and to play. In recent years, a concept of youth has been proposed that also draws on this theme of commitment. Although the ultimate scientific or practical value of this proposed phase remains unclear, it too can be seen as marking movement into early adulthood.

SUGGESTED READINGS

Bardwick, Judith M. *The Psychology of Women: A Study of Biocultural Conflicts.* New York: Harper & Row, 1971.

Douvan, Elizabeth, and Joseph Adelson. *The Adolescent Experience.* New York: Wiley, 1966.

Kandel, Denise, and Gerald S. Lesser. *Youth in Two Worlds.* San Francisco: Jossey-Bass, 1972.

Keniston, Kenneth. *Youth and Dissent.* New York: Harcourt Brace Jovanovich, 1971.

Mead, Margaret. *Culture and Commitment: A Study of the Generation Gap.* Garden City, N.Y.: American Museum of Natural History Press, 1970.

Our society has no rite or social ceremony to mark the passage from adolescence to adulthood. Although one may become a legal adult at eighteen or twenty-one, there is no one age at which a person becomes mature. We will, therefore, arbitrarily define adulthood as the years from twenty until death. In order to look more closely at this phase of development, we will further divide adulthood into three periods: (1) early adulthood, from twenty to forty; (2) middle adulthood, from forty to sixty; and (3) later adulthood, from sixty until death. Most people assume that growth and development halt once an individual reaches adulthood. However, as these chapters will show, adulthood is a time of change, of growth, and of development. Although the child does make the man, the experiences of a lifetime make the man of sixty the same and yet very different from the adult of twenty-five.

UNIT VII
Adulthood: Functioning in Society

The early adult years are a time of clarifying goals and of deciding how and where to live one's life.

20

EARLY ADULTHOOD: SELECTING THE OPTIONS

As she enters the adult world, Lauren has many more choices to make than her grandmother faced. Her grandmother knew that women married and became mothers, and her goals were simply and clearly set. Lauren, on the other hand, is free to choose a traditional marriage and to devote the major part of her adult life to being a wife and mother. But she may also choose to marry and remain childless or to reject marriage altogether without feeling that she has failed as a human being. Lauren also has a third choice, one that more and more young women are selecting. She can marry and have both a family and a career, perhaps choosing a contract marriage, in which both she and her husband share in the obligations of making a home and rearing a family.

The choices that confront Lauren show that early adulthood is a time when individuals are confronted with the tasks of becoming adult. It is generally a time of becoming independent, a time to choose a vocation or career, and a time to choose a marriage partner and begin a family. Adolescents see an adult as someone who no longer plays and who is no longer playful; nevertheless, adolescents generally look forward to becoming adults themselves. Perhaps one reason that adolescents look forward to entering the adult world of commitments and responsibility is that they look forward to the freedom and social respect associated with adulthood rather than to adulthood itself.

In this chapter we will describe the developmental and psychological characteristics that are typical of early adulthood. We will see that achieving independence and self-sufficiency is the central developmental task of these years. We will find that one's identity seems to remain fairly stable from adolescence into early adulthood and that younger adults are generally at their peak of physical and mental ability and performance. We will look at marriage and parenthood, divorce and remarriage as transition points in development that can make heavy demands on an individual. Throughout the chapter, we will emphasize that there are important differences in the ways individuals experience and cope with the tasks of early adulthood and that some of these differences depend on whether one is male or female, on one's concepts of appropriate sex-role behavior, on social class, on education, and on one's unique developmental history. Finally, we will see that there is no longer a single model for these early adult years and no longer one best road to maturity.

THE CONCEPT OF MATURITY

Almost all personality theories have described the development of maturity in early adulthood (see Figure 20.1). Each of these views offers a unique perspective, yet there are some human characteristics that all these theories consider as mature. For example, all regard the ability to be intimate, to give and accept love, and to be affectionate and sexually responsive as a necessary component of maturity. All stress the ability to be sociable, to have friends, to be devoted to and nurturant of other important people. They also agree that some clear, vivid sense of who one is, of what one's aims and powers are, and of what is best for oneself typifies a mature individual. One probable result of these characteristics is an interest in productive work and an ability to do it.

In each of these theories, the mature person constantly changes and adapts. He or she is a person who successfully and flexibly copes with the responsibilities and demands of adulthood. Maturity is not an end state, but a life-long process of becoming.

One way to look at maturity, then, is to think of it in terms of being able to cope successfully with the typical events and decisions that most people face at characteristic times in their lives. Throughout this book we have considered life as divided into developmental phases. In this sense, a mature adult would be one who successfully deals with the demands to grow, develop, and change during the phase of adult development. In terms of Erik Erikson's (1963) concept of developmental stages, a mature individual is one who successfully resolves the crisis at each stage of development in the ideal direction. Thus, maturity in early adulthood, in Erikson's terms, means (1) having resolved the possible developmental crises of childhood and adolescence, (2) having ability for and interest in relating closely to another person (intimacy), and (3) having the ability and desire to be productive and to nurture and devote oneself to others, as to children and to productive work (generativity). But no matter how it is defined, maturity in adulthood is cumulative and changing. It involves a continuing adjustment to the constantly changing expectations and responsibilities of adult-

hood. A mature adult is able to cope successfully with the tasks, problems, and decisions that generally confront people of his age.

There is another, related way of looking at maturity. A mature person is likely to feel good about himself. In this view, maturity is determined more by a person's subjective assessment of how things are going than by society's judgment that he is doing things appropriate to his age. Adulthood is not only a time of doing things, it is also a time when an individual looks critically at himself, at the direction his life is taking, and at the ways other people see him. In the mature person, there is often a fairly close fit between the way he sees himself, the way he would ideally like to be, and the way other people see him (Birren, 1964). A young man like Matt, for example, may have unrealistic career goals for himself, and he may also perceive himself to be much more aggressive with women than he actually is. In the process of maturing, he will bring his career expectations and ideals more in line with career goals that he could realistically hope to achieve. For Matt, maturing also involves becoming more aware of his own shyness and caution in approaching women.

Thus, maturity means that a person can be sensitive, aware, and realistic in assessing himself, in choosing his ideals or goals, and in perceiving how others see him. To be mature, then, does not necessarily mean that one has to get married, work hard at a career, or have children. Maturity means being aware of who one is now, of where one wants to go in life,

Figure 20.1 Summary descriptions of some major theoretical viewpoints on personality development and maturity during adulthood.

Sigmund Freud takes the view that mature, adult personality functioning is characterized by patterns of behaving that effectively deal with one's sexual urges and environment. According to Freud, the mature adult has a stabilized self-concept, or ego identity, and has developed a number of adaptive ways of handling his desires, wishes, and fantasies. In Freud's theory, having more or less successfully passed through previous stages of personality development, in the final, genital stage, the person becomes able to love others on a more altruistic basis. In addition to providing love and care, marriage traditionally fulfills a principal biological function of this stage: reproduction. In Freud's view, if an individual has developed into a reality-oriented and socialized adult, he also will have formed social attachments that allow him to enjoy the pleasure and companionship of others in both work and play.

Alfred Adler believes that, in the development of personality, the mature adult is one who becomes able to free himself from self-imposed restrictions and to face reality as necessary. In Adler's view, the individual must develop a style of life that is his own, and this unique identity then unifies his personality and organizes and directs his behavior. According to Adler, the direction of this behavior is ideally toward others, and this social interest shows itself in the desire for interaction and in a concern for others. In this view, marriage and parenthood, the development of interpersonal relationships, and the formation of friendships are all expressions of this social interest.

Harry Stack Sullivan emphasizes that the mature adult is one who can deal effectively with potential sources of anxiety and who engages in satisfying interpersonal relationships. In this view, the individual's self-concept or identity also is seen as organizing and directing his actions, as well as having a stabilizing influence on his interpersonal relationships. According to Sullivan, the ability of the mature adult to be intimate and to have mutually satisfying relationships is usually shown clearly in marriage and parenthood. However, friendship and relationships with others also generally are considered important, because they provide further sources of pleasure as well as additional opportunities for personal growth and change.

Erik Erikson holds that a mature level of personality development depends on successful resolution of the crises of previous stages. In his view, successful resolution results in the formation of a clear sense of identity, which gives the individual a sense of perspective and direction and a feeling of unity and purpose. Erikson's theory emphasizes that development continues during adulthood; it does not stop. Thus, marriage and the formation of an intimate, loving relationship, as well as parenthood and a concern with productivity, involve and are a result of ongoing psychosocial processes of development. At each step, successful psychosocial resolution also contributes to the adult's ability to engage in a widening radius of mutually satisfying and close friendships.

Erich Fromm stresses that the personality development of the mature individual is characterized by his living in harmony with nature and society. According to Fromm, this involves transcending one's limits by creativity and by devoting oneself to society without conforming. Thus, the individual's sense of himself, his identity, is seen as coming from the development of a creative and constructive control over nature and from participation in society. In Fromm's view, marriage and parenthood can be seen as epitomizing the possibility of productive self-realization. In addition, being a creatively active adult, according to Fromm, is likely to lead to the formation of many deep bonds of brotherhood and friendship.

Walter Mischel considers the adult who shows mature ways of behaving to be one who has successfully learned the roles of adulthood and who effectively performs them. In this view, self-esteem during adulthood continues to derive in part from others' praise and acceptance of what one says and does. Marriage and parenthood can in turn be considered two complex roles that build on previous experience but also require learning new behavior. Throughout the adulthood years, according to this view, new friendships and other relationships can also be expected to develop as a result of an individual's continuing participation with others in various social, recreational, and vocational activities.

and it means working toward one's goals. In a real sense, the popular phrase "getting it all together" refers to young adults' struggle to become mature.

PHYSICAL CHARACTERISTICS

The early years of adulthood usually represent the peak of attractiveness and of physical agility, speed, and strength. The healthy young adult stands erect and walks with a firm step. There are curves where there should be curves and firmness where one should be firm.

For most people, these are the years when their bodies, inside and out, are at their best. Despite this sense of physical perfection, some of the physical hallmarks of aging begin, almost imperceptibly, in early adulthood. Around the age of twenty, slow, continuing changes affect the workings of the human body. Muscle tone and strength are generally at their peak between the ages of twenty and thirty and decrease after that. Height begins to decrease slowly but measurably around twenty-five. Hearing losses usually begin during adolescence. And, even if a person's weight remains constant, the proportion of fatty tissue in his body begins to increase.

Considering society's overwhelming focus on youth and beauty, it might be expected that these small but noticeable changes in body appearance would have a negative effect on the way that an individual feels about himself. However, this does not appear to be the case. A recent survey by Ellen Berscheid, Elaine Walster, and George Bohrnstedt (1973), which investigated Americans' attitudes toward their bodies, found that there was no difference between people under twenty-five years old and people twenty-five to forty-four years old in their overall liking for their bodies. Apparently, despite our focus on youth, today's young adults are not bothered much by these small changes in their physical appearance.

One reason for the lack of concern over the physical changes of early adulthood may be that, aside from an occasional gray hair or a new wrinkle beside the eyes, the early adult years are typically the years of peak physical fitness and performance. Reaction times generally improve from childhood until the age of nineteen and then remain constant until around twenty-six. In any competitive situation or in any situation that demands a fast response, younger adults usually come out ahead. Such factors may explain why only the young excel in some sports. James Birren (1973) has noted that, in such competitive sports as basketball, boxing, skiing, and

Figure 20.2 Physical fitness and performance typically reach their highest level of development during early adulthood.

baseball, it takes early-adulthood strength and speed to stay on top. Other sports such as bowling or golf depend much more on concentration and decision making and not at all on speed, so that adults can excel in these activities well into the later years.

NEW DEVELOPMENTAL TASKS

Early adulthood is the first time in an individual's life when he is truly on his own, when no one else makes his decisions for him. Once a person is twenty, he is increasingly expected to assume the responsibilities of an adult, and his behavior is expected to conform to that required by the adult world. In a way, the demands in early adulthood to change, to become adult, and to grow up are not radically different from the pressures to grow up that adolescents feel. As we saw in Chapter 19, a critical difference between adulthood and adolescence is that the young adult must be independent and responsible. This means that, as individuals move into the early adult years, they may feel a loss of security and support that was given to them as adolescents by their family and friends.

In contrast to the general search for self, goals, and values that dominates adolescence, early adulthood is characterized by one's direction toward specific goals. The younger adult is much more in control of his own life and much more self-directing than the adolescent. One dominant concern of early adulthood is the focusing of one's life (Havighurst, 1972). During his twenties, the young adult makes the choices that will give him social identity. For example, Matt takes a job, chooses a marriage partner, and selects a neighborhood to live in.

During his thirties, an individual has generally made the decisions that focus his life, and he usually turns to developing his skills and deepening his base of experiences. As a worker, he generally grows in skill and experience and finds such growth rewarded by promotions. Young scientists produce research papers, teachers teach effectively, mothers become effective and skilled in child rearing.

This is not to say that worries, conflicts, and goals are not prevalent in young adulthood. They are. Young adults tend to be anxious about heterosexual relationships, their emotionality, their appearance, and their social acceptability (M. Powell and Ferraro, 1960). They also are likely to be concerned about their vocations and about decisions they face regarding marriage and children (Smoller-Weimer, 1974). For example, the single woman in her twenties generally fixes on the goal of marriage, whereas the

single woman in her thirties stresses occupational goals. The goals of the married woman in her twenties are likely to focus on being a housewife and having a home, whereas the thirty-year-old married woman's goal is to stay in a job. Married or single, young men in their twenties and thirties stress vocational goals, and they would like to get a promotion or get into another job.

The truth is that not all people get married and not all people settle into careers or have children at exactly the same age. Exactly what is considered appropriate behavior for a particular age group depends to some extent on who one is, the era one lives in, and one's social class. Each person has expectations regarding the kinds of behavior that are appropriate at various ages. Bernice Neugarten (1968) suggests that men and women have "social clocks" in their heads to help them judge other people's behavior, as well as their own, as being early, late, or on time. What constitutes the appropriate time for certain developmental events may change with the passing of generations. In 1940 the young woman who was not married by the age of twenty-five faced the threat of spinsterhood. By 1966 it was the twenty-one-year-old who faced such a fate. In the 1970s the appropriate age for marriage once again seems to be older, and young women who want to marry can postpone fears of spinsterhood for a time.

According to Neugarten, early adulthood is both quantitatively and qualitatively different for people in different socioeconomic classes. Early adulthood

Figure 20.3 The nature and timing of the developmental tasks involved in establishing a personal and social identity during early adulthood are likely to be perceived somewhat differently depending on a person's sex and social class and the era in which he lives.

lasts longer for a person in the upper middle class than for a member of the working class: The upper middle class regards forty as the end of early adulthood, whereas the working class believes that it ends at thirty-five. Further, the upper-middle-class person sees young adulthood as a time of exploration and groping, of "feeling one's way" and trying out jobs and careers, marriage and adulthood. To the working-class man, young adulthood is not a time of experimentation; instead it is a time when issues are settled. Sometimes this is explained as an obligation ("The responsibility is hung on you"), and there is some regret. Others in the working class see these decisions as necessary for independence; it is time to "be a man." The working man is likely to regard young adulthood as a time when youth is gone and one gets down to the serious business of living, of job, marriage, children, and responsibility.

When people are asked, "When is the best time to marry?" or "When is the best time to finish school?" there is widespread agreement within social classes on the answers. As Neugarten reports, in the middle class, most say that the best age for a man to marry is between twenty-five and thirty-five, whereas, among the working class, the best age for a man to marry is somewhat younger. The ages at which such major events as marriage actually occur also shows a great deal of regularity within social classes. The higher the social class, the older an individual is likely to be when he leaves school, gets his first job, gets married, and has children.

IDENTITY AND INTERPERSONAL BEHAVIOR

The direction of growth and development of a young adult's personal and interpersonal skills is primarily the result of his experiences and not simply the product of growing older. In general, gradual stabilization rather than radical change seems to be the rule, and many of the changes that occur are similar to those discussed in Chapter 19 with regard to the adolescent's capacity for commitment.

As Robert White (1966) has suggested, under reasonably favorable circumstances there is a stabilizing of one's identity. The individual's sense of who he is becomes sharper and clearer and also becomes more consistent and free of transient influences. Accumulated personal experience increasingly determines his identity, and he progressively gains autonomy from the daily impact of social judgment and his successes and failures.

A second growth trend is toward a freeing of personal relationships. Whereas a child may treat a teacher as if she were his mother and other children as if they were brothers and sisters, the adult is able to be increasingly responsive to another person's true nature. An adolescent is likely to think primarily of himself in social interactions; that is, he is generally concerned only with the impression he makes or with what he is trying to say. In early adulthood a person begins to be able to interact with others as people in their own right. Typically, a young adult becomes less defensive and anxious and more flexible, more sensitive to the verbal and nonverbal behavior of others, and more friendly, warm, and respectful.

A third area of change is in the direction of deepening interests. Life-long interests can, and often do, develop early in life, but the young adult tends to move toward a fuller engagement with those objects of interest. He feels an increased effectiveness and a growing command over his sphere of interest. At this time, an individual deepens existing interests or develops new interests as ends in themselves rather than as means to ends. As a person's interests and commitments become clearer and deeper, he is likely to have a heightened sense of self-confidence.

The humanizing of values is often a fourth area of development among young adults. During these years, a person may become increasingly aware of the human meaning of values as opposed to their absolute meaning. The young adult may use his own experiences and motives to affirm and promote a value system that seems best to him, and his value system becomes increasingly personal.

A final area of change involves the expansion of caring. Individuals typically outgrow the self-centeredness of their childhood and adolescent phases. An individual's self becomes "extended," and the welfare of another person, a group, or some valued object becomes as important as his own welfare. This caring becomes apparent only when there is involvement in and feeling for the welfare of others and not just a profession of interest.

Self-concept and Self-esteem

Because an individual's self-concept is so closely related to his physical appearance and to his social roles and abilities and because all these change in adulthood, it would seem likely that his self-concept would change as well. A young adult often feels himself oriented outward, toward the environment, and his self-concept becomes related to trying to master the world. Young adults tend to answer questions about themselves in terms of their social roles, as compared to older individuals, who tend to

describe their experiences in terms of emotional tones or attitudes. When people are asked to draw themselves, men's self-portraits get bigger and bigger until they are about thirty years old, and women's self-portraits increase in size until they are forty (Birren, 1964). Because the drawings are presumed to reflect a person's self-concept, the implication is that the young adult senses his increasing power and importance in life.

Among workers, the young male's concept of himself as a worker and his drive for a career are likely to be more important than any other concept he has of himself. The social-class differences discussed in Chapter 19 are likely to affect occupational self-concepts. For example, the young adult with an advanced education is likely to have a view of himself as more frustrated and striving than the adult whose formal education ended early. Thus, the well-educated young adult with a good job is less likely to be satisfied with his position or his productivity than his less well-educated counterpart. Whereas the better-educated person generally regards middle adulthood as the best time of life, workers in an industrial setting prefer the years twenty to thirty-five for themselves, and they think of the years up to twenty as being best for others (Meltzer, 1962). A twenty-one-year-old man explained why he thought the years twenty to thirty-five would be the best of his life: "Because my life will be determined by how much I work and what lengths I will be willing to go to insure a good life."

As we have seen in earlier discussions of personality, learning what it means to think, act, and feel male or female is a critical part of adolescent and childhood development. The adult personalities of men and women clearly indicate that our social stereotypes about male and female roles have a profound impact on the kinds of adults that boys and girls are likely to become.

For example, Norah Rosenau (1974) found that young adults have comparable sex-role stereotypes regarding ideal self-concept when she asked them to list the characteristics that (1) they would ideally want for themselves, (2) they would want in a person of the opposite sex, (3) they think a person of the opposite sex would want to have of himself or herself, and (4) a person of the opposite sex would want in a person of the individual's own sex. Figure 20.5 shows men's and women's typical responses in the four categories. The pattern of these responses indicates that sex-role stereotypes have more influence on women's ideas of gender roles than on men's. Women are more likely

Figure 20.4 The work and social roles and relationships of young adults provide an important source of self-esteem.

What Men Would Like to Be

creative
happy
honest
independent
intelligent
sensitive to others
understanding

What Women Would Like to Be

attractive
friendly
independent
intelligent
loving

Men's Ideal Woman

creative
friendly
sensitive

Women's Ideal Man

good-looking
intelligent
loving
understanding

What Men Think Women Would Like to Be

honest
independent
intelligent
sensitive to others

What Women Think Men Would Like to Be

brave
dominant
rich

What Men Think Women Would Like Them to Be

friendly
good-looking
honest
intelligent
sensitive to others

What Women Think Men Would Like Them to Be

beautiful
dependent
physically well-proportioned

Figure 20.5 Chart showing the characteristics that young men and women list as ideal for themselves and for a person of the opposite sex and the characteristics that they think the opposite sex considers ideal for both men and women. (Adapted from Rosenau, 1974)

than men to see the ideal woman in stereotypic terms, and they also tend to believe that men are more eager to assume the traditional dominant male role than men actually are. It would appear, therefore, that young adults of both sexes tend to lack sensitivity and understanding when it comes to the opposite sex's ideal self.

Beyond sex differences in ideal self-concepts, likenesses are evident. Both men and women would like to see themselves as intelligent, independent, and loving or understanding. People are human beings first and sexual beings second. This emphasis on the importance of an "individual" or "human" identity over a "male" or "female" identity is, after all, the basic force of the Women's Liberation Movement.

One's gender role is a central part of one's self-concept, and it is also important in determining how good a person feels about himself or herself as an adult. Like adolescents, men and women typically find their sense of self-esteem from different sources. For example, men are prized and prize themselves for what they accomplish, whereas women tend to esteem themselves only inasmuch as they are esteemed and regarded highly by others (Bardwick, 1971). Because in most cases our society values accomplishment over interpersonal success and admiration, women tend to have lower self-esteem than men. Also, as was reported in Chapter 19, women, especially those who are better educated, are more likely than men to fear success. Men tend to work hard to achieve some internal standard of excellence and to gain satisfaction from successful accomplishment. Most women, by contrast, are motivated to work more for praise and esteem from others than for their own satisfaction (Oetzel, 1966).

Sexuality

Sexual relationships and sexual performance continue to be important concerns during early adulthood (Saxton, 1972). The early data presented in the Kinsey reports indicated that the average American male establishes a pattern of orgasm and ejaculation that remains fairly consistent from adolescence through later adulthood and that is relatively independent of marital status. However, the relative frequency of the behaviors that result in orgasm and ejaculation do change over the years. Whereas masturbation is the dominant type of male sexual behavior before puberty and in early adolescence, sexual intercourse is more prominent in early adulthood (Kinsey, Pomeroy, and Martin, 1948; Masters and Johnson, 1966).

Sexual intercourse in marriage is almost universally regarded as a right, or even a duty. Especially during the first years of marriage between young adults, a couple is likely to have intercourse frequently. In addition to its physiological benefit and its value as one of life's great pleasures, marital intercourse can be an affirmation of affection and desire for each other that holds a marriage together.

A recent survey by Robert Bell and Norman Lobsenz (1974) of the sexual practices and attitudes of 2,372 moderately well-educated American wives revealed that most young adult wives enjoy a high level of sexual pleasure in marriage. Wives in their twenties tended to derive more pleasure from the physical aspects of love-making, whereas the thirty-year-olds tended to regard the emotional aspects as more important. The majority of wives reported that they had orgasms "most of the time" or at least "some of the time." Orgasmic satisfaction was related to a woman's feelings of contentment with her marriage: Happier women reported a higher frequency of orgasms. Frequency of intercourse was also related to sexual satisfaction and marital happiness, as is true of men. Although frequency of intercourse and orgasms were related to marital happiness, it is not clear whether good sexual relations make a good marriage or a good marriage leads to good sex. Probably both are true.

Most of the women in Bell and Lobsenz's survey were satisfied with the frequency of coitus. Of the women surveyed, those between twenty-six and thirty had coitus just over nine times a month, whereas women between thirty-one and forty reported that they had intercourse around seven times a month. Those who said that coitus was too infrequent explained that it was not due to their husbands' lack of interest but due to the pressures of jobs, child rearing, and housework, which left them with little time and energy. Wives who reported that intercourse was too infrequent also tended to talk less with their husbands about their sexual relationship.

Young-adult wives were more likely than teen-age wives or wives in their forties to experiment with love-making techniques, and those women who reported such experiments tended to be more satisfied with their marriages. Wives in their twenties and thirties reported more experience with oral-genital sex and were somewhat more concerned with the "environment of sex"—what they looked like, where they engaged in it—than teen-age or middle-aged wives. Generally, wives under thirty found it easy to talk to their husbands about their sexual desires and needs, and most said that their husband usually initiates the love-making.

Intellectual Skills

A person's intellectual skills, or at least his own perception of them, are likely to affect both his self-concept and his self-esteem. The young adult will find that these years are a time of improved performance in all areas of intellectual ability. In the areas of verbal skills, stored facts, and information proces-

Figure 20.6 (*opposite*) Although many more young adults today are pursuing jobs and careers in fields traditionally considered appropriate for only males or females, such instances are still atypical enough to bring about an occasional second look and wry smile.

Figure 20.7 Sexual expression and satisfaction are matters of concern to all young adults, married or unmarried, and some degree of experimentation in sexual practices and techniques is almost universal.

sing, young adults do better than they ever have before. Young adults also reach their peak performance on tests involving psychomotor skills, especially speed and coordination.

According to Paul Baltes and K. Warner Schaie (1974), young adults are better than they ever have been, but not necessarily better than they ever will be, in three other major areas of intellectual functioning: (1) verbal comprehension and number skills, which are acquired through education and socialization; (2) the ability to shift easily from one way of thinking to another, as when a person must provide an antonym or a synonym to a given word, depending on whether the word is printed in upper- or lower-case letters; and (3) the ability to organize and process visual materials, such as finding a simple figure in a complex one or identifying a picture that is incomplete.

However, age is not the only factor that affects intellectual skills during adulthood. For example, our species is becoming smarter with each new generation (Baltes and Schaie, 1974). We are also better educated and healthier, and both education and health are at least as important as age in determining an individual's intellectual ability (Birren and Morrison, 1961; Botwinick, 1967).

Beyond measures of intellectual skill, there also are questions as to how well young adults learn and remember, how well they think and solve problems, and how creative they are. In terms of learning and memory, performance in early adulthood generally is at its peak. Thus, on any kind of learning or memory task, young adults usually perform better than they ever have before. In addition, if success at a task depends on how fast one does it, they probably do the best that they will ever do.

In the case of thinking, early adulthood is likely to be the time when a person has the maximum flexibility to form new concepts and is most easily able to shift the ways he thinks to solve problems. This is most likely to be shown when problem solving involves discovering the details of categories and finding solutions when the information is at hand. But again, age is not the only determinant; intelligence, education, and memory also contribute heavily to thinking ability.

As for creativity, which involves finding original and unique solutions, the early adult years often provide the most fertile ground for creative thought. For example, maximum creativity in the arts and sciences may occur during the thirties (Lehman, 1953). The most influential books tend to be produced by writers in their late thirties, and many popular children's books and short stories are written by people in their early thirties. The twenties is the usual age to write poetry, whereas drama seems to be a favorite mode of expression for people in their thirties. Inventions and discoveries tend to be made by people in their thirties. The production of novels, paintings, poetry, plays, and inventions reaches a peak during these years, but this does not mean that creativity ends with one's fortieth birthday. As we will see, the creative individual is likely to continue to produce works of high quality throughout his life.

MARRIAGE

Nearly everyone gets married. In the United States, somewhere between 95 and 98 percent of the population choose to make this legal commitment to another person (Carter and Glick, 1970). Generally, this major developmental decision takes place in these early adult years. Although people live, die, marry, and divorce in the name of love, a number of other factors are important in determining who one marries and how well that marriage lasts.

Choosing a mate, or choosing not to choose one, is one of the most significant decisions that a person will ever make. The person one chooses to marry will have a great influence on one's life style, one's lifetime experiences, and even one's lifetime happiness. Despite the importance of marriage and its impact on one's life, the decision to marry usually is made quickly, easily, and rather casually. However,

Figure 20.8 Early adulthood is usually a time when a person reaches the peak in many of his intellectual skills and is a period when he may have a maximum capacity to be productive.

most decisions to marry do consider social level, temperamental compatibility, and similarity of outlook on life.

Most people do not fall in love at first sight, and many are likely to marry the girl or boy next door. Residential proximity has a profound impact on the choice of a mate. For example, in 1932 a review of 5,000 marriage-license applications showed that one-fourth of the couples lived within two city blocks of each other at the time of their marriage application and that one-third of the couples lived within five blocks of each other (Bossard, 1932). This finding makes sense; it would be silly to drive across town for a date or a mate when someone equally interesting lives down the street. It helps, then, to be not only physically desirable but also geographically near.

People also tend to marry people who are like themselves. Individuals look for mates who have a suitable background; that is, a background that matches their own ethnically, religiously, and socially (Murstein, 1971). Although interracial and interfaith marriages and some forms of interclass marriages are more likely to be accepted today, in the past society has condemned, if not outlawed, such marriages.

People also tend to choose marriage partners who share their interests, values, and ways of behaving. This kind of selectivity reflects a human tendency to seek out persons who validate one as a human being and who approve of the way that one lives. If engaged couples are questioned separately, a striking agreement between the two partners appears on such issues as smoking and drinking, as well as in their attitudes toward working women, the number of children they want, and where they should live (Burgess and Wallin, 1953). In general, residential proximity and similarity of background tend to be important in starting a relationship, and whether it stands the test of time and marriage is also likely to depend on a similarity in the couple's values, attitudes, and interests (Z. Rubin, 1973). Apparently, then, the course of choosing a mate follows a pattern somewhat like the course of friendship discussed in Chapter 19.

When one looks at young adults' attitudes toward love and the person they would like to marry, interesting sex differences appear. Zick Rubin (1973) notes that men are likely to fall in love more quickly than women, to be more easily satisfied with the woman's qualities, and to be more romantic. Women, in general, tend to be more practical about whom they marry. To put it succinctly, young adult women are picky. But in a traditional relationship, they may have more to gain in marriage, in terms of economic and emotional security and social status, than men. Willard Waller (1938) said it well, if bluntly, nearly forty years ago: "A man, when he marries, chooses a companion and perhaps a helpmate, but a woman chooses a companion and at the same time a standard of living." However, with women's increasing equality on the job market, this is perhaps becoming less of a truism.

The State of Being Married

For couples who do not live together before marriage, and they remain in the majority, marriage means not only adjusting to all the social roles associated with marriage but also adjusting to living with another person. The honeymoon may be over once the dirty dishes and laundry have to be washed and the bathroom scrubbed. The smallest things can have a profound impact on a marriage: Susan may roll the toothpaste tube from the bottom; her husband may just squish it out and leave the top uncapped. The romance and sexual attraction of dating and courtship are not enough to hold a relationship together through the realities of everyday living. If young adults have had good parental models to help them learn what a good relationship is like, they are at an advantage. If they also have the willingness and the patience to develop emotional intimacy and to communicate their feelings to their partner, the relationship will have more potential for enduring growth (C. Rogers, 1972).

New marriages can be described in terms of a few general characteristics (Cox, 1968). Newly married couples soon discover that their individual freedom is reduced, that they must make financial adjustments, and that they face problems involving the maturity or lack of maturity of their partner. By marrying in early adulthood, at a time when this freedom may still be critical to one's individual growth, people often find the restrictions of marriage difficult to handle. Adding children to the marriage generally exaggerates whatever problems already exist.

One problem that confronts a new marriage is the problem of power. In the traditonal, male-dominated relationship, the husband holds the power, and the wife usually bows meekly to his superior decision-making abilities. Another kind of relationship is becoming more common today, one in which the power is divided more equally between the man and the woman. When Robert Blood and Donald Wolfe (1960) surveyed 909 white middle-class Detroit families, they found that, if the husband and wife had more or less equal education and if both worked, the

Perfect Wife Quiz

1.   Do you allow your husband an appropriate amount of the family income, to spend as he chooses, without accounting?   0   1   2   3   4

2.   Do you still "court" him with an occasional gift of flowers; by remembrance of birthdays and anniversaries; by unexpected attentions?
                                        0   1   2   3   4

3.   Are you cooperative in handling the children, taking your full share of responsibility and also backing him up?   0   1   2   3   4

4.   Do you make it a point never to criticize him before others?   0   1   2   3   4

5.   Do you share at least half your recreation hours with him?   0   1   2   3   4

6.   Do you show interest in and respect for his intellectual life?   0   1   2   3   4

7.   Do you show as much consideration and courtesy to his relatives as you do to your own?   0   1   2   3   4

8.   Do you enter sympathetically into his plans for social activities, trying to do your full share as a hostess in your own home and, when a guest in the homes of others, trying to make him appear to the best possible advantage?
                                        0   1   2   3   4

Perfect Husband Quiz

1. Do you try to make the home interesting, attractive, cheerful, a place of rest and relaxation—devoting as much thought and study to that as you would to a job "downtown"?

0 1 2 3 4

2. Do you encourage your wife to go out frequently with her women friends, though it means leaving you home alone? 0 1 2 3 4

3. Do you serve meals that are enticing in variety and attractiveness?

0 1 2 3 4

4. Do you handle household finances in a businesslike way?

0 1 2 3 4

5. Do you keep yourself attractive (though not offensively so!) in appearance, in order that your wife may be proud to have everyone know you are her husband?

0 1 2 3 4

6. Are you a "good sport," cheerful and uncomplaining, punctual, not nagging, not insisting on having your own way or the last word, not making a fuss over the trifles or requiring her to solve minor problems that you should handle alone?

0 1 2 3 4

7. Do you bolster your wife's ego by not comparing her unfavorably with more successful women but making her feel that she is the most successful woman you ever met?

0 1 2 3 4

8. Do you prevent your mother and other relatives from intruding unduly, and show courtesy and consideration to her own relatives?

0 1 2 3 4

Figure 20.9 (top) A spoof on quizzes from Radical Therapist, (left) for a perfect wife and (right) for a perfect husband. Scoring on each item is as follows: 0 = "never," 1 = "sometimes," 2 = "an average amount," 3 = "usually," and 4 = "regularly." The "perfect" score on the eight items is a total of 32.

Figure 20.10 (opposite, bottom) Physical proximity, similarity of ethnic and social background, temperamental compatibility, and similarity of interests, values, and behavior are all factors that tend to influence the choice of whom one marries.

relationship tended to be equalitarian. If this couple had children, however, the wife lost power in the relationship. If the husband had a clearly high-status job, he tended to dominate the relationship. In husband-dominated families, the husband tended to disapprove of his wife's working, thereby minimizing her chance to gain some power in the relationship.

Blood and Wolfe found that the power structure in the early-adulthood marriage is established very early, usually within the first year. The power automatically goes to the person who has the greater resources, which include financial ability, education, know-how, status, and competence. This means that the person who is least dependent on the relationship holds the power. The partner who can say "Think what things would be like if I were not here—no sex, no clean clothes, no food, no money, no house" runs things.

It is common for the young wife to work during the early years of a marriage, at least until the couple decides to start a family. Today, the period between marriage and parenthood is becoming longer as couples devote more time to getting to know each other and to enjoying life together. In addition, a growing number of women are continuing to work even after they begin a family. Some work because their income is economically important; college-educated wives may feel that they have important careers to develop; some wives simply find work rewarding. Among couples with well-educated working wives, more and more are choosing not to have children at all or to divide the responsibilities of child care more evenly between the husband and wife. There no longer seems to be a single, rigid model for the right kind of marriage (C. Rogers, 1972). Instead, the trend is toward establishing a relationship that optimizes the personal satisfaction and growth of each individual.

Divorce and Remarriage. Not all marriages are happy. Divorce offers a way out of an unhappy marriage, and it is becoming more acceptable. Therefore, increasing numbers of young adults find themselves making decisions about divorce and remarriage. These changes in life style place additional demands on a person to change and develop.

Failures in marriage might better be defined in terms of psychological unhappiness and dissatisfaction than in legal terms. A number of factors tend to make couples unhappy but not necessarily divorced. As might be expected, the more dissimilar the personalities of the partners, except for such socially accepted differences as assertiveness or passivity, the more unhappy the marriage will be. When a man and woman do not accurately see what the other is like, there is apt to be a great deal of marital discord and dissatisfaction. In addition, the less the husband and wife agree about their roles, the lower their marital satisfaction will be. Finally, an unwillingness to change and adapt to the changing demands, roles, and responsibilities of the marital relationship usually goes along with an unsatisfactory relationship (Murstein, 1971).

Some relationships seem to last in spite of it all; others do not. In the young adult years, marriages seem especially subject to failure, and, if the couple has children, the chances of failure increase. If the partners are both under twenty at the time of marriage, they are twice as likely to become divorced (Lasswell and Lasswell, 1973). Couples with higher incomes and more education are also more likely to seek divorce.

Increasingly, and this is especially true for younger adults, couples who are unhappy in marriage are less likely to persist in a dismal relationship. The United States has the highest divorce rate in the world; about 40 percent of all American marriages end in divorce. But in sunny, single California, the divorce rate in 1971 reached 70 percent. However, these statistics do not account for remarriages and divorces; therefore, the number of first marriages that end in divorce is about 25 percent nationwide.

Most people do learn from failure, at least in marriage. Second marriages generally are as happy as those first marriages that endure. Statistics show that 75 percent remarry within five years of their divorce (Kimmel, 1974). Apparently, people are not disillusioned with marriage but only with the relationship they were in. More and more, the trend in our society is toward serial or sequential marriages.

The reasons for remarrying are similar to the reasons for marrying in the first place. People remarry for love. Also, especially for women, it is socially more acceptable to be remarried than to be unmarried (Rollin, 1973). Women with children are likely to be intent on finding a husband. Even divorced men who looked forward to a swinging life are likely to tire of it and find themselves wanting to remarry. People who marry again seem to work hard at it. Young adults who have divorced and remarried report lack of motivation as a major reason for their first failure.

New Styles of Marriage and Intimacy.   In the view of some younger adults, traditional marriage has failed and must be replaced with other styles of

intimacy. Alternative life styles such as singlehood, cohabitation, mate swapping, contract marriage, communal living, and group marriage that some individuals are experimenting with today are not new forms of human relationships. What is new is the increasing openness to and awareness of these different styles of expressing human sexuality, intimacy, and affection.

"Singlehood," when the individual chooses to remain unmarried, is a new style of life and living that is rapidly emerging in Western societies. Nearly 13 million of the United States' 48 million single adults are between twenty and thirty-four years old (U.S. Bureau of the Census, 1972b). Although, as was stated earlier, most divorced people remarry, the number of persons under thirty-five who have divorced but not remarried has doubled in the past ten years. Singlehood has become more attractive because it offers both sexes an extended period of time in which to find themselves as well as to enjoy themselves.

"Cohabitation," or living together without marriage, as Judith Lipetz and Keith Davis (1972) point out, is not a new phenomenon, but its present visibility, the frequency of these relationships among college-educated individuals, and their tendency to be emotionally rather than financially based is new. Many couples who live together eventually do marry each other. Most see living together as a kind of trial marriage, a time for getting to know each other, a time for seeing if the relationship can bear the closeness and realities of everyday life. For many young people, it involves the same kind of commitment and involvement as a legal marriage. Sometimes partners become dissatisfied with this kind of arrangement because it lacks the apparent stability, security, and futurity of the married relationship. If the relationship does not work out, the partners are legally free, although generally not emotionally free, to leave.

"Mate swapping," also called "swinging," is perhaps a new approach to extramarital sex in this society. It has been estimated that 2-1/2 million couples in the United States exchange partners on a somewhat regular basis—that is, three or more times a year—and that some 8 million couples have tried it at least once (Denfeld and Gordon, 1973). People who support this life style say that it enriches their marriage, that it provides variety, and that it contributes to individual growth, which makes marriage mutually satisfying. People who disapprove of mate swapping say that it is immoral or that it is imper-

Figure 20.11 Other styles of marriage
and living are being tried by those
young adults who do not see traditional
marriage as the best way to satisfy their
needs for affection, intimacy, sexuality,
and a sense of community.

sonal. Because the emphasis of mate swapping is on impersonality, advocates of swinging counter that this very effect keeps it from becoming a threat to the marriage.

For those young couples who try to keep their relationships open and flexible, "contract marriages" are becoming popular (Sheresky and Mannes, 1972). In this form of marriage, the couple draws up a contract or statement that specifies the obligations of each partner and communicates their expectations about the relationship to each other. The goal of a contract marriage is to increase mutual understanding of each partner's interests, values, and attitudes.

"Communal living" is generally associated with the young and unmarried. There are, however, a number of communes made up of married couples who feel that only this style of living can make marriage and families satisfying. One thing most communes seem to have in common is the desire to achieve intimacy within the context of an extended family unit (Kanter, 1973).

"Group marriage," which may involve any number of married couples, is a relatively rare form of marriage in American society. Larry and Joan Constantine (1973), who studied ten such marriages, found that six people appear to be the optimal group size and that people enter this kind of relationship for the same reason that others enter a monogamous marriage: for love, security, sex, child rearing, and companionship.

Parenthood

Although young married couples today tend to postpone beginning a family, eventually most young adult couples do have children. Statistics tell us that over 90 percent of the women in the United States have at least one child (Lasswell and Lasswell, 1973). However, fewer couples now have children because they have to for religious or economic reasons. Increasingly, couples have children because they want to.

Becoming a mother and father has an important impact on both wife and husband and demands major adjustments in the marital relationship. The birth of the first child turns a twosome into a threesome, adds extra chores (especially for the mother), and reduces the time and energy that husband and wife have for each other. Before parenthood, there is only one relationship: between the husband and the wife. After the first child arrives, there are four: husband-wife, father-child, mother-child, and mother-father-child. With each additional child, there is a geometric increase in family relationships and responsibilities.

However, the aspect of parenthood that seems crucial to marital happiness is not the number of children a couple has, nor the spacing between the children, but that the couple has the number of children that they wanted to have (Christensen, 1968).

Recent social changes are also influencing the transition to parenthood and the resulting experience. For example, Alice Rossi (1968) notes that, first, there is now less cultural pressure on women to assume the role of motherhood. As a result, motherhood can be a more voluntary and pleasurable experience than it used to be. Second, the increased time between marriage and parenthood, when the wife generally works, and the tendency for more mothers to continue working allows more time for an equalitarian relationship to develop between the husband and wife, so that decisions and household responsibilities are shared. This sharing of responsibilities is likely to carry over into the role of parent, giving the woman more autonomy and the man more respon-

Figure 20.12 Styles of parenthood among young adults reflect differing roles, views, and practices.

sibility in the child-rearing process. Third, parent-hood remains irreversible. It is possible to have ex-spouses but not ex-children. Unwanted children are likely to be neglected children and not gratifying for the parents.

A woman's experience as a mother may result in less liking for herself rather than in helping her grow and mature (Bradburn and Caplovitz, 1965). The exception to this trend appears to be working and nonworking mothers who are happy with their roles. Mothers who like their jobs and who like working, whether their job is that of homemaker or career woman, are likely to like their children and them-selves more than women who dislike what they are doing (M. Yarrow et al., 1962).

The traditional role played by fathers generally is thought of as simply providing the pay check so that the child has food to eat and clothes to wear. Although many fathers do see their children as an economic responsibility and many children see their

fathers as the provider of the allowance, fathers play an important role in the child's emotional and social development (Nash, 1965). As earlier discussions have stressed, fathers can play a major role in caretaking. More and more fathers are taking an active and involved interest in their children's growth and development. This may be especially true in families where the mother works.

SOCIAL LIFE AND CHANGE

As we have seen, a young adult begins to focus his life and to make lifetime decisions about career, marriage, and family. These years are also a time of experimentation and expansion, a time for making friends, and a time for developing new leisure inter-ests, as well as for deepening old interests and friendships.

Many of the factors important in the development of love relationships that lead to marriage are also important in the development of friendships. People

who live close together are more likely to be friends, and so are people who share similar interests, attitudes, and values. However, not much is known about the friendship patterns of adults. What little is known indicates that most married couples have two close friends who live nearby and that, at any age in adulthood, men are more likely than women to initiate friendships for the couple (Babchuk, 1965). In addition, it is especially characteristic of young-married friendships that all the friends tend to be of the same age.

Because vocational opportunities for advancement may require the well-educated younger couple to be highly mobile, the friendships that they make in this period of life are not likely to be lasting. In contrast, less well-educated couples are more likely to have permanent friendships that revolve around the husband's job and that involve old high-school or even elementary-school friends.

Married individuals also are more likely to have same-sex friends than opposite-sex friends. One simple reason for this is that, whereas society encourages single and divorced individuals to develop cross-sex ties, it generally regards opposite-sex friends as a threat to a marriage (Booth and Hess, 1972). Both married and unmarried people who work have opportunities to develop same-sex friendships with fellow employees. However, if a woman does not work outside the home, she is likely to find herself relatively friendless, aside from relationships with other women who gather for bridge or coffee.

The fact that much of the young adult's life is bound up with his work is likely to have major implications for his leisure activity. Ideally, work should be play. Unfortunately, the work we do usually is not our ideal, and so we have to find other outlets for our needs for recreation and play. The importance of recreation and play for the developing child and adolescent has been discussed throughout this book. Time for recreation and play is also important to the adult like Lauren in helping her use up her surplus energy, to meet her needs for relaxation, and to serve her need for creativity and self-expression. Depending on his particular needs at the time, an adult may choose either physical or passive recreation. For example, if a man has been lifting beams all day on some housing project, he may prefer to spend a leisurely evening relaxing with a beer in front of the television. On the other hand, if David has been trying to develop a series of equations to solve a complex engineering problem, he may look forward to playing tennis with a friend or to jogging

along the beach. Exercise, as well as listening to music, reading, or watching television, can be relaxing for an adult. In early adulthood, particularly among men, there seems to be a preference for physical and active leisure occupations, such as tennis, skiing, and basketball. Younger adults who read as a leisure activity are likely to prefer being amused by what they read, and they generally read on diverse topics.

Younger adults do not use all their leisure in play. Some go back to school, some work in the garden, and others spend long hours practicing musical instruments or developing skills in some sport. However, what is work to one person may be recreation or play to another. A leisure activity is anything an individual freely chooses to do. James Birren (1964) has estimated that adults today have twice as many free hours as they had in 1900. This means that the kind of leisure activity an adult chooses is becoming more and more important in determining his self-concept and his satisfaction with life.

SUMMARY

1. Early adulthood is a time when individuals are confronted with the task of becoming adult, of being independent and self-sufficient, and of achieving maturity. Becoming mature in turn means becoming aware of who one is now, of where one wants to go in life, and it means working toward one's goals.

2. In these years an individual typically reaches his peak of attractiveness, physical agility, speed, and strength. Although aging is going on, its effects are relatively inconsequential for most people.

3. During their twenties, many young adults make choices in such matters as a vocation or marriage, which will give them social identity. During their thirties, they turn their attention to developing their

skills and base of experience. However, the way that these early adult years are perceived and the kinds of choices that are considered possible are likely to vary depending on an individual's sex, socioeconomic level, and other considerations.

4. Stabilizing, clarifying, and deepening one's identity, self-concept, and self-esteem, rather than radical change, is likely to be the rule during early adulthood. Sex-role stereotypes, socioeconomic class differences, sexual activity, and intellectual skills all continue to interact with and reflect an individual's self views. In addition, sexual and intellectual development are likely to reach their highest level of expression during these years.

5. Marriage is a major developmental decision that is often made during early adulthood. Once married, adjustments must be made to new social roles and to living with another person. When these adjustments prove too difficult, divorce provides an increasingly acceptable way out of the relationship. For those who do not choose traditional marriage, other styles of marriage and living, such as cohabitation and communal living, have become popular. Regardless of the form that parental life may also take, further adjustments must be made once a couple has children.

6. Young adulthood is also usually a time of experimentation and expansion in making friends and developing new leisure interests, as well as a time for deepening old interests and friendships. People's friends are likely to live close by and to share similar interests, attitudes, and values, and married individuals' friends are likely to be of the same sex. Young adults may choose either physical or passive recreation and play, but, whatever its form, leisure activity usually remains important as a way to use up surplus energy and to meet one's needs for relaxation, creativity, and self-expression.

SUGGESTED READINGS

Berscheid, Ellen, Elaine Walster, and George Bohrnstedt. "The Happy American Body: A Survey Report," *Psychology Today,* 7 (November 1973), 119–123+.

Comfort, Alex (ed.). *The Joy of Sex: A Gourmet Guide to Lovemaking.* New York: Crown, 1972.

Kinkade, Kathleen. *A Walden Two Experiment.* New York: Morrow, 1973.

Maslow, Abraham H. *Toward a Psychology of Being.* Princeton, N.J.: Van Nostrand, 1962.

Rogers, Carl. *Becoming Partners: Marriage and Its Alternatives.* New York: Delacorte, 1972.

Figure 20.13 Active, physical recreation and exercise are a major and preferred form of leisure activity for most young adults, although social interaction is also important.

A mature sense of competence and self-confidence is often reflected in the high productivity and satisfaction of the middle years of adulthood.

21

MIDDLE ADULTHOOD: MAKING THE MOST OF IT

Our uncertainty about middle age is reflected in the jokes that we tell. For example, the middle-aged woman is sometimes a common object of humor: "Middle age is when a woman's youth changes from present tense to pretense" and "Forty doesn't tell on a woman. It is her best friends who do" (Birren, 1975). In our society youth is often regarded as the most promising time of life, and many young people seem to feel that, once they reach forty, they may as well find a rocking chair to spend their remaining days in.

Although our society may be oriented toward youth, it is controlled by the middle-aged adult. In fact, the term "the Command Generation" has been coined to describe middle age and the position of the forty- to sixty-year-old in American society. Middle-aged adults like Susan and Matt are now likely to be in charge of and responsible for not only themselves but also the young and the old. The advantage of all this responsibility is that it brings rewards in terms of power, prestige, and money. If for everything there is a season and if young adulthood is a time to plant, then middle adulthood is the time to pluck up what has been planted. The middle adult years are likely to be a period of both maximum productivity and maximum rewards.

One change that marks the middle adult years is that chronological age no longer serves as the positive marker that it was at an earlier age, when growing older meant becoming bigger, smarter, and more powerful. Instead of marking change and progress with chronological age, middle-aged people typically use their positions within various life contexts: self, career, family, community. In this chapter we will examine what it means to be middle-aged and will focus on those characteristics of middle age that differentiate it from other periods of development. After discussing the meaning of maturity in middle adulthood, we will look at the physical changes that affect the middle-aged person and the new developmental tasks that confront him. We will note that, although a person's self-concept is likely to remain stable, he may think that it has greatly changed. We will find that, as children leave home, their parents must learn to cope with changing family life and with grandparenthood. Finally, we will examine social life in the middle years and see that friendship and leisure patterns also change.

MATURITY IN MIDDLE ADULTHOOD

Maturity was defined in Chapter 20 as the ability to deal successfully with the changing tasks and responsibilities of adulthood. Thus, a mature individual in the middle adult years is usually seen as one who accepts and adjusts to the new demands of these years. Having learned to handle demands to change in childhood, adolescence, and young adulthood, the middle-aged person generally has a substantial and effective set of strategies for dealing successfully with the stresses and complexities that now confront him.

As noted in the last chapter, a mature individual also can be seen as one who achieves a fairly close fit between the way that he sees himself, the way that he would ideally like to be, and the way that he thinks others see him. In the middle years, then, maturity involves being aware of and realistic about the changes occurring inside and outside oneself and about one's ideals and goals in life.

During middle age, an individual typically becomes increasingly aware of the emotional, social, and cultural distance between himself and the younger generation. It is a time when men and women often attempt to bridge the gap by trying to communicate and work effectively with children and young adults, but it also is a time when most people realize that their interests and values are clearly different from those of the younger generation. The middle-aged person realizes that the young cannot understand his position simply because they have not lived as long or as much. Many middle-aged adults realize that they no longer want to be young again, and some tend to look at youth with thin-set lips of annoyance (Britton and Britton, 1972).

By contrast, the gap that middle-aged persons feel between themselves and older adults seems small. They come to feel that the old understand and appreciate their commitments and responsibilities. There also is likely to be a sympathy, and sometimes a fear, that draws middle-aged adults closer to the old.

Men and women generally become aware of middle age for different reasons. As Bernice Neugarten (1968) has suggested, women tend to define their place in the life cycle by events within the family. For a married woman, middle age is closely linked to the time that she sends her children out into the adult world. An unmarried woman is likely to become aware of middle age as she begins to reflect on the kind of family that she might have had. Men, by contrast, are more likely to become aware of middle age because of cues outside the family setting. For example, a man may find himself deferred to or ceremoniously treated by others for the first time in his life. Because middle age is generally thought of as the time of achieving occupational goals, men who have not succeeded in line with their expectations are likely to have a heightened awareness of middle age (Kay, 1974).

An individual's social class also has an important influence on his awareness of middle age. Middle age typically occurs later for middle-class men and women than for working-class people. An upper-middle-class man, say a business executive, is "in the prime of life" at forty and considers middle age as beginning around fifty. By contrast, life goes more quickly for the unskilled worker. For him, people are "in their prime" at thirty-five and middle-aged at forty (Neugarten and Peterson, 1957).

Middle age is also often marked by a change in life values and in the way that time is perceived. Instead of looking at life in terms of time-since-birth, as the young generally do, most individuals begin to look at life in terms of time-left-to-live. Generally, an awareness grows that time is finite, that there is only a certain amount of time left. Instead of taking the youthful view that anything is possible, the middle-aged person generally begins to structure his life, his ideals, and his aspirations in terms of priorities.

Maturity in the middle adult years also refers to the individual's ability to deal effectively with the complexities and competing demands typical of middle-aged life. The mature individual usually has developed a set of strategies that allow him to respond effectively to stress and change and to make judgments and decisions (Birren, 1969; Neugarten, 1968). For example, adults often find that they have too much to do and not enough time to do it. A young adult in this situation, even a mature one, is likely to get bogged down intellectually and emotionally. The mature individual in the middle years, however, seems to know when to pull back. David is more likely to be aware of the signs that tell him he is doing too much: the headaches, the stomach aches, the quick temper, the fact that nothing looks good to eat. A mature person is likely to say, "I cool myself down by accepting the fact that other people around me have to do their own learning and make their own mistakes. I stand back and simply don't let my insides get as involved as they used to . . . '' (Birren, 1975). Thus, one strategy that mature individuals use is to be less emotionally involved in a stressful situation.

Maturity in middle age also tends to be characterized by a sense of self-confidence and competence. This I-know-I-can-handle-it attitude helps individuals deal effectively with the demands and events in their lives. Because expectations are important in determining the outcome of events, the person who feels that he can respond successfully increases the chances that he will. Mature individuals are characteristically less self-conscious about the impression that they are making on others, as well as more self-assured and confident about their values and their ability to control and direct their lives (Birren, 1969).

PHYSICAL CHANGES

Adolescents may look forward to the social strength and power that adulthood brings, but as youthful appearance fades, adults begin to look backward (Terrien, 1965). Inside and out, the middle adult years are characterized by noticeable changes in the way that the body looks and works. All those little changes that began in early adulthood continue to change steadily. Muscles do not work as strongly, as quickly, or as long as they used to. A less active life results in morning aches and pains and in middle-aged spread. The skin no longer stretches so tightly over the body, the face has a few wrinkles, and laugh lines lurk at the corners of the eyes. The hair does not grow as fast as it once did, and it may become thinner and may begin to gray.

However, middle-aged declines in muscle strength and speed of reaction are likely to be of only marginal significance in a person's everyday life. Middle-aged people are not likely to be bothered much by these losses, because they have learned to compensate for them (Belbin, 1967). That is, a person learns to pay attention to the features of a task in order to determine what he must do to maintain or even improve his performance in view of his changing physical abilities. He begins to carry only two bags of groceries at a time instead of four, and at work he tries to avoid jobs where speed is an important factor and instead looks for jobs where he can go at his own speed.

Among women, menopause is the medical marker of middle age. During menopause, which typically occurs between the ages of forty-five and fifty-five, ovulation, menstruation, and reproductive capacity cease (Kinsey *et al.,* 1953). With menopause, the body's production of the sex hormones estrogen and progesterone drops off to a negligible level. In the

Figure 21.1 Although some physical abilities decline during the middle adult years, most changes are slight and unnoticeable because most people almost automatically compensate for them.

past, menopause took its toll on a woman's youthfulness and attractiveness. Today estrogen, or hormone-replacement, therapy is being used by more and more women to eliminate such menopausal symptoms as hot flashes, loss of hair, loss of skin elasticity, and changes in the breasts and genitals (Kirby, 1973). Among men there is no known similar abrupt cessation of reproductive ability. Rather, the level of the male hormone testosterone drops off gradually during the middle years.

During middle age, many people, especially men, tend to become concerned about their health. The most common major disorders in otherwise healthy middle-aged Americans are overweight (16.3 percent), hypertension (7.8 percent), and arthritis (4.4 percent) (Bierman and Hazzard, 1973). The death rate also begins to accelerate in the middle adult years, especially among individuals in their late fifties. The most common cause of death in these years is cardiovascular disease (39 percent); the second most common cause of death is cancer (24 percent); and the third, hypertension (7 percent) (U.S. National Center for Health Statistics, 1971).

There are, however, great individual differences in the rates of aging and in the way that people age. One can easily say that a woman looks young for her age or old for her age. In addition, not all physical changes that people connect with middle age are either necessary or due to the normal processes of aging; some may be due to pathology, others, to disuse. There are, of course, a number of things that an individual can do to decrease his susceptibility to the common changes of middle age (Hrachovec, 1972). For example, good nutrition, exercise, avoidance of cigarettes and too much direct sunlight, and an absence of emotional stress can retard or eliminate many of the expected changes in health and appearance.

Because American society stresses a youthful appearance, a variety of ways have been developed to make fading men and women feel, think, and look young again. Cosmetic surgery is big business, as is the world of health spas, gymnasiums, and weight-control centers. Make-up techniques, hair creams and dyes, treatments for balding, wigs, ointments and creams, and vitamin therapies all promise to make the middle-aged look young again.

With all the emphasis on looking and feeling young, it would seem likely that middle-aged men and women, who no longer look or feel as young as they used to, would be less happy than younger adults about themselves and their physical appearance. Gen-

erally, however, people over forty-five report just as much overall happiness with their bodies as people under forty-five (Berscheid, Walster, and Bohrnstedt, 1973). In both age groups, men are likely to be somewhat more satisfied with their bodies than women are, which indicates that physical appearance tends to be more important for women than for men.

NEW DEVELOPMENTAL TASKS

Whereas the developmental tasks of young adulthood involved becoming adult, the tasks of middle adulthood involve being adult. Being adult means being part of the age group that runs society and therefore means being in power, in command, and responsible. The middle years of adulthood are characterized by a concern with expanding and asserting one's adulthood and, potentially, with developing a new life style. The developmental tasks unique to these years include maintaining oneself as an effective worker, which may involve additional schooling or retraining;

Figure 21.2 The productivity and creativity of the middle adult years is often directed toward family, social, and community activities, as well as toward job and career activities.

continuing to relate oneself to one's spouse; assisting teen-age children in becoming responsible adults; relating to aging parents and parents-in-law; establishing and maintaining an economic standard of living congruent with needs; achieving adult civic and social responsibility; maintaining friendships and social ties; and sustaining and developing leisure-time activities (Havighurst, 1972).

Individuals in their forties usually devote a great deal of energy to the outer world. During this decade, they are likely to achieve peak levels of effectiveness and assertiveness. Often, as parents in their forties, they must deal with the task of setting adolescent children free to become independent people. With fewer family responsibilities, middle-aged women are likely to be drawn into new responsibilities outside the home. Adults in their forties also tend to get involved in community activities and citizenship responsibilities.

The tasks that confront individuals in their fifties are typically the most interesting and challenging of the adult years. Although this tends to be a fairly stable period in terms of an individual's resources, influence, and productivity, many persons may feel that they are losing ground (Havighurst, 1972). The fifties often tend to be a period of dealing with doubts about occupational, social, intellectual, and physical powers, and they are likely to be a period of striving to maintain what was achieved in the last decade. This may be a decade of life when individuals try to prove themselves, giving rise to such stereotypical examples as the balding middle-aged man who has an affair with a younger, attractive woman to prove his sexual potency. Just as familiar is the woman who tries to maintain her beauty by getting a face-lift. For some people the task may be simply to hang on desperately to what they have already achieved. For others, the major concern of these years is not merely to hang on but to create a relatively new and satisfying life style.

Whereas individuals in their forties tend to think of the future as infinite, individuals in their fifties often

change their attitude toward the future (Jaques, 1967). People begin to think of life in terms of time left to live and begin to realize the inevitability of their own deaths. In fact, many individuals deal with the meaning of death in middle age instead of postponing this developmental concern until later life. In this sense, Erik Erikson's (1963) final stage of integrity may develop gradually over several decades, beginning in middle age. Realizing that their remaining time is short, many persons begin to structure their lives in terms of priorities. Some shift the focus of their lives from one set of roles to another, more satisfying set (Havighurst, 1972). In creating a new life style, for example, some men become active in church activities, clubs, or in community matters. A scientist may shift to a radically different area of research; a merchant may enter the priesthood; an executive may sell a thriving company or give up a successful career to go back to school, to get into another line of work, or to travel. A woman, her family responsibilities over, may develop a career, become active in a service organization, or go back to school.

Other tasks that generally have to be dealt with during the fifties are the accelerating changes in body appearance and health described earlier, as well as changes in feelings of sexual potency and in sexual relationships. As William Masters and Virginia Johnson (1974) note, this decade is characteristically a time of tenderness, contentment, and tranquility in sexual relationships, and some individuals find this change disturbing when compared to the sexual fires of youth.

As at any age, approaching developmental tasks successfully in middle adulthood can sometimes be quite different from handling them successfully. For example, an adult may achieve occupational success in the middle years but may be unable to deal with that success (Birren, 1964). Some people turn to alcohol just at the moment of success and ruin what they had worked so hard and long to achieve. Others who had been successful at finding a spouse find that their marriage falls apart once the children are gone.

IDENTITY AND INTERPERSONAL BEHAVIOR

Understandably, the way that an individual characteristically responds to the events in his life and to his successes and failures in responding to the changes and challenges of middle age affects his sense of identity. However, the successful adult usually adapts to these challenges, maintaining a stable identity.

Self-concept and Self-esteem

In general, there tends to be considerable stability in the way that an individual sees and evaluates himself in relation to his environment from young adulthood into the middle years. For example, when E. Lowell Kelly (1955) gave personality tests to engaged couples and then tested these couples again after fourteen to nineteen years of marriage, their personal views

Figure 21.3 Changes in physical abilities or in life goals present new developmental tasks, sometimes requiring major shifts in life style. For example, Bob Cousy switched his involvement in basketball from playing to coaching.

and concepts generally changed little. Apparently neither more than a decade of marriage nor time itself led to widespread changes in an individual's self-concept or self-esteem. Even so, there was some tendency for both men and women at the second testing to be somewhat less energetic, less concerned with their appearance, narrower in their interests, and somewhat more ill-natured.

As individuals move into middle adulthood, they also are likely to feel that they have changed greatly over the years, but studies indicate that large changes are uncommon. For example, Diana Woodruff and James Birren (1972) asked a group of middle-aged people who had taken a personality test as adolescents to fill out this same test again but to answer it twice: once to describe themselves now and once to duplicate the way that they thought they had answered it twenty-five years before. There was almost no real change between their scores as adolescents and their scores in middle age. That is, they described themselves in adolescence and in middle age in almost the same terms.

However, the second test, in which middle-aged adults gave retrospective pictures of their adolescent self, tended to be relatively negative; they viewed their past self as much less competent and as handling life less well than they actually had as adolescents. These adults generally experienced a subjective, but apparently nonexistent, discontinuity between their adolescent and adult views of themselves. These

results suggest that, as they grew older, this group of adults may have manufactured a kind of identity gap.

The sex-role stereotypes of our society also appear to affect the development of one's self-concept throughout life. In Chapter 20 we discussed the influence of these stereotypes on concepts of the other sex and on self-concepts. Like younger adults, middle-aged men and women are likely to display different patterns of assertiveness and passivity, emotionality, and social sensitivity as a result of their particular social and cultural environment (Kimmel, 1974).

Although some women become more achievement-oriented and assertive in their middle adult years, and although the relationships between men and women in our society are changing, Bernice Neugarten and David Gutmann (1968) note that middle-aged men and women still tend to perceive women as being dependent and passive as compared to men. When asked to tell a story about an ambiguous picture in which there is an older woman and man and a younger woman and man, both middle-aged women and men (ages forty to fifty-four) typically see the older woman as being sensitive to, or checked by, outer demands and pressures. The older man is generally described as being in command of the situation and as a dominant figure. The implication is that women see themselves as being submissive to men in their middle years and that men hold a similar view of their power over women. Apparently our sex-role stereotypes continue to be important during the middle years, and they appear to determine the ways that men and women view themselves in relation to other people and the environment.

Middle-aged men and women also are likely to look to different sources for a sense of self-worth and self-esteem (Bardwick, 1971). In the middle years, men are likely to continue to see themselves as being worthy or unworthy in terms of their careers or work achievements and their sexual potency. By contrast, as women enter their middle years and as family responsibilities become less important, they are likely to have to redefine their sources of self-esteem.

The self-esteem of a middle-aged woman like Lauren, who now becomes active in social activities, in work, or in further education, is likely to be determined more by her productivity and sense of achievement and less by her interpersonal success and by how well others like her. In this sense, a woman who finds a new role and who begins to define her identity apart from her family is likely to become more "masculine" in terms of both self-concept and her sources of self-esteem. Developing these new sources of self-esteem tends to be especially important for the middle-aged woman, because an important source of her earlier self-esteem, her attractiveness, is likely to have begun to erode.

Changes in Sexuality

Until middle age, the relationship of a woman's youthful beauty and a man's strength and virility to sexual ability are taken for granted. Consequently, as youthful beauty and strength fade, many men and women begin to question their ability and adequacy in sexual performance (I. Rubin, 1968). Telling middle-aged people that youthful beauty and strength have little, if any, relationship to sexual ability or to the ability to give and receive sexual pleasure does not stop them from worrying about it.

Historically, menopause has always been thought of as the time when a woman loses not only her ability to reproduce but her sex drive and her femininity as well. Fantasy about the relationship of menopause to sexuality saturates our society. Old wives' tales warn: "After menopause a woman is no longer a woman," "Menopause makes women crazy," or "Menopause marks the end of a woman's sexual desires and sexual attractiveness." The reality of menopause is altogether different. Neugarten and her associates (1963) have found that younger women are likely to characterize menopause in terms of shared negative cultural fantasies, whereas middle-aged women consider menopause a far different experience. Middle-

aged women are likely to see menopause as bringing positive changes. Only four middle-aged women out of one hundred reported fearing the experience, and college-educated women were least anxious about menopause. The postmenopausal woman typically feels better, more confident, calmer, and freer than before. Thus, from a developmental standpoint, menopause is far from being "the change of life." Most middle-aged women do not see menopause as creating a major discontinuity in their lives. Instead, they feel that "You get what you are looking for." In other words, if one expects to have difficulty during menopause, one is more likely to experience uncomfortable symptoms.

The best thing about menopause, as most women see it, is that they no longer have to worry about getting pregnant or about menstruation. Many women also report that their relationships with their husbands improve. Most middle-aged women feel that menopause has no effect on sexual relations, and some report that sexual relations become more important and more enjoyable (Neugarten *et al.*, 1963). Basically, then, middle-aged women tend to view menopause as a temporarily unpleasant period that is followed by a period of being happier and healthier.

Psychologically, a man's sexuality is more likely to be affected by age than a woman's. Because a man's sense of worth may depend on his sense of "being a man," perceived changes in health, strength, and sexual drive are more likely to affect his self-concept and, therefore, his sexuality. How well a man copes

Figure 21.4 Although doubt and worry over sexual attractiveness and fulfillment may occur at some point for most people during middle adulthood, sexual interest and physical and affectional expressions of sexuality generally remain a stable and enjoyable part of life.

with possible changes in his sexual desire depends not only on his general ability to adapt to changes in his life but also on his past sexual relationships, his attitude toward aging, and his self-concept (Masters and Johnson, 1966, 1970).

Thus, the loss of sexual responsiveness is likely to be due to psychological factors, not physiological ones. Nevertheless, the incidence of sexual inadequacy in the human male increases sharply after the age of fifty (Masters and Johnson, 1970). According to Masters and Johnson (1974), the single most important factor in reduced sexual responsiveness among middle-aged men appears to be the monotony of a repetitive sexual relationship, which generally means boredom with the wife. Other factors that may have a negative effect on a man's sexual responsiveness are preoccupation with his career or with economic pursuits, mental or physical fatigue, overindulgence in food or drink, or "fear of failure." In general, however, the richer and the more regular a man's sexual life has been, the more likely it is that his sexual interest and activity will be maintained throughout the middle years.

Intellectual Skills
Many middle-aged men and women fear the loss of their mental abilities. Often their memory for little things does not seem to be as good as it once was. It sometimes takes them longer to finish a task or solve a problem because they become distracted. As we will see, these common changes in intellectual skills are no reason for a person to believe that his mind is slipping.

Instead, if a person is healthy, his verbal and reasoning skills are likely to get even better. For example, individuals continue to store new information just as they always have. In fact, there may be considerable increases in a person's vocabulary during middle age (Birren, 1973). An individual's ability to organize and to process visual information, as in finding a simple figure in a complex one, also gets better in middle adulthood. In addition, the ability to think flexibly, to shift the set of one's mind to solve a problem, is likely to be as good as it was in early adulthood. Only when an individual is asked to do a task that involves coordinated eye-hand movements does he tend to do less well than he used to. Overall, this means that people are likely to show improvement in their thinking, comprehension, and informational skills into middle age but that some of their motor skills are not likely to be as good as they once were (Baltes and Schaie, 1974). Thus, if successful performance depends on speed, middle-aged David will probably do worse than a younger person. However, this poor performance is likely to be due more to his relatively slower responses than to any changes in his intellectual abilities.

Differences in intellectual functioning among people also are likely to become even more marked throughout middle adulthood. Thus, individuals who were high in intellectual skills in their younger years are likely to become even more skilled. As in young adulthood, the amount of education that an individual has had, his social class, his health, how active he is, and how stimulating his current environment is are likely to be more important than age in determining just how well or how poorly he functions intellectually (Botwinick, 1967).

Despite the fact that many middle-aged people believe that their memory is not as good as it was and fear that they cannot learn new skills as easily as they used to, a person's ability to remember and to learn shows little decline in middle age. If middle-aged individuals are given as much time as they need to learn or remember, they are likely to do about as well as younger adults (Canestrari, 1963). Again, health, education, and individual differences make a difference. In addition, how motivated an individual is to learn or remember, how interesting or meaningful the information is, and how much recent educational experience he has had are likely to be more important than age in affecting learning and memory abilities (Arenberg, 1973).

Many people presume that middle-aged adults are somehow more rigid than younger adults. They believe that a middle-aged person holds a particular point of view and resists change when the situation calls for it. This assumption appears to be strengthened by the finding that a person over fifty-five is more likely to agree with clichés than younger adults and adolescents are (Riegel and Riegel, 1960). However, what appears to be a rigid approach to problem solving is less likely to be due to a "rigid" or "cautious" attitude than to the way that the middle-aged adult's abilities have been affected by his past experiences. For example, a middle-aged adult tends to solve problems and to think as well as a younger adult, but his greater number of past associations and experiences may interfere with how flexibly he solves problems. In addition, well-established ways of solving problems, which tend to look rigid in laboratory-test situations, may serve individuals well as they confront the problems of everyday life.

The ability to be creative also does not belong solely to youth. Adults in their middle years are often equally creative. In fact, when creativity is examined in terms of total productivity rather than in terms of quality, creativity peaks at an older age. For example, the decade of the forties is generally the most productive period of life in the humanities, sciences, and arts (Dennis, 1966). Although an individual's productivity in the arts declines somewhat during the middle years, the productivity of persons working in the sciences and humanities remains fairly stable. The

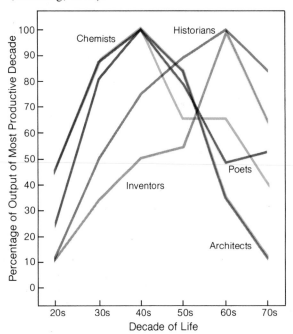

Figure 21.5 Graph showing productivity for certain professions, expressed as a percentage of the output of the most productive decade (designated as 100 percent). Poets, architects, and chemists usually achieve maximum professional productivity during their forties, whereas inventors and historians do so during their sixties. The data summarized here should be considered illustrative, because the subjects were not uniform in degree of eminence. Also, the units of productivity (for example, a sonnet versus a history of Rome) are not equivalent. (After Dennis, 1966)

Figure 21.6 Continued productivity during the middle adult years is illustrated by such well-known people as conductor Leonard Bernstein and novelist André Malraux.

earlier decline in productivity in the arts is likely to be due in part to the fact that scholarly or scientific creativity requires more time and a greater amount of study than artistic genius does.

MARRIAGE AND FAMILY LIFE

The life cycle of the family began in the early adult years with marriage followed by a time of bearing and rearing children. Now, as Susan and her husband enter their middle years, they usually face the tasks of relating to adolescent children, encouraging them to become independent and responsible adults, and adjusting to being alone together once the children have left home. As Evelyn Duvall (1971) points out, in many ways the family cycle resembles the life cycle of individual development. In each phase of the family cycle, changes occur that require individuals to adjust to new roles and to develop new ways of seeing themselves in the context of changing interpersonal relationships.

Because people live longer today and because they have fewer children, the postparental period of family life makes up one-quarter to one-half of a person's married life. This later-life period of marriage is characterized by its own unique set of psychological and social challenges.

Parental and Postparental Life

The middle years of parental and married life are a time of both relative stability and considerable stress. The family tends to be stable in size, and each member's roles and responsibilities generally are clearly defined (Kimmel, 1974). However, this can also be a time of periodic stress and strain for both parents. Some of the concerns that are likely to cause friction between parents and their adolescent children revolve around the selection of a line of work or a college, dating and perhaps selecting a mate, sexuality, an increase in independence and mobility, drugs, and alcohol. Solidarity, with periodic conflict, generally characterizes the relationship between parents and their adolescent children (Bengtson, 1971).

The adolescent's search for identity and independence is not only a developmental issue for an adolescent, it is also a developmental issue for his middle-aged parents. Parents must deal with the task of letting their children go. This can be an especially difficult developmental issue for the mother who may have defined her own identity in terms of her parental role. Many women are reluctant to encourage their offspring to leave home and find their own identities because, once the grown children are gone, the women will have to redefine themselves. However, Irwin Deutscher (1973) reports that the transition to postparental life is neither as abrupt nor as difficult as it generally is thought to be. Most parents gradually prepare for the day when their offspring get married or leave home to live by themselves. In fact, preparing for and anticipating postparental life is the most stressful point in the marriage relationship. By the time the event arrives, many parents have already handled the problem.

Parents prepare themselves in a number of ways. First, an important American value, the belief that change is both inevitable and good, lessens the impact of this transition. As one father put it: "Of course you hate to give up your daughter, but I think we all understand that it is the way of life. You can't stand still; you can't be the same forever. Life moves on and that is the more natural thing" (Deutscher, 1973). Second, middle-class parents often have a chance to play the postparental role when their sons and daughters leave home for college. Other parents get an opportunity to try out what life alone together will be like when their son or daughter goes into military service. College and the military not only wean young adults away from their parents, they also wean parents away from their offspring. Finally, many young people spend so little time at home that the adjustment to postparental life is gradual.

The transition to the childless home is likely to be easier for women who perceive their sons and daughters as "on time" in such developmental events as college entrance and marriage. If a woman thinks that her offspring are well on the way to being educated, married, and fully developed as individuals, she is likely to feel free to pursue goals for herself. As Donald Spence and Thomas Lonner (1971) note, this means that the fewer long-range goals a mother has for her offspring, the sooner she will perceive herself as having completed the parental phase of her life. Fathers, especially those who work long hours, who are heavily involved in their careers, or who travel extensively, are likely to find the transition less difficult than mothers. Thus, parents who are aware of their periodic opportunities to experience what postparental life will be like and who take full advantage of them will find it easier to be alone with each other.

Most couples find that being alone is a great pleasure. Generally, marital satisfaction decreases during the early adult years of childbearing and child rearing and reaches its lowest point in the middle years just before sons and daughters leave home for

good (Rollings and Feldman, 1970). Once their offspring are out of the house, however, a couple generally become quite satisfied with their marriage. The majority find themselves entering a new era of freedom: freedom from financial responsibilities, freedom to be mobile, freedom from household responsibilities and chores, and freedom to be the person one wants to be (Deutscher, 1968). Most couples also report that, once their children are gone, they laugh more together, they have more calm discussions with each other, they have more stimulating discussions, and they work together more often on projects. Wives, especially, are likely to feel much more satisfied with their marriage once the children have left home. Apparently companionship in the relationship, which tends to be reduced when children are growing up, is critical to a woman's satisfaction with her marriage.

Although the newly childless home presents an important transition point in the lives of middle-aged men and women, it does not mark the end of family involvement; instead, family involvement with sons and daughters enters a new phase.

Parenthood. Middle-aged adults are really parents to two generations: They have their own children to care for, and they also tend to become responsible for their aging parents. When the young adult leaves home, the parent-child bond does not end. In fact, young adults are likely to be in contact with their parents more often than with their siblings (Adams, 1970). Middle-aged parents also are likely to continue giving financial and emotional support to their grown children.

One of the major developmental tasks that is likely to confront middle-aged Matt and his sister Susan is becoming a parent to their own parents. Just as children and adolescents call on their middle-aged parents in time of need, aging parents are more likely to call on their middle-aged children than on anyone else. Marvin Sussman and Lee Burchinal (1968) note that the help middle-aged adult children give to their aging parents varies from economic support to personal care; from help with transportation to sharing of outings and holidays; from gifts of money and food to help with housekeeping and home chores. In general, research indicates that the relationship between a middle-aged adult and his aging parent is generally most satisfactory when it is characterized by independence and friendship rather than by dependence and authority (Adams, 1970).

In this developmental task, as in all others, individuals have their own styles of meeting the problems that arise. For example, the ability of middle-aged adults to adjust to having an aging parent living in their home depends greatly on the middle-aged adult's expectations and feelings about whether this adjustment will be easy or difficult.

Grandparenthood. Today, more parents are becoming grandparents during middle adulthood. Being a middle-aged grandparent means adjusting to an additional role and integrating it into one's self-concept. The younger grandparent may find life more enjoyable than it ever has been (Duvall, 1971). There are fewer responsibilities, and there is likely to be more money to spend on oneself, as well as more leisure time. However, individuals differ in the amount of satisfaction that they derive from being grandparents. Also, depending on the individual, the meaning of being a grandparent will be different, as will his style of relating to his grandchildren.

When Bernice Neugarten and Karol Weinstein (1968) asked a group of seventy grandparents how satisfied they were as grandparents, most expressed only comfort, satisfaction, and pleasure. As few as one-third reported that the experience of being a grandparent brought them discomfort, disappointment, or lack of positive reward. When asked what being a grandparent meant to them, some said that they felt a sense of biological renewal ("It's through my grandchildren that I feel young again") or biological continuity with future generations. This aspect of grandparenthood tended to be more important for grandmothers than for grandfathers.

Some also found that grandparenthood provided emotional self-fulfillment in a way that being a parent did not. This aspect of grandparenthood is likely to be especially important for men, who feel that they are better grandfathers than they were fathers. Being a grandparent meant being a teacher or a resource person to some individuals. In this role grandparents are likely to see themselves as contributing to their grandchild's welfare by giving him money or emotional support. Some people regarded grandparenthood as an extension of the self, so that the grandchild was expected to accomplish what the grandparent always dreamed of accomplishing.

Finally, there were some grandparents for whom the existence of grandchildren had little meaning or effect on their lives. These grandparents tended to feel a psychological distance from their grandchildren. Sometimes the distance developed because they were too busy themselves to cultivate the relationship; at other times it was because they disapproved of their own child's marriage or the younger couple's decision to have a child. Some grandparents who reported a psychological distance, however, said that it was physical distance that minimized the meaning of grandparenthood.

Neugarten and Weinstein further note that, beyond the meaning that individuals attribute to grandparenthood, grandparents find a variety of ways of relating to their grandchildren. There are three fairly traditional "styles" of being a grandparent. One is the formal kind of grandparent, who tends to leave the role of parent to the child's parent but who likes to offer special treats. The second type, the surrogate parent, typically a grandmother, takes care of the child at the parent's request and is most likely to be found in a home where the mother works. The third kind of traditional grandparent becomes the reservoir of family wisdom and sees himself as being in authority and as teaching special skills. There are also two less traditional ways in which grandparents can relate to grandchildren. The fun-seeker is the grandparent who plays with the child simply to have fun. This style of grandparenthood is informal, and both the grandparent and the grandchild derive pleasure from the relationship. The "distant figure" style characterizes the grandparent who relates to the child only on special occasions such as birthdays or religious holidays. These less-traditional styles of grandparenthood occur more often today than in the past and are more commonly found among younger grandparents, whereas older grandparents are likely to adopt one of the traditional "formal" styles.

Divorce and Remarriage

Many middle-aged couples wait until their children grow up and leave home and then end their marriage. Although the divorce rate is not quite so high in middle adulthood as it is in early adulthood, it remains substantial throughout the years just after the children are likely to have left home (U.S. Bureau of the Census, 1972a). During the middle adult years, research suggests that the divorce rate is higher for blacks and for low-income individuals without college educations. Less-wealthy people are also more likely to separate, because separation is not so financially devastating as divorce is (Carter and Glick, 1970). The demands on the individual to adjust and change, as well as the impact of divorce on individual development, typify the kinds of adjustments and developmental changes that people often face during their middle adult years. In some cases, because a

person generally has been out of single life for a good many years, the process of developing new dating and interpersonal skills may be lengthier and more stressful in the middle years than it is in early adulthood.

In middle age, as in the early adult years, most people who get a divorce remarry. The rate of marriage remains higher for divorced men and women than for single persons at any age (Kimmel, 1974). The major change in the middle years is that marriage rates among women drop below those for men. That is, whereas in the early adult years the women are most likely to marry, in the middle years it is the men who marry. This situation comes about partly because the death rates for men begin to increase and because there are simply more available middle-aged women than men. In addition, as we noted in Chapter 20, most people tend to marry people who are like themselves. This adds to the problem of the single woman who wants to marry, because women who have never married by forty are likely to have adequate incomes and to be well educated, whereas their masculine counterparts tend to be relatively poor and uneducated.

SOCIAL-LIFE CHANGES

Social interaction tends to differ in both type and extent as adults move into their middle years. Adolescents generally form closely knit groups or cliques with their peers, but, as they become adults, peer-group involvement loses its intensity. Over the adult years of development, individuals tend to become more involved in organizational activities, and they

Figure 21.7 Family relationships and responsibilities often change dramatically during the middle adult years. Adjustments to being alone and caring for grandchildren and aging parents are some of the new tasks that face many adults during this period.

also increase their civic and political participation. For example, middle-aged people generally spend more time than young adults in informal discussions about politics and in reading newspapers, and they are more likely to vote in national elections (U.S. Bureau of the Census, 1965). Throughout the middle adult years, individuals participate actively in politics by making contributions, circulating petitions, and becoming candidates for public office.

As they move from early adulthood into late middle age, more and more individuals tend to see themselves as interacting with others less often. However, Aida Tomeh (1967) reports that, in spite of this overall decline in social interaction, married adults are more likely than single persons to have more frequent informal social contacts with friends and acquaintances, particularly after age forty-five.

While a married couple's child or children live at home, the social activities of both mother and father are likely to be determined by their children's activities and friends: Boy Scouts, Campfire Girls, Parent-Teacher Association, Sunday-school teaching, Little League. When their offspring marry, however, parents are free to develop their own circle of friends (Bischof, 1969). Once their offspring leave, the mother is more able to develop attachments and responsibilities outside the home. Understandably, the transition from activities and attachments inside the home to activities and friendships outside tends to be easier for a woman who develops outside interests and friendships before her offspring leave home (Deutscher, 1973).

A divorced person who remarries finds many new friendships, not only because the spouse has friends but also because married people just tend to have more friends than single people do. Individuals who do not remarry generally have a small circle of friends, and their friends are also likely to be unmarried (Bischof, 1969). On the other hand, middle-aged adults who have never married find that their need for companionship, which a spouse would generally fill, must be met by one or more friends. Thus, most middle-aged women who have never married have a close friend or confidant whom they have traveled and partied with and who they turn to for help and emotional support.

As a result of various life changes, individuals often have more time on their hands than they ever have had before. The person who never had trouble finding some pleasurable activity to occupy his free time now has more time to do what he wants to do.

The person who has been too busy with job or career to develop interests outside of work may find learning to use leisure a difficult adjustment. Yet another person may look at his new leisure as a freedom that challenges him to develop a different and more satisfying life style.

Among other things, leisure and recreation activities tend to become less physically active in the middle adult years (Birren, 1964). For example, when women elementary-school teachers were asked how often they participated in various recreational activities, middle-aged women generally participated less than younger women in strenuous physical activities and social activities. Middle-aged women preferred to go to concerts, read nonfiction, and just relax.

Both men and women in their middle years increasingly tend to prefer quiet work and tend to participate less in activities, jobs, and hobbies that require quick adjustment, that produce excitement, and that may involve danger. Thus, a youthful mountain climber like David may become a backpacker in his middle years. A young adult who enjoys hang-gliding or motorcycling may prefer to watch others doing it when he enters middle age. However, increasing numbers of middle-class men, concerned about the effect on their health of sedentary life, have begun jogging, playing tennis, and engaging in other strenuous activities (DeVries, 1970).

As John Kelly (1972) has pointed out, when one looks closely at various choices of leisure activity, it becomes clear that in most cases recreational activities also are related to work. For example, an auto mechanic may read a copy of *Car and Driver* magazine, a physician may read a medical journal, or an individual might go to school during the evenings to get a better job. Americans apparently have trouble separating work from recreation and leisure.

This preference for work is deeply rooted in the history of our country and culture and is especially likely to be reflected in the values of middle-class middle-aged men and women. For example, when Eric Pfeiffer and Glenn Davis (1971) asked people if they would still work if they did not have to work for a living, 80 percent of the women and 90 percent of the men said that they would continue to work. Most of these people reported that they got more satisfaction from work than from leisure and that they did not want more free time. The people who had been employed also said that they had had "more fun" lately than those who had not been working. It appears, then, that many middle-aged people have

little interest in using their free time for purely recreational activities.

In many ways the preferences of middle-aged individuals for certain leisure or recreational activities and for particular life styles also tend to be related more to social class and to personal adjustment than to age or to sex (Havighurst, 1961). In terms of education and income, for example, the more of each of these that an individual has, the more he tends to participate in activities that are unconnected with his work and the more positively he tends to view leisure (Neulinger and Raps, 1972). Presumably money frees a person to do what he wants to do where he wants to do it, and education tends to make him aware of more and varied ways of passing his leisure time.

SUMMARY

1. Most people enter middle adulthood with a substantial and effective set of strategies for dealing with the changes, responsibilities, and demands that confront them. A realistic self-awareness is often further associated with self-confidence and a sense of competence.

2. Middle adulthood is characterized by noticeable changes in the appearance and functioning of the body. Whereas menopause is the medical marker of middle age for women, there is no known comparable marker for men. Attention to one's physical appearance may increase, in an attempt to maintain a youthful and attractive look, and most middle-aged people learn to compensate for any declines or losses in physical ability.

3. Typically, the developmental tasks of middle adulthood revolve around expanding and affirming one's resources, influence, productivity, and social relationships. For some it may also require the development of a new life style as their children grow up and leave home or as other events take place.

4. Many middle-aged people feel they have changed greatly over the years, but research indicates that large changes in one's self-concept or self-esteem are uncommon and that middle adulthood is generally a period of continuity and stability. In addition, whereas there may be some decline in sexual activity and intellectual skills from the high level of expression of the earlier years, such changes are often minor.

5. During the middle adult years, many married couples must face such tasks as encouraging their adolescent children to become adults, adjusting to being alone together again, and caring for aging parents. The postparental years can bring new pleasure and fulfillment (as in becoming a grandparent) or dissatisfaction and disappointment (if there is friction with children or spouse). For an increasing number of people, divorce and remarriage also take place, which involves new choices and responsibilities.

6. As adults move through the middle years, their social life tends to change in both type and extent. Friendship patterns often move from attachments inside the home to activities and friendships outside the family. Individuals tend to become more involved in organizational activities and to increase civic and political participation. Frequently there is also an increase in leisure time, allowing the individual to participate in new activities and to gain new satisfactions.

Figure 21.8 Leisure and recreational activities frequently change during the middle adult years, becoming less strenuous but still providing new personal-social interactions and satisfactions.

SUGGESTED READINGS

Anderson, Robert. *Solitaire and Double Solitaire*. New York: Random House, 1972.

Comfort, Alex. *The Process of Aging*. New York: New American Library, 1964.

LeShan, Eda. *The Wonderful Crisis of Middle Age*. New York: McKay, 1973.

Mead, Margaret. *Blackberry Winter: My Earlier Years*. New York: Morrow, 1972.

O'Neill, Nena, and George O'Neill. *Shifting Gears: Finding Security in a Changing World*. New York: Evans, 1974.

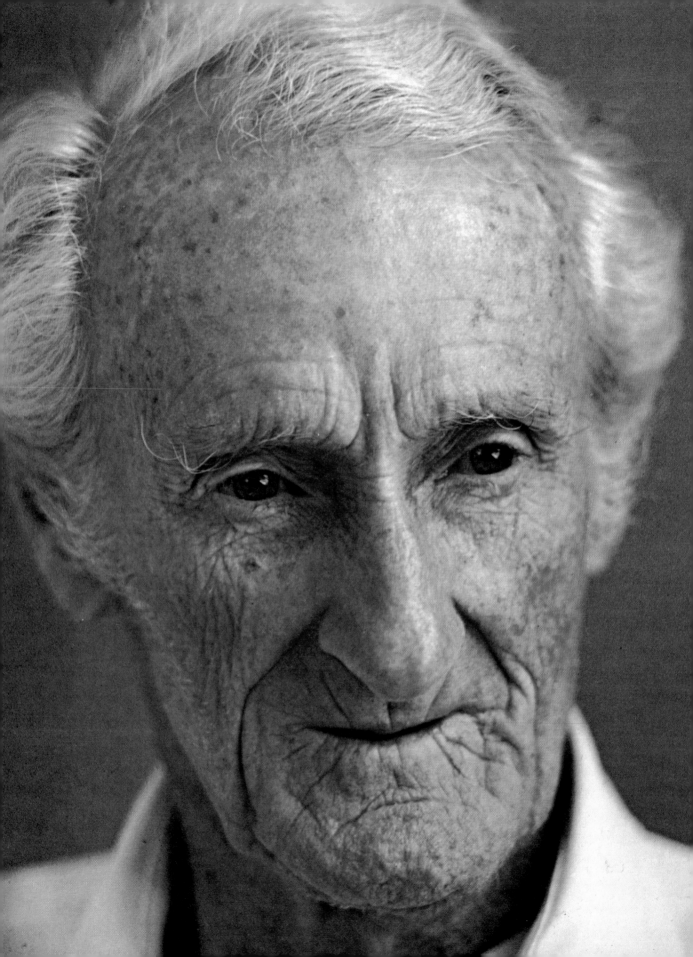

Aging is inevitable, but the rates and styles of growing old reflect people's life-long experiences.

22

LATER ADULTHOOD: LIVING SUCCESSFULLY

Human development continues into the last years of life. Just as change and development characterize the early and middle adult years, the years after sixty place their own unique demands on the individual to grow, develop, and change. Although Matt is different now from the child, the adolescent, and the adult that we have followed throughout this book, he remains the same person, and he continues to develop and change. He has more memories and a longer history than he once did, but he still lives in the present. At seventy-three, Matt's physical ability is somewhat diminished, but he retains the human capacity and desire to control his environment. He has lost some of those he loved, but he still needs to love and to be loved. His friends are fewer, but he still has the capacity for friendship.

Until recently, most people never had to worry about later adulthood or about growing old. They simply did not live that long. In the Middle Ages, to be forty was to be old. This new period of life is technology's gift to humankind. Continuous improvements in health care, diet, and the physical environment allow more people to reach their seventies, eighties, and even nineties than ever before. The twentieth century's gift of years are a welcome present to those who learn to manage and exploit them for what they can be. The later years of life can be fantastic or awful, depending on what a person is willing to make of them. Although our society is youth-oriented, the hard facts and figures are that America is graying. Whereas in 1900 only 3 percent of the population of the United States was age sixty-five or older, today 21 million people, or 10 percent of the total American population, are over the age of sixty-five. Although there are 2.5 times as many under sixty-five today as in 1900, there are 6.5 times as many over sixty-five (Weg, 1973a).

In this final chapter, we will see that the major developmental tasks of later adulthood are to clarify, deepen, and accept one's own life and to use one's experiences to manage personal change. We will find that some older people are happiest if they keep active, whereas others are happiest if they take a more passive and disengaged approach. We will see that the later years tend to accentuate early- and middle-life characteristics and abilities rather than alter them. We will look at the changes of later life and discover that reasonably healthy older people continue to have a rich sexual life and that the more a person uses his mind and memory, the better and longer he will be able to think, learn, and remember. An examination of family life will show that the husband's retirement is a major transition point, that the major loss in this period is the death of a spouse, and that older people who remarry are generally happy. As we will discover, the last developmental task of life is dealing with death, and this final transition comes easiest to those who can accept it.

MATURITY IN LATER ADULTHOOD

What growing and being older means to a person in the later years is largely determined by the culture he lives in. In Asia, the older a person is, the wiser he is thought to be and the more he is respected, esteemed, and listened to by those around him. According to Eastern philosophy, both life and death are part of the life cycle and within human experience. In Western societies, by contrast, death is regarded as being outside of life. Because they emphasize individuality and control in life and because aging and death are outside their control, most people in Western societies are inclined to look at aging and death as an outrage to their existence. Far from believing that older means wiser, we too often think of older as having one foot in the grave.

Figure 22.1 (*top and middle*) Although the observable effects of normal aging are relatively inconspicuous because they occur gradually over time, the cumulative changes of several decades are unmistakable.

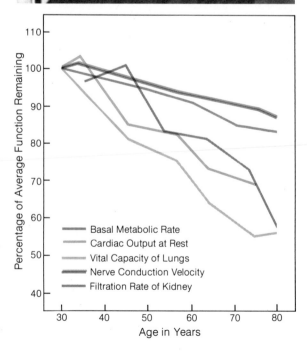

Figure 22.2 (*bottom*) Graph showing the percentage of change with age in cardiac output and certain other physiological functions, using 100 percent at age thirty as the standard. (Adapted from Nathan W. Shock, "The Physiology of Aging," copyright© 1962 by Scientific American, Inc. All rights reserved)

Many popular stereotypes reinforce our fears about growing older. These stereotypes are more myth than reality. One myth is that a person's chronological age determines his physical age. However, the saying that one is only as old as he feels has a good deal of truth in it. People who say that they feel young at seventy tend to age more slowly and more gracefully than people who say that they are old at seventy. Another myth is that all older people become senile. In truth, senility has nothing to do with the normal process of development and aging. Healthy older people still have active, inquiring minds. A third related myth is that older people are unproductive. The fact is that about one-third of older people have some income from employment, and a good number are still active in a variety of civic affairs. A final myth is that older people resist change. However, the ability and willingness to change in later years has more to do with life-long habits and behavior patterns than with age. People who challenged themselves to change and adapt earlier in life will continue to do so in their later years; those who never did still will not (R. Butler and Lewis, 1973).

If we look at a mature person in his later years, we usually find that he is able to accept his own and only life cycle. He may have achieved maturity by achieving "ego integrity," the final stage of Erik Erikson's (1963) theory of development, which is described in Chapters 2 and 20. Because the mature individual has had a great deal of experience with change, he knows what to accept, what to oppose, when to sit quietly, and when to fight, and he is able to accept his own limitations. As Erikson notes, the mature person is also likely to be one who can accept his own death. Failure to achieve integrity may leave the individual in a state of despair; he feels that he would like to live his life over again but that he does not have the time.

A person's expectations about growing older also seem to be important in how successfully he handles the stresses and changes of later life (Birren, 1975). Men who look forward to retirement adjust to it more easily and enjoy it more than men who find the idea distasteful. Those few who look forward to growing older also tend to grow old more gracefully than those who fear old age.

Maturity in later adulthood, as in the middle years, also means relying on others for help. Perhaps more than before, mature individuals are willing to be dependent on others when it is necessary. At this time, at least one intimate friend with whom a person can share the details of his life is especially helpful. Hopefulness, as opposed to helplessness, also charac-

terizes the mature adult who is living successfully and aging happily. Hope helps mobilize a person's energies and increases his ability to cope with change. When a person feels that all hope is gone, he is likely to lose the will to live. In the later years, the death of a loved one, the sudden loss of power, status, or purpose in life, or the loss of physical abilities can result in death if an individual reacts to the stress with a sense of hopelessness and helplessness (Seligman, 1974). Because Matt continues to hope and to believe that he has some control over the direction of his life, he is not only likely to handle the events of later life successfully but also to live longer.

PHYSICAL CHANGES

To most people, getting older means continuing to lose beauty, strength, and vigor. Although physical changes characterize the entire phase of adulthood, these changes rarely have much effect on a person's everyday life in the early and middle adult years. It is only in later life that the cumulative changes tend to catch up with the individual and begin to interfere with his everyday effectiveness and his daily patterns and habits (Weg, 1973b).

Although there are great individual differences in the rates of aging, most people can estimate an individual's age, give or take a few years, just by looking at him. During later adulthood, the hair turns white and becomes sparse. Whereas hair tends to get thinner on top of the head, it starts to grow for the first time on the chins of older women. The skin loses its natural moisture and elasticity, and it becomes more and more wrinkled. Many people lose their teeth, which causes the lower part of the face to become shortened and brings the nose, which lengthens as the skin's elasticity decreases, nearer to the chin. Eyelids thicken, and hollows develop beneath the eyes. As the skeletal structure changes, the spine bows, and people in their sixties become shorter (Weg, 1973b). The chests of men and women are no longer as full or as broad as they were thirty years before. Shoulders become narrower, and the pelvis broadens. As his muscles atrophy and his joints become stiff, a person's strength and movement become impaired. The dense part of the bone becomes spongy and fragile, so that bones break more easily in the later years.

Other changes also take place inside the older adult's body; they have no effect on his appearance but have a profound effect on his ability to function and to adapt to stress and change. For example, although the heart's structure undergoes little change, its capacity to work decreases. It probably works as well as it ever did when the person is resting, but, when he is exposed to stress, as during exercise or fear, his heart does not react as fast or as well. After stress, it takes longer for the older heart to return to its normal level of beating and pumping (Shock, 1962).

Many other gradual changes begin to make a difference in later years. The circulatory system no longer carries the blood as well as it did. As circulation becomes slowed by thickening artery walls, blood pressure rises. In addition, by the time a person is eighty-five, his lungs can hold only about three-fifths of the volume of oxygen that they held when he was twenty-five. Because his lungs hold less oxygen, an older adult generally has less energy for activity and less reserve to deal with stresses (Weg, 1973a). Because signals travel more slowly along the motor nerves, his reactions also become slower. Digestion is no longer as good, and neither is the process of eliminating body waste. All his senses work less well; vision, hearing, touch, taste, and smell all are much less sensitive than they once were. As a result, some older people may become irritable, moody, temperamental, or even paranoid because they no longer can perceive and interpret their surroundings as acutely and as rapidly as they once did.

Older people frequently complain that they sleep badly. Typically, people in their later years awaken more often during the night and sleep fewer hours (Feinberg, 1969). Because they sleep less, older people also tend to spend less time in deep sleep. However, many people make up for their lost sleep at night by taking cat naps during the day.

As physical changes become noticeable, the alterations in body appearance during later years tend to be more disturbing for women than for men. Older women complain more than men about their bodies, and they also worry about their bodies more (Plutchik, Weiner, and Conte, 1971). Despite various physical changes, however, a person may retain robust health and a zest for living into his eighties and beyond, and in the remaining sections of this chapter, we will consider in more detail some of the factors that contribute to a vigorous late adulthood.

NEW DEVELOPMENTAL TASKS

The developmental tasks of the later years are much more personal than the tasks of earlier life phases. Childhood, adolescence, and early adulthood are years for gathering and increasing strength and experience, which can be put to productive social use during middle adulthood. By contrast, the major developmental task of the later years is to clarify, deepen, and accept one's own life and to use a lifetime of experiences to deal with personal changes or loss.

As already noted, the changes of later adulthood are many. They include adjusting to decreasing physical strength and health, adjusting to retirement and possibly to reduced income, perhaps adjusting to the death of a spouse, establishing satisfactory but certainly less gracious physical living arrangements, and, ultimately, dealing with one's own death. In their later years, individuals also must face changes in their social roles. When Elaine Cumming and William Henry (1961) asked people over fifty about their active social roles—such as living with another person, keeping in contact with relatives, and being a church-goer, a friend to another person, or a shopper—they found that the number of roles for both men and women remained fairly stable until they reached sixty-five. After that, most people had fewer social roles. Men tended to lose their formal roles such as the role of worker or organization member. Women were likely to lose these formal roles and also to lose their roles as spouse and household member. Success in dealing with these changes tends to have less to do with wealth or poverty, education or ethnic background than with a person's characteristic style of handling change.

When people reach their sixties, they usually also have to decide whether they are going to continue to be as active as they were in their middle years. Although psychological "disengagement" typically begins in the fifties (Havighurst, Neugarten, and Tobin, 1968), it is not until individuals are in their sixties that they may begin to change their social behavior and level of activity. Some people refuse to slow down (Cumming and Henry, 1961). For example, a man who is confronted with retirement may find new jobs and activities. A woman who becomes a widow may refuse to withdraw from social events and instead seek out new friendships and a new life style with other widows. One person may find that the sixties are full of conflict: He wants to stay active, but his body and his social environment pressure him to slow down. Another may be ready and willing to give up social activities and roles, but this person is likely to be someone who has never wanted to be socially active.

When people reach their seventies, the task is still to make the best out of life. Many people achieve a new and satisfying outlook on life during this decade. "Self-fulfillment," "integrity," "self-actualization" are terms that various theories use to characterize the

Figure 22.3 Later adulthood often requires an adjustment to increased free time and the development of new roles, activities, and patterns of social interaction.

older individual who is dealing with his developmental tasks in the best possible way. Although some people withdraw completely from social participation, others remain active even if their activities are curtailed (Havighurst, 1972). Thus, it does not appear to be activity or the lack of it that makes an older individual more or less able to handle change. Instead, success in handling the social aspect of aging usually depends on how an older adult feels about being active or inactive. Some older people are "active" and doing quite well; others are "disengaged" and also doing fine.

IDENTITY AND INTERPERSONAL BEHAVIOR

The Romans described the relationship between body and mind as "Sound mind, sound body." This relationship is especially true in the later years of life. The older person who takes no pleasure in life or in living typically has little desire to adjust to the changes in his body functions. On the other hand, as long as an individual has his health, he is likely to maintain his emotional, interpersonal, and intellectual skill and curiosity. As we will see in this section, changes in views of oneself, in interpersonal relationships, and in intellectual skills are less likely to be related to an individual's age than to his health and the amount of stress and social change that he experiences.

Self-concept and Self-esteem

Throughout the adult years, most people keep their personal style of relating to the world. The social aspects of an individual's identity continue to remain stable as he moves from middle age into later adulthood (Neugarten, Crotty, and Tobin, 1964). If anything, people become more like what they have always been. For example, a man who was somewhat aggressive and hostile in middle age is likely to become somewhat more hostile in his later years. A woman who has always been dependent on others will tend to become somewhat more dependent in later adulthood. When large changes appear in a person's behavior, they are likely to be due to changes in health or to social and psychological losses such as the death of a spouse (Birren *et al.*, 1963). Under normal conditions, an older individual may less frequently come into contact with the social world, but, when he does interact with others, his behavior will be consistent with his social interactions of earlier years.

However, in later adulthood both men's and women's ideas about appropriate sex-role behavior generally change. Bernice Neugarten and David Gutmann

(1968) found that, regardless of their social class, older men and women, as compared to middle-aged individuals, see themselves as reversing their roles in family authority. Most people over sixty-five think of an older man as being submissive, whereas they think of the older woman as being dominant and an authority figure. The behavior of some older men and women also appears to undergo a change that is consistent with this reversed image of sex roles. Some older men become more accepting and open about their needs to nurture and to be nurtured. Older women sometimes become more tolerant of their own needs to be assertive and selfish.

On the other hand, the sexes also become more alike in some ways. For example, both men and women tend to become more eccentric, to become more preoccupied with their own personal lives, and to be concerned with their own personal needs. However, this decreasing interest and involvement in the world and increasing "disengagement" is more likely to characterize an older person who has experienced stresses such as illnesses, widowhood, or retirement than one who has escaped them (Tallmer and Kutner, 1969).

Despite the changes of later years, older adults are like younger people in many ways. The picture that an adolescent or a young adult has of an older person like David or Lauren may bear little resemblance to their own self-concept. Although the young often fail to realize it, there are as many similarities as differences in self-concept among the generations. When Inge Ahammer and Paul Baltes (1972) asked adolescents, adults, and older people how desirable it is to be affiliative, achieving, nurturing, and autonomous at their own ages, both adolescents and older people felt that being affiliative was more desirable than middle-aged people did. Middle-aged adults were more concerned about achievement than were the other two generations. All three generations thought it was equally desirable to be nurturing and autonomous. When these different generations were asked to report what other generations are like, the misperceptions were consistent. Older adults were consistently misjudged by others on those aspects of self-concept that remain the same across generations. That is, both adolescents and middle-aged people saw older adults as wanting to be more nurturing and less autonomous than they themselves actually wanted to be. Clearly, the self-concept that an older person generally would like to have of himself as an autonomous and fairly independent person is quite different from the view that the younger and middle generations have of him.

Of course, what an individual considers a desirable

self-concept is not necessarily the concept that he actually has of himself. It might be expected that older people, as they experience changes in health and social roles, do need more nurturing and that they do become less autonomous. However, as Robert Atchley (1972) points out, two factors make it possible for the older individual to continue to see himself as he always has. For one thing, older people often depend less on feedback from others and more on their own judgment. They frequently pay no attention to the cues from other people that they are old or dependent, and some older people simply reject the image of being old. Also, despite all the changes in social roles that an older individual may have experienced, he generally continues to think of himself in terms of former roles. A widow may still think of herself as Mrs. So-and-So, and a man may still think of himself as a carpenter or a lawyer after he retires. Taken together, one's own judgment and thinking in terms of old roles make it possible for many older people to keep their middle-aged self-concepts.

Because our society seldom regards the later years as desirable, it might be expected that older people would have lower self-esteem than they had in middle age. However, the same kinds of processes that help preserve an older individual's self-concept also help him maintain his sense of self-esteem. For example, as long as a person refuses to realize that he is older, he does not have to accept the negative status that many associate with age. Thus, many people over seventy tend to identify themselves as "middle-aged" rather than as "old" (Kuhlen, 1964). Self-deception in the later years, then, serves some purpose. It makes it possible for an individual to sense a continuity with the rest of his life that is not supported by either the reality of his body or others' view of him.

Sexuality

Older people are not supposed to be sexy, interested in sex, or sexually active. American humor reinforces the notion that the years past sixty are sexless: "Definition of old age: The time of life when a man flirts with girls but can't remember why"; "Description of the sexual life cycle of a man: Tri-weekly. Try weekly. Try weakly"; "Young men want to be faithful and are not. Old men want to be faithless and cannot" (Puner, 1974). When adolescents and young adults were asked to complete the sentence "Sex for most old people is . . . ," most responded by saying "negligible," "unimportant," or "past" (Golde and Kogan, 1959).

Because as we grow up our society teaches us that sexual interest and desire do not exist in later life,

Figure 22.4 Many older adults share attitudes and beliefs similar to those espoused by the younger generation, although both generations are likely to have a somewhat distorted picture of each other.

some older people do seem to respond by losing their interest in sex and by giving up sexual activity. For these people, the ''sexless older years'' are the result of a self-fulfilling prophecy. Some other people look forward to growing older because age provides them with an acceptable excuse for ending sexual relations. Usually these people have always thought of sex as being dirty or unpleasant.

However, most people continue to be sexual beings throughout their lives. A majority of older people still want to have intercourse almost as much as they ever did, and many continue to be sexually active well into their later years, as long as they have an interested partner. Although the lack of a partner may lead many older people to turn to masturbation in their later years, the myth of the dirty old man who is an exhibitionist or a child molester is completely unsupported. Exhibitionism is rare among people over forty, and older people are the least likely of any to be involved in child molesting (I. Rubin, 1968).

Some changes do occur in the sexual organs and in sexual performance during later adulthood. William Masters and Virginia Johnson (1966) found that these changes lead to differences in the experience of sexuality and sex but need not lead to impotence. Among women, the vaginal tissues gradually atrophy, vaginal lubrication decreases, and the uterus and cervix get smaller. Among men, there is a steady decline in the production of testosterone. It may take an older man two or three times longer to achieve an erection, but he can preserve it without ejaculating much longer than he could in earlier years. Older men also usually experience less-intense orgasms, and it takes longer for them to be restimulated after an ejaculation.

Thus, although the capacity for sexual response gradually slows down, reasonably healthy men and women have the capacity for sexual activity well into their later years. When Adriaan Verwoerdt, Eric Pfeiffer, and Hsioh-Shan Wang (1969) asked older

men and women about their sexual activity and interest over a ten-year period, older men generally reported more sexual activity than older women. The reason for this may lie in the fact that an older woman is less likely than an older man to have a spouse, therefore a woman is less likely to have a sex partner. It also was not unusual for men in their eighties and nineties to report continued sexual activity. Although the amount of sexual interest declined with age, nearly one-half of the individuals in their eighties and nineties reported mild or moderate sexual interest. Both older men and women also said that their sexual interest was generally higher than their actual sexual activity.

However, gender is not the only factor that may influence sexual activity. For example, older people of lower socioeconomic status tend to continue sexual activity longer than people in upper socioeconomic groups (Newman and Nichols, 1960). Other studies also indicate that the more sexually active men or

women are during youth, the more likely they are to continue being sexually active into the later years (Kinsey, Pomeroy, and Martin, 1948). These and other studies support the rule "Use it or you'll lose it," indicating that active and satisfying sex can last as long as life itself. According to Masters and Johnson (1968), only four criteria appear to be necessary: an interesting and receptive partner, regular sexual activity, reasonably good physical health, and a healthy mental attitude toward aging. Thus, as in the middle years, the richer and happier a person's sexual life has been, the longer it continues.

Intellectual Skills

One common stereotype about old age is that intelligence invariably declines, but, as we noted earlier, the idea that all older adults are senile is purely myth. As we have seen throughout this book, individuals generally manage to become what they expect to become. People who assume that life after sixty is downhill all the way will usually find their assumptions to be correct. Along with a person's expectations, his general health and how much he challenges himself throughout life determine how well his mind works in his later years. In general, the more often a person puts himself in stimulating learning situations and the more he uses his mind and memory, the better and longer he will be able to learn, think, and remember.

In some areas of intellectual functioning, individuals tend to improve well into their later years. For example, a person's verbal skills, in terms of word use and comprehension, will be better at sixty-five than they were at forty or at twenty-five. His visual skills, such as finding a simple figure in a complex one, also keep on getting better right into old age (Baltes and Schaie, 1974).

In later adulthood people also generally are about as flexible and as good at shifting from one way of thinking to another as they were in middle age. However, on tasks that involve eye-hand coordination, such as solving a puzzle or copying words, older people do progressively worse over the years. Older people also are quite likely to do worse on any task where speed is important. Being slower is perhaps the most characteristic thing about being older (Botwinick, 1967).

As noted earlier, the more stimulating an individual's life has been and continues to be, the more likely he is to make gains in intellectual skills during his later years. For example, in one study, men who had been bright as children showed great increases in

Figure 22.5 Contrary to popular belief, sexual interest, desire, and activity are a natural part of living that can last as long as life itself.

intellectual ability during their adult years, whereas
women who had been bright as children tended to
make fewer gains in intellectual ability as they grew
older. This difference seems to have come about
because most of the men had stimulating jobs that
forced them to think, whereas most of the women
became housewives and had fewer opportunities for
intellectual growth and stimulation (Correll, Rokosz,
and Blanchard, 1966; Kangas and Bradway, 1971).

It also is not true that memory declines in the later
years. For example, David's ability to learn and to
remember is likely to be just as good as it ever was as
long as he continues to stimulate himself to learn and
to remember. And again, health, education, and
motivation affect his ability. The meaningfulness of
the material to be learned also affects how well older
people learn and remember. Younger people, especially those who are well educated, are willing to
learn almost anything, no matter how irrelevant it
seems. Older people, by contrast, are more likely to
be unwilling or unable to learn something that they
judge to be meaningless, irrelevant, or trivial.

The amount of time that David has to learn
something is also important in determining how well
he learns it. Because older people generally tend to be
slower, they tend to learn more slowly. Given enough
time, older people generally learn and remember as
well as the young (Monge and Hultsch, 1971).

Just as having more time increases an older person's ability to learn, so the opportunity to practice
helps. Thus, as Harvey Taub and Margaret Long

Figure 22.6 Continued productivity
during the later adulthood years has
been illustrated by such well-known
people as cellist Pablo Casals, painter
Marc Chagall, and humanitarian
Eleanor Roosevelt.

(1972) found, older people typically benefit as much from practice as younger people do. When older individuals are allowed to go at their own speed and when they are given the opportunity to do a task rather than just watch it being done, they also learn better (Canestrari, 1963).

The capacity for creative thought and creative work also persists into the later years. People who are creative in youth are likely to be creative throughout their lives. Tolstoy, Voltaire, Marc Chagall, Pablo Casals, and Pablo Picasso are outstanding examples of older people who continue to produce literature, art, and music of high quality into their seventies, eighties, or beyond. Even more than in middle age, creativity and productivity are likely to be the result of accumulated experience and knowledge, as well as the result of a perspective that comes when one realizes that he has relatively few years left. Wayne Dennis (1966) found that, in terms of their productivity, historians and inventors, for example, tend to be most productive around the age of sixty. Supreme Court justices and statesmen are also usually older.

Some people become creative for the first time in their later years. Grandma Moses is one outstanding example, but many older men and women use retirement as an opportunity to develop their talents. Some take up painting, some learn silvercrafting, and others start to knit or write for the first time in their lives. Curiosity, flexibility, and a certain joy for life are important characteristics of the creative person at any age (R. Butler and Lewis, 1973). As long as individu-

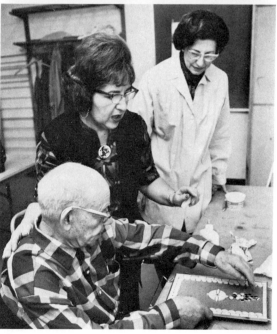

Figure 22.7 A person's expectations about growing older and the interests, values, and psychological resources that he has developed have a major influence on how successfully and happily he lives and ages.

als are healthy and as long as they challenge themselves to learn and to think, the myths of intellectual decline, fading memory, and worn-out genius are likely to remain just that.

In general, the most important measure of an older person's abilities is how well he functions in everyday life. As long as a person's abilities meet his needs, any decline in intellectual skills should make little difference. This point is exemplified by the eighty-two-year-old woman who operated a small business for her absent-minded and unreliable middle-aged boss. She opened and closed the shop, waited on customers, kept the accounts, took inventories, placed orders, and completed tax forms. In addition, she maintained her own apartment and never failed to remember the birthdays of her relatives and close friends. Everyone counted on her to help organize the scheduled events at her church. On the other hand, when asked as part of an adult intelligence test "How are north and west alike?" she received no credit for her reply: "Well, honey, I don't know how it is up your way, but around here the coldest winds come out of the north."

FAMILY LIFE

Each individual experiences his own life cycle of development, and he participates in a family that also develops over time and has its own collective life cycle. As a person grows older, the family grows and contracts with births, deaths, and marriages of brothers, sisters, nieces, and nephews. The older person like Lauren who has never had children will experience a very different kind of family life and sense of family integrity and continuity from that known by Susan, who has watched children grow up to have their own children. Grandparents may become great-grandparents; the death of a spouse may lead to remarriage or to learning to live a single life. With retirement, Susan and her husband may sell a house that has grown too large and move into a retirement community. As Frederick Brand and Richard Smith (1974) have recently noted, these communities, made up of houses, condominiums, or apartments inhabited exclusively by older people, require new adjustments. A couple may find themselves far from grown children and grandchildren and far from old friends. They must learn to live in a new town, in a new climate, and among new people. Some appear to thrive in these new communities, where planned activities may fill every minute of what might have been vacant hours. Others find that the lack of younger people cuts off an important source of intellectual stimula-

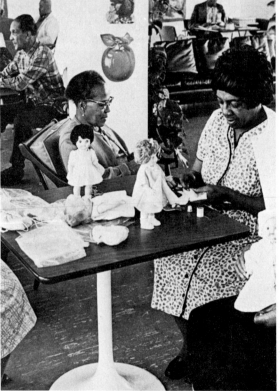

tion. However, the fact that so many older people adjust so readily to such an abrupt change in life style makes it apparent that their intellectual and personal skills are in good working order.

Marital Life

Being married is a demanding and problematic state at any age, and the later years are no exception. Often, the most significant transition point in later marital life is the husband's retirement. The man finds himself suddenly without his job or career and without daily contacts with his fellow workers. If his wife has been working and retires at about the same time, she also loses both income and independence. On the other hand, if the wife continues to work for several years, the couple faces a role reversal that can create additional problems. No matter what happens, the couple is faced with new problems and new demands to adjust. There are likely to be complaints and worries about how fast the money is going, disagreements over relationships with children, disagreements about moving into a smaller house or apartment, and health problems (Stinnett, Carter, and Montgomery, 1972). However, a married couple who reaches the later adulthood years together has probably lived through enough stress to weather this period.

More older persons are married and living with their spouses than ever before. The great majority of these older people say that they are "happy" or "very happy" with their marriages (Riley and Foner,

Figure 22.8 Family relationships and responsibilities continue to expand and contract during later adulthood, as new and old members come and go.

1968). The divorce rate among older couples is extremely low, partly because truly unhappy couples are likely to have divorced or separated years before and partly because being married is generally more desirable to an older person than living alone.

Many older people think that their marriage is at least as good, if not better, than in previous years (Bossard and Boll, 1955). Generally, marriages that were good to begin with tend to remain good or to improve, and marriages that were unhappy in their earlier years tend to become more unhappy as the couples advance into their later years. If the couple shared little companionship or satisfaction in the earlier years, their happiness in later life is more likely to decline. Happy older people generally say that companionship and being able to express true feelings to each other are the most rewarding aspects of their relationship (Stinnett, Carter, and Montgomery, 1972).

As in the earlier years of marriage, marital happiness is related to frequency of sexual satisfaction. In fact, in one study 28 percent of the older women who were happily married reported that they made love with their husbands more than once a week. When one considers that the average frequency of intercourse among older people is about once a month or less, it is clear that being happily married and having developed a good interpersonal relationship has a profound impact on an older person's sexual activity (Busse and Eisdorfer, 1970).

It appears that the more the relationship meets a person's needs for love, fulfillment, respect, and communication, as well as his need to find meaning in life and to sense a continuity with the past, the happier the marriage is in later life. Older couples who have happy marriages tend to have a more positive outlook on life and to be more active than those who are single or unhappily married. Apparently, once the couple adjusts to having the children gone and the husband retired, the marriage relationship is better than ever. For some it may even be the first time that they have been able to spend time together, to go at their own pace, and to enjoy each other's companionship.

On the other hand, an older adult is likely to remain in close contact with at least one of his children. Among American old people, 84 percent live an hour or less away from a child, and 30 percent are ten minutes or less from their nearest child. They see their children frequently, and, perhaps most characteristically in the middle classes, aged parents continue to help their children. Most older people,

however, generally get more than they give (Hill, 1965). For example, about two-thirds report that they receive support from their families in the form of money or gifts. And nearly one-third depend on children or other relatives to help with housework, meals, or shopping. Also, the older a person is, the more likely he is to live with his children. Thus, about 28 percent of older people live with a middle-aged child, usually a daughter.

Although most older people live close to their children and to other family members, about 10 to 20 percent of them have no relatives or family alive or living close to them (Riley and Foner, 1968). These people also tend to have inadequate financial resources. Thus, those older individuals who most need emotional and financial support are least likely to have them in times of need.

Widowhood

Three times as many women as men experience the trauma and grief of losing a spouse, which marks a transition to a new position in the human life cycle. Of women sixty to sixty-four, 25 percent currently are widows, but only 6 percent of the men are widowers. Half of the women aged seventy to seventy-four are widows, and it is not until fifteen years later, when they are eighty-five or older, that half the men are widowers (U.S. Bureau of the Census, 1972b). The loss of a spouse is a major psychological and developmental issue. Many women who lose their husbands also lose their best friend, their bedmate, their only source of emotional support and intellectual stimulation, their social status, and often their financial security.

Dealing with the death of a spouse places heavy demands on the older individual to adjust. Grieving over the spouse's death seems to be a critical and necessary part of the process of handling the crisis and of adjusting. A number of older people find it impossible to deal with widowhood. It is not uncommon for a widowed person to die soon after the spouse's death. Some even commit suicide, and the suicide rate among widowed people is higher than it is among married people, as is the rate of mental disorder (Bernardo, 1973).

As Marjorie Lowenthal and Clayton Haven (1968) have noted, the intensity and amount of grief that an older person feels when he or she loses a spouse and the amount of time required to complete the grief process can be somewhat reduced if there are others around to help the person through the adjustment period. If the grieving person is supported by a warm and loving family, if he or she has been able to anticipate and prepare for the loss, and if there is something left to live for, the grieving process will be shorter and easier. In addition, if the individual can rationalize the loss or make it meaningful through some religious or philosophical belief, or if the bereaved person has a confidant he can talk openly to, the adjustment will be easier, and the loneliness will not be so profound.

The widowed person often must develop a new social identity. Most individuals learn to see themselves in a new way and learn to relate to other people differently, especially people of the opposite sex (Kimmel, 1974). Widowhood is often a time for learning to live alone, perhaps for the first time. Many find it a time of being socially marooned. Friends and even relatives are likely to avoid the widowed person. They stay away because they do not know how to act or what to say or because it makes them feel pain over the loss or because they need to deny the reality that they are also getting old. Clearly, this can be a difficult period of adjustment, but once the grieving is over and they learn to deal with their new status, many widows and widowers also find a new sense of freedom.

Remarriage

Older widows seek out other widows, whereas older widowers remarry. After the death of his wife, the older man generally finds many women his age to choose from, whereas the widowed woman has little choice. In addition, society approves when an older man marries a younger woman but frowns on the reverse. Each year approximately 35,000 men over sixty-five marry compared to 16,000 women over sixty-five, despite the fact that women in this age group outnumber men by 3 million (R. Butler and Lewis, 1973).

Remarriage makes it possible to avoid such unpleasant alternatives to widowhood as living alone, living with a friend or friends, or moving in with children. Equally important, most couples who do marry late in life have highly successful marriages. Walter McKain (1972) found that, of one hundred late-life marriages between couples who had little income and little education, only six failed.

In many ways the courtship experiences of older adults resemble those of younger and middle-aged adults. Older couples tend to have similar incomes and social and religious backgrounds. The older man is generally a little older than his bride. However, there is one major difference: Over half of the older

people who remarry have known their new spouses for a long time before being widowed, many for most of their lives (McKain, 1972). Some are already related by marriage, some are childhood sweethearts, others are neighbors or old friends. The courtship usually is short and sweet, and the marriage, simple. Widowers rarely wait more than a year or two before remarrying. Widows are more likely to take their time, usually about seven years (McKain, 1972).

Not all older couples who are in love and who get pleasure from one another's company marry. Like the young, increasing numbers of older people are seeking alternatives to marriage. Living together is becoming more common among older people who cannot afford to get married because the marriage could mean a reduction in social security benefits or in a widow's pension. Even if all older men were to marry, the problem of older women would not be solved. Because society is not likely to accept polygamous marriages, many older women must live alone unless other ways to meet their needs for intimate companionship are developed.

SOCIAL-LIFE CHANGES

The major characteristic of the social interaction and social participation of older people is that they do less. And the older a person is, the less likely he is to be socially active. Thus, one of the toughest problems that older people have to deal with is the feeling of not being needed. However, most older people are not completely isolated. Only about 17 percent of the men and women between sixty and seventy-four have contact only with relatives who visit them or with people who live in their building (Lowenthal and Haven, 1968). After the age of seventy-five, people are more likely to be socially isolated, and older women are generally more isolated than men.

Despite decreasing social participation, people over sixty continue to participate in the political process. Older people vote as often as the middle-aged and more often than other age groups. They actively discuss political issues and generally are well informed, because they watch the news on television and read newspapers (Glenn, 1969). The fact that there are more older people than ever before, combined with the fact that they are more likely to vote than any other age group, means that older adults, if they were organized, could wield a great deal of political power. The Gray Panthers, an organization of older political activists, indicates that some older people are beginning to assert themselves politically.

When people reach later adulthood, they are more

likely than at any other age in their lives to seek out people who are like themselves. This is especially true among older people who live in an area where there are large numbers of older people and among older people in the lower socioeconomic class. On the other hand, middle-class older people may tend to include younger people among their friends and usually have more friends than older working-class people. Older people with a middle-class background also tend to be less dependent on their immediate neighborhoods for their friendships (Rosow, 1968).

Research suggests that, if an older person has at least one very close person with whom he can talk about the details of his life, he will adjust more easily to the stresses that usually accompany the later years (Lowenthal and Haven, 1968). This confidant does not have to be a mate, and it does not matter whether the person is male or female. However, an older person's confidant is most likely to be a spouse, a child, or a friend. A man most frequently names his wife as his best friend. Women are much more likely than men to name a child or a friend as their confidant, but they seldom name their husband, even if he is still alive.

It has also been found that some older people are more likely than others to have a close friend. For example, people just entering later adulthood (those between the ages of sixty and sixty-five) and people over seventy-five are less apt to have a confidant than older adults between sixty-five and seventy-four (Lowenthal and Haven, 1968). The fact that women are more likely than men to have a close friend during the later years may help give them their advantage over men in survival and adaptability. And older married people, who outlive the widowed, separated, or divorced, are also more likely to have a confidant.

In general, it is retirement that ushers in a number of changes in people's social life. But money, more than retirement itself, determines what an older person does with his time. Retirement makes it possible for older people like Matt or Lauren to spend more time in leisure activities, if he or she can afford them. Retirement generally cuts a couple's income in half; thus, a greater proportion of their income must go for food, housing, and medical expenses. Most older people have little money for leisure and recreation. Studies have found that older people of higher socioeconomic status tend to be more active, to have more leisure activities outside the home, to participate more in community activities, to have more friends, and to be more concerned citizens than older people of low socioeconomic status (Havighurst and Feigenbaum,

1968). The reason that poorer older people stay around their homes more is not because of lack of interest but because of lack of money.

The idea of retirement, which means that a person can have as much free time as he chooses, makes many people anxious. Thus, retirement makes some men feel useless and leads them to question who they are in a kind of second identity crisis. This is more likely to happen to the man whose life has centered about his work (Vogel and Schell, 1968). However, well-educated professional women who have devoted themselves to work may be even more reluctant than men to retire (Streib and Schneider, 1971).

Most people, however, have identities other than their work identity, and only about 30 percent of older people report difficulty in adjusting to their own retirement. People who look forward to retirement, who choose to retire early, and who have many identities tend to be the ones who adjust most easily to retired life. Also, people with many friends who are actively involved in family, church, and other social organizations generally find the transition to retirement an easy one.

Despite the likelihood of reduced income, the retired person is relatively free to decide what interests he will pursue and what leisure activities will occupy his time. What the older adult finds interesting and which leisure activities occupy his time is heavily influenced by the interests and activities of his middle age (Zborowski, 1962). If a person has developed many ways to spend his free time during

Figure 22.9 Apart from decreases in some forms of social participation, most older people remain active, alert, and interested in pursuing some activity and in enjoying the friendship and company of other people of similar age and background.

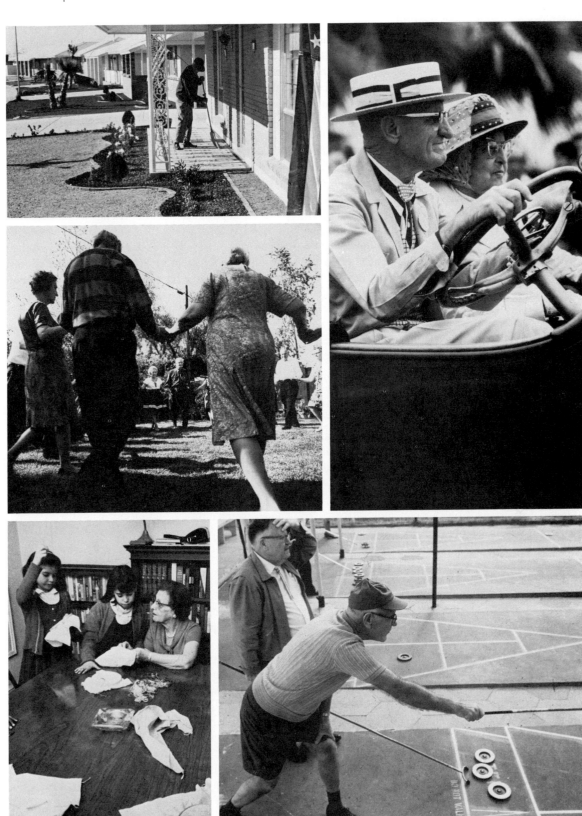

earlier adulthood, he will probably continue these leisure activities as long as his health remains good.

During later years, the tendency begun in middle age to participate less actively and to watch others increases. As James Birren (1964) notes, older people tend to spend less time in groups; their participation in both activity-oriented and intellectually oriented clubs declines. Older women are especially likely to spend more time around the home and in solitary activities. During later years, religious feelings and beliefs become more important for those people who had religious convictions earlier in life. Thus, although an older person may not go to church often because it is difficult to get transportation or because he may be ill, he tends to read religious literature and to be more interested in his religion (Moberg, 1968).

DISEASE, AGING, AND LONGEVITY

As we have stressed throughout this chapter, some older people appear to sail through their later years active, vigorous, and the picture of robust health. Others seem to spend those years in physicians' offices and in hospitals. To judge by the healthy, old age is merely a different period of life; to judge by the ill, it is a dismal period. Researchers interested in developmental changes over the life span are beginning to concentrate on this final period and to advance a number of different ideas as to why some people seem to age faster and perhaps die sooner than others.

Disease

Age tends to make the older person more susceptible to disease, and disease tends to make people age faster. The circle is a vicious one: Both processes work together and result in the loss of health and finally in death. Thus, the saying "Nobody ever dies of old age" has more than a glimmer of truth in it. In fact, when the causes of death were determined for some 12,000 individuals, the examiner found no cases of natural death and was always able to discover a pathological condition responsible for the death (Zur Aschoff, 1937). In this country, cardiovascular disease (50 percent), cancer (15 percent), and hypertension (15 percent) are the leading causes of death among older people (U.S. National Center for Health Statistics, 1971).

Even if disease does not kill them, old people are ill more frequently than the young. Because 86 percent have chronic health problems of one kind or another, they visit the doctor more frequently than the young do, go to the hospital more often and stay there longer, and spend more days each year sick at home

(Weg, 1973a). Older people chiefly complain of some ill-defined discomfort, rheumatism, arthritis, and digestive problems. Despite this ill health, 81 percent of older adults move around on their own, and only 5 percent live in institutions.

Older people are particularly affected by the close relationship between stress and disease. The more life changes that a person of any age undergoes in a short period of time, the more likely he or she is to experience a serious illness. Thomas Holmes and Richard Rahe (1967) have found that this relationship between stress and disease holds in spite of education, wealth, intellectual skills, or social class. They note that six of the thirteen most stressful life changes are characteristic of later life: death of a spouse, death of a close family member, personal injury or illness, retirement, change in the health of a family member, and sex difficulties. Because major life stresses and change tend to pile up in the later adult years, it is more likely that the older individual's abilities to handle change may be tested beyond his limits and that a serious and even terminal illness may result.

Aging and Longevity

Because science has not yet discovered the fountain of youth, the inevitable fact of life is death. Aging means that one may name a year when one will no longer be alive. In biological terms, aging refers to the increasing inability of a person's body to maintain itself and to perform its operations as it once did. The result is that, with the passing of time, there is a greater probability of dying by natural causes. Although this definition describes the biological process, it does not explain why people age.

At present, there are a number of major theories of aging that attempt to explain the why of aging (Timaras, 1972). As yet, none has been accepted as the primary cause of aging by all the scientists who study these processes. The first is the "wear and tear" theory, which maintains that the human body simply wears out with constant use, as a complex machine would. The "waste product" theory proposes that damaging substances build up within the cells and interfere with their function. The "homeostatic imbalance theory" supposes that the mechanisms that maintain vital physiological balances in the body do not work as well in times of stress. The "auto-immune" theory maintains that, as an individual ages, his body's immune system, which is normally directed against foreign substances, begins to attack his own body cells. The body ages because it can no longer distinguish between its own cells and germs or viruses. According to the "free radical" theory, the aging process is related to the presence of fragments of molecules whose original bonds have become unstuck from other molecules. These fragments seek new substances to latch onto, thereby throwing body functions out of order.

The "cellular" or "error in copying" theory maintains that the messages that control the orderly behavior of the cells gradually become so full of errors that the cells can no longer function normally. The errors that supposedly build up during the repeated copying of the cells' genetic message are somewhat like the nicks that build up on a frequently played phonograph record. The "genetic" theory supposes that the program spelled out at conception in the genetic material eventually runs out, simply ending cell function. The "pacemaker" theory proposes that aging is controlled by specific pacemakers in the body, probably located in the brain.

Although there is no consensus as to which, if any, of these theories is correct, other factors are generally agreed to play a role in determining how long a person can expect to live (Kimmel, 1974). As our earlier discussions would lead one to expect, the environment in which he lives, the food he eats, how active he is, the stability of his social roles and social environment, his marital status, his attitude toward aging, and how long he expects to live affect an individual's chances of living a long life.

The twentieth-century gift of technology mentioned earlier is a primary factor in determining longevity. In general, the more technologically advanced a society is, the longer the life expectancy at birth is. However, technology simply makes it possible for people to live longer and does not increase the life span appreciably. Thus, life expectancy for today's adults has not increased much since the turn of the century. An American who was sixty-five in 1900 could expect to live for thirteen more years. Today's life expectancy for sixty-five-year-olds is fifteen years, only an additional two years.

Heredity is another primary factor in determining how long an individual can expect to live. Longevity tends to run in families (Kallman and Jarvik, 1959), and children of long-lived parents are more likely to live longer than children of short-lived parents.

There also is a marked difference between the life expectancies of men and women. Generally, women outlive men in societies where they no longer perform hard physical labor, where their chances of dying in childbirth are small, and where sanitation is adequate. In our society, although more boy babies are born than girl babies, girls begin to outnumber boys after age eighteen. In the later adulthood years, there are 135 women for every 100 men. The life expectancy of an American baby boy born in 1970 is 68.1 years, contrasted with 75.4 years for a baby girl (U.S. National Center for Health Statistics, 1974).

In this country, a person's ethnic background also affects the length of time that he can expect to live. Black men and women have a lower life expectancy than white men and women (U.S. National Center for

Figure 22.10 Aging and disease tend to go together among the elderly. Older people have more chronic illnesses, are ill longer, and visit the doctor more often than younger adults do.

Health Statistics, 1974). Black men generally live seven and one-half years less than white men, or 60.5 years, and the life expectancy for black men declined by one full year during the 1960s. However, black men who reach the age of seventy-five begin to show a greater survival rate than whites. Although white and black women both gained a year in life expectancy during that same decade, black women can still expect to live six and one-half years less than white women.

In terms of life expectancy, Mexican-Americans fare even worse than blacks (R. Butler and Lewis, 1973). A Mexican-American has a typical life span of around 56.7 years. In comparison to American Indians, however, Mexican-Americans do well. The average American Indian can expect to live for forty-four years. Obviously, poverty, poor housing, and lack of medical care and education have profound effects not only on the physical and intellectual development of blacks, Mexican-Americans, and American Indians, but also on their life expectancy.

Extreme longevity is customary in three communities in the world, and it is common to live beyond the age of one hundred in these places: Vilacabamba in Ecuador, Hunza in Kashmir, and Abkhazia in the Soviet Republic of Georgia. By looking at these groups of long-lived people, one can see that environmental factors are closely related to their longevity. Their diets have much in common. All three areas are predominantly agrarian, and the people's diets contain almost no saturated fats, which are generally found in meat and dairy products. This absence of saturated fat is likely to delay the progress of arteriosclerosis and the incidence of cardiovascular disease. People in these communities also eat less than Americans do, and reduced caloric intake is known to be related to longevity.

Although all of these people may have uninteresting diets by some American standards, other aspects of their lives are far from bland. Alexander Leaf and John Launois (1973) observed that these older people continue to enjoy an occasional smoke or drink and that they continue to be interested in sex. One 110-year-old man from the Caucasus said that he thought that youth meant engaging in sexual activity and then admitted that he had considered himself a youth until he was 98. The majority of these long-lived people were married, and those women who had borne many children tended to live longer. Several women had borne more than twenty children. A one-hundred-year-old who had been married to his seventh wife for only three years pointed out the

Figure 22.11 The environment in which one lives, the food one eats, how active one is, and whether or not one smokes are all environmental factors that appear to partly determine the rate at which one ages and how long one lives.

importance of a happy marriage: "My first six wives were all wonderful women, but this present wife is an angry woman, and I have aged at least ten years since marrying her. If a man has a good and kind wife, he can easily live 100 years" (Leaf and Launois, 1973).

Another common element of life in these societies is that the people are used to prolonged physical labor, and they remain very active throughout life. People over one hundred continue to tend flocks, clean house, and care for grandchildren. In these societies there is no such thing as retirement. In addition to being highly active, these long-lived people retain their social roles and responsibilities throughout life, thus facing few of the stressful transition points that have been discussed in this chapter. In their societies there is little demand or need to be highly adaptive because there are few changes to adapt to. An additional factor that may contribute to their longevity is their joy for living and their emphasis on the importance of a worry-free and calm state of mind. Finally, as Leaf and Launois note, these people expect to live a long time, and, perhaps as a result, they generally do.

In our own country, a number of characteristics that appear to be common among people who live long and well recall the life style of these people from Ecuador, Kashmir, and the Soviet Union. Findings from interviews with individuals between the ages of 87 and 103 indicate that these people have parents who lived a long time, that they are happily married, and that they are sexually active. In fact, a good marriage appears to add five years to life.

Another characteristic of long-lived Americans is that their physical abilities and reaction times tend to remain above those considered normal for the later years, as do their intellectual skills and abilities. These people are physically and socially active. They refuse to give in to social or physical change. They remarry if they are widowed, they develop hobbies, and they take long walks and get plenty of exercise (Palmore and Jeffers, 1971). Long-lived Americans are also unlikely to be anxious, they generally have always been independent, and they have a joy for living. All are religious but not extremely orthodox. They tend to be moderate eaters of normal weight, and they have never slept long hours. Some drink, and some never have. Some smoke occasionally (C. Rose and Bell, 1971). Unlike the non-Americans who live to be centegenarians, long-lived Americans by necessity tend to be highly adaptable. Finally, all prefer to live in the present, with all its problems, rather than in the past (Jewett, 1973).

Figure 22.12 Older couples who can draw on the support and comfort provided by a satisfying marriage are usually not only happier but also likely to live longer than single or unhappily married older people.

How long people live, however, may be a less important issue than how well people live. Perhaps a better and more reasonable goal than avoiding aging is stretching out the productive middle years of life into later adulthood.

The Terminal Period of Life

The event that people look forward to least in life is death. Yet, what gives life its urgency is the fact that it does not go on forever. Although death can occur at any age, most people do not have to face dying until their later years. But at any age, the last developmental task is dealing with one's own death.

Just as it is difficult for a person to see his own aging, so is it difficult for a person to conceive of his own death (Shneidman, 1971). Although we all know that it must happen, we do not actually believe that it will ever happen to us. As stated in the introduction to this chapter, our culture encourages us to avoid thinking about death: Other people pass on, pass away, or depart, but they never die. As this reluctance to put death into words would indicate, the fear of death is common human experience. Strangely enough, many younger people and middle-aged adults fear death more than the older person does. Older people, by contrast, are more likely to fear the process of dying. Some older people find that living through the deaths of friends and lovers is more painful than the thought of their own deaths. As at every other period of life, individuals vary in the way that they approach the end of life (Weisman, 1972). Some welcome it, some simply accept it, some deny it, some disdain it, and some are filled with fear.

When a person faces dying, the developmental changes that occur are for the first time since birth timed more by one's distance from death than by his age. Not too long before they die, some people seem to act differently. The individual who is close to death becomes less personally involved with the outer world and may suddenly become much more withdrawn and distant.

Elisabeth Kübler-Ross (1969) has suggested that, whether death comes slowly or quickly, most people pass through succeeding phases as they deal with their dying. At first the dying person denies the possiblity of his own death; then he becomes filled with rage and tries to bargain for his life (perhaps with God), becomes depressed, and finally accepts his fate. Once he accepts his death, a person awaits death quietly and looks back over the years, accepting his life for what it has been.

Thus, the tendency of older people to reminisce about their lives is an important aspect of dealing with the end of life and a way for an individual to come to terms with his own life. At any age, a person enjoys looking back at his past and telling stories about it, but older people are likely to do this for a special reason (R. Butler, 1968). It helps them integrate their lives and gives them a sense of continuity with their own past. Thus, Matt, Lauren, David, and Susan now have a personal sense of the entire life cycle and of human development that they did not have as younger people.

Successful preparation for death is still a mystery and probably will always be one. By some objective standards, a person has successfully prepared himself for a developmental task if he handles it well. The problem with death is that it is impossible to determine whether or not anyone has been successful. Dying is a personal and unique experience, and birth and death are the only two events in life that each

individual must experience alone. Perhaps the most sensible preparation for the end of life, then, is a life well lived from beginning to end.

SUMMARY

1. What growing and being older means to a person in the later years is largely determined by the culture he lives in. In America, many popular stereotypes reinforce our fears about growing older. In reality, productive living and functioning in later adulthood depend as much on life-long habits and behavior patterns as on anything else.

2. Although aging goes on throughout life, it is often only in later life that the cumulative effects of aging tend to catch up with the individual and to begin to interfere with his everyday effectiveness.

3. The major developmental task of the later years is to clarify, deepen, and accept one's own life and to use a lifetime of experience to deal with personal changes or loss. This often includes adjusting to retirement and reduced income, the death of a spouse, and new social roles and living arrangements. And for everyone it ultimately includes dealing with the end of one's own life.

4. An individual's personal style of relating to the world is likely to be retained, if not accentuated, during later adulthood. When large changes do appear in an individual's views of himself, his interpersonal relationships, or his sexual or intellectual behavior, they are likely to be due to changes in health or due to social or psychological losses.

5. In general, the more that family life meets an individual's needs for fulfillment, meaning in life, and a sense of continuity with the past, the more satisfying the later years are likely to be. The loss of one's spouse is a major developmental crisis and must potentially be faced by all older people as they continue aging. Following widowhood, many older people remarry, finding it a satisfying alternative.

6. Although their social life may eventually decrease in type and extent, most older people do not become completely isolated; many, if not most, actively discuss politics and vote, most enjoy the company of other people, and most are likely to have a close friend or confidant with whom they can talk about their lives.

7. Disease and aging tend to go together in older people, forming a vicious circle that is likely to result in faster aging, loss of health, and finally death. A number of theories have been proposed to explain why people age, and research on longevity indicates that it is complexly determined and involves both environmental and genetic factors. Dying is a last and inevitable developmental task for everyone, and preparation for the end of life may begin at any age and take many forms.

SUGGESTED READINGS

Birren, James. "The Abuse of the Urban Aged," *Psychology Today*, 3 (March 1970), 36–38+.

Curtin, Sharon. *Nobody Ever Died of Old Age.* Boston: Little, Brown, 1972.

Kübler-Ross, Elisabeth. *On Death and Dying.* New York: Macmillan, 1969.

Neugarten, Bernice L. "Age: Grow Old Along With Me! The Best Is Yet to Be," *Psychology Today*, 5 (December 1971), 45–48+.

Puner, Morton. *To the Good Long Life.* New York: Universe Books, 1974.

Figure 22.13 The relationships of young and old, present and past, symbolize the continuity of human development.

FILM APPENDIX

PRENATAL DEVELOPMENT

In the relatively short span of forty weeks, a tiny human cell develops into a complex newborn baby. This film traces the course of the human organism's development, stressing two major themes: the remarkable sequence of growth and development that takes place during the prenatal period and the influences that may affect it.

The film begins with Dr. Bernard Towers (Department of Pediatrics and Anatomy at the University of California, Los Angeles), who notes that, although for a long time only genetic factors were considered important during prenatal development, genetic and environmental factors are clearly interactive throughout these first nine months of life as well as later, as discussed in Chapter 3.

Prenatal Development outlines, in one sequence after another, the fertilization of the egg, genetic transmission, the formation and functioning of the umbilical cord and placenta, and the development and functioning of organs and systems. To help highlight the rapid rate and increasing complexity of the development that takes place in these and other respects during the prenatal period, the film also shows the developing embryo/fetus at four, eight, twelve, sixteen, twenty, and twenty-eight weeks.

To demonstrate the ongoing influence on the developing organism of the prenatal environment furnished by the mother, the film is interspersed with a number of illustrations from these developmental sequences. Thus, research conducted with animals and with humans illustrates how the developing fetus can be affected by the mother's diet, drug intake, and psychological state during pregnancy. For example, Dr. Stephen Zamenhoff and Dr. Edith Van Marthens (Mental Retardation Research Center at the University of California, Los Angeles) describe research on malnutrition that indicates that nerve cells in the brain of a fetus may stop developing depending on the nature, degree, and timing of malnutrition that it experiences. In addition, the film notes that the defects produced by malnutrition may extend to other organ systems, at least in the case of rats, and that this can result in female offspring then providing an inadequate prenatal environment for their own fetuses.

As we have seen in Chapter 4, the first trimester of pregnancy is generally conceded to be particularly important. The film also considers this point, using drug intake by the mother as an example and briefly covering the use of the tranquilizer thalidomide as a case in point. Dr. Towers extends this filmed coverage of the possible harmful effects of drug intake on the developing fetus and discusses the need for caution as well as more information.

In the final segment of the film, Dr. Klaus Staisch, an obstetrician at the University of California, Los Angeles, is shown monitoring the heart rate of a mother as she listens to pleasant music. This sequence shows how a mother's emotional state during pregnancy influences not only her physiological reactions but also her unborn baby's reactions. Dr. Staisch notes and the film shows that, as the mother becomes stimulated by the music, there is an increase in her heart rate closely followed by an increase in her baby's heart rate. Dr. Towers then summarizes some of the implications of such findings on the importance of the prenatal environment, and the film closes with the observation that the tie between prenatal and subsequent development is likely to be profound.

INFANCY

This film illustrates points brought out in several chapters of the text. Through images of infants in natural settings and in experimental settings, we can see what psychologists see when they study infants. In an animation sequence, an infant displays the capabilities with which he came into the world: reflexes; sucking behavior; visual, auditory, and other sensory capacities; and coordinated patterns of behavior for meeting certain environmental situations.

The film then considers what the infant has to learn about his new world, how well prepared he is, and how he goes about the process of active discovery. Dr. Keith Moore (University of Washington), a developmental psychologist, explains and demonstrates attempts to answer the question of what the very young infant must learn and what he can already perceive and understand. In Dr. Moore's laboratory, a young infant watches a large patterned box approach him; the box is on a track and rolls to a stop within a few inches of the baby's face. Dr. Moore notes that infants as young as one or two weeks have been subjects in this experiment and have exhibited the same pattern of behavior as the infant shown in the film: They all put their hands up between their faces and the closely approaching box, pull their heads back, and open their eyes wide. The infants do not react this way when the box is going to miss them. These results indicate that the babies know the consequences of what is happening—that this thing approaching them may hit them and that they should

protect themselves from it as well as they can. This sequence of behaviors is a complex reaction, and it is most unlikely that it could have been learned. This study adds to the growing number that show the sophisticated equipment that newborns bring into the world.

Although the newborn infant's capacities are proving to be greater than once imagined, he clearly has a lot to learn. The next sequence in *Infancy* shows that the human infant is an avid, active learner. Dr. Lewis Lipsitt and Dr. Einar Siqueland are shown in their Brown University laboratory. We see an infant sucking on a pacifier attached to a television screen while Dr. Lipsitt and Dr. Siqueland explain that the baby's sucking controls the appearance of a picture on the screen. And, in fact, we see the pattern on the screen produced by the baby's sucking. Dr. Siqueland explains that infants only three weeks old will suck to obtain novel stimuli to look at. The study shows not only a very important aspect of human learning—active stimulus-seeking—but also an important methodological tool for psychologists who want to study infant learning.

Dr. Lipsitt then suggests that the infant's capacity for actively participating in his learning (an idea supported by the text's descriptions of infancy) contributes to the development of attachment. There have been a number of studies of attachment in animals; the Harlow studies are mentioned in the film and in the text. The text also describes attachment in humans and discusses how the attachment bond is formed and what its consequences are for further development. In the film, Dr. Lipsitt discusses how the attachment bond grows as a result of the interaction between baby and mother. The baby's actions—crying, cooing, smiling, scanning, and the like—cause the mother to react and to modify her behavior, and her actions cause the baby to modify his reactions in turn. Dr. Lipsitt notes that, because the mother permits and otherwise encourages the baby's reactions, the attachment bond grows during infancy.

The film then points out that there is a cognitive element to attachment: The baby must realize that he has only one mother. The text describes the experiment that permitted babies to see multiple views of their mother and that also showed them a disappearing image of her. By testing infants of various ages, T. G. R. Bower discovered that, at about twenty-four weeks, children came to understand that they have but one mother and that they get very upset when her image appears to dissolve.

The disappearing-mother experiment illustrates a special case of *object identity* and *object permanence*, the acquisition of which is an important step forward in cognitive development. The film shows Dr. Moore demonstrating, in a series of test situations, how the infant must develop a number of conceptions about transformations in the physical characteristics of objects and about the possible displacement of objects in space and time. Dr. Moore points out that the development of a full understanding of object identity and object permanence may take about two years.

The film closes with a sequence that shows how active curiosity and exploratory behavior play a major role in all aspects of an infant's development. As he begins to crawl, then walks and talks, the infant learns more about his world and increasingly becomes a more emotionally and socially responsive human.

COGNITIVE DEVELOPMENT

This film presents two theoretical ways of looking at how people come to know and understand—how they think. It deals first with Jean Piaget's theory of cognitive development, describing his four proposed stages: the sensorimotor period, the preoperational period, the stage of concrete operations, and the stage of formal operations. In Piaget's theory, two processes are basic to each stage and to all of cognitive development: *assimilation* and *accommodation*. In an example, a child assimilates the knowledge that a species of bird he has not seen before fits into his category "bird" and accommodates his scheme of "colorful, winged, flying creatures" to include not only "bird" but "butterfly."

After describing Piaget's theory, the scene shifts to a preschool at Pacific Oaks, California, whose curriculum incorporates many of Piaget's notions about young children's cognitive abilities and about how they learn. We see the children playing freely with a variety of objects and structures. They play with sand, water, and clay, for example, to develop the understanding of *conservation* of liquid and mass when they are ready to. They play with blocks and sticks of various shapes and sizes, which are constructed with obvious external clues to their size relationships so that the children also will have experience in *classifying* objects.

We see a teacher working with one of the children, directing her attention to some blocks in a three-sided mirrored box. The child, who is egocentric at this age, can thereby see the arrangement of blocks from

several different viewpoints simultaneously. In keeping with Piaget's ideas, this school emphasizes self-initiation and direction of one's own learning, and the children are encouraged to interact freely with one another, learning that their peers do not necessarily share their point of view and elaborating their skills in social interaction.

The film next switches to another preschool, whose curriculum is based on behavior-learning principles. Developmentalists of this persuasion share a number of points of view, and the film draws on these to represent this approach to cognitive development. In general, cognitive growth and the development of new capabilities are viewed primarily as a result of learning. Thus, cognitive development steadily becomes more complex partly because people learn more concepts and master more complex sets of rules that reflect how the world is put together and how it operates.

While we watch the children in this preschool, Professor Siegfried Engelmann (University of Oregon) explains the principles on which this school operates and how these principles differ from those of Piaget. His comments are interspersed with live-action instruction sequences in the classroom. Only formal-instruction sequences were selected and shown for this school, in order to highlight some of the differences that are likely to exist among preschools of various theoretical perspectives.

Professor Engelmann explains that in this approach there is little concern with stages, and he expresses the belief that, if properly taught, even young children may be able to understand such concepts as conservation. As shown in the film, materials and activities are specific and are designed for a particular kind of presentation. The teacher is responsible for initiating and directing a very explicit unit of instruction, and the instruction is direct and clearly articulated. In his comments, Professor Engelmann emphasizes the importance of making sure that only the right cues are taught and that the learner is able to generalize what he learns. Finally, he points out that there may be a number of ways to enhance creative thinking and that it is based first on a solid foundation of relevant concepts.

Although the two theoretical views of cognitive development presented in this film are at odds in a number of respects, both positions have wide acceptance in the discipline of psychology. The text, in particular Chapters 7, 11, and 14, also draws heavily on one or both points of view at whatever point they are most useful.

LANGUAGE DEVELOPMENT

Language learning is an extraordinary accomplishment, as this film shows. The narration, accompanied by a series of animated drawings of children at various ages, discusses the cultural universality of the sequence of language learning. As discussed in the text, virtually all children learn the basics of their native language and speak it in a relatively fluent manner by about four or five years of age.

In the early phase of that sequence (which consists of the prespeech sounds that infants make before the end of the first year), the sounds of children from different language communities cannot be distinguished from one another. The film plays back recorded vocalizations typical of infants, from their first cries at birth to cooing to babbling. There is a very good recording of *echolalic babbling,* the complex sequence of nonword sounds that have the pitch and intonation of adult speech. (The infant sounds recorded here sound much like English, but the baby is not speaking words.)

During the second half of the first year, the sounds made by infants in various language communities begin to diverge. The film narrative points out that, at about this point in development, deaf infants, whose vocalizations have been identical to those of hearing infants, cease vocalization.

The film narrative then traces language development from the first word to the two-word sentence, which is discussed at length in the text. As the film illustrates, two-word sentences are telegraphic: Little words, such as prepositions and articles, and verb endings are left out. Nevertheless, the word order and intonation of the youngster usually convey his meaning. Also, at this point a young child usually begins to use language more to communicate and to share experiences with others. The development of three-word sentences is marked by the child's use of rules in combining words into sentences. Sentence structure is more complex now, and noun phrases or verb phrases often replace other words: "See car" becomes "See red car." Some grammatical rules, however, will not become fully developed for several more years.

Dr. Merilee Oakes, a psychologist at the University of Southern California, then discusses some of the processes that have been suggested as involved in language development. She notes that imitation by the child and reinforcement by parents and others may be one important basis of language acquisition. She then goes on to explain that children also construct their own primitive grammar and that in doing so they utter novel statements that they are unlikely to have heard from anyone else. Dr. Oakes then describes several grammatical changes in language comprehension and production, including the type of error discussed as *overregularization.*

Through still shots and narration, the film points out that children from many different cultures seem to acquire the rules for their native language in much the same sequence and at about the same time. And in any culture, the child's language and cognitive abilities usually develop interdependently. Against a background of scenes of teaching the deaf in the classroom and at home, the film discusses some of the results of Dr. Ursula Bellugi-Klima's recent studies. It is pointed out, for example, that deaf children seem to master American Sign Language at the same rate and in the same sequence as children learn normal language.

The film then switches to the laboratory of Dr. David Premack at the University of California, Santa Barbara. A chimpanzee is shown in the early stages of being trained to use magnetized chips as word symbols. Dr. Premack points out that it has been possible not only to teach chimpanzees a large number of words but also to get them to use such word symbols to form simple sentences and to answer questions. Such research suggests that the ability to acquire and use language is closely tied to cognitive development, in other species as well as in human beings.

The film closes with comments from Dr. Oakes on a final aspect of language development: Those who emphasize the biological basis of language development and those who stress the role of learning and the child's linguistic environment are probably both correct in some respects.

EMOTIONAL DEVELOPMENT: AGGRESSION

This film focuses on the development of aggression for several reasons. One is that the field of emotional development is too broad and too diverse in subject matter to be looked at in its entirety in one film. In addition, psychologists know more about the nature of aggression, its development, and its interrelations with other emotions. As the text makes clear, aggression is also one of the most troublesome and misunderstood of emotional behaviors. The film examines some of the circumstances that foster the development of aggression and stresses that aggressive behavior is largely learned in a social context.

The film opens by noting that aggression is pervasive and universal. But, whereas an explanation that relates aggression to *anger,* to *frustration,* or to an *instinct* may be partly correct, it fails to explain adequately why different people show different kinds and amounts of aggression and why not all people behave aggressively when angered or frustrated.

Dr. Gerald Patterson (the University of Oregon), a psychologist, then discusses the related idea that aggression may be inevitable and that little can be done about it. He questions this view and then notes that there are a number of ways to encourage or discourage aggression and its development. The film next focuses on how children learn the skills involved in aggressive acts, when such skills will be used, why they keep occurring, and how they can be changed.

In discussing how aggressive skills are learned, Dr. Stephen Johnson, a developmental psychologist at the Oregon Research Institute, explains that people generally learn to be aggressive when they see other people get what they want by being aggressive. This is illustrated by *modeling,* the principle of which is that people learn much of their behavior simply through observation and imitation of others. Dr. Johnson then notes that, once learned, aggressive behavior is likely to occur when a situation is *emotionally arousing* and frustrating. However, he also cites research with children that shows that not all children behave aggressively when frustrated; only those who have already learned to behave aggressively when frustrated do so.

Aggressive behavior frequently keeps occurring because of two types of *reinforcement: coercion* and *attention.* We see two young boys fighting over a toy while Dr. Johnson points out that, in a *coercive* interaction like this one, the aggressive behavior of one person is rewarded when the other person gives in. Also, the person who gives in is rewarded when the other person stops being aggressive and thus stops inflicting pain. The film then demonstrates the reinforcement value of *attention* by showing a scene in a nursery school in which the teacher attends to a child who is pinching and hitting. As this scene unfolds, we see that it often does not matter whether attention is positive or negative: For young children, adult attention per se is usually a powerful form of reinforcement that is likely to encourage any behavior that it follows, good or bad.

All these principles of aggressive behavior are then illustrated in an unrehearsed filmed sequence of aggression and counteraggression in the nursery school. After the full sequence is shown, selected sections are replayed and analyzed in terms of the specific principles involved.

In the final portion of the film, Dr. Johnson discusses three ways in which aggressive behaviors can be changed and their development discouraged. He notes that, although complicated, the best thing to do is to teach alternatives to aggression, such as showing people how to cooperate and negotiate conflicts. A second method consists of ignoring minor instances of aggression, and a third involves providing a brief and mild negative consequence for aggressive behavior, such as removing a child for a short time from a pleasant setting. Dr. Patterson then notes that aggression in adults may be developed and maintained in many of the same ways as in children and that it might be better to replace such behavior with more-beneficial human skills.

SEX-ROLE DEVELOPMENT

The major role of parents, peers, play, and society in the socialization process and the development of sex-role differences is emphasized throughout the text. This film provides a strong visual supplement to the text. It examines the influence that sex roles and stereotypes have on almost every facet of an individual's development, illustrates how they are developed from one generation to the next, and considers some of the ways in which people are currently trying to find better alternatives for human development.

The film opens with a fast-moving sequence of examples of common sex-role stereotypes and then illustrates how such stereotypes are taught to children through books, by television, through play and use of toys, by peer behavior, and by adult expectations. Dr. Peter Bentler, a psychologist at the University of California, Los Angeles, briefly supplements this presentation by noting how quickly such stereotypes become established and how arbitrary they can be. An animated sequence depicts the development, elaboration, and strengthening of sex-role differences from birth through adulthood.

Dr. Bentler next discusses some of the consequences of sex-role stereotyping. For example, it has been shown that both men and women will rate the quality of a piece of work as poorer if it is attributed to a woman rather than to a man. He then goes on to note that, whereas there may be some truth in certain sex-role stereotypes, a particularly important concept is that of *androgyny,* which involves creatively combining characteristics of both the male and female sex roles so that people can behave more flexibly and effectively in any given situation.

In a final segment, the film explores the implications and impact of traditional sex-role influences by looking at two examples of a nontraditional, androgynous style of socializing children. The first example illustrates the role of parental influences in a family with a three-year-old son. As they go about their daily activities, the parents freely discuss their ideas about sex roles. The parents point out, for example, that they feel strongly about not making distinctions between ''boy'' and ''girl'' behavior and that rearing boys and girls in stereotyped ways robs them of a wide variety of experiences that enrich the process of growing up. The second example illustrates the influences of teachers, peers, and playmates and involves a nursery school that is trying to provide experiences for children that eliminate some of the artificial boy–girl differences created by society. As the film follows the activity and interaction of the children and teachers in this setting, it becomes clear that the aim is not to make boys and girls the same but rather to encourage the development of each child as an individual.

The film closes with an illustration of how children must learn to deal with a world in which sex-role stereotypes abound, and Dr. Bentler raises and discusses the question of whether some sex-role stereotypes might be necessary in human development and in social functioning.

MORAL DEVELOPMENT

This film depicts a classical experiment originally conducted by Dr. Stanley Milgram to discover the conditions under which obedience to authority takes place. The subjects of Milgram's experiment were told that they were to participate in a learning experiment and were asked to deliver electric shocks to a learner (actually the experimenter's confederate) after wrong answers. (No shocks were actually delivered.) If the subjects expressed reservations about giving another person pain, they were urged by the experimenter to continue.

Dr. Lawrence Kohlberg and his colleagues saw in this experimental situation a vivid illustration of a moral dilemma much like the ones used in their studies of moral reasoning. In Milgram's study, the subject must ask himself: ''Should I fulfill my obligation to the experimenter, who is counting on me to help complete his important psychological study, even though it means inflicting pain on a fellow subject, who has, however, also volunteered to participate and thus has also obligated himself?''

The moral reasoning of the six subjects seen in the film (actually actors) falls into Kohlberg's six stages of moral reasoning. Their behavior (for example, continuing the experiment without questioning the experimenter, hesitating and being persuaded to continue, or refusing to administer any shocks at all) is not meant to reflect behavior typical of any given stage of reasoning. That is, it is not the action that exemplifies a particular stage of moral reasoning but the reason for the action.

In order to best present Kohlberg's view, *Moral Development* shows the six subjects in ascending order of presumed developmental progression, from Stage 1 to Stage 6. In discussing these six stages, Dr. David Rosenhan, a psychologist at Stanford University, who also plays the role of the experimenter in this film, notes that in Kohlberg's view each successive stage is presumed to require greater *cognitive organization* and more sophisticated concepts of morality than the stage that precedes it. The film shows each of the six subjects during the experiment. Afterward, they are interviewed by Dr. Rosenhan about their moral reasoning in the dilemma. The subject in the first stage says in part, ''I was only doing what you told me to do . . . I was supposed to do it. I *had* to do it.'' The moral reasoning of each subject in turn is then probed, revealed, and characterized by Dr. Rosenhan, in terms of its respective stage. The moral reasoning of each subject can be compared to that elicited in other dilemmas employed in Kohlberg's studies of moral reasoning.

By using only young adults rather than children to represent Kohlberg's different stages of moral reasoning, the film makes the point that, although progression through the stages is assumed to be invariant (Stage 1 reasoning always precedes that of Stage 2, and so on), movement from stage to stage is by no means automatic. That is, both cognitive and social factors determine how or whether an individual moves through the different stages.

The final segment of the film also stresses social factors, but it does so from a learning point of view. Dr. Rosenhan notes that, from this perspective, moral reasoning is as much a product of social-environmental factors as it is a product of cognitive development. He then explains that those who stress the role of learning in moral development are likely to be as concerned, or more so, with what people *do* as with what they *say* when they report on their reasons for a particular moral decision.

To illustrate the kinds of social influences that are likely to be important in moral learning and development, actors reenact a later variation of the original Milgram experiment, in which the experimenter has three confederates; besides the so-called learner, there are three "teachers." The two confederate teachers have been coached so that, at intervals during the experiment, each refuses to continue shocking the learner. In spite of the experimenter's urgings and commands to continue, they stop. Under these circumstances, nearly all the subjects discontinued the shocks before reaching the end of the experiment. In summary, Dr. Rosenhan explains that, from a learning standpoint, results like this can be interpreted in a number of ways. For example, in this kind of situation a participant's actions are more *public* and *detectable,* and he can see that there are no *punishing consequences* if he *imitates* the actions of the two confederates who stop.

AGING

The popular meaning of "aging" is the focus of this film. Thus, although aging goes on from the moment of conception, in everyday use people think of aging as being something peculiar to later adulthood or old age. In addition, as the text points out, most people tend to think of aging with fear and of the aged individual with a certain degree of distaste. In a major sense, one purpose of this film is to help dispel such common misconceptions about aging and old age.

The film opens with Dr. Harry J. Baker, eighty-four years old, recalling his past. Shots of family pictures document developmental steps in Dr. Baker's life, from childhood through school and working years to retirement. It becomes evident that he is in good health and feels satisfaction with his life. With this introduction as a background, the film then considers in succession a series of commonly held misconceptions or negative stereotypes about what life and people are like during the later adulthood years. In contrast to these negative, stereotyped views, we discover that later adulthood, for most people, is not a period of isolation and neglect by one's family, that most older people are not sick and dependent, that retirement does not cause most older people to feel idle and worthless, and that people over sixty-five do not constitute a homogeneous group that can be characterized as conservative or rigid.

The next section of the film stresses the individuality of older people, the variety of their needs and desires, and the joys and satisfactions that are often found during later adulthood. Dr. Vern Bengtson, a sociologist at the University of Southern California, introduces this section of the film by discussing some of the life styles followed by older individuals. We see sequences from Leisure World, a retirement community in Laguna Hills, California, designed for older people. As other older individuals are shown engaging in various activities, the film suggests that there is no one good way of living or of growing old.

To further document this point, the film then presents three satisfying and relatively continuous life styles as illustrated through three personal interviews. Marion Fox is seventy-three years old and shows the life style or pattern of a *reorganizer.* She has reallocated her time among her new friends and activities, and her involvement makes her happy: "I'm enjoying it." Frank Schaeffer, age seventy-five, does not believe that "because people are old, they should give up," and his style is that of *holding on.* He still plans ahead, maintains a high level of activity and work, feels satisfied, and feels that he is doing "something worthwhile." John Ehrle, age sixty-three, has followed a *rocking chair* style in later life. Although he does not do some things any more, he remains interested in the world: "The activity I'm enjoying is doing nothing."

The final segment of the film considers the possibly broad implications of two phenomena for American society. First, biological research may unlock many of the secrets of physical aging and help to lengthen the human life span. Second, by the year 2000, almost 30 million of us will be sixty-five or older.

CONTRIBUTORS

JAMES F. CALHOUN, assistant professor of psychology and director of the Psychological Center at the State University of New York at Stony Brook, received his Ph.D. from the University of Illinois. Dr. Calhoun's research interests are environmental modification and personalized systems of instruction. He has contributed supplementary materials throughout the text.

FRANK FALKNER, a professor of pediatrics at the University of Cincinnati and director of the Fels Research Institute, received his medical training at Cambridge University and the London Hospital Medical College. His professional interests include the nature and course of physical development in children and adolescents. Dr. Falkner contributed to the chapters on prenatal and newborn development and to those on physical development.

JOHN P. HILL received his Ph.D. from Harvard University and now serves as professor and chairman in the Department of Human Development and Family Studies at Cornell University. His research interests at present include the impact of cognitive change on social development in adolescence. Dr. Hill contributed much of the information for the adolescence chapters.

ROBERT B. MCCALL, who received his Ph.D. from the University of Illinois, is senior scientist and chief of the Perceptual-Cognitive Development Section of Fels Research Institute as well as an associate professor of psychology at Antioch College in Ohio. Among his research interests are attention, memory, exploration, and play in infants; methods of collecting and analyzing longitudinal data; and developmental changes in mental performance. Dr. McCall is responsible for the chapters on prenatal development and the development of the newborn.

BERT MOORE is an assistant professor of psychology at Wellesley College. He received his Ph.D. from Stanford University, and his professional interests include prosocial behavior and cognitive strategies in self-control. Dr. Moore, along with his wife Joy and Bill Underwood, is responsible for the chapters on personality development.

JOY WILLIAMS MOORE, who is currently an assistant professor of psychology at Wellesley College, received her Ph.D. from the University of California at Berkeley. Dr. Moore is interested in the development of self-regulation and in the interpersonal cognitive structures underlying personality development. She is responsible, with her husband Bert and Bill Underwood, for the chapters on personality development.

MARGARET E. NEISWENDER is currently a research assistant and NICHD Fellow at the Andrus Gerontology Center of the University of Southern California. Her professional interests include the development of affectional and interpersonal relationships and changes in self-perception during later adulthood. Ms. Neiswender is responsible for the three chapters in the adulthood unit.

SANDRA SCARR-SALAPATEK, a professor of child psychology at the University of Minnesota, earned her Ph.D. at Harvard University. Her professional interests are behavior genetics and human development. Dr. Scarr-Salapatek is responsible for the three chapters in the introductory unit.

ROBERT E. SCHELL, director of research and training at the Center for Research, Education, Applied Training, and Evaluation in San Diego, received his Ph.D. from the University of Illinois. His main research interests are language development in children, educational/learning problems of children, and moral and social development in children and adults. Dr. Schell served on this book as chief academic adviser and coordinator and is also responsible for the chapter on moral development.

SOLOMON SCHIMMEL, an assistant professor of psychology at Brandeis University, received his Ph.D. from Wayne State University. His professional interests include cognitive development in children and determinants of concept learning in children and adults. He attributes much of his own knowledge on the subject to his young son. Dr. Schimmel is responsible for the chapters on cognitive development.

LAURA ELLEN SCHREIBMAN received her Ph.D. from the University of California at Los Angeles and is an assistant professor of psychology at Claremont Men's College. Among her interests are the experimental analysis of psychopathology, especially in children, behavior therapy for deviant children, and training programs for teachers and parents of deviant children. Dr. Schreibman, with Judith Stevens-Long, contributed to the chapters on physical development.

DAN I. SLOBIN, a professor of psychology at the University of California at Berkeley, received his Ph.D. from Harvard University. His research interests include the cross-linguistic study of children's language development, which brings together the intersecting fields of cognitive and developmental psychology, linguistics, and anthropology. Dr. Slobin is responsible for the chapters on language development.

JUDITH STEVENS-LONG received her Ph.D. from the University of California at Los Angeles and is an assistant professor of psychology at California State University in Los Angeles. Professionally, Dr. Stevens-Long has an interest in experimental psychopathology, especially in regard to autistic children, and in the psychology of learning. She contributed to the physical development chapters with Laura Ellen Schreibman.

BILL UNDERWOOD received his Ph.D. from Stanford University. As an assistant professor of psychology at the University of Texas, his interests include prosocial behavior, affect, and aggression. Dr. Underwood, along with Bert and Joy Williams Moore, is responsible for the chapters on personality development.

BIBLIOGRAPHY

A

Abercrombie, M. L. J. "Learning to Draw," in K. J. Connolly (ed.), *Mechanisms of Motor Skill Development.* New York: Academic Press, 1970, pp. 307–325.

Abravanel, E. "The Development of Intersensory Patterning with Regard to Selected Spatial Dimensions," *Monographs of the Society for Research in Child Development,* 33 (1968), whole no. 2.

Acheson, R. M. "Effects of Nutrition and Disease on Human Growth," in J. M. Tanner (ed.), *Human Growth.* New York: Pergamon Press, 1960, pp. 73–92.

————. "Maturation of the Skeleton," in F. Falkner (ed.), *Human Development.* Philadelphia: Saunders, 1966, pp. 465–502.

Adams, B. N. "Isolation, Function and Beyond: American Kinship in the 1960's," *Journal of Marriage and the Family,* 32 (1970), 575–597.

Adamsons, K., Jr. "The Role of Thermal Factors in Fetal and Neonatal Life," *Pediatric Clinics of North America,* 13 (1966), 599–619.

Ahammer, I. M., and P. B. Baltes. "Objective Versus Perceived Age Differences in Personality: How Do Adolescents, Adults, and Older People View Themselves and Each Other?" *Journal of Gerontology,* 27 (1972), 46–51.

Ahrens, R. "Beitrag zur Entwicklung des Physiognomie- und Mimikerkennens," *Zeitschrift für Experimentelle und Angewandte Psychologie,* 2 (1954), 412–454, 599–633.

Ainsworth, M. D. S. *Infancy in Uganda: Infant Care and the Growth of Love.* Baltimore: Johns Hopkins University, 1967.

Ainsworth, M. D. S., and B. A. Witting. "Attachment and Exploratory Behavior of One-year-olds in a Strange Situation," in B. M. Foss (ed.), *Determinants of Infant Behavior.* Vol. 4. London: Methuen, 1969, pp. 111–136.

Aldrich, C. A., and E. S. Hewitt. "A Self-Regulating Feeding Program for Infants," *Journal of the American Medical Association,* 135 (1947), 340–342.

Allinsmith, W. "The Learning of Moral Standards," in D. R. Miller and G. E. Swanson (eds.), *Inner*

Conflict and Defense. New York: Holt, Rinehart and Winston, 1960, pp. 141–176.

Ambrose, A. (ed.). *Stimulation in Early Infancy.* New York: Academic Press, 1969.

Ambrose, J. A. "The Development of the Smiling Response in Early Infancy," in B. M. Foss (ed.), *Determinants of Infant Behavior.* Vol. 1. London: Methuen, 1961, pp. 179–201.

Anderson, R. C. "Can First Graders Learn an Advanced Problem-Solving Skill?" *Journal of Educational Psychology,* 56 (1965), 283–294.

Apgar, V., and L. S. James. "Further Observations on the Newborn Scoring System," *American Journal of Diseases of Children,* 104 (1962), 419–428.

Arenberg, D. "Cognition and Aging: Verbal Learning, Memory, and Problem Solving," in C. Eisdorfer and M. P. Lawton (eds.), *The Psychology of Adult Development and Aging.* Washington, D.C.: American Psychological Association, 1973, pp. 74–97.

Ariès, P. *Centuries of Childhood: A Social History of Family Life.* R. Baldick (tr.). New York: Vintage Books, 1962.

Aronfreed, J. *Conduct and Conscience: The Socialization of Internalized Control over Behavior.* New York: Academic Press, 1968.

———. "The Concept of Internalization," in D. A. Goslin (ed.), *Handbook of Socialization Theory and Research.* Chicago: Rand McNally, 1969, pp. 263–323.

Aronson, E., and S. Rosenbloom. "Space Perception in Early Infancy: Perception within a Common Auditory-Visual Space," *Science,* 172 (1971), 1161–1163.

Asch, S. E., and H. Nerlove. "The Development of Double Function Terms in Children: An Exploratory Investigation," in B. Kaplan and S. Wapner (eds.), *Perspectives in Psychological Theory: Essays in Honor of Heinz Werner.* New York: International Universities Press, 1960, pp.47–60.

Atchley, R. C. *The Social Forces in Later Life: An Introduction to Social Gerontology.* Belmont, Calif.: Wadsworth, 1972.

Ausubel, D. P. *Theory and Problems of Child Development.* New York: Grune & Stratton, 1958.

———. *Educational Psychology: A Cognitive View.* New York: Holt, Rinehart and Winston, 1968.

B

Babchuk, N. "Primary Friends and Kin: A Study of the Associations of Middle Class Couples," *Social Forces,* 43 (1965), 483–493.

Bacon, M., and M. B. Jones. *Teenage Drinking.* New York: T. Y. Crowell, 1968.

Baer, K. E. von. *De ovi mammalium et hominis genesi.* Lipsiae: Sumptibus Vossii, 1827.

Baltes, P. B., and K. W. Schaie. "Aging and IQ: The Myth of the Twilight Years," *Psychology Today,* 7 (March 1974), 35–40.

Bandura, A. *Principles of Behavior Modification.* New York: Holt, Rinehart and Winston, 1969a.

———. "Social-Learning Theory of Identificatory Processes," in D. A. Goslin (ed.), *Handbook of Socialization Theory and Research.* Chicago: Rand McNally, 1969b, pp. 213–262.

———. *Aggression: A Social Learning Analysis.* Englewood Cliffs, N.J.: Prentice-Hall, 1973.

Bandura, A., and F. J. McDonald. "Influence of Social Reinforcement and the Behavior of Models in Shaping Children's Moral Judgments," *Journal of Abnormal and Social Psychology,* 67 (1963), 274–281.

Bandura, A., and R. H. Walters. *Social Learning and Personality Development.* New York: Holt, Rinehart and Winston, 1963.

Bandura, A., D. Ross, and S. A. Ross. "Imitation of Film-Mediated Aggressive Models," *Journal of Abnormal and Social Psychology,* 66 (1963), 3–11.

Bardwick, J. M. *Psychology of Women: A Study of Bio-Cultural Conflicts.* New York: Harper & Row, 1971.

Bardwick, J. M., and E. Douvan. "Ambivalence: The Socialization of Women," in V. Gornick and B. K. Moran (eds.), *Woman in Sexist Society: Studies in Power and Powerlessness.* New York: Basic Books, 1971, pp. 147–160.

Barker, R. G., H. F. Wright *et al.* *One Boy's Day: A Specimen Record of Behavior.* New York: Harper & Row, 1951.

Barry, H., III, M. K. Bacon, and I. L. Child. "A Cross-Cultural Survey of Some Sex Differences in Socialization," *Journal of Abnormal and Social Psychology,* 55 (1957), 327–332.

Baruch, D., with medical collaboration by H. Miller. *One Little Boy.* New York: Dell, 1964.

Battle, E., and J. B. Rotter. "Children's Feelings of Personal Control as Related to Social Class and Ethnic Group," *Journal of Personality,* 31 (1963), 482–490.

Bayley, N. "Consistency and Variability in the Growth of Intelligence from Birth to Eighteen Years," *Journal of Genetic Psychology,* 75 (1949), 165–196.

———. "Individual Patterns of Development," *Child Development,* 27 (1956), 45–74.

———. *Manual for the Bayley Scales of Infant Development.* New York: Psychological Corporation, 1969.

Bayley, N., and E. S. Schaefer. "Relationships between Socioeconomic Variables and the Behavior of Mothers toward Young Children," *Journal of Genetic Psychology,* 96 (1960), 61–77.

Beatty, R. A., and S. Gluecksohn-Waelsch. *Edinburgh Symposium on the Genetics of the Spermatozoan.* Edinburgh/New York, 1972.

Belbin, R. M. "Middle-age: What Happens to Ability," in R. Owen (ed.), *Middle Age.* London: Cox and Wyman, 1967, pp. 98–106.

Bell, R. Q. "A Reinterpretation of the Direction of Effects in Studies of Socialization," *Psychological Review,* 75 (1968), 81–95.

Bell, R. R., and J. B. Chaskes. "Premarital Sexual Experience among Coeds, 1958 and 1968," *Journal of Marriage and the Family,* 32 (1970), 81–84.

Bell, R. R., and N. Lobsenz. "Married Sex: How Uninhibited Can a Woman Dare to Be?" *Redbook,* 143 (September 1974), 75+.

Bell, S. M. "The Development of the Concept of Object as Related to Infant-Mother Attachment," *Child Development,* 41 (1970), 291–311.

Bell, S. M., and M. D. S. Ainsworth. "Infant Crying and Maternal Responsiveness," *Child Development,* 43 (1972), 1171–1190.

Bellugi, U. "Linguistic Mechanisms Underlying Child Speech," in E. Zale (ed.), *Proceedings of the Conference on Language and Language Behavior, Ann Arbor, Michigan, 1966.* New York: Appleton-Century-Crofts, 1968.

———. "Learning the Language," *Psychology Today,* 4 (December 1970), 32–35+.

Belmont, L., and F. A. Marola. "Birth Order, Family Size, and Intelligence," *Science,* 182 (1973), 1096–1101.

Bem, S. L. "The Measurement of Psychological Androgyny," *Journal of Consulting and Clinical Psychology*, 42 (1974), 155–162.

Bengtson, V. L. "Inter-age Perceptions and the Generation Gap," *Gerontologist*, 11 (1971), 85–89.

Bereiter, C., and S. Engelmann. *Teaching Disadvantaged Children in the Preschool*. Englewood Cliffs, N.J.: Prentice-Hall, 1966.

Berko, J. "The Child's Learning of English Morphology," *Word*, 14 (1958), 150–177.

Berlyne, D. E. *Conflict, Arousal, and Curiosity*. New York: McGraw-Hill, 1960.

Bernardo, F. "Widowhood Status in the United States: Perspective on a Neglected Aspect of the Family Life-Cycle," in M. E. Lasswell and T. E. Lasswell (eds.), *Love, Marriage, Family: A Developmental Approach*. Glenview, Ill.: Scott, Foresman, 1973, pp. 458–464.

Bernstein, B. "Linguistic Codes, Hesitation Phenomena and Intelligence," *Language and Speech*, 5 (1962), 31–47.

———. "Elaborated and Restricted Codes: Their Social Origins and Some Consequences," in A. G. Smith (ed.), *Communication and Culture*. New York: Holt, Rinehart and Winston, 1966, pp. 427–442.

Berscheid, E., E. Walster, and G. Bohrnstedt. "Body Image," *Psychology Today*, 7 (November 1973), 119–131.

Bever, T. G. "The Cognitive Basis for Linguistic Structures," in J. R. Hayes (ed.), *Cognition and the Development of Language*. New York: Wiley, 1970, pp. 279–362.

Bierman, E., and W. Hazzard. "Adulthood, Especially in the Middle Years," in D. W. Smith and E. Bierman (eds.), *The Biologic Ages of Man*. Philadelphia: Saunders, 1973, pp. 154–170.

Biller, H. B. "A Multiaspect Investigation of Masculine Development in Kindergarten Age Boys," *Genetic Psychology Monographs*, 78 (1968), 89–138.

Birren, J. E. *The Psychology of Aging*. Englewood Cliffs, N.J.: Prentice-Hall, 1964.

———. "Age and Decision Strategies," *Interdisciplinary Topics in Gerontology*, 4 (1969), 23–36.

———. "The Experience of Aging," in R. E. Davis and M. E. Neiswender (eds.), *Aging: Prospects and Issues*. Los Angeles: Andrus Gerontology Center, 1973, pp. 1–11.

———. *Coping with the Stresses of Aging: Blueprint for Health*. Chicago: Blue Cross Association, 1975.

Birren, J. E., and D. F. Morrison. "Analysis of the WAIS Subtests in Relation to Age and Education," *Journal of Gerontology*, 16 (1961), 363–369.

Birren, J. E., R. N. Butler, S. W. Greenhouse, L. Sokoloff, and M. R. Yarrow (eds.). *Human Aging: A Biological and Behavioral Study*. Washington, D.C.: U.S. Government Printing Office, 1963.

Bischof, L. *Adult Psychology*. New York: Harper & Row, 1969.

Blank, M. "Cognitive Functions of Language in the Preschool Years," *Developmental Psychology*, 10 (1974), 229–246.

Blank, M., and W. H. Bridger. "Cross-Modal Transfer in Nursery-School Children," *Journal of Comparative and Physiological Psychology*, 58 (1964), 277–282.

Blatt, M. "The Effects of Classroom Discussion Programs Upon Children's Level of Moral Judgment." Unpublished doctoral dissertation, University of Chicago, 1969.

Blau, Z. S. "Maternal Aspirations, Socialization, and Achievement of Boys and Girls in the White Working Class," *Journal of Youth and Adolescence*, 1 (1972), 35–57.

Blood, R. O., and D. M. Wolfe. *Husbands and Wives: The Dynamics of Married Living*. New York: Free Press, 1960.

Bloom, L. *Language Development: Form and Function in Emerging Grammars*. Cambridge, Mass.: M.I.T. Press, 1970.

———. *One Word at a Time: The Use of a Single Word Utterance Before Syntax*. Janua Linguarum, Series Minor, 154 (1973).

Blos, P. *On Adolescence, A Psychoanalytic Interpretation*. New York: Free Press, 1962.

Booth, A., and E. Hess. "Cross-Sex Friendship," *Journal of Marriage and the Family*, 34 (1972), 38–47.

Borow, H. "Development of Occupational Motives and Roles," in L. W. Hoffman and M. L. Hoffman (eds.), *Review of Child Development Research*. Vol. 2. New York: Russell Sage Foundation, 1966, pp. 373–422.

Bossard, J. H. S. "Residential Propinquity as a Factor in Marriage Selection," *American Journal of Sociology*, 38 (1932), 219–224.

Bossard, J. H. S., and E. S. Boll. "Marital Unhappiness in the Life Cycle," *Marriage and Family Living*, 17 (1955), 10–14.

Botwinick, J. *Cognitive Processes in Maturity and Old Age*. New York: Springer, 1967.

Bower, T.G.R. "The Visual World of Infants," *Scientific American*, 215 (December 1966), 80–92.

———. "The Development of the Object Concept," in J. Mehler (ed.), *Handbook of Cognitive Psychology*. Englewood Cliffs, N.J.: Prentice-Hall, 1970.

———. "The Object in the World of the Infant," *Scientific American*, 225 (October 1971), 30–38.

Bowlby, J. "Some Pathological Processes Set in Train by Early Mother-Child Separation," *Journal of Mental Science*, 99 (1953), 265–272.

Boyle, R.P. "The Effect of the High School on Students' Aspirations," *American Journal of Sociology*, 71 (1966), 628–639.

Brackbill, Y. (ed.). *Infancy and Early Childhood*. New York: Free Press, 1967.

———. "Cumulative Effects of Continuous Stimulation on Arousal Level in Infants," *Child Development*, 42 (1971), 17–26.

Brackbill, Y., J.E. Wagner, and D. Wilson. "Feedback Delay and the Teaching Machine," *Psychology in the Schools*, 1 (1964), 148–156.

Brackbill, Y., G. Adams, D.H. Crowell, and M.L. Gray. "Arousal Level in Neonates and Preschool Children Under Continuous Auditory Stimulation," *Journal of Experimental Child Psychology*, 4 (1966), 178–188.

Bradburn, N.M., and D. Caplovitz. *Reports on Happiness: A Pilot Study of Behavior Related to Mental Health*. Chicago: Aldine, 1965.

Brand, F., and R. Smith. "Life Adjustment and Relocation of the Elderly," *Journal of Gerontology*, 29 (1974), 336–340.

Bridger, W.H. "Sensory Habituation and Discrimination in the Human Neonate," *American Journal of Psychiatry*, 117 (1961), 991–996.

Bridges, K.B. "A Study of Social Development in Early Infancy," *Child Development*, 4 (1933), 36–49.

Brittain, C.V. "Adolescent Choices and Parent-Peer Cross Pressures," *American Sociological Review*, 28 (1963), 385–391.

Britton, J.H., and J.O. Britton. *Personality Changes in Aging: A Longitudinal Study of Community Residents*. New York: Springer, 1972.

Brodbeck, A.J., and O.C. Irwin. "The Speech Behavior of Infants Without Families," *Child Development*, 17 (1946), 145–156.

Bronfenbrenner, U. "The Split-Level American Family," *Saturday Review*, 50 (October 7, 1967), 60–66.

———. *Two Worlds of Childhood: U.S. and U.S.S.R.* New York: Russell Sage Foundation, 1970.

———. "An Emerging Theoretical Perspective on Research and Social Policy." Paper presented at the biennial meeting of the Society for Research in Child Development, March 31, 1973.

Bronstein, I.P., S. Wexler, A.W. Brown, and L.J. Halpern. "Obesity in Childhood: Psychologic Studies," *American Journal of the Disturbed Child*, 63 (1942), 238–251.

Brook, C.G.D. "Evidence for a Sensitive Period in Adipose-Cell Replication in Man," *Lancet*, 2 (1972), 624–627.

Broverman, D.M., I.K. Broverman, W. Vogel, R.D. Palmer, and E.L. Klaiber. "Physique and Growth in Adolescence," *Child Development*, 35 (1964), 857–870.

Brown, P., and R. Elliott. "Control of Aggression in a Nursery School Class," *Journal of Experimental Child Psychology*, 2 (1965), 103–107.

Brown, R. *A First Language: The Early Stages*. Cambridge, Mass.: Harvard University Press, 1973.

Brown, R., C. Cazden, and U. Bellugi-Klima. "The Child's Grammar from I to III," in J.P. Hill (ed.), *Minnesota Symposia on Child Psychology*. Vol. 2. Minneapolis: University of Minnesota Press, 1968, pp. 28–73.

Bruch, H. *The Importance of Overweight*. New York: Norton, 1957.

Brück, K. "Temperature Regulation in the Newborn Infant," *Biologia neonatorum*, 3 (1961), 65–119.

Bruner, J.S. "The Course of Cognitive Growth," *American Psychologist*, 19 (1964), 1–15.

———. "Nature and Uses of Immaturity," *American Psychologist*, 27 (1972), 687–708.

Bryan, J.H., and N.H. Walbek. "Preaching and Practicing Generosity: Children's Actions and Reactions," *Child Development*, 41 (1970), 329–353.

Buell, J., P. Stoddard, F.R. Harris, and D.M. Baer. "Collateral Social Development Accompanying Reinforcement of Outdoor Play in a Preschool Child," *Journal of Applied Behavior Analysis*, 1 (1968), 167–173.

Buffery, A.W.H., and J.A. Gray. "Sex Differences in the Development of Spatial and Linguistic Skills," in C. Ounsted and D.C. Taylor (eds.), *Gender Differences:*

Their Ontogeny and Significance. London: Churchill Livingstone, 1972, pp. 123–157.

Burgess, E. W., and P. Wallin. *Engagement and Marriage.* Philadelphia: Lippincott, 1953.

Burnstein, E. "Fear of Failure, Achievement Motivation, and Aspiring to Prestigeful Occupations," *Journal of Abnormal and Social Psychology,* 67 (1963), 189–193.

Buss, A. H., and T. C. Brock. "Repression and Guilt in Relation to Aggression," *Journal of Abnormal and Social Psychology,* 66 (1963), 345–350.

Busse, E. W., and C. Eisdorfer. "Two Thousand Years of Married Life," in E. Palmore (ed.), *Normal Aging: Reports from the Duke Longitudinal Study, 1955–1969.* Durham, N.C.: Duke University Press, 1970, pp. 266–269.

Butler, N. R., and H. Goldstein. "Smoking in Pregnancy and Subsequent Child Development," *British Medical Journal,* 4 (1973), 573–575.

Butler, R. N. "The Life Review: An Interpretation of Reminiscence in the Aged," in B. L. Neugarten (ed.), *Middle Age and Aging.* Chicago: University of Chicago Press, 1968, pp. 486–496.

Butler, R. N., and M. I. Lewis. *Aging and Mental Health: Positive Psychosocial Approaches.* St. Louis: Mosby, 1973.

Butterfield, E. C. "An Extended Version of Modification of Sucking with Auditory Feedback." Working paper No. 43, Bureau of Child Research Laboratory, Children's Rehabilitation Unit, University of Kansas Medical Center, October 1968.

Byrne, D., *et al.* "Attitude Similarity-Dissimilarity and Attraction: Generality Beyond the College Sophomore," *Journal of Social Psychology,* 79 (1969), 155–161.

C

Caldwell, B. M. "The Effects of Infant Care," in M. L. Hoffman and L. W. Hoffman (eds.), *Review of Child Development Research.* Vol. 1. New York: Russell Sage Foundation, 1964, pp. 9–87.

Call, J. D. "Games Babies Play," *Psychology Today,* 3 (January 1970), 34–37+.

Campbell, J. D., and M. R. Yarrow. "Perceptual and Behavioral Correlates of Social Effectiveness," *Sociometry,* 24 (1961), 1–20.

Canestrari, R. E. "Paced and Self-paced Learning in Young and Elderly Adults," *Journal of Gerontology,* 18 (1963), 165–168.

Carlsmith, L. "Effect of Early Father Absence on Scholastic Aptitude," *Harvard Educational Review,* 34 (1964), 3–21.

Caro, G., and C. T. Pihlblad. "Aspirations and Expectations: A Reexamination of the Bases for Social Class Differences in the Occupational Orientations of Male High School Students," *Sociology and Social Research,* 49 (1965), 465–475.

Carter, H., and P. Glick. *Marriage and Divorce: A Social and Economic Study.* Cambridge, Mass.: Harvard University Press, 1970.

Cattell, P. *The Measurement of Intelligence of Infants and Young Children.* New York: Psychological Corporation, 1940.

Celotta, B. K. "Knowledge of the Human Figure as Measured by Two Tasks," *Developmental Psychology,* 8 (1973), 377–381.

Chall, J. S. *Learning to Read: The Great Debate.* New York: McGraw-Hill, 1967.

Charlesworth, R., and W. W. Hartup. "Positive Social Reinforcement in the Nursery School Peer Group," *Child Development,* 38 (1967), 993–1002.

Chodorow, N. "Being and Doing: A Cross-Cultural Examination of the Socialization of Males and Females," in V. Gornick and B. K. Moran (eds.), *Woman in Sexist Society: Studies in Power and Powerlessness.* New York: Basic Books, 1971, pp. 173–197.

Chomsky, N. *Language and Mind.* Enl. ed. New York: Harcourt Brace Jovanovich, 1972.

Christensen, H. T. "Children in the Family: Relationship of Number and Spacing to Marital Success," *Journal of Marriage and the Family,* 30 (1968), 283–289.

Clark, B. S. "The Acquisition and Extinction of Peer Imitation in Children," *Psychonomic Science,* 2 (1965), 147–148.

Clark, E. V. "What's in a Word? On the Child's Acquisition of Semantics in His First Language," in T. E. Moore (ed.), *Cognitive Development and the Acquisition of Language.* New York: Academic Press, 1973, pp. 65–110.

Coates, B., E. P. Anderson, and W. W. Hartup. "Interrelations in the Attachment Behavior of Human Infants," *Developmental Psychology,* 6 (1972), 218–230.

Cohen, L. B. "Attention-getting and Attention-holding Processes of Infant Visual Preferences," *Child Development,* 43 (1972), 869–879.

Coleman, J. S. *The Adolescent Society: The Social Life of the Teenager and Its Impact on Education.* New York: Free Press, 1961.

Coleman, J. S., *et al. Equality of Educational Opportunity.* Washington, D.C.: U.S. Department of Health, Education, and Welfare, Office of Education, 1966.

Coleman, R. P., and B. L. Neugarten. *Social Status in the City.* San Francisco: Jossey-Bass, 1971.

Condon, W. S., and L. W. Sander. "Synchrony Demonstrated between Movements of the Neonate and Adult Speech," *Child Development,* 45 (1974), 456–462.

Conel, J. L. R. *The Cortex of the Four-Year Child.* Vol. 7. *The Postnatal Development of the Human Cerebral Cortex.* 7 vols., 1939–1963. Cambridge, Mass.: Harvard University Press, 1963.

Conger, J. J. *Adolescence and Youth: Psychological Development in a Changing World.* New York: Harper & Row, 1973.

Constantine, L., and J. M. Constantine. "The Group Marriage," in M. E. Lasswell and T. E. Lasswell (eds.), *Love, Marriage, Family: A Developmental Approach.* Glenview, Ill.: Scott, Foresman, 1973, pp. 446–454.

Correll, R., S. Rokosz, and B. Blanchard. "Some Correlates of WAIS Performance in the Elderly," *Journal of Gerontology,* 21 (1966), 544–549.

Cosentino, F., and A. B. Heilbrun Jr. "Anxiety Correlates of Sex-Role Identity in College Students," *Psychological Reports,* 14 (1964), 729–730.

Costanzo, P. R., and M. E. Shaw. "Conformity as a Function of Age Level," *Child Development,* 37 (1966), 967–975.

Cox, F. D. *Youth, Marriage, and the Seductive Society.* Rev. ed. Dubuque, Iowa: William C. Brown, 1968.

Cratty, B. J. *Movement Behavior and Motor Learning.* 2nd ed. London: Kimpton, 1967.

Crites, J. O. "Parental Identification in Relation to Vocational Interest Development," *Journal of Educational Psychology,* 53 (1962), 262–270.

Cruise, M. O. "A Longitudinal Study of the Growth of Low Birth Weight Infants: 1. Velocity and Distance Growth, Birth to 3 Years," *Pediatrics,* 51 (1973), 620–628.

Cumming, E., and W. E. Henry. *Growing Old, The Process of Disengagement.* New York: Basic Books, 1961.

D

D'Andrade, R. G. "Sex Differences and Cultural Institutions," in E. E. Maccoby (ed.), *The Development of Sex Differences.* Stanford, Calif.: Stanford University Press, 1966, pp. 174–204.

Davis, J. A. *Great Aspirations.* Vol. 1. Chicago: National Opinion Research Center, University of Chicago, 1963.

Dawe, H. C. "An Analysis of Two Hundred Quarrels of Preschool Children," *Child Development,* 5 (1934), 139–157.

Dayton, G. O., Jr., M. H. Jones, P. Aiu, R. A. Rawson, B. Steele, and M. Rose. "Developmental Study of Coordinated Eye Movements in the Human Infant: I. Visual Acuity in the Newborn Human: A Study Based on Induced Optokinetic Nystagmus Recorded by Electro-Oculography," *Archives of Opthalmology,* 71 (1964), 865–870.

Debakan, A. *Neurology of Infancy.* Baltimore: Williams & Wilkins, 1959.

de Mause, L. "The Evolution of Childhood," in L. de Mause (ed.), *The History of Childhood.* New York: Psychohistory Press, 1974, pp. 1–73.

Dement, W. "The Effect of Dream Deprivation," *Science,* 131 (1960), 1705–1707.

Denenberg, V. H. "Animal Studies on Developmental Determinants of Behavioral Adaptability," in O. J. Harvey (ed.), *Experience Structure and Adaptability.* New York: Springer, 1966.

Denenberg, V. H., and K. M. Rosenberg. "Nongenetic Transmission of Information," *Nature,* 216 (1967), 549–550.

Denfeld, D., and M. Gordon. "Mate Swapping: The Family that Swings Together Clings Together," in

M.E. Lasswell and T.E. Lasswell (eds.), *Love, Marriage, Family: A Developmental Approach.* Glenview, Ill.: Scott, Foresman, 1973, pp. 432–440.

Denney, D.R., N.W. Denney, and M.J. Ziobrowski. "Alterations in the Information-Processing Strategies of Young Children Following Observation of Adult Models," *Developmental Psychology,* 8 (1973), 202–208.

Dennis, W. "Infant Development Under Conditions of Restricted Practice and of Minimum Social Stimulation," *Genetic Psychology Monographs,* 23 (1941), 143–191.

———. "Causes of Retardation Among Institutional Children: Iran," *Journal of Genetic Psychology,* 96 (1960), 47–59.

———. "Creative Productivity between the Ages of 20 and 80 Years," *Journal of Gerontology,* 21 (1966), 1–8.

Dennis, W., and M.G. Dennis. "The Effect of Cradling Practices upon the Onset of Walking in Hopi Children," *Journal of Genetic Psychology,* 56 (1940), 77–86.

Dennis, W., and P. Najarian. "Infant Development Under Environmental Handicap," *Psychological Monographs,* 71 (1957), 436.

Dennis, W., and Y. Sayegh. "The Effect of Supplementary Experiences upon the Behavioral Development of Infants in Institutions," *Child Development,* 36 (1965), 81–90.

Deutscher, I. "The Quality of Postparental Life," in B.L. Neugarten (ed.), *Middle Age and Aging.* Chicago: University of Chicago Press, 1968, pp. 263–268.

———. "Socialization for Postparental Life," in M.E. Lasswell and T.E. Lasswell (eds.), *Love, Marriage, Family: A Developmental Approach.* Glenview, Ill.: Scott, Foresman, 1973, pp. 510–517.

Devereux, E.C. "The Role of Peer Group Experience in Moral Development," in J.P. Hill (ed.), *Minnesota Symposia on Child Psychology.* Vol. 4. Minneapolis: University of Minnesota Press, 1970, pp. 94–140.

DeVries, H. "Physiological Effects of an Exercise Regime Upon Men Aged 52 to 88," *Journal of Gerontology,* 25 (1970), 325–336.

Dewey, J. *Democracy and Education: An Introduction to the Philosophy of Education.* New York: Macmillan, 1916.

Dishotsky, N.I., W.D. Loughman, R.E. Mogar, and W.R. Lipscomb. "LSD and Genetic Damage," *Science,* 172 (1971), 431–440.

Dobbing, J. "Effects of Experimental Undernutrition on Development of the Nervous System," in N.S. Scrimshaw and J.E. Gordan (eds.), *Malnutrition, Learning, and Behavior.* Cambridge, Mass.: M.I.T. Press, 1968, pp. 181–202.

———. *The Later Development of the Brain and Its Vulnerability.* Scientific Foundations of Pediatrics. London: Heineman Medical Books, 1974.

Douglas, J.W.B. "The Age at Which Premature Children Walk," *Medical Officer,* 95 (1956), 33–35.

Douvan, E. "Social Status and Success Strivings," *Journal of Abnormal and Social Psychology,* 52 (1956), 219–223.

Douvan, E., and J. Adelson. *The Adolescent Experience.* New York: Wiley, 1966.

Douvan, E., and M. Gold. "Modal Patterns in American Adolescence," in L.W. Hoffman and M.L. Hoffman (eds.), *Review of Child Development Research.* Vol. 2. New York: Russell Sage Foundation, 1966.

Duck, S.W. *Personal Relationships and Personal Constructs: A Study of Friendship Formation.* New York: Wiley-Interscience, 1973.

Dulit, E. "Adolescent Thinking à la Piaget: The Formal Stage," *Journal of Youth and Adolescence,* 1 (1972), 281–301.

Dunphy, D.C. "The Social Structure of Urban Adolescent Peer Groups," *Sociometry,* 26 (1963), 230–246.

Duvall, E.M. *Family Development.* 4th ed. Philadelphia: Lippincott, 1971.

Dwyer, J., and J. Mayer. "Psychological Effects of Variations in Physical Appearance During Adolescence," *Adolescence,* 3 (Winter 1968–1969), 353–380.

———. "Overfeeding and Obesity in Infants and Children," *Bibliotheca Nutritio et Dieta,* No. 18 (1973), pp. 123–152.

E

Eckerman, C.O., and H.L. Rheingold. "Infants' Exploratory Responses to Toys and People," *Developmental Psychology,* 10 (1974), 255–259.

Eibl-Eibesfeldt, I. *Ethology: The Biology of Behavior.* E. Klinghammer (tr.). New York: Holt, Rinehart and Winston, 1970.

Eichenwald, H. F., and P. C. Fry. "Nutrition and Learning," *Science,* 163 (1969), 644–648.

Eichorn, D. *Biological Correlates of Behavior.* Chicago: National Society for the Study of Education, 1963.

Eid, E. E. "Follow-Up Study of Physical Growth of Children Who Had Excessive Weight Gain in First Six Months of Life," *British Medical Journal,* 2 (1970), 74–76.

Eimas, P. D., E. R. Siqueland, P. Jusczyk, and J. Vigorito. "Speech Perception in Infants," *Science,* 171 (1971), 303–306.

Eisenberg, R. B. "The Development of Hearing in Man: An Assessment of Current Status," *Journal of the American Speech and Hearing Association,* 12 (1970), 119–123.

Eisenberg, R. B., E. J. Griffin, D. B. Coursin, and M. A. Hunter. "Auditory Behavior in the Human Neonate: A Preliminary Report," *Journal of Speech and Hearing Research,* 7 (1964), 245–269.

Elder, G. H., Jr. *Adolescent Socialization and Personality Development.* Chicago: Rand McNally, 1968.

Emmerich, W. "Continuity and Stability in Early Social Development: II. Teacher Ratings," *Child Development,* 37 (1966), 17–27.

Engen, T., and L. P. Lipsitt. "Decrement and Recovery of Responses to Olfactory Stimuli in the Human Neonate," *Journal of Comparative and Physiological Psychology,* 59 (1965), 312–316.

Erikson, E. H. *Childhood and Society.* 2nd rev. ed. New York: Norton, 1963.

———. *Identity, Youth, and Crisis.* New York: Norton, 1968.

Ervin-Tripp, S. "Discourse Agreement: How Children Answer Questions," in J. R. Hayes (ed.), *Cognition and the Development of Language.* New York: Wiley, 1970, pp. 79–108.

Espenschade, A. S., and H. M. Eckert. *Motor Development.* Columbus, Ohio: Merrill, 1967.

F

Fagan, J. F., III. "Infants' Recognition Memory for a Series of Visual Stimuli," *Journal of Experimental Child Psychology,* 11 (1971), 244–250.

Fagan, J. F., III, R. L. Fantz, and S. B. Miranda. "Infants' Attention to Novel Stimuli as a Function of Postnatal and Conceptual Age." Paper presented at the biennial meeting of Society for Research in Child Development, Minneapolis, Minnesota, 1971.

Falkner, F. T. (ed.). *Human Development.* Philadelphia: Saunders, 1966.

Fantz, R. L. "The Origin of Form Perception," *Scientific American,* 204 (May 1961), 66–72.

———. "Visual Perception from Birth as Shown by Pattern Selectivity," *Annals of the New York Academy of Sciences,* 118 (1965), 793–814.

Farb, P. *Word Play: What Happens When People Talk.* New York: Knopf, 1974.

Faust, M. S. "Developmental Maturity as a Determinant in Prestige of Adolescent Girls," *Child Development,* 31 (1960), 173–184.

Feffer, M. H. "The Cognitive Implications of Role Taking Behavior," *Journal of Personality,* 27 (1959), 152–168.

Feffer, M. H., and V. Gourevitch. "Cognitive Aspects of Role-Taking in Children," *Journal of Personality,* 28 (1960), 383–396.

Fein, G. G., and K. A. Clarke-Stewart. *Day Care in Context.* New York: Wiley, 1973.

Feinberg, I. "Effects of Age on Human Sleep Patterns," in A. Hales (ed.), *Sleep Physiology and Pathology.* Philadelphia: Lippincott, 1969, pp. 39–52.

Feldman, W. M. *The Principles of Ante-Natal and Post-Natal Child Physiology Pure and Applied.* London: Longmans, Green, 1920.

Ferguson, C. A., and D. I. Slobin (eds.). *Studies of Child Language Development.* New York: Holt, Rinehart and Winston, 1973.

Feshbach, S. "Aggression," in P. H. Mussen (ed.), *Carmichael's Manual of Child Psychology.* Vol. 2. New York: Wiley, 1970, pp. 159–259.

Flacks, R. *Youth and Social Change.* Chicago: Markham, 1971.

Flavell, J. H. *The Developmental Psychology of Jean Piaget.* New York: D. Van Nostrand, 1963.

———. "Role-taking and Communication Skills in Children," *Young Children,* 21 (1966), 164–177.

———. "Concept Development," in P. H. Mussen (ed.), *Carmichael's Manual of Child Psychology.* Vol. 1, 3rd ed. New York: Wiley, 1970, pp. 983–1060.

———. "Stage-Related Properties of Cognitive Development," *Cognitive Psychology*, 2 (1971), 421–453.

———. "An Analysis of Cognitive-Developmental Sequences," *Genetic Psychology Monographs*, 86 (1972), 279–350.

Flavell, J. H., et al. *The Development of Role-taking Communication Skills in Children.* New York: Wiley, 1968.

Flavell, J. H., D. R. Beach, and J. M. Chinsky. "Spontaneous Verbal Rehearsal in a Memory Task as a Function of Age," *Child Development*, 37 (1966), 283–299.

Floyd, J. M. "Effects of Amount of Reward and Friendship Status of the Other on the Frequency of Sharing in Children," *Dissertation Abstracts*, 25 (1965), 5396–5397.

Forgus, R. H. "The Effects of Early Perceptual Learning on the Behavioral Organization of Adult Rats," *Journal of Comparative Physiological Psychology*, 47 (1954), 331–336.

Fort, J. *The Pleasure Seekers: The Drug Crisis, Youth and Society.* New York: Grove Press, 1970.

Frank, L. K. *On the Importance of Infancy.* New York: Random House, 1966.

Fraser, C., U. Bellugi, and R. Brown. "Control of Grammar in Imitation, Comprehension, and Production," *Journal of Verbal Learning and Verbal Behavior*, 2 (1963), 121–135.

Freedman, D. G. "Constitutional and Environmental Interactions in Rearing of Four Breeds of Dogs," *Science*, 127 (1958), 585–586.

———. "Smiling in Blind Infants and the Issue of Innate vs. Acquired," *Journal of Child Psychology and Psychiatry*, 5 (1964), 171–184.

Freud, S. *Psychopathology of Everyday Life.* New York: Macmillan, 1917.

———. "Three Essays on the Theory of Sexuality," in *The Standard Edition of the Complete Psychological Works of Sigmund Freud.* Vol. 7. London: Hogarth, 1953, pp. 125–245 (orig. pub. 1905).

———. *Jokes and Their Relation to the Unconscious.* J. Strachey (ed. and tr.). New York: Norton, 1960.

Friedman, S. "Habituation and Recovery of Visual Response in the Alert Human Newborn," *Journal of Experimental Child Psychology*, 13 (1972), 339–349.

Friedman, S., L. A. Bruno, and P. Vietze. "Newborn Habituation to Visual Stimuli: A Sex Difference in Novelty Detection," *Journal of Experimental Child Psychology*, 18 (1974), 242–251.

Fries, M. E. "Some Hypotheses on the Role of the Congenital Activity Type in Personality Development," *International Journal of Psychoanalysis*, 35 (1954), 206–207.

Friesen, D. "Academic-Athletic-Popularity Syndrome in the Canadian High School Society: 1967," *Adolescence*, 3 (1968), 39–52.

Fryer, J. G., and J. R. Ashford. "Trends in Perinatal and Neonatal Mortality in England and Wales 1960–69," *British Journal of Preventive and Social Medicine*, 26 (1972), 1–9.

Furth, H. G. "Research with the Deaf: Implications for Language and Cognition," *Psychological Bulletin*, 62 (1964), 145–164.

———. *Piaget and Knowledge.* Englewood Cliffs, N.J.: Prentice-Hall, 1969.

Furth, H. G., B. M. Ross, and J. Youniss. "Operative Understanding in Reproductions of Drawings," *Child Development*, 45 (1974), 63–70.

G

Gardner, H. "Metaphors and Modalities: How Children Project Polar Adjectives Onto Diverse Domains," *Child Development*, 45 (1974), 84–91.

Garvey, C., and R. Hogan. "Social Speech and Social Interaction: Egocentrism Revisited," *Child Development*, 44 (1973), 562–568.

Gelman, R. "Conservation Acquisition: A Problem of Learning to Attend to Relevant Attributes," *Journal of Experimental Child Psychology*, 7 (1969), 167–187.

———. "The Nature and Development of Early Number Concepts," in H. W. Reese (ed.), *Advances in Child Development and Behavior.* Vol. 7. New York: Academic Press, 1972, pp. 115–167.

Gesell, A. L. *The Mental Growth of the Pre-School Child: A Psychological Outline of Normal Development from Birth to the Sixth Year, Including a System of Developmental Diagnosis.* New York: Macmillan, 1925.

———. "Maturation and Infant Behavior Patterns," *Psychological Review*, 36 (1929), 307–319.

Gesell, A., H. M. Halverson, H. Thompson, F. L. Ilg, B. M. Costner, L. B. Ames, and C. E. Amatruda. *The First Five Years of Life: A Guide to the Study of the Pre-School Child, from the Yale Clinic of Child Development.* New York: Harper & Row, 1940.

Gewirtz, J. L. "The Course of Infant Smiling in Four Child-rearing Environments in Israel," in B. M. Foss (ed.), *Determinants of Infant Behavior.* Vol. 3. London: Methuen, 1965, pp. 205–260.

Gibson, E. J. *Principles of Perceptual Learning and Development.* New York: Appleton-Century-Crofts, 1969.

Gibson, E. J., and R. D. Walk. "The Visual Cliff," *Scientific American,* 202 (April 1960), 64–71.

Ginzberg, E., S. W. Ginsburg, S. Axelrad, and J. L. Herma. *Occupational Choice: An Approach to a General Theory.* New York: Columbia University Press, 1951.

Gleason, J. "Do Children Imitate?" *Proceedings of the International Conference on Oral Education of the Deaf,* 2 (1967), 1441–1448.

Glenn, N. "Aging, Disengagement, and Opinionation," *Public Opinion Quarterly,* 33 (1969), 17–33.

Gluck, L., and M. V. Kulovich. "Fetal Lung Development: Current Concepts," *Pediatric Clinics of North America,* 20 (1973), 367–379.

Glucksberg, S., R. M. Krauss, and R. Weisberg. "Referential Communication in Nursery School Children: Method and Some Preliminary Findings," *Journal of Experimental Child Psychology,* 3 (1966), 333–342.

Goldberg, S., and M. Lewis. "Play Behavior in the Year-Old Infant: Early Sex Differences," *Child Development,* 40 (1969), 21–31.

Golde, P., and N. Kogan. "A Sentence Completion Procedure for Assessing Attitudes Toward Old People," *Journal of Gerontology,* 14 (1959), 355–363.

Golomb, C. "Children's Representation of the Human Figure: The Effects of Models, Media, and Instruction," *Genetic Psychology Monographs,* 87 (1973), 197–251.

Goodenough, F. L. *Anger in Young Children.* Minneapolis: University of Minnesota Press, 1931.

Gottlieb, S. "Modeling Effects Upon Fantasy," in J. L. Singer (ed.), *The Child's World of Make-Believe: Experimental Studies of Imaginative Play.* New York: Academic Press, 1973, pp. 155–182.

Gouin-Décarie, T. *Intelligence and Affectivity in Early Childhood.* E. P. Brandt and L. W. Brandt (trs.). New York: International Universities Press, 1965.

Gould, L. "X: A Fabulous Child's Story," *MS,* 1 (December 1972), 74–76+.

Govatos, L. A. "Relationships and Age Differences in Growth Measures and Motor Skills," *Child Development,* 30 (1959), 333–340.

Graham, D. *Moral Learning and Development: Theory and Research.* New York: Wiley, 1972.

Green, E. H. "Friendships and Quarrels Among Preschool Children," *Child Development,* 4 (1933), 237–252.

Green, F. P., and F. W. Schneider. "Age Differences in the Behavior of Boys on Three Measures of Altruism," *Child Development,* 45 (1974), 248–251.

Greenfield, P. M., and J. Bruner. "Culture and Cognitive Growth," *International Journal of Psychology,* 1 (1966), 89–107.

Griffiths, R. *The Abilities of Babies.* New York: McGraw-Hill, 1954.

Grosser, D., N. Polansky, and R. Lippitt. "A Laboratory Study of Behavioral Contagion," *Human Relations,* 4 (1951), 115–142.

Grusec, J. E., and S. L. Skubiski. "Model Nurturance, Demand Characteristics of the Modeling Experiment, and Altruism," *Journal of Personality and Social Psychology,* 14 (1970), 352–359.

Gunn, B. "Children's Conceptions of Occupational Prestige," *Personnel and Guidance Journal,* 42 (1964), 558–563.

Gusinow, J. F., and L. E. Price. "Modification of Form and Color Responding in Young Children as a Function of Differential Reinforcement and Verbalization," *Journal of Experimental Child Psychology,* 13 (1972), 145–153.

Gutteridge, M. V. "A Study of Motor Achievements of Young Children," *Archives of Psychology,* No. 244 (1939).

H

Haaf, R. A., and R. Q. Bell. "A Facial Dimension in Visual Discrimination by Human Infants," *Child Development,* 38 (1967), 893–899.

Haan, N., M. B. Smith, and J. Block. "Moral Reasoning of Young Adults: Political-Social Behavior, Family Background, and Personality Correlates," *Journal of Personality and Social Psychology,* 10 (1968), 183–201.

Haber, R. N., and M. Hershenson. *The Psychology of Visual Perception.* New York: Holt, Rinehart and Winston, 1973.

Hagen, J. W., and G. H. Hale. "The Development of Attention in Children," in A. D. Pick (ed.), *Minnesota Symposia on Child Psychology.* Vol. 7. Minneapolis: University of Minnesota Press, 1973, pp. 117–140.

Haith, M. M. "The Response of the Human Newborn to Visual Movement," *Journal of Experimental Child Psychology,* 3 (1966), 235–243.

Hale, G. A., and J. S. Morgan. "Developmental Trends in Children's Component Selection," *Journal of Experimental Child Psychology,* 15 (1973), 302–314.

Hall, D. W. "The Vocational Development Inventory: A Measure of Vocational Maturity in Adolescence," *Personnel and Guidance Journal,* 41 (1963), 771–775.

Hall, G. S. "Notes on the Study of Infants," *The Pedagogical Seminary,* 1 (1891), 127–138.

Hall, K. R. "Social Organization of the Old-World Monkeys and Apes," in P. C. Jay (ed.), *Primates: Studies in Adaptation and Variability.* New York: Holt, Rinehart and Winston, 1968, pp. 7–32.

Hamerton, J. L., S. M. Briggs, F. Gianelli, and C. O. Carter. "Chromosome Studies in Detection of Parents with High Risk of Second Child with Down's Syndrome," *Lancet,* 281 (1961), 788–791.

Hammer, E. F. "Creativity and Feminine Ingredients in Young Male Artists," *Perceptual and Motor Skills,* 19 (1964), 414.

Harlow, H. F. "The Nature of Love," *American Psychologist,* 13 (1958), 673–685.

Harlow, H. F., and M. K. Harlow. "Learning to Love," *American Scientist,* 54 (1966), 244–272.

———. "Effects of Various Mother-Infant Relationships on Rhesus Monkey Behaviors," in B. M. Foss (ed.), *Determinants of Infant Behavior.* Vol. 4. London: Methuen, 1969, pp. 15–36.

Harlow, H. F., and R. R. Zimmermann. "Affectional Responses in the Infant Monkey," *Science,* 130 (1959), 421–432.

Harrel, R. F., E. Woodyard, and A. I. Gates. *The Effect of Mothers' Diets on the Intelligence of Offspring: A Study of the Influence of Vitamin Supplementation of the Diets of Pregnant and Lactating Women on the Intelligence of Their Children.* New York: Columbia University Press, 1955.

Harrison, C. W., J. R. Rawls, and D. J. Rawls. "Differences between Leaders and Nonleaders in Six- to Eleven-Year-Old Children," *Journal of Social Psychology,* 84 (1971), 269–272.

Hartley, R. E. "Children's Concepts of Male and Female Roles," *Merrill-Palmer Quarterly,* 6 (1960), 83–91.

Hartley, R. E., and F. P. Hardesty. "Children's Perceptions of Sex Roles in Childhood," *Journal of Genetic Psychology,* 105 (1964), 43–51.

Hartshorne, H., and M. A. May. *Studies in Deceit.* New York: Macmillan, 1928.

Hartup, W. W. "Friendship Status and the Effectiveness of Peers as Reinforcing Agents," *Journal of Experimental Child Psychology,* 1 (1964a), 154–162.

———. "Patterns of Imitative Behavior in Young Children," *Child Development,* 35 (1964b), 183–191.

———. "Peer Interaction and Social Organization," in P. H. Mussen (ed.), *Carmichael's Manual of Child Psychology.* Vol. 2. New York: Wiley, 1970, pp. 361–456.

———. "Aggression in Childhood: Developmental Perspectives," *American Psychologist,* 29 (1974), 336–341.

Hartup, W. W., and B. Coates. "Imitation of a Peer as a Function of Reinforcement from the Peer Group and Rewardingness of the Model," *Child Development,* 38 (1967), 1003–1016.

Hathaway, M. L., and D. W. Sargent. "Overweight in Children," *Journal of the American Dietetic Association,* 40 (1962), 511–515.

Hauck, B. B. "Differences between the Sexes at Puberty," in D. Evans (ed.), *Adolescents: Readings in Behavior and Development.* Hinsdale, Ill.: Dryden, 1970.

Havighurst, R. J. "The Nature and Values of Meaningful Free-time Activity," in R. W. Kleemeier (ed.), *Aging and Leisure.* New York: Oxford University Press, 1961, pp. 309–344.

————. *Developmental Tasks and Education*. 3rd ed. New York: McKay, 1972.

Havighurst, R. J., and K. Feigenbaum. "Leisure and Life-Style," in B. L. Neugarten (ed.), *Middle Age and Aging: A Reader in Social Psychology.* Chicago: University of Chicago Press, 1968, pp. 347–353.

Havighurst, R. J., B. L. Neugarten, and S. S. Tobin. "Disengagement and Patterns of Aging," in B. L. Neugarten (ed.), *Middle Age and Aging: A Reader in Social Psychology.* Chicago: University of Chicago Press, 1968, pp. 58–71.

Haynes, H., B. L. White, and R. Held. "Visual Accommodation in Human Infants," *Science,* 148 (1965), 528–530.

Hebb, D., W. E. Lambert, and G. R. Tucker. "Language, Thought and Experience," *Modern Language Journal,* 55 (1971), 212–222.

Hécaen, H., and J. de Ajuriaguerra. *Left-Handedness.* New York: Grune & Stratton, 1964.

Helson, R. "Personality of Women with Imaginative and Artistic Interests: The Role of Masculinity, Originality, and Other Characteristics in Their Creativity," *Journal of Personality,* 34 (1966), 1–25.

Herron, R. E., and B. Sutton-Smith. *Child's Play.* New York: Wiley, 1971.

Hershenson, M. "Visual Discrimination in the Human Newborn," *Journal of Comparative and Physiological Psychology,* 58 (1964), 270–276.

Hess, E. H. "Imprinting in Birds," *Science,* 146 (1964), 1128–1139.

Hess, R. D. "Social Class and Ethnic Influences on Socialization," in P. H. Mussen (ed.), *Carmichael's Manual of Child Psychology.* Vol. 2. 3rd ed. New York: Wiley, 1970, pp. 457–557.

Hetherington, E. M. "Effects of Paternal Absence on Sex-Typed Behaviors in Negro and White Preadolescent Males," *Journal of Personality and Social Psychology,* 4 (1966), 87–91.

————. "Effects of Father Absence on Personality Development in Adolescent Daughters," *Developmental Psychology,* 7 (1972), 313–326.

Hetherington, E. M., and J. Deur. "The Effects of Father Absence on Child Development," in W. W. Hartup and N. L. Smothergill (eds.), *The Young Child: Reviews of Research.* Vol. 2. Washington, D.C.: National Association for the Education of Young Children, 1972, pp. 303–319.

Hicks, D. J. "Imitation and Retention of Film-Mediated Aggressive Peer and Adult Models," *Journal of Personality and Social Psychology,* 2 (1965), 97–100.

————. "Girls' Attitudes Toward Modeled Behaviors and the Content of Imitative Private Play," *Child Development,* 42 (1971), 139–147.

Hill, R. "Decision-Making and the Family Life Cycle," in E. Shanas and G. Streib (eds.), *Social Structures and the Family: Generational Considerations.* Englewood Cliffs, N.J.: Prentice-Hall, 1965, pp. 113–139.

Hoffman, M. L., and H. D. Saltzstein. "Parent Discipline and the Child's Moral Development," *Journal of Personality and Social Psychology,* 5 (1967), 45–57.

Hollingshead, A. *Elmtown's Youth: The Impact of Social Classes on Adolescents.* New York: Wiley, 1949.

Hollos, M. *Growing up in Flathill: Social Environment and Cognitive Development.* Oslo: Universitetsforlaget, 1974.

Hollos, M., and P. A. Cowan. "Social Isolation and Cognitive Development: Logical Operations and Role-Taking Abilities in Three Norwegian Social Settings," *Child Development,* 44 (1973), 630–641.

Holmes, T. H., and R. H. Rahe. "The Social Readjustment Rating Scale," *Journal of Psychosomatic Research,* 11 (1967), 213–218.

Holstein, C. "The Relation of Children's Moral Judgment Level to That of Their Parents and to Communication Patterns in the Family," in R. C. Smart and M. S. Smart (eds.), *Readings in Child Development and Relationship.* New York: Macmillan, 1972, pp. 484–494.

Holt, J. C. *How Children Fail.* New York: Pitman, 1964.

Honzik, M. P. "Developmental Studies of Parent-Child Resemblance in Intelligence," *Child Development,* 28 (1957), 215–228.

Hooker, D. *The Prenatal Origin of Behavior.* Lawrence: University of Kansas Press, 1952.

Horner, M. "Fail: Bright Women," *Psychology Today,* 3 (November 1969), 36–38+.

Horney, K. *The Neurotic Personality of Our Time.* New York: Norton, 1937.

Houston, B. K. "Review of the Evidence and Qualifications Regarding the Effects of Hallucinogenic Drugs on Chromosomes and Embryos," *American Journal of Psychiatry,* 126 (1969), 251–254.

Hrachovec, J. P. *Keeping Young and Living Longer.* Los Angeles: Sherbourne, 1972.

Hunt, M. M. "Special Sex Education Survey," *Seventeen,* 29 (July 1970), 94–97+.

Hutt, C. J. *Males and Females.* Baltimore: Penguin, 1972.

Huttenlocher, J., K. Eisenberg, and S. Strauss. "Comprehension: Relation Between Perceived Actor and Logical Subject," *Journal of Verbal Learning and Verbal Behavior,* 7 (1968), 527–530.

I

Inhelder, B., and J. Piaget. *The Growth of Logical Thinking From Children to Adolescence: An Essay on the Construction of Formal Operational Structures.* A. Parsons and S. Milgram (trs.). New York: Basic Books, 1958.

Irwin, O. C. "Infant Speech," *Scientific American,* 181 (September 1949), 22–24.

J

Jack, L. M. "An Experimental Study of Ascendant Behavior in Preschool Children," *University of Iowa Studies: Study of Child Welfare,* 9 (1934), 7–65.

Jakobson, R. *Child Language, Aphasia and Phonological Universals.* The Hague: Mouton, 1968.

James, W. *The Principles of Psychology.* Vol. 1. New York: Dover, 1950 (orig. pub. 1890).

Jaques, E. "The Mid-Life Crisis," in R. Owen (ed.), *Middle Age.* London: Cox and Wyman, 1967, pp. 22–36.

Jarvik, L. F., and D. Cohen. "A Biobehavioral Approach to Intellectual Changes with Aging," in C. Eisdorfer and M. P. Lawton (eds.), *The Psychology of Adult Development and Aging.* Washington, D.C.: American Psychological Association, 1973, pp. 220–280.

Jensen, A. R. "How Much Can We Boost IQ and Scholastic Achievement?" *Harvard Educational Review,* 39 (1969), 1–123.

Jensen, A. R., and W. D. Rohwer Jr. "Syntactical Mediation of Serial and Paired-Associate Learning as a Function of Age," *Child Development,* 36 (1965), 601–608.

Jensen, K. "Differential Reactions to Taste and Temperature Stimuli in Newborn Infants," *Genetic Psychology Monographs,* 12 (1932), 361–479.

Jersild, A. *In Search of Self: An Exploration of the Role of the School in Promoting Self-Understanding.* New York: Columbia University Press, 1952.

Jersild, A., and F. B. Holmes. *Children's Fears.* New York: Columbia University Press, 1935.

Jewett, S. "Longevity and the Longevity Syndrome," *The Gerontologist,* 13 (1973), 91–99.

Joffe, J. M. "Genotype and Prenatal and Premating Stress Interact to Affect Adult Behavior in Rats," *Science,* 150 (1965), 1844–1845.

Jones, M. C. "The Later Careers of Boys Who Were Early- or Late-Maturing," *Child Development,* 28 (1957), 113–128.

———. "Psychological Correlates of Somatic Development," *Child Development,* 36 (1965), 899–911.

Jones, M. C., and N. Bayley. "Physical Maturing among Boys as Related to Behavior," *Journal of Educational Psychology,* 41 (1950), 129–248.

Jones, N. B. (ed.). *Ethological Studies of Child Behavior.* London: Cambridge University Press, 1972.

K

Kagan, J. "The Concept of Identification," *Psychological Review,* 65 (1958), 296–305.

———. "Acquisition and Significance of Sex Typing and Sex Role Identity," in M. Hoffman and L. Hoffman (eds.), *Review of Child Development Research.* Vol. 1. New York: Russell Sage Foundation, 1964, pp. 137–367.

———. "Do Infants Think?" *Scientific American,* 226 (March 1972), 74–83.

Kagan, J., et al. *Change and Continuity in Infancy.* New York: Wiley, 1971.

Kagan, J., and H. A. Moss. *Birth to Maturity, A Study in Psychological Development.* New York: Wiley, 1962.

Kagan, J., and S. R. Tulkin. "Social Class Differences in Child Rearing During the First Year," in H. R. Schaffer (ed.), *The Origins of Human Social Relations: Proceedings. Centre for Advanced Study in the Developmental Sciences Study Group.* New York: Academic Press, 1971, pp. 165–186.

————. "Mother-Child Interaction in the First Year of Life," *Child Development,* 43 (1972), 31–41.

Kagan, S., and M. C. Madsen. "Cooperation and Competition of Mexican, Mexican-American, and Anglo-American Children of Two Ages Under Four Instructional Sets," *Developmental Psychology,* 5 (1971), 32–39.

Kahl, J. A. *The American Class Structure.* New York: Holt, Rinehart and Winston, 1961.

Kallman, F. J., and L. F. Jarvik. "Individual Differences in Constitution and Genetic Background," in J. E. Birren (ed.), *Handbook of Aging and the Individual.* Chicago: University of Chicago Press, 1959, pp. 216–263.

Kamin, L. J. "Heredity, Intelligence, Politics, and Psychology." Invited address, Eastern Psychological Association, Washington, D.C., March 1973.

Kandel, D. B., and G. S. Lesser. *Youth in Two Worlds.* San Francisco: Jossey-Bass, 1972.

Kangas, J., and K. Bradway. "Intelligence at Middle Age: A Thirty-eight Year Follow-Up," *Developmental Psychology,* 5 (1971), 333–337.

Kanter, R. M. *Communes: Creating and Managing the Collective Life.* New York: Harper & Row, 1973.

Kay, E. "The World of Work: Its Promises, Conflicts and Reality," in American Medical Association, *The Quality of Life: The Middle Years.* Acton, Mass.: Publishing Sciences Group, 1974, pp. 63–69.

Keasey, C. B. "Social Participation as a Factor in the Moral Development of Preadolescents," *Developmental Psychology,* 5 (1971), 216–220.

Keller, S. "The Social World of the Urban Slum Child: Some Early Findings," *American Journal of Orthopsychiatry,* 33 (1963), 823–831.

Kelly, E. L. "Consistency of the Adult Personality," *American Psychologist,* 10 (1955), 659–681.

Kelly, G. A. *The Psychology of Personal Constructs.* New York: Norton, 1955.

Kelly, J. R. "Work and Leisure: A Simplified Paradigm," *Journal of Leisure Research,* 4 (1972), 50–62.

Kendler, T. S. "An Ontogeny of Mediational Deficiency," *Child Development,* 43 (1972), 1–19.

Keniston, K. *Young Radicals: Notes on Committed Youth.* New York: Harcourt Brace Jovanovich, 1968.

Kessen, W., M. M. Haith, and P. H. Salapatek. "Human Infancy: A Bibliography and Guide," in P. H. Mussen (ed.), *Carmichael's Manual of Child Psychology.* Vol. 1. 3rd ed. New York: Wiley, 1970, pp. 287–445.

Kimmel, D. *Adulthood and Aging.* New York: Wiley, 1974.

Kinsey, A. C., W. B. Pomeroy, and C. E. Martin. *Sexual Behavior in the Human Male.* Philadelphia: Saunders, 1948.

Kinsey, A. C., W. B. Pomeroy, C. E. Martin, and P. H. Gebhard. *Sexual Behavior in the Human Female.* Philadelphia: Saunders, 1953.

Kirby, I. J. "Hormone Replacement Therapy for Postmenopausal Symptoms," *Lancet,* 2 (1973), 103.

Klinger, E. "Development of Imaginative Behavior: Implications of Play for a Theory of Fantasy," *Psychological Bulletin,* 72 (1969), 277–298.

Knobloch, H., and B. Pasamanick. "The Developmental Behavioral Approach to the Neurologic Examination in Infancy," *Child Development,* 33 (1962), 181–198.

Koch, H. L. *Twins and Twin Relations.* Chicago: University of Chicago Press, 1966.

Koch, K. *Wishes, Lies and Dreams: Teaching Children to Write Poetry.* New York: Chelsea House, 1970.

Kohl, H. *Thirty-six Children.* New York: New American Library, 1968.

Kohlberg, L. "The Development of Children's Orientations Toward a Moral Order: I. Sequence in the Development of Moral Thought," *Vita Humana,* 6 (1963), 11–33.

————. "A Cognitive-Developmental Analysis of Children's Sex-Role Concepts and Attitudes," in E. E. Maccoby (ed.), *The Development of Sex Differences.* Stanford, Calif.: Stanford University Press, 1966, pp. 82–173.

————. "Stage and Sequence: The Cognitive-Developmental Approach to Socialization," in D. A. Goslin (ed.), *Handbook of Socialization Theory and Research.* Chicago: Rand McNally, 1969, pp. 347–480.

Kohlberg, L., and C. Gilligan. "The Adolescent as a Philosopher: The Discovery of the Self in a Postconventional World," *Daedalus,* 100 (1971), 1051–1086.

Kohlberg, L., and R. B. Kramer. "Continuities and Discontinuities in Childhood and Adult Moral Development," *Human Development,* 12 (1969), 93–120.

Kohn, M. L. "Social Class and Parent-Child Relationships: An Interpretation," *American Journal of Sociology,* 68 (1963), 471–480.

Kozol, J. *Death at an Early Age.* New York: Bantam Books, 1970.

Krebs, R. L. "Some Relationships Between Moral Judgment, Attention, and Resistance to Temptation." Unpublished doctoral dissertation, University of Chicago, 1968.

Kübler-Ross, E. *On Death and Dying.* New York: Macmillan, 1969.

Kuhlen, R. G. "Developmental Changes in Motivation During the Adult Years," in J. E. Birren (ed.), *Relations of Development and Aging.* Springfield, Ill.: Charles C Thomas, 1964, pp. 209–246.

Kummer, H. "Two Variations in the Social Organization of Baboons," in P. C. Jay (ed.), *Primates: Studies in Adaptation and Variability.* New York: Holt, Rinehart and Winston, 1968, pp. 293–313.

Kurtines, W., and E. B. Greif. "The Development of Moral Thought: Review and Evaluation of Kohlberg's Approach," *Psychological Bulletin,* 8 (1974), 453–470.

L

Labov, W. "Contraction, Deletion, and Inherent Variability of the English Copula," *Language,* 45 (1969), 715–762.

———. *Language in the Inner City: Studies in the Black English Vernacular.* Philadelphia: University of Pennsylvania Press, 1973.

Landers, W. F. "Effects of Differential Experience on Infants' Performance in a Piagetian Stage IV Object-Concept Task," *Developmental Psychology,* 5 (1971), 48–54.

Lasswell, M. E., and T. E. Lasswell (eds.). *Love, Marriage, Family: A Developmental Approach.* Glenview, Ill.: Scott, Foresman, 1973.

Laurendeau, M., and A. Pinard. *Causal Thinking in the Child: A Genetic and Experimental Approach.* New York: International Universities Press, 1962.

LaVoie, J. C. "Type of Punishment as a Determinant of Resistance to Deviation," *Developmental Psychology,* 10 (1974), 181–189.

Leaf, A., and J. Launois. "Every Day Is a Gift When You Are Over 100," *National Geographic,* 143 (1973), 93–119.

Lesser, G. S. *Children and Television: Lessons From Sesame Street.* New York: Random House, 1974.

Leventhal, A. S., and L. P. Lipsitt. "Adaptation, Pitch Discrimination, and Sound Localization in the Neonate," *Child Development,* 35 (1964), 759–767.

Levitin, T. E., and J. D. Chananie. "Responses of Female Primary School Teachers to Sex-Typed Behaviors in Male and Female Children," *Child Development,* 43 (1972), 1309–1316.

Levy, D. M. *Behavioral Analysis: Analysis of Clinical Observations of Behavior as Applied to Mother-Newborn Relationships.* Springfield, Ill.: Charles C Thomas, 1958.

Lewis, M., with the collaboration of S. Goldberg and H. Campbell. "A Developmental Study of Information Processing Within the First Three Years of Life: Response Decrement to a Redundant Signal," *Monographs of the Society for Research in Child Development,* 34 (1969), whole no. 133.

Liebert, R. M., and R. A. Baron. "Some Immediate Effects of Televised Violence on Children's Behavior," *Developmental Psychology,* 6 (1972), 469–475.

Lind, J. "The Infant Cry," *Proceedings of the Royal Society of Medicine,* 64 (1971), 468.

Lipetz, J., and K. Davis. "Living Together: An Alternative to Marriage," *Journal of Marriage and the Family,* 34 (1972), 305–311.

Lipsitt, L. P. "Learning in the Human Infant," in H. W. Stevenson, E. H. Hess, and H. L. Rheingold (eds.), *Early Behavior: Comparative and Developmental Approaches.* New York: Wiley, 1967a, pp. 225–247.

———. "Stages in Developmental Psychology." Comments from a round-table discussion at the meeting of the Eastern Psychological Association, Boston, April, 1967b.

Little, J. K. "The Occupations of Non-College Youth," *American Educational Research Journal,* 4 (1967), 147–153.

Livesley, W. J., and D. B. Bromley. *Person Perception in Childhood and Adolescence.* New York: Wiley, 1973.

Locke, J. *An Essay Concerning Human Understanding.* Collated and annotated by Alexander Campbell Fraser. Oxford: Clarendon Press, 1894 (orig. pub. 1690).

Lefkowitz, M. M., L. D. Eron, L. O. Walder, and L. R. Huesmann. "Television Violence and Child Aggression: A Followup Study," in G. A. Comstock and E. A. Rubinstein (eds.), *Television and Social Behavior, vol. 3: Televison* *and Adolescent Aggressiveness.* Washington, D.C.: U.S. Government Printing Office, 1972, pp. 35–135.

Lehman, H. C. *Age and Achievement.* Princeton, N.J.: Princeton University Press, 1953.

Leifer, A., and D. F. Roberts. "Children's Responses to Television Violence," in J. P. Murray, E. A. Rubenstein, and G. A. Comstock (eds.), *Television and Social Behavior, vol. 2: Television and Social Learning.* Washington, D.C.: U.S. Government Printing Office, 1972, pp. 43–180.

Lenneberg, E. "Understanding Language Without Ability to Speak: A Case Report," *Journal of Abnormal and Social Psychology,* 65 (1962), 419–425.

———. *Biological Foundations of Language.* New York: Wiley, 1967.

Leopold, W. F. *Grammar and General Problems in the First Two Years, Vol. 3: Speech Development of a Bilingual Child: A Linguist's Record,* 1939–1949, 4 vols. Evanston, Ill.: Northwestern University Press, 1949.

Lorenz, K. "Die Angeborenen Formen Möglicher Erfahrung," *Zeitschrift Für Tierpsychologie,* 5 (1942–1943), 235–409.

Lovell, K., and E. Ogilvie. "A Study of the Conservation of Weight in the Junior School Child," *British Journal of Educational Psychology,* 31 (1961), 138–144.

Lowenthal, M. F., and C. Haven. "Interaction and Adaptation: Intimacy as a Critical Variable," *American Sociological Review,* 33 (1968), 20–30.

Luckey, E. B., and G. D. Nass. "A Comparison of Sexual Attitudes and Behavior in an International Sample," *Journal of Marriage and the Family,* 31 (1969), 364–379.

Lyle, J. "Television in Daily Life: Patterns of Use," in E. A. Rubinstein, G. A. Comstock, and J. P. Murray (eds.), *Television and Social Behavior, vol. 4: Television in Day-to-Day Life: Patterns of Use.* Washington, D.C.: U.S. Government Printing Office, 1972.

M

Maccoby, E., and C. Jacklin. *The Psychology of Sex Differences.* Stanford, Calif.: Stanford University Press, in press.

Maier, H. W. *Three Theories of Child Development: The Contributions of Erik H. Erikson, Jean Piaget, and Robert R. Sears, and Their Applications.* New York: Harper & Row, 1965.

Manheimer, D. I., G. D. Mellinger, and M. B. Balter. "Marijuana Use Among Urban Adults," *Science,* 166 (1969), 1544–1545.

Martin, M. F., D. M. Gelfand, and D. P. Hartmann. "Effects of Adult and Peer Observers on Boys' and Girls' Responses to an Aggressive Model," *Child Development,* 42 (1971), 1271–1275.

Maslow, A. H. *Motivation and Personality.* New York: Harper & Row, 1954.

Masters, W. H., and V. E. Johnson. *Human Sexual Response.* Boston: Little, Brown, 1966.

———. "Human Sexual Response: The Aging Female and the Aging Male," in B. L. Neugarten (ed.), *Middle Age and Aging.* Chicago: Chicago University Press, 1968, pp. 269–279.

———. *Human Sexual Inadequacy.* Boston: Little, Brown, 1970.

———. "Emotional Poverty, a Marriage Crisis of the Middle Years," in American Medical Association, *The Quality of Life: The Middle Years.* Acton, Mass.: Publishing Sciences Group, 1974, pp. 101–108.

Maudry, M., and M. Nekula. "Social Relations Between Children of the Same Age During the First Two Years of Life," *Journal of Genetic Psychology,* 54 (1939), 193–215.

Mayer, J. *Overweight: Causes, Cost, and Control.* Englewood Cliffs, N.J.: Prentice-Hall, 1968.

McCall, R. B. "Attention in the Infant: Avenue to the Study of Cognitive Development," in D. N. Walcher and D. L. Peters (eds.), *Early Childhood: The Development of Self-Regulatory Mechanism.* New York: Academic Press, 1971, pp. 107–140.

McCall, R. B., M. I. Appelbaum, and P. S. Hogarty. "Developmental Changes in Mental Performance," *Monographs of the Society for Research in Child Development,* 38 (1973), whole no. 150.

McCandless, B. R. "Rate of Development, Body Build, and Personality," *Psychiatric Research Reports,* 13 (December 1960), 42–57.

McCarthy, D. "Language Development in Children," in L. Carmichael (ed.), *Manual of Child Psychology.* 2nd ed. New York: Wiley, 1954, pp. 492–630.

McClearn, G. E. "Genetic Influences on Behavior and Development," in P. H. Mussen (ed.), *Carmichael's Manual of Child Psychology.* Vol. 1. 3rd ed. New York: Wiley, 1970, pp. 39–76.

McDougall, W. *Outline of Psychology.* New York: Scribner's, 1923.

McGraw, M. B. *Growth, A Study of Johnny and Jimmy.* New York: Appleton-Century-Crofts, 1935.

———. "Later Development of Children Specially Trained During Infancy: Johnny and Jimmy at School Age," *Child Development,* 10 (1939), 1–19.

McKain, W. "A New Look at Older Marriages," *The Family Coordinator,* 21 (1972), 61–69.

McLaughlin, L. J., and J. F. Brinley. "Age and Observational Learning of a Multiple-Classification Task," *Developmental Psychology,* 9 (1973), 9–15.

McMichael, R. E., and R. E. Grinder. "Children's Guilt After Transgression: Combined Effect of Exposure to American Culture and Ethnic Background," *Child Development,* 37 (1966), 425–431.

McNeill, D. "Developmental Psycholinguistics," in F. Smith and G. A. Miller (eds.), *The Genesis of Language: A Psycholinguistic Approach.* Cambridge, Mass.: M.I.T. Press, 1966, pp. 15–84.

———. *The Acquisition of Language: The Study of Developmental Psycholinguistics.* New York: Harper & Row, 1970a.

———. "The Development of Language," in P. H. Mussen (ed.), *Carmichael's Manual of Child Psychology.* Vol. 1. 3rd ed. New York: Wiley, 1970b, pp. 1061–1161.

Mead, M. *Coming of Age in Samoa: A Psychological Study in Primitive Youth for Western Civilisation.* New York: Dell, 1968.

Mehrabian, A. *Silent Messages.* Belmont, Calif.: Wadsworth, 1971.

Meichenbaum, D. H., and J. Goodman. "Training Impulsive Children to Talk to Themselves: A Means of Developing Self-control," *Journal of Abnormal Psychology,* 77 (1971), 115–126.

Meltzer, H. "Age Differences in Status and Happiness of Workers," *Geriatrics,* 17 (1962), 831–838.

Menyuk, P. *The Acquisition and Development of Language.* Englewood Cliffs, N.J.: Prentice-Hall, 1971.

Menyuk, P., and N. Bernholtz. "Prosodic Features and Children's Language Production," *M.I.T. Research Laboratory of Electronics Quarterly Progress Reports,* no. 93 (1969), 216–219.

Menzel, E. W., Jr., R. K. Davenport Jr., and C. M. Rogers. "The Effects of Environmental Restriction upon the Chimpanzee's Responsiveness to Objects," *Journal of Comparative and Physiological Psychology,* 56 (1963), 78–85.

Meredith, H. V. "Change in the Stature and Body Weight of North American Boys During the Last 80 Years," in L. P. Lipsitt and C. C. Spiker (eds.), *Advances in Child Development and Behavior.* Vol. 1. New York: Academic Press, 1963, pp. 69–114.

———. "A Synopsis of Pubertal Changes in Youth," *Journal of School Health,* 37 (1967), 171–176.

Merminod, A. (ed.). *The Growth of the Normal Child During the First Three Years of Life.* Basel/New York: S. Karger, 1962.

Metropolitan Life. "Patterns of Venereal Disease Morbidity in Recent Years," *Metropolitan Life Statistical Bulletin,* (April 1969), 5–7.

Michaels, R. H., and G. W. Mellin. "Prospective Experience with Maternal Rubella and the Associated Congenital Malformations," *Pediatrics,* 26 (1960), 200–209.

Milgram, S. "Behavioral Study of Obedience," *Journal of Abnormal and Social Psychology,* 67 (1963), 371–378.

Millar, W. S. "A Study of Operant Conditioning Under Delayed Reinforcement in Early Infancy," *Monographs of the Society for Research in Child Development,* 37 (1972), whole no. 147.

Miller, D. R., and G. E. Swanson. *Inner Conflict and Defense.* New York: Holt, Rinehart and Winston, 1966.

Miller, N. E., and J. Dollard. *Social Learning and Imitation.* New Haven, Conn.: Yale University Press, 1941.

Miller, W., and S. Ervin. "The Development of Grammar in Child Language," in *Cognitive Development in Children.* Chicago: University of Chicago Press, 1970, pp. 309–334.

Milner, E. "A Study of the Relationship Between Reading Readiness in Grade One School Children and Patterns of Parent-child Interaction," *Child Development* 22 (1951), 95–112.

Minkowski, A. *Regional Development of the Brain in Early Life.* Oxford: Blackwell, 1967.

Minuchin, P., et al. *The Psychological Impact of School Experience.* New York: Basic Books, 1969.

Mischel, W. "Theory and Research on the Antecedents of Self-imposed Delay of Reward," in B. A. Maher (ed.), *Progress in Experimental Personality Research.* Vol. 3. New York: Academic Press, 1966, pp. 85–132.

———. *Personality and Assessment.* New York: Wiley, 1968.

———. "Sex-Typing and Socialization," in P. H. Mussen (ed.), *Carmichael's Manual of Child Psychology.* Vol. 2. New York: Wiley, 1970, pp. 3–72.

Mischel, W., and H. Mischel. "A Cognitive Social-Learning Approach to Morality and Self-Regulation," in T. Lickona (ed.), *Man and Morality.* New York: Holt, Rinehart and Winston, in press.

Moberg, D. O. "Religiosity in Old Age," in B. L. Neugarten (ed.), *Middle Age and Aging: A Reader in Social Psychology.* Chicago: University of Chicago Press, 1968, pp. 497–508.

Money, J., and A. A. Ehrhardt. *Man and Woman, Boy and Girl: The Differentiation and Dimorphism of Gender Identity from Conception to Maturity.* Baltimore: Johns Hopkins University Press, 1972.

Monge, R. H., and D. Hultsch. "Paired-Associate Learning as a Function of Adult Age and the Length of the Anticipation and Inspection Intervals," *Journal of Gerontology,* 26 (1971), 157–162.

Montagu, M. F. A. "Constitutional and Prenatal Factors in Infant and Child Health," in M. J. E. Senn (ed.), *Symposium on the Healthy Personality.* New York: Josia Macy Jr. Foundation, 1950, pp. 148–175.

Mooney, H. F. "Popular Music Since the 1920s," in R. S. Denisoff and R. A. Peterson (eds.), *Sounds of Social Change: Studies in Popular Culture.* Chicago: Rand McNally, 1972, pp. 181–197.

Morgan, G. A., and H. N. Ricciuti. "Infants' Responses to Strangers During the First Year," in B. M. Foss (ed.), *Determinants of Infant Behavior.* Vol. 4. London: Methuen, 1969, pp. 253–272.

Moro, E. "Das Erste Trimenon," *Münchener Medizinische Wochenschrift,* 65 (1918), 1147–1150.

Moskowitz, A. I. "The Two-Year-Old Stage in the Acquisition of English Phonology," *Language,* 46 (1970), 426–441.

Mundy-Castle, A. C., and J. Anglin. "The Development of Looking in Infancy." Unpublished paper presented at Society for Research in Child Development, Santa Monica, Calif., 1969.

Murphy, D. P. *Congenital Malformation: A Study of Parental Characteristics With Special Reference to the Reproductive Process.* 2nd ed. Philadelphia: Lippincott, 1947.

Murstein, B. I. "A Theory of Marital Choice," in B. I. Murstein (ed.), *Theories of Attraction and Love.* New York: Springer, 1971, pp. 100–151.

Mussen, P. H. "Early Sex-Role Development," in D. A. Goslin (ed.), *Handbook of Socialization Theory and Research.* Chicago: Rand McNally, 1969, pp. 707–731.

Mussen, P. H., and M. C. Jones. "Self-Conceptions, Motivations, and Interpersonal Attitudes of Late and Early-Maturing Boys," *Child Development,* 28 (1957), 243–256.

Muuss, R. E. "Adolescent Development and the Secular Trend," *Adolescence,* 5 (1970), 267–284.

N

Nash, J. "The Father in Contemporary Culture and Current Psychological Literature," *Child Development,* 36 (1965), 261–297.

Needham, J. *A History of Embryology.* 2nd rev. ed., with the assistance of A. Hughes. Cambridge: Cambridge University Press, 1959.

Nelson, K. "Structure and Strategy in Learning to Talk," *Monographs of the Society for Research in Child Development,* vol. 38 (February, April 1973), whole nos. 1 and 2.

Nelson, R. C. "Knowledge and Interests Concerning Sixteen Occupations Among Elementary and Secondary School Students," *Educational and Psychological Measurement,* 23 (1963), 741–754.

Neugarten, B. L. "Adult Personality: Toward a Psychology of the Life Cycle," in B. L. Neugarten (ed.), *Middle Age and Aging: A Reader in Social Psychology.* Chicago: University of Chicago Press, 1968, pp. 137–147.

Neugarten, B. L., and D. L. Gutmann. "Age-Sex Roles and Personality in Middle Age: A Thematic Apperception Study," in B. L. Neugarten (ed.), *Middle Age and*

Aging: A Reader in Social Psychology. Chicago: University of Chicago Press, 1968, pp. 58–71.

Neugarten, B. L., and W. A. Peterson. "A Study of the American Age-Grade System," *Proceedings of the Fourth Congress of the International Association of Gerontology,* 3 (1957), 497–502.

Neugarten, B. L., and K. K. Weinstein. "The Changing American Grandparent," in B. L. Neugarten (ed.), *Middle Age and Aging: A Reader in Social Psychology*. Chicago: University of Chicago Press, 1968, pp. 280–286.

Neugarten, B. L., W. J. Crotty, and S. S. Tobin. "Personality Types in an Aged Population," in B. L. Neugarten *et al.* (eds.), *Personality in Middle and Late Life: Empirical Studies*. New York: Atherton, 1964, pp. 158–187.

Neugarten, B. L., V. Wood, R. J. Kraines, and B. Loomis. "Women's Attitudes Toward the Menopause," *Vita Humana,* 6 (1963), 140–151.

Neulinger, J., and C. S. Raps. "Leisure Attitudes of an Intellectual Elite," *Journal of Leisure Research,* 4 (1972), 196–207.

Newman, G., and C. R. Nichols. "Sexual Activities and Attitudes in Older Persons," *Journal of the American Medical Association,* 173 (1960), 33–35.

O

Oetzel, R. M. "Annotated Bibliography," in E. E. Maccoby (ed.), *Development of Sex Differences*. Stanford, Calif.: Stanford University Press, 1966, pp. 223–321.

Office of the Surgeon General. *Television and Growing Up: The Impact of Televised Violence*. Washington, D.C.: U.S. Government Printing Office, 1972.

Opie, I., and P. Opie. *Children's Games in Street and Playground: Chasing, Catching, Seeking, Hunting, Racing, Duelling, Exerting, Daring, Guessing, Acting, Pretending*. Oxford: Clarendon, 1969.

Ornstein, R. *The Psychology of Consciousness*. New York: Viking, 1973.

Osborn, D. K., and R. C. Endsley. "Emotional Reactions of Young Children to TV Violence," *Child Development,* 42 (1971), 321–331.

Osgood, C. *Method and Theory in Experimental Psychology*. New York: Oxford University Press, 1953.

Osler, S. F., and E. Kofsky. "Stimulus Uncertainty as a Variable in the Development of Conceptual Ability," *Journal of Experimental Child Psychology,* 2 (1965), 264–279.

Osofsky, J. D., and B. Danzger. "Relationships Between Neonatal Characteristics and Mother-Infant Interaction," *Developmental Psychology,* 10 (1974), 124–130.

P

Palermo, D. S., and D. L. Molfese. "Language Acquisition from Age Five Onward," *Psychological Bulletin,* 78 (1972), 409–428.

Palmore, E., and F. C. Jeffers (eds.). *Prediction of Life Span: Recent Findings*. Lexington, Mass.: Heath, 1971.

Papoušek, H. "Conditioning During Early Postnatal Development," in Y. Brackbill and G. G. Thompson (eds.), *Behavior in Infancy and Early Childhood: A Book of Readings*. New York: Free Press, 1967, pp. 259–274.

Papst, M. "Das Verhalten von Kindern in einfachen strategischen Spielen," *Zeitschrift für Psychologie,* 172 (1966), 17–39.

Parry, M. H. "Infants' Responses to Novelty in Familiar and Unfamiliar Settings," *Child Development,* 43 (1972), 233–237.

Patterson, G. R. "Reprogramming the Families of Aggressive Boys," in C. E. Thoresen (ed.), *Behavior Modification in Education*. Chicago: University of Chicago Press, 1972, pp. 154–194.

Patterson, G. R., R. A. Littman, and W. Bricker. "Assertive Behavior in Children: A Step Toward a Theory of Aggression," *Monographs of the Society for Research in Child Development,* 32 (1967), whole no. 113.

Pavlov, I. P. *Conditioned Reflexes: An Investigation of the Physiological Activity of the Cerebral Cortex*. G. V. Anrep (ed. and tr.). London: Oxford University Press, 1927.

Peck, R. F., and R. J. Havighurst. *The Psychology of Character Development*. New York: Wiley, 1960.

Peel, E. A. *The Nature of Adolescent Judgment*. New York: Wiley-Interscience, 1971.

Peskin, H. "Pubertal Onset and Ego Functioning," *Journal of Abnormal Psychology,* 72 (1967), 1–15.

Pfeiffer, E., and G. C. Davis. "The Use of Leisure Time in Middle Life," *Gerontologist,* 11 (1971), 187–195.

Piaget, J. *The Language of the Child.* M. Warden (tr.). New York: Harcourt Brace Jovanovich, 1926.

———. *Judgment and Reasoning in the Child.* M. Warden (tr.). New York: Harcourt Brace Jovanovich, 1928.

———. *The Moral Judgment of the Child.* M. Gabain (tr.). Boston: Routledge & Kegan Paul, 1932.

———. *Play, Dreams and Imitation in Childhood.* C. Gattegno and F. M. Hodgson (trs.). New York: Norton, 1951.

———. *The Child's Conception of Number.* C. Gattegno and F. H. Hodgson (trs.). Boston: Routledge & Kegan Paul, 1952a.

———. *The Origins of Intelligence in Children.* M. Cook (tr.). New York: International Universities Press, 1952b.

———. *The Construction of Reality in the Child.* M. Cook (tr.). New York: Basic Books, 1954.

———. Six Psychological Studies. A. Tenzer and D. Elkind (trs.). New York: Random House, 1967.

———. "Piaget's Theory," in P. H. Mussen (ed.), *Carmichael's Manual of Child Psychology.* Vol. 1. 3rd ed. New York: Wiley, 1970, pp. 703–732.

———. *The Science of Education and the Psychology of the Child.* D. Coltman (tr.). New York: Viking, 1972.

Piaget, J., and B. Inhelder. *Le Développement des Quantités Chez L'Enfant; Conservation et Atomisme.* Neuchatel: Delachaux et Niestlé, 1941.

———. *Mémoire et Intelligence.* Paris: Presses Universitaires de France, 1968.

———. *The Psychology of the Child.* Boston: Routledge & Kegan Paul, 1969.

Piscopo, J. "Obesity: An Interdisciplinary Approach to a Major Health Problem," *The Physical Educator,* 27 (March 1970), 27–29.

Plutchik, R., M. B. Weiner, and H. Conte. "Studies of Body Image: I. Body Worries and Body Discomforts," *Journal of Gerontology,* 26 (1971), 344–350.

Powell, G. F., J. A. Brasel, and R. M. Blizzard. "Emotional Deprivation and Growth Retardation Simulating Idiopathic Hypopituitarism. I. Clinical Evaluation of the Syndrome," *New England Journal of Medicine,* 276 (1967), 1271–1278.

Powell, M., and C. D. Ferraro. "Sources of Tension in Married and Single Women Teachers of Different Ages," *Journal of Educational Psychology,* 51 (1960), 92–101.

Pratt, K. C. "The Neonate," in L. Carmichael (ed.), *Manual of Child Psychology,* 2nd ed. New York: Wiley, 1954, pp. 215–291.

Prechtl, H. F. R. "Problems of Behavioral Studies in the Newborn Infant," in D. S. Lehrman, R. A. Hinde, and E. Shaw (eds.), *Advances in the Study of Behavior.* Vol. 1. New York: Academic Press, 1965, pp. 75–98.

Prentice, N. M. "The Influence of Live and Symbolic Modeling on Promoting Moral Judgment of Adolescent Delinquents," *Journal of Abnormal Psychology,* 80 (1972), 157–161.

Project Talent Office, University of Pittsburgh. *One Year Follow-Up Study.* Bulletin No. 5. Washington, D.C.: U.S. Government Printing Office, 1966.

Psathas, G. "Ethnicity, Social Class, and Adolescent Independence from Parental Control," *American Sociological Review,* 22 (1957), 415–423.

Pulaski, M. "The Rich Rewards of Make Believe," *Psychology Today,* 7 (January 1974), 68–74.

Puner, M. *To the Good Long Life: What We Know About Growing Old.* New York: Universe Books, 1974.

R

Rainwater, L. "Crucible of Identity: The Negro Lower-Class Family," *Daedalus,* 95 (1966), 172–216.

Ramey, C. T., and L. L. Ourth. "Delayed Reinforcement and Vocalization Rates of Infants," *Child Development,* 42 (1971), 291–298.

Ramsey, G. V. "The Sexual Development of Boys," *American Journal of Psychology,* 56 (1943), 217–233.

Redl, F. "The Impact of Game Ingredients on Children's Play Behavior," in B. Schaffner (ed.), *Group Processes: Transactions of the Fourth Conference.* New York: Josiah Macy Jr. Foundation, 1959.

Reiss, I. L. *The Social Context of Premarital Sexual Permissiveness.* New York: Holt, Rinehart and Winston, 1967.

———. "How and Why America's Sex Standards Are Changing," in H. Gagnon and W. Simon (eds.), *The Sexual Scene.* Chicago: Aldine, 1970, pp. 43–57.

———. *Heterosexual Relationships Inside and Outside Marriage.* Morristown, N.J.: General Learning Press, 1973.

Rest, J. "The Hierarchical Nature of Moral Judgment: A Study of Patterns of Comprehension and Preference of Moral Stages," *Journal of Personality,* 41 (1973), 86–109.

Rest, J., E. Turiel, and L. Kohlberg. "Level of Moral Development as a Determinant of Preference and Comprehension of Moral Judgments Made by Others," *Journal of Personality,* 37 (1969), 225–252.

Rheingold, H. L. "The Social and Socializing Agent," in D. A. Goslin (ed.), *Handbook of Socialization Theory and Research.* Chicago: Rand McNally, 1969, pp. 779–791.

Rheingold, H. L., and C. O. Eckerman. "The Infant Separates Himself from His Mother," *Science,* 168 (1970), 78–83.

Rheingold, H. L., J. L. Gewirtz, and H. W. Ross. "Social Conditioning of Vocalizations in the Infant," *Journal of Comparative and Physiological Psychology,* 52 (1959), 68–73.

Riegel, K. F., and R. M. Riegel. "A Study on Changes of Attitudes and Interests During Later Years of Life," *Vita Humana* 3 (1960), 177–206.

Riley, M. W., and A. Foner. *Aging and Society, Vol. 1: An Inventory of Research Findings.* New York: Russell Sage Foundation, 1968.

Robinson, H. B., and N. M. Robinson. *The Mentally Retarded Child: A Psychological Approach.* New York: McGraw-Hill, 1965.

Roff, M., S. B. Sells, and M. M. Golden. *Social Adjustment and Personality Development in Children.* Minneapolis: University of Minnesota Press, 1972.

Roffwarg, H. P., J. N. Muzio, and W. C. Dement. "Ontogenic Development of the Human Sleep-Dream Cycle," *Science,* 152 (1966), 604–619.

Rogers, C. R. *Becoming Partners: Marriage and Its Alternatives.* New York: Delacorte, 1972.

Rohwer, W. D., Jr. "Learning, Race, and School Success," *Review of Educational Research,* 41 (1971), 191–210.

Rollin, B. "The American Way of Marriage: Remarriage," in M. E. Lasswell and T. E. Lasswell (eds.), *Love, Marriage, Family: A Developmental Approach.* Glenview, Ill.: Scott, Foresman, 1973, pp. 489–494.

Rollings, B. C., and H. Feldman. "Marital Satisfaction Over the Family Life Cycle," *Journal of Marriage and the Family,* 32 (1970), 20–28.

Rose, C. L., and B. Bell. *Predicting Longevity: Methodology and Critique.* Lexington, Mass.: Heath, 1971.

Rose, S. P. R. *The Conscious Brain.* New York: Knopf, 1973.

Rosen, B. C. "The Achievement Syndrome: A Psychocultural Dimension of Social Stratification," *American Sociological Review,* 21 (1956), 203–211.

———. "Race, Ethnicity, and the Achievement Syndrome," *American Sociological Review,* 24 (1959), 47–60.

Rosenau, N. "Sex Differences in Ideal Self-Concepts." Unpublished manuscript, Andrus Gerontology Center, Los Angeles, 1974.

Rosenberg, M. *Society and the Adolescent Self-image.* Princeton, N.J.: Princeton University Press, 1965.

Rosenhan, D. L. "The Natural Socialization of Altruistic Autonomy," in J. R. Macaulay and L. Berkowitz (eds.), *Altruism and Helping Behavior: Social Psychological Studies of Some Antecedents and Consequences.* New York: Academic Press, 1970, pp. 251–268.

Rosenthal, R. "Self-Fulfilling Prophecy," *Psychology Today,* 2 (1968), 44–51.

Rosenthal, R., and L. Jacobson. *Pygmalion in the Classroom.* New York: Holt, Rinehart and Winston, 1968.

Rosenthal, T. L., and B. J. Zimmerman. "Organization, Observation, and Guided Practice in Concept Attainment and Generalization," *Child Development,* 44 (1973), 606–613.

Rosenzweig, M. R., E. L. Bennett, and M. C. Diamond. "Brain Changes in Response to Experience," *Scientific American,* 226 (February 1972), 22–29.

Rosow, I. "Housing and Local Ties of the Aged," in B. L. Neugarten (ed.), *Middle Age and Aging: A Reader in Social Psychology.* Chicago: University of Chicago Press, 1968, pp. 382–389.

Ross, H. S., H. L. Rheingold, and C. O. Eckerman. "Approach and Exploration of a Novel Alternative by 12-Month-Old Infants," *Journal of Experimental Child Psychology,* 13 (1972), 85–93.

Rossi, A. "Transition to Parenthood," *Journal of Marriage and the Family,* 30 (1968), 26–39.

Rousseau, J. J. *Emile.* New York: Dutton, 1911 (orig. pub. 1762).

Rubin, I. "The 'Sexless Older Years'—A Socially Harmful Stereotype," *Annals of the American Academy of Political and Social Science,* 376 (1968), 86–95.

Rubin, K. H., and F. W. Schneider. "The Relationship between Moral Judgment, Egocentrism, and Altruistic Behavior," *Child Development,* 44 (1973), 661–665.

Rubin, Z. *Liking and Loving.* New York: Holt, Rinehart and Winston, 1973.

Rutter, M. "Parent-Child Separation: Psychological Effects on the Children," *Journal of Child Psychology and Psychiatry and Allied Disciplines,* 12 (1971), 233–260.

Ryle, G. *The Concept of Mind.* New York: Barnes and Noble, 1949.

S

Salapatek, P. H., and W. Kessen. "Visual Scanning of Triangles by the Human Newborn," *Journal of Experimental Child Psychology,* 3 (1966), 155–167.

Salk, L. "Mothers' Heartbeat as an Imprinting Stimulus," *Transactions of the New York Academy of Sciences,* 24 (1962), 753–763.

Saltz, E. *The Cognitive Bases of Human Learning.* Homewood, Ill.: Dorsey Press, 1971.

Sameroff, A. J. "The Components of Sucking in the Human Newborn," *Journal of Experimental Child Psychology,* 6 (1968), 607–623.

Saxton, L. *The Individual, Marriage, and the Family.* 2nd ed. Belmont, Calif.: Wadsworth, 1972.

Scarr, S., and P. Salapatek. "Patterns of Fear Development During Infancy," *Merrill-Palmer Quarterly,* 16 (1970), 53–90.

Scarr-Salapatek, S. "Genetics and the Development of Intelligence," in F. D. Horowitz *et al.* (eds.), *Review of Child Development Research.* Vol. 4. Chicago: University of Chicago Press, 1975.

Schachtel, E. G. *Metamorphosis: On the Development of Affect, Perception, Attention, and Memory.* New York: Basic Books, 1959.

Schaffer, H. R. *The Growth of Sociability.* Baltimore: Penguin, 1971.

Schaffer, H. R., and P. E. Emerson. "The Development of Social Attachments in Infancy," *Monographs of the Society for Research in Child Development,* 29 (1964a), whole no. 94.

———. "Patterns of Response to Physical Contact in Early Human Development," *Journal of Child Psychology and Psychiatry,* 5 (1964b), 1–13.

Schaie, K. W. "A General Model for the Study of Developmental Problems," *Psychological Bulletin,* 64 (1965), 92–107.

Schell, R. E., and J. W. Silber. "Sex-Role Discrimination Among Young Children," *Perceptual and Motor Skills,* 27 (1968), 379–389.

Schimmel, S. "Conditional Discrimination, Number Conception, and Response Inhibition in Two and Three-year-old Children." Unpublished doctoral dissertation, Wayne State University, 1971.

Schnall, M., E. Alter, T. Swanlund, and T. Schweitzer. "A Sensory-Motor Context Affecting Performance in a Conservation Task: A Closer Analogue of Reversibility than Empirical Return," *Child Development,* 43 (1972), 1012–1023.

Schonbuch, S. S., and R. E. Schell. "Judgments of Body Appearance by Fat and Skinny Male College Students," *Perceptual and Motor Skills,* 24 (1967), 999–1002.

Schonfeld, W. A. "Body-Image in Adolescents: A Psychiatric Concept for the Pediatrician," *Pediatrics,* 31 (1963), 845–855.

———. "Body-Image Disturbances in Adolescents with Inappropriate Sexual Development," *American Journal of Orthopsychiatry,* 34 (1964), 493–502.

Schwartz, G., and D. Merten. "The Language of Adolescence: An Anthropological Approach to the Youth Culture," *American Journal of Sociology,* 72 (1967), 453–468.

Schwartz, M., and J. Schwartz. "Evidence Against a Genetical Component to Performance on IQ Tests," *Nature,* 248 (March 1974), 84–85.

Schwartz, S. H., K. A. Feldman, M. E. Brown, and A. Heingartner. "Some Personality Correlates of Conduct in Two Situations of Moral Conflict," *Journal of Personality,* 37 (1969), 41–57.

Scott, E. M., R. Illsby, and A. M. Thomson. "A Psychological Investigation of Primigravidae. II. Maternal Social Class, Age, Physique and Intelligence," *Journal of Obstetrics and Gynaecology of the British Empire,* 63 (1956), 338–343.

Scott, J. P. "Genetics and the Development of Social Behavior in Mammals," *American Journal of Orthopsychiatry,* 32 (1962), 878–893.

———. "The Development of Social Motivation," *Nebraska Symposium on Motivation,* 15 (1967), 111–132.

———. *Early Experience and the Organization of Behavior.* Belmont, Calif.: Brooks/Cole, 1968.

Scrimshaw, N. S. "Early Malnutrition and Central Nervous System Function," *Merrill-Palmer Quarterly,* 15 (1969), 375–388.

Scrimshaw, N. S., and J. E. Gordon (eds.). *Malnutrition, Learning, and Behavior.* Cambridge, Mass.: M.I.T. Press, 1968.

Sears, R. R. "Relation of Early Socialization Experiences to Aggression in Middle Childhood," *Journal of Abnormal and Social Psychology,* (1961), (1961), 466–492.

Sears, R. R., E. E. Maccoby, and H. Levin. *Patterns of Child Rearing.* Evanston, Ill.: Row, Peterson, 1957.

Sears, R. R., L. Rau, and R. Alpert. *Identification and Childrearing.* Stanford, Calif.: Stanford University Press, 1965.

Seligman, M. E. P. "Submissive Death: Giving Up on Life," *Psychology Today,* 7 (May 1974), 80–85.

Selman, R. L. "The Relation of Role Taking to the Development of Moral Judgment in Children," *Child Development,* 42 (1971), 79–91.

Semb, G. (ed.). *Behavior Analysis and Education.* Lawrence: University of Kansas Press, 1972.

Shapiro, L. R., M. C. Hampton, and R. L. Huenemann. "Teenagers: Their Body Size and Shape, Food, and Activity," *The Journal of School Health,* 37 (1967), 166–170.

Sheldon, W. H., *et al. The Varieties of Human Physique: An Introduction to Constitutional Psychology.* New York: Harper & Row, 1940.

———. *Atlas of Men: A Guide for Somatotyping the Adult Male at All Ages.* New York: Harper & Row, 1954.

Sheresky, N., and M. Mannes. *Uncoupling: The Art of Coming Apart.* New York: Viking, 1972.

Sherif, M., and C. W. Sherif. *Groups in Harmony and Tension: An Integration of Studies on Intergroup Relations.* New York: Harper & Row, 1953.

———. *Reference Groups: Explorations into Conformity and Deviation of Adolescents.* New York: Harper & Row, 1964.

Sherman, J. A. *On the Psychology of Women: A Survey of Empirical Studies.* Springfield, Ill.: Charles C Thomas, 1973.

Shneidman, E. S. "You and Death," *Psychology Today,* 5 (June 1971), 43–45.

Shock, N. W. "The Physiology of Aging," *Scientific American,* 206 (January 1962), 100–110.

Shultz, T. R. "Development of the Appreciation of Riddles," *Child Development,* 45 (1974), 100–105.

Shultz, T. R., and F. Horibe. "Development of the Appreciation of Verbal Jokes," *Developmental Psychology,* 10 (1974), 13–20.

Siegler, R. S., D. E. Liebert, and R. M. Liebert. "Inhelder and Piaget's Pendulum Problem: Teaching Preadolescents to Act as Scientists," *Developmental Psychology,* 9 (1973), 97–101.

Sigel, I. E., and E. Mermelstein. "Effects of Nonschooling on Piagetian Tasks of Conservation." Unpublished paper, 1966. (Cited in J. H. Flavell, "Concept Development," in P. H. Mussen (ed.), *Carmichael's Manual of Child Psychology.* 3rd ed. New York: Wiley, 1970.)

Simon, W., and J. H. Gagnon. "On Psychological Development," in D. A. Goslin (ed.), *Handbook of Socialization Theory and Research.* Chicago: Rand McNally, 1969, pp. 733–752.

Simpson, R. L. "Parental Influence, Anticipatory Socialization, and Social Mobility," *American Sociological Review,* 27 (1962), 517–522.

Sinclair, C. B. *Movement of the Young Child: Ages Two to Six.* Columbus, Ohio: Merrill, 1973.

Singer, J. L. *The Child's World of Make-Believe: Experimental Studies of Imaginative Play.* New York: Academic Press, 1973.

Siqueland, E., and C. A. Delucia. "Visual Reinforcement of Non-Nutritive Sucking in Human Infants," *Science,* 165 (1969), 1144–1146.

Skinner, B. F. *The Behavior of Organisms: An Experimental Analysis.* New York: Appleton-Century-Crofts, 1938.

————. "Pigeons in a Pelican," *American Psychologist,* 15 (1960), 28–37.

————. *About Behaviorism.* New York: Knopf, 1974.

Skodak, M., and H. M. Skeels. "A Final Follow-Up Study of One Hundred Adopted Children," *Journal of Genetic Psychology,* 75 (1949), 85–125.

Slobin, D. I. "Children and Language: They Learn the Same Way All Around the World," *Psychology Today,* 6 (July 1972), 71–74+.

————. "Cognitive Prerequisites for the Development of Grammar," in C. A. Ferguson and D. I. Slobin (eds.), *Studies of Child Language Development.* New York: Holt, Rinehart and Winston, 1973, pp. 175–208.

————. "On the Nature of Talk to Children," in E. H. Lenneberg and E. Lenneberg (eds.), *Foundations of Language Development: A Multidisciplinary Approach.* UNESCO-IBRO, in press.

Smedslund, J. "The Acquisition of Conservation of Substance and Weight in Children. V. Practice in Conflict Situations Without External Reinforcement," *Scandinavian Journal of Psychology,* 2 (1961), 156–160.

Smith, C. "Effects of Maternal Undernutrition upon the Newborn Infant in Holland (1944–45)," *Journal of Pediatrics,* 30 (1947), 229–243.

Smith, H. "A Comparison of Interview and Observation Measures of Mother Behavior," *Journal of Abnormal and Social Psychology,* 57 (1958), 278–282.

Smoller-Weimer, A. "Proceedings of the 27th Annual Scientific Meeting of the Gerontological Society," *Gerontologist,* 14 (1974), 69.

Sontag, L. W., and H. Newbery. "Normal Variations of Fetal Heart Rate During Pregnancy," *American Journal of Obstetrics and Gynecology,* 40 (1940), 449–452.

Sorensen, R. C. *Adolescent Sexuality in Contemporary America: Personal Values and Sexual Behavior, Ages Thirteen to Nineteen.* New York: World Press, 1973.

Spelt, D. K. "The Conditioning of the Human Fetus *in utera,*" *Journal of Experimental Psychology,* 38 (1948), 338–346.

Spence, D., and T. Lonner. "The 'Empty Nest': A Transition Within Motherhood," *Family Coordinator,* 20 (October 1971), 369–375.

Sroufe, L. A., and J. P. Wunsch. "The Development of Laughter in the First Year of Life," *Child Development,* 43 (1972), 1326–1344.

Staats, A. "Linguistic-Mentalistic Theory Versus an Explanatory S-R Learning Theory of Language Development," in D. I. Slobin (ed.), *The Ontogenesis of Grammar: A Theoretical Symposium.* New York: Academic Press, 1971, pp. 103–150.

Staats, A., B. A. Brewer, and M. Gross. "Learning and Cognitive Development: Representative Samples, Cumulative-Hierarchical Learning, and Experimental-Longitudinal Methods," *Monographs of the Society for Research in Child Development,* 35 (1970), whole no. 8.

Staffieri, J. R. "A Study of Social Stereotype of Body Image in Children," *Journal of Personality and Social Psychology,* 7 (1967), 101–104.

Staub, E. "A Child in Distress: The Influence of Age and Number of Witnesses on Children's Attempts to Help," *Journal of Personality and Social Psychology,* 14 (1970), 130–140.

————. "A Child in Distress: The Influence of Nurturance and Modeling on Children's Attempts to Help," *Developmental Psychology,* 5 (1971), 124–132.

Stein, A. H., S. R. Pohly, and E. Mueller. "The Influence of Masculine, Feminine, and Neutral Tasks on Children's Achievement Behavior, Expectancies of Success, and Attainment Values," *Child Development,* 42 (1971), 195–207.

Stendler, C., D. Damrin, and A. C. Haines. "Studies in Cooperation and Competition: I. The Effects of Working for Group and Individual Rewards on the Social Climate of Children's Groups," *Journal of Genetic Psychology,* 79 (1951), 173–197.

Stephens, M. W., and P. Delys. "External Control Expectancies Among Disadvantaged Children at Preschool Age," *Child Development,* 44 (1973), 670–674.

Stephenson, R. M. "Mobility Orientation and Stratification of 1,000 Ninth Graders," *American Sociological Review,* 22 (1957), 204–212.

Stevenson, H. W. *Children's Learning.* New York: Appleton-Century-Crofts, 1972.

Stewart, W. A. (ed.). *Non-standard Speech and the Teaching of English.* Washington, D.C.: Center for Applied Linguistics, 1964.

Stinnett, N., L. Carter, and J. Montgomery. "Older Persons' Perceptions of Their Marriages," *Journal of Marriage and the Family,* 34 (1972), 665–670.

Stirnimann, F. "Über das Farbempfinden Neugeborener," *Annales Paediatrici,* 163 (1944), 1–25.

Stolz, H. R., and L. H. Stolz. *Somatic Development of Adolescent Boys: A Study of the Growth in Boys During the Second Decade of Life.* New York: Macmillan, 1951.

Streib, G., and C. Schneider. *Retirement in American Society; Impact and Process.* Ithaca, N.Y.: Cornell University Press, 1971.

Stuart, H. C., and D. G. Prugh (eds.). *The Healthy Child: His Physical, Psychological, and Social Development.* Cambridge, Mass.: Harvard University Press, 1960.

Sullivan, H. S. *The Interpersonal Theory of Psychiatry.* H. Perry and M. Gawel (eds.). New York: Norton, 1953.

Super, C. M., J. Kagan, F. J. Morrison, M. M. Haith, and J. Weiffenbach. "Discrepancy and Attention in the Five-Month Infant," *Genetic Psychology Monographs,* 85 (1972), 305–331.

Super, D. E. "Vocational Development in Adolescence and Early Childhood: Tasks and Behaviors," in D. E. Super, R. Starishevsky, N. Matlin, and J. P. Jordaan (eds.), *Career Development: Self-Concept Theory.* Princeton, N.J.: College Entrance Examination Board, 1963, pp. 79–95.

Super, D. E., and P. L. Overstreet. *The Vocational Maturity of Ninth-Grade Boys.* New York: Columbia University Press, 1960.

Sussman, M., and L. Burchinal. "Kin Family Network: Unheralded Structure in Current Conceptualizations of Family Functioning," in M. Sussman (ed.), *Marriage and the Family.* 3rd ed. Boston: Houghton Mifflin, 1968, pp. 72–81.

Sutton-Smith, B. "Child's Play—Very Serious Business," *Psychology Today,* 5 (December 1971), 66–69.

Sutton-Smith, B., and J. M. Roberts. "Rubrics of Competitive Behavior," *Journal of Genetic Psychology,* 105 (1964), 13–37.

Sutton-Smith, B., and B. G. Rosenberg. *The Sibling.* New York: Holt, Rinehart and Winston, 1970.

T

Tallmer, M., and B. Kutner. "Disengagement and the Stresses of Aging," *Journal of Gerontology,* 24 (1969), 70–75.

Tanner, J. M. *Education and Physical Growth: Implications of the Study of Children's Growth for Educational Theory and Practice.* London: University of London Press, 1961.

————. *Growth of Adolescence, with a General Consideration of the Effects of Hereditary and Environmental Factors upon Growth and Maturation from Birth to Maturity.* 2nd ed. Oxford: Blackwell, 1962.

————. "Physical Growth," in P. H. Mussen (ed.), *Carmichael's Manual of Child Psychology.* Vol. 1. 3rd ed. New York: Wiley, 1970, pp. 77–155.

————. "Sequence, Tempo and Individual Variation in Growth and Development of Boys and Girls Aged Twelve to Sixteen," in J. Kagan and R. Coles (eds.), *Twelve to Sixteen: Early Adolescence.* New York: Norton, 1972, pp. 1–24.

Tanner, J. M., R. H. Whitehouse, and M. J. R. Healy. *A New System for Estimating Skeletal Maturity from the Hand and Wrist, with Standards Derived from a Study of 2,600 Healthy British Children.* Parts I and II. Paris: Centre International de l'Enfance, 1962.

Taub, H. A., and M. K. Long. "The Effects of Practice on Short-Term Memory of Young and Old Subjects," *Journal of Gerontology,* 27 (1972), 494–499.

Taylor, D. C. "Differential Rates of Cerebral Maturation Between Sexes and Between Hemispheres," *Lancet,* 2 (1969), 140–142.

Terrien, F. "Turn Backward on Time," in C. Vedder (ed.), *Problems of Middle Age.* Springfield, Ill.: Charles C Thomas, 1965, pp. 29–39.

Thomas, A., S. Chess, and H. G. Birch. "The Origin of Personality," *Scientific American,* 223 (August 1970), 102–109.

Thomas, A., S. Chess, H. G. Birch, M. E. Hertzig, and S. Korn. *Behavioral Individuality in Early Childhood.* New York: New York University Press, 1963.

Thompson, W. R. "Influence of Prenatal Maternal Anxiety on Emotionality in Young Rats," *Science,* 125 (1957), 698–699.

Thompson, W. R., and J. Grusec.
"Studies of Early Experience," in
P. H. Mussen (ed.), *Carmichael's
Manual of Child Psychology.* Vol.
2. 3rd ed. New York: Wiley, 1970,
pp. 565–656.

Thoresen, C. E., and M. Mahoney.
Behavioral Self-Control. New
York: Holt, Rinehart and Winston,
1974.

Timaras, P. S. *Developmental Physiology and Aging.* New York:
Macmillan, 1972.

Tinbergen, N. *The Study of Instinct.*
Oxford: Clarendon Press, 1951.

———. *The Animal in Its World:
Explorations of an Ethologist,
1932–1972.* Field Studies, vol. 1.
Cambridge, Mass.: Harvard University Press, 1972.

Tomeh, A. K. "Informal Participation
in a Metropolitan Community," *Sociological Quarterly,* 8 (1967),
85–102.

Tonkova-Yampol'skaya, R. V. "De-
velopment of Speech Intonation in
Infants During the First Two Years
of Life," in C. A. Ferguson and
D. I. Slobin (eds.), *Studies of Child
Language Development.* New York:
Holt, Rinehart and Winston, 1973,
pp. 128–138.

**Trainham, G., and J. C.
Montgomery.** "Self-Demand Feeding for Babies," *The American
Journal of Nursing,* 46 (1946),
767–770.

Trivers, R. L. "The Evolution of Reciprocal Altruism," *The Quarterly
Review of Biology,* 46 (1971),
35–57.

Tyler, L. E. "The Antecendents of
Two Varieties of Vocational Interests," *Genetic Psychology Monographs,* 70 (1964), 177–227.

U

U.S. Bureau of the Census. "Voter
Participation in the National Elec-
tion: November 1964," *Current
Population Reports,* Series P-20,
no. 143, 1965.

———. "Marital Status and Living
Arrangements: March 1972," Cur-
rent Population Reports, Series
P-20, no. 242. Washington, D.C.:
U.S. Government Printing Office,
1972a.

———. *1970 Census of Population.
Subject Reports: Marital Status.*
Washington, D.C.: U.S. Govern-
ment Printing Office, 1972b.

**U.S. National Center for Health
Statistics.** *Vital Statistics of the
United States, 1968.* Vol. 2, Part
B: Mortality. Rockville, Md.: U.S.
Department of Health, Education,
and Welfare, 1971.

———. *Vital Statistics of the United
States, 1973.* Vol. 2, Part A: Mortality. Rockville, Md.: U.S. Department of Health, Education, and
Welfare, 1974.

Uzgiris, I. C. "Situational Generality
of Conservation," *Child Development,* 35 (1964), 831–841.

V

Van Leeuwenhoek, A., and J. Ham.
"Observationes de natis e semine
genetali animalculis," *Philosophical
Transactions of the Royal Society
of London,* 12 (1677). No. 142,
1040. (Cited in J. Needham, *A History of Embryology.* 2nd rev. ed.,
with the assistance of A. Hughes.
Cambridge: Cambridge University
Press, 1959, p. 267.)

Verinis, J. S., and S. Roll. "Primary
and Secondary Male Characteristics:
The Hairiness and Large Penis Stereotypes," *Psychological Reports,*
26 (1970), 123–126.

**Verwoerdt, A., E. Pfeiffer, and H.
Wang.** "Sexual Behavior in Senes-
cence. II. Patterns of Sexual Activity and Interest," *Geriatrics,* 24
(1969), 137–154.

Vlietstra, A. G., and J. C. Wright.
"Sensory Modality and Transmodal
Stimulus Properties in Children's
Discrimination Learning and Trans-
fer," *Annual Report, Kansas Cen-
ter for Research in Early Childhood
Education.* Lawrence: University of
Kansas, 1971.

Vogel, B. S., and R. E. Schell. "Vocational Interest Patterns in Late
Maturity and Retirement," *Journal
of Gerontology,* 23 (1968), 66–70.

Von Frisch, K. *The Dance Language
and Orientation of Bees.* L. E.
Chadwick (tr.). Cambridge, Mass.:
Belknap Press of Harvard University Press, 1967.

Vygotsky, L. S. *Thought and Language.* E. Hanfmann and G. Vakar
(trs.). Cambridge, Mass.: M.I.T.
Press, 1962.

Wahler, R. G. "Child-Child Interactions in Free Field Settings: Some Experimental Analyses," *Journal of Experimental Child Psychology,* 5 (1967), 278–293.

Wallach, M. A. "Creativity," in P. H. Mussen (ed.), *Carmichael's Manual of Child Psychology.* Vol. 1. 3rd ed. New York: Wiley, 1970.

Waller, W. W. *The Family: A Dynamic Interpretation.* New York: Cordon, 1938.

Walster, E., V. Aronson, D. Abrahams, and L. Rottmann. "Importance of Physical Attractiveness in Dating Behavior," *Journal of Personality and Social Psychology,* 4 (1966), 508–516.

Walters, C. E. "Prediction of Postnatal Development from Fetal Activity," *Child Development,* 36 (1965), 801–808.

Walters, R. H., and R. D. Parke. "Influence of Response Consequences to a Social Model on Resistance to Deviation," *Journal of Experimental Child Psychology,* 1 (1964), 269–280.

Walters, R. H., R. D. Parke, and V. A. Cane. "Timing of Punishment and the Observation of Consequences to Others as Determinants of Response Inhibition," *Journal of Experimental Child Psychology,* 2 (1965), 10–30.

Waterlow, J. C. "Note on the Assessment and Classification of Protein-Energy Malnutrition in Children," *Lancet,* 2 (1973), 87–89.

Watson, E. B., and G. H. Lawrey. *Growth and Development of Children.* 5th ed. Chicago: Year Book Medical Publishers, 1967.

Watson, J. S. "The Development and Generalization of 'Contingency Awareness' in Early Infancy: Some Hypotheses," *Merrill-Palmer Quarterly,* 12 (1966), 123–135.

———. "Cognitive-Perceptual Development in Infancy: Setting for the Seventies," *Merrill-Palmer Quarterly,* 17 (1971), 139–152.

———. "Smiling, Cooing and 'the Game'," *Merrill-Palmer Quarterly,* 18 (1972), 323–339.

Weg, R. B. "The Aging and the Aged in Contemporary Society," *Journal of Physical Therapy,* 53 (1973a), 749–756.

———. "The Changing Physiology of Aging," *American Journal of Occupational Therapy,* 27 (1973b), 213–217.

Weir, R. H. *Language in the Crib.* The Hague: Mouton, 1962.

Weisman, A. "Psychosocial Death," *Psychology Today,* 6 (November 1972), 77–79+.

Werner, H. *Comparative Psychology of Mental Development.* E. B. Garside (tr.). New York: International Universities Press, 1948.

———. "The Concept of Development from a Comparative and Organismic Point of View," in D. B. Harris (ed.), *The Concept of Development: An Issue in the Study of Human Behavior.* Minneapolis: University of Minnesota Press, 1957, pp. 125–148.

White, B. L. "An Experimental Approach to the Effects of Experience on Early Human Behavior," in J. P. Hill (ed.), *Minnesota Symposia on Child Psychology.* Vol. 1. Minneapolis: University of Minnesota Press, 1967, pp. 201–226.

———. *Human Infants: Experience and Psychological Development.* Englewood Cliffs, N.J.: Prentice-Hall, 1971.

White, B. L., and R. Held. "Plasticity of Sensorimotor Development in the Human Infant," in J. F. Rosenblith and W. Allinsmith (eds.), *The Causes of Behavior II: Readings in Child Development and Educational Psychology.* 2nd ed. Boston: Allyn & Bacon, 1966, pp. 60–70.

White, R. W. "Competence and the Psychosexual Stages of Development," in M. R. Jones (ed.), *Nebraska Symposium on Motivation.* Lincoln: University of Nebraska Press, 1960, pp. 97–141.

———. *Lives in Progress: A Study of the Natural Growth of Personality.* 2nd ed. New York: Holt, Rinehart and Winston, 1966.

White, S. "Age Differences in Reaction to Stimulus Variation," in O. J. Harvey (ed.), *Experience Structure & Adaptability.* New York: Springer, 1966, pp. 95–122.

———. "The Learning Theory Tradition and Child Psychology," in P. H. Mussen (ed.), *Carmichael's Manual of Child Psychology.* Vol. 1. 3rd ed. New York: Wiley, 1970, pp. 657–701.

Whiting, B. B. *Six Cultures: Studies of Child Rearing.* New York: Wiley, 1963.

Whiting, J. W. M. "Resource Mediation and Learning by Identification," in I. Iscoe and H. W. Stevenson (eds.), *Personality Development in Children.* Austin: University of Texas Press, 1960, pp. 112–126.

Wickelgren, L. W. "Convergence in the Human Newborn," *Journal of Experimental Child Psychology,* 5 (1967), 74–85.

Widdowson, E. M. "Mental Contentment and Physical Growth," *Lancet,* 260 (1951), 1316–1318.

Wiesel, T. N., and D. H. Hubel. "Effects of Visual Deprivation on Morphology and Physiology of Cells in the Cat's Lateral Geniculate Body," *Journal of Neurophysiology,* 26 (1963), 978–993.

Wiggins, J. S., N. Wiggins, and J. C. Conger. "Correlates of Heterosexual Somatic Preference," *Journal of Personality and Social Psychology,* 10 (1968), 82–90.

Winder, C. L., and L. Rau. "Parental Attitudes Associated with Social Deviance in Preadolescent Boys," *Journal of Abnormal Social Psychology,* 64 (1962), 418–424.

Windle, W. F. *Biology of Neurologia.* Springfield, Ill.: Charles C Thomas, 1968.

Winer, G. A. "An Analysis of Verbal Facilitation of Class-Inclusion Reasoning," *Child Development,* 45 (1974), 224–227.

Wohlford, P., J. W. Santrock, S. E. Berger, and D. Liberman. "Older Brothers' Influence on Sex-Typed, Aggressive, and Dependent Behavior in Father-Absent Children," *Developmental Psychology,* 4 (1971), 124–134.

Wohlwill, J. F. "The Concept of Experience: S or R?" *Human Development,* 16 (1973), 90–107.

Wolf, T. M. "A Developmental Investigation of Televised Modeled Verbalizations on Resistance to Temptation," *Developmental Psychology,* 6 (1972), 537.

Wolff, G. "Increased Bodily Growth of School-Children Since the War," *Lancet,* 228 (1935), 1006–1011.

Wolff, K. F. *Theoria generationis.* Halle, Germany, 1759. (Cited in J. Needham, *A History of Embryology.* 2nd rev. ed., with the assistance of A. Hughes. Cambridge: Cambridge University Press, 1959, p. 291.)

Wolff, P. H. "The Role of Biological Rhythms in Early Psychological Development," *Bulletin of the Menninger Clinic,* 31 (1967), 197–218.

———. "The Natural History of Crying and Other Vocalizations in Early Infancy," in B. M. Foss (ed.), *Determinants of Infant Behavior.* Vol. 4. London: Methuen, 1969, pp. 81–109.

Woodruff, D. S., and J. E. Birren. "Age Changes and Cohort Difference in Personality," *Developmental Psychology,* 6 (March 1972), 252–259.

Y

Yakovlev, P. I., and A. R. Lecours. "The Mylogenetic Cycles of Regional Maturation of the Brain," in A. Minkowski (ed.), *Regional Development of the Brain in Early Life.* Oxford: Blackwell, 1967.

Yarrow, L. J. "Maternal Deprivation: Toward an Empirical and Conceptual Re-evaluation," *Psychological Bulletin,* 58 (1961), 459–490.

———. "Research in Dimensions of Early Maternal Care," *Merrill-Palmer Quarterly,* 9 (1963), 101–114.

Yarrow, M. R., P. M. Scott, and C. Z. Waxler. "Learning Concern for Others," *Developmental Psychology,* 8 (1973), 240–260.

Yarrow, M. R., P. Scott, L. de Leeuw, and C. Heinig. "Child-Rearing in Families of Working and Nonworking Mothers," *Sociometry,* 25 (1962), 122–140.

Z

Zankov, L. V., and D. M. Mayants. "Memorizing and Recalling Objects in Hearing and Deaf-mute Children." Moscow, 1940.

Zaporozhets, A. V. "The Development of Perception in the Preschool Child," in P. H. Mussen (ed.), "European Research in Cognitive Development," *Monographs of the Society for Research in Child Development,* 30 (1965), 82–101.

Zborowski, M. "Aging and Recreation," *Journal of Gerontology,* 17 (1962), 302–309.

Zelnik, M., and J. F. Kantner. *Sexuality, Contraception, and Pregnancy Among Young Unmarried Females in the U.S.* Unpublished manuscript, 1972. (Cited in I. L. Reiss. *Heterosexual Relationships Inside and Outside Marriage.* Morristown, N.J.: General Learning Press, 1973, p. 15.)

Zur Aschoff, L. "Normalen und Pathologischen Anatomie des Criesenalters," *Medisinische Klinik,* 33 (1937), 257–291.

GLOSSARY

A

accommodation. According to Piaget, the modification of existing schemes to incorporate new knowledge that does not fit them.

action-instrument. In the two-word stage of language development, the indication of knowledge of the use of instruments, as in "Cut knife."

action-location. In the two-word stage of language development, the expression of the location of an action, as in "Sit chair."

action-recipient. In the two-word stage of language development, the indication of who is to benefit from an action, as in "Cookie me."

acuity. The ability to see objects clearly and to resolve detail.

adaptation. A key principle in ethological theories, referring to the way that behavior changes or develops to meet environmental demands and to insure survival and reproduction.

addition. According to Flavell, a sequence in intellectual development in which the later-emerging skill is added to the earlier one and supplements but does not replace it. An example is the addition of counting ability to one's knowledge of number concepts.

afterbirth. The placenta, its membranes, and the rest of the umbilical cord, all expelled in the final stage of labor.

agent, action, and object. In the two-word stage of language development, the expression of an agent's action on an object, using only two of the components of the thought, as in "Daddy ball" for "Daddy throw ball."

aggressiveness. Verbal or physical behavior that is inappropriate or harms someone.

alleles. The different forms that a gene can take at a given site on a chromosome.

amniocentesis. A means of detecting fetal abnormality by the insertion of a hollow needle through the maternal abdomen and the drawing out of a sample of amniotic fluid on which chromosomal analyses can be performed.

amnion. The inner membrane of the sac that surrounds and protects the developing fertilized ovum.

androgens. Male hormones.

androgynous. The capability of expressing both masculine and feminine behaviors and attitudes, depending on their appropriateness to the particular situation.

Apgar score. Developed by Apgar and James in 1962, a much-used and practical scoring system for assessing, on a scale from 0 to 2, appearance, heart rate, reflex irritability, activity, muscle tone, and respiratory effort in newborns. The totaled score may vary from 0 to 10 (10 being best).

artificialism. A kind of precausal thinking that refers to explanations involving either God or man as the artisan of all natural things.

assertiveness. Verbal or physical behavior that is appropriate and that injures no one.

assimilation. According to Piaget, the incorporation of new knowledge through the use of existing schemes.

asynchrony. The maturation of different body parts at different rates. This disproportion becomes most pronounced during puberty.

attachment. The primary social bond that develops between an infant and its caretaker.

attribution. In the two-word stage of language development, the modifying of nouns with attributes, as in "Red truck."

autonomy. A feeling of self-control and self-determination. According to Erikson's theory of psychosocial development, this feeling develops around the ages of two to four and manifests itself in the child's increasing demands to determine his own behavior.

B

babbling. The sound sequences of alternating vowels and consonants, such as "babababa." Produced by the infant, they may be a form of motor practice that facilitates later speech development.

basal metabolism. The rate of energy required to maintain the body's functioning while resting.

behavior. An observable act that can be described or measured reliably.

behavior modification. An approach to changing behavior that involves a wide variety of techniques based on learning principles such as conditioning and reinforcement.

body ideal. The body type defined by one's culture as ideally attractive and sex appropriate.

C

canalization. The temporary deviation from and subsequent return to a child's normal growth curve.

cephalocaudal development. The progression of physical and motor development from head to foot. For example, a baby's head develops and grows before his torso, his arms, and his legs.

cerebral dominance. Refers to the fact that one cerebral hemisphere is dominant over the other in the control of body movements, as in handedness.

cervix. The pinhead-sized opening that separates the vagina from the uterus.

chorion. The outer membrane of the sac that surrounds and protects the developing fertilized ovum.

chromosomes. The beadlike strings of genes present in every cell of the body. Except in the gametes, they occur in pairs that reproduce and split during cell formation.

classical conditioning. A procedure in which conditioned reflexes are established by the association of one stimulus with another stimulus that is known to cause an unconditioned reflex. Also known as Pavlovian conditioning or respondent conditioning.

clinical study. A study consisting of in-depth interviews and observations. It can be controlled or can be varied for each subject.

cognition. The process of gaining knowledge about the world through sensing, perceiving, using symbols, and reasoning; the actual knowledge that an individual has about the world.

cognitive theorists. Theorists such as Jean Piaget and Jerome Bruner who describe intellectual development and Roger Brown who describes early language behavior. They see children's thinking as different but no less effective than that of adults.

cohorts. The members of a certain age group; a group of people of the same age.

conception. The uniting of the sperm and the egg, which signals the beginning of life.

concrete-operational stage. A subperiod of the representational stage, in Piaget's theory of cognitive development, which begins when children understand new kinds of logical operations involving reversible transformations of concrete objects and events.

conditioned reflex. In classical conditioning, one of two kinds of reflexes in which the reflex is one that comes to be elicited by a previously neutral stimulus.

conjunctive concept. A concept in which all the attributes of a category must be present in order for the object to be included in the category.

conservation. The understanding that certain perceptual changes do not actually alter physical quantities. For example, rearranging a row of objects does not affect their number.

constructionist. A description of Piaget's theory that a child's actions on objects in his environment yield knowledge of the effects of his actions and the properties of the objects and that these actions thus construct his understanding of reality.

continuous reinforcement. In operant conditioning, a schedule in which each correct response is reinforced.

control. The intentional modification of any condition of an investigation. These modifications may include the selection of subjects for study, the experiences they have in the study, and the possible responses that they can give to that experience.

conventional level. The level of moral reasoning in which value is placed in maintaining the conventional social order and the expectations of others.

convergence. The mechanism by which the slightly different images of an object seen by each eye come together to form a single image.

cooperative (reciprocal) play. Play in which the child begins to adjust his behavior to the activities and desires of his peers.

correlation coefficient. The numerical expression of how closely two sets of measurements correspond. Correlation coefficients range from $+1.00$ (perfect positive correlation) to -1.00 (perfect negative correlation).

co-twin control. A method of studying the relative contributions of maturation and experience in which the experimenter gives one of a pair of twins some experiences believed to be important in learning a skill and withholds or delays those same experiences for the other twin.

cross-sectional studies. Studies that compare different age groups at some specific point in time.

D

deoxyribonucleic acid (DNA). The complex chemical containing the genetic code that guides development.

dependence. Reliance on others for comfort, nurturance, or assistance in accomplishing some task or activity.

detachment. The infant's desire to try out new experiences and to expand his competence. Developing in the second year, it coexists and interacts with the attachment system.

differentiation. The developmental trend in which an infant's abilities become increasingly distinct and specific.

disjunctive concept. A concept in which a member of a category may possess some, but need not possess all, of several different attributes to be included in the category.

displacement. The ability to communicate information about objects, people, and events in another place or another time; one of three formal properties of language.

dominant gene. The gene whose corresponding trait appears in the individual when it is paired with a different gene for that trait.

Down's syndrome. A condition that can result from an extra sex chromosome in the fertilized egg, or when extra material from Chromosome 21 becomes attached to another chromosome. Formerly called mongolism, it produces various physical abnormalities and mental retardation in the affected child.

E

ecological. The approach to studying development which takes into account the limiting and determining effects of the physical and social environment.

ectoderm. The layer of cells in the embryo from which the skin, sense organs, and nervous system will develop.

ego. An aspect of personality, in Freud's theory, which guides a person's realistic coping behavior and mediates the eternal conflicts between what one wants to do (id) and what one must or must not do (superego).

egocentrism. In cognitive development, the tendency of an individual to think that others see things from the same point of view and that they also experience his own behavior, thought, and feelings in relation to these things.

embryonic period (embryo). The six weeks, following the two-week germinal period, during which the organism begins to take shape and its various organ systems begin to form.

emotional dependence. Dependence on others, which has as its aim the obtaining of their comfort and nurturance.

endoderm. The layer of cells in the embryo from which the visceral organs and digestive tract develop.

equilibration. The most general developmental principle in Piaget's theory, which states that an organism always tends toward biological and psychological balance and that development is a progressive approximation to an ideal state of equilibrium that it never fully achieves.

estrogens. Female hormones.

expectancy. Anticipation of a given stimulus determined by one's previous experiences with related stimuli. Deviation from expectancy is a factor in selective attention.

experimentation. A type of study designed to control the arrangement and manipulation of conditions in order to systematically observe particular phenomena.

expression. The second component of a baby's sucking, during which the nipple is pressed against the roof of the mouth with the tongue applying heavy pressure at the front of the mouth and then progressively moving toward the rear.

extinguish. To gradually eliminate a response by withholding reinforcement.

F

Fallopian tube. The tube that connects the ovaries with the uterus.

fetal period (fetus). The developing organism from approximately eight weeks after conception to birth.

field study. A study of naturally occurring behavior in which the researcher controls only some aspects of the situation.

formal-operational period. The last of the major stages in Piaget's theory of intellectual development. It begins around age twelve when the individual starts to develop a formal logic that consists of "if . . . then" statements and to engage in thinking that is characterized by the ability to consider what is possible, as well as what is.

G

gametes. The mature reproductive cells; the sperm and the egg.

genes. The microscopic elements carried by the chromosomes. They contain the codes that produce inherited physical traits and behavioral dispositions.

genetic epistemology. The developmental study of what is known and how it comes to be known; most closely associated with Piaget's theory.

genotype. The specific combination of alleles that characterize one's genetic make-up.

germinal period. The first two weeks after conception when the fertilized egg is primarily engaged in cell division.

gestation period. The total period of prenatal development calculated from the beginning of the mother's last menstruation (280 days, 40 weeks, or 9 calendar months).

gestational age. The age of the fetus calculated from the date of conception.

gonococcus. The bacterium that produces gonorrhea.

gonorrhea. A venereal disease.

grammar. The structural principles of a language; syntax.

grasping reflex. The tendency during the first few weeks of life for an infant to clutch any small object placed in his hand.

guilt. A negative feeling that stems from deviation from one's own internalized moral standards.

H

habituation. A decrement in responding associated with repeated stimulation; analogous to becoming bored with a stimulus.

heritability. An estimate, based on a sample of individuals, of the relative contribution of genetics to a given trait or behavior.

heterozygous. The condition in which cells contain different genes for the same trait. The dominant gene will determine the appearance of the trait.

homozygous. The condition in which cells have matching genes for a trait.

hostile aggression. Behavior that aims at hurting another person.

I

id. An aspect of personality, in Freud's theory, in which all unconscious impulses reside.

identification (language). In the two-word stage of language development, the verbal extension of a simple pointing response, as in "See doggy."

identification (socialization). A developmental process through which a child comes to be like specific people whom he has grown to respect, admire, or love.

imitation. The principle and the processes by which an individual copies or reproduces what has been observed.

implanted. Attached; after floating freely for several days, the fertilized ovum becomes implanted in the uterine wall.

imprinting. The phenomenon occurring during a sensitive period of an animal's infancy, in which the animal follows a certain type of moving object, usually its mother, and forms a strong, long-lasting social attachment to it.

inclusion. According to Flavell, a sequence in intellectual development in which the earlier item becomes incorporated as an integral part of the later item. An example is the inclusion of children's early naming skills into all later language development.

induced abortion. The premature removal of the fetus by deliberate interference.

instrumental aggression. Behavior that aims at retrieving or acquiring an object, territory, or privilege.

instrumental conditioning. See *operant conditioning.*

instrumental dependence. Dependence that involves seeking assistance as a means of accomplishing some task or activity.

integration (hierarchic). The developmental trend of combining simple, differentiated skills into more complex skills.

interval reinforcement. In operant conditioning, the schedule of the partial reinforcement in which a person is reinforced for his first correct response after a specified period of time has passed.

K

kwashiorkor. The severe, often fatal, disease caused by prolonged protein deficiency.

L

lanugo. The fine hair appearing on parts of some newborns' bodies that may remain several weeks before disappearing.

lateralization. The developmental process in which one hemisphere of the brain becomes dominant.

location. In the two-word stage of language development, the signaling of the location of an object with such words as "here" and "there."

locus of control. The perceived location of the control over an individual's life. It can be internal, as when one believes he controls his own life, or it can be external, as when one believes his life is controlled by forces outside himself.

longitudinal studies. Studies that follow the same subjects over a specified period of time.

M

maternal deprivation. The loss or lack of mothering.

mediating mechanisms. Mechanisms assumed to intervene between a stimulus situation and a response and to explain the resulting behavior.

mediation. According to Flavell, a sequence in intellectual development in which an earlier-developed item serves as a bridge to a later one. An example is the necessity of knowing how to count before one can understand that five coins remain the same no matter how they are arranged.

meiosis. The cell division that produces gametes, each containing twenty-three single rather than twenty-three pairs of chromosomes.

menarche. First menstruation.

menstrual age. The age of the fetus when calculated from the beginning of the mother's last menstruation.

menstrual cycle. The discharge of blood and tissue from the uterus, which occurs monthly from puberty to menopause, except during pregnancy.

mesoderm. The layer of cells in the embryo from which the muscular, circulatory, and skeletal systems will develop.

miscarriage. The spontaneous expulsion from the uterus of a fetus less than twenty-eight weeks old.

modeling. A principle and a process by which an individual learns by observing the behavior of others.

modification. According to Flavell, a sequence in intellectual development in which the later-emerging behavior represents a differentiation or a generalization of a more stable form of an earlier skill. An example is children's coming to realize that quantities do not change if only certain perceptual properties do.

moral conduct. A form of complex behavior involving three aspects: reasoning, feeling, and action.

moral development. The nature and course of development of an individual's moral thoughts, feelings, and actions.

Moro reflex (response). A reflex which is most easily elicited during the infant's first three months of life and which consists of a thrusting out of the arms in an embracelike movement when the baby suddenly loses support for his neck and head.

mutagenic. Altering the genetic structure of cells, which results in the production of new forms.

myelin. A white, fatty substance that covers some nerve fibers.

N

naturalistic observation. A form of study in which there is observation of behavior without any interference from the investigator.

nature. The genetic-biological determinants used to explain developmental changes.

negation. In the two-word stage of language development, the use of a negative construction to contradict or to avoid a misunderstanding.

negative pressure. The first component of a baby's sucking. A vacuum is produced by closing the oral cavity in the back of the mouth, sealing the lips around the object to be sucked, and lowering the jaws.

neonate. A technical term for a newborn baby.

nonexistence. In the two-word stage of language development, the expression of object disappearance or cessation of activity, as in "All-gone ball."

norm. An outline that describes the development of an important attribute or skill and the approximate ages at which it appears in the average child.

novelty. A possible factor in selective attention, involving a different or unique aspect of a stimulus.

nurture. The environmental determinants used to explain developmental changes.

O

object identity. In cognitive development, the understanding that an object remains the same even though it may undergo various transformations.

object permanence. In cognitive development, the understanding that an object continues to exist even though it disappears or is out of sight.

operant conditioning. A procedure by which the frequency of a response can be increased or decreased, depending on when, how, and to what extent it is reinforced. Associated with B. F. Skinner, it is also called instrumental conditioning.

ovaries. The female reproductive glands, which release ova.

overextension. A generalization in the apparent meaning of a word so that it includes a number of dissimilar objects or events.

overregularization. A kind of temporary error in language development in which the apparent attempt is to simplify or to make language more regular than it actually is. In English, this is likely to be shown when a child overregularizes the past tense of verbs ("breaked") and the plural forms of nouns ("foots").

ovum. A human egg cell; the largest cell in the human body.

P

partial reinforcement. In operant conditioning, the reinforcement of a selected response on an interval or ratio schedule.

perception. An important aspect of cognitive development, involving the transformation of sensations into information.

phase (in development). A concept that indicates that development is continuous across the life span; the divisions are culturally determined.

phenotype. The nature of a trait as it appears in the individual; it reflects the contributions of both genetic and environmental factors.

phenylketonuria (PKU). The inherited inability to metabolize phenylalinine, a component of some foods. It occurs when the two recessive genes for PKU are paired.

placenta. The organ that transmits nourishment and waste between the mother and the fetus.

placing. A reflex movement, which is most easily elicited during the first three months of an infant's life, consisting of a baby's lifting his foot onto a surface.

polygenic. Indicates that several genes have an equal and cumulative effect in producing a trait.

possession. In the two-word stage of language development, the expression of ownership, as in "Daddy coat."

practice play. Play in which the infant finds pleasure and satisfaction in repeating what he already knows.

precausal. A kind of thinking in which a child maintains that some events are either completely or partly caused by psychological, subjective factors. An example is a child's ideas about the origins of dreams.

premoral level. The level of moral reasoning in which value is placed in physical acts and needs, not in persons or social standards.

preoperational stage. A subperiod of the representational period, in Piaget's theory of cognitive development, which begins when children start to record experiences symbolically, involves the use of language to record experiences, and involves the appearance of the ability to think in terms of classes, numbers, and relationships.

principled level. The level of moral reasoning in which value resides in self-chosen principles and standards that have a universal logical validity and can therefore be shared.

productivity. The ability to combine individual words into an unlimited number of sentences; one of the three formal properties of language.

proximodistal development. The progression of physical and motor development from the center of the body toward the periphery. For example, a baby learns to control the movements of his shoulders before he can direct his arms or fingers.

puberty. The main biological event of adolescence, characterized by the attainment of biological sexual maturity.

Q

questions. In the two-word stage of language development, the transformation of all sentence types into questions by the use of rising intonation or question words, as in "Where ball?"

R

rapid eye movement (REM). A type of eye movement that occurs during a certain period of sleep and that is accompanied by changes in respiratory, muscle, and brain-wave activity.

ratio reinforcement. In operant conditioning, the partial reinforcement schedule in which a person is reinforced only after he has responded correctly a certain number of times.

reaction range. The limits set by genetic conditions on an individual's possible behavior.

reaction time. The interval of time that elapses between the instant a stimulus is presented and the individual's reaction to it.

recessive gene. The subordinate member of a pair of genes whose corresponding trait fails to appear.

reciprocal play. See *cooperative play*.

recurrence. In the two-word stage of language development, the indication of the presence, absence, or repetition of things and actions, as in "Book again."

reductionism. A general point of view that holds that complex phenomena can be understood and explained by breaking them into simpler components.

reflex. An unlearned or naturally occurring reaction to a stimulus.

reinforcement. In operant conditioning, the presentation or withdrawal of an event following a response, which increases or decreases the likelihood of that response occurring again.

releasing stimuli. Those events that regularly evoke certain behavior in all members of a species; a key concept in ethological theories.

reliability. The dependability and consistency of a measure, observation, or finding.

replication. In studies, the attempt to repeat the essential features of an investigation and its findings.

representational skills. Those cognitive skills or ways in which an individual represents and constructs an understanding of his world and the people, objects, and events in it.

representational stage. A stage in Piaget's theory of cognitive development that begins with the preoperational and ends with the concrete-operational period.

respiratory distress syndrome. The lung condition (formerly called hyaline disease of the lungs) in which the fetus is unable to maintain necessary surfactin levels and dies.

respondent conditioning. See *classical conditioning*.

reversibility. The mental operation or understanding, according to Piaget's theory of cognitive development, in which one can think of a transformation that would reverse a sequence of events or restore the original condition.

rickets. The condition caused by a calcium deficiency during infancy and childhood and characterized by the softening and malformation of the bones.

role taking. The ability to take the role or point of view of another person; a requirement in cognitive and other forms of development.

rooting reflex. A reflex that is most easily elicited during the baby's first two weeks of life, consisting of the baby turning his head in the direction of any object that gently stimulates the corner of his mouth.

S

schedules of reinforcement. In operant conditioning, the timetables for reinforcing behavior; they have different effects on the rate of responding.

schemes. Piaget's term for action patterns that are built up and coordinated throughout the course of cognitive development. In the infant, they are like concepts without words. Throughout development, such schemes are presumed to be involved in the acquisition and structuring of knowledge.

self-actualizing. According to Maslow, the human tendency to realize one's full potential in work and love. It develops after the basic needs of food, security, and esteem are met.

self-concept. The sum of ideas one has about oneself.

self-demand feeding. A feeding schedule in which a baby is fed according to when he is hungry, not according to a schedule designed by others.

self-esteem. A concept or description involving the way that one evaluates himself.

self-regulation. The regulation of one's own conduct.

semanticity. The learning of the meaning of words, and the process of communicating meaning. One of the three formal properties of language.

sensation. A necessary aspect for cognitive development involving the reception, through the various sense organs, of stimulation from the external world.

sensitive periods. Periods of development during which an organism is most likely to be susceptible to a particular influence.

sensorimotor stage. The first major stage in Piaget's theory of cognitive development, which begins at birth and extends through the first two years of life. It is characterized by the development of sensory and motor functions and by the infant's coming to know the world as a result of interacting with and affecting it.

separation anxiety. The distinctly negative reaction of an infant to separation and his attempts to regain contact with his attachment figure.

sequence (in development). A concept used to explain the relationship among developmental changes in behavior, indicating that some behaviors precede others in a meaningfully related way.

sex role. The pattern of behavior and attitudes considered to characterize each sex.

sex-role stereotypes. Simplified, fixed concepts about the behaviors and traits typical of each sex.

shame. A negative feeling response that is a reaction to the disapproval of others.

small-for-dates. The condition in which a baby is underweight for his gestational age.

social-learning theory. A set of concepts and principles from behavior-learning theory, frequently used in describing and explaining personality characteristics and social behavior.

socialization. The process of psychologically growing into a society, in which an individual acquires the behaviors, attitudes, values, and roles expected of him.

sociometric analysis. A method for charting how often a child is chosen by his peers as a preferred friend or companion.

spermatozoon. A single sperm cell.

spontaneous abortion. The expulsion, from the uterus, of a fetus older than twenty-eight weeks.

stage (in development). A concept used to explain the orderly relationship among developmental changes in behavior and indicating that the organization of behavior is qualitatively different from one stage to the next.

stepping. A reflex movement, which is most easily elicited during the infant's first two weeks of life, that consists of straightening the legs out at the knees and hip, as if to stand, when the infant is held with his feet touching a surface.

stimulus generalization. A process or phenomenon in which a response learned in reaction to one stimulus can be elicited by separate but similar stimuli.

stranger anxiety. The negative response and withdrawal that occurs in reaction to strangers, usually developing a month or two after specific attachments begin.

sublimation. The altering, in socially acceptable ways, of forbidden impulses. According to Freud, it is one of the processes important in the development of rational behavior.

substitution. According to Flavell, a sequence in intellectual development in which the later-emerging item replaces the earlier one completely or almost completely. An example is children's recognition of the true nature of their dreams.

successive approximations. In operant conditioning, a procedure in which behaviors that resemble more and more closely the final desired response are reinforced.

superego. An aspect of personality, in Freud's theory, defined as the conscience; develops as the child internalizes parental and societal values and standards.

surfactin. The liquid that coats the air sacs of the lungs and permits them to transmit oxygen from the air to the blood.

symbolic play. Play that becomes more symbolic and complex as the ability to imagine and pretend develops.

syntax. See *grammar*.

syphilis. A venereal disease due to systemic infection with treponema pallidum.

T

term (prenatal development). The gestational age of 266 days from conception. Formerly, babies born before term were considered premature.

testicles. The male reproductive glands, which release sperm.

theory (developmental). A set of logically related statements about the nature of development that help psychologists understand, predict, and explain human behavior.

totalism. Defined by Erikson as an organization of one's self-concept that has rigid, absolute, and arbitrary boundaries.

transfer. A process or phenomenon in which the learning of one task results in improvement of learning or performance in another related, but different, task.

transitivity. A concept that requires the joining together of two or more instances of an abstract relation; for example, if A is larger than B and B is larger than C, then A is larger than C.

trimester. A period of approximately three months; often used in discussing pregnancy.

Turner's syndrome. A condition resulting from a missing sex chromosome in the fertilized egg. It produces children with physical abnormalities and mental retardation.

U

unconditioned reflex. In classical conditioning, one of two kinds of reflexes; it is inborn and occurs naturally to a stimulus.

unconscious impulses. In Freud's theory, those irrational impulses that reside in the id and that the individual is unaware of.

uniformism. A concept indicating immersion into the peer group and the acceptance of its norms as infallible and regulatory.

V

variability. Variation due to individual differences as well as other sources of influence.

variables. Those factors in an investigation that can vary in quantity or magnitude, or in some qualitative aspect, and that may or may not affect the results of the investigation.

vernix. The white greasy material that covers and lubricates the newborn for passage through the birth canal.

visual accommodation. The ability to alternate focus for objects at different distances.

vital capacity. The air-holding capacity of the lungs.

INDEX

504

INDEX

Chodorow, N., 246
Chomsky, N., 32, 34–36, 43, 144, 224
Christensen, H. T., 404
chromosomes, 48, 67, 69
  abnormalities of, 76–77
chumship, 372
Clark, B. S., 258
Clark, E. V., 153–154
Clarke-Stewart, K. A., 14
classical conditioning, 28, 138
clinical studies, 56–57
cliques, adolescent, 372–373
  see also groups
Coates, B., 174, 258
cognition, 124–125, 131
  see also cognitive development; thought
cognitive development, 123–141
  in adolescence, 275, 349–353
  aggression and, 294
  altruism and, 291, 293
  attachment and, 171–172
  attention and, 130–132, 205–207, 268–269
  autonomy and, 179
  in early childhood, 203–220
  egocentrism and, 211–213, 279–281
  environmental influences, 136–141, 238–239
  family influences, 53–54
  fear and, 167–168
  in infancy, 33, 123–141
  language and, 143, 144, 145, 148–149, 156–158, 205–206, 211, 213, 215–216, 275–278
  in later childhood, 267–283
  moral reasoning and, 310–313, 318–320, 253–355
  multiple caretaking and, 177
  perceptual functioning in, 125–130, 204–205
  play and, 216–218, 278, 300–302
  problem solving and, 273–275
  representational skills in, 136, 213–219, 275–279
  sequences in, 15–16, 112
  social development and, 168, 219–220
  stages of, 34
  training skills and, 209, 275
cognitive-developmental theory. See Kohlberg, L.; Piaget, J.
cognitive level, 25, 32
cognitive theories, 24–25
  see also Chomsky, N.; Kohlberg, L.; Piaget, J.
cohabitation, 402, 441
Cohen, D., 48
Cohen, L. B., 131

cohesiveness, group, 298
Coleman, J. S., 357, 375, 376
Coleman, R. P., 366
collectivism vs. individualism, in achievement motivation, 366–368
commitment, in adolescence, 379–381
communal living, 402, 404
communication
  animal vs. human, 144
  in infancy, 112, 143–161
  in newborns, 99, 100–101
  nonverbal, 146, 152
  skills, 279–281
  see also language; language development
community
  adolescence and, 377
  middle adulthood and, 413, 423
compensatory education, 239
competence, 178–179, 201
competence motivation, 42, 178–180
competition
  group, 298
  physical, 199
competitiveness, 261, 262
concept learning, 30–31, 125
  in early childhood, 207–211
  effects of environment on, 139
  and language development, 154
  in later childhood, 269–275, 276
conception, 66–67, 69
concepts, 123
  cognitive level and, 32
  formation of, 132–136, 207–211
  language and, 153
  relational, 267, 269–270
  types of, 209–211
concrete-operational stage, of intellectual development, 34, 269, 349, 352
conditioning
  attention and, 131
  classical, 28, 138
  fetal, 75
  of guilt, 316
  in infancy, 138–139, 145, 147–148
  operant, 28–30
  of sex roles, 288
Condon, W. S., 101
Conel, J. L. R., 115, 198
conflict
  in Erikson's theory, 39
  in Freud's theory, 38–39
  intergroup, 298
conformity
  to authority, 368, 377
  to peers, 297–298, 370, 371, 377
  popularity and, 373
  see also socialization
Conger, J. C., 335
Conger, J. J., 357, 358
conjunctive concepts, 209–210

S

W

Y

Z

CREDITS AND ACKNOWLEDGMENTS

A special thanks to:

Emily Beebee, Mary Bess Holloway (proofreading); Howard Cohen, John McCarthy (research); Kitty R. Anderson (production art); Genevieve Clapp, Davey Estrada (indexing); Rolande Angles, Amy Barnett, Leslie Bolinger, Margaret Kassner, Teri Marshall, Laura Szalwinski (typing and editorial services).

Cover—(top) Rhoda Kellogg, *Psychology of Children's Art*, © 1967 by CRM, Inc., (bottom) Mia Tegner, Scripps Institute of Oceanography.

UNIT I/THE MEANING OF DEVELOPMENT
2—Rhoda Kellogg, *Psychology of Children's Art*, © 1967 by CRM, Inc.

Chapter 1/The Concept of Development
4—Harry Crosby; 7—(top left) Historical Pictures Service, Chicago, (top right) William MacDonald, (center left) Lewis Hine, The George Eastman House, (center right and bottom right) Harry Crosby, (bottom left) Scala Fine Arts Publishers; 11—(top and center) courtesy Dr. L. B. Shettles, (bottom) Irven DeVore/Anthro-Photo; 12—Jason Lauré; 13—Dick Corten; 15—Jerome Wexler/Photo Researchers; 17—Allan Roberts; 19—Andy Lucas; 20—(left) Ken Heyman, (center) from *Film Guide to Developmental Psychology Today Films*, © 1973 by CRM, Inc., (right) Lorenzo Gunn/Gordon Menzie Photography; 21—(left) Robert Isaacs, (right) Pete Robinson.

Chapter 2/Theories of Development
22—Robert Van Doren; 25—*The Wild Child*, © 1973 by F. Truffaut; 27—Andy Lucas; 29—Robert Isaacs; 31—Andy Lucas; 32—George S. Zimbel/Monkmeyer Press; 33—(top) John Oldenkamp, (center and bottom right) Steven Wells, (bottom left) Arthur Tress/Magnum Photos; 35—Alan Mercer; 37—Andy Lucas; 38—Terry Lamb; 40—Andy Lucas; 41—(top) William MacDonald, (top center left) Steve McCarroll, (top center right) Charles Harbutt/Magnum Photos, (bottom center left) Jane Bown, (bottom center right) John Oldenkamp, (bottom left) copyright © 1967, Educational Development Center, Inc., (bottom right) Harry Crosby; 42—Andy Lucas.

Chapter 3/Determinants of Development
44—Patsy Rowe; 47—John Dawson, after S. L. Washburn and Ruth Moore, *Ape Into Man*, Little, Brown & Co., 1974; 49—Andy Lucas, after M. Honzik, "Developmental Studies of Parent-Child Resemblance in Intelligence," *Child Development*, vol. 28, 1957, pp. 215-228. By permission of The Society for Research in Child Development, Inc.; 51—Joyce Kitchell; 53—(left) Alan Mercer, (right) Ken Heyman; 55—(top left) Harry Crosby, (top right) Suzanne Szasz, (center left) Bob Smith/Rapho-Guillumette, (center right) Rogier Gregoire, (bottom) Rogers/Monkmeyer Press; 57—(top) Builder Levy, (bottom) Jason Lauré; 58-59—Andy Lucas; 60—(top) William MacDonald, (bottom) Chris Engholm.

UNIT II/THE BEGINNING OF LIFE
62—Rhoda Kellogg, *Psychology of Children's Art*, © 1967 by CRM, Inc.

Chapter 4/Prenatal Development
68—Kitty Anderson; 72—John Dawson; 75—(bottom) Elizabeth Wilcox; 77—(top) John Dawson, (bottom) Department of Neurosciences, University of California, San Diego; 79—C. Quinton Kimball/NKS.

Chapter 5/The World of the Newborn
82—Elizabeth Wilcox; 84—Mr. A. K. Tunstill, Department of Medical Photography, Sheffield Area Health Authority, (teaching); 86—(top) Jason Lauré, (bottom) Andy Lucas, adapted from Roffwarg, Dement, and Fisher, *Behaviour in Infancy and Early Childhood*, Y. Brackbill and S. G. Thompson (eds.), Free Press, 1967, New York; 87—Andy Lucas, after H. P. Roffwarg, J. N. Muzio, and W. C. Dement, "Ontogenetic Development of the Human Sleep-Dream Cycle," *Science*, vol. 152. Copyright © 1966 by The American Association for the Advancement of Science; 88—Andy Lucas, after A. Gesell and F. L. Ilg, *The Feeding Behavior of Infants: A Pediatric Approach to the Mental Hygiene of Early Life*, J. B. Lippincott Co., 1937; 90—William MacDonald; 91—Mr. A. K. Tunstill, Department of Medical Photography, Sheffield Area Health Authority, (teaching); 93—courtesy Dr. Robert L. Fantz; 94—(left) courtesy Dr. William Kessen, Yale University, (right) Andy Lucas, from Philip Salapatek and William Kessen, "Visual Scanning of Triangles by the Human Newborn," *Journal of Experimental Child Psychology*, vol. 3, pp. 156-167, © 1966 by Academic Press, Inc.; 96—Andy Lucas, from A. J. Sameroff, "An Apparatus for Recording Sucking and Controlling Feeding in the First Days of Life," *Psychonomic Science*, vol. 2, 1965; 97—Andy Lucas, after S. Friedman, "Differential Dishabituation as a Function of Magnitude of Stimulus Discrepancy and Sex of the Newborn Infant," from an unpublished paper; 99—Ken Heyman; 100—(left) Steve McCarroll, (right) Professor John Lind, Karolinska Institutet, Stockholm.

UNIT III/INFANCY: THE DAWN OF AWARENESS
102—Rhoda Kellogg, *Psychology of Children's Art*, © 1967 by CRM, Inc.

Chapter 6/Physical Growth: Fundamentals
104—Rogier Gregoire; 106—Joyce Kitchell; 107—Tom Suzuki; 108—adapted from C. M. Jackson (ed.), *Morris' Human Anatomy*, 7th ed. Copyright © 1923 by P. Blakiston's Son & Co. Used by per-

mission of McGraw-Hill Book Company; 109—Andy Lucas, adapted from Eric H. Lenneberg, *Biological Foundations of Language,* 1967, John Wiley & Sons, N.Y.; 111—(top and center left) Steve McCarroll, (bottom left and bottom right) from *Film Guide to Developmental Psychology Today Films,* © 1973 by CRM, Inc.; 113—Andy Lucas, adapted from A. Prader, J. M. Tanner, and G. A. Von Harnack, "Catch–up Growth Following Illness or Starvation: An Example of Developmental Canalization in Man," *Journal of Pediatrics,* vol. 62, 1963; 115—Joyce Kitchell; 116–117—Steve McCarroll; 118—(top) Marcia Keegan, (bottom) Andy Lucas, adapted from C. B. Hindley, A. M. Filliozat, G. Klackenberg, D. Nicolet-Meister, and E. A. Sand, "Differences in Walking in the European Longitudinal Samples," *Human Biology,* vol. 38, 1966. By permission of Wayne State University Press; 119—courtesy of Burton L. White; 120—William MacDonald.

Chapter 7/Cognition: From Sensing to Knowing
122—William MacDonald; 125—Andy Lucas; 127—Steve McCarroll; 128—Eric Aronson; 129—(top) William MacDonald, (bottom) from *Film Guide to Developmental Psychology Today Films,* © 1973 by CRM, Inc.; 130—Andy Lucas; 131—Joyce Kitchell, adapted from R. Ahrens, *Zeitschrift für Experimentelle und Angewandte Psychologie,* 1954; 133—Andy Lucas; 134—Steve McCarroll; 135—George Zimbel/Monkmeyer Press Photo Service; 137—William MacDonald; 138—Jason Lauré; 139—William MacDonald; 140—(left) Doug Wilson/Black Star, (right) William MacDonald.

Chapter 8/Language: Beginnings
142—Harry Crosby; 145—John Dawson; 146—Andy Lucas; 147—Joyce Kitchell; 149—William MacDonald; 150—Andy Lucas, adapted from Tonkova-Yampol'skaya, *Phonology,* 1973; 151—Andy Lucas, after P. Menyuk, *The Acquisition and Development of Language,* © 1971. Reprinted with permission of Prentice-Hall, Inc., Englewood Cliffs, N.J.; 152–157—Joyce Kitchell; 159—(top and bottom) from *Film Guide to Developmental Psychology Today Films,* © 1973 by CRM, Inc., (center) Roger Mayne.

Chapter 9/Personality: From Attachment to Sociability
162—from *Film Guide to Developmental Psychology Today Films,* © 1973 by CRM, Inc.; 166—Thomas McAvoy, Time-Life Picture Agency, © Time, Inc.; 167—Andy Lucas, adapted from A. T. Jersild and F. B. Holmes, *Children's Fears,* Child Development Monograph No. 20, New York, Columbia Univer-

sity, 1935; 169—Andy Lucas; 170—Harry F. Harlow, University of Wisconsin Primate Laboratory; 171—Andy Lucas, adapted from H. R. Schaffer and P. E. Emerson, "The Development of Social Attachment in Infancy," *Monographs of the Society for Research in Child Development,* vol. 29, 1964. By permission of The Society for Research in Child Development, Inc.; 173—(top) Alan Mercer, (bottom) Office of Economic Opportunity; 175—John Dawson; 176—(top) Harry Crosby, (bottom) William MacDonald; 177—Tom Blau/Camera Press, Ltd.; 179—(top) William MacDonald, (bottom) Suzanne Szasz; 180—(left) Rogier Gregoire, (right) William MacDonald; 181—William MacDonald.

UNIT IV/EARLY CHILDHOOD: THE FORMATIVE YEARS
184—Rhoda Kellogg, *Psychology of Children's Art,* © 1967 by CRM, Inc.

Chapter 10/Physical Change: Growth and Skills
186—William MacDonald; 188—Joyce Kitchell; 189—Andy Lucas; 191—(left) Joan Sydlow/Monkmeyer Press, (right) Paul Conklin, courtesy of Office of Economic Opportunity; 193—(top left) John Oldenkamp, (top right and bottom) William MacDonald; 195—John Oldenkamp; 196—Myron Papiz; 197—A. J. Hayhurst; 198—Andy Lucas, adapted from R. C. Lewis, A.M. Duval, and A. Iliff, "Standards for the Basal Metabolism of Children from Two to Fifteen Years of Age," *Journal of Pediatrics,* vol. 23, 1943; 200—(top) John Oldenkamp, (bottom) Vista.

Chapter 11/Cognition: Changes in Thinking
202—John Oldenkamp; 205—Andy Lucas; 206—Andy Lucas, adapted from Sheldon White, "Evidence for a Hierarchical Arrangement of Learning Processes," L. P. Lipsitt and C. C. Spiker (eds.), *Advances in Child Development and Behaviour,* vol. 2, Academic Press, 1965, illustrations from *The Golden Book of Bird Stamps* by Sonia Bleeker, illustrated by James Gorden Irving and Janet Rumley. Copyright © 1949 by Western Publishing Company, Inc. Reprinted by permission of the publisher; 208—William MacDonald; 210—Joyce Kitchell; 211—Andy Lucas; 212—Joyce Fitzgerald; 214—(top) Sol Schimmel, (bottom) Dorothy Levens, Vassar College, N. Y.; 216—from *Film Guide to Developmental Psychology Today Films,* © 1973 by CRM Books, Inc.; 217—(top left) C. Quinton Kimball/NKS, (top right) John Oldenkamp, (bottom) from *Film Guide to Developmental Psychology Today Films,* © 1973 by CRM, Inc.; 219—Andy Lucas after Claire Golomb, *Genetic Psychology*

Monographs, vol. 87, 1973; 220—(left) John Oldenkamp, (right) William MacDonald; 221—Myron Papiz.

Chapter 12/Language: Understanding and Using
222—Steve McCarroll; 225—Andy Lucas, adapted from Roger Brown, *A First Language: The Early Stages,* 1973, Harvard University Press; 227—Joyce Kitchell; 228-230—William MacDonald; 231—Andy Lucas; 233—William MacDonald; 234—Andy Lucas, adapted from E. H. Lenneberg, *Biological Foundations of Language,* New York, John Wiley & Sons, 1967; 235—from *Film Guide to Developmental Psychology Today Films,* © 1973 by CRM, Inc.; 236—Office of Economic Opportunity; 238—Robert Isaacs; 240—(top) Barbara Young/Photo Researchers, (bottom) Ken Heyman.

Chapter 13/Personality: Establishing Social Interactions
242—William MacDonald; 244—From *Tootle* by Gertrude Crampton, illustrated by Tiber Gergeby, © 1945 by Western Publishing Co., Inc. Reprinted by permission of the publisher; 247—(top) Burk Uzzle/Magnum Photos, (bottom) Paul Sequeira; 249—(top left) Robert Smith/Black Star, (bottom left) Myron Papiz, (right) John Oldenkamp; 251—(top) William MacDonald, (bottom) Operation Head Start; 253—Andy Lucas; 254—(left) Ken Heyman, (right) Harry F. Harlow, University of Wisconsin Primate Laboratory; 255—Harry F. Harlow, University of Wisconsin Primate Laboratory; 256—John Rees/Black Star; 257—courtesy of Albert Bandura from A. Bandura, D. Ross, and S. A. Ross, "Imitation of Film-Mediated Aggressive Models," *Journal of Abnormal and Social Psychology,* 1963; 258—Andy Lucas, after W. W. Hartup and Brian Coates, *Child Development,* vol. 38, © 1967 by The Society for Research in Child Development, Inc. All rights reserved; 259—Andy Lucas, after M. B. Parten, "Social Participation Among Preschool Children," *Journal of Abnormal and Social Psychology,* vol. 24, © 1932-1933 by American Psychological Association; 260—Jane Bown; 262—Ken Heyman.

UNIT V/LATER CHILDHOOD: GROWING UP
264—Rhoda Kellogg, *Psychology of Children's Art,* © 1967 by CRM, Inc.

Chapter 14/Cognition: Advances in Thinking
266—Rogier Gregoire; 269—Andy Lucas, adapted from J. W. Hagen, "The Effect of Distraction on Selective Attention," *Child Development,* vol. 38, 1967.

By permission of the Society for Research in Child Development, Inc.; 270—(top) Robin Forbes/Ford Foundation, (bottom) from *Film Guide to Developmental Psychology Today Films,* © 1973 by CRM, Inc.; 271—Jane Bown; 272—From the book *How The Mouse Was Hit on the Head by a Stone and So Discovered the World.* Copyright © 1971 by Etienne Delessert. Reprinted by permission of Doubleday & Company, Inc.; 274—Cheryl Solheid, after Bärbel Inhelder and Jean Piaget, "The Oscillation of a Pendulum and the Operations of Exclusion," from *The Growth of Logical Thinking: From Childhood to Adolescence,* translated by A. Parsons and S. Milgram, © 1958 by Basic Books, Inc.; 276—after H. Gardner, "Metaphors and Modalities: How Children Project Polar Adjectives Onto Diverse Domains," *Child Development,* vol. 45, 1974. By permission of the Society for Research in Child Development, Inc.; 277—From Richard Lewis, *Miracles,* Simon & Schuster, © 1966 by R. Lewis. Reprinted with permission of publisher; 279—Cheryl Solheid, adapted from Furth, Ross, and Youniss, 1974.

Chapter 15/Personality: Expanding Social Interactions
284—Michael Alexander; 288—Andy Lucas, after Francis P. Hardesty and Ruth E. Hartley, "Children's Perceptions of Sex Roles in Childhood," *Journal of Genetic Psychology,* vol. 105, 1964; 289—(left) Ken Heyman, (right) John Oldenkamp; 290—Jane Bown; 292—Suzanne Szasz; 294—(top) William MacDonald, (bottom) Myron Papiz; 295—Irene B. Bayer/Monkmeyer; 296—(top) Ken Heyman, (bottom) Harry Crosby; 297—Andy Lucas, from P. R. Costanzo and M. E. Shaw, "Conformity as a Function of Age Level," *Child Development,* vol. 37, 1966. By permission of the Society for Research in Child Development, Inc.; 299—(left) William MacDonald, (top right) Harry Crosby, (bottom right) Steve McCarroll; 301—Robert Isaacs; 304—Harry Crosby.

Chapter 16/Morality: From Rules to Conduct
306—Peter Hudson; 309—Steve McCarroll; 311—Andy Lucas; 312—Andy Lucas, after Lawrence Kohlberg, "The Development of Children's Orientations Toward a Moral Order," *Vita Humana,* vol. 6, 1963. Reprinted by permission of S. Karger AG, Basel; 313—Andy Lucas, after L. Kohlberg, "The Child as a Moral Philosopher," *Psychology Today,* September 1968; 314—Myron Papiz; 315—Andy Lucas, adapted from L. Kohlberg, "The Child as a Moral Philosopher," *Psychology Today,* September 1968; 317—(top) William MacDonald,

(bottom) Bill Duncan; 318—Harry Crosby; 319— from the film *Development,* © 1973 by CRM, Inc.; 322—Miami News Photo.

UNIT VI/ADOLESCENCE: BUILDING AN IDENTITY
324—Aurilla Rivera, courtesy of Ms. Judy Earle.

Chapter 17/Physical and Sexual Maturation
326—John Oldenkamp; 328—Joyce Kitchell; 329— Andy Lucas; 330—Andy Lucas, after L. M. Tanner, *Growth at Adolescence,* 2nd edition, Blackwell Scientific Publications, Oxford, 1962; 332—(top) Mike Gutstadt, (bottom) UPI-COMPIX; 334—Andy Lucas, adapted from J. M. Tanner, *Growth at Adolescence,* 2nd edition, Blackwell Scientific Publications, Oxford, 1962; 336—courtesy of the California Milk Advisory Board; 337—Wayne Miller/Magnum Photos; 339–340—Michael Alexander; 341—Kenneth Murray/Nancy Palmer Photo Agency.

Chapter 18/Identity and Experience
344—Rogier Gregoire; 348—(top) Victor Friedman, (bottom) Rogier Gregoire; 350—(top) Michael Alexander, (bottom) Richard B. Klein/Nancy Palmer Photo Agency; 351—Joyce Kitchell; 353—John Oldenkamp; 354—Paul Ganster; 356—(left) Westinghouse Broadcasting Company, (right) Michael Alexander; 358—(top) Bruce Roberts/Rapho-Guillumette, (bottom) Burk Uzzle/Magnum Photos; 359–360—Michael Alexander; 362—(top) Michael Alexander, (bottom) Rogier Gregoire.

Chapter 19/Social Relations and Influence
364—Michael Alexander; 367—(top left) Alan Mercer, (top right) UPI-COMPIX, (bottom left) Jane Bown, (center right) Wayne Miller/Magnum Photos, (bottom right) Paul Sequeira; 369—(top) Michael Alexander, (bottom) Wayne Miller/Magnum Photos; 372—(left) courtesy of VISTA, (right) Rogier Gregoire; 373—Andy Lucas, adapted from R. D. Franklin and H. H. Remmers, "Youth's Attitudes Towards Courtship and Marriage," Report of Poll 62 of the Purdue Opinion Panel. Purdue Research Foundation, 1961; 374—(top) courtesy of VISTA, (bottom) Ken Heyman; 375—Rogers/Monkmeyer Press; 377—(top) Steve McCarroll, (bottom) Michael Alexander; 378—(top) Ann Zane Shanks/Photo Researchers, (bottom) Steve McCarroll; 380—(top left) Victor Friedman, (top right) Burk Uzzle/Magnum Photos, (bottom left) Elihu Blotnick/BBM Associates, (bottom right) UPI-COMPIX; 382—(top left) Peace Corps/ACTION, (bottom left) Peter Keen/courtesy of *Aramco World* magazine, (right) Hugh Wilkerson.

UNIT VII/ADULTHOOD: FUNCTIONING IN SOCIETY
384—gift of Mrs. Murray S. Danforth, Museum of Art, Rhode Island School of Design, Providence, R.I.

Chapter 20/Early Adulthood: Selecting the Options
386—Craighead/Photophile; 390–391—Gordon Menzie/Photophile; 392—(top left) Ton Thal, (top right) Ken Heyman, (bottom left) William MacDonald, (center right) M. M. Warren/Photo Researchers, (bottom right) UPI-COMPIX; 395—(top) courtesy of VISTA; 396—(top) UPI-COMPIX, (bottom) Wide World Photos; 397—Michael Alexander; 398—(top) Michael Alexander, (bottom) Ken Heyman; 400—Arthur Schatz for *Life* magazine, © 1972 by Time Inc.; 400–401—quiz reprinted by permission of *Rough Times* (formerly *Radical Therapist*) from the April 1972 issue; 403—(left) Ken Heyman, (right) Michael Alexander; 405—(left) John Oldenkamp, (right) William MacDonald; 406—(top) John Oldenkamp, (center) Ralph Watwood, (bottom) Harry Crosby.

Chapter 21/Middle Adulthood: Making the Most of It
408—Harry Crosby; 411—Burt Glinn/Magnum Photos; 413—(top left) Yvonne Freund, (bottom left and right) Ken Heyman; 414–415—UPI-COMPIX; 416—(top) Charles Gatewood, (center) Steve McCarroll, (bottom) Kirk Breedlove/Photophile; 418—Andy Lucas, after Wayne Dennis, "Creative Productivity Between the Ages of 20 and 80 Years," *Journal of Gerontology,* vol. 21, 1966; 419—(top) Schmick/Monkmeyer Press, (bottom) Dourdin/Rapho-Guillumette; 422—Alan Mercer; 424—(top) Gordon Menzie, (bottom) Ken Heyman.

Chapter 22/Later Adulthood: Living Successfully
426—Harry Crosby; 428—(top and center) UPI-COMPIX, (bottom) Andy Lucas; 431—Harry Crosby; 433—Nacio Jan Brown/BBM Associates; 434—Joe Molnar; 436—(top) Henle/Monkmeyer Press, (center) Izis/Rapho-Guillumette, (bottom) UPI-COMPIX; 437—(top) Michael Monnie/Photophile, (bottom) Ken Heyman; 438—(top) Neale M. Albert, (bottom) Department of Housing and Urban Development; 439—(top) Alan Mercer, (bottom) C. Quinton Kimball/NKS; 443—(top left) Burk Uzzle/Magnum Photos, (center left) Harry Crosby, (top right) Chuck Bellin/Photophile, (bottom left) Ken Heyman, (bottom right) Paul Fusco/Magnum Photos; 445—Department of Housing and Urban Development; 446—(top) UPI-COMPIX, (bottom) Alan Mercer; 447—Harry Crosby; 448—Elliott Erwitt/Magnum Photos.

DEVELOPMENTAL PSYCHOLOGY TODAY Second Edition

Book Team

Harvey A. Tilker, Ph.D., *Publisher*

Mary Salgueiro, *Publishing Coordinator*

Elizabeth Hall, *Editor*

Rebecca Smith, *Associate Editor*

Pamela Morehouse, *Designer*

Alice Harmon, *Associate Designer*

Cheryl Solheid, *Art Assistant*

Alastair McLeod, Ph.D., *Graphics Adviser*

Shelagh Dalton, *Photo Editor*

Lyn Smith, *Permissions*

Sandra Marcus, *Production Supervisor*

John C. Ochse, *Psychology Product Manager*